Politics and Society in Contemporary Africa

Contents

PART 4   INTERNATIONAL RELATIONS

PART 5   POLITICAL FUTURES

Tables

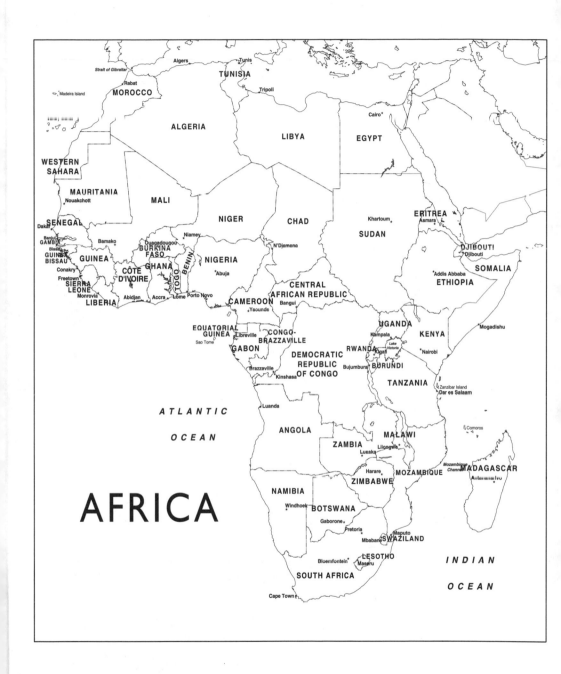

AFRICA

Introduction

The excitement of the struggle for independence that permeated the African continent in the second half of the twentieth century gained new momentum in the 1990s as most African countries undertook political reform measures and instituted multiparty governments. Nevertheless, at the close of the century, ongoing traumas regarding economic survival, effective political rule, and civil war continued to take a heavy toll. And a series of devasting political and human disasters rocked the continent—in Rwanda, Somalia, Liberia, Sierra Leone, and elsewhere.

Africans, their governments, and the international community still grapple today with economic adversity, political uncertainty, and social inequities. How have these constraints on growth and opportunity influenced the African political experience? What political and economic choices have been made and what are their implications? What options exist in these circumstances? What steps can Africans in Algeria, Angola, Nigeria, or Congo take to restore shaken societies to confidence as they move into the twenty-first century? The answers lie not in a single isolated variable but in the complex interconnections between politics and society, between domestic and external forces, and among historical legacies, available resources, and future prospects.

The purpose of this introduction to African politics and society is to depict in broad strokes the complexities and diversities of the African world since independence and to investigate new paths to understanding its intricate dynamics. Besides offering an initial acquaintance with contemporary Africa, we seek to provide a basic knowledge of political events and a closer comprehension of major problems, processes, and trends. By suggesting different ways of looking at issues, we raise a range of explanations for past occurrences and possible directions for theory. This book, therefore, constitutes a preliminary exploration into the multiple forces that make up present-day Africa.

In Chapter 1 we analyze different approaches to the study of African politics and present the main elements of an interactive method for the investigation of political structures, processes, and change. In Part 1 we concentrate on the building blocks of African politics. Chapter 2 is devoted to the study of government institutions. We examine the colonial legacy, the manner of transition to independence, and the structural foundations of the new states. We also trace institutional changes since independence and pinpoint the differences that have emerged among African states since the 1960s. Chapter 3 is focused on the varying social groups that operate within the African setting. We look not only at cultural, kin, religious, racial, and geographic agglomerations but also at socioeconomic formations and their competing interests. Chapter 4 is concerned with the interaction of class, ethnicity, and the state in various African countries, highlighting differing patterns of cooperation, conflict, violence, and political exchange.

Part 2 centers on the study of the political process. In Chapter 5 we present a typology of regime forms and discuss their evolution. In Chapter 6 we examine how leaders have attempted to govern: We look at ideologies and at the linkages between rulers and ruled. Chapter 7 is devoted to political conflicts evident since independence. In Chapter 8 we analyze the mechanisms, the direction, and the nature of political change, summarizing common political themes, indicating diverging trends, underlining the diverse dynamics of state-society relationships, and focusing on contemporary political reforms and crises.

Part 3 concerns the political economy. In Chapter 9 we analyze the differing contexts of development and underdevelopment and examine several major policy issues. Building on this base, in Chapter 10 we study the relationship of Africa to the world economy, probing the ways in which global economic currents impinge on African choices and the differing strategies adopted by African governments and groups to enhance their capacity to manage and progress in such settings.

In Part 4 we delve into the international facets of the African experience since independence. In Chapter 11 we look at how external and domestic constraints have guided relations within Africa and in Chapter 12 we review Africa's ties with the outside world and its activities in the international arena. Diverging foreign policies are therefore conceived of as the outcome of the exercise of choice within the context of powerful common constraints.

In Chapter 13, the beginning of Part 5, we examine the special case of white minority rule and black opposition in South Africa, highlighting the parameters of the political transition that took place in the 1990s. We look at the peculiar structures and processes of this dual society in order to understand the explosive situation that prevailed in the southern part of the continent and the factors leading to the profound changes in recent years. The significance of the transition in South Africa and the importance of the new South Africa at the beginning of the twenty-first century still merit a separate chapter. In Chapter 14 we draw together the lessons gleaned from the study of the many dimensions of politics on the continent, reviewing major patterns, discussing ongoing trends, and advancing some tentative ideas as to the choices ahead for Africans in the twenty-first century as they continue to deal with the exigencies of scarcity, institutional fragility, dependency, and sociocultural diversity.

In each chapter we present the historical background, give an overview of developments since independence, and depict the differing manifestations of each topic and issue. Because it is impossible to go into detail for all fifty-four states in Africa, we conduct a comparative analysis of processes that exemplify emerging patterns on the continent. On this basis, special attention is devoted to Nigeria, Ghana, Guinea, Côte d'Ivoire, Cameroon, and Senegal in West Africa; Algeria and Morocco in North Africa; Chad and Mali in the Sahel; Ethiopia and Sudan in the Horn of Africa; Congo (formerly Zaire*) and Zambia in central Africa; Kenya, Tanzania, and Uganda in East Africa; and Angola, Mozambique, and Botswana in southern Africa. We conclude each chapter by extracting the major patterns that emerge from the data; we discuss various explanations and raise further questions for thought and action.

In this textbook, unlike others on African politics, we concentrate on the period since independence in order to expose existing problems in greater detail and to explore the possibilities that emanate from the need to confront these difficult realities. The politics of contemporary Africa are as vibrant as they are diverse. Since independence, new dimensions of political life have unfolded that defy conventional wisdom and demand a reformulation of concepts and expectations. We offer this volume as an introduction into this often confusing, constantly challenging, always fascinating, and ultimately questioning world.

---

*In May 1997, Zaire became the Democratic Republic of Congo, which we refer to as Congo (not to be confused with the Republic of Congo, or Congo-Brazzaville) throughout this book.

1

The Diversity
of African Politics:
Trends and Approaches

The African continent encompasses a rich mosaic of peoples, cultures, ecological settings, and historical experiences. Africa's vast expanse of 11,677,240 square miles (30,244,050 square kilometers) stretches from the Mediterranean in the north to the meeting point of the Atlantic and Indian oceans in the south. The 730 million people of Africa (roughly 10 percent of the globe's population) are as diverse as the terrain they inhabit. The blacks and Arabs who live on the continent (together with small concentrations of Asians and whites) speak more than eight hundred languages, belong to hundreds of ethnic groups, and over the years have embraced many animist belief systems as well as all the great religions (most notably, Christianity and Islam). Although 70 percent of the continent's people live in the rural areas and make their living as farmers and pastoralists, rapidly growing ancient and new cities are also sprinkled over the map of Africa. Subsistence agriculture is sustained alongside hi-tech industries; the world's greatest mineral reserves are to be found in regions of the most abject poverty; universities thrive where illiteracy still prevails.

The political map of Africa captures the complexity that is the essence of the continent. Africa's fifty-four states are the product of conquest and separation, amalgamation and continuity. Ethiopia and Egypt are among the oldest political entities known to human history. But most of Africa consists of new states carved out by the imperial powers. Nigeria, with its population of more than 100 million, contrasts sharply with tiny Comoros or Gambia. Massive Congo is bordered by the small and extremely troubled republics of Rwanda and Burundi. Swaziland is a nation-state (that is, ethnically homogeneous); it is surrounded by some of the most heterogeneous, multiethnic countries in the world today. Africa sustains monarchies and dictatorships, military regimes and civilian governments,

5

revolutionary systems and democracies, populist administrations and authoritarian modes of rule.

African politics constitute a microcosm of political forms and contents, experiences and patterns, trends and prospects. To focus on the contemporary politics of this continent is therefore to contemplate some of the most basic issues of human survival, organization, change, and growth. This book provides an introduction to the central themes of political life in independent Africa.

■ INDEPENDENT AFRICA: TRENDS AND PATTERNS

The first wave of independence in Africa commenced in the 1950s with the emergence of North Africa and then Ghana from colonial rule. The year 1960, generally considered the year of African independence, witnessed the dismantling of the French colonial empire as well as the attainment of sovereignty by Nigeria—sub-Saharan Africa's most populous country. By the mid-1960s, more than thirty new states had undergone the process of decolonization.

The second, and generally more violent, wave of independence began in 1974, following the revolution in Portugal. The lusophone (Portuguese-speaking) states of Guinea-Bissau, Cape Verde, Mozambique, and Angola finally overcame 400 years of colonial domination. In 1975, Spain withdrew from the western Sahara, setting in motion a period of still unresolved strife over control of the territory. In 1980 the struggle against white rule in Rhodesia was crowned with success: The independence of Zimbabwe brought the British colonial presence in Africa to an end. Namibia gained independence in 1990. And South Africa, the last, and most recalcitrant, remnant of an internal colonial presence in contemporary Africa, completed its transition to a multiracial democracy in the spring of 1994.

The heady expectations that accompanied the transfer of power have, in the first postcolonial generation, of necessity given way to a much more sober view of domestic and international realities. The meaning of independence, nevertheless, has varied from place to place on the continent. Different states, individuals, and groups have undergone quite distinct experiences in a variety of spheres, rendering Africa far more heterogeneous at the end of the twentieth century than it was on the eve of the transition from colonial rule.

In economic terms, the performance of many African countries has fallen far short of the vision of progress and well-being held forth by the leaders of anticolonial movements (see Table 1.1). In 1985, for example, twenty-two countries could not feed their growing population; agricultural production in the first part of the 1980s had actually declined. Economic growth rates per capita during the 1970s and 1980s, with a few exceptions, were stagnant if not negative. In most instances, these trends continued during the 1990s. The foreign debt of most African states has increased precipitously since the late 1970s. Yet, some countries recorded substantial economic achievements (Botswana, Algeria, Gabon, and Côte d'Ivoire, for example) and others have taken significant steps to avert further economic deterioration (Ghana, Zimbabwe). Certain amenities, such as clean water, electricity, latrines, and feeder roads, are now generally more available than at the close of the colonial era. Some Africans have enriched themselves in the course of these years; for others the exigencies of absolute poverty have continued to shape their existence.[1] Although economic trends have highlighted a widespread malaise, the economic paths of African countries and specific groups have diverged markedly during this short time span.

Social gains in some areas have come together with social dislocation and glaring inequalities in others (see Table 1.2). Most African countries initially made impressive advances in education and primary health care. Nevertheless, infant mortality rates are high (in some cases 50 percent of those born do not survive until the age of five), and life expectancy is just over fifty years. Access to much-needed services is uneven. The gap between the city and the countryside persists and has, in many places, been exacerbated. Elite-mass strains are pronounced. In Nigeria, for example, successful entrepreneurs and professionals fly around in private jets, while peasants line up for a portion of rice. Many rural areas have not been electrified; urban dwellers frequently have their own generators. In the countryside, wealthier landowners sometimes control large tracts of land, while small farmers scratch out a living from depleted soil.

Social groups throughout the continent have become more aware, over the years, of their own particular circumstances. Ethnic groupings, incipient classes, and a variety of local communities, professional associations, trade unions, women's organizations, and religious movements have organized to forward their specific interests. In some instances, formal channels of participation have facilitated ongoing communication; in others, indirect avenues have been established to raise demands and to distribute benefits (patron-client relationships are a good example); and in other cases politicization has increased while access to the political center has been severely circumscribed. The opportunities for involvement in decisionmaking have therefore varied.

Conflicts have been an integral part of the independence experience, as have the ongoing quests for national coherence. Political violence, unquestionably, has proliferated. Ethnic and nationality conflicts (in Ethiopia, Chad, Nigeria, Congo, Sudan, and Angola) persist. Civil dissension has risen in Liberia, Somalia, and Congo. Burundi and Rwanda have been plunged into the most unspeakable human tragedy. Religious riots, virtually

Table 1.2 Basic Social Characteristics of African States

	Life Expectancy at Birth 1996	Annual Growth of Population (percentage) 1989–1996	Urban Population as Percentage of Total Population 1996	Population per Physician 1990–1994	Population per hospital bed 1990–1994	Percentage of Total Primary Age Group Enrolled in School 1993–1995	Percentage of Female Primary Age Group Enrolled in School 1993–1995	Percentage of Total Secondary Age Group Enrolled in School 1993–1995
Algeria	70	2.4	56.4	1218	475	107	100	62
Angola	46	3.1	31.6	23725	774	72	—	—
Benin	55	2.9	39.2	16435	4281	72	52	16
Botswana	51	2.7	62.7	5159	635	115	117	56
Burkina Faso	46	2.8	16.4	—	3392	38	30	8
Burundi	47	2.7	7.8	17153	1519	—	—	—
Cameroon	56	2.9	45.5	11996	392	88	84	27
Cape Verde	66	2.1	55.9	4271	631	131	129	27
Central African Republic	49	2.3	39.5	25920	1140	—	—	—
Chad	48	2.5	22.5	—	1373	55	36	9
Comoros	59	2.6	31	8816	362	74	71	22
Congo (B)	51	3	59.2	15150	306	114	109	53
Congo (DRC)	53	3.2	29	3713	702	72	59	26
Cote d'Ivoire	54	3.2	44	11739	1268	69	58	23
Djibouti	50	3.4	82.3	6155	394	38	33	13
Egypt	65	2.1	44.9	546	476	100	93	74
Equatorial Guinea	50	2.3	43.4	3556	—	—	—	—
Eritrea	55	2.7	17.4	—	—	57	51	19
Ethiopia	49	2.3	15.8	35051	4141	31	24	11
Gabon	55	2.8	51.1	1998	313	142	140	—
Gambia	53	3.9	29.7	—	1639	73	67	22
Ghana	59	2.8	36.4	—	685	—	—	—
Guinea	46	2.7	29.9	6568	1816	48	34	12
Guinea-Bissau	44	2	22.1	—	671	64	47	—
Kenya	58	2.7	29.5	21970	602	85	85	24
Lesotho	58	2.2	24.8	24095	—	99	105	28
Liberia	49	2.2	45.6	—	—	—	—	—
Libya	68	2.6	85.8	934	240	110	110	—

(continues)

Table 1.2 (continued)

	Life Expectancy at Birth 1996	Annual Growth of Population (percentage) 1989–1996	Urban Population as Percentage of Total Population 1996	Population per Physician 1990–1994	Population per hospital bed 1990–1994	Percentage of Total Primary Age Group Enrolled in School 1993–1995	Percentage of Female Primary Age Group Enrolled in School 1993–1995	Percentage of Total Secondary Age Group Enrolled in School 1993–1995
Madagascar	58	2.7	27	8385	1072	72	70	14
Malawi	43	2.9	13.9	45737	645	135	128	18
Mali	50	2.8	27.4	19448	—	34	27	9
Mauritania	53	2.5	52.5	15770	1486	78	72	15
Mauritius	71	1.1	40.7	1183	325	107	106	62
Morocco	66	2	52.5	2753	898	83	71	39
Mozambique	45	3.5	35.1	—	1153	60	50	7
Namibia	56	2.7	37	4328	—	133	134	62
Niger	47	3.2	18.7	53986	—	29	22	7
Nigeria	53	2.9	40.4	5208	599	89	79	30
Rwanda	41	-0.5	5.8	31029	505	—	—	—
São Tomé and Principe	64	2.8	43.7	1885	212	—	—	—
Senegal	50	2.6	44.4	18226	1371	65	57	16
Seychelles	71	1.4	55.2	172	—	96	—	—
Sierra Leone	37	2.4	34	—	—	—	—	—
Somalia	49	1.9	26	—	1472	—	—	—
South Africa	65	1.7	49.5	—	—	117	116	84
Sudan	54	2.1	32.3	—	919	54	48	13
Swaziland	57	3.1	32	9277	—	122	119	27
Tanzania	50	3	24.9	—	1123	67	66	5
Togo	50	3.1	31.2	11395	664	118	97	27
Tunisia	70	1.9	62.6	1763	568	116	112	61
Uganda	43	3.2	12.8	—	1092	73	67	12
Zambia	44	2.9	3.3	10917	—	89	86	28
Zimbabwe	56	2.5	32.5	7384	1959	116	114	47

Source: African Development Indicators 1998/99 (Washington DC: World Bank, 1998).

unheard of in the 1960s, are in evidence today in Nigeria, which has just undergone another transition to civilian rule. Several interstate conflicts erupted in the 1980s: the Chad-Libya dispute, the Zaire (now Congo)-Angola skirmishes, and the border wars between Burkina Faso and Mali are just some examples. Most recently, Congo and Rwanda, as well as Ethiopia and Eritrea, have experienced similar tensions. In Senegal and Mauritania in 1989, mutual pogroms, primarily in the two capitals, took place against nationals of the neighboring country, followed by arrests and deportations. From a most personal point of view, in some countries individual security has been threatened. In Nigeria, highway robbery is commonplace; army units threaten public security in contemporary Congo. But violent confrontations have been less widespread than could have been expected given the multiplicity of ethnic and linguistic groups and the growing socioeconomic discrepancies apparent throughout the continent. Indeed, with a few notable exceptions, some form of national consciousness has evolved over the years. And in many countries, norms of social interaction have been formulated and a modicum of civic order established.

Socioeconomic malaise is reflective of endemic political problems. In the early postcolonial years, most African leaders, in an effort to gain control, centralized power. Kwame Nkrumah of Ghana and Ahmed Sekou Touré of Guinea were among the first leaders to establish one-party states; they were followed by most of their peers. Centralization came with the personalization of power and with a heavy reliance on bureaucratic structures. The trend toward unitary government was almost uniform in the first two decades of independence. Yet, during this period Nigeria developed a sophisticated federal system; Gambia, Botswana, and Mauritius were able to sustain multiparty politics; in the 1980s Senegal returned to competitive elections; and, more recently, close to thirty countries have experimented with measures to liberalize their regimes. These trends constitute important examples of a possible shift away from the convention of centralized nonparticipatory politics.

African leaders have also experimented with many ideologies and political philosophies. African socialism, adopted in such countries as Tanzania, Ghana, Mali, Guinea, and Zambia, proliferated in the 1960s. In the mid-1970s Afro-Marxist regimes, more closely aligned with Marxist-Leninist principles, developed in Ethiopia, Mozambique, and Angola. In the early part of the 1980s, Jerry Rawlings in Ghana and Thomas Sankara in Burkina Faso introduced an African brand of radical populism. Throughout the past thirty years democratic ideas have proliferated alongside decidedly personalistic concepts of rule, and although ideological fads have come and gone, pragmatic values have prevailed in many countries.

Ideologies aside, authoritarian politics dominated the domestic scene in the first postcolonial phase. Competition over access to and control of state resources nurtured an instrumental view of politics in which the public domain was seen as a channel for individual or partisan enrichment. Zero-sum patterns of interaction (one side's gain is another side's loss) led to the muzzling of loyal oppositions and to an intolerance of dissenting opinions. Armed resistance to incumbent governments developed in some countries (Ethiopia, Rwanda, Sudan, Zaire/Congo).

Under these conditions, the military became an important mechanism for bringing about political change. Virtually every African state has been subjected to an attempted coup. Until recently, the armed forces ruled in almost half the states of the continent. At least a third of the countries in the sub-Saharan region have had several military takeovers. The move from civilian to military rule and back again has become an essential part of the rhythm of politics in postcolonial Africa. In some countries, however—Cameroon, Zambia, Kenya, Côte d'Ivoire, Botswana, Senegal, Malawi—the army has not taken over, and some have witnessed orderly political succession. Patterns of political transition, therefore, have varied widely.

Governmental capacities have not improved markedly during these years. In many countries, top-heavy administrations run by civilian or military leaders wield very little authority, and the power of their governmental institutions has remained weak. Instability—a surface expression of a more profound inability to maintain political control—is indeed a common theme throughout the postcolonial period. It should not, however, obscure important instances of stable government nor minimize the prevalence of efforts to form meaningful frameworks for political interchange.

Perhaps the greatest achievement of African states since independence, especially in light of events in Eastern Europe in the 1990s, has been the fact that they have endured. Even in cases of apparent collapse, most notably Chad and Uganda at the beginning of the 1980s and Liberia, Rwanda, and Congo in the 1990s, governmental structures have persisted.[2] But survival has frequently not meant enhanced political efficacy. By the late 1990s, the most pressing political challenge facing African governments and citizens—forging a modus vivendi between the wielders of state power and their subjects, aligning government institutions more closely to socioeconomic processes, and regularizing state-society relations—has not been met in many countries.

The corollary of domestic political uncertainty has been greater external dependence on foreign powers and international economic agencies. The International Monetary Fund (IMF) and the World Bank have been involved in extensive operations to bail African as well as other economies out of their economic morass. But the price for this support has been the forfeiture (with some partial exceptions) of control over certain facets of economic decisionmaking, as well as growing external indebtedness and mounting social inequalities.

In these circumstances, the role of continental institutions has vacillated. The Organization of African Unity (OAU), an important pivot of inter-African relations in the late 1960s and 1970s, almost collapsed at the beginning of the 1980s. It is slowly being reorganized in an attempt to deal more directly with the problems of economic rehabilitation, but its record on crisis management has remained uneven. As gross inequalities between African states have come to the fore, many efforts at regional cooperation have stumbled. The Economic Community of West African States (ECOWAS) was in some distress twenty years after its creation in 1975. Its experiences, and those of other groupings such as the Southern African Development Community (SADC), suggest that the road to fruitful regional collaboration, however enticing, is still a long one.

The African world at the end of the 1990s is thus quite different from that at mid-century. The common trends of economic adversity, political unrest, and external dependence have evoked a variety of responses and generated a great deal of experimentation. African politics have become "dehomogenized" in the process.[3] The rules of the political game in Nigeria, Kenya, Cameroon, Côte d'Ivoire, or Zambia differ from each other and from those in Botswana, Ethiopia, or Congo. Some African countries have exhibited a remarkable stability (Côte d'Ivoire and Botswana, to name but two); others have been shaken by constant political turmoil (Uganda and Ghana). As the independence generation has withdrawn from the political scene, the surface similarities of yesteryear have given way to more readily apparent differences. The specific social makeup of each African state is putting its stamp on the politics of that country. In this sense, at least, an Africanization and localization of politics has begun to take place.

Common problems and experiences, therefore, should not obscure the fact that there is not one but many Africas. The continuity of separate heritages, coupled with different experiences and patterns of change, have worked to differentiate African states from one another.[4] Behind the general processes, therefore, it is possible to discern intricate variations that have developed over the years. We shall examine not only the achievements and failures of African politics but also the diverse political mechanisms that have evolved.

■ APPROACHES TO THE STUDY OF AFRICAN POLITICS

It is clear that there is no consensus among analysts on how to probe the complex interconnections between politics and society in Africa. Old certainties on the relevance of legal, formal-institutional (legislatures, executives, parties, judiciaries), psychocultural, and purely historical frameworks have largely disappeared, seemingly inadequate and incomplete in their insight into the new hegemonic (monolithic, state-dominant) orders that gained ascendancy at the time of independence in most of Africa. Thus, social scientists have had little alternative but to undertake a search for new conceptual frameworks that would afford a fuller insight into the dynamic processes unfolding on the continent.

In broad terms, this quest has revolved around several well-defined approaches. The first, centered on the concept of modernization, emerged in the early 1960s. Echoing the heady mood of the initial years of independence, modernization theories presented a hopeful general framework of progressive development toward "modern" statehood, conceived largely in a Western mold. By the close of the decade, however, it was apparent that these notions were at best only a partial guide to understanding the political and economic conditions prevailing on the continent. The second approach—dependency—came to the fore in the 1970s. Preoccupied with explicating the causes of Africa's underdevelopment, studies grounded in dependency analysis highlighted the external constraints imposed on African societies and focused attention on emergent class conflicts. As the somewhat grim and deterministic implications of dependency ideas became more explicit, as their theoretical limitations were realized, and as conditions in Africa reached crisis proportions, a third approach—the statist—gained currency. To comprehend the extent of the African malaise in the early 1980s, it became necessary to reassess the role of the state and to pinpoint the effects of political frailty and mismanagement.

At the present time an integrative tendency is taking shape that seeks to bring together within a broader societal framework what has been proven to be useful in the modernization, dependency, and statist conceptual frameworks. It stresses the choices that policymakers and social groups have made and the complex dynamics of their interrelationship. This framework, which we term the political interaction approach, utilizes appropriate ideas from a variety of contemporary thinkers and theories to forge an eclectic method for understanding the relations between the historical, political, social, and economic dimensions of the contemporary African experience. Our textbook is cast in this mold. By expanding the field of political vision beyond the formal and the visible to the reciprocal and dynamic, it offers additional insights into the rhythm of politics on the continent.

◼ The Modernization School

Early studies of African nationalism and African politics were written mostly from a modernization, or political development, perspective. The basic premise behind this approach was that African societies are in the process of becoming "modern" rational entities in which efficiency and scientific logic replace traditional values and belief systems. In economic terms, modernization was seen as commensurate with mechanization, rapid industrialization, and growth; in social terms, its goals were defined as increasing individual mobility, controlling the political importance of communal identities, and establishing procedures for equitable resource allocations. In political terms, modernization implied institutional expansion, the rationalization of the government apparatus, power concentration, some measure of political participation, and an augmentation of capacities in order to meet growing demands.[5] Modernization was seen as providing a foundation for African countries to achieve, first, some measure of stability and autonomy and, ultimately, a pattern of convergence with the Western industrialized world.

Modernization theories were formulated in the West and were closely related to developments in U.S. political science in the 1950s. Its analysts assumed that a focus on transformation from traditional to modern environments would lead to a generalizable theory of political development. The concerns of many of the first works on African politics, therefore, centered on one or several of the six challenges of political development that were identified as facing countries in their attempt to achieve modernization.[6] The first challenge was defined as one of identity: fostering a common sense of purpose among culturally diffuse groups.[7] The second challenge was viewed as one of legitimacy: arriving at a consensus on the valid exercise of authority (the most visible instrument for legitimation, the political party, became the object of intense research).[8] The third was that of participation, the need to guide public demands for inclusion in the decisionmaking process into constructive—and controllable—channels. The fourth was one of penetration: the quest to secure an effective government presence throughout a given territory. The fifth challenge was one of distribution: balancing the public's demand for goods and services with the government's obligations to provide such general welfare objectives as economic growth, resource mobilization, and national defense.[9] The final challenge addressed in this literature was that of integration: the creation of a coherent set of relationships among the many groups and interests competing for access and control within the new state framework.

In the modernization perspective, the task of politics was to create the conditions for equitable growth by ensuring social quiescence and stable government. If African countries faltered on this path, then surely these shortcomings could be attributed either to poor judgment, to mistaken ideologies, to the conflict between competing goals, or to an inability to overcome cultural impediments deeply rooted in African societies. When, by the mid-1960s, it was abundantly clear that many of the objectives of the modernization vision were not being fulfilled, its upholders turned their attention to isolating the sources of political inefficiency, explicating contradictions in development processes, and examining the role of the military in the political arena. They engaged, at this juncture, in documenting the manifestations of political decay.[10]

Early studies of African politics varied widely, both in terms of quality and in terms of explanatory theories. Nevertheless, they had in common a tendency to favor domestic rather than external explanations for political occurrences, and certain dominant sociocultural rather than structural and economic factors in political analysis (for this reason, they are sometimes referred to, perhaps mistakenly, as pluralist approaches). The utility of the modernization models was, however, increasingly questioned in an Africa frustrated by its incapacity to maintain previous gains, let alone progress toward the desired goals of societal betterment.

Critiques of the modernization school have clustered around several key themes. First, studies conducted within this framework could account for only a segment of the realities they sought to convey. Emphasis on industrialization, theoretically of some interest, seemed of peripheral relevance given the central role that agriculture plays in African economic life. Social change and education are undoubtedly important targets, but once again, the focus on these issues tended to overlook the ongoing roles of traditional institutions and norms. Although parties were a part of the transition to independence, more vital aspects of that political era, especially processes of bureaucratization, were frequently neglected. Social currents, inequalities, and conflicts were often glossed over. These theories of political development may, therefore, have fostered misplaced emphases and failed to reflect many crucial processes taking place on the ground.

A second set of criticisms, no less compelling, related to the priorities built into these theories. The stress on economic growth, without a concomitant delineation of the beneficiaries of this economic activity, was subjected to severe scrutiny by the late 1960s. The bias toward equilibrium and harmony was similarly challenged. The tendency of some development theories to support elitist and status quo orientations was found to be particularly troubling.[11] And the supposition that the Western model of development was both feasible and desirable smacked of a type of arrogance not easily acceptable in countries that had only recently emerged from colonial rule.

A third series of criticisms revolved around the tools of analysis generated by scholars of political development. Few instruments were designed to examine how transformations could take place or to evaluate the implications of ongoing processes. Thus, many analyses were extremely static. The external context of African politics was virtually overlooked. Issues critical to Africans, such as racial justice, pan-Africanism, negritude, and socialism, were not treated with the degree of seriousness that they deserved.[12]

In retrospect, however, modernization theories did provide a foundation for the analysis of postcolonial African politics. They helped to identify some of the principal problems faced by African political systems and nurtured a series of basic works on the dilemmas of independence.[13] But by the late 1960s, it became painfully apparent that these approaches, centered as they were on the achievement of ideal goals, did not reflect complex realities on the continent and could not keep up with the rapid and problematic pace of events. At the beginning of the second decade of independence, the search for alternative conceptual frameworks—overviews more likely to provide an intellectual challenge to an increasingly unacceptable status quo—became inevitable.

■ The Dependency and Underdevelopment Schools

Theories of dependency and underdevelopment came into vogue as a reaction both to the premises and the origins of political development theory and were based on the opposite assumption that African progress has been, and continues to be, impeded by forces (international and/or domestic) bent on the ongoing exploitation of the continent and its resources. These primarily capitalist interests could only be held at bay if the global system underwent a fundamental change that would alter the structural relations between the Third World and the industrialized world (underdevelopment) or between the masses and the dominant classes within Africa (dependency). Thus, in stark contrast to the modernization approach, these theorists have focused not on the process of development but on the roots of underdevelopment. They have shunned what they claimed to be empty objectivity in favor of an avowedly committed and activist approach and have rejected the seeming benevolence that underlies modernization analysis. They have asserted that if Africans have remained impoverished, then this condition is a result of circumstances that have enabled others to benefit at their expense.

Underdevelopment theory originated in Latin America and mirrored the Third World concerns of its designers. Dependency approaches, which contain an underdevelopment component, were rooted in neo-Marxist political theory. The tools employed by this school were quite different than those developed by the so-called pluralists. In the first place, these studies adopted a purposefully historical perspective in an effort to trace unequal relations within Africa and between the continent and the rest of the world over time. Second, the units of analysis of the dependency and underdevelopment approaches were not the individual and the state, but classes and/or the global system. Third, these studies were concerned primarily—but by no means exclusively—with the political economy. Economic structure and economic trends were highlighted, and the object of analysis moved more squarely to material matters such as trade relations, capital flows, and modes and relations of production. Finally, these analyses began with an assumption of inequality and disequilibrium. They sought to uncover the sources and illuminate the manifestations of Africa's scarcity in these terms.

In this view, the beginnings of Africa's systematic impoverishment were linked to European imperialism, which, these analysts posit, not only brought Africa into the global economy but did so in a structurally unequal manner. Colonial economic policies perpetuated this institutionalized vulnerability to external economic forces and constrained the freedom of movement of Africa's new leaders on the eve of independence.[14]

Much attention has been given to the economic factors that continue to delimit Africa's options. In brief, the present pattern of global economic relations results in asymmetrical exchange: The benefits of these ties are shared unequally between core (the industrialized center of the world economy) and periphery (the less-industrialized countries of the Third World). Because of the superior information, technological know-how, wealth, and market advantages at its disposal, the core remains at a decided advantage in its exchange encounters with the African countries in the periphery.

The question of change is consequently central to dependency theory. For Immanuel Wallerstein, "it is not possible theoretically for all states to 'develop simultaneously.'"[15] In his opinion, because global relations are closed and rigorously structured, if one country or area advances, then the progress of others must, perforce, be impeded. In fact, economic prospects in today's world may be less predetermined than such an approach would admit. Writers imbued in the more classical Marxist tradition, which influences much of the dependency literature, have suggested that capitalism is still an important precondition for the emergence of socialism and that capitalist global and domestic relations are therefore a necessary, if painful, step in the process of transformation.

Whatever their approach to change, dependency and underdevelopment theorists have viewed politics as a reflection of global and economic relations. Explanations for political actions have been couched in historical and material terms. Political analyses shifted from the domestic to the international and from the idiosyncratic to the structural. In contrast to modernization approaches, then, dependency and underdevelopment theories present politics in terms of resources and control rather than management.

Dependency theory has furnished potent insights into the nature of constraints on African development. Its vitality lies, first and foremost, in the importance it attributes to external factors in the explication of Africa's present predicament. By highlighting international structural variables, dependency analysts have placed specific policy actions in proper perspective. The second strength of this approach rests in its insistence on studying politics within a socioeconomic context. It has effectively outlined some historical, economic, and external limitations that operate in the African political environment. Third, dependency and underdevelopment theories have, relentlessly and accurately, illuminated the premise of inequality that underlies African political activity. Such theories have, therefore, added important dimensions to the analysis of African politics, even if they have not been accepted as a guiding theoretical framework, but have succumbed to severe criticisms from both Marxist and non-Marxist scholars.

The first weakness of underdevelopment theory (but not necessarily of its dependency counterpart) stems from the uniformity it imposed on the study of contemporary Africa. The distinction between exploiters and exploited, core and periphery, good and evil, did not always permit refined analyses of variations, degrees, and specific trends and patterns. Dependency scholars, in response to such criticism, spawned a growing literature on the meaning of various kinds of bourgeoisies. Studies of the peasantry came into vogue.[16] Arguments about precapitalist, capitalist, and mixed modes of production raged. But insufficient attention was devoted to the determined nationalism of many African leaders, to the ongoing significance of ethnicity, or to the intricacies of the political upheavals that engaged the continent during the course of the 1970s and 1980s. As a result, even the analysis of foreign relations frequently lacked finesse: There developed an inability to identify the changing patterns of links between African states and specific countries in the industrialized world. Thus, although it highlighted previously neglected factors in the study of African politics, dependency theory nevertheless remained aloof from many of the significant processes taking place on the continent. Its adherents' grasp of African realities was as skewed, albeit for very different reasons, as that of the modernization writers whom they treated with such contempt.

A second major difficulty with the dependency and underdevelopment schools relates directly to their assessments of African futures. Although it successfully dispelled the false optimism of the modernization approach, dependency theory has been almost uniformly pessimistic in its evaluation of the prospects for the continent (an anomaly, given the reformist thrust of its practitioners). In this view, Africa is entrapped in a morass not of its own making, and from which it is virtually incapable of extricating itself.[17] Barring revolution or total global structural transformation, dependency theory provided precious few indications of possible guidelines for action in local arenas. By dichotomizing conflicts and envisaging outcomes in static terms, this mode of thinking has had the effect of limiting choice, even at the margins.

A third criticism stems directly from the fact that underdevelopment notions are fundamentally atheoretical and also, quite surprisingly, apolitical. Dependency ideas possess greater explanatory power but have sacrificed a close study of ongoing events and processes in favor of debates over theory. African political processes are external in their derivation, execution, and implications. By removing autonomy from African actors, this approach inevitably stymies analytic growth and forecloses further inquiry. In this respect, the work of some dependency analysts, returning to more detailed research in the Marxist mold, has remained closer to the African experience.[18]

Hence, for quite different reasons and in very different ways, both the dependency and underdevelopment schools, although pointing to significant trends, have been unable either to advance significantly the understanding of the complexities of Africa's present predicament or to trace accurately the dynamics of the processes the continent experienced in the 1990s.

■ The Statist School

Both the underdevelopment and the modernization schools have undergone considerable internal revision since the late 1970s. The modernization school has taken external and historical factors into consideration in its analyses, underdevelopment scholars have become more sensitized to the importance of internal sociocultural forces, and dependency theorists have moved from abstract debates to the application of models in the field.[19] By the late 1970s, therefore, both Marxist and liberal researchers, working from parallel, albeit inverted, paradigms, made an attempt to reorient their work so that it would focus more squarely on specific processes occurring within Africa. They were joined by a group of (mostly African) scholars who concentrated on studying African events from an African nationalist point of view.[20] These efforts began to yield a wealth of new material that, significantly, converged on one central aspect: the importance of the state and state actions in grasping the roots of the political and economic crises of the third decade of independence. What emerged as a result is a third, coldly realistic and Africa-centric school of analysis.

In the statist approach to the study of African politics, the state is viewed as a primary motor force behind social and economic occurrences on the continent, and state leaders are held responsible for the political and economic deterioration of the early 1980s. Unlike its predecessors, the modernization and dependency schools, and in contrast to ongoing materialist studies, this school has broken out of existing molds and placed political factors at the center of investigation and analysis. For scholars working within this framework, state structures are the key to coming to grips with contemporary African processes.

Those writing in this mode have concentrated on studying the state apparatus, its expansion, its uses (and abuses) of power, and its relations with domestic groups and the international economy.[21] They have presumed that the state is more than a descriptive entity; that it is an actor with interests, capacities, achievements and, of course, frailties. These analysts do see the postcolonial state as autonomous, at least to some extent, and hence as an entity in its own right.

Political scientists working within this framework have sought to uncover the characteristics of African states in the independence period. They have studied patterns of institutionalization, examined leadership styles, and devoted a great deal of attention to isolating the mechanisms of patron-client relations and identifying patterns of personal rule. The trends highlighted by writers in this school are of no mean consequence: The gradual enfeeblement of the state apparatus in many parts of Africa has been noted, as have the repressive predilections that have accompanied the reduction of systemic power.

The concept of politics that emerges from these studies is extremely instrumental. Power holders, it is claimed, have created structures of domination that have enabled them to misuse their offices to reap personal gains at the expense of the pressing needs of the bulk of the population. If Africa is undergoing a process of impoverishment, then the leaders of the new states bear much of the blame for this state of affairs. The food crisis of the early 1980s, the debt crisis of the mid-1980s, the civil wars of the 1990s, and the ensuing crisis of governability are the outcome of an extractive view of politics that has guided African ruling classes for over a generation.[22] The neo-patrimonial statists have thus combined the domestic emphasis of modernization theory and elements of the structural and external analysis of dependency theory to depict a view of Africa that is simultaneously well documented and brutal.

The main contribution of the statist approach has been its stress on the inner workings of power politics within Africa. Nevertheless, the structural statist framework has not been able to come to terms with some issues that are central to its overall thrust. The definition and conceptualization of the state has proven to be elusive, and the distinction between it and specific governments frequently confused. State-society relations have not been studied with the precision they warrant. The relationship of state, class, and ethnicity, especially when the state is in disrepair, is still obscure. What is more problematic is that the emphasis on personal rule and systems of domination has hampered a close analysis of the role of the state in the actual (and not just the formal) political economy. The limits of state power have yet to be defined and its relative economic and social significance adequately assessed.

The statist approach has, therefore, somewhat ironically, highlighted the external supports and the personal character of the postcolonial African state at the expense of a closer analysis of state organization and interactions with other social institutions. Although patrimonial relations and authority structures have been scrutinized at some length, the connection between public institutions and specific social groups has yet to be fully explored. Indeed, statist analysts have generated innovative and significant questions; their somewhat deterministic outlooks do not shed much light on African trends in the years to come.

The focus on the state in patrimonial terms just when the state in Africa may be undergoing significant changes highlights a problem common to all schools of political analysis in Africa: the propensity of political scientists to employ a top-down approach to the study of politics on the continent. Political processes and political conflicts have been interpreted as revolving exclusively around formal state structures, either separately or in their international context. Politics in Africa (as elsewhere), however, cannot be reduced so easily to the activities of actors on the national scene. State institutions intersect with nonformal structures: social organizations relate, or do not interact, with governments depending on changing conditions; and power constellations are not entirely state-centric. A new synthesis, which builds on the strengths of previous approaches and, at the same time, goes beyond the weaknesses they have exhibited, has slowly begun to take shape.

■ THE POLITICAL INTERACTION FRAMEWORK

This synthesis, which casts the political net widely to capture the choices that people actually do face, goes beyond the limitations of existing schools of thought, each of which contains important insights developed at various points in Africa's recent history, and attempts to concentrate more directly on the complex processes and factors at work on the continent.[23] We call this analytic framework, which is by no means a separate school, a political interaction perspective.

This framework presumes that the state-society relationship is central to understanding the political dynamic of Africa today. Individuals and governments are constrained by a variety of demographic, technological, ideological, global, historical, and social factors. Changing conditions define available options at any given historical moment.[24] It is within this range that decisions are made, not only by political leaders and state officials, but also by external actors and domestic social organizations. By looking at the interaction of social forces, economic activities, formal institutions, and prevalent values, we may better grasp the meaning and direction of the diverse patterns that have evolved in Africa since independence.

The political interaction approach, therefore, focuses on identifying the multiple factors at work on the African political scene and tracing their diverse dynamics over time. Those adopting this perspective commence their inquiry with an examination of the key components of African politics, assuming that its sphere is far broader than the formal state domain and the international state system. Official institutions, as in the statist approach, are, indeed, significant actors, but so too are individuals, social groups, traditional authority structures, trading networks, and multinational corporations. The study of the interests, organization, and capacities of these entities affords a better view of the processes by which they interrelate. Political competition encompasses struggles over material and normative resources, over identity and interests, over institutions and symbols.

Power—the capacity to control these valued goods—and authority—the right to do so—may legitimately be vested in a variety of structures. Power vectors and the search for empowerment take on different meanings in this context. Structure and process are a precondition for understanding outcomes: economic policies and circumstances, social dynamics, and foreign relations. By studying the many dimensions of political interaction and modes of interchange, it may be possible to trace more accurately shifting political patterns in Africa and their ramifications for social and economic processes and political options in the years to come.

In the political interaction framework, political factors account for many social and economic realities but are themselves informed by historical, demographic, cultural, ecological, ideological, and international factors. Politics are, therefore, perceived as a set of transactions, the manifestation of the exercise of choice by multiple actors within existing parameters. This perspective, unlike the managerial view of the modernization school, the exploitative emphasis of dependency approaches, and the instrumental notions of statist writers, highlights the fluidity of politics and attempts to trace the vacillating political course. Thus, although this research strategy, through its focus on the diversity of civil society, may together with existing theories help to account for the changing fortunes of many countries on the continent, it is less concerned with assessing the reasons for past errors than with uncovering the components of ongoing processes and elucidating future opportunities, constraints, and patterns.

■ The Constraints on Choice

The world of African politics and political interaction is delimited by constraints imposed by the environment and history. Some of the most fundamental limitations to which African countries are subject arise from their geographical location in the tropics. Tropical climates affect all parts of Africa except the Republic of South Africa and the Mediterranean countries north of the Sahara. As Andrew Kamarck suggests, sub-Saharan Africa may be divided into three distinct tropical climatic zones.[25] A belt of wet tropical climates extends across the coastal states of the Gulf of Guinea through Congo to the highlands of Uganda and Kenya; it also includes parts of the coasts of Kenya, Mozambique, and Tanzania. These areas usually have annual rainfalls of between 75 and 120 inches (187 and 300 cm) per year; rain typically falls in all months. Constant heat and extreme humidity are common. In contrast, a dry tropical climatic belt stretches across the continent from Mauritania to northern Sudan. Here, rainfall is irregular at best and insufficient to support agriculture. Between these two belts is a zone (from Gambia through Somalia) characterized by alternate wet and dry climates. There is considerable variation within this zone, not only between different areas, but also from one year to the next.

Unpredictability, in fact, is one of the principal characteristics of all tropical climates and one of their major constraining features. Rainfall from one year to the next frequently varies by as much as 300 percent and typically falls in torrents in concentrated periods; occasionally, no rain comes at all.

No place in these three zones of sub-Saharan Africa, except the high est mountain ranges, experiences frost—nature's great executioner. In consequence, pests and diseases proliferate. Fungi are a particularly acute agricultural problem given the humid climate. African countries are frequently victims of locust plagues. Tsetse flies not only have prevented the introduction of cattle and of animal traction in many parts of the continent but also carry the deadly disease trypanosomiasis (a principal form of which is sleeping sickness). This illness debilitates victims, prevents individuals from engaging in sustained strenuous activity, and eventually results in early death. Other diseases to which African populations are particularly vulnerable include malaria, schistosomiasis (a parasitic infestation with approximately 200 million sufferers), onchocerciasis (river blindness, from which approximately 20 million suffer), leprosy (which affects 4 million people in Africa), and, most recently, AIDS, especially in East and central Africa (although the disease is spreading throughout the continent). Attempts at eradication have made few inroads into the incidence of the diseases, all of which considerably reduce the human productive potential of the continent.

A further ecological constraint on Africa's development is poor tropical soils. Rich soil is dependent upon living organisms to provide humus. In tropical climates the heat of the sun tends to kill these organisms. Heavy tropical rains destroy the particle structure of the topsoil, which is then eroded by strong winds. As a result, the main plant foods in the soil are removed, leaving a clay (laterite) that hardens on exposure to air and sun. In many parts of Africa the soil is inadequate to sustain permanent agriculture.

Proliferation of pests and diseases has inhibited attempts to improve African livestock and plants through crossbreeding with imports from overseas (which have proved to be especially vulnerable to local diseases). The multitude of species and of climatic zones has also made agricultural research more difficult than has been the case in temperate areas, which enjoy greater uniformity of soils and climates. Africans, then, are faced by ecological constraints that are far more severe than those in most Western countries.

Africa has traditionally been a continent of sparse population. This has had profound impact on its economic evolution. Most economic historians are agreed that population pressure has been an enormously important factor in stimulating invention and new modes of productive activity. In most parts of Africa until the last quarter of this century, land has been plentiful, and population pressure provided little stimulus toward an agricultural revolution. This demographic pattern has also had a profound impact on economic and political structures. Many African countries remain—by Western European and Asian standards—underpopulated. Distances between settlements are great, which increases the costs of delivery of government services and communications. Underpopulation also means that domestic markets in most countries are small (the principal exception is Nigeria, with its population estimated at more than 100 million; only nine other sub-Saharan African countries—Congo, Ethiopia, Ghana, Kenya, Mozambique, South Africa, Sudan, Tanzania, and Uganda—have populations in excess of 15 million).

Yet, although the continent's total population is relatively low, the population growth rate is the highest in the world. Improved health care has greatly lowered infant mortality, but families have not responded by reducing the number of children that they desire. The average African woman will bear seven children. Population grew in sub-Saharan Africa in the period from 1965 to 1980 by 2.7 percent per year; in the 1980s and 1990s, the average population growth rose to 3.2 percent per year. Aggregate figures, however, obscure significant differences across the continent: some countries are already experiencing dramatically higher rates of growth. In Kenya, for instance, the population grew until quite recently at roughly 4 percent annually, with the consequence that the country's total population has more than doubled since independence. In order merely to sustain existing levels of per capita incomes, African economies will have to achieve exceptionally high rates of economic growth.

▪ Historical Inheritance

The constraints of the environment have been compounded by those of history. The newly independent states of Africa, despite their many differences, shared a common and troubled inheritance at the point of transition from colonial rule. The first, most obvious, and profound characteristic of Africa on the eve of independence was the artificiality of its political boundaries. The political map of present-day Africa was carved out by European countries during the scramble for Africa in the late nineteenth and early twentieth centuries. Since the European powers assembled at the Congress of Berlin in 1884–1885 to delineate spheres of influence and lay down the ground rules for imperial expansion, the political frontiers of Africa have undergone only minor adjustments. The African state system is therefore a product of external logic, and it primarily reflects the ambitions and capabilities of European powers rather than any geographical or social realities of the African continent.

African countries vary drastically in terms of their economic resource base, demographic composition, and potential for development. Chad, Niger, and Mali, for example, are sparsely populated, landlocked states containing large stretches of desert; they do not have the access to the sea, the strong population concentrations, or the vibrant local economies of South Africa or Côte d'Ivoire. Tiny Gambia cannot but be affected by the shadow of its larger neighbor, Senegal. In Burkina Faso poverty prevails, whereas mineral-rich Gabon boasts the highest per capita income in the sub-Saharan region. These units are the uneasy products of arbitrary foreign interventions.

The second shared legacy of Africa on the eve of independence is associated with the first: The new states of Africa contain a multiplicity of societies whose institutions predate the colonial intrusion. The indigenous African inheritance is a rich one. The great empires of Ghana, Mali, and Songhai in the western Sudan flourished during the medieval period and controlled the trans-Saharan trade routes for many centuries. At the same time, in southern Africa political authority was sufficiently centralized to oversee the construction of the magnificent stone edifices of Zimbabwe. Migrants from the Nile Valley established the early lacustrine kingdoms in East Africa, and the Hausa city-states of northern Nigeria were already well in place before Europeans first reached the African coast. More centralized entities proliferated in the sixteenth and seventeenth centuries: the forest states of West Africa (most notably Asante, Dahomey, Oyo, and Benin), the Kongo empire, the Lozi and Barotse states in central Africa, and the Mwenomutapa in present-day Mozambique.

When the Europeans arrived in Africa, they encountered indigenous states alongside well-organized segmentary societies with no overarching leadership structures (for example the Kikuyu and the Igbo). These groups had long established patterns of interaction within their own cultural settings and with their more elaborately structured neighbors. The colonial conquest disrupted these flows. The new boundaries not only divided existing political entities but, more significantly, compelled groups that frequently had no history of ongoing ties to relate to each other. The very plural composition of the colonial units was, in many instances, subsequently nurtured by the administration. As a result, African states at independence were socially amorphous and frequently severly divided; the structures of the colonial state superseded but did not displace the complex social, cultural, and political institutions of indigenous Africa.

The continuity of African institutions need not, however, obscure certain important influences of the colonial presence. The third historical constraint on African countries on the eve of independence was the burden of economic weakness. Colonial rule was accompanied by the systematic introduction of economic changes. Cash cropping altered the agricultural base of African economies. Although most rural dwellers continued to produce for subsistence needs and local markets, farmers began to grow for export as well. Groundnuts in Senegal, cotton in northern Nigeria, sisal in Tanganyika (Tanzania), cocoa in the Gold Coast (Ghana) and western

Nigeria, and tea and coffee in Kenya and Uganda brought African producers into the cash economy. The transformation of rural Africa came together with the growth of urban services, transportation facilities, and petty manufacturing. The colonial economies were, however, malintegrated. Heavy investments in the small export sector came at the expense of the underdeveloped and largely ignored indigenous economies in which most Africans operated. Taxation, forced labor, and a variety of levies affected virtually everyone. Those outside the money economy felt the economic strain of colonial rule but did not always share in its benefits. At the termination of the colonial era, economic resources—human, capital, technological—were still scarce. These constraints were accompanied, at the end of the phase of direct foreign administration, by the additional onus of severe structural inequalities.

African economies at the end of the colonial period were not only weak, they were also exposed. The fourth legacy for Africa at this conjuncture was a history of external dependence. The conquest of Africa in the nineteenth century underlined the continent's global vulnerability. Its uneven development in the early part of the twentieth century reflected the interventions of external economic interests and colonial administrators. During the brief period of colonial domination, African territories were first brought into the world economy and then systematically subordinated to the needs of the industrialized north. The colonial experience rendered African economies particularly open to external shocks. Political independence did not alleviate this external reliance. Decolonization marked the termination of responsibility for the day-to-day affairs of African territories; it by no means implied the cessation of foreign influence. The new states of Africa were, and in most instances still are, internationally weak. They have little room to maneuver in the global arena. Like all weak states, they suffered, to one degree or another, from an inability to design their futures independent of foreign considerations.

This external dependence was compounded by a fifth inheritance: the creation within African states of a small, Western-educated elite quite distinct from the bulk of the population. European colonialism came to Africa together with Christianity and formal education. Each colonial power, in its own way, developed a local stratum that could provide the personnel necessary to carry out the imperatives of external rule. Educational institutions helped to transmit much-needed skills and to lay the foundations for the development of human resources capable of managing the multiple needs of societies in the process of rapid change. Colonial education, although introducing new criteria for social mobility, was highly selective. In French West Africa, postprimary education was the domain of a select few. In Ghana, which boasted some of the finest educational institutions in Africa, more than 70 percent of the population was illiterate on the eve of independence. The Belgian Congo had almost no university graduates when Belgian authorities withdrew hastily in 1960.

Those Africans fortunate enough to acquire a Western education were drawn to the colonial centers and subsisted at its margins. Many became the core of the postcolonial civil service. Others established positions in business and the professions. They enjoyed European salaries and lifestyles. It is not insignificant that they were disproportionately represented in the anticolonial movements that proliferated after World War II. The new elites became the direct inheritors of the colonial mantle. They were, however, too few to have a forceful impact on their surroundings, too different to have strong roots in their society, and too bound to Western institutions to undertake a significant transformation of their environment. In the social realm, much as in the economic, the colonial experience offered new opportunities while simultaneously curtailing the prospects for their realization.

This pattern was especially pronounced in the political and administrative spheres. The sixth historical legacy for African countries at independence was the fragility of their state institutions. The colonial framework was not only alien, it was also underdeveloped. The administrative apparatus of the colonial state was the minimum necessary to ensure a semblance of control. The British, French, Belgian, and Portuguese authorities, in very different ways, encouraged an institutional dualism that has in many cases survived to the present day. Mechanisms for the extraction of resources were refined, those for distribution rudimentary. Military and police forces were everywhere carefully elaborated as instruments of rule; participation in political life was actively discouraged. Thus although the colonial state was highly centralized, its apparatus was not necessarily suited to the needs of independence.

At independence, African countries also displayed a seventh, and particularly burdensome, inheritance: the absence of a shared political culture.[26] Colonial rule, although it varied in intensity, severity, and intrusiveness from one part of Africa to another, was fundamentally authoritarian. Government was imposed but not participatory, instructive rather than consultative. In French-speaking West Africa and throughout most of English-speaking Africa, where the transition to independence was relatively smooth, Western-styled democratic constitutions were designed on the eve of the transfer of power. These efforts to democratize Africa stood in stark contrast to the authoritarian patterns of government laid down during colonial rule. They were also introduced just as protest against foreign domination peaked. Many of the leaders of the anticolonial movements had neither the tools nor the time to guide their followers through the complex move from defiance to constructive interaction.

The task of these leaders was further complicated by the fact that they stood at the head of relatively weak political parties that had only recently been established. Not one major governing party at independence had been formed prior to World War II. If the colonial administrative apparatus evoked resistance, the new parties provided quite feeble alternative rallying

of action since independence have been limited and that unpredictability increases the complexity of decisions. Economic scarcity, fragile institutions, ambiguous power networks, structural dependence, and gross inequalities have severely circumscribed the range of maneuverability within the African political domain. Nevertheless, political occurrences reflect what people choose to do in a world not of their own making. They also shed light on the persistent search for relevant and effective ways of preserving human dignity and advancing the quest for meaningful development. Political interaction thus highlights the challenge inherent in the African world at the beginning of the twenty-first century: the need to exercise imagination and ingenuity in unraveling priorities and designing options for societies under pressure. The dynamics of power in Africa have been recalcitrant to existing conceptual approaches. The new synthetic perspective offered in these pages is built on substantial research; with it, we seek to extend the understanding of Africa since independence.

The attempt to come to terms with the constraints and diversity of African political processes is at the heart of this undertaking. Heterogeneity and complexity in conditions of uncertainty have marked the recent history of the continent. This theme underlies key events and patterns and provides the critical framework within which ongoing processes are unfolding. The difficult and compelling realities of Africa furnish the subject matter and the challenge now facing the continent and its inhabitants.

■ NOTES

1. An excellent overview may be found in Richard Sandbrook, *The Politics of Africa's Economic Stagnation* (Cambridge: Cambridge University Press, 1985), esp. pp. 1–62.

2. Robert H. Jackson and Carl G. Rosberg, "Why Africa's Weak States Persist: The Empirical and the Judicial in Statehood," World Politics 35, no. 1 (1982): 1–25, offer external explanations for this durability. Other interpretations also have been suggested: see Donald Rothchild and Naomi Chazan, eds., *The Precarious Balance: State and Society in Africa* (Boulder: Westview Press, 1988).

3. Roger Charlton, "Dehomogenising the Study of African Politics—The Case of Inter-State Influence on Regime Formation and Change," *Plural Societies* 14, no. 1/2 (1983): 32–48.

4. Richard Hodder-Williams, *An Introduction to the Politics of Tropical Africa* (London: George Allen and Unwin, 1984), is insistent on this point.

5. For some overviews of this literature, see Richard A. Higgott, *Political Development Theory: The Contemporary Debate* (London: Croom Helm, 1983), and Samuel P. Huntington, "The Change to Change: Modernization, Development and Politics," *Comparative Politics* 4, no. 3 (1971): 55–79. For a critical discussion, see Irene L. Gendzier, *Managing Political Change: Social Scientists and the Third World* (Boulder: Westview Press, 1985).

6. Leonard Binder et al., *Crises and Sequences in Political Development* (Princeton: Princeton University Press, 1971). In this text, the term "challenges" is preferred to "crises."

7. For two examples, see Ronald Cohen and John Middleton, eds., *From Tribe to Nation in Africa: Studies in Incorporation Processes* (Scranton, PA: Chandler Publishing, 1970), and Leo Kuper and M.G. Smith, eds., *Pluralism in Africa* (Berkeley: University of California Press, 1971).

8. For a good summary of this literature, see Aristide Zolberg, *Creating Political Order: The Party States of West Africa* (Chicago: Rand McNally, 1966).

9. For one example, see Roger Genoud, *Nationalism and Economic Development in Ghana* (New York: Praeger, 1969).

10. This term was promulgated by Samuel P. Huntington. See his *Political Order in Changing Societies* (New Haven: Yale University Press, 1968) and "Political Development and Political Decay," *World Politics* 17, no. 3 (1965): 386–430.

11. See Huntington, *Political Order in Changing Societies*, for one example of these tendencies.

12. Richard Sandbrook, "The Crisis in Political Development Theory," *Journal of Development Studies* 12, no. 2 (1976): 165–185.

13. Some of the most notable examples of these early studies include: Aristide Zolberg, *One Party Government in the Ivory Coast* (Princeton: Princeton University Press, 1964); James S. Coleman, *Nigeria: Background to Nationalism* (Berkeley: University of California Press, 1958); Ruth Schachter Morgenthau, *Political Parties in French-Speaking Africa* (London: Oxford University Press, 1964); Crawford Young, *Politics in the Congo* (Princeton: Princeton University Press, 1965).

14. Theotonio Dos Santos, "The Structure of Dependence," in Charles K. Wilbert, ed., *The Political Economy of Development and Underdevelopment* (New York: Random House, 1973), p. 109.

15. Immanuel Wallerstein, "Dependence in an Interdependent World," *African Studies Review* 17, no. 1 (1974): 7. Also see Walter Rodney, *How Europe Underdeveloped Africa* (Washington, DC: Howard University Press, 1974).

16. For a good collection of such essays, see Dennis L. Cohen and John Daniel, eds., *Political Economy of Africa: Selected Readings* (London: Longman, 1981).

17. For a good critique, see Tony Smith, "The Underdevelopment of Development Literature," *World Politics* 31, no. 2 (1979).

18. See, for some examples, Nicola Swainson, *The Development of Corporate Capitalism in Kenya 1918–1977* (Berkeley: University of California Press, 1980); Colin Leys, *Underdevelopment in Kenya* (Berkeley: University of California Press, 1974); and John Saul, *The State and Revolution in Eastern Africa* (New York: Monthly Review Press, 1979).

19. This more careful revision of existing approaches is apparent, for example, in such works as Crawford Young, *Ideology and Development in Africa* (New Haven: Yale University Press, 1982), and Sara Berry, *Fathers Work for Their Sons: Accumulation, Mobility and Class Formation in an Extended Yoruba Community* (Berkeley: University of California Press, 1985). Also see Frederick Cooper, "Africa and the World Economy," *African Studies Review* 24, no. 2/3 (1981): 1–86.

20. Ali A. Mazrui and Michael Tidy, *Nationalism and New States in Africa* (London: Heinemann, 1984).

21. The most sophisticated analysis in this approach may be found in Thomas M. Callaghy, *The State-Society Struggle: Zaire in Comparative Perspective* (New York: Columbia University Press, 1984). Also see Christopher Clapham, *Third World Politics: An Introduction* (Madison: University of Wisconsin Press, 1985), and Sandbrook, *The Politics of Africa's Economic Stagnation*. For a general collection see Peter B. Evans, Dietrich Reuschemeyer, and Theda Skoçpol, eds.,

Bringing the State Back In (New York: Cambridge University Press, 1985). Also, for a more patrimonial view, see Robert H. Jackson and Carl G. Rosberg, *Personal Rule in Black Africa: Prince, Autocrat, Prophet, Tyrant* (Berkeley: University of California Press, 1984).

22. For some general examples, see Ken C. Koteka and Robert W. Adams, *The Corruption of Power: African Politics* (Washington, DC: University Press of America, 1981), and Henry Bretton, *Power and Politics in Africa* (Chicago: Aldine Publishing, 1973). Also see Patrick Chabal, ed., *Political Domination in Africa* (London: Cambridge University Press, 1986); and William Reno's concept of the "shadow state" in his *Corruption and State Politics in Sierra Leone* (Cambridge: Cambridge University Press, 1995) and his discussion of extraction via warlordism in *Warlord Politics and African States* (Boulder: Lynne Rienner, 1998).

23. Donald Rothchild and Robert L. Curry, Jr., *Scarcity, Choice and Public Policy in Middle Africa* (Berkeley: University of California Press, 1978). See also Robert Bates, "Agrarian Politics," in Myron Weiner and Samuel P. Huntington, eds., *Understanding Political Development* (Boston: Little, Brown, 1987), pp. 160–195, for a collective choice approach, which is based on somewhat different premises.

24. Myron Weiner, "Introduction," in Weiner and Huntington, *Understanding Political Development*, p. xxviii.

25. Andrew M. Kamarck, *The Tropics and Economic Development* (Baltimore: Johns Hopkins University Press, 1976), Chapter 2.

26. This point is highlighted in William Tordoff, *Government and Politics in Africa* (Bloomington: Indiana University Press, 1984), pp. 2–3.

27. Ali A. Mazrui, *The African Condition: A Political Diagnosis* (London: Cambridge University Press, 1980).

28. Adrian Leftwich, *Redefining Politics* (London: Routledge and Kegan Paul, 1983), pp. 26–27. Also see Richard A. Higgott, "From Modernization Theory to Public Policy: Continuity and Change in the Political Science of Political Development," *Studies in Cooperative International Development* 5, no. 4 (1987): pp. 26–57.

Part I

THE STRUCTURES OF POLITICS

2

State Institutions and the Organization of the Public Arena

In the first part of this book we examine the types of organizations devised by Africans at various levels to mobilize themselves, their allies, and their resources to deal with their constantly changing surroundings, and we introduce the basic concepts of contemporary African politics: state, social groups, ethnicity, and class. Who are the main political actors in Africa today? What interests do they have and what resources do they control? How are they structured? In what ways are they connected? And what are their capabilities and their weaknesses? In Chapter 2 we focus on the consolidation and alteration of formal government institutions, and in Chapter 3 we deal with the structures of social and economic life. Because state and society are analytical categories that intersect and frequently overlap, Chapter 4 is devoted specifically to the investigation of the many forms of state-society relations that have evolved in Africa in the postcolonial period. These relationships provide the basis for understanding how decisions are made, why certain policies are adopted, how they affect various groups, and with what results.

Politics in Africa take place most obviously, though hardly exclusively, in and around the associations and agencies that make up the state. The organization of the public domain has an important bearing on political, social, and economic processes and is itself affected and molded by these forces. The discussion of political structures in contemporary Africa begins, therefore, with an analysis of formal institutions and the changes they have undergone in recent years.

In this chapter we explore the ways in which the institutional frameworks of governance have been shaped and used since independence. First, we briefly examine different approaches to the study of the state and state institutions; second, we survey the institutional legacy of the colonial period; third, we look at the various constructions of the public arena immediately after the transfer of power and trace the changes that have been introduced since then; fourth, we assess some emerging patterns of state organization and offer explanations for these configurations; and, finally, we discuss some of the implications of these processes for political interactions and policymaking in various parts of the continent. Almost all African countries followed a course of centralization and bureaucratic expansion in the first few years of independence, effectively excluding most social groups from participation in public affairs. Why did this authoritarian thrust develop? What impact has it had on the ability of formal agencies to penetrate society and to carry out policy successfully? Who has benefited from these arrangements? What are the prospects for their alteration?

Despite the overwhelming propensity toward statism (the concentration of political, economic, and social activity around the state), various leaders chose to structure the public domain in different ways. The pattern of state organization that developed in Côte d'Ivoire and Kenya, for example, has not been identical to that favored by the Tanzanian government. The type of patrimonial politics (authority placed in a leader, rather than in legally backed structures) devised by Mobutu Sese Seko in Zaire (now Congo) differed substantially from the party-centric national organizations developed in the then Afro-Marxist states of Angola and Mozambique in the first fifteen years of their independence. The varieties of states that have evolved have had important repercussions on the capacities of public institutions: The nature and extent of state consolidation (stateness) on the continent vary markedly from Cameroon and Côte d'Ivoire, on the one hand, to Chad and Uganda, on the other. Understanding the forms of official organization provides essential insights into the channels and types of political and socioeconomic interchange.

■ THE CONCEPT OF THE STATE IN AFRICA

The concept of the state is inevitably elusive. Although most observers of Africa have employed the term freely, they have differed considerably in their interpretation of its significance and its main characteristics. Despite the fact that state structures and agencies generally had deep roots in African society in the precolonial and the colonial periods, and that central state institutions were the object of conflict and struggle during decolonization, observers paid little attention during the first years of independence to the state or to state organs. Indeed, during most of the 1960s, the African state was virtually ignored. The state was perceived as an arena of sovereignty, of territoriality, and perhaps of nation-building, but it was not seen as an interconnected set of institutions with an existence of its own. Studies of parties, ideologies, and even of the civil service were carried out separately, and little effort was made to grasp the state as a critical actor in the public domain.[1]

In the 1970s, the importance of the state was recognized, at least in part, by those who viewed these institutions as agents in the global arena. At this juncture, the state was conceptualized (and refined) as an instrument of capitalist exploitation.[2] The close connections between class formation, capitalism, and the character of the state in Africa generated a variety of social definitions of African states. Because the state was perceived as synonymous with the ruling class, special emphasis was placed on understanding the process of class formation, its characteristics, and its implications.[3]

Neo-Marxist scholars pioneered the effort, in the late 1970s, to dissociate the state from the ruling class by pointing out that although there is an affinity between the state and dominant groups, the two terms are hardly coterminous.[4] Thus, state institutions may reflect and in fact even produce social forces and conflicts; they are, however, quite clearly distinct empirically. This shift in emphasis occurred at the same time as other scholars began to take a renewed interest in public structures, their functions, and their capacities.

Throughout the recent literature there is substantial agreement on the definition of the state as "the organized aggregate of relatively permanent institutions of governance."[5] The state is seen as a set of associations and agencies claiming control over defined territories and their populations.[6] The main components of the state are, consequently, decisionmaking structures (executives, parties, parliaments), decision-enforcing institutions (bureaucracies, parastatal organizations, and security forces), and decision-mediating bodies (primarily courts, tribunals, and investigatory commissions). The precise character and capacities of the state in any particular country are determined by the pattern of organization of these institutions at specific points in time.

The definition of the state as an institutionalized legal order separates this notion, conceptually, from those of regime and government. The structures of the state, through the organization of people and resources and the establishment of policy outlines and priorities, are essentially institutions of power. From Max Weber on, the state has been viewed as a set of instruments of domination. Regime, in contrast, refers to the rules, principles, norms, and modes of interaction between social groups and state organs.[7] The concept of regime is, therefore, concerned with the form of rule. It deals with how political relations are carried out, with the procedures and mechanisms of political exchange. If the idea of the state is associated primarily with the organization of power, regime focuses on how state power is exercised and legitimated. Government, in turn, relates to the specific occupants of public office who are in a position to make binding decisions at any given time.[8] State, regime, and government may or

structures. Indeed, in no African state was an entirely new set of government bodies constructed at independence. Rather, those institutions perpetuating formalized political competition within the ruling coalition were reshaped or eradicated, whereas those that enhanced central leadership were sustained and elaborated.

The first step in this process revolved around limiting the opportunities for opposition. Shortly after securing political power, the new rulers moved in a determined manner to dismantle many of the constitutional protections put in place at the time of independence. One way to curb opposition was to emasculate quasi-federal provisions in preindependence constitutions. In Kenya, Uganda, and Ghana the new leaders denounced regionalism and regional structures, claiming that these not only hindered national unity but also that their acceptance prior to independence was an expedient that was no longer tolerable. Thus, the Nkrumah government reduced the regional (middle) tier of government to a purely advisory position:

> It would be wasteful, cumbersome and altogether unsound administratively [argued government spokesmen] to have in the proposed local government structure another tier, in the form of Regional Assemblies, where would be exercised powers and functions which have normally been exercised by local authorities. This would mean taking a retrograde step and departing from the principle which the Government has always observed of permitting Local Authorities to develop more and more into responsible bodies with extensive functions.[26]

The effect of such moves was twofold: the placement of local government directly under the aegis of central institutions (with the notable exception of Nigeria, which has always maintained a federal-type structure); and the elimination of regional political bases that could enhance the power and autonomy of local leaders in competition with ruling coalitions at the national level.

Another way to reduce opposition was to outlaw rival political organizations based on particularistic, sectarian, or ethnic interests. Ghana, once again, together with Guinea, paved the way for such actions by declaring local political parties illegal and contrary to national interests. In Kenya, Jomo Kenyatta hounded opposition leaders and accused them of fueling regional and separatist tendencies. In Senegal, Muslim religious authorities were either co-opted or discredited; in Sierra Leone, traditional institutions were manipulated; and in Guinea, chieftaincy was declared illegal. With alternate power constellations officially enfeebled, reconstructed opposition parties were on tenuous ground when they sought to mobilize support or criticize government actions.

The opportunities to voice discontent were also substantially reduced. The notion of a loyal opposition was alien to the colonial and decolonization experiences of most African leaders; once in power, they typically assumed that hesitations and reservations threatened their positions. Steps were taken to enforce newly formulated sedition laws. The independent press was curtailed or shut down. Vocal opponents of ruling parties and of their methods of government were either incarcerated or exiled. By the early 1960s, for example, in Kenya, Algeria, Ghana, and Guinea, most leaders of contending parties during decolonization were either in jail or had left the country to carry out their political struggles from abroad. Where the insecurity of the new regimes was especially apparent, the notion of opposition itself was considered to be immoral. Unity was equated with uniformity, disagreement with treason.

The enfeeblement of opposition in many cases also involved the actual dismantling of the multiparty system. The trend toward the creation of one-party states is perhaps the best known and the most noted of the political changes introduced at independence.[27] In the quest for consolidation, political competition, it was suggested, had to be controlled and some monopoly of the governing political apparatus assured. African leaders throughout the continent, arguing from different perspectives, thus supported the transition to single-party dominance. Felix Houphouët-Boigny in Côte d'Ivoire claimed that the elimination of opposition merely sanctioned the unity that actually existed. Kwame Nkrumah defended the move to one-party rule by suggesting that the multiparty system was divisive and antithetical to the needs of economic development and national integration. Sekou Touré in Guinea, by correlating the proposed nation with the party, thought that alternative political poles undermined the national purpose. And in Tanzania, Julius Nyerere saw the one-party concept as essentially democratic and reflective of African culture and deep-rooted norms of consensus.[28]

Many methods were employed to bring about the consolidation of one-party dominance. In some cases, persuasion was used to encourage the fusion of opposition and ruling parties, as in Senegal and Kenya during the first years of independence. In other instances, legal means were employed to make it virtually impossible for opposition parties to subsist. Kwame Nkrumah employed such techniques in Ghana, as did Ahmadou Ahidjo in Cameroon. In other countries, coercion was the key: Opposition leaders were harassed in Guinea and Uganda, and attempts to voice discontent were put down forcefully in Angola and Mozambique. In many places, the leaders did not have to do much of anything: They could, as in Côte d'Ivoire, assume that the electorate would not find it beneficial to support weak parties with no access to state resources and, by tacit collaboration, would allow the single-party monopoly to evolve. In all cases, the process of impedance of multiparty competition resulted in the creation of palpably monopolistic formal political institutions.

These moves were reinforced by purposeful changes in the laws guiding political activities and possibilities. In Ghana, for example, the British, determined to forestall rash actions on the part of a majoritarian-backed chief executive or central legislature, provided a highly inflexible amendment procedure in the 1957 constitution. Two-thirds approval of all members of the national and regional assemblies was required to alter clauses in the constitution. The government of the Convention People's Party (CPP), describing this limitation as unnecessary, made use of its overwhelming support in parliament to allow for amendment by a simple majority. In a similar fashion, the Kenyan and Zambian leaderships, faced with amendment procedures that seemed to inhibit government-sponsored political and economic change, moved to alter amendment procedures.

The message, in these and other instances, was quite clear. Those legal safeguards standing in the way of firm central control were regarded as unacceptable. To drive home this point, many governments undertook to rewrite preindependence constitutions to reflect the shifts in the political sphere and to provide themselves with greater power. Kenya, Uganda, Malawi, Zambia, Ghana, Côte d'Ivoire, and Sierra Leone stand out in this respect.

These very elaborate means of thwarting opposition also had the effect of profoundly altering the function of participatory and representative institutions. National assemblies and parliaments, packed with ruling party supporters, were downgraded in many cases from legislative bodies to decree-sanctioning organs. Although careful efforts were made to maintain some notion of representation, parliamentary debates mostly offered opportunities to express support or to allow for a certain measure of bargaining. They rarely permitted real engagement in policy formulation or even constructive commentary on the direction of government policies.[29]

The process of impedance, in all its various forms, was one that concentrated directly (if not exclusively) on the fragile and fluid political institutions constructed at independence. The limitation or outright elimination of competition, coupled with the assertion of single-party dominance, had the effect of circumscribing access to the central government and reducing formal pressure on its resources.

The other side of the institutional readjustment process focused on measures designed to augment the power apparatus. These reinforcement procedures centered on three main structures: the administration, the security services, and the executive. The administrative institutions of Africa at independence were the main reservoir of skilled personnel in every African country. The knowledge concentrated in these bodies was essential to devise and implement economic policies and to maintain order. In these circumstances, rulers sought not to undermine the administrative infrastructure but to remold these functional bodies so that they would promote their interests.

With independence, therefore, the process of Africanization was expedited and the size and functions of the administrative agencies were augmented dramatically. Young graduates were rapidly absorbed into the civil service, endowed with broad responsibilities, and in the name of parity, granted the same terms of service and perquisites previously accorded to colonial administrators. Service ministries, such as education, health, and community welfare, were greatly expanded. Every country developed a foreign service and established economic planning bureaus and state-owned parastatal corporations. With independence came the need for currency changes and new fiscal arrangements and consequently also for enlarged finance ministries. It seemed that at every turn, administrative bodies multiplied.

This process also encompassed the military and police services. The new rulers in Sudan, Zimbabwe, Congo, Kenya, Uganda, Mauritania, and elsewhere were keenly aware of the fact that various ethnoregional elements did not accept their legitimacy. These political leaders came to rely heavily on the army and security forces inherited from the colonial period to maintain order in their countries. Moreover, the perceived threat of disruption or secession was a serious one that demanded the Africanization, the enlargement, and the modernization of the new armies. With very few exceptions, such as Gambia and Botswana, the coercive apparatus grew alongside the bureaucratic.

The expansion of the administrative apparatus also proved to be a crucial means for personal advancement. The facilitation of bureaucratic institutions allowed select individuals to gain direct access to state resources and to enjoy the not inconsiderable privileges associated with administrative office. In countries such as Tanzania, Zimbabwe, Côte d'Ivoire, Kenya, Senegal, Mali, Cameroon, and Congo, the increase in the number of state personnel also involved an increase in administrative costs. As David Abernathy notes,

> At the time of independence, top-level salary scales set initially with European conditions in mind were accepted by the incoming African regimes as appropriate scales for those Africans fortunate enough to occupy the most responsible administrative posts. When there was talk in Africa of "reforming" the civil service, the issue was how to move local citizens more rapidly and effectively into the existing hierarchical structure, or how to expand the structure laterally to assume new developmental functions. What was never seriously addressed . . . was the appropriateness of a situation in which the top civil servant earned at least 40 and sometimes over 100 times more than the per capita GDP of the country.[30]

The requirements of governance, it appeared, dovetailed quite well with the personal interests of technocrats, educated groups, and party militants. Association with the state complex began to emerge as one, if not the, key avenue to social advancement and class differentiation.

The bureaucratic growth that accompanied the consolidation of power had important implications for the organization of the state. The downgrading of political opportunities and the substantial opening of administrative and coercive ones made for an institutional imbalance not dissimilar to the one that existed throughout the colonial period. It also created a different type of problem for political leaders. Because the bureaucratic apparatus was growing rapidly, its members held privileged positions, and their political loyalties were not always clear, governments approached the proliferating administration with some measure of suspicion.

In order to keep an eye on the administration (in some instances to take over key offices), the party was often used as a means of bureaucratic supervision. The process of politicization, therefore, followed upon that of bureaucratic facilitation. Party functionaries were injected into the civil service, police, army, and local government. It was inevitable that party and government tended to overlap in many different ways. Thus, although Tanzanian leaders went so far as to proclaim the party (then the Tanzanian African National Union, TANU) as the preeminent public institution in the country, in reality the division between party and state was not always so clear-cut. The administrative apparatus was always central in policy implementation, even though the party had some role in policy formulation.[31] Such an uneasy separation also characterized Nkrumah's Ghana in the early 1960s.

In other countries, the party actually absorbed state structures. This was the case with the transformation-minded regimes of Mozambique, Guinea, and Angola. In Angola, the ruling Popular Movement for the Liberation of Angola (MPLA) has played a central role in setting out basic principles for governmental and societal action and for mobilizing popular support behind a regime that was under military attack from the National Union for the Total Independence of Angola (UNITA) forces until 1991, when the two parties began to negotiate a cease-fire and settlement. Up to this time, the MPLA Politburo and Central Committee placed themselves as the key policymaking bodies. Matters of implementation were dealt with in the National Assembly and the ministries, where MPLA party members remained very prominent.

In still other states, the growth of the administrative apparatus resulted in a contrary trend: the subordination of the party to government institutions. In Côte d'Ivoire, for one, emphasis was placed on building up bureaucratic mechanisms, whereas the party was relegated to more symbolic tasks. In Kenya during the 1960s, membership in the Kenya African National Union (KANU) became an important vehicle for the attainment of bureaucratic position. In Algeria, too, though officially supreme, the ruling party has been less central as a regulatory institution. "Since independence the FLN has possessed neither the authority nor the technical competence to orient and supervise the administrative apparatus of the state. . . . Neither armed forces nor bureaucracy have been subject to its authority. In a sense, therefore, the Party and its ramifications could be regarded as part of the bureaucracy, performing essentially a public relations function on its behalf. . . . Its job was to explain and justify decisions taken elsewhere, not to reason why."[32] In these cases, technocrats were at least somewhat insulated from political pressures.

Whatever the precise pattern of party-state relations, a clear feature of governmental reorganization during the early years of independence was the intrusion of party political elements into the decision-enforcing institutions of government. This had two significant implications. First, although the political role of the party as a means of participation and competition was downplayed, the party became a channel to the administration, thus making the administrative apparatus subject to particularistic political demands. Second, in this situation the location of decisionmaking was unclear. To be sure, administrative units could reach conclusions on technical matters or in specific areas, but they were dependent on government decisionmakers. On the other hand, as the lines of distinction between party and bureaucracy were nebulous, the party could not function on a regular basis as the center of policy formulation. Under these conditions, the executive took on particular significance in the decisionmaking sphere.

The final element in the process of strengthening already existing administrative institutions at the expense of participatory ones centered on the concentration of the state power apparatus in the hands of individual leaders. The personalization of decisionmaking was a concomitant of the overall trend toward centralization. Leadership became a substitute for regularized channels of policymaking. This was the case in Guinea, Senegal, Ghana, Kenya, Tanzania, and Uganda—indeed, throughout the continent. Even when, because of the complex nature of decisionmaking, other agencies were naturally involved in issuing key policy rulings, it usually was the president (endowed with increased executive powers) who had the final say.[33]

These executive presidents were undoubtedly informed by the opinions of party officials, personal advisers, technical experts, senior bureaucrats, friends, and specific local and at times foreign interests. But unlike their counterparts in the West or, for that matter, in portions of Asia and Latin America, African leaders during the first generation of independence were not subject to checks and balances, nor were they necessarily restrained (at least at the outset) by organized pressures from below. The centrality of leaders in decisionmaking did not, however, imply that they possessed total power. Rather, it suggested that under the new institutional arrangements they became the hub that connected the party with the army and the civil service with the politicians.

The process of facilitation, geared almost exclusively toward augmenting the power apparatus, had the effect of strengthening the extractive machinery of the new states at independence. State-linked structures were reinforced, whereas political institutions rooted in society were stymied. A system of domination came to replace the inherently fluid and dispersed institutional networks prevalent at the close of the colonial period.

The reorganization of public structures during the first years of independence, regardless of political philosophies and the personal inclinations of particular leaders, therefore assumed the characteristics of what has been termed the typical postcolonial state. Until the democratic wave swept across Africa in the 1990s, such a state was characterized by the limitation of political pluralism to very small enclaves, the strong emphasis on statism and bureaucratic structures, the politicization of administrative institutions, and personalistic forms of decisionmaking.[34] It has frequently been referred to as a neopatrimonial state, one in which relationships to a person (rather than an officeholder) thrived within a purportedly legal-rational administrative system.[35] Although monopolistic, the postcolonial state had only tenuous power and legitimacy and very little authority. Centralization became a means for consolidation but did not necessarily imply full control. In fact, the highly concentrated system of rule created at this time was as noted for what it excluded as for what it sought to encompass. Social groups, local communities, and even party diehards were often kept outside the official domain. The consolidation of state institutions in the first postcolonial phase, therefore, implied a combination of power concentration and power diffusion. It was this broad pattern of distancing the state from societal constraints, of pushing society out, that constituted the initial response of African governments to the problems of control that they faced when they took office; it was also within this general framework that specific adjustments were made in individual countries in the ensuing years.

■ Phase 2: The Elaboration of State Power

The reorganization of government structures at independence laid the groundwork for the growth of the institutional order in different African states since the early postcolonial years. During the 1960s and the 1970s, African leaders further molded the various components of government— the public administration, the coercive apparatus, the legal order, and political institutions.[36] Paradoxically, these actions had the dual effect of expanding state structures while at the same time frequently limiting the effectiveness of these agencies.

Administration. The growth of the public bureaucracy in African states has been one of the most notable formal features of African politics in the past three decades. The nature of this expansion, and its significance for politics and development, have been the subject of not inconsiderable controversy. Some have seen the proliferation of the administration as evidence of the emergence of a monopolistic class that has preyed on society and systematically extracted its resources. Some have viewed this process as a sign of inefficiency: as a further indication of the absence of rational norms of public behavior. Other observers bemoan the lack of experience and skills that continues to plague the public sector, pointing to the dearth of qualifications as the immediate cause of poor implementation. And many commentators have highlighted the unclear connection between administrative and political institutions as a grave problem of governability. A common thread runs through these debates: a comprehension both of the extensiveness and the inadequacy of administrative structures in the postcolonial period.[37]

The 1960s were marked by rapid bureaucratic enlargement. This trend began with persistent calls for the Africanization of the civil service on the eve of independence. Very few African governments were able to stem these demands. Hastings Kamuzu Banda in Malawi and Felix Houphouët-Boigny in Côte d'Ivoire did, in fact, moderate Africanization procedures until suitably trained candidates could be found to fill professional positions. In most cases, however, local cadres were given intensive courses to enable them to take over positions held by departing expatriates, and younger civil servants were promoted rapidly in administrative, if not always in technical and professional, posts. Higher education and vocational training institutions were strengthened. Graduates were quickly assimilated into the civil service and granted relatively senior positions.

The results, in quantitative terms, were startling. In each year during the 1960s, the civil service in Africa grew on an average of 7 percent. By 1970, 60 percent of wage earners were government employees. A decade later, at least 50 percent of government expenditures were allocated to salaries. In some countries, a full 80 percent of government revenues were spent on supporting the civil service.[38] Tanzania provides one illustration of this immense growth. The total number of established state posts increased from 65,708 in 1966 to 191,046 in 1976 and to an estimated 295,352 in 1980. Rwekaza Mukandala puts this growth in perspective: "While the GDP expanded at an annual rate of 3.88 percent between 1966 and 1976 . . . and total wage employment increased at an average annual rate of around 2.84 percent between 1966 and 1976, the civil service expanded at an average annual rate of 13.3 percent, a rate more than treble that of GDP and total wage employment."[39]

The outcome of this spurt was not only to distort expenditure patterns, but also, almost inevitably, to create a privileged group that gradually developed corporate interests of its own. Civil servants stood out in comparison to other groups in African countries; they were also well placed to advance themselves financially. The manner of bureaucratic expansion enhanced their status and opened opportunities for the personal aggrandizement of state officials at the expense of other groups.

became obstacles to effective growth. The first two decades of independence witnessed administrative expansion and, concomitantly, highlighted the extent of institutional frailty in most African states.[47]

The coercive apparatus. The fortification of administrative institutions in the 1960s and 1970s came hand in hand with the growth of enforcement agencies and, most significantly, the army and the police. Armed forces were retained at first as a symbol of sovereignty and national independence; then they were sustained and expanded to quell disturbances, ensure compliance, and provide necessary props for frail regimes. With few exceptions (Botswana, Lesotho, Gambia, Swaziland), African leaders engaged in the construction and expansion of the military during the first two decades of independence. The small military forces of the mid-1960s (Nigeria's army, for example, numbered 11,500; Côte d'Ivoire's, 4,000; Togo's, 1,450; Zambia's, 3,000; Kenya's, 4,755; Tanzania's, 1,800; Uganda's, 5,960) and relatively low financial outlays for these units (defense as a percentage of GNP ranged from Tanzania's 0.3 percent and Nigeria's 0.9 percent to Côte d'Ivoire's 2.4 percent and Kenya's rather high 9.8 percent) reflected the limited and largely ceremonial roles of the earlier colonial armies.[48] By the late 1970s, however, military size and expenditures had risen significantly. In 1978, the Nigerian armed forces stood at 231,000, mirroring the rapid expansion that took place during the Nigeria-Biafra civil war and the problems attendant upon demobilization. The armed forces in Côte d'Ivoire increased to approximately 9,000; in Togo to 4,800; in Zambia to 20,000; in Kenya to 13,700; and in Tanzania to 26,700 (further expanded in 1980–1981 to 44,850, as additional troops were mobilized to aid the Tanzanian incursion into Uganda and to maintain order in that country after the ouster of Idi Amin Dada).[49]

A rise in military expenditures naturally accompanied these increases in troops. For Africa as a whole, military expenditures as a proportion of GNP rose from 1.8 percent in 1963 to 2.6 percent in 1968 and then to 3.4 percent in 1971, decreasing slightly to 2.9 percent in 1980.[50] As military power grew, Africa's share of world arms imports climbed from 4.6 percent in 1971 to 18.8 percent in 1980, indicating an annual growth rate in arms expenditures of 33.4 percent. The effects of this heavy burden of military expenditures continue to be distributed quite unevenly among African states. As indicated in Table 2.1, approximately 50 percent of the countries on the continent had military outlays of more than 2 percent of GNP in 1995. A large number of poor countries, usually coinciding with areas of internal insurrection and major political instability, carried especially heavy military burdens (for example Angola, Ethiopia, Mozambique, and Zimbabwe).

It is possible to point to an overall process of militarization in this phase of the elaboration of state power. This trend was visible also in the

Table 2.1 Relative Burden of Military Expenditures in Sub-Saharan Africa, 1995

Military Expenditures as Percentage of GNP	GNP Per Capita (1995 dollars)	Countries
5%–6.99%	Under $200	Mozambique, Sierra Leone
	$200–$499	Rwanda, Sudan
	over $1000	Botswana
2%–4.99%	under $200	Burundi, Chad, Ethiopia
	$200–$499	Burkina Faso, Central African Republic, Gambia, Guinea-Bissau, Kenya, Mauritania, Togo, Uganda, Zambia
	$500–$999	Angola, Congo-Brazzaville, Zimbabwe
	over $1000	Djibouti, Gabon, Namibia, South Africa, Swaziland
1%–1.99%	under $200	Malawi, Tanzania
	$200–$499	Benin, Equatorial Guinea, Ghana, Guinea, Mali, Niger
	$500–$999	Cameroon, Cape Verde, Côte d'Ivoire, Lesotho, Senegal
Under 1%	under $200	Congo
	$200–$499	Madagascar
	$500–$999	Nigeria
	over $1000	Mauritius

Source: U.S. Arms Control and Disarmament Agency, *World Military Expenditures and Arms Transfers 1996.*

expansion of paramilitary structures.[51] In the early years of independence, new rulers, uneasy about the loyalty of their British- or French-trained officer corps or the remnants of national liberation armies, bolstered the police force and sometimes even established their own armed guard alongside the military establishment. In many parts of French-speaking Africa the gendarmerie was used to maintain order, and throughout the continent border guards and elite presidential units were created.

The growth of the coercive branch of government resulted in the formation of highly organized groups with distinct professional and corporate interests. The definition of new tasks generated calls for higher salaries, improved living conditions, an expanded array of consumer goods, and expensive military equipment. This trend first became evident in 1963 and 1964, when soldiers in Togo, Tanzania, Kenya, and Uganda mutinied to support their calls for improved service conditions. Leaders in these countries, despite some embarrassment, requested troops from the ex-colonial metropole to quell these military insurrections. Salaries were consequently increased and conditions in the armed forces improved. The coercive apparatus thereby became a potential political force not only in these but in most African countries. Indeed, the mutinies of the early 1960s presaged a series of military interventions that have been part and parcel of African political history in the postcolonial era (military coups will be discussed in Chapter 8).

These circumstances generated an additional set of issues of coordination and control. The first problem that developed around the military related, as in the administration, to questions of internal cohesion and specialization. In some countries, where the size of the military was small, external military support available, and economic conditions relatively stable, it was possible to retain a high degree of professionalism and discipline. Côte d'Ivoire and Senegal are two cases in point. But in most countries, the growth of military institutions, coupled with their politicization, led to friction between the senior officer corps and the lower ranks and between various branches of the armed services. This tendency was especially apparent in countries like Ghana, Benin, and Nigeria, which had undergone several military interventions. It was further exacerbated by interethnic and interregional strife within the military, especially in countries where recruitment patterns were ethnically slanted (Congo, 1960; Nigeria, 1966; Uganda, 1972).

The question of military cohesion was closely tied to patterns of civil-military relations. The dilemma of rulers in this regard was pronounced. They had to learn how to navigate between their need for coercive enforcement and the dangers attendant upon the threat of military politicization. Some leaders—Houphouët-Boigny in Côte d'Ivoire, Kenneth Kaunda in Zambia, and Leopold Sedar Senghor in Senegal—were able to balance prudently these countervailing pressures and remain in office. Others, such as Hilla Limann in Ghana or Shehu Shagari in Nigeria, were less successful in this regard and were compelled to suffer the consequences (both were overthrown in military coups).[52]

The relations between decisionmakers and the armed forces also had an impact on the links between these agencies and their social environment. Well-disciplined military personnel not prone to preying on innocent citizens to supplement their incomes have succeeded in gaining respect in some African states. On the other hand, faulty lines of command, inadequate salaries, and raw ambition have allowed soldiers in other countries to become, themselves, the cause of indiscriminate lawlessness. This was the case in many parts of Nigeria in 1966 and in Uganda during the 1970s and early 1980s. "Such is the anarchy," wrote one observer, "that even the very notion of a Ugandan army is blurred." The army, described as divided, disorganized, and frightened, "came to undermine the very state which built it up and relied upon it."[53] This was also the pattern that developed in Liberia in 1989, in Somalia and Ethiopia in the early 1990s, and in Rwanda and Congo in the late 1990s.

Patterns of military growth and of civil-military relations vary substantially from one country to another. In certain places—most notably,

Côte d'Ivoire, Botswana, Senegal, and Malawi—the military has not been an important political factor. In other countries, the political scene has almost continuously been integrally linked to the status and orientation of soldiers (Ghana and Nigeria stand out in this regard). In almost all countries, the coercive apparatus emerged as an essential branch of formal governmental structures. This trend was less a statement on the centrality of the armed forces to the conduct of state affairs than a commentary on the fragility of civilian institutions and the insecurity of many leaders on the continent.[54]

The legal order. Administrative and military expansion and entrenchment in the 1960s and 1970s was part of the process of strengthening the power apparatus at the expense of broadly based political institutions. Judicial structures, in contrast, although developing at a steady pace, remained somewhat separate from the rapid growth that took place in the decision-enforcing spheres. The legal systems of African countries at independence were generally constructed on two foundations evolved during the colonial period. The first was customary law, which varied from locale to locale. Long-standing rules developed by local communities regarding land tenure, marriage, divorce, and petty offenses were codified and continued to govern many aspects of daily life. In Muslim areas, the Shari'a law prevailed. On top of this preexisting legal system, colonial rulers superimposed a second set of judicial institutions to serve as courts of appeal and to adjudicate disputes resulting from infringements on colonial decrees. These structures were modelled faithfully on the lines of metropolitan judicial institutions.

On the eve of independence, these courts, much as the civil service and the military, underwent a process of Africanization. The judicial system in each country was charged with upholding customary law as well as provisions in the new independence constitutions. Inevitably, therefore, the courts became the focus of a great deal of activity. At the local level, litigation increased as land claims were disputed and inheritance laws were altered. In English-speaking countries in particular, access to resources also involved an ability to work through the court system. Here the courts became a crucial vehicle for contesting decisions of traditional authorities and gaining control of desired assets. In Congo, the nationalization of land also increased activity around the courts. The judicial system also attempted to act as the watchdog of decisionmakers. This implied that the courts had a say in evaluating the behavior of politicians and civil servants. The tension between the courts and the politicians was not inconsiderable.

In Ghana, for example, Kwame Nkrumah sought on several occasions to ignore unfavorable court decisions. When these actions aroused indignation, first specific laws and then the constitution in its entirety were changed. Kofi Busia defied a court order overturning his dismissal of over five hundred civil servants, thereby laying himself open to charges of interfering with the judicial process. In Uganda, both Idi Amin and Milton Obote bypassed the courts and directly attacked the authority of judges. In Nigeria, the courts were seen as a means, albeit indirect, of supervising politicians and attaining some measure of redress from unbridled bureaucrats. The centralizing efforts of Robert Mugabe in Zimbabwe involved a confrontation between the government and the courts over civil rights issues. In all these cases the judicial system became the object of attempted manipulation.

The court system has not, moreover, been entirely free of political favoritism or, for that matter, a measure of elitism. Although local courts and religious judicial authorities have, over the years, remained relatively accessible, dealings with the complex legal systems inherited from the colonial period have required more skills and expertise. Rural dwellers or impoverished urban populations have either avoided the national court systems or found themselves outclassed in intricate court cases. When feelings of exclusion ran high (Ghana and Uganda during the late 1970s are two examples), judges were denounced alongside politicians. Even in these cases, however, it was rarely the judiciary in its entirety that was repudiated but rather the individual actions of specific justices and lawyers.

Changes in judicial structures per se have, in general, been few and far between. Only on rare occasions did the judicial structure itself become the object of a major revamping. This was the case in Ghana in 1979 and again in 1982, when public tribunals and popular commissions were set up to bypass the formal judicial system and dispense justice quickly.[55] The assault on the courts did not, however, succeed in displacing existing institutions, nor did it undermine the essential faith of citizens in Ghana and elsewhere in the established judicial system.

At issue in many African states, therefore, was not the judicial system specifically, but the notion of the rule of law in general. Authoritarianism was frequently accompanied by repression. If rulers such as Idi Amin in Uganda, Jean-Bedel Bokassa in the Central African Republic, and Macias Nguema in Equatorial Guinea became notorious for their flagrant violations of the law, human rights violations were not unknown in other parts of the continent (and have continued through the 1990s, as in Nigeria, where human rights activists were executed in 1995). Political detainees were held without trial in Kenya, Malawi, Guinea, Liberia, Gabon, Zambia, Tanzania, Congo, and Ethiopia, to name but a few. Government officials and policymakers openly flaunted import restrictions, foreign currency controls, and even curfew laws that they themselves had imposed. The resiliency of judicial structures was maintained, but the system of public accountability in many countries did become frayed. The growth of administrative and coercive structures therefore adversely affected the separation of powers and judicial autonomy in most parts of Africa.[56]

The political machinery. The heavy emphasis on administrative and coercive institutions during the phase of power elaboration had its effects on the organization and functions of the political machinery as well. The history of African politics during the first two decades of independence (and often beyond) was one of the systematic subordination of the political apparatus in the bulk of the continent to the executive. The margin for political maneuvering at the national level was severely constrained.

The single-party systems that were created in the early period of independence gradually took on distinct forms in subsequent years. Some parties were quickly changed into auxiliaries of the administration and their representative functions undermined. This was the case in Côte d'Ivoire throughout the 1960s, the 1970s, and most of the 1980s and in Cameroon during the same period. In these cases, the party was viewed as a channel for the dispensation of patronage, as a medium for political communication, and, above all, as a legitimating device. Here single-party politics became machine politics, and the regime a one-party plebiscitary one. The legislatures in these countries became forums for discussion but had little, if any, voice in decisionmaking.

In other instances, more stress was placed on finding ways for permitting political participation within a single-party setup. Tanzania, Kenya, and Algeria pioneered a system of limited competition within the one-party framework, enabling a rotation of members of parliament in regularly scheduled elections. In these African states, the single parties did assume at least a linkage role between local constituents and the central government.[57] Consideration of constituency concerns became part of the legislative scene. Nevertheless, parliaments had next to no decisionmaking functions.

In still other cases—Ghana under Nkrumah, Uganda under Obote, Guinea under Sekou Touré, Sierra Leone under Siaka Stevens—the party deteriorated into a hollow shell whose functions were unclear and whose utility was uncertain. In these instances, the single party was used primarily as an instrument of control and, again, patronage, frequently justified in ideological terms. Parliamentary activity virtually ground to a halt. Eventually, the combination of low party dominance and decreased participation transformed these countries into what has been termed no-party states.

To be sure, a few countries in Africa succeeded in establishing and sustaining a multiparty system since independence. In Botswana, one party has remained in power throughout this period, but opposition parties were able to organize, compete in elections, and have their voices heard in a parliament possessing some real legislative role. In Mauritius, a vibrant multiparty system developed that allowed for a change in governing parties at the ballot box. In these instances, as well as in Namibia, the single party was eschewed in favor of a more demonstratively competitive system. Executive government was also attenuated by checks imposed by parliaments.

During the course of the 1970s, with the creation of Afro-Marxist regimes in Angola, Mozambique, Guinea-Bissau, and Ethiopia, another revolutionary mobilizing pattern was laid down. In these cases, the party became the focal point of policymaking efforts. In Angola, the Popular Movement for the Liberation of Angola (MPLA) initiatives made a significant contribution to regime performance and perhaps survival. In 1981, for example, the MPLA proclaimed a year of "discipline and control," thereby asserting itself as a key monitoring agency in the part of the country under its control. In Ethiopia, a formal Soviet-styled communist party was proclaimed on 10 September 1984 in an effort by the country's former leader, Lieutenant Colonel Mengistu Haile Mariam, to consolidate his rule and to strengthen his control over society. The party was meant to provide a vehicle for the ruling clique's unsuccessful attempt to transform Ethiopian society from a "feudal-bourgeois" regime to a genuinely communist one. In these countries, the party supplanted the legislature as a forum for voicing opinions on significant issues.

The party framework, and, by extension, legislative structures in Africa, therefore evolved in many different ways and exhibited varying degrees of stability. During the phase of power elaboration, the party apparatus became an auxiliary of the administrative coercive institutions, and parliaments forfeited many of their policymaking and supervisory roles. At best, the political machinery was subordinated to executive structures; in at least 50 percent of African states, parties and parliaments were dissolved in the aftermath of a military coup.

The fact that power elaboration under military rule further deemphasized the political apparatus drives home the extreme vulnerability of political institutions in Africa during the 1960s, 1970s, and most of the 1980s. These were the first to be monopolized by insecure leaders and the first to be abandoned by incoming military rulers. The organization of the political realm was thus the most arbitrary, haphazard, and unpredictable component of power elaboration during the first two decades after independence.

This trend accentuated what had become obvious during the initial organization of government institutions after the transfer of power: that in most of Africa government institutions lacked a well-defined popular foundation. Authoritarian structures evolved and were refined by personal rulers who became substitutes for regularized organizations and decisionmaking procedures. The bases of power were still not clearly laid out even when the parameters of the unacceptable had been tested and delineated. As one observer stated at the end of the second postcolonial decade, "the state still faces a crisis of legitimacy before the tribunal of African pluralism."[58]

The entrenchment of administrative institutions at the expense of regularized channels of political involvement left many African leaders in a situation in which their control was uncertain, their reach arbitrary, and their reliance on force greater than at the time of independence.[59] The process of administrative proliferation and political enfeeblement had rendered many African institutions weak and others insufficiently effective.

▓ Phase 3: The Reconsideration of State Power

By the late 1970s and early 1980s most, if not all, African states were undergoing an organizational crisis. The first and most widely noted characteristic of this crisis was the fraying character of state-society relations. Many governments, particularly in those countries that had experienced numerous regime changes since independence, had not been able to gain the trust of large portions of their populations. Government directives were seen as intrusive and even destructive; policies tended to favor groups close to those in power; distrust of officials abounded. Decrees were frequently skirted, laws flaunted, and although bureaucrats were courted, they were also regarded as oppressors.[60] A second feature of the dilemma of African states at this juncture was the extensive nature of the administrative and coercive apparatus. Government structures were overstaffed and costly (large portions of wage labor contined to be employed in the public sector).[61] The propensity of unwieldy institutions to overconsume taxed already scarce resources and further reduced the capacity of state institutions to achieve their development objective. A third dimension of the crisis of government institutions related to the widespread use of public funds and positions for the personal enrichment of civil servants, politicians, and their immediate supporters. In many African states, the distinction between the private and the public realms was completely blurred.[62]

Fourth, the abuse of public office had a debilitating effect on the support accorded to state leaders and officeholders. Autocratic rule was a poor substitute for legitimacy and authority; consent and consensus were undermined. In the absence of state supremacy, politics came to involve competition among a small and fractured elite for control over a dwindling state pie.[63] This rent-seeking behavior, coupled with the lack of legitimate authority, fostered a counterproductive elitism that perpetuated gross inequality and induced divisions among those social groups that had achieved privileged positions throughout the state.

The final, and most pernicious, dimension of the state crisis was the inability of many formal institutions to fulfil even the most basic tasks. To be sure, most African governments recorded impressive gains in education, health, and social welfare during the first two decades of independence. But by the late 1970s, anemic rates of development and a relative reduction in social services and infrastructural maintenance indicated a diminution in administrative capabilities,[64] which still could be seen in the late 1990s.

Not all African countries experienced the crisis of state institutions to the same degree and in the same ways. Ghana and Uganda, for example, appeared to be on the verge of disintegration in the 1980s, but underwent rehabilitation in the 1990s. Congo (Zaire) and Nigeria were stagnating in the 1980s and have deteriorated since. But even states with relatively strong records, such as Côte d'Ivoire, Zambia, and Kenya, felt the adverse effects of dwindling resources, growing violence, and decreased capabilities. In the first two decades of independence, state institutions had become more salient: their capacities had rarely increased accordingly.

What explains the relative weakness of governmental structures in the first decades of independence? The answer would appear to include at least six critical elements: scarcity of resources, politicized patterns of social differentiation, overexpanded state structures, insufficient state legitimacy, inadequate state power, and the lack of adaptation of alien institutions to local conditions.[65] The challenge of state organization was therefore particularly pronounced as the postcolonial phase of African independence began to come to an end.

The heavily centralized statism that marked the first decades of independence has been subjected to close scrutiny in recent years. And although many of the authoritarian and repressive tendencies of the first independence generation persisted throughout the 1990s, most countries undertook some reviews of the structure of the public sphere and others proceeded to make institutional adjustments as well.

The first and most obvious target of this reordering has been the administrative apparatus. Foreign donors and international monetary agencies (especially the IMF and the World Bank) tied capital support to plans for the contraction of the administrative and public sector. In line with these programs of structural adjustment (SAPs), the size of ministries has been purposely cut, and in some countries governments have systematically divested themselves of unprofitable or costly state enterprises. The quantitative reduction of the administrative apparatus was undertaken in Côte d'Ivoire, Congo (Zaire), Ghana, Zambia, Senegal, Guinea, Nigeria, and Cameroon, to mention but a few.

This process has been accompanied by a concomitant trend toward increased reliance on market mechanisms. Although state-owned enterprises still act as entrepreneurs, more economic activity has been fostered in the private sector, and state economic controls have been relaxed. The dismantling of marketing boards in many West and central African states is a case in point. The governmental arena has cut back on its economic involvement in many places without totally relinquishing its regulatory roles. The reduction of bureaucratic involvement in the economy frequently has come hand in hand with plans for the devolution of central authority to local agencies. Decentralization schemes have been devised in countries like Uganda, Senegal, and Ghana, and similar plans are being drawn up in other countries. They have yet to be fully implemented in practice.

The political side of this process has involved some opening of participatory opportunities. Certain single-party systems allowed for greater competition in the early 1980s (Côte d'Ivoire, for one) and others actually permitted multiparty competition (Senegal, Benin, and Tanzania). Some military governments withdrew in favor of (short-lived) multiparty regimes, as in Ghana and Nigeria in the late 1970s and early 1980s. Others, particularly in francophone countries (Mali, Togo, Niger), underwent a process of civilianization in the dominant party mode. Populist governments—Ghana and Burkina Faso—experimented in the 1980s with new, and rather destructive, types of direct participation and related populist institutional arrangements. And in countries where the founding fathers survived the first decades of independence and military coups, the initial generation gave way, at times voluntarily, to a new crop of rulers (Cameroon, Senegal, Tanzania, Zambia, Sierra Leone, and Kenya).[66] If political patterns were no more regularized in the 1990s than in the 1970s and 1980s, they were at least more heterogeneous and innovative. And in the last decade of the twentieth century, multiparty government was reinstated in many countries in Africa.

The rethinking that has begun to take place has also included a reassessment of the size and role of the armed forces in a select number of African states. For example, Nigeria grappled, especially after the 1983 coup, with trimming down its military establishment and with reorganizing the internal chain of command. In 1999, it carried out a long-delayed return to an elected presidency. Ghana in 1984 and 1985 also reduced the size of its army and began to deal more systematically with the growing problem of military indiscipline. And although many leaders, still heavily dependent on coercive devices and wary of antagonizing the armed forces, have been reluctant to interfere in this sphere, the issue of the military, and of military participation in politics, has become a topic of serious political discussion. This observation has also held true for questions related to the judicial process. The rise of populist leaders accentuated the concern with questions of public accountability and problems of severe social inequality. The underlying principles that guided, or misdirected, public affairs during the first postcolonial generation were at least aired more thoroughly in African capitals.

The experimentation of the 1980s and 1990s varied in intensity and direction. Although many past patterns persisted and were even highlighted, the notion of exclusive state domination was gradually undergoing reconsideration. There appeared to be a movement in many countries toward "renewed yet partial liberalism at the level of politics and . . . capitalism at the level of economics, indicating a greater openness at both levels as inherited institutions decay."[67] At the same time, however, too many countries were experiencing upheavals that were symptomatic of institutional unraveling and a reliance on the use of force.

The question of viable constructions of the public arena was, perhaps, more urgent at the end of the fourth decade of African independence than at the beginning of the postcolonial era. From this ongoing evaluation may yet emerge a formula for the decolonization of the state.[68] As past experiences mesh with present possibilities and future prospects, the question of institutional remolding remains a pressing and ongoing issue on the African political agenda. The process of introspection and reevaluation which followed the realization of the crisis of public structures in the 1980s constituted an important step in the sober confrontation with this fundamental challenge.

■ STATES AND STATE VARIETY IN AFRICA: SOME IMPLICATIONS

The task of molding public institutions in Africa has been a fundamental and ongoing concern of African governments over the years. Different countries and ruling coalitions have approached this challenge in a variety of ways. By the mid-1980s, some African countries had succeeded in establishing a workable set of structures that endured over time. But by the early 1990s, even these seemingly stronger states (Kenya, Côte d'Ivoire, Cameroon, Algeria), were experiencing difficulties. Nevertheless, they contrasted sharply with a small group of countries (Liberia, Congo, Rwanda, Somalia) that had failed to coalesce viable institutions of governance. And most countries were still, nearly forty years after independence, grappling with the complex problems of shaping public organizations that would accommodate the resources and needs of societies constrained by scarcity and external dependence.[69] Until recently, authoritarianism was a common theme in these efforts.

The main question raised at the outset of this chapter dealt with the connection between statism and governmental capacities. During the first postindependence phase, as this analysis has shown, the range and scope of public institutions expanded palpably. The growth of state agencies should not, however, be confused with a concomitant increase in their effectiveness or their penetrative capacities. Indeed, current analyses have highlighted the frailties of many public institutions in recent years. This tendency has led certain observers to write off the state entity as an important factor in African political life and to predict the decomposition of the public structures inherited from the colonial period.[70] Despite the vicissitudes of administrative organs, coercive agencies, political parties, and judicial structures, state institutions (even when enfeebled) have survived, as has the idea of stateness. "The African state's resilience is remarkable and its relative influence on society is still greater than that of any other organization."[71] Indeed, "at a minimum we have seen that the threat of anarchy . . . is unfounded,"[72] although Congo, Sudan, Rwanda, Liberia, and Somalia are in precarious situations. Public institutions are significant as funnels of resources (both domestic and international), as repositories of expertise, and as coordinators of a variety of activities. For all their weaknesses, the state institutions imposed during the colonial period and subsequently redesigned since independence have become an inseparable part of life on the continent. The question facing the current generation of African leaders is, thus, not so much one of averting state collapse as one of adjusting public organizations in such a way that previous mistakes will not be repeated and that institutional devices will be more in tune with local conditions and needs.[73]

In light of the crisis of control, African elites—those who have benefited the most from statism—have begun to reassess some of their methods. They have examined ways of increasing the efficiency of the state, decentralizing power, and/or reducing the size of state institutions. The overall thrust of these suggestions has been away from overconcentration and toward a reaggregation that takes into account not only the extent of public resources but also social and economic realities. If the dynamic of statism prevailed through the heady years immediately after independence, the pendulum in the late 1980s and 1990s began to shift in the direction of less direct control and perhaps more supervision and regulation.

The question of the amount of government, in the final analysis, may therefore be giving way to a more careful consideration of the varieties of organization in the public domain. Just as formal structures provide frameworks within which social and economic processes take place, their organizational abilities, in turn, are molded by these forces. Different economic resources, historical legacies, foreign attachments and interests, social composition, types of stratification, and political skills have affected the capacity and prospects of public institutions.[74]

The experiences of the first decades of independence have underlined the danger inherent in the lopsided development of the power apparatus at the expense of political mechanisms. They have also stressed the pitfalls of power elaboration divorced from social currents, economic conditions, and existing concepts of authority.[75] The initial frameworks of public life in Africa suffered perhaps from too great a detachment from local processes and broad societal concerns, while enabling particularistic interests to take undue advantage of public resources. In the coming decades, imposed models and forms may continue to yield, as in recent years, to institutional reformulations more attuned to changing circumstances within the continent. The shape of public institutions, nevertheless, and the nature of their activities, will continue to define the central reference point of economic, social, and external processes.

■ NOTES

1. For a review of the concept of the state, see J. P. Nettl, "The State as a Conceptual Variable," *World Politics* 20, no. 4 (1968): 559–592. See also Stephen D. Krasner "Approaches to the State: Alternative Conceptions and Historical Dynamics," *Comparative Politics* 16, no. 2 (1984): 223–245.

2. Peter Anyang' Nyong'o, "The Economic Foundations of the State in Contemporary Africa: Stratification and Social Classes," *Présence Africaine* no. 127/128 (1983): 195. Also see Andre Gunder Frank, *Crisis: In the Third World* (London: Heinemann, 1981), pp. 245–249.

3. Joel Samoff, "Class, Class Conflict, and the State in Africa," *Political Science Quarterly* 97, no. 1 (1982): 105–128; Issa Shivji, "The State in the Dominated Social Formations of Africa: Some Theoretical Issues," *International Social Science Journal* 32, no. 4 (1980): 730–742.

4. Claude Ake, *A Political Economy of Africa* (London: Longman, 1981), pp. 126–127.

5. Raymond Duvall and John R. Freeman, "The State and Dependent Capitalism," *International Studies Quarterly* 25, no. 1 (1981): 106.

6. This is essentially a paraphrase of the definition suggested by Max Weber. See Theda Skoçpol, "Bringing the State Back In: Current Research," in Peter B. Evans, Dietrich Rueschmeyer, and Theda Skoçpol, eds., *Bringing the State Back In* (Cambridge: Cambridge University Press, 1985): pp. 7–8.

7. Stephen D. Krasner, *Structural Conflict: The Third World Against Global Liberalism* (Berkeley: University of California Press, 1985), p. 4. The concept of regime may be applied both on the domestic and the international levels.

8. Ruth Berins Collier, *Regimes in Tropical Africa* (Berkeley: University of California Press, 1982), pp. 7–10, views states as pacts of domination and regimes as modes of domination.

9. Joel S. Migdal, "Strong States, Weak States: Power and Accommodation," in Myron Weiner and Samuel P. Huntington, eds., *Understanding Political Development* (Boston: Little, Brown, 1987), pp. 396–397. Also see Joel Migdal, *Strong Societies and Weak States: State-Society Relations and State Capabilities in the Third World* (Princeton: Princeton University Press, 1988).

10. See Crawford Young, "Africa's Colonial Legacy," in Robert J. Berg and Jennifer Seymour Whitaker, eds., *Strategies for African Development* (Berkeley: University of California Press, 1985), esp. pp. 26–27.

11. Otwin Marenin, "The Managerial State in Africa: A Conflict Coalition Perspective," in Zaki Ergas, ed., *The African State in Transition* (London: Macmillan, 1987).

12. Skoçpol, "Bringing the State Back In," p. 21. Much of this type of analysis may also be found in Theda Skoçpol, *The State and Social Revolutions* (London: Cambridge University Press, 1980), esp. pp. 24–33.

13. David P. Laitin, "Hegemony and Religious Conflict: British Imperial Control and Political Cleavages in Yorubaland," in Evans, Rueschmeyer, and Skoçpol, *Bringing the State Back In*, p. 287.

14. See Victor Azarya and Naomi Chazan, "Disengagement from the State in Africa: Reflections on the Experience of Ghana and Guinea," *Comparative Studies in Society and History* 19, no. 1 (1987): 106–131.

15. Guillermo O'Donnell, "Comparative Historical Formations of the State Apparatus and Socio-Economic Change in the Third World," *International Social Science Journal* 32, no. 4 (1980): 717–718.

16. G. van Benthem van den Berghe, *The Interconnection Between Processes of State and Class Formation: Problems of Conceptualization* (The Hague: Institute of Social Studies Occasional Papers, no. 52, August 1975), p. 15.

17. Victor Azarya, "Reordering State-Society Relations: Incorporation and Disengagement," in Donald Rothchild and Naomi Chazan, eds., *The Precarious Balance: State and Society in Africa* (Boulder: Westview Press, 1987).

18. A.I. Asiwaju, "The Concept of Frontier in the Setting of States in Pre-Colonial Africa," *Présence Africaine* 127/128 (1983): 44–45, and Adekunle Ajake, "The Nature of African Boundaries," Afrika Spectrum 18, no. 2 (1982/1983): 177–190.

19. Nelson Kasfir, "Designs and Dilemmas: An Overview," in Phillip Mahwood, ed., *Local Government in the Third World: The Experience of Tropical Africa* (New York: John Wiley, 1983), p. 34.

20. Richard Hodder-Williams, *An Introduction to the Politics of Tropical Africa* (London: George Allen and Unwin, 1984), p. 86.

21. The discussion of this period is necessarily brief in this context. For an overview, see Thomas Hodgkin, *Nationalism in Colonial Africa* (New York: New York University Press, 1957) and his *African Political Parties* (Harmondsworth: Penguin, 1961).

22. Yves Person, "L'état nation en Afrique," *Le Mois en Afrique* 190/191 (1981): 27–35; Bakary Traoré, "De la genése de la nation et de l'état en Afrique noire," *Présence Africaine*, no. 127/128 (1983): 149–160.

23. Robert Price, "Neo-Colonialism and Ghana's Economic Decline: A Critical Assessment," *Canadian Journal of African Studies* 18, no. 1 (1984): 188–190.

24. I. William Zartman, "Issues of African Diplomacy in the 1980s," *Orbis* 25, no. 4 (1982): 1026.

25. Thomas M. Callaghy, "Politics and Vision in Africa: The Interplay of Domination, Equality and Liberty," in Patrick Chabal, ed., *Political Domination in Africa* (London: Cambridge University Press, 1986), pp. 30–51.

26. Quoted in Donald Rothchild, "On the Application of the Westminster Model to Ghana," *Centennial Review* 4, no. 4 (Fall 1960): 478. On this, also see his "Majimbo Schemes in Kenya and Uganda," in Jeffrey Butler and A.A. Castagno, eds., *Boston University Papers on Africa* (New York: Praeger, 1967), pp. 291–318.

27. Aristide Zolberg, *Creating Political Order: The Party States of West Africa* (Chicago: Rand McNally, 1966).

28. Julius K. Nyerere, "Democracy and the Party System," in Julius K. Nyerere, *Freedom and Unity* (Dar es Salaam: Oxford University Press, 1966), pp. 196–197. Also see Ahmed Sekou Touré, *The Doctrine and Methods of the Democratic Party of Guinea*, Part I (Conakry: Democratic Party of Guinea, n.d.), p. 52.

29. Michael F. Lofchie, "Representative Government, Bureaucracy and Political Development: The African Case," in Marion Doro and Newell Stultz, eds., *Governing in Black Africa* (Englewood Cliffs, NJ: Prentice Hall, 1970), pp. 278–294.

30. David B. Abernathy, "Bureaucratic Growth and Economic Decline in sub-Saharan Africa" (Paper presented at the African Studies Association, Boston, December 1983), p. 11.

31. Dean E. McHenry, *Tanzania's Ujamaa Villages* (Berkeley: Institute of International Studies, 1979), p. 68.

32. Hugh Roberts, "The Algerian Bureaucracy," *Review of African Political Economy*, no. 24 (1982), p. 53, as quoted in William Tordoff, *Government and Politics in Africa* (Bloomington: Indiana University Press, 1984), p. 108.

33. Highlighted in Tordoff, *Government and Politics in Africa*, pp. 105–106.

34. For a full exposition of this notion, see Thomas M. Callaghy, *The State-Society Struggle: Zaire in Comparative Perspective* (New York: Columbia University Press, 1984).

35. Christopher Clapham, *Third World Politics: An Introduction* (Madison: University of Wisconsin Press, 1985), pp. 47–48.

36. Collier, *Regimes in Tropical Africa*, p. 9.

37. Gatian F. Lungi and John O. Oni, "Administrative Weakness in Contemporary Africa," *African Quarterly* 24, no. 4 (1979): 3–16.

38. See Irving Leonard Markovitz, "Bureaucratic Development and Economic Growth," *Journal of Modern African Studies* 14, no. 2 (1970): 183–200, and Lungi and Oni, "Administrative Weakness."

39. Rwekaza Mukandala, "Trends in Civil Service Size and Income in Tanzania, 1967–1982," *Canadian Journal of African Studies* 2 (1983): 254.

40. For a full discussion, see Richard Sklar, "The Nature of Class Domination in Africa," *Journal of Modern African Studies* 17, no. 4 (1979): 531–552.

41. A good summary may be found in Tordoff, *Government and Politics in Africa*, pp. 139–144.

42. Paul Collins, "The State and Industrial Capitalism in West Africa," *Development and Change* 14, no. 3 (1983): 403–430; J. O. Udoji, "Reforming the Public Enterprises in Africa," *Quarterly Journal of Administration* 4, no. 3 (1970): 217–234; David B. Jones, "State Structure in New Nations: The Case of Primary Agricultural Marketing in Africa," *Journal of Modern African Studies* 20, no. 4 (1982): 553–570.

43. See, especially, Richard Crook, "Bureaucracy and Politics in Ghana: A Comparative Perspective," in Peter Lyon and James Manor, eds., *Transfer and Transformation: Political Institutions in the New Commonwealth* (Leicester: Leicester University Press, 1983). See also J.R. Nellis, "Is the Kenyan Bureaucracy Developmental? Political Considerations in Development Administration," *African Studies Review* 14, no. 3 (1971): 389–401.

44. John Ayoade, "States Without Citizens: An Emerging African Phenomenon," in Rothchild and Chazan, *The Precarious Balance*, p. 115. Also see Robert Price, *Society and Bureaucracy in Contemporary Ghana* (Berkeley: University of California Press, 1975), and Goran Hyden, "Social Structure, Bureaucracy and Development Administration in Kenya," *African Review* 1, no. 3 (1972): 118–129.

45. For one example, see Victor Le Vine, *Political Corruption: The Ghana Case* (Stanford: Hoover Institution, 1975).

46. David Abernathy, "Bureaucracy and Economic Development in Africa," *African Review* 1, no. 1 (1974): 93–107.

47. Goran Hyden, *No Shortcuts to Progress* (Berkeley: University of California Press, 1983), pp. 60–63, and A.H.M. Kirk-Greene, "The New African Administration," *Journal of Modern African Studies* 10, no. 1 (1972): 93–108.

48. Statistics from Claude E. Welch, ed., *Soldier and State in Africa* (Evanston: Northwestern University Press, 1970), pp. 268–269.

49. Calculated from Colin Legum, ed., *African Contemporary Record 1981–82* (New York: Africana Publishing Co., 1981), B279, B309, C62–65, and *African Contemporary Record 1978–79* (New York: Africana Publishing Co., 1980), B736.

50. U.S. Arms Control and Disarmament Agency, *World Military Expenditures and Arms Trade 1963–1973* (Washington, DC: U.S. Government Printing Office, 1975), p. 16; *World Military Expenditures and Arms Transfers 1968–1977* (Washington, DC: U.S. Government Printing Office, 1979), p. 27; and *World Military*

Expenditures and Arms Transfers 1971–1980 (Washington, DC: U.S. Government Printing Office, 1983), p. 33.

51. A general overview may be found in Eboe Hutchful, "Trends in Africa," *Alternatives* 10 (1985): 115–137.

52. For a good overview, see Olatunde Odetola, *Military Regimes and Development. A Comparative Analysis in African Societies* (London: George Allen and Unwin, 1982).

53. Jacques de Barrin, "Behind the Facade of Uganda's Democracy," *Manchester Guardian Weekly* 131, no. 4 (22 July 1984): 12.

54. Dennis Austin, "The Ghana Armed Forces and Ghanaian Society," *Third World Quarterly* 7, no. 1 (1985): 99.

55. E. Gyimah-Boadi and Donald Rothchild, "Rawlings, Populism and the Civil Liberties Tradition in Ghana," *Issue* 12, no. 3/4 (1982): 64–69.

56. Richard L. Sklar, "Developmental Democracy," *Comparative Studies in Society and History* 29, no. 4 (1987): esp. pp. 694–698.

57. Ruth Berins Collier, "Parties, Coups and Authoritarian Rule: Patterns of Political Change in Tropical Africa," *Comparative Political Studies* 11, no. 1 (1978): 62–94; Joel D. Barkan and John J. Okumu, "Linkage Without Parties: Legislators and Constituents in Kenya," in Kay Lawson, ed., *Political Parties and Linkage* (New Haven: Yale University Press, 1980), pp. 289–324.

58. Ali A. Mazrui, "Political Engineering in Africa," *International Social Science Journal* 25, no. 2 (1983): 244. Also see Robert H. Jackson and Carl G. Rosberg, *Personal Rule in Black Africa: Prince, Autocrat, Prophet, Tyrant* (Berkeley: University of California Press, 1982), p. 23.

59. Aristide Zolberg, "The Structure of Political Conflict in the New States of Tropical Africa," *American Political Science Review* 62, no. 1 (1968): 70–87.

60. Hyden, No Shortcuts to Progress, p. 19. Also see Donald Rothchild and Victor A. Olorunsola, eds., *State Versus Ethnic Claims: African Policy Dilemmas* (Boulder: Westview Press, 1983), esp. p. 7.

61. Donald Rothchild and E. Gyimah-Boadi, "Ghana's Economic Decline and Development Strategies," in John Ravenhill, ed., *Africa in Economic Crisis* (London: Macmillan, 1986). For a fuller, though earlier, discussion see Michael Lofchie, ed., *The State of the Nations* (Berkeley: University of California Press, 1971).

62. Nelson Kasfir, "Introduction: State and Class in Africa," *Journal of Commonwealth and Comparative Politics* 21, no. 3 (1983): 4.

63. Richard Sandbrook, *The Politics of Africa's Economic Stagnation* (London: Cambridge University Press, 1985), pp. 112–113.

64. See John S. Saul, *The State and Revolution in Eastern Africa* (New York: Monthly Review Press, 1979). See also Marenin, "The Managerial State," pp. 6–10.

65. For an earlier and fuller discussion of these points, see Donald Rothchild and Michael Foley, "The Implications of Scarcity for Governance in Africa," *International Political Science Review* 4, no. 3 (1983): 311–326.

66. For a discussion of state populism, see Donald Rothchild and Letitia Lawson, "The Interaction Between State and Civil Society in Africa: From Deadlock to New Routines," in John W. Harbeson, Donald Rothchild, and Naomi Chazan, eds., *Civil Society and the State in Africa* (Boulder: Lynne Rienner, 1994), pp. 263–266.

67. Timothy M. Shaw, "The State of Crisis: African and International Capitalism in the Late Twentieth Century," in Rothchild and Chazan, *The Precarious Balance*, p. 307.

68. Crawford Young, "The African Colonial State and its Political Legacy," in Rothchild and Chazan, *The Precarious Balance*, p. 60; also see his *The African*

Colonial State in Comparative Perspective (New Haven: Yale University Press), 1994.

69. Sandbrook, *The Politics of Africa's Economic Stagnation*, pp. 35–36.

70. Hyden, *No Shortcuts to Progress*, pp. 45–47; and James S. Wunsch and Dele Olowu, eds., *The Failure of the Centralized State* (Boulder: Westview Press, 1990), passim. For an excellent set of case studies, see I. William Zartman, ed., *Collapsed States: The Disintegration and Restoration of Legitimate Authority* (Boulder: Lynne Rienner, 1995).

71. Azarya, "Reordering State-Society Relations," p. 18.

72. Irving Leonard Markovitz, *Power and Class in Africa* (Englewood Cliffs, NJ: Prentice Hall, 1977), pp. 3–12.

73. Bernard Schaffer, "Organization Is Not Equity: Theories of Political Integration," *Development and Change* 8, no. 1 (1977): 19–44.

74. Philip Lemaitre, "Who Will Rule Africa in the Year 2000?" in Helen Kitchen, ed., *Africa: Mystery or Maze* (New York: Council on Foreign Relations, 1979).

75. Peter Skalnik, "Questioning the Concept of the State in Indigenous Africa," *Social Dynamics* 9, no. 2 (1983): 28; Jean-François Bayart, "Les sociétés africaines face à l'état," *Pouvoirs* 25 (1983): 23–39. Also see Jean-François Bayart, *The State in Africa: The Politics of the Belly* (London and New York: Longman, 1993).

3

Social Groupings

Political life in Africa is conducted through a complex web of social forces, institutional settings, and interpersonal relationships. If government structures furnish the context for official interactions in the public domain, social groups constitute the fundamental building blocks of political action and interchange. In Chapter 2, we demonstrated that it is difficult to understand the state in Africa, and consequently to assess its capacity to formulate and implement policy, without probing its social underpinnings. Most studies of contemporary Africa, cast either in the modernization, dependency, or statist molds, have emphasized the importance of class and ethnicity in determining the social roots of public institutions. African social and material life, however, revolves, in the first instance, around a medley of more compact organizations, networks, groupings, associations, and movements that have evolved over the centuries in response to changing circumstances. Although they frequently serve disparate interests, vary widely in composition, operate in many different ways, and have altered substantially over time, these groups have consistently formed a broad tapestry of social, political, and economic communication. The political interaction approach suggests that it is vital to begin with a closer look at these arenas of social exchange.

Our purpose in this chapter is to examine the cultural, social, and economic frameworks of African political life and the manner and extent of their transformation in the postcolonial era. First, we introduce basic concepts of societal organization in Africa and identify the factors that affect group autonomy and cohesion. Then we portray, in some detail, the various primary and associational organizations that exist in different parts of the continent and the changes they have undergone in the past three decades. On this basis, patterns of differentiation emerging at independence are identified and major trends analyzed.

The discussion is organized around several key questions: What are the main concerns of Africa's various social and economic groups? How do they organize to pursue these goals? How do they deal with each other? What is their connection with formal government institutions? And what are the implications of their activities for politics and policy?

Virtually no corner of Africa has been left untouched by broader economic influences. As Africans have undergone a process of commercialization and as new problems and opportunities have arisen, existing structures have been reshaped or new groups formed to promote interests, obtain access to resources, and enhance cultural meaning. There is much of the old in the new, and although the social bases of African life have been altered, their capitalist roots remain fragile.[1] Social life in African countries may thus lack uniformity; it does, however, possess an underlying coherence.[2]

Societal constructions in Africa, because of the intricate kinds of interpenetration on which they are built, usually cover an area that is broader than the official, the public, the formal. These groups have accumulated varying amounts and types of resources, and consequently political power, independent of government institutions. Thus, state agencies may, in many cases, exercise a degree of direct or indirect control in the social realm. But because of the complex social structures in African countries, governments do not have a monopoly over power, let alone authority or legitimacy. The location of power concentrations and the extent of power dispersion depends, to a great extent, on the nature and degree of interactions between social groups and public institutions. The way these relationships are organized lies at the foundation of the dynamics of politics on the continent.

By examining the intricacies of social reality, choice, and action, it is possible not only to delve into important aspects of group behavior but also to obtain a better grasp of the persistent elements of the African experience that have been achieved during periods of extraordinary instability and structural change.[3] Such a study also helps to delineate the location and effects of power vectors in given African countries. To focus on the structure of socioeconomic organization is therefore to gain important insights into the main features of the African political landscape.

■ SOCIAL GROUPS AND SOCIAL PROCESS

The main basis of political and socioeconomic activity in Africa is the group, rather than the individual or broader social constellation. Membership in groups has been an outgrowth of perceived or real common bonds. These ties may be ones of blood, affinity, identity, utility, or worship. People join organizations not only because they were born into them but also because a certain association or community can advance their interests and concerns and aid them in coping with their surroundings. As more groups have sprung up on the African scene, individuals have tended to attach themselves to a number of organizations simultaneously. Group frameworks are therefore at the core of the African social fabric: although some social action may be conducted by classes or ethnic groups writ large, the reality of social organization consists of participation in smaller groupings limited in membership and/or geographic scope.

The group-based concepts of African social structures have their roots in traditional forms of social organization. The political culture of group action was deeply embedded in precolonial Africa. Both status and prestige at that time were dependent on group affiliation and on the relative position of each group in the social hierarchy. In the colonial period, the associational basis of social life continued and often intensified. Colonial administrations in most parts of the continent viewed coherent groups as desirable precisely because they facilitated control. This orientation encouraged the persistence of existing social structures and, frequently, traditional political units. In some cases these frameworks were allowed to maintain their separate identities, as in the past, but were incorporated simultaneously into the colonial structures. In other instances, people who were engaged in wage labor or in the colonial economy used their proceeds to invest in kin groups or in their local communities. New means were therefore used to enhance status in existing groups.[4]

Colonial attitudes also guided the ways in which Africans could organize to take advantage of opportunities presented by the penetration of Western education and different modes of economic production. In the rural areas, the introduction of cash crops fueled the growth of farmer organizations and migrant associations. The expansion of commerce nurtured trader groups, whereas gender differences took on organizational shape in the form of women's associations and market women's cooperatives.[5] From the urban perspective, group life allowed Africans to control fragments of daily existence. It constituted a significant channel for individual mobility and a psychological cushion against the dislocations of a changing environment.[6] Trade unions, secret societies, savings clubs, ethnic and religious associations, literary societies, sports clubs, and old-boys' networks sprung up in virtually every African city.

The constrictions placed on formal political activity by the colonial authorities meant that voluntary organizations and social and economic groups also became political frameworks in which anticolonial ideas were articulated and leaders schooled, and upon which political support was drawn. Almost every nationalist leader started his political career in a voluntary or economic organization. Felix Houphouët-Boigny in the Syndicat Agricole Africain, Nnamdi Azikiwe in the Ibo State Union, and Julius Nyerere in the Tanganyika Teachers' Association are just some examples. These early organizations also became the cornerstones of party structures and political movements.[7]

In the postcolonial period, this pattern has not only been maintained but has actually flourished, especially in the 1980s. The range of groups in any political context today varies widely. In Ghana, literally hundreds of separate associations were recorded in the last decade alone. Nigeria, too, has witnessed a plethora of social and economic groupings under military rule, particularly in recent years. A steep rise in the formation of such groups has been traced in Côte d'Ivoire; similar levels have been visible in Congo, Zambia, Kenya, and Senegal (to mention but a few).[8] Even in Mozambique and Angola, new local associations have begun to emerge. By the beginning of the fourth decade of independence, vibrant organizations at the grassroots and intermediary levels have become a central vehicle of social interaction.

The aims of these groups reflect the mixture of interest, identity, and consciousness that motivate their members and define their roles.[9] Their primary purpose is to cater to the needs of their members. Ability to dispense goods and services is a decided asset. The strength of these networks grows in direct relationship to the resources they can obtain, control, and distribute.[10] A second objective of these organizations centers on group maintenance. They provide small-scale settings for meaningful participation in a context frequently devoid of possibilities for popular involvement. Most groups have clearly defined codes and norms of behavior. Leaders are subject to scrutiny. Regulations for access to office and for the rotation of persons in positions of responsibility exist. Tools of enforcement and the dispensation of justice have been developed. Decisionmaking is often consultative. Many groups, therefore, have evolved their own concepts of power and authority and devised the means to put them into action.

A third, and related, set of goals focuses on group interaction with broader economic, social, and political frameworks. Specific associations actively pursue formal power or access to those in such positions. They cooperate or conflict with other associations over their place in the market and the social hierarchy. They seek to affect policy, the composition of power holders, and the content of the system itself. They act, therefore, not only as channels of information and communication and as barometers of popular feeling, but also as contenders for power and as key determinants of the political process.[11]

The ability of groups to pursue their objectives is linked to general contextual factors, such as prevailing economic conditions, transnational links and influences, and above all, existing official power constellations.[12] Their capacities are also determined by factors internal to their organization, such as historical continuity, access to or control of autonomous resources (particularly land or labor), location, size, and social organizing principles. For these reasons, social entities vary significantly in scope, ability to act, intensity of operations, internal structure, and impact on others.

The socioeconomic scene in African countries is composed of a multiplicity of interlocking yet distinct organizations.[13] In any given African country, it is possible to discern three main layers of social structures. The first consists of groups based on identity and affinity. Kinship associations, hometown organizations, and cultural units fall into this category. The second, or associational, level of social organization revolves around principles of affiliation. Here it is possible to place professional and occupational groups, such as lawyer associations, medical societies, trade unions, and farmer cooperatives, as well as religious communities, student groups, and neighborhood or village development groups. The third level of social organization is of an interlocking yet amorphous sort: it links specific groups and organizations to each other and to the state. Ethnicity and class are the main categories at this level of social organization (see Chapter 4). Individuals move between the various levels of social organization in the course of a lifetime. Their security, well-being, and development are tied to the nature of the groups to which they belong and how they interrelate.

■ THE ORGANIZATION OF SOCIAL LIFE

In the following pages the main primary and associational structures prevalent on the African scene will be examined in greater detail. The origins of each type of grouping will be traced, its main characteristics examined, the changes it has undergone in recent years explored, and its relations with other social and political entities elaborated.

■ Primary Groups

The first broad category of social structures in Africa consists of indigenous institutions that have deep historical roots, such as clans, lineages, cultural associations, and village communities. As many of these organizations are ascriptive—one is born into them—they are frequently referred to as primary groups. These divisions distinguish African societies along vertical lines: they highlight the differences between groups but do not order them hierarchically. Four main subtypes fall into this rubric: groups based on kinship; territoriality or location; traditional political affiliation; and cultural affinity.

The most continuously significant ascriptive structures throughout Africa have remained those based on *kinship*. Kinship is the bedrock of African social relationships. The extended family, the lineage, and in some cases the more inclusive clan define a person's immediate social networks and obligations. In most cases, descent and inheritance are calculated through the male line: patrilineality has delineated the shape of kinship links. In some parts of Africa, matrilineal descent arrangements still prevail. Among the Akan-speaking peoples of Ghana, for example, inheritance procedures and kin group connections have been determined for centuries through the female line. The mother's brother has been the important person in a child's life; the uncle-nephew relationship has evolved as the most significant. In other instances, mixed descent patterns have developed, in which both female and male ties are salient. Marriage bonds, which are still in many places polygynous, further broaden the social network of kin ties.

Kinship not only defines a person's identity but also a set of values, norms, responsibilities, and life-styles. The kin group is an individual's initial community. Relations with other members of the group are governed by rules deeply embedded in local cultures. Nevertheless, two normative referents appear to be common to most kin connections: the notion of kinship solidarity and the reverence for age and seniority.

Kinship ties are frequently also economic ties. In the past, access to land was granted to lineages and extended families. In many places this pattern has continued to the present. Through kinship, one also gained control of labor, perhaps the single most important determinant of survival prospects and possibilities for well-being. The kin bond was, and continues to be, the cornerstone upon which other economic relations are constructed.

Despite many changes during the colonial period and the first years of independence—including a move toward a more nuclear family in the urban areas and the development of inequalities based on education and income within the extended family—kin ties have rarely been consciously severed or kin obligations easily ignored. It is commonplace, for example, to see agricultural cultivation carried out in rural areas according to principles of household division of labor practiced for years. In areas where a rural exodus has been the norm, if only on a seasonal basis, the rural household still acts as a refuge into which wage laborers withdraw and to which they retire to live out their old age. Kinship responsibilities, moreover, extend to new settings and to new occupations. Illiterate fathers educate their sons, who in turn are expected to provide material support and channels of access for their families in later years. There is rarely a bureaucrat, university lecturer, or migrant worker who does not feel the need to meet the expectations of his or her relatives.

The flexibility of kin groups means that uncertainty and insecurity may be met by adherence to age-old patterns redefined to meet new circumstances and constantly changing surroundings. Although not all kin have equal recourse to group resources (women, in particular, often encounter ongoing discrimination), the adhesive of kinship gives meaning when other institutions are being transformed or fail.

Kinship has frequently been linked to ties of *locality*. The local community is delineated in geographical or territorial terms (even though many residents are related). Place of origin—whether it is a village, town, or a ward of a city—is a bond of not insignificant consequence. If the kinship unit is by definition exclusive, the geographical community tends to be more all-inclusive.[14] The local collectivity was associated, historically, with the framework of production and interchange, with the sources of livelihood. Here different kin groups interacted, social positions were established and at times sanctified, needs met, and interests pursued. If the kin group was the hub of identity, the community was the foundation of material life and exchange.

Homogeneous communities are, in many parts of Africa, a thing of the past. Nevertheless, the notion of locality and local identification is still very strong. In the rural areas, the sense of community has been maintained in the twentieth century through the town association, the local improvement society, or the village development committee. Local government, whether formalized or not, is the business of the indigenous inhabitants. Thus, even in major metropolises such as Nairobi, Lagos, or Accra, the affairs of the community are managed by families that can trace their roots back to the original inhabitants of the area.[15]

Migrants, in turn, maintain strong ties to their places of origin. Hometown organizations in English-speaking Africa, and *associations des originaires* in French-speaking countries, are among the most prominent frameworks in the urban areas. Members aid in the absorption of newcomers, provide them with shelter and food, and help them find jobs in the city. Hometown groupings also raise funds for village improvement, initiate projects, and support local festivals. Although the demands of cohabitation in new settings do foster specific interests, these usually do not dispel ties to one's place of origin. The territorial bond provides a psychological and practical anchor for those who continue to live in the local community as well as for those millions of Africans who have left their place of origin over the years.

Kinship and territoriality were in the past, and in many cases are still today, closely connected to *traditional political institutions* and authority structures. The village community or the extended family were either themselves the framework of political affiliation or were component units of wider political entities, such as states or empires. In precolonial Africa, a variety of political forms were established, ranging from village headmen and councils, through chiefdoms that included a number of villages, to elaborate state entities such as Asante and Benin in West Africa or Buganda and Zulu in East and southern Africa. These political institutions incorporated fragments of clans or lineages, entire social groups, or a wide array of unrelated peoples loosely connected by bonds of authority or territoriality. In each political unit specific concepts of governance and methods of acquiring and using power were developed.

These indigenous structures evolved their own notions of status, prestige, social privilege, and patterns of leadership. The pastoral polities of northeastern Africa therefore differed in organization and guiding rules from the more egalitarian and age-based political structures of the Kikuyu in East Africa or the Igbo of present-day Nigeria. The foundations of legitimacy, authority, and power varied; so did processes of political participation, leadership succession, and decisionmaking.[16]

When the Europeans first reached the shores of Africa, they encountered a multiplicity of rulers and institutions with which they had to come to terms. The political structures and practices of indigenous Africa were frequently co-opted, manipulated, distorted, or in extreme cases even dismantled. In very few instances, however, was the authority of local leaders so undermined or their access to economic resources so circumscribed that they did not survive the processes of colonization and decolonization. Traditional political structures, though often greatly altered or transformed, remain in place in most parts of the continent. Chiefs, paramount chiefs, or other traditional officeholders still control much land and have access to communal labor. These authorities allocate shares of jointly owned lands to kin groups and define community holdings. They may still levy taxes, collect other forms of revenue, and serve as judges and arbiters of local disputes.

The position of the chief varies from country to country. In the Akan-speaking areas of Côte d'Ivoire, for example, those traditional leaders who are still in place are often state functionaries or local civil servants. In neighboring Ghana, in contrast, the importance of local authorities, many of whom are highly educated, actually increased during the 1960s, 1970s, and 1980s, when political turmoil at the national level enhanced the appeal of indigenous institutions and augmented their power. Traditional political structures flourish in Nigeria and regions of Senegal; their role is still debated in Sierra Leone; and in Guinea, although their formal position was abolished at the time of independence, they have reemerged in recent years.[17]

Chiefs collectively may constitute a pressure group and pursue their own interests at the state level. They also stand accountable to their local communities and must abide by accepted rules and practices. Affiliation with traditional, yet altered, political structures is still a part of daily life in contemporary Africa. In situations of political fluctuation or opportunity, these structures offer the security of familiarity and control and may also furnish channels for mobility and growth.

The final type of primary grouping is one that has developed around notions of *cultural identity*. Language groups and cultural associations are, in contrast to the other types of primary groups, very much twentieth-century constructs. Organizations such as the Egbe Omo Oduduwa among the Yoruba, the Asante Kotoko Society, or other cultural clubs were created as a response to growing contacts between different groups in the colonial period. They provided a focus of linguistic definition and historical grounding as well as another vehicle for collective action. These culturally based organizations have often evolved into ethnic associations, as they highlight the subjective perception of cultural belonging and, by extension, distinctiveness. Around these groupings, which blossomed among urban migrants during the colonial period and have continued to thrive ever since, there developed political forms of ethnic action and agitation in the postcolonial period. Usually fueled by members of the elite vying for position among themselves, sectarian-based political mobilization has become an important tool in competing for positions of power or wealth within the formal domain. The ethnic patron, or "big man," has been able to manipulate sentiments of cultural identity and local interests to fulfill personal ambitions. At the same time, however, this framework has provided an important vehicle for group mobility and differentiation.

In some cases, cultural identity has taken on a regional dimension as well. During the colonial period, the imperial powers divided up their colonies for administrative purposes. The French set up *cercles* and *sous-divisions*; the British, districts and provinces; the Belgians, large administrative regions. At independence, many of these administrative regions were geographically redefined and others were deprived of resources or official political roles. Nevertheless, in several countries administrative regions have been retained and, in fact, institutionalized. Liberia, despite the turmoil it has undergone in the past two decades, is still divided into counties. In Nigeria, the three regions of the independence constitution have been transformed by stages into thirty-six states that have fairly significant administrative responsibilities. Ghana's unitary governments have maintained and even further subdivided the colonial regions. In Congo, provincial governments are still significant funnels of official resource allocation (as well as of rebellion), as are the *wilayas* in Algeria. In some areas, especially where regional divisions overlap cultural identities, a sense of regional identity has developed. In Ethiopia, Sudan, Congo, Mozambique, Angola, Senegal, Côte d'Ivoire, and Chad, the regional unit per se has assumed a special position, as a focus for both affiliation and action.

The kin, territorial, political, and cultural structures evident on the African scene have in common an ascriptive and/or delimited geographic definition of membership. Particular subnational, symbolic schemes bind members together. These groups adhere to patterns of authority established by traditional or revised custom, and members have a clear notion of belonging to a community linked together around common norms and values. The locations of these groups span, and at times transcend, the boundaries of a given country. The commitment to the primary tie has promoted some perception of a commonality of goals and interests. In political terms, demands have been raised, votes given, and support withdrawn depending on government responses to these concerns.

Together, primary groupings lay the foundation for an understanding of the nature of social pluralism in given African countries. The degree of heterogeneity evident in any country (or, conversely, the degree of homogeneity) defines the social connection among various groups and determines many of the types of social conflict. This ascriptive pole, therefore, outlines the national structure and the predominant lines of vertical cleavage in a particular country.

Vertical boundaries are based on intricate and constantly changing notions of inclusion and exclusion. Asantes in Ghana may see themselves as Akan in relation to the Ewe (another broad linguistic group), as Asante in relation to the Fante (an Akan-speaking ethnic group), or as Mampong in relation to people from Offinsu (two political and geographical units). Each of these identities evokes situational considerations, material aspirations, and symbolic concerns. Without question, lines of cooperation and conflict do refer back to historical patterns of interaction and social memory. But what is more emphatic in recent years is that the self-perceptions and interest delineation of such groups are significantly molded by government composition, policies, and performance.[18] How people view themselves is thus often a mixture of objective criteria as well as some reflection of how others categorize and behave toward them.

The web of relations around interlocking frameworks varies substantially from place to place. During the colonial and postcolonial periods, kin connections have endured and frequently been transformed. They have rarely, however, been discarded.[19] Similarly, the bond of the local community has been retained and, in many cases, has increased in periods of grave economic and political uncertainty. Cultural links, on the other hand, have vacillated according to circumstances. And traditional political institutions have persisted when these authorities have succeeded in retaining access to resources and/or when formal government structures have been incapacitated. The significance of each of these entities, however, has increased when ties of kinship and territoriality have overlapped. This was the case, for example, among the Igbo of Nigeria in the late 1960s, the Oromo in Ethiopia, the Ovimbundu in Angola in the 1980s and 1990s, and the southern Sudanese throughout the latter part of the twentieth century.

Primary groupings and collective forms of identity in Africa, despite alterations in definition and relative position, have ongoing meaning for their participants. These frameworks are highly institutionalized, and within their confines presumptive rules of behavior—well known to members—do prevail. They are also flexible. Ascriptive structures have consequently usually maintained a high degree of cohesion.[20] In the wider setting, these groups offer channels for lateral interaction and for engagement with central government authorities, as well as for withdrawal from the state realm. With very few exceptions, however, they do not preclude other forms of association. Entities of this sort, precisely because they are particularistic, are not by definition all-embracing: They may stand alone, but more often than not they comprise the source of basic identities without impeding other forms of affiliation and action.

■ Social and Economic Organizations

Social and economic organizations, unlike primary groups, have emerged explicitly around associational interests. This horizontal constellation of basic social structures covers a diversity of groups established to secure occupational, social, ideological, leisure, self-improvement, and service goals. Membership in these associations is frequently on a voluntary basis. These structures usually, though by no means exclusively, sprang up initially around urban centers and were originally connected with the growth of colonial state institutions and official markets. For this reason, these associations have generally operated within broader geographic frameworks than primary groups and have helped to determine the organization of social and economic life in individual countries.

Occupational groups. The most visible of these horizontal groupings developed around occupational concerns and include various associations of workers, farmers, teachers, lawyers, engineers, police, soldiers, entrepreneurs, and traders. *Professional associations* bring together educated people to pursue joint substantive concerns and to vie for collective benefits. Prominent among these organizations are the bar associations (which incorporate lawyers within each country and also on regional and continental bases) and associations of doctors, nurses, teachers, journalists, architects, engineers, chartered accountants, insurance agents, and university lecturers. Of the many occupational organizations, the professional ones tend to be among the best organized and most cohesive.

The origins of the professional associations of contemporary Africa lie in the colonial period, when the first educated Africans banded together to exchange information and to promote their interests within the frameworks created by colonial rule. By definition, professional organizations have been limited to a select circle of people who have had Western education and possess special qualifications; the several hundreds of thousands of professionally trained people in Africa constitute only a small fraction of the population of the continent.[21] Although there is considerable internal equality among members of these associations, there is also a fair amount of distance between them and other social organizations in each country. The resources of these groups are a function of their bargaining power—of the perquisites they can gain, the salaries they can negotiate, and the fees that they can demand for their services.

As more Africans entered the ranks of the highly educated and as their qualifications became more specialized, the size and diversity of these organizations increased. The growth of these associations also augmented their capacity to lobby for more benefits. Professional organizations provide basic social services and thereby help to shape urban life-styles. They have consequently secured both special access to official resources and privileged positions in many countries.

Because professional status has been linked to government activities in many cases, and because many professionals are public service employees, professional associations have been heavily represented in the formal political arena. Some of these organizations were active in the initial phases of decolonization and, indeed, spearheaded anticolonial movements.[22] Others defined the terms of decolonization. Since independence, these organizations have been constantly involved in public affairs. They are salient and forceful pressure groups on any African government and have been at the forefront, not only of support for particular regimes, but also of opposition, protest, and dissent.[23] They constitute a highly visible barometer of public opinion in the state. They have therefore been the object of numerous official attempts to control them. When they have come together independently under an umbrella organization, such as the Association of Recognized Professional Bodies in Ghana, they have been transformed into a formidable political force capable of toppling unpopular governments or inducing significant change in policy orientations (as, most notably, in the early 1990s, when such coalitions were instrumental in inducing major political reforms in many countries).

Closely related to these professional groupings, yet nevertheless distinct, are organizations of people employed, in one way or another, by the state. The most important associations of this sort are those of *civil servants*. Similar bodies exist for the police, and in almost every African country the military also acts as an interest group, even where the armed forces are in power. Membership in these groups—whether institutionalized or loosely organized—is defined by place of work. Although state employees have in common direct access to and even control over state resources, the interests of these subgroups do not always coincide. Bureaucrats may be viewed as a cohesive social segment united by long-range security interests that are frequently at odds with those of more transitory political cadres. Each of these groups, therefore, is separable analytically, and each can act distinctly from the state apparatus that it purports to serve.[24]

Associations of civil servants, military, and loosely knit groupings of politicians have proliferated as state institutions have expanded and parastatal corporations have grown. These organizations are highly instrumental in nature: They attempt to preserve the status of their members and advance their corporate interests. As these groups do not themselves engage in economic production but in the control of formal resources, they have built up a culture of power. "The power cult is everywhere embedded in the total culture of elite groups."[25] Power, in the view of members of these groups, is integrally linked to the state nexus; its location, conceptually and physically, is at the center of government institutions. Such groups have become the social embodiment of the formal sector.

Beginning in the 1980s, with the depletion of state resources, stringent adherence to programs of bureaucratic streamlining, and wage constraints many public employees witnessed a reduction in their standards of living and a diminution of their incomes. They suffered palpably from food shortages in the urban areas and, in countries such as Ghana, Nigeria, Côte d'Ivoire, Gabon, Cameroon, Kenya, and Congo, began to move into the private sector. With the increasing trends in the 1990s toward privatization, the civil service may no longer be the only major repository of skills in many African states.

A third, government-linked, occupational group is that of *chiefs,* or traditional authorities. In various parts of the continent, the position of chiefs has been formalized, and in some cases they have enjoyed income from the state. In Sierra Leone, for example, "the office of paramount chief, although used as an instrument of social control by the central government, has nevertheless been ardently sought because it has represented an important avenue to wealth and social prestige."[26] In Nigeria, most traditional authorities, known as natural rulers, have been organized in houses of chiefs and have received government sanction and salaries (but formally the role of the great emirs of northern Nigeria has been curtailed). In Ghana, despite attempts by Kwame Nkrumah to downplay chieftancy, chiefs as a group have been protected by subsequent constitutions and have been able to wield power through formal and informal organizations.

Entrepreneurs, particularly owners of industrial enterprises, have also established organizations to forward their common concerns and to forge avenues of access to official agencies. Many entrepreneurs, a fairly new social category on the continent, come from the ranks of politicians or government employees. Others began as petty traders and small businesspeople and succeeded in establishing vast manufacturing concerns. The opportunity for entrepreneurial expansion has been heavily dependent on government policy. In countries that have stressed state ownership of industries, such as Guinea, Ethiopia, Algeria, Somalia, Mozambique, and Angola, businesspeople as a group have not risen to the fore. In states that have relied on foreign firms and capital, such as Cameroon and Congo, local industrialists were few and far between until the beginning of the 1980s. On the other hand, in mixed enterprise or systems of nurture capitalism, as in Kenya, Nigeria, Ghana, Morocco, Zambia, and Senegal, private entrepreneurs have blossomed. In Ghana, they account for at least 50 percent of industrial ownership; in Nigeria, after the indigenization decrees of the late 1970s, they constituted even higher proportions of ownership of large-scale businesses.[27] These industrialists have come together in chambers of commerce and employers' associations to protect the private sector and to lobby government for favorable credit terms, flexible trade policies, import provisions, and licensing arrangements. Thus, especially in the 1980s and 1990s, and with the expansion of the informal economy, an indigenous monied bourgeoisie of not insignificant proportions has emerged. This closely knit group has transnational links, often bypasses state frontiers, and possesses many of its own sources of capital.

When taken together, associations of professionals, government employees, chiefs, and entrepreneurs constitute elite groupings that are bound to each other by interlocking membership, income, status, and life-style. These elite organizations are composed of individuals who have had access to education, the state apparatus, and concomitant wealth. Members of these organizations are frequently closely related personally. They live in the better parts of each capital city, send their children to the best schools at home or in Europe, and enjoy the most modern amenities of the Western world.[28] Their children are disproportionately represented in institutions of higher education. They themselves move easily from public to private enterprises, and their standard of living is maintained through astute political action.[29] This system has been sustained because elite groups have not been totally exclusionary: They continuously held forth the promise of membership to young people who have followed the path of education or government service. Because of the close interpenetration of these groups and their reliance on government resources, they have come to constitute, despite internal factionalization and cleavage, what may best be described as the dominant class or the managerial bourgeoisie. Their interests are heavily represented in the formal state apparatus; public institutions, in turn, provide an opportunity for them to further pursue their objectives, and government policies frequently reflect their concerns.

Elite culture during the first decades of independence revolved around the close connection among education, state power, and personal wealth. Informed by kinship and ethnic affinity—although hardly confined to these links—elites nurtured an extractive view of politics that dominated the national scene during the first postcolonial years. Norms of public behavior and social interaction were initially laid down by these groups, which, in the name of development and social progress, frequently enhanced their own status and wealth. They molded patterns of domination, social stratification, and separation.[30] Without these organizations, it would have been impossible to maintain basic services or to administer a country; their corporate interests have also made them a major drain on public resources. In recent years, however, much of the attention of professional groups and even state employees shifted from the political domain, where opportunities had been constricted, to that of the market. At this juncture, the beginnings of a new definition of interests, and perhaps identity, began to surface among these groups, possibly paving the way for different forms of interaction.

Unlike elite occupational interests, other occupational associations have usually been more amorphous organizationally, and only segments have been consolidated in discrete groupings. *Trade unions* were among the first nonelite bodies to coalesce during the colonial period. Workers' organizations were formed around sources of wage labor: in the mining regions of the Zambian copper belt, Katanga, and South Africa, the ports and the railways in East and West Africa, and major urban concentrations. Although trade unions were banned in many parts of the continent in the prewar period, they have multiplied since 1945.

During early independence these unions were consolidated, and frequently trade union congresses, or *associations des syndicats,* were established. The experience of organized labor since independence has been one of increased government regulation and periodic dissension.[31] Officials have attempted to standardize criteria for membership, control wages, and exact loyalty from labor leaders. Despite concerted efforts to subordinate trade unions to state policies and to co-opt leaders, as more people have entered the labor force, and as individual unions have pressed for better conditions for their members, unions have persisted and have been reorganized and in many cases reinvigorated.

The social organizing principles of workers' organizations, which still encompass only a small proportion of African laborers, center on the pragmatic struggle for improved work conditions, salaries, and less frequently, prices and subsidies. Because trade unions have sprung up in economic centers and during crucial economic occurrences, their visibility has been particularly high. Around trade unions and workers' organizations there have developed new forms of consciousness and radical subcultures. In contrast to the avowed nationalism of Nigerian elites, for example, laborers in Nigeria's cities have evolved a form of urban populism heavily imbued with ethnicity and religion.[32] In Ghana, the railway workers of Sekondi-Takoradi stood at the forefront of opposition to elite privilege and bureaucratic domination. Through strikes and demonstrations, song and dance, in popular literature and the theater, workers have expressed contempt for patterns of public power abuse and corruption and have backed, if only implicitly, movements for radical transformation.[33] Not only have they frequently created a mood of discontent, but they have also found their own methods of protest. The forms of protest at the workplace include withdrawal and desertion, neglect, slowdown, sabotage, and theft.[34] Trade unions, consequently, have been in a position to make government officials more accountable; they have not, however, with the notable exception of Zambia, been able to bring about substantial political transformation.

Trade union organization and worker action in various parts of Africa have, indeed, been marked by a great deal of ambiguity. Union organizers have often found themselves caught between their dependence on those in power at the state level and the demands and needs of their members.

Worker reliance on elite social groups and on the state as the major wage employer has therefore constrained their options and has usually fostered an uneasy alliance with public officials.

One cushion of wage laborers in these circumstances has been to engage in petty commerce or trade in conjunction with their salaried employment. *Trade networks* have a long history in most parts of Africa. Along the West African coast, women have monopolized petty trade throughout the twentieth century, controlling the markets in Lagos, Ibadan, Accra, Kumasi, Abidjan, and Monrovia, to name but a few. Hausa and Dioula traders (mostly male) have operated in the savannah regions, frequently roaming down to the coast to sell their wares. In central and East Africa, women traders have been joined by Asians and Swahilis along the coast and by other male traders in the interior.[35]

Trader organizations have multiplied as commerce has grown. In many cases, they possess a well-defined internal structure. Market-women groups, for example, elect their own leaders and employ elaborate sanctions to discipline members. Leaders of the Kumasi marketing pools, to illustrate from one case, "settle disputes, primarily over credit and commercial procedure, and represent traders in external negotiations and at ceremonies such as funerals. Leaders of the predominantly female foodstuffs group represent the market as a whole."[36] Through their organizations, traders divide routes, commodities, market stalls, and even entire transportation systems. The marketplace is thus an important hub of social as well as economic life in many parts of Africa. The vibrancy of particular markets is an excellent indicator of social conditions and productive capacities in particular countries.

Traders, and especially market women, have been the object of public criticism and, at times, of official scapegoating, especially when commodities are scarce and food prices skyrocket. In Ghana in 1979, the main Accra market, Makola, was razed in an effort to eradicate trade malpractices. Goods quickly became unavailable and prices rose even more. In 1983, when the markets were deregulated, the supply of goods became more predictable. In Ghana, therefore, "if the chief liability for traders has been government interference, their chief asset has been the creation of, and participation in, a distribution system suited to Ghana's needs."[37] As most salaried people and many rural producers take part directly or through their families in some form of trade or petty manufacturing, they were able to survive and even thrive during the economic crisis of the 1980s. These associations, together with artisan groups, therefore constitute the core of contemporary nonstate yet market-oriented processes of social reconstruction. Although they are affected by government policies, they are not dependent on the state. In this category, small craft guilds, rotating credit associations, apprenticeship systems, and organizations of small manufacturers have also developed. Microindustrial units are, like their commercial counterparts, tied to market processes and reinforce the significance of this form of social organization.

Trading networks link local producers with the market and often with the state. At least 70 percent of Africa's population is engaged, in one form or another, in agricultural production. Most agricultural activity takes place in *peasant households*, where a small-scale, family economy prevails. Each cluster of agricultural producers has rights to land and labor but is, at the same time, also involved in a wider system of production that defines its status and options.[38]

The evolution of African rural production patterns has been dictated by ecological possibilities and local traditions and customs as well as by official orientations. For this reason, the molding of farming cultures has differed quite significantly from place to place. Thus, in southern Rhodesia (present-day Zimbabwe) there emerged a group of small-scale cash farmers who were gradually stripped of their access to land and labor and thereby proletarianized during the course of the twentieth century. In Ghana, capitalist cocoa farmers developed export production at the household level with the assistance of seasonal workers provided by labor-exporting groups on the fringe of the forest zones. In Tanzania, a stratified pattern of development was evident, with various farmers coexisting on an unequal basis in the countryside. In Rwanda, an independent form of labor consciousness coalesced around *ubureetwa*, a method of labor clientship used widely during the colonial period. In each African country, then, and in each subregion, different types of rural differentiation emerged.[39]

In any given rural area it was possible to identify, by the beginning of the postcolonial period, clusters of petty bourgeois farmers who expropriated large tracts of land and brought in seasonal migrant laborers; a middle peasantry, usually with one farm and its own family labor; an indebted peasantry, which borrowed money and engaged in sharecropping; and landless migrant laborers.[40] Rural variety and rural inequalities, therefore, defy the tendency to aggregate agriculturalists into an overarching category of "peasant." The culture of peasants is marked, in most parts of the continent, by local orientations and semi-autonomous interest structures.[41]

The degree of institutionalization of farmer interests varies. Some governments have sought to control rural inhabitants by establishing large producer organizations, such as the United Ghana Farmers Council during the Nkrumah period. Although many similar efforts have been made to force the diversity of rural life into some uniform grid controlled by governments, these efforts have not been particularly successful.[42] Farmers have often organized their own self-help groups. Such producer and marketing cooperatives have blossomed in many parts of the continent since independence, with the dual effect of politicizing farmer organizations and creating spheres of independent activity autonomous of state control.

Small farmers are poorly represented in central government. Nevertheless, they hold the key to development prospects. They may totally oppose government measures and bypass or ignore official channels. They may bargain with officials. They may receive some support from particular regimes, or they may even enjoy substantial encouragement, as in the case, at various junctures, of Niger, Kenya, and Tanzania.[43] Networks of peasant producers usually do not interact laterally with each other, but deal, separately, with other social groups and local and state bureaucrats. Peasants, because of their proximity to vital resources, do have power; in most parts of Africa, however, they are difficult to organize and therefore are only marginally represented in the formal sector. The effect is to diminish their immediate impact on policy, although hardly their long-range political influence.

The processes of capitalist penetration and state aggrandizement have fostered fragmentation and growing inequalities in the rural areas. The political cultures of these groups reveal their diffuse worldviews. Exclusion from activities at the state level, coupled with the capacity to evade formal control, have generated many combinations of fatalism and defiance throughout rural Africa.[44] As an ineffectively mobilized group, farmers have continued to maintain their own spheres of activity while nevertheless interacting more regularly with official institutions and with each other. Their networks, like those of traders and petty manufacturers, extend beyond the reach of government agencies.

Occupational structures (of professionals, state employees, workers, traders, entrepreneurs, and farmers) cover a wide range of interests and concerns, although they differ from one another in the extent of their organizational coherence, the degree of their access to and the kinds of resources they control, the cultures they have elaborated, their historical legacies, and hence their capacities. By the close of the fourth decade of independence, these interlocking networks had been commercialized, thus emerging as the most readily apparent of the essential frameworks of daily economic life.

Women's and students' associations. A second major horizontal constellation has evolved around the universal distinctions of age and gender. *Women's organizations* have played a prominent role in African political history in the twentieth century, especially in the western part of the continent. The roots of gender-based social groups lie in the development of a sexual division of labor in many African societies in the precolonial period. The colonial intrusion added new dimensions to the differentiation between the sexes. During this period, wage labor and export production came to be considered men's work. Women continued to produce food and to market their goods locally. Some women's organizations did provide support and even financial backing for anticolonial movements. Since independence, however, women as a collectivity have generally been neglected and underrepresented in central institutions. The public (state) and private (household) distinctions have assumed gender overtones as well.[45] Development policies have frequently excluded women, and when specific projects were designed for their benefit, these projects often resulted in women's further marginalization.[46]

Some facts regarding the condition of African women in the postcolonial period are pertinent here. Women predominate in the subsistence sector in most parts of the continent. It is estimated that their activities account for 78 percent of food production, 80 percent of food processing, 80 percent of fuel preparation, 80 percent of water supplies, 90 percent of brewing, and 50 percent of animal husbandry.[47] Between 60 and 80 percent of field hands in sub-Saharan Africa are women, as are 50 percent of cattle tenders.[48]

Women also play an important role in petty trade. Sixty percent of internal trade in Africa is conducted by women. Despite their centrality in the local economy, women are grossly underrepresented in wage labor. They make up only 15 percent of workers in the wage sector. Even where women do take part in modern wage employment, they tend to congregate in the lower income categories. The incomes of 50 percent of female wage earners in Kenya are below the poverty line.[49] Specific efforts to improve women's access to and status in wage employment have been slow.

The lopsided participation of African women in economic life reveals a picture of severe gender disparities. This divergence has increased the dependence of women on men for cash income. Many women find themselves more burdened, more impoverished, and more on their own economically than in the past. This trend is reflected in figures on literacy and school enrollment, two vital indicators of the current and potential status of women in Africa. Female literacy is 67 percent in Lesotho and only 6 percent in Chad. With the exception of Botswana and Lesotho, females are less literate than males throughout the continent. When coupled with higher mortality rates and inferior health facilities, it appears that the process of impoverishment falls disproportionately on females.

The position of women in various parts of Africa is determined to a large extent by cultural norms and traditional practices. Although African women frequently share common concerns, specific forms of inequality vary from country to country and from one culture to another. New problems have cropped up since independence. The image of women has suffered tremendously from scapegoating in the media. Working women have been particularly exposed to derision in the press. Incidences of rape, prostitution, and child-dumping have increased alarmingly in recent years. In the mid-1990s, Tutsi women suffered mass rapes in Rwanda, often followed by death at the hands of their Hutu tormenters.

Disparities of personal and social status have inevitably led to a call for greater gender equality. In Muslim societies of the Sahel this has taken on the form of a demand for the liberation of women from certain conditions imposed by religion. In the agrarian countries of West Africa it has been expressed in a call for greater property rights in general and access to land in particular. There is a growing recognition in women's quarters that women's depressed status in society is closely related to the ambiguity of their place in the public arena. Although they still possess spheres of autonomy (especially financial), they have witnessed a reduction in their political positions in comparison to their status in traditional society. The symbolic features of women's existence, therefore, capture many of the anomalies of contemporary life in Africa. Women, like some farmers, workers, and local communities, resist subordination to official institutions. Still, the "reality that African women have constructed lingers and remains a vision for a world without the state leviathan."[50]

The many different views of African women on their condition have been given expression in a myriad of women's organizations that fall into several distinct categories. First are the official women's associations. Each African country has its own umbrella organization (the All Women's Association of Ghana, the Organization of Mozambique Women, etc.). At times, there is a women's branch of the ruling party that either fills this role or exists side by side with the general association. Official women's groups tend to reflect the position of their regimes on women's matters.

A second type of women's association is based on employment. Every major trade union in Africa has a women's branch (which usually follows government guidelines). Professions that have a high representation of women (nurses, teachers) also have an allied women's organization. Traders have established their own institutions to meet their needs, as have female farmers in recent years.

Voluntary associations constitute the third form of women's organization. These groups provide services for women, extend nonformal training, operate childcare facilities, and furnish support networks. Many of these organizations (the YWCA and the Ahmaddiyah, for example) are tied to international women's associations or to religious institutions (churches, mosques).

A fourth kind of women's organization is of a grassroots sort. These local associations have sprung up in rural and urban areas to meet specific needs of working women. They differ from the voluntary groups in their more spontaneous origins, their localized roots, their self-help orientation, and their avowed (nonestablishment) activism. A fifth type of group, to be found in some major cities, falls into the radical feminist category. Highly educated women have banded together to militate for basic changes in social attitudes toward their gender. Many of these women are aggregated in the continent-wide Association of African Women for Research and

Development. A final, and quite distinct, kind of women's group has been that connected to later liberation movements; among this type, the women's sections of the African National Congress (ANC) in the new South Africa and of the South-West African People's Organization (SWAPO) in Namibia are still extremely strong.

There are literally thousands of women's associations in Africa today (many individuals hold multiple membership in several groups). Each women's organization reflects the social composition, age, geographical location, occupational constellation, and ideological predilection of its participants. The split between mass-based and government-backed groups has become more apparent. So, too, has the disparity between elite and nonelite women. With the crystallization of African women's organizations, a growing understanding of the profundity of the implications of the gender division of labor in many portions of Africa has emerged. Their experiences and their responses to their condition highlight a crucial, and all too often neglected, theme in African social organization.

Much in the same mold as women's organizations, although quite different in its political implications, is the *youth sector,* which consists of a series of associations that have frequently bisected other types of horizontal formations and primary groups. The notion of differentiation by age has deep roots in African cultures. Seniority has, traditionally, been closely associated with political office and positions of responsibility. Norms of deference, as well as rights and obligations, were defined in many societies in terms of age and status associated with elders. Youth, therefore, was conceived of as rebellious and critical; in many places its role as a limited watchdog was institutionalized (the *asafo* companies in West Africa, made up of "brigades of young men," are a case in point).[51]

Youth groups spearheaded the formation of protest movements in the colonial period (the Gold Coast Youth Conference and the Nigerian Youth Movement, for example) and constituted the preliminary frameworks around which many anticolonial movements were constructed in the postwar era. In the initial years of independence, these youth wings were incorporated into the ruling parties, and official youth organizations were established. At the same time the creation of national universities witnessed the establishment of student unions at all major universities.

Over the years, organizations such as the National Association of Nigerian Students (NANS) or the National Union of Ghanaian Students (NUGS) have engaged in highly visible political activity. They have lobbied to protect student disbursements and the unusually luxurious conditions of student life in many portions of Africa; they have also set themselves up as units to monitor the quality of public life in most African countries. Students have therefore emerged as a vital barometer of the status of particular regimes, being among the first groups to voice discontent and to indicate levels of dissatisfaction with government policies.[52]

Although not an economic force, student groups have played an important role in shaping popular attitudes.[53]

Youth organizations have not been confined to student activity. In many local communities small youth associations—often the successors of traditional constructs—have resurfaced in recent years. Some youth groups are attached to church groups and Muslim communities. Separate youth organizations have also been established to cater to the interests of elite youth in the cities (the Boy Scouts and Girl Guides are major examples). These associations, much like their student counterparts, represent certain interests and worldviews and help to define the individual member's social position and standing.

Women's and youth associations differ from other forms of social and economic organization in that they cut across conventional structures of affiliation and identity and establish settings for linking otherwise disparate groups. Their numbers, cohesion, and modes of activism reflect the content of many broader societal concerns in particular African states and establish patterns of lateral transaction. For these reasons they mirror, perhaps better than many of their counterparts, some fundamental societal values, norms, problems, and practices.

Other voluntary organizations. During the twentieth century, Africans have also created a variety of associations that provide outlets for leisure and service activities. In the urban areas, many sports clubs, improvement associations, literary societies, alumni associations (generally known as old boys' and old girls' networks), debating groups, credit clubs, and neighborhood development institutions have developed. These organizations furnish frameworks for discussion, debate, support, and interaction. Recreation groups help to structure leisure activities, just as credit associations (known as *esusu* in Nigeria) offer loans and provide some financial security.[54] Cities have also been the setting for the formation of street gangs, drug rings, gambling groups, and organized crime networks, which are a rarely studied byproduct of rapid urbanization. In the past two decades, some of these voluntary associations have also spread to the rural areas. Small towns and villages now boast stadiums or athletic fields where soccer has become a favorite activity. Many local communities have their own reading societies and self-help organizations. Thus, many voluntary groups fill in the spaces that other institutions have not been able to bridge.

The most recent innovation on the associational scene has been the emergence, in the past two decades, of civil liberties and human rights groups, such as local branches of Amnesty International or Africa Watch, as well as separate African organizations (the Civil Liberties Organization in Nigeria, for example). These associations monitor infringements of individual rights and have played a central role in the current wave of democratization.

When taken together, social and economic groups of various sorts have emerged to deal with virtually every aspect of human existence in Africa. Although they vary widely in size, scope, and degree of institutionalization, they do furnish a resilient and pliant network that supports social, material, and cultural life throughout the continent. These associations, based on interest articulation and affiliation, have several features in common. First, their expansion and growth have been closely linked to the creation of colonial and postcolonial centers and to the spread of market mechanisms. They are, therefore, more salient in and around administrative and economic centers (in contrast with the local focus of primary groupings). Second, many of these groups, although by no means all, are marked by the ethnically crosscutting composition of their membership. And third, these horizontal groups have quite different political connections and, hence, impact on state policies. Elite groups tend to be better organized, their membership more cohesive, and their representation in state institutions more pronounced than other forms of horizontal organization. The web of relations between various groups mirrors patterns of subordination and social cleavage even when it is not possible to point to coherent class formations. Indeed, these institutions emerge both as vehicles for joint activity and as manifestations of social and political differentiation.

▮ Religious Communities

The symbolic sphere is best articulated by a medley of religious structures that have been shaped around historical experiences and contacts and have provided mechanisms for dealing with the exigencies of daily life for centuries. Participation in religious organizations is the most prevalent form of associational life in Africa today.[55] Africans belong to religious frameworks ranging from organized churches, Muslim brotherhoods, secret sects, messianic movements, spiritualist movements, and prayer gatherings to antiwitchcraft groups and animistic cults.

Traditional African religions, which are still followed in many parts of the continent, are based on particularistic worldviews and involve worship of ancestors and natural objects. Each African society evolved its own set of deities; around these gods there developed explanations for natural and social phenomena and well-defined concepts of power and legitimacy. Muslim invaders and traders who came in contact with Africans along the trans-Saharan and East African trading routes introduced their great tradition into Africa at an early date. The diffusion of Islam was accomplished either by conquest, by the Islamization of African rulers (first in ancient Ghana and Mali and then in other areas), or most notably, by the gradual adaptation of Islamic practices in many African societies, usually as a result of economic contacts. In this process of the piecemeal spread of Islam, the religion became Africanized, undergoing modifications to suit local conditions.[56]

By the time Europeans began to arrive on the shores of the continent, the Islamic presence had been established in the Sahel, along the East African coast, in the Sudan, and throughout most of West Africa. The nineteenth-century *jihads* (holy wars) in west Africa led to the formation of large Islamic states and entrenched the position of some Muslim orders at the apex of politico-religious entities (such as the Fulani empire in northern Nigeria, Massina in Senegal, and Kong in Côte d'Ivoire).

Christianity has existed in Africa for some time (most notably in Ethiopia), but its spread is related to the white encounter. The religious expression of colonialism came in the form of Christian missionaries and proselytizing societies. The Portuguese, and then the Dutch, the British, the Germans, the French, and the Belgians, were accompanied in their initial intrusions into Africa by clerics and religious leaders. Christianity, with the backing of the colonial powers, spread rapidly through non-Muslim areas of Africa at the same time as Islam continued to expand as a barrier against cultural and religious imperialism.[57] Even in Muslim areas, however, religious leaders sometimes cooperated with colonial authorities and benefited economically from the association (as in the case of the Mourides of Senegal) or resisted colonial penetration and stood apart from the colonial worldview.[58] The "role of religion as a symbolic medium of contact and conflict is striking in the colonial history of Africa."[59]

Anticolonialism and religious activity were intertwined, although the two processes did not always intersect. Each may be viewed "as a combined cultural/ideological/social/political response to the situation."[60] Thus, although religious activity in the later colonial period was intrinsically political, as it was in South Africa in the 1990s, it was not necessarily anticolonial. Indeed, nationalism in Africa, in contrast to Asia, for example, was fundamentally secular. When the colonial rulers departed the continent, however, they left behind a religious legacy whose impact in terms of cultural change and conflict was immeasurable.

The early years of independence seemingly reflected the secular spirit of anticolonialism. Religious commitment was a fact of life for individual Africans, but it rarely emerged as a major factor in national affairs during the 1960s. At this time, religious institutions, like many of their socioeconomic and political counterparts, underwent a process of Africanization. Umbrella religious organizations, such as National Christian Councils, African branches of the World Council of Churches, national Catholic organizations, and Muslim councils, were set up in many African capitals. Also, separate religious communities proliferated. Orthodox churches and spiritual movements continued to grow. Mosque construction increased, and progressive Muslim orders, such as the Ahmaddiyah, expanded.

Starting in the 1970s and 1980s, as secular political structures were enfeebled and economic conditions worsened, a widespread religious renaissance began to take place. Although periods of religious fervor and revivalism are not new in African history, this most recent demonstration of religious activity reaffirms the close connection between religious identity, power, and politics on the continent. Religious institutions became important vehicles for the expression of popular discontent and for the elaboration of alternative survival strategies.[61]

The assertion of religious consciousness has been most noticeable in the Islamic portions of the continent. In some countries—such as Senegal, Mauritania, Sudan, Somalia, and, most notably, Libya—state institutions have assumed religious trappings and explicitly shed many of their secular characteristics.[62] Islamic frameworks have also supplied important channels for the expression of discontent with secular authorities. In northern Nigeria, Islam has become a crucial vehicle for voicing dissatisfaction with the government. In Senegal, the Mouride *marabouts* (holy men) became self-appointed spokesmen for peasant political dissent; they transformed themselves into trade union leaders of a new sort. Some Muslim communities have withheld allegiance from official bodies and created alternative constructs of a totally independent order. In portions of West Africa and the Sahel, fundamentalist Islamic sects have sprouted up. The Arab societies of North Africa have likewise seen the rise of fundamentalist movements, especially in Algeria in the 1990s, in protest against ruling elites. In these areas, an Islamic network may be basically reordering political allegiances.[63]

Christian activism has also become more apparent during the past decade. Fundamentalist denominations have enjoyed a new resurgence. Millenarian sects and spiritual movements, such as the Watchtower Society, have flourished. Traditional secret societies are still operative. In some countries, such as Tanzania, Kenya, and Congo, established churches have provided employment and food at times of scarcity. These have also been vocal in opposing the violations of the rule of law by government officials, actively denouncing administrative conduct in countries such as Ghana, Zambia, and Kenya.[64] In extreme cases, such as in Nigeria, churches have become the basis for intense rioting and violence; and in portions of southern and South Africa, churches have furnished settings for the grouping of the devout in communities consciously withdrawn from broader political currents.

Africa at the beginning of the twenty-first century is thus also divided along religious lines. Relations between Muslims and Christians within and across international boundaries are affected by their external associations as well as by their differing symbolic orientations. The increasingly close connections between African Muslims and the central lands of Islam, especially through the *hajj* (pilgrimage) to Mecca, have influenced their attitudes toward the Western world.[65] Christian affiliations with international ecumenical bodies have also had an impact on political orientations. Religious ties, therefore, add new dimensions to both inter- and intra-African relations. The proliferation of religious organizations reflects the uncertainty inherent in political and economic trends on the continent. It also provides compelling evidence of the ongoing significance of religious life in African culture and history.

■ SOCIAL NETWORKS AND SOCIAL TRENDS

African society has responded to the challenges of external dependence, economic uncertainty, and political change by the activation of existing organizations and the formation of new groups to deal with the many facets of economic, cultural, and political existence. African social orders are marked by the fact that their component units are related to, yet also distinct from, each other. Each group or association occupies a particular social "space," yet, at the same time, interacts with other groups on both a hierarchical and lateral basis. Economic, cultural, material, and social fields are made up of these organizational spaces, which tend to come together mostly at the apex—much less so at the base. The picture that emerges is one of social richness but rarely of societal uniformity.

The diversity yet interconnectedness of African social systems is a function of many factors. In a continent of many little traditions, specific social groups developed their own mechanisms of dealing with their environments. Colonial conquest, and with it new forms of economic production and of state consolidation, not only evoked responses and adjustments from existing groups but also sparked the creation of new associations and networks. During decolonization further contacts were made and alliances forged. And the period of independence has reinforced this pattern of autonomy and interpenetration. African societies are, indeed, an intricate mosaic.

The composition of Africa's incipient and still ambiguous civil society and the shape of its social structures vary substantially from place to place and country to country. Cultural legacies and differing manners of social and economic organization have yielded quite distinct patterns. Thus, in Senegal, for example, Islamic brotherhoods control major facets of daily existence, as they do in northern Nigeria. In southern Nigeria, Ghana, and Sierra Leone, professional and voluntary organizations proliferate. These are much weaker and more amorphous in countries like Congo, Tanzania, and Malawi, where church groups and informal networks play a more significant role. African states vary culturally, too, from the relatively homogeneous (but severely fractured) Somalia and Swaziland to the extremely diffuse situation in Tanzania. In some instances (Ghana, Botswana, Zimbabwe) one ethnolinguistic group has a clear plurality; in others (Nigeria, Ethiopia, Congo), there are several relatively large groups, often in competition with each other.

The structure of social relations in each African country has differed in light of group composition and possibilities for action. These vary quite distinctly from one country to another. In Ghana, for example, the horizontal axis of social and economic organizations has provided the dynamic framework within which mobility has occurred. A great many social and economic structures have developed at the interface between the local community, market, and formal institutions. In Tanzania, hierarchical structures have been less salient and intermediate levels of social organization less cohesive and elaborate. Here transactions are more limited. Nigeria, in turn, presents a different picture: a highly differentiated system of interactions has emerged, which has been sustained by a multiplicity of unequal flows. In Congo, this pattern solidified even more: a minute group of public officials was able to penetrate the countryside, perpetuating, until recently, the position of a small political "aristocracy."[66] Weak intermediary organizations (with the exception, perhaps, of some churches and newly formed cooperatives) and extreme vulnerability have increased the dependency of most social groups on state officials. In Côte d'Ivoire a more gradated structure of civil society has developed, with a strong group of dominant professionals and bureaucrats at the core and numerous associations spanning the urban and extending to the rural areas. By way of contrast, social structures in Uganda and Chad in the 1980s were based on intense primary-group identities but on many fewer crosscutting social and economic networks.

Official institutions have in the past, and continue today, to try to mold social allegiances and reshape social groupings. Even when formal agencies do not engage directly in social engineering, the organizational configuration of public structures opens opportunities for certain kinds of action and forecloses other possibilities. Specific groups, however, have access to their own resources and constituencies and may at times provide alternative services as well. In some cases, therefore, they seek representation in the formal realm; in some they stand in opposition to existing officeholders, and in others they may develop avenues of exchange that either evade or subvert official channels. Social groups have positioned themselves both as vehicles of interaction with official bodies and as substitutes or alternatives to formal networks.[67] The degree and nature of these exchanges may range from one extreme of total separation, mutual mistrust, and lack of cooperation (Congo in the 1990s) to intricate patterns of power diffusion (Tanzania), intermittent power networks (Ghana), and varying degrees of power concentration (Botswana, Nigeria, Zambia, or Malawi). In few countries has a strong civil society emerged.

In every country, however, the span of social networks is far broader than the reach of formal institutions. Indeed, state structures have tended to reflect the interests and concerns of a small, elite minority (professionals, bureaucrats, some ethnic groups) whose vertical hold remains rather tenuous. At the same time, social and economic contacts have proliferated. More significantly, the rates and types of exchanges between rural and urban areas continue to grow. With communication expanding, the stark separation between the city and the countryside is giving way to a more complex picture of multiple interactions. There has been a gradual, yet palpable, transition from purely hierarchical to lateral transactions in the past few decades. In political terms, this trend means that state power is not unlimited. Although individuals and social groups cannot easily detach themselves from their national environments, governments, in turn, may not be able to skirt demands from well-organized social forces without losing access to the vital resources controlled by these associations. As the outlines of civil societies are emerging in many African countries, previous patterns of state-society relations may also be undergoing change.[68]

Specific groups have molded a variety of means to mobilize their resources and to fulfill their aspirations. These associations are the bedrock of political life on the continent. Their activities do not always intersect with those of state institutions. Class and ethnicity have been the main vehicles for linking these groups to formal structures. In Chapter 4 we look more closely at how these overarching formations have evolved and at the kinds of relations they have fostered.

■ NOTES

1. Many thanks are due to Frank Holmquist, who suggested this formulation.

2. Jean-François Bayart, "La revanche des sociétés africaines," *Politique Africaine* 11 (1983): 95–127. Also see Margaret Peil, *Consensus and Conflict in African Society: An Introduction to Sociology* (London: Longman, 1977).

3. Jane I. Guyer, "Comparative Epilogue," in Jane I. Guyer, ed., *Feeding Africa's Cities* (Manchester: Manchester University Press, 1989), pp. 242–243.

4. Peter C.W. Gutkind and Peter Waterman, eds., *African Social Studies: A Radical Reader* (London: Heinemann, 1977). Also see Sara Berry, *Fathers Work for Their Sons: Accumulation, Mobility and Class Formation in an Extended Yoruba Community* (Berkeley: University of California Press, 1985), p. 7 and elsewhere.

5. For a good overview, see Chris Allen and Gavin Williams, eds., *Sociology of "Developing Societies": Sub-Saharan Africa* (New York: Monthly Review Press, 1982).

6. Immanuel Wallerstein, "Voluntary Associations," in James Coleman and Carl Rosberg, eds., *Political Parties and National Integration in Tropical Africa* (Berkeley: University of California Press, 1966), pp. 318–339; Kenneth Little, *West African Urbanization: A Study of Voluntary Associations in Social Change* (Cambridge: Cambridge University Press, 1967); John M. Hamer, "Preconditions and Limits in the Formation of Associations: The Self-Help and Cooperative Movement in Sub-Saharan Africa," *African Studies Review* 24, no. 1 (1981): 113–128. In contrast, Sandra T. Barnes and Margaret Peil, "Voluntary Association Membership in Five West African Cities," *Urban Anthropology* 6, no. 1 (1977): 83–106, do not see voluntary associations as necessarily integrative.

7. Roger Tangri, *Politics in Sub-Saharan Africa* (London: James Currey, 1985), p. 127. For an excellent case study see Yaw Twumasi, "Prelude to the Rise of Nationalism in Ghana, 1920–1949: Nationalists and Voluntary Associations," *Ghana Social Science Journal* 3, no. 1 (1976): 35–46.

8. For example, see Margaret Peil, *Nigerian Politics: The People's View* (London: Cassel, 1976), p. 162; John Hanna, ed., *Students and Politics in Africa* (New York: Africana Publishing Co., 1975). For an overview, see Naomi Chazan, "The New Politics of Participation in Tropical Africa," *Comparative Politics* 14, no. 2 (1982): 169–189; and Michael Bratton, "Beyond the State: Civil Society and Associational Life in Africa," *World Politics* 41 no, 3 (1989): 407–430.

9. Otwin Marenin, "Essence and Empiricism in African Politics, In Tolumnu Barongo, ed., *Political Science in Africa* (London: Zed Press, 1985), p. 230 and passim.

10. M. K. Schutz, "Observations on the Functions of Voluntary Associations; with Special Reference to West African Cities," *Human Relations* 30, no. 9 (1977): 803–816.

11. This definition goes beyond that of Richard Hodder-Williams, *An Intro-duction to the Politics of Tropical Africa* (London: George Allen and Unwin, 1984), p. 164.

12. Barnes and Peil, "Voluntary Association Membership," p. 91. Also see Crawford Young, *The Politics of Cultural Pluralism* (Madison: University of Wisconsin Press, 1976).

13. For a categorization, see Naomi Chazan, "Africa's Democratic Challenge," *World Policy Journal* (Spring 1992): 279–307.

14. Maxwell Owusu, "Policy Studies, Development and Political Anthropology," *Journal of Modern African Studies* 13, no. 3 (1975): 367–382.

15. Margaret Peil, "The Common Man's Reaction to Nigerian Urban Government," *African Affairs* 74, no. 296 (1975): 300.

16. For an excellent and still timely typology, see Paula Brown, "Patterns of Authority in West Africa," in Irving Leonard Markovitz, ed., *Politics and Society in Africa* (New York: Free Press, 1970).

17. René Lemarchand, ed., *African Kingships in Perspective* (London: Frank Cass, 1977); Roger Tangri, "Paramount Chiefs and Central Governments in Sierra Leone," *African Studies Review* 3, no. 2 (1980): 183–196; Harry Silver, "Going for Brokers: Political Innovations and Structural Integration in a Changing Ashanti Community," *Comparative Political Studies* 14, no. 2 (1981): 233–263; and Maxwell Owusu, "Chieftancy and Constitutionalism in Ghana: The Case of the Third Republic," *Studies in Third World Societies* 24 (1983): 29–53.

18. For a case study, see Naomi Chazan, "Ethnicity and Politics in Ghana," *Political Science Quarterly* 47, no. 3 (1982): 461–485.

19. Berry, *Fathers Work for Their Sons*, p. 193.

20. Peter Ekeh, "Colonialism and the Two Publics in Africa: A Theoretical Statement," *Comparative Studies in Society and History* 17, no. 1 (1975): 91–112.

21. *Afriscope* 7, no. 4 (1977): 24–25.

22. Immanuel Wallerstein, *The Road to Independence: Ghana and the Ivory Coast* (The Hague: Mouton, 1964).

23. For one case study, see Naomi Chazan and Victor Le Vine, "Politics in a 'Non-Political' System: The March 30, 1978 Referendum in Ghana," *African Studies Review* 22, no. 1 (1979): 177–208.

24. The literature is somewhat divided on this point. See, for an excellent discussion of the nomenclature, Richard L. Sklar, "The Nature of Class Domination in Africa," *Journal of Modern African Studies* 17, no. 4 (1979): 544–547.

25. Abner Cohen, *The Politics of Elite Culture: Exploration in the Dramaturgy of Power in a Modern African Society* (Berkeley: University of California Press, 1981), p. 9.

26. Tangri, "Paramount Chiefs and Central Government," p. 183.

27. Paul Bennell, "Industrial Class Formation in Ghana: Some Empirical Observations," *Development and Change* 15 (1985): 593–612; Richard Rathbone, "Businessmen in Politics: Party Struggle in Ghana, 1949–1957," *Journal of Development Studies* 9, no. 3 (1973): 391–402; Sayre P. Schatz, "Government Lending to African Businessmen: Inept Incentives," *Journal of Modern African Studies* 6, no. 4 (1968): 519–529; Paul Kennedy, "Capitalism in Ghana," *Review of African Political Economy* 8 (1977): 21–38.

28. For early examples, see P. C. Lloyd, ed., *The New Elites of Tropical Africa* (London: Oxford University Press, 1966).

29. Philip Foster, "Education and Social Inequality in Sub-Saharan Africa," *Journal of Modern African Studies* 18, no. 2 (1980): 201–236; Remi Clignet, "Education and Elite Formation," in John Paden and Edward Soja, eds., *The African Experience*, vol. 1 (Evanston, IL: Northwestern University Press, 1970), pp. 304–330.

30. Ali A. Mazrui, *Political Values and the Educated Class in Africa* (London: Heinemann, 1978).

31. Yves Person, "Les syndicats en Afrique noire," *Le mois en Afrique* 172/173 (1980): 22–46; Richard Sandbrook and Robin Cohen, eds., *The Development of an African Working Class: Studies in Class Formation and Action* (London: Longman, 1975).

32. Lawrence P. Frank, "Ideological Competition in Nigeria: Urban Populism Versus Elite Nationalism," *Journal of Modern African Studies* 17, no. 3 (1979): 433–452; Bernard Magubane and Nzongola Ntalaja, "Proletarianization and Class Struggle in Africa," *Contemporary Marxism*, no. 6 (1983).

33. Richard Jeffries, *Class, Power and Ideology in Africa: The Railwaymen of Sekondi* (Cambridge: Cambridge University Press, 1978). Also see Peter C. W. Gutkind, "Change and Consciousness in Urban Africa: African Workers in Transition," *Cahiers d'études Africaines*, 81–83 (1981): 299–346.

34. Robin Cohen, "Resistance and Hidden Forms of Consciousness Amongst African Workers," *Review of African Political Economy* 19 (1980): 822.

35. Guyer, "Comparative Epilogue," passim.

36. Gracia Clark, "Pools, Clients and Markets" (Paper presented at the Twenty-sixth Annual Meeting of the African Studies Association, Los Angeles, October 1984), p. 7. Also see her edited volume, *Traders and the State in Africa* (Boulder: Westview Press, 1989).

37. Claire Robertson, "The Death of Makola and Other Tragedies," *Canadian Journal of African Studies* 17, no. 3 (1983): 477.

38. For background, see Martin A. Klein, ed., *Peasants in Africa: Historical and Contemporary Perspectives* (Beverly Hills: Sage Publications, 1980); John C. Saul and Roger Woods, "African Peasantries," in Dennis L. Cohen and John Daniel, eds., *Political Economy of Africa* (London: Longman, 1981), pp. 112–118; and Claude E. Welch, "Peasants as a Focus in African Studies," *African Studies Review* 20, no. 3 (1977): 2–5.

39. M. Catherine Newbury, "Ubureetwa and Thangata: Catalysts to Peasant Political Consciousness in Rwanda and Malawi," *Canadian Journal of African Studies* 14, no. 1 (1980): 97–111; Szymon Chodak, "Birth of an African Peasantry," *Canadian Journal of African Studies* 12, no. 3 (1971): 327–349.

40. Rhoda Howard, *Colonialism and Underdevelopment in Ghana* (London: Croom Helm, 1978). Also see Sharon Stichter, *Migrant Laborers* (London: Cambridge University Press, 1985).

41. Contrast with Goran Hyden, *Beyond Ujamaa in Tanzania: Underdevelopment and an Uncaptured Peasantry* (London: Heinemann, 1980). Also see Joshua B. Forrest, "Defining African Peasants," *Peasant Studies* 9, no. 4 (1982): 242–249.

42. Keith Hart, *The Political Economy of West African Agriculture* (London: Cambridge University Press, 1982), especially p. 105.

43. Jonathan Barker, "Political Space and the Quality of Participation in Rural Africa: A Case from Senegal" (University of Toronto, Development Studies Programme, Working Paper no. C4, July 1984), and his, "Can the Poor in Africa Fight Poverty?" *Journal of African Studies* 7, no. 3 (1980): 161–166.

44. See Michael Watts, *Silent Violence* (Berkeley: University of California Press, 1983).

45. Kathleen Staudt, "Women's Politics and Capitalist Transformation in Sub-Saharan Africa," Women in Development Working Paper 54 (1984), p. 2.

46. Achola O. Pala, "La femme africaine dans le développement rurale," *Cahiers économiques et sociaux* 16, no. 3 (1978): 306–333; *Review of African Political Economy* 27/28 (1983), Special Issue on Women in Africa.

47. Margaret Snyder, "The African Woman in Economic Development: A Regional Perspective," in *The African Women in Economic Development Conference Proceedings* (Washington, D.C.: African American Scholars Council, 1975), p. 11.

48. "Masculin-féminin: L'autre apartheid," *Jeune Afrique plus* 2 (September-October 1983): 57–58.

49. Ibid., p. 57. For more details, see Jane Parpart and Kathleen Staudt, eds., *Women and the State in Africa* (Boulder: Lynne Rienner, 1989).

50. Staudt, "Women's Politics," p. 21; Jette Bukh, *The Village Woman in Ghana* (Uppsala: Scandinavian Institute of African Studies, 1979).

51. Naomi Chazan, "The Manipulation of Youth Politics in Ghana and the Ivory Coast," *Geneva-Africa* 15, no. 2 (1976): 38–63.

52. "Student Power: The Credit and Debit Side," *New African* 154 (1980): 11–18; Nono Lutula Piame-Ololo, "La jeunesse et la politique en Afrique noire," *Le mois en Afrique* 215/216 (1983–1984): 11–17.

53. William John Hanna, *University Students and African Politics* (New York: Africana Publishing Co., 1975).

54. For one case study, see Claude Meillassoux, *Urbanization of an African Community: Voluntary Associations in Bamako* (Seattle: University of Washington Press, 1968).

55. Sandra T. Barnes, "Voluntary Associations in a Metropolis: The Case of Lagos, Nigeria," *African Studies Review* 18, no. 2 (1975): 75–88.

56. O.K. Finagnon, "Notes sur les forces religieuses dans les états africains," *Le mois en Afrique* 213/214 (1983): 110–114; Kofi Asare Opoku, *West African Traditional Religion* (Accra: University of Ghana Press, 1978).

57. D. C. O'Brien, "La filière musulmane: Confréries soufies et politique en Afrique noire," *Politique africaine* 1, no. 4 (1981): 7–30.

58. D. C. O'Brien, "A Veritable Charisma: The Mouride Brotherhood 1967–1975," *Archives européenes de sociologie* 18 (1977): 84–106.

59. Johannes Fabian, "Religion and Change," in Paden and Soja, *The African Experience*, vol. 1, p. 383. Also see Raymond F. Hopkins, "Christianity in Sub-Saharan Africa," *Social Forces* 44, no. 4 (1966): 555–562.

60. Terence O. Ranger, "Religious Movements and Politics in Sub-Saharan Africa" (Paper presented at the Twenty-eighth Annual Meeting of the African Studies Association, New Orleans, November 1985), p. 39.

61. Paul Lubeck, "Conscience de classe et nationalisme islamique à Kano," *Politique africaine* 4 (1981): 40. Also see Martial Sinda, "L'état africain post-colonial: Les forces sociales et les communautés religieuses dans l'état post-colonial en Afrique," *Présence africaine* 127/128 (1983): 240–260.

62. Mar Fall, "L'état sénégalais et le renouveau récent de l'islam: Une introduction," *Le mois en Afrique* 219/220 (1984): 154–159. Also see John N. Paden,

Religion and Political Culture in Kano (Berkeley: University of California Press, 1973).

63. Christian Coulon, "Le réseau islamique," *Politique africaine* 9 (1983): 68–83. Also see Guy Nicholas, "Islam et 'constructions nationales' au sud du Sahara," *Revue française d'études politiques africaines* 165/166 (1979): 86–107. *Politique africaine*, no. 4 (1981), features a special issue on Islam in Africa.

64. For some examples, see Peil, *Consensus and Conflict in African Society*, p. 239; and Allen and Williams, *Sociology of "Developing Societies": Sub-Saharan Africa*, pp. 93–120.

65. Guy Nicholas, "Sociétés africaines, monde arabe et culture islamique," *Le mois en Afrique*, no. 173/174 (1980): 47–64; Babiatu Amman, "New Light on Muslim Statistics for Africa," *Bulletin on Islam and Christian-Muslim Relations in Africa* 2, no. 1 (1984): 11–20.

66. This term is taken from Thomas M. Callaghy, *The State-Society Struggle: Zaire in Comparative Perspective* (New York: Columbia University Press, 1984).

67. Berry, *Fathers Work for Their Sons*, pp. 16–17, 194; Szymon Chodak, "Social Stratification in Sub-Saharan Africa," *Canadian Journal of African Studies* 7, no. 3 (1973): 401–417. Also see Immanuel Wallerstein, "Class and Status in Contemporary Africa," in Gutkind and Waterman, *African Social Studies*, pp. 277–283; and Naomi Chazan, "Engaging the State: Associational Life in Africa," in Atul Kohli, Joel Migdal, and Vivienne Shue, eds., *The State-in-Society: Struggles and Accommodations in the Third World* (London: Cambridge University Press, 1994).

68. See John W. Harbeson, Donald Rothchild, and Naomi Chazan, eds., *Civil Society and the State in Africa* (Boulder: Lynne Rienner, 1994).

4

Ethnicity, Class, and the State

Our political interaction approach emphasizes the complexity of the group demands that the African state faces. It assumes a constant engagement of rival interests in the contemporary political arena, an interaction among various groups mobilized to secure public resources from those in authority. These groups—based on ethnicity, region, race, gender, religion, generation, class, and so forth—may be distinct in terms of origins and appeals, but they share common features in the way they organize to engage in a dynamic interplay of conflict and collaboration. In some instances cultural communities succeed in uniting people for some of the primary purposes of existence—cultural fulfillment, belongingness, psychological and physical security, and social intercourse; where this occurs, such communities can play an important role in gathering group members around an intermediary for the purpose of making collective demands on state decisionmakers. The range of these demands varies considerably. Not only do group representatives lay claim to a full share of public political power, protections, economic resources, administrative positions, contracts, awards, and scholarships but they make appeals, sometimes more conflict-laden in their effects, for broad grants of political autonomy and independence.

It is this accent upon organized group action in the political arena and upon expressed collective claims to resources, participation, and security that makes a political interaction approach so appropriate to the study of the many political identities on the African scene. It is in this vein that Joel Samoff's remark that "all people have multiple identities—which identity is salient depends on the situation" has significance for our purposes.[1] Our objective here will be to differentiate these multiple identities, attempting thereby to understand the nature of the struggle that each one engages in for various public benefits. In particular, we will concentrate upon the

in economic roles such as worker, professional, businessperson, or administrator, develops crosscutting ties of economic class, gender, religion, region, and so forth, that modify the exclusivity of primary group obligations. Insofar as the ethnic group, as a culturally based social organization, interacts with other ethnic, economic, and social groups, it promotes the salient interests—political power, economic resources, public positions, status, protection—of the dominant coalition among the membership at a particular time. The membership must negotiate a common position within the group and continually act so as to maintain the unity and strength of the heterogeneous unit before it can engage in meaningful bargaining encounters at the top of the system. No matter how successful these coalition-building efforts may prove, intragroup differences are likely to persist, allowing rivals the option to interact with factions on separate bases rather than to deal with the ethnic collectivity as a whole.

In addition to class differences, the postindependence political behavior of African ethnic groups reveals a persistence of internal or subethnic schisms along the lines of clan, age-set, geographical, and sometimes gender differences. Thus, an understanding of intra-Shona conflicts among the Karanga, Zezuru, Manica, and other clans for power and patronage in Zimbabwe is critical to gaining a comprehensive insight into the complicated politics of that country. And clan politics is highly significant in Somalia, where, following Mohammed Siad Barre's ascendancy, the powerful Mijerteyn clan felt dissatisfied in relation to this former president's own Marehan clan and his mother's clan, the Ogaden. Similarly, Kenya's interethnic conflicts are not as straightforward as is sometimes assumed; not only is predominantly Kikuyu Central Province divided by the three rival districts of Muranga, Nyeri, and Kiambu, but clan and generational differences remain as intense as ever.[6] Moreover, Kenya's other major ethnic groups—the Luo, Kamba, Kalenjin, and Luhya—are also torn by divided interests and leadership and are not, as is so frequently assumed, united internally.[7]

To be sure, the existence of such internal divisions must not blind us to the fact that ethnic identities, which may vary under different circumstances, can be highly effective politically, even with only a limited attachment on the part of their members to their goals and values. Thus, for example, in the early 1960s, various groups among the Yoruba contested power in the then Western Region of Nigeria. Each faction (in particular, the Oyo Yoruba around Chief Samuel Ladoke Akintola and the Ijebu Yoruba who looked to Chief Obafemi Awolowo) vied for political power in the region. It was to build linkages between these competing interests within the larger Yoruba community that Chief Awolowo played an instrumental role in organizing a pan-Yoruba cultural organization, the Society of the Descendants of Oduduwa, which subsequently led to the founding of a Yoruba-led political party, the Action Group. However, the "divisive rivalry between traditional Yoruba groups"[8] continued into the 1960s and, combined with ideological differences and competing alliance politics, culminated in the 1962 proclamation of a state of emergency in the Western Region and the subsequent trial and imprisonment of Chief Obafemi Awolowo for possessing arms and ammunition illegally. Some fifteen years later, commenting on Chief Awolowo's consolidation of various Yoruba ethnic subgroups for electoral purposes in 1979, Richard Joseph asserted: "By sweeping Yorubaland so convincingly, Chief Awolowo became leader of the Yorubas with a completeness whose significance can be fully comprehended only when placed in the context of the historical rivalries among the Yoruba subgroups."[9]

The impact of this internal diversity upon intergroup exchange is also noteworthy. Rather than a simple dichotomized relationship between bargaining partners, internal differences require a more complicated two-level process of negotiations, within the heterogeneous ethnic group at the regional and central levels and among the ethnic bloc intermediaries and central leaders at the top. A Kalenjin leader in Kenya must forge a united position among diverse representatives for Kipsigis, Marakwet, Nandi, Pokot, Elgeyo, Tugen, and other interests prior to dealing with the leaders of other important ethnic peoples in public forums (the Kikuyu, Luo, Embu, Meru, Masai, Luhya, Mijikenda, etc.). It is the two-level aspect of this political process that so often frustrates state leaders as they seek to negotiate with ethnoregional go-betweens who may or may not be able to keep their constituents in line and deliver on the terms of bargains.[10]

Yet another characteristic of the ethnic group germane to our analysis is its role in promoting the common, as opposed to the like, interests of its members. Like interests may be said to be in evidence where individuals "severally or distributively pursue a like object, each for himself"; common interests may be said to exist where individuals "seek a goal or objective which is one and indivisible for them all, which unites them with one another in a quest that cannot be resolved merely into an aggregate of individual quests."[11] In this sense, the interest group whose members seek to improve their economic conditions must be distinguished from the ethnically based social organization whose members join forces to advance the unspecialized goals of the community "for itself." Thus, if railway or construction workers organize to promote the occupational or class interests of individuals similarly situated in society, the members of an ethnic group combine to protect and improve what they broadly define as communal concerns—in particular, the security, identity, and well-being of a people as a whole. Although the ethnic group strives to fulfill its own potentialities in relationship to other sociocultural organizations, its commitment to a common set of goals is not to be taken as indicating a denial of the like interests of its members. The existence of a common set of goals does not preclude a limit on an individual member's commitment to group purposes. The group finds its meaning through interaction with other such social organizations, but the common interests of its members by no means preclude the emergence of crosscutting class or other interests, creating a diversity of identities that may have the effect of reducing group cohesiveness.

■ THE ETHNIC INTERMEDIARY'S CRITICAL ROLE

So far we have described the ethnic group in Africa as a phenomenon that has grown in significance in the twentieth century. What colonial administrators previously grouped together as "tribal" identities for administrative purposes became the basis for urban-led demands in the postindependence period. As such, the ethnic group has become a useful instrument for mobilizing and aggregating interests in competition with other ethnic, occupational, and business groups for state-controlled political and economic resources. Thus ethnicity, like socioeconomic class, has proved to be a state-linked category that places claims upon the state and to which the state normally responds. Ethnic group participation in this dynamic struggle over scarce state resources is a continuing element in contemporary African political life. It reflects the political imperatives of the times and cannot be wished away by the exhortations of rulers; on the contrary, it is part and parcel of today's political process. African ethnicity, as Abner Cohen observes, is "basically a political and not a cultural phenomenon, and it operates within contemporary political contexts and is not an archaic survival arrangement carried over into the present by conservative people."[12]

The task of promoting collective ethnic political and economic interests at the center naturally requires leadership, and in this instance authority positions are assumed by what we will call ethnic intermediaries. An intermediary's role on the contemporary African scene exists within a broader category of relationships characterized as political clientelism (discussed also in Chapter 6). "Unlike 'class' and 'ethnicity,' both of which are group phenomena," René Lemarchand and Keith Legg remark, "clientelism refers to a personalized and reciprocal relationship between an inferior [client] and a superior [patron] commanding unequal resources."[13] If patron-client ties often prove coextensive with ethnic cleavages in society, it is also important to keep in mind that local patron/leaders can also engage in reciprocal relations with subordinates outside the ethnic community, extending protection, services, and material benefits to members of other identity groups in exchange for support and assistance. Here, however, we will emphasize the overlaps between ethnicity and clientelism at the national level. Such a focus will allow us to concentrate upon the process utilized by the ethnic intermediary when articulating communal interests to decisionmaking elites at the political center.

Because state institutions in Africa are fragile and command only limited public acceptance, informal networks of personal relationships emerge in society to link a relatively powerful and well-placed patron with a less powerful client or clients for the purpose of advancing their mutual interests. Political clientelism, which involves ties of reciprocity between actors controlling unequal political, economic, or social resources, takes various forms; we can therefore distinguish traditional clientelist structures bringing together actors of unequal status at the local level from what René Lemarchand and others call "machine-like clientelism," political exchange patterns at the top of the political system that link powerful and partially autonomous state and ethnoregional leaders for the purposes of governance and resource distribution. Certainly a range of interconnecting clientelist relations exists between the local and systemwide levels. As Lemarchand notes, "clientelism can lead to a *pyramiding of client-patron ties*, and, through the recruitment of new brokers, to an expansion of local or regional reciprocities on a more inclusive scale."[14] Hence, a focus on clientelism at the system level embraces local-level clientelist relations.

In terms of the nature of the relationship, a patron is linked vertically to subordinates on a basis of unequal status and exchange, distributing limited political and economic benefits to clients largely dependent on the patron's protection in a scarcity-prone and sometimes hazardous environment. Moreover, the patron is linked horizontally to other patrons and state officials on a more or less equal basis to assure access to a share of the public resources controlled by the state. In negotiations at the center, the patron/intermediary's influence and bargaining power is dependent in no small part on that person's ability to maintain stable, informal ties with clients at the periphery. If a patron's local constituency base is successfully challenged by a new patron—an ever-present possibility where material resources are generally scarce and opportunities limited—the informal ties of reciprocity may unravel and rivals may take over the leadership role. Yet, as James Scott cautions, based on an extended experience with patron-client relationships in Southeast Asia, the probability that structures will prove resilient is not to be discounted.[15] In fact, sub-Saharan Africa's experience with political clientelism both at the local and state levels bears out Scott's contentions on the likely durability of such linkages.

It is quite clear, then, that the patron/ethnic intermediary plays a leading role in promoting the interests of his or her ethnic constituents. Even within the context of the African one-party or no-party system, ethnic intermediaries remained active, engaging state leaders in a continual process of informal political exchanges. Ethnic intermediaries, themselves members of the dominant political class, must strive to maintain a loyal following within their ethnic constituencies if they are to be able to negotiate effectively at the top with other ethnic and state leaders, whether in the legislature, the cabinet, or the party executive committee. The styles and preferences of these dominant political class members are critical to the regularity and persistence of these interactional relationships. Where the state leadership makes effective use of the political exchange process to facilitate mutual accommodations, constructive state-ethnoregional relations may materialize. At other times, intermediaries may "play the ethnic card" to mobilize group members to band together to protect group interests; in worst-case scenarios, where the group feels threatened in terms of its cultural identity or security, as in Rwanda in 1994, this can lead to the launching of a preemptive strike, bringing with it terrible consequences for all concerned.[16]

To be sure, something of a gap exists between the felt dissatisfactions of the general public and the ethnic intermediary's selection and shaping of public demands prior to channeling these into the formal political process. Not only are African peasants essentially unorganized and dependent upon their representatives for articulating their claims, but the ethnic intermediaries, who maintain close ties with the dominant political class living mostly in urban areas, have interests and life-styles that diverge from those of their constituents. Nevertheless, it is these ethnic intermediaries, the go-betweens for the rural constituencies at the political center, who are in a position to manipulate symbols and thereby to communicate collective claims to those in authority. Consequently, what the various ethnic intermediaries determine as their primary objectives and the effectiveness with which they make their claims are critical to the demand process and the manner in which scarce economic and political resources are distributed. The ethnic intermediary's appeals, both for specific goods and services and for general developmental assistance, often prove an effective catalyst for increased governmental attention and support. It is inevitable that the intermediary will be selective in how demands are organized and presented to those in control. The intermediary cannot possibly convey all of the public's wishes at the same time and expect to have a significant impact; hence, task effectiveness necessitates setting priorities, requiring that the ethnic intermediary structure collective claims in a generalized, coherent, and sophisticated manner. As a result, political judgment on what demands to present, as well as the ability to cope with local factional dissent and the counterclaims of state and other leaders at the national level, become critical to the intermediary's performance. If the intermediary's choice of demands masks class privilege without taking account of his or her constituents' concerns, that person is likely to find it difficult to maintain support in his or her home area over time (as became evident in many electoral contests in Kenya and Tanzania).

Ethnic intermediaries make use of the classic tactics of group delegates the world over in pressing their claims on public authorities at the political center. Varying enormously in terms of influence, access, and types of relationships with both state elites and other ethnic intermediaries, these group representatives operate in all kinds of political contexts: authoritarian, constitutional, pluralist, military, and civilian. In highly authoritarian or military-led regimes, the provincial commissioner or military governor quite commonly acts as the main official point of contact with the central executive leader or his ministerial heads. Thus, during various military regimes in Ghana and Nigeria, commanders of the armed forces carefully reconciled a central perspective with the advocacy of subregional interests at the center.[17] Similarly, in Sudan, the man who served as president of the High Executive Council for the Southern Region during part of the 1981–1982 period, Major General Gasmallah Rassas, behaved in a manner similar to that of his civilian predecessor, traveling to Khartoum and negotiating with President Gaafar Nimeiri or the appropriate ministers for increased public allocations for his region.[18] Civilian provincial commissioners have acted in a very similar manner. The four civilian presidents or acting presidents of the High Executive Council of Sudan's southern region from 1972, when the first Addis Ababa agreement was signed, to 1983 all acted to represent ethnoregional interests at the political center. And in postrevolutionary Ethiopia, provincial commissioners appointed by the *derg*, more often than not originally hailing from the area over which they had come to exercise authority, acted as ethnoregional intermediaries, making demands on the state for an increased share of public resources and services.[19]

In a somewhat more systematic fashion, a more broadly embracing, two-directional process of state-ethnoregional linkages emerged during postindependence times in such countries as Uganda, Zambia, Cameroon, Côte d'Ivoire, and Kenya. Although Uganda's President Milton Obote and Zambia's President Kenneth Kaunda both denied the legitimacy of reciprocity in the relations between state elites and ethnoregional intermediaries, they nonetheless accepted the reality of this informal relationship and acted to apply a principle of proportionality in such areas as fiscal allocations, elite recruitment, and coalition formation in the upper levels of the party and government. Thus, Obote declared that a "National Assembly . . . as an assembly of peace conference delegates and tribal diplomatic and legislative functionaries"[20] was unacceptable, but he went on engaging in political exchange relationships with these ethnoregional ambassadors nonetheless. Similarly, Kaunda expressed distaste for the idea of provincial "champions"; yet he was careful, in forming his cabinets, to "delicately [balance] between the tribal poles of the Bemba in the north and Barotse (Lozi) in the south."[21] Also, true to his commitments to equitable allocations among subregions, his government pursued a principled policy of redistribution, aimed at securing an equalization of rural and urban services and more equal incomes within a relatively short time span.[22] State-ethnoregional relations remained informal and without official recognition or sanction in these two cases, but the outcomes reflected a pragmatic adjustment to the reality of a weak state.

Finally, in the cases of Côte d'Ivoire and Kenya, a system akin to a cartel of state and ethnoregional elites may be said to have developed under Felix Houphouët-Boigny and Jomo Kenyatta. In such political coalitions, all major ethnic groups are assured some minimal participation in the governing process—whether by formal rules (for example, the provisions in Nigeria's 1979 and 1992 constitutions on the "federal character" of national decisionmaking bodies) or by informal rules (in hegemonic Côte d'Ivoire, Kenya, and Cameroon). This participation is encouraged by the inclusion of major ethnoregional intermediaries in the cabinet and/or the party national executive committee. Such inclusion encourages bargaining by prominent communal representatives over major issues within the key centers of power, thereby promoting collaboration rather than group competition. Other informal rules on the maintenance of an elite cartel of state and ethnoregional intermediaries appear with some regularity: the decision not to drop a minister who has been reelected to parliament; the replacement of retiring ministers and high party officials with others from the same subregion; and the preservation, when succession occurs, of a balance in high government and party appointments.

In both Côte d'Ivoire and Kenya, the founding fathers were careful to consolidate their rule through practices of ethnic inclusion and hegemonic exchange. Especially in the 1960s and early 1970s, where the rules of the political game in Côte d'Ivoire involved an "acknowledge[ment]," but not a public display of ethnic politics, the late President Houphouët-Boigny "tried to achieve some ethnic balance in his cabinets in order to mollify the resentment of Baoulé dominance."[23] Rather than challenging the validity of ethnic appeals, Houphouët-Boigny prudently provided for the incorporation of all major ethnic groups in the cabinet and on a basis roughly proportional to their position in the National Assembly. Informal practices shifted in the 1980s with a greater emphasis on regional identity, educational achievement, and loyalty to Houphouët-Boigny and the Parti Democratique de la Côte d'Ivoire. Even so, ethnic identity factors remained important for recruitment into high government and party positions, and continue to be important under Houphouët-Boigny's successor, President Konan Bédié.[24]

In a similar way, Kenya's Jomo Kenyatta ensured considerable stability for his regime by establishing a one-party cabinet coalition of ethnoregional notables. With the central party organization of the ruling Kenya African National Union exercising only loose control over affairs at the branch level, ethnoregional party notables were able to build strong bases of power in their constituencies and then, as in the case of such prominent ethnoregional champions as Ronald Ngala and Paul Ngei, to negotiate over the nature of their participation in the central cabinet.[25] Kenyatta's system of competitive bargaining underwent significant change under his successor, Daniel arap Moi, who appointed a number of his protégés to high party and cabinet positions. This change in leadership style had adverse political and economic consequences, and Kenya in the 1980s and 1990s—as illustrated by the violence in the Rift Valley and the bitter struggles between the government and the opposition in the December 1997 elections—did not experience the same level of stability and development that marked the earlier period.

Operating for the most part out of the public view, the ethnic intermediaries use a variety of formal and informal channels—contacts with politicians and bureaucrats, support for sympathetic parties or candidates, pressure on legislators, logrolling, threats of noncooperation and noncompliance, and so forth—to influence decisionmakers to act positively on their demands. In Ghana, for example, ethnoregional spokespeople, especially those hailing from the less-advantaged subregions, made extensive use of parliamentary forums in the years immediately after independence to push the government to accelerate the development of their home areas. However, with the demise of party competition under President Kwame Nkrumah, the ethnic power brokers found face-to-face contacts as advisers to "the Redeemer" to be the surest means of securing a full share of state patronage for their constituents. Then, with the advent of President Kofi Busia and the return to parliamentary government, the power brokers became, in the early years of the Busia administration at least, "largely synonymous with cabinet members."[26] With the eclipse of party government following Colonel I. K. Acheampong's military intervention in 1972, the opportunities for an open articulation of demands largely disappeared, and the style of putting forth group claims became concealed. However, ethnoregional intermediaries—often traditional leaders, civil servants, or highly placed military officers—continued to communicate their constituents' wishes (as they interpreted them) to those in authority positions, though in a less dramatic fashion. Thus, the Upper Regional House of Chiefs openly appealed in 1976 for the establishment of a university and a brewery in that relatively disadvantaged area.

Further confirmation of this relation between changing political structures and the process of ethnic interest articulation became evident as Ghana passed through subsequent cycles of parliamentary government (the Hilla Limann administration), military rule (the second Jerry Rawlings administration), and a return to presidential and parliamentary governance (under President Rawlings). In Ghana's pluralistic society, the elections of 1992 and 1996 were viewed by many as being tantamount to ethnic censuses, with the results showing a high correlation between ethnoregional distributions and party vote outcomes. Such perceptions had destructive effects, for the fear of political disadvantage and possible exclusion from the decisionmaking process contributed to demonstrations by Ashanti supporters of the New

Patriotic Party in Kumasi following the 1992 election, and to subsequent tensions in the northeast.[27] More evidence of communal insecurity emerged as Rawlings' second term came to a close and politicians jockeyed for position in the next administration.

Thus, the prospect of elections and their results can be conflict producing. They can be manipulated by parliamentarians and other ethnic intermediaries to give advantage to the special interests of their groups on such issues as the introduction of a value-added tax or interregional terms of trade and structural adjustment policies. What proved constant through all these switches was the critical role played by the ethnic broker, even if the means used to advance the interests of rural constituents at the political center changed noticeably with each switch in authority system. By dint of their political skill, knowledge, initiative, contacts, and resources, the ethnic intermediaries have been the ones who inevitably gave direction to the diffuse claims of their constituents for state resources. Should the dominant political elite become inattentive to the intermediary's appeals, the precariousness of his or her personal position is likely to become apparent. Nevertheless, until recently, the role itself could be expected to survive, with another ethnic intermediary more than likely to seize the patron/intermediary mantle on behalf of those same constituents.

The African ethnic intermediary has had to forge unity to promote the collective interests of his/her group. Similarly, the representative for occupational and other economic interests competes in the political marketplace for a full share of status, political power, and publicly controlled resources. In the case of class and occupational leaders, a distinction may usefully be made between the open political and economic action of union leaders and some representatives of opposition organizations (for example, the outspoken criticism by the president of the Ghana Bar Association with respect to alleged abuses of civil liberties under the regimes of I. K. Acheampong and Jerry Rawlings;[28] or the critical role of doctors and other professional people in agitating against the regime of President Gaafar Nimeiri in Sudan in 1985) and the behind-the-scenes lobbying and interest-influencing by manufacturing and commercial interests. In Kenya and Zimbabwe, for example, the move from colonialism to formal independence brought with it a change of tactics on the part of business leaders, who avoided open political action in postindependence times in favor of quiet contacts with parliamentarians and bureaucrats. This raises an important question: If the ethnic intermediary resembles the class spokesperson in participating in the struggle for benefits, how is the ethnic intermediary distinguishable from a class leader? It is clear that ethnicity and crosscutting class identities overlap and become intermeshed, and it is essential for us to point to the kinds of situations in which each of these state-linked categories appears to be primary. But first it is necessary to examine the emergent class cleavages in African societies.

■ AFRICAN CLASS CLEAVAGES AND SOCIAL CONFLICTS

The analysis of African political conflicts in class terms is relatively recent and often represents a reaction to what is perceived as the ethnocentrism and determinism implicit in modernization theory. Social scientists as well as political leaders in the 1950s and early 1960s frequently denied that conflicts based on class identities were occurring and spoke instead of mass-elite divisions or cultural pluralism. A Kenya government paper on African socialism declared, not atypically, in 1965: "The sharp class divisions that once existed in Europe have no place in African Socialism and no parallel in African society. No class problem arose in the traditional African society and none exists today among Africans."[29] Such denials of class relations in African societies did not go unchallenged, however. Scholars from the Marxist, neo-Marxist, and structural dependency schools argued that both colonialism and the incorporation of African societies into a world capitalist system (and the class divisions this entailed) contributed to the formation of modern classes based on their relationship to the means of production and their conflicts with other classes on issues of private and public policy.

Although such a process of class formation remains "incomplete" and, because of underdevelopment and the penetration of external capitalism, involves "weak class differentiation," class relations, as viewed by these schools, are nonetheless the critical element in determining objective reality.[30] Consciously thinking in class rather than ethnic terms, Marxist regimes were inclined to dismiss references to ethnic domination as irrelevant and counterrevolutionary. Hence, where conservative, capitalist-oriented regime analysts often tend to downplay the significance of class affinities, their radical, Marxist-oriented counterparts frequently tended to reduce ethnic attachments to relative unimportance.[31] A more comprehensive political interaction orientation must, for the sake of effectiveness, give heed simultaneously to the impact of each variable or combination of variables in different time and place contexts.

It is certain that much of the responsibility for current class cleavages in the typical contemporary African country arises from colonial policies and programs, particularly the colonial administration's emphasis upon attracting European civil servants, professionals, farmers, and businesspeople to Africa. Colonial development efforts largely concentrated upon the relatively high-income urban enclaves, leaving the majority of people in the rural areas neglected and with limited opportunity for advancement. This differentiated rate of economic change, reinforced by subsequent policy decisions in many of the newly independent African countries, became the basis for contemporary uneven development—both between various identity groups and the subregions of a country. Such a process had important implications for class relations, as these disparities were related to income, occupation, gender, and status. Subregional interests entered differently into the productive process, not only in terms of the goods they produced and the distribution of benefits and services that took place, but also in their linkages outward to the industrial centers of the West. Precapitalist and capitalist features of the production process, therefore, tended to exist side by side in the same state.[32] As Robert Bates observed, modernization helped to shape a new stratification system that produced competition between traditional and modern classes for scarce state-controlled resources.[33]

Given the constraints that colonial development priorities placed on subsequent African leaders, it is important to examine the challenge these leaders encountered in uniting their countries around the time of independence. For this purpose, we will look at interregional disparities in Zambia, surveying the inequalities of opportunity between the relatively advantaged line-of-rail provinces (Copperbelt, Central, and Southern) and the five relatively disadvantaged off-line-of-rail provinces (Northern, Luapula, North-Western, Eastern, and Western).[34] Inequality of opportunity between residents of the line-of-rail provinces and the rest was evident with respect to both economic and social variables. Not only were the greatest number of employment opportunities found near the railway strip (which could carry the products to domestic and international markets), but the average wages for such African employees tended to be higher. In 1969, the line-of-rail accounted for 84 percent of the total number of employees in Zambia (more than half of them in the Copperbelt alone). Manufacturing activity was heavily concentrated along the rail line, with 98 percent of the 31,938 employees in manufacturing-related activities finding work in Copperbelt, Central, or Southern provinces. This imbalance was reflected as well with regard to average African earnings in the public and private sectors. Average earnings of K935 ($2,618) in Copperbelt Province was well above the national average of K789 ($2,209); annual earnings in North-Western Province (K404, $1,131), Northern Province (K430, $1,204), and Western Province (K483, $1,352) were well below the average.[35]

Disparities with respect to amenities and social services between the line-of-rail and off-line-of-rail provinces were also striking. For example, 94 percent of all dwellings equipped with electricity were found in the three line-of-rail provinces. Moreover, rural deprivation, as a holdover from colonial times, was apparent in such social services as health and education. Unlike the urban dweller, who is often relatively close to adequate medical assistance, the average villager, and particularly those in the off-line-of-rail areas, traveled some 9 or 10 miles (16 km) to the most rudimentary dispensary and considerably further to a modern, well-equipped hospital. As a member of parliament depicted the plight of the rural villager, "Looking, Sir, at our health in the rural areas, Sir, our dispensaries are very far apart. You have got to walk about 70 miles [112 km] to reach the nearest dispensary in the rural areas where there is no public transport. And most of the rural health centres, Sir, are manned by untrained people."³⁶ If urban hospitals were unable to cope with the pressure of a heavy patient load from all over the country, rural clinics and dispensaries lacked the staff and facilities to give any but the most elementary kind of medicine.

Finally, in the face of what former President Kaunda described as "a revolutionary urge for education among all our people," hopes for universal primary education remained unfulfilled, and rural opportunities, particularly in the off-line-of-rail provinces, continued to be more circumscribed than in the more-advantaged areas.³⁷ Ministry of Education data for 1966 showed that enrollment in the high-quality fee-paying government primary schools heavily favored pupils from the line-of-rail provinces, as 94 percent of the student body in these schools came from these relatively advantaged subregions.³⁸ Moreover, data on all fee- and non-fee-paying schools showed that the population-teacher ratios in the three line-of-rail provinces were roughly half those of the rest of the country. Whereas the ratios for Copperbelt, Central, and Southern provinces were 212, 255, and 246, respectively, those for North-Western and Eastern were 383 and 384, respectively, and that for Luapula ran to a high of 493.³⁹

The implications for Zambia, and many other African countries, are clear. Colonial efforts affected various parts of the country differently, resulting in a stratification of opportunities that could not be altered easily by African policymakers, even where they were determined to balance the imbalances of the past. The consequence was to perpetuate grave disparities in production, distribution, and social welfare. Urban enclaves, as well as some advantaged rural areas, gained access to scarce resources, which set them apart from the majority of rural dwellers. As Kaunda himself warned, Zambia faced the danger of creating two nations within one. It is quite evident, then, that class stratification in Africa is complicated by its historical origins. A stratification between center and periphery overlaps with the more standard types of socioeconomic class divisions found within the modern sector. And because of the extent of these various kinds of inequalities, the possibilities for conflict abound.

If class and ethnic relations are both fluid and overlapping, they may nonetheless be described as resting on different attributes and types of behavior.⁴⁰ Birth-ascribed systems, which frequently have a basis of existence external to the societies they are united with politically, make comprehensive claims on the loyalties and activities of their memberships. More often than not, status is assigned and mobility across ranks is difficult. In a class (or non-birth-ascribed) system, group membership is determined largely by relationship to the productive process and the relations of classes to one another, although in independent Africa proximity to state power has played a central role. The claims of the members in a class-stratified system tend to be less total, and movement up ranks, although infrequent, is possible.

Such variables as income, occupation, and education are indicators of separate and possibly conflicting interests and life-styles around which class identities might develop; however, no connection necessarily exists between the presence of acquired attributes and the actual formation of class groups. Hence, the emergence of a full-blown class system requires a conscious recognition of membership on the part of individuals with similar backgrounds and experiences who share common economic and political objectives.

In the most general terms, class analysts, despite their many differences, do tend to make similar distinctions among broad classes and class fractions (that is, the elements within a class). The bourgeoisie, who own and control the means of production, rank at the top of the class continuum. The bourgeoisie includes the various dominant elements of the new African emerging order: the political elite and leading bureaucratic and parastatal officials; the local auxiliaries of multinational companies; businesspeople, landlords, large plantation and cash-crop farmers, high-ranking service personnel (corporate lawyers and accountants). Not only is it useful to distinguish the state bourgeoisie from the private bourgeoisie with respect to their exercise of political power and their access to political decisionmakers but the state bourgeoisie itself may be classified in terms of the special roles played by its various fractions (making, executing, and interpreting public rules). And if an "auxiliary bourgeoisie" facilitates multinational investment activities in African countries, these so-called compradors may be distinguished from the emergent national capitalists. Despite government "ambivalence" in a number of countries, the national capitalists, especially recently, have gained considerable success on their own in establishing successful trading, retailing, and even some manufacturing businesses.[41] In the rural areas, nascent bourgeois interests are increasingly apparent, reflecting the penetration of capitalism into the countryside. Thus, large capitalist farmers maintain a privileged relationship with state officialdom and superior access to state-controlled financial credit and farm inputs and to civil service personnel, resulting in social conflict with the less-advantaged classes in their midst.

Normally lower in terms of social and economic status than the bourgeoisie, the petty bourgeoisie, proletariat, and peasant classes are heterogeneous groups. The market women of West Africa, a diversified group most fittingly described as petty bourgeois, are something of an exception to this generalization, for they may amass considerable wealth over the years. The petty bourgeois class, one of the least studied in the African context, is clearly a very diverse grouping of people in terms of income, education, and occupation. Their class interests may clash with the dominant bourgeoisie or mesh in various ways, allowing them, in a number of cases, to play an important, if not an indispensable, role in the productive process. They typically engage in smaller retailing and trading activities and perform a variety of middle-level functions in the areas of finance, construction, transportation, communication, and education. The petty bourgeoisie frequently aspire to greater social mobility than do the peasants or workers, seizing whatever opportunities are available to improve the quality of their lives. Elementary school teachers, for example, may rise quickly to high positions in central or local government or, indicative of the transient character of their station, fall largely from sight and resign themselves to a modest retirement on a small farm.

But if petty bourgeois class interests intermittently clash with those of the bourgeoisie, it is the interests of the proletariat and the peasants that are most likely to appear in open conflict with those of the dominant African bourgeoisie. As the late Claude Ake noted,

> The subordinate classes exercise considerable influence on the character of African socio-economic formations by their latent radicalism. In most of Africa the class contradictions are all too visible in the different lifestyles and living conditions of the bourgeoisie and the subordinate classes. And the bourgeoisie is constantly reminded of the potential danger of the contradiction by occasional outbursts of violence, crimes against property, workers' militancy, and the subversion by workers and peasants of some "development" policies.[42]

Worker and peasant resistance takes a variety of forms, ranging from violent opposition to sabotage, theft, and organized protest. Fully cognizant of the repressive power of the African state and the bourgeois interests identified with it, the subordinate classes adjust to their relative weakness by adopting tactics that they regard as appropriate to the situation at hand.

Like their bourgeois counterparts, the African peasants and the working class are incompletely formed and internally differentiated in terms of status and power.[43] As seen in Chapter 3, such incomplete class formation may result, in African circumstances, in the emergence of weakly integrated interests. With respect to the proletariat, this incomplete formation is partly attributable to the low level of industrial activity in most of contemporary Africa. And because the number of urban job openings in the formal sector has fallen short of the pressing need for employment, a rapid increase in employment in the informal sector, with its labor-intensive, small-scale activities, has occurred.[44] This has had the effect of creating a fast-growing unemployed or underemployed labor force—described by some as a lumpenproletariat "class"—which lives precariously at the margins of the urban wage-labor system. It is not surprising that the interests of those living off the informal sector clash with those holding down secure and relatively better paying positions in the formal sector, especially where those receiving wages have only minimal education and skill levels.

The African proletariat, then, is just becoming aware of its separate class interests. Consciousness of what unites the working class is held back by the socioeconomic conditions of underdevelopment and by the uneven penetration of capitalism on the continent. Moreover, the strike weapon and other modes of resistance are less easily employed against a nationalist government, which controls many of the levers of political power and manipulates many of the symbols of community consensus. A number of urban wage laborers are careful to preserve their ties with their kin in their home villages, returning frequently for celebrations and funerals and sending part of their earnings back to their relatives at home. They also save a portion of their meager salaries to purchase land in their home areas for retirement purposes.

Nevertheless, to note the nascent character of the African proletariat is not to blind us to the African trade unionists' capacity for effective collective action. To attend union rallies is to gain an appreciation of relatively effective organization and popular consensus under difficult circumstances. A weak ruling class has at times made significant concessions to organized union demands, seeking to blunt the dynamics of class action by accommodations on issues of wages, transportation, and working conditions. As Richard Jeffries maintains, there certainly are reasons to doubt whether such concessions have resulted in the creation of a "privileged" working class, as is sometimes contended, but skilled union labor has gained a limited advantage as compared to unskilled workers in Ghana's informal sector as a consequence of organization.[45] It is clear, then, that the African subordinate working class is increasingly conscious of its unequal circumstances vis-à-vis the bourgeoisie. However, the combined conditions of narrow industrialization, abundant manual and semiskilled labor competing for scarce positions, and state-corporate antipathy to collective demands make it difficult for trade union leaders to translate their legitimate claims into public or private policies.

The other subordinate class or social stratum, the peasants, includes the vast number of citizens in the new African state who, as small farmers, "have similar economic motivation because they have similar economic opportunities."[46] Scattered throughout the rural areas, these small farmers (who produce either for their own consumption or for the wider national or international market) are identifiable in terms of such variables as occupation, income, and education. They also tend to be predominantly female; women comprise approximately 70 percent of Africa's subsistence agricultural workforce.[47] They inevitably represent a class-in-themselves, even if they lack the collective consciousness and organization to be a class-for-themselves. This low level of group consciousness results in a lack of political power vis-à-vis other classes and interests on the national scene. Moreover, small farmers are virtually powerless to influence pricing policies at the regional and international levels.

The tendency to remain politically unmobilized, except on specific occasions, has other consequences for the peasants as well. In their competition with large-scale individual or corporate farmers or urban interests for state support, the often politically ineffective small farmers are clearly at a disadvantage in terms of pricing, credit, and support policies and programs. Until recently, food prices were frequently held down, to the advantage of urban consumers, and currency and import policies worked to the benefit of large, mechanized agricultural producers.[48]

Moreover, the state in Africa, influenced by dominant class interests in the vicinity of the capital city, has all too often tended to skew its resource allocation policies in such a way as to favor its constituency, to the disadvantage of the small farmers. Priorities on roadbuilding, hospitals, piped water, and social services have frequently emphasized the needs of the relatively advantaged, precisely because these groups are the most mobilized and have the best access to decisionmakers. As the relatively disadvantaged peasants and subregions show lower expectations and make less far-reaching demands, they allow central state authorities greater latitude in expenditure policies than do other classes and subregional interests.[49] It remains to be seen, however, whether a policy of providing the peasants and other relatively disadvantaged groups with minimal allocations will frustrate the achievement of longer-term system goals of stability, equity, and increasing state capacity. The small farmers, who largely underwrite the expansion of industry, parastatals, state farms, bureaucracy, military, and urban life-styles, will be allowed to flounder at everyone's peril.

Although the peasants are at a political disadvantage in organizing for effective class action, this is not to say that they are always powerless to influence policy. Governments, recognizing the potential power of the peasants, have striven to gain their cooperation. Peasant representatives have been co-opted by governments that are seeking rural support. Thus, as these representatives are included in party ranks or selected to district- or national-level positions, they are well suited to bring influence to bear upon public officials.[50] But state neglect of the rural farmers has persisted despite this co-optation process. It is not surprising, therefore, that peasants have responded to what they regard as an overburdensome state by resisting state regulations in a variety of subtle but damaging ways: refusing to plant cash crops; avoiding regulations on soil erosion; evading tax payments; illegally chopping out firewood; burning cash crops; and absenting themselves from required chores on state farms. Ugandan smallholders, resentful of government mismanagement and mistreatment during the period of Idi Amin's rule, moved steadily away from participation in the official market for monetary agriculture and toward the sale of their cash crops through informal channels or, as an alternative, retreated into subsistence farming.[51] Although it is perhaps too much to contend that peasants can or want to cut themselves off fully from market incentives or state regulations, it is certainly the case that smallholders have a limited autonomy that they can use to distance themselves from external control.[52]

Resistance by peasants is most manifest when expressed in the form of open rebellion. At times, such revolutionary proclivities came into view in the anticolonial struggles where educated elites were able to mobilize the countryside against the colonial state and its supporters in the urban administrative centers. However, in postcolonial times similar rebellions by peasantries lacking in consciousness and solidarity were more difficult to organize. Arguing against any inherent revolutionary potential upon the part of the peasants, Claude Welch writes:

> African governments may not be perceived by substantial portions of their populaces as holding legitimate authority. Such weaknesses, however, cannot be directly translated into strength for insurgent efforts. The syncretic nature of African societies imposes serious limits on the extent to which any government, or any peasant movement, can achieve significant alteration. Social divisions afflict both. Would-be guerrillas confront significantly greater organizational and logistical problems than do the incumbents. Unless serious rifts open in the armed forces of the particular state, prospects for peasant success appear to be low.[53]

"Peasant success" is clearly different from "peasant movements" of resistance, and where the interests of peasants coincide with ethnicity, as in Sudan and Burundi, the result is likely to be powerful demands, if not successful revolts. Even so, it seems possible to contend that the peasants' lack of class consciousness limits successful class action, whether it be influencing political decisionmakers as to appropriate public policies and programs or actively opposing state manipulation and exploitation.

Because of the incomplete nature of class development and consciousness among peasants, a number of analysts have raised questions about the applicability of the classical Marxist model to African conditions. This questioning has led in due course to a search for alternative classifications more relevant to the African experience. For example, Richard Sklar, emphasizing the dominant political class capacity for autonomous action, describes class relations as "determined by relations of power." "Class formation," he writes, "is a consequence of determinants that are specifically political as well as economic. However 'dependent' . . . the economy of an underdeveloped country may be, the autonomy of its bourgeoisie may yet be firmly established upon a foundation of indigenous political organization."[54] Sklar is consciously taking note of the political dimension of African class relations, stressing the basic conflicts of interest between the rulers and the ruled. And Michael Cohen, specifically rejecting a stratification system along traditional Marxist lines as ignoring the "political origins of social mobility," concludes, on the basis of his work in Côte d'Ivoire, that "classes are categories of people sharing common political and economic interests arising from their access to public authorities and the public resources and opportunities which they control."[55] It is clear that a process of redefinition is taking place here, one that tries to take account of the fluid and undetermined nature of class relations evident in the current context. Because this fluidity parallels the malleable nature of ethnic relations, it is important for us to examine the interrelationship of these variables and the implication of these overlaps for political interaction.

■ CLASS AND ETHNICITY
AS SITUATIONAL VARIABLES

Class and ethnicity are by no means hard-and-fast categories, unchanging in new circumstances. Both are products of the state, which must respond, to some extent, to their various demands for public resources. They certainly rest upon somewhat different attributes and types of behavior; yet, in practice, they often overlap and become intertwined with one another. Patron-client ties, interest articulation, language, and occupation patterns are not static but respond to the impact of new political and economic developments in the postindependence environment. The effect of these realignments is to shape and give meaning to both class and ethnic attachments. Hence, rather than being interpreted as fixed, rigid, and exclusive categories, class and ethnicity seem more accurately viewed situationally—in terms of the social, economic, and political context in which the various groups interact and attempt to achieve their collective purposes.

In light of these overlaps, determining which, if any, of these variables is salient at any particular time is largely a matter of the context in which they operate. As Nelson Kasfir observes, "Class and ethnicity, as well as regionalism or religion, are organizing principles of social action that may act alone, may reinforce, or may work against each other, depending on the social situation."[56] Ethnoregional leaders, often members of the dominant class themselves, may make different uses of class and ethnic appeals to gain support for their claims upon the state. As they mobilize these identities for their political purposes, they help to shape which particular identity, or mix of identities, comes to the fore.

Because these elites mobilize identities to secure political and economic resources from the state, they inevitably vest the state with considerable power to influence the nature of class and ethnic identities. The state's capacity to allocate resources and to mediate societal conflicts makes it a central link in the political process. It is able to use the coercive powers at its disposal to set informal guidelines as to relations between interest groups and the state and among these groups themselves. The state's ability to determine the rules for competition and conflict gives state elites a vantage point from which to legitimate the organizations of collective interests and allow them access to decisionmakers. Will the state define the basis of organization along class or ethnic lines? Will it identify individuals primarily in terms of class or ethnic affiliations? The answers to these questions are critical in terms of the way individuals align themselves and participate as social actors. As Henry Bienen points out, "The fluidity, heterogeneity, and complexity of processes of identity and group formation suggest that state interventions may be very important for outcomes."[57]

Not the least of these outcomes is the impact of state action in distinguishing between class and ethnicity or, as an alternative, blurring the distinction between these two forms of attachment. As we have already discussed distinctions between class and ethnic action, we will concentrate here on patterns of overlapping identities. In a situation of horizontal stratification, where parallel structures exist and there is a presumption of equality among these groupings,[58] powerful ethnoregional patrons organize their home-base constituents, ethnic compatriots, and others alike to make demands at the political center for protection and for a wide range of benefits. Whether in a one-party, military, or mixed type of system, they engage within their hierarchically organized system in a process of informal and quiet exchanges with state elites and intermediaries for other ethnoregional interests. The relatively advantaged frequently concede limited material benefits to ensure political stability and the acceptance of state regulations; the relatively disadvantaged, seeking increased material resources to enable them to gain greater equality with the more advantaged areas, may be prepared to trade compliance with state rules for improved material distributions.

But either way, this is a transactional process that sees the subjective principle of social action, ethnicity, reinforcing the objective one of class. Describing one extreme process of hegemonic exchange, Richard Joseph asserts: "The grid of Nigerian political society is an intricate and expanding network of patron-client ties, which serve to link communities in a pyramidal manner. At the summit of such networks can be found individual office-holders in the federal and state capitals."[59] The same point may be made about other countries, such as Cameroon and Uganda, where the cabinet at the political center traditionally brought together a coalition of various ethnoregional and other interest group leaders, on a roughly proportional basis. In doing so, the class and ethnic principles of social action are combined under the rubric of "ethnoregional" and then used by the unit's intermediary at the center to advance the collective interests of the people living in the territory as a whole.

In a situation of vertical stratification, however, the ethnic groups are ranked in terms of power, status, and wealth, and mobility between strata is normally difficult. In the extreme cases of Rwanda, Burundi, and Zanzibar around the time of decolonization, privileged minorities, in control of state institutions and determined to preserve colonially inherited patterns of social stratification, perceived themselves as pitted against an underprivileged ethnic-class majority determined to restructure opportunities in a fundamental manner. In Rwanda, the rather unstructured Hutu uprising of November 1959 and the dominant Tutsi minority's reprisals that followed revealed a reciprocity of fear and aggressive behavior of terrifying dimensions. Quoting Grégoire Kayibanda's remark that between these peoples "there is no intercourse and no sympathy, [they] are ignorant of each other's habits, thoughts and feelings," René Lemarchand stresses the polarization of expectations in the period after the uprising and "the all-pervasive climate of fear and suspicion which gripped the country at the approach of the [1960] elections."[60] These events in Rwanda, which reappeared with the genocidal frenzy of 1994, also exacerbated latent fears in neighboring Burundi; there, many Tutsi, fearing "the advent of a Rwanda-like republican order based on majority rule," engaged in violent acts against their Hutu kinsmen and kinswomen.[61] In a similar vein, Michael Lofchie described Zanzibar's African nationalism as a reaction to the perceived "threat of [minority] Arab domination posed by the ZNP [Zanzibar Nationalist Party]."[62]

It is important to reiterate that these are extreme examples of totalist perceptions and by no means typical of the pragmatic perceptions that generally prevail in middle Africa, but they do point up the possibility that worst-case scenarios can surface in Africa, as elsewhere. In such a context, political exchange relationships are inevitably irregular. Because interactions tend to be seen in more threatening or totalist terms, the proportionality principle is a less-ready guide to political coalition formation, elite recruitment, or resource allocation. The dominant elite is even more reliant than in horizontally stratified societies on the coercive capacity of the state to maintain political order. It often shuns explicit redistributive policies, preferring instead to opt for market actions in the form of a trickling down of benefits to the relatively disadvantaged classes and ethnoregional units. Quite frequently, socioeconomic class coincides with ethnic identity in these vertically stratified societies. Hence, the dominance of an ethnic-class elite over the state and its institutions is regarded by the dominant strata as essential to its general strategy of control: for example, the institutionalization of grand apartheid in former President Pieter W. Botha's South Africa.

In such racially stratified colonial societies as Kenya, Northern Rhodesia (Zambia), Southern Rhodesia (Zimbabwe), and apartheid South Africa, a small racial-class cluster of white Europeans predominated in the top ranks of the economy and administrative services of the society, with the Asians and/or "Coloreds" (people of mixed racial background) performing indispensable roles as adjuncts of the colonial system, assuming a variety of tasks as artisans, clerks, professionals, and shopkeepers. The pyramid of power and privilege was filled out by the African masses, who acted as laborers on the farms and in the mines.[63] Moreover, in Rwanda, as Catharine Newbury emphasizes, the role of colonialism in facilitating Tutsi use of the state apparatus to refine and increase their exploitation over the majority Hutus resulted in a heightened racial-class consciousness on the part of both groups. The Hutu, exploited in terms of weakened land rights, increasing demands on Hutu labor, and reduced access to dramatically altered structures of power, acted to seize control of the state as independence approached. As Newbury concludes, elements of both class and ethnicity were in evidence during the 1950s: "For the majority of the population, ethnic status and class overlapped—that is, most of the people who were poor and exploited were categorized as Hutu."[64]

In brief, then, representatives of various groups can mobilize their constituents by appeals to either class or ethnic identity, or they can take account of the overlaps between these organizing principles of social action. The grounds upon which a support base is built are largely dependent upon the social situation prevailing in each specific context. Hence, effective policymaking requires sensitivity to the social dynamics at work and the forces giving rise to constituency demands. It is clear that there is no overriding need to disentangle class and ethnic identifications in all instances. An effective political interaction approach requires a recognition of all politically mobilized identities—whether single or multiple—and the different parts they may play in the articulation and processing of demands and the implementation of policy. In Chapter 9 we will look more closely at the role of the state in responding to demands and determining policies.

■ NOTES

1. Joel Samoff, "Pluralism and Conflict in Africa: Ethnicity, Interests, and Class in Africa" (Paper presented to the International Political Science Association, Rio de Janeiro, 9–14 August 1982), p. 19.

2. Introduction, in Fredrick Barth, ed., *Ethnic Groups and Boundaries* (Boston: Little, Brown, 1969), pp. 13–14.

3. Aidan W. Southall, "The Illusion of Tribe," *Journal of Asian and African Studies* 5, no. 1/2 (January-April 1970): 33.

4. Crawford Young, *The Politics of Cultural Pluralism* (Madison: University of Wisconsin Press, 1976), pp. 171–173.

5. Warren Weinstein, "Conflict and Confrontation in Central Africa: The Revolt in Burundi 1972," *Africa Today* 19, no. 4 (Fall 1972): 27.

6. On the frustrations the younger generation of educated Africans feel over lack of opportunity, see Aristide Zolberg, "The Structure of Political Conflict in the New States of Tropical Africa," *American Political Science Review* 62, no. 1 (March 1968): 75–76. Expressions of such frustration have been vented in student demonstrations against political authorities. See *West Africa*, 18 April 1983, pp. 933–934.

7. Cherry Gertzel, *The Politics of Independent Kenya 1963–68* (London: Heinemann, 1970), p. 17.

8. See Richard L. Sklar, "Nigerian Politics: The Ordeal of Chief Awolowo, 1960–65," in Gwendolen M. Carter, ed., *Politics in Africa: 7 Cases* (New York: Harcourt Brace and World, 1966), p. 18.

9. Richard A. Joseph. "Democratization Under Military Tutelage," *Comparative Politics* 14, no. 1 (October 1981): 92.

10. Robert D. Putnam, "Diplomacy and Domestic Politics: The Logic of Two-Level Games," *International Organization* 42, no. 3 (Summer 1988): 427–460.

11. Robert MacIver, *On Community, Society and Power* (Chicago: University of Chicago Press, 1970), p. 48.

12. Abner Cohen, *Custom and Politics in Urban Africa* (Berkeley: University of California Press, 1969), p. 190.

13. René Lemarchand and Keith Legg, "Political Clientelism and Development: A Preliminary Analysis," *Comparative Politics* 4, no. 2 (January 1972): 151.

Also see René Lemarchand, "Political Clientelism and Ethnicity in Tropical Africa: Competing Solidarities in Nation-Building," *American Political Science Review* 64, no. 1 (March 1972): 86, and Henry Bienen, "Political Parties and Political Machines," in Michael F. Lofchie, ed., *The State of the Nations* (Berkeley: University of California Press, 1971), Chapter 9.

14. Lemarchand, "Political Clientelism and Ethnicity," p. 76 (italics in the text). See also John Duncan Powell, "Peasant Society and Clientelist Politics," *American Political Science Review* 54, no. 2 (June 1970): 413.

15. James C. Scott, "Patron-Client Politics and Political Change in Southeast Asia," *American Political Science Review* 64, no. 1 (March 1972): 100.

16. David A. Lake and Donald Rothchild, "Containing Fear: The Origins and Management of Ethnic Conflict," *International Security* 21, no. 2 (Fall 1996): 41–75.

17. Robin Luckham, *The Nigerian Military* (Cambridge: Cambridge University Press, 1971), p. 296.

18. See his comments in *Sudanow* 6, no. 11 (November 1981): 15.

19. For a fuller discussion, see Donald Rothchild, "State-Ethnic Relations in Middle Africa," in Gwendolen M. Carter and Patrick O'Meara, eds., *African Independence: The First Twenty-Five Years* (Bloomington: Indiana University Press, 1985), pp. 74–82.

20. A. Milton Obote, *Proposals for New Methods of Election of Representatives of the People to Parliament* (Kampala: Milton Obote Foundation, 1970), pp. 6–7.

21. Richard Hall, *The High Price of Principles* (New York: Africana Publishing Co., 1969), p. 195.

22. See Donald Rothchild, "Rural-Urban Inequities and Resource Allocation in Zambia," *Journal of Commonwealth Political Studies* 10, no. 3 (November 1972): 234–239.

23. Robert A. Mortimer, "Ivory Coast: Succession and Recession," *Africa Report* 28, no. 1 (January-February 1983): 5, 7.

24. On latent ethnic tensions in Côte d'Ivoire, see J. F. Medard, "La regulation socio-politique," in Y. A. Faure and J. F. Medard, eds., *Etat et Bourgeoisie en Côte D'Ivoire* (Paris: Karthala, 1982), p. 75; and Tessy D. Bakary, "Political Polarization over Governance in Côte d'Ivoire," in I. William Zartman, ed., *Governance as Conflict Management: Politics and Violence in West Africa* (Washington, DC: Brookings Institution Press, 1997), pp. 87–88.

25. Robert H. Jackson, "Planning, Politics, and Administration," in Goran Hyden, Robert Jackson, and John Okumu, eds., *Development Administration: The Kenyan Experience* (Nairobi: Oxford University Press, 1970), pp. 177–178. On the Moi period, see Victoria Brittain, "Five Months That Took Kenya to the Brink," *Manchester Guardian Weekly* 17, no. 6 (8 April 1982).

26. Naomi Chazan, *An Anatomy of Ghanaian Politics* (Boulder: Westview Press, 1983), p. 96.

27. Emmanuel Gyimah-Boadi, "Managing Electoral Conflicts: Lesson from Ghana," in Timothy D. Sisk and Andrew Reynolds (eds.), *Elections and Conflict Management in Africa* (Washington, DC: United States Institute of Peace Press, 1998), p. 103.

28. See the "Statement by Ghana Bar Association on the Promulgation of the Constitution of the Fourth Republic," March 13, 1993; reprinted in Kwame A. Ninsin, ed., *Ghana's Political Transition 1990–1993* (Accra: Freedom Publications, 1996), pp. 167–170.

29. Republic of Kenya, *African Socialism and Its Application to Planning in Kenya* (Nairobi: Government Printer, 1965), p. 12. Also see remarks made by President

Houphouët-Boigny of Côte d'Ivoire in Michael Cohen, *Urban Policy and Political Conflict in Africa: A Study of the Ivory Coast* (Chicago: University of Chicago Press, 1974).

30. R. N. Ismagilova, *Ethnic Problems of the Tropical Africa* (Moscow: Progress Publishers, 1978), pp. 44, 96.

31. This tendency leads John S. Saul to suggest "that Marxist scientists and African revolutionaries can only make progress when they take ethnicity . . . seriously as a real rather than ephemeral and/or vaguely illegitimate variable in Africa." "The Dialectic of Race and Class," *Race and Class* 20, no. 4 (1979): 371.

32. Ibid., p. 358.

33. Robert H. Bates, "Modernization, Ethnic Competition, and the Rationality of Politics in Contemporary Africa," in Donald Rothchild and Victor A. Olorunsola, *State Versus Ethnic Claims* (Boulder: Westview Press, 1983), p. 154.

34. Some of the material on Zambia in this section is drawn from Rothchild, "Rural-Urban Inequities and Resource Allocation in Zambia," pp. 222–224.

35. Colin Legum and John Drysdale, eds., *Africa Contemporary Record 1968–1969* (London: Africa Research, 1969), p. 252.

36. Republic of Zambia, Official Report, *Debates of the Second National Assembly* 25, no. 3 (25 February 1971): 1549. Statement by Mr. Noyoo (Lusaka: Government Printer, 1971).

37. Republic of Zambia, *His Excellency the President's Address to Parliament on the Opening of the Third Session of the Second National Assembly*, 8 January 1971 (Lusaka: Government Printer, 1971), p. 4.

38. Calculated from Republic of Zambia, Ministry of Education, "Digest of Statistical Information for School Year, 1966" (mimeo.). Fee-paying requirements were terminated for schools in January 1971.

39. *Population and Housing Census in Zambia in 1969*, report on a mission to Zambia from 16 September to 23 October 1967, by Vaino Kannisto (Lusaka: United Nations, October 1967), p. 15.

40. Gerald D. Berreman, "Race, Caste, and Other Invidious Distinctions in Social Stratification," *Race* 13, no. 4 (April 1972): 398–399.

41. Andrew A. Beveridge and Anthony R. Oberschall, *African Businessmen and Development in Zambia* (Princeton: Princeton University Press, 1979), Chapter 7; Peter Marris and Anthony Somerset, *African Businessmen* (London: Routledge & Kegan Paul, 1971); and Nicola Swainson, *The Development of Corporate Capitalism in Kenya, 1918–1977* (Berkeley: University of California Press, 1980), pp. 288–290.

42. Claude Ake, *A Politial Economy of Africa* (Essex: Longman, 1981), p. 186. See also Claude Ake, *Democracy and Development in Africa* (Washington, DC: Brookings Institution Press, 1996), p. 47.

43. Henry Bienen, "The State and Ethnicity: Integrative Formulas in Africa," in Rothchild and Olorunsola, *State Versus Ethnic Claims*, p. 104.

44. International Labour Office, *Employment, Incomes and Equality: A Strategy for Increasing Productive Employment in Kenya* (Geneva: ILO, 1972), pp. 93–94.

45. Richard Jeffries, *Class, Power and Ideology in Ghana: The Railwaymen of Sekondi* (Cambridge: Cambridge University Press, 1978), pp. 172–173.

46. Nelson Kasfir, "Relating Class to State in Africa," *Journal of Commonwealth and Comparative Politics* 21, no. 3 (November 1983): 5.

47. World Bank, *Sub-Saharan Africa: From Crisis to Sustainable Growth* (Washington, DC: World Bank, 1989), p. 103.

48. Robert H. Bates, *Markets and States in Tropical Africa* (Berkeley: University of California Press, 1981), p. 55.

49. Donald Rothchild, *Managing Ethnic Conflict in Africa: Pressures and Incentives for Cooperation* (Washington, DC: Brookings Institution Press, 1997), p. 185.

50. On the possibilities for peasant-bourgeois collaboration under populist bourgeois-dominated regimes, see Richard Sklar, "The Nature of Class Domination in Africa," *Journal of Modern African Studies* 17, no. 4 (December 1979): 549.

51. The effects of this retreat in terms of aggregate productivity are discussed in Donald Rothchild and John W. Harbeson, "Rehabilitation in Uganda," *Current History* 80, no. 463 (March 1981): 135.

52. See Jonathan Barker, "Politics and Production," in Jonathan Barker, ed., *The Politics of Agriculture in Tropical Africa* (Beverly Hills: Sage Publications, 1984), p. 18.

53. Claude E. Welch, Jr., "Obstacles to 'Peasant War' in Africa," *African Studies Review* 20, no. 3 (December 1977): 129. Also see his introduction to this special issue, p. 4.

54. Sklar, "The Nature of Class Domination," p. 550.

55. Michael A. Cohen, *Urban Policy and Political Conflict in Africa* (Chicago: University of Chicago Press, 1974), p. 194.

56. Kasfir, "Relating Class to State in Africa," p. 6.

57. Bienen, "The State and Ethnicity," p. 106.

58. Donald Horowitz, "Three Dimensions of Ethnic Politics," *World Politics* 3, no. 2 (January 1971): 232; and his *Ethnic Groups in Conflict* (Berkeley: University of California Press, 1985), pp. 22–23.

59. Richard A. Joseph, "Class, State, and Prebendal Politics in Nigeria," *Journal of Commonwealth and Comparative Politics* 1, no. 3 (November 1983): 28.

60. René Lemarchand, *Rwanda and Burundi* (London: Pall Mall Press, 1970), pp. 169, 179. Also see Gérard Prunier, *The Rwanda Crisis: History of a Genocide* (New York: Columbia University Press, 1995).

61. René Lemarchand, *Burundi: Ethnocide as Discourse and Practice* (Washington, DC: Woodrow Wilson Center Press, 1994), pp. 60–67.

62. Michael Lofchie, "The Plural Society in Zanzibar," in Leo Kuper and M. G. Smith, eds., *Pluralism in Africa* (Berkeley: University of California Press, 1969), p. 312.

63. Donald Rothchild, *Racial Bargaining in Independent Kenya* (London: Oxford University Press, 1973), Chapters 2, 3.

64. M. Catherine Newbury, *The Cohesion of Oppression: Clientship and Ethnicity in Rwanda (1860–1960)* (New York: Columbia University Press, 1988), Chapter 10. Also see her article, "Background to Genocide: Rwanda," *Issue* 23, no. 2 (1995): 12–17.

Part 2

POLITICAL PROCESS AND POLITICAL CHANGE

5

Regimes in Independent Africa

Political processes—the ways in which political rules, norms, methods, and modes of interaction are established, maintained, and change—have evolved in Africa in a historical environment of economic adversity and external dependence and in a structural context of fragility and diffusion. Patterns of political conduct determine priorities, preoccupations, and possibilities. Development strategies and foreign policies (the substance of politics) are therefore the concrete outcome of how politics are conceived, practiced, and transformed. The dynamics of politics in Africa is about the procedures and mechanisms by which state agencies and social groups cooperate, conflict, intertwine, and consequently act.

Leaders have had to devise strategies of legitimation and find appropriate means of maintaining social order while being beholden to particular groups, frequently without the benefit of viable domestic structures supported by widespread sentiments of national loyalty and without the ability to avert the influences of regional and global forces. Individuals and social groups, in turn, have sought to protect their security, assure their access to resources, improve their well-being, and strive for a semblance of order and perhaps even justice in the absence of political predictability. How have politics worked in these circumstances? Assuming that rulers have neither resorted exclusively to the use of force nor been entirely ineffective, how have they balanced their quest for power with their need for support?[1] What methods have citizens used to voice demands, increase government responsiveness, and curb excesses? What rules have guided the political game, how have they operated, and what have been their consequences? What efforts have been made to alter the conduct of political life and what has been their effect? What political trends emerge, and what are their implications for understanding the content of policies and their consequences?

Our purpose in Part 2 of this text is to explore political processes in contemporary Africa, to understand how politics works. The treatment of African political dynamics has suffered from many attempts to generalize from approaches designed to deal with one aspect of politics into overarching frameworks for understanding politics in general. Some scholars have sought to study political patterns through the lens of ideology, some have found the concepts of political psychology or rational choice to be effective guides to overall political trends. It has been suggested, alternatively, that leadership styles, corporatist arrangements, party systems, or even the distinction between civilian and military governments capture the main flow of politics on the continent. Although each of these emphases makes an important contribution to comprehending the practice of politics (and is, consequently, incorporated into the ensuing discussion), not one of these methods can, by itself, illuminate all of the many complex facets of the African political dynamic. In this book, therefore, we focus squarely on the search for viable formulas for the conduct of politics. We look at the kinds of regimes that have developed in Africa and then explore how their modes of institutionalization have affected the various dimensions of the political process—decisionmaking, policy application, societal reactions, and consequent change. Such a strategy highlights options and choices and enables a better comparison of political processes both within Africa and between Africa and other parts of the world.

The starting point for this discussion is the presentation of regime forms. In this chapter, we lay out the characteristics of the main types of regimes that have emerged on the continent and analyze their different norms, patterns, and behavioral manifestations. In Chapter 6, we look at the high politics of the political center—at the ways in which various regimes make decisions and the means they have devised to carry them out. In Chapter 7, we delve into the deep politics of society, examining social responses to regime policies and performance through an analysis of the major forms of conflict, the strategies and tactics of dissent and insurrection, and official reactions to challenges from below. In Chapter 8, we deal with political change: we trace the methods by which continuity has been maintained or regimes altered and assess both the degree and direction of political transformation since independence, highlighting the reforms of the 1990s.

The overriding themes of the first phase of postcolonial politics in Africa have been personal rule, political domination, and resistance to such hegemonic impulses.[2] The generally weak structures linking social groups and government agencies have highlighted the role of individual leaders as the pivot of official political thought and action. In this rather ambiguous political world, different regimes have set down their own guidelines and identifiable norms have prevailed. Choices have been made by both rulers and their constituencies, leading in some cases to chronic turmoil and in others to a measure of continuity and order. The path of African politics has consequently been far from inexorable "as the courage, the determination, the humor and often the political wisdom of anonymous populaces demonstrate."[3]

The key political problem has, therefore, revolved around the type of institutionalization that has prevailed (rather than the absence of any regularized patterns). Many African regimes have been unable to establish political procedures that could be simultaneously efficient and representative. In fact, political processes have been marked by varying amounts of repression, inequality, instability, dishonesty, ineffectiveness, and disorder. Many governments have lacked legitimacy and have consequently been assailed by discontented groups unwilling to extend support to often corrupt rulers. Laws have been subverted by officials and ignored by irate citizens, and in many instances politics have been not only uncertain but also grimly brutal.

Even if the conduct of politics has followed tortuous paths in the decades since independence, the parameters of the politically permissible have, implicitly and informally, been laid down. Limits have been placed on the ability of leaders to act with impunity, just as recalcitrant populations have found their quest for autonomy largely curtailed. The crux of the political conundrum in independent Africa—the issue of good government—has consequently emerged with renewed force. The lesson gleaned from the past political record is that "power is always tied to legitimacy," that the effective conduct of public affairs requires some measure of political accountability (of rulers responsible to citizens who hold them to account).[4] Increasingly, Africa's political leaders and scholars are linking sovereignty and responsible governance, arguing that a balance must be struck between a state's right to exercise autonomous power and the need for state responsiveness to the legitimate demands of its citizens for security and well-being.[5] How some governments have instituted steps to ensure accountability and why others have been woefully lacking in this regard is the common thread that unites our discussion of African political processes.

■ REGIME EVOLUTION IN POSTCOLONIAL AFRICA

Political processes in Africa have been complex, heterogeneous, and frequently both perplexing and uncertain. Political procedures and patterns of change combine to draw a diverse picture of politics. These images portray cases of mismanagement and gross inhumanity, of irresponsibility and official pillaging, alongside those of experimentation, disappointment, vacillation, and ongoing confrontation. They also convey instances of efficient management and responsiveness, of the creation of widely accepted notions of political behavior, and sometimes of allied organizations for their maintenance. In each of these many instances, political processes have assumed definite shapes and possessed recognizable dynamics.

The criteria for the classification of regime types have varied widely.[6] The crudest distinction and the least helpful has been based on the division between civilian and military regimes, highlighting a confusion between means of regime change and their outcomes. Employing a similar conceptual foundation, some typologies have relied on the differentiation of leadership styles: mobilizing, conciliatory, coercive, autocratic. Others have favored categories derived from ideology or policy orientations: Marxist, socialist, capitalist, and the like. More sophisticated distinctions have been drawn on the basis of degrees of competition, participation, control, and choice.[7] We propose to distinguish between regimes by reference to the dynamic interactions between rulers and ruled and the norms governing these exchanges.

If the concept of regime indeed refers to the rules of the political game and its concomitant institutions, to the ways in which society is linked to the apparatus of the state, then regime types should be defined in these terms. The intent of rulers is far less important than the latent principles that have guided their exercise of power. Regimes in Africa may vary according to several main criteria: the structure of the relationship between the administrative, the political, the coercive, and the legal apparatus; the degree of elite cohesion; the extent of societal exclusion and/or inclusion; rules and modes of social-governmental interaction; spheres of operation; longevity of institutional arrangements; and workability. On this basis, it is possible to identify six distinct kinds of regimes that have emerged in Africa since independence.

The first part of the 1960s was marked by the rise of single-party governments and the consolidation of authoritarian patterns of rule, some of which have persisted to the present day, either in administrative-hegemonic or party-mobilizing forms.[8] The latter part of the 1960s witnessed the introduction of the military component and, with it, both the entrenchment of administrative regimes and the injection of instability into the progression of political change. The 1970s began with the rise of authoritarian rulers and personal-coercive modes of rule (and ended with the demise of many of them); the middle part of the decade was characterized by the addition of an Afro-Marxist, party-centralist dimension to the African political map; and the latter years were accompanied by the brief resurrection of pluralist experiments. The transition to the 1980s was unquestionably the most turbulent. Putsches, abdications, elections, repeated military takeovers, and populist uprisings seemed to take place in rapid succession throughout the continent, magnifying the heterogeneity of political conflicts and further accentuating the growing economic malaise. In some cases where regimes broke down, populist forms of government were created. By the 1990s, some brakes had been placed on these gyrations, and democratic systems began to take hold in former one-party contexts; the varieties of authoritarianism had also multiplied, its limitations accentuated, and the search for alternatives intensified. At the end of the 1990s, some countries, such as Congo (Zaire), Sierra Leone, and Liberia experienced a new, and pernicious, form of regime breakdown. (See Table 5.1.)

From the 1960s through the late 1980s, then, the general thrust of African politics was in an authoritarian direction; it then changed toward pluralist-type regime experiments. Within these broad paths, however, no uniformities are evident. This is a reflection of different definitions of the responsibilities of rulers to ruled, of the regularization of alternative courses of action and norms of political conduct, and, it is clear, of variations in stability and continuity. The examination of each of these regime types lays the foundation for a better understanding of political processes.

■ REGIME TYPES AND THEIR VARIATIONS

The regime forms that have emerged in independent Africa have multiplied as various experiments were attempted and lessons gleaned from past experience. The conduct of politics has also undergone a process of localization, accounting for further heterogeneity. The seven major kinds of regimes outlined in the following pages have themselves, therefore, been quite fluid (see Table 5.1).

Table 5.1   Typology of Regimes, 1951–1999

Regime Type	Examples
Administrative-hegemonic	Kenya, Zaire (under Mobutu), Togo, Côte d'Ivoire, Cameroon, Zambia, Malawi, Morocco, Nigeria
Pluralist	Botswana, Mauritius, Senegal, Namibia
Party-mobilizing	Ghana (Nkrumah), Mali (Keita), Guinea (Sekou Touré), Zambia, Algeria (Boumedienne), Tanzania, Zimbabwe
Party-centralist	Angola, Mozambique, Ethiopia, Guinea-Bissau, Congo-Brazzaville, Benin (1970s–1980s)
Personal-coercive	Uganda (Amin), Central African Republic (Bokassa), Equatorial Guinea (Nguema)
Populist	Ghana (Rawlings, 1981–1983), Libya (Qaddafi), Burkina Faso (Sankara), Uganda (Museveni), Democratic Republic of Congo (formerly Zaire)
Regime breakdown	Congo (after Mobutu), Sierra Leone (late 1990s), Liberia (1990s)

Administrative-Hegemonic Regimes

Kenya, Congo, Togo, Côte d'Ivoire, Cameroon, Zambia, Malawi, Morocco, Nigeria, and most other African countries, at various junctures, fall into this category. These regimes were first established in the early 1960s and later sometimes adopted by military leaders. In this type of regime, the three key institutions are the executive, the bureaucracy, and the coercive apparatus (at times with a one-party dominant auxiliary organ subordinated to the presidency). Main policy decisions are centralized around the leader and his close advisers. Specific technical and professional decisionmaking is carried out in the bureaucracy (sometimes with foreign advice), and the military is generally controlled. More significant, the bureaucratic structures and the judiciary maintain a certain autonomy vis-à-vis each other. Political operations, however, are strictly guided by the executive. This type of bureaucratic-personal organization has encompassed both military and civilian governments. Thus, pragmatic one-party states in which the position of the party has been marginalized (Kenya and Côte d'Ivoire until the 1990s); firmly entrenched one-party states permitting a plurality of presidential candidates (Paul Biya's Cameroon); one-party dominant systems allowing for some form of legitimate party competition (Senegal during the late 1960s and 1970s); and military governments attendant to certain social interests (Nigeria, Niger, Congo at certain points) all fall within this rubric.

The administrative-hegemonic regimes, however exclusionary on the surface, nevertheless involve major actors in the decisionmaking process. Policymakers have assumed that to the extent to which key interest group (ethnic, regional, class, occupational, and gender) leaders are part of the policymaking process, they will be more likely to cooperate with government institutions and their regulations. A number of African rulers certainly have shown themselves to be highly alert to the need for some inclusiveness in the deliberations of state. In the Cameroon Republic, former President Ahmadou Ahidjo, despite his heavy-handed and secretive authoritarian tendencies, was careful to use his ministerial appointments as a means of balancing ethnoregional, linguistic, religious, and economic interests. Deeply concerned to preserve national unity, this northern Muslim took steps to preserve an "equilibrium" by appointing Paul Biya, a Catholic from the south-central region, as prime minister, and to maintain a rough ethnoregional balance in ministerial, bureaucratic, and parastatal appointments.

When Ahidjo retired in 1982, Biya succeeded him as president, and the policy of ethnic balancing became, if anything, more pronounced. Biya appointed Bello Bouga Malgari, a northerner, as his prime minister; this upheld the north-south balance at the top and assured that another northern Muslim would eventually succeed to the presidency. But the presidential transition was not destined to be an entirely smooth one. In 1983, the coalition received a jolt as a deepening Biya-Ahidjo quarrel led to growing north-south schisms and then to an attempted coup d'état against the Biya government in April 1984. Although the coup was crushed and the main plotters (the great majority of whom were northerners, according to the armed forces minister)[9] were executed, Biya took special pains to preserve his national coalition by insisting that people from the south as well as the north were involved in the attempt to topple his regime. In the same vein, President Biya took steps in the direction of "gender balancing" in 1996 by naming women to 20 percent of the new positions in the Political Bureau and the Steering Committee.[10]

Similarly, in Kenya, the late President Jomo Kenyatta consolidated power by incorporating leaders not only from his Kikuyu ethnic group but also from other ethnoregional units. And although Kenyatta ruled largely through the bureaucracy, he allowed for a measured pluralism in the cabinet and high party organs. Robert H. Jackson writes:

> The art of statecraft in Kenya is largely a careful exercise in maintaining the support of key ethnic and other interests through the judicious allocation of scarce public resources, while at the same time preventing overt opposition or hostility to government from those less favored through the skillful threat or application of coercion. Government itself is highly plural, with bargaining and competition occurring among Cabinet members acting on behalf of supporting groups and between the ministries themselves.[11]

This strategy was passed on intact to Kenyatta's successor, Daniel arap Moi, a Kalenjin from the Rift Valley. At the outset, Moi appeared careful to preserve the networks of reciprocity carefully built up by his predecessor. Later, however, he made adjustments to secure his control, preferring to work closely with his own protégés rather than to perpetuate a broad-based working relationship with key social groups. Major figures such as Kamba leader Paul Ngei, Luo strongman Oginga Odinga, Kikuyu influential Charles Njonjo, and leading Rift Valley intermediaries Masinde Muliro and Jean Marie Seroney were soon distanced from power, and in 1983, the influence of the Kalenjin group in the cabinet and security services was significantly increased. But in 1992 and 1997, Kenya did hold multiparty parliamentary and presidential elections; and although Moi and his party, the Kenya African National Union, managed to hold on to power, it was clear that the president's monopoly on power was at an end and that henceforth he would have to compete with strong opposition parties, backed by powerful ethnoregional bases of support.[12]

The administrative-hegemonic regimes in Africa have therefore developed some type of ordered relationship with at least some key social interests. This phenomenon, however, has been predicated, not only in Kenya and Cameroon but also in Côte d'Ivoire and Malawi, on the concomitant nurturing of elite cohesion. Strategies of social control have been avowedly elitist in orientation. Leaders have used state resources and state offices as a means of constructing a state managerial class with a common interest in bolstering the public apparatus. The conscious promotion of elite interests was visible in the selective training and recruitment of civil servants in Côte d'Ivoire, Malawi, and Kenya, as well as in the effort made to enable parliamentarians in Nigeria and Cameroon to maintain their status locally through the skewed allocation of resources. These regimes have therefore been marked by the relative solidity of their dominant class, even if instability has been apparent as a result of growing competition (especially in Nigeria and Kenya in the 1980s and 1990s).

Certain rules of social-governmental exchange have flowed from these arrangements. The underlying norm in these regimes has been a willingness to enter into bargaining relations with domestic and international interests. In Kenya, Côte d'Ivoire, Malawi, and Nigeria (before 1993 and almost certainly after the 1999 elections), and now in Gabon, Uganda, and Congo-Brazzaville, leaders have retained strong notions of power concentration while acquiescing to the need to make concessions to well-placed interests. On the domestic side, this organizing principle has involved the careful construction of networks of patrons and clients. In international matters, foreign concerns have been encouraged to invest in these countries, and the government has attempted to impose some controls or to enhance its revenue through the utilization of external bargaining techniques. In this framework, there has been a notion of some, however reluctant, redistribution of resources to powerful local groups as well as foreign interests. Conflicts have tended to be conducted primarily within the elite or among factions organized by members of the ruling circle. Bargaining, however, has its limits: It is carried out to preserve elite interests and rarely includes significant concessions to workers or small farmers. Policy outcomes consequently have a built-in class bias. The notion of centralization through reciprocity has meant that inequalities between those denied access to public resources and those who benefited unduly from access to public resources become inevitable.

The administrative-hegemonic regimes, through some flexibility and responsiveness to predominant class and ethnic forces, have established a certain degree of stability. The workability of this form of state construction has, however, not always been clear-cut. In Kenya, Congo, Niger, and Cameroon, some limited pluralism has been entertained, but the cost of hegemonic exchange has been high in terms of efficiency and equity. As one observer remarked about Cameroon, "The very nature of the coalition, with its tendency to favor ethnic, regional and economic interests at the expense of competence, operates to bring mediocrity to the top of the political heap."[13] More to the point, at times gross inequalities have been tolerated and certain social groups purposefully marginalized (as in Congo, for example) in order to maintain the grasp of the ruling coalition.[14] More concerted efforts at inclusion have, nevertheless, enabled the achievement of some continuity in this select group of relatively resilient regimes in Africa. A differentiation between more stable administrative-hegemonic and more strife-ridden administrative-competitive regimes, on the one hand (Nigeria, for one), and patrimonial-administrative regimes, on the other hand (Togo, Liberia, and Congo), emerged in the 1980s.

Pluralist Regimes

The pluralist regime type in Africa had a far more precarious history prior to the 1990s. This category includes Botswana, Gambia (until 1994), Mauritius, Senegal, and, increasingly, many other countries in the 1990s.[15] In 1996, for example, free elections were held in Benin, Ghana, and Sierra Leone, and multiparty contestations took place in fourteen other countries as well; international observers also deemed the Uganda election to be fair, although it was organized on a no-party basis.

Experiments of this sort were first attempted in most countries at independence and have since been tried and faltered in Sudan and Nigeria. The relationship of public bodies to each other in this construct has been based on a notion of the separation of powers, with multiparty political institutions and fairly vibrant representative structures. In these few countries an effort has been made not only to pursue interest-group involvement but also to allow for a fair amount of autonomous nongovernmental activity. At least some notion of checks and balances has been retained, and therefore the very centralized political structures apparent in administrative regimes are not present in this more loosely organized context.

Nevertheless, in the more resilient pluralist countries, regimes have possessed a strong elitist strain. Although internal disagreement between civil servants and parliamentarians has been noted, the position of the dominant group has been protected through the judicious use of resource allocation. "Big men" in government have been dependent on their constituencies and, hence, subjected to some popular scrutiny at regular intervals. In Senegal and Mauritius, turnover of parliamentarians has been fairly frequent, but mechanisms for overseeing bureaucratic behavior have been far less well developed. The sphere of political inclusion is broader in this arrangement and tends to be more clearly concerned with local issues; actual involvement in the administrative decisionmaking process has been, evidently, contained.

The principles guiding pluralist regime activities have been a mixture of bargaining, compromise, and reciprocity. These notions are evident in relations between decisionmakers and parliamentarians, as well as in the interactions between social groups and government institutions. The underlying value of a measure of reciprocity is central to the continued operation of these constructs. Once again, competition has generally taken on elite and factional forms, although in Senegal religiously based opposition has also been in evidence. Over time, the spheres of activity of government and social institutions in pluralist systems became less well defined than in their administrative-hegemonic counterparts. In Nigeria and Ghana in the early 1980s, for example, the strong emphasis on freedom of expression and the fortification of social autonomy left the role of government institutions, especially in economic matters, somewhat nebulous. The stress on supervisory mechanisms highlighted questions of process but left the substantive division of labor between the executive, the legislative, private entrepreneurs, and local communities rather hazy. Overlapping spheres of activity made decisionmaking cumbersome and permitted excesses. This situation has not been the case in Botswana, where pluralism has been more controlled, or in Senegal, where the privileged position of the bureaucracy has been carefully safeguarded.[16]

Pluralist regimes in Africa have not succeeded in most instances in maintaining themselves for a reasonable period of time. Efforts at instituting political arrangements that incorporate large segments of the population have been repeatedly tried and, in most cases, failed. In Ghana, Uganda, and Nigeria these attempts have not altered the predominance of the administrative machinery, contained factional disputes, or resolved dilemmas of decisionmaking. Moreover, leaders operating within these frameworks have faced problems of elite control, even if their social composition has been ostensibly broader. The workability of pluralist constructions, therefore, had proven itself for the most part in relatively small and homogeneous countries (Botswana) and in countries in which bureaucratic privilege has not been threatened by autonomous and well-organized social groups, especially at the intermediate level. Until the 1990s pluralist regimes, with their attention to the political as well as the administrative apparatus, did not fare well in many parts of the continent, and sometimes changed to administrative-competitive forms. Experimentations with variations on this kind of arrangement, however, resurfaced in the early 1990s. Michael Bratton and Nicolas van de Walle note that "of the 40 African regimes that opened up politically in the first years of the 1990s, a majority (28) did so in conjunction with mass political protest."[17] During this period of democratic transitions, Africa's experience with multiparty elections has varied considerably. Whereas elections proceeded smoothly in Benin and Ghana in 1996, those in Zambia and Côte d'Ivoire led to opposition charges of government manipulation.[18] Thus, in Bratton and van de Walle's words, there has been "confirmation of seemingly contradictory propositions; mass protest led to *both* advances and setbacks."[19]

The past difficulties encountered by pluralist experiments certainly should not be taken to imply the inapplicability of democratic modes of rule to Africa. In many parts of the continent, pluralism has been associated with clientelism and elite privilege. Ongoing efforts to break the connection between elitism and pluralism (as in the organization of the

Ghanaian elections in 1992 and 1996 and the current reforms in Niger, Benin, South Africa, and other countries) may yield other, more equitable and participatory forms of pluralist regimes.[20]

Party-Mobilizing Regimes

The party-mobilizing type of regime bears the imprint of some of the participatory elements of regimes in the pluralist category together with the monopolistic tendencies of administrative-hegemonic regimes.[21] Within this category, it is possible to place Ghana under Nkrumah, Mali under Modibo Keita, Guinea under Sekou Touré, Zambia under Kenneth Kaunda, Algeria under Houari Boumedienne, Tanzania under Julius Nyerere, and, in the early years, Zimbabwe under Robert Mugabe. In all these instances, regimes in this category reflect the organizational preferences of founding fathers with strong socialist predispositions.

The ordering of public institutions in these regimes has rested on a combination of strong one-party domination coupled with bureaucratic expansion firmly under the control of an executive president. Unlike administrative-hegemonic regimes, the center of gravity in these regimes is an ideological party. The politico-administrative pattern of institutionalization fostered in these countries has encouraged the centralization of power around the leader and the party. Thus, the Politburo of Guinea's Parti Democratique de Guinée (PDG), operating on the basis of democratic centralism until the regime was dissolved in a bloodless coup in 1984, retained a decisive capacity to shape public policies, discipline party members, and process appointments to high executive and civil service positions. Similarly, in Tanzania, the party (TANU, subsequently renamed Chama Cha Mapinduzi-CCM) and particularly its National Executive Committee gained a preeminent position in the country's decisionmaking process. Nevertheless, the CCM's formal supremacy in Tanzania in the articulation of public policy did not obviate the growth of a powerful bureaucratic apparatus, primarily charged with the implementation of policy.[22] Tanzania's constitution was amended in 1992 to allow multiparty elections, which were held for the first time in 1995. However, the government placed restrictions on the formation of opposition parties, and it prohibited parties based on ethnic, religious, or regional appeals. Some oppostion members, decrying the 1995 elections as rigged by the CCM, refused to participate in the new government.

In these and other cases, coercive devices have been used to consolidate party-state control. In Guinea and in Ghana during the First Republic, political opponents were jailed regularly and supervisory legal structures subordinated to party interests. In this way, power concentration enhanced the position and the cohesion of a dominant party elite. This group itself was closely knit, but it frequently was in conflict with powerful ethnic or economic interests beyond governmental control.

Strategies of social control in mobilizing regimes have relied heavily on national and party identification and affiliation. Although these regimes have shared a concern with mobilizing common people into politics, certain groups or factions were purposely excluded from the party's central organs, and non-party-linked social groups, especially in elite occupational categories, were undermined and even eliminated. In Guinea, the quest for uniformity precluded the legal maintenance of separate social institutions (even market women were not allowed to operate), and in Tanzania middle-level social groups were discouraged. Mobilization, therefore, was politically selective, if not ethnically or regionally partial.

The principles underlying this regime type highlight notions not only of unity but also of uniformity. For this reason, party-mobilizing regimes have placed a great deal of emphasis on ideology—typically socialist until the 1990s—as a means of appealing to their populations and fostering support for monopolistic policies. The identification between the leader, the party, the nation, and the administrative apparatus was asserted strongly, if not always convincingly. Elite and functional conflicts persisted; in some countries passivity and indifference set in.

These regimes consequently were less inclined to bargain openly with external and domestic interests. President Nyerere and his party supporters took strong measures to present a unified face to the world and to downplay local discontent. Similarly, Nkrumah and Sekou Touré strove to achieve a measure of autonomy globally and to curb dissidence domestically. In fact, party-mobilizing regimes proved relatively successful in curtailing most kinds of immediate political dissent but were susceptible to more widespread disaffection that could lead to profound domestic conflict.[23]

Although the principles of socialist unity were guarded fairly systematically internally, they were bent, however reluctantly, internationally. Both Guinea and Tanzania made their own accommodations with international capitalism. Thus, Sekou Touré agreed in 1973 that Guinea would own only 49 percent of the shares in the Fria bauxite interests (and was to receive 65 percent of profits), and Tanzanian parastatals and National Development Corporation subsidiaries have accommodated transnational economic concerns, even though Tanzania in the 1980s initially refused to comply with IMF preconditions for the extension of its international credit (a decision it changed in mid-decade).[24]

In this situation, the spheres of activity of government institutions were fairly all-embracing. The public arena intruded into the daily lives of citizens and attempted to affect directly social organizations and institutions. Moreover, these regimes assumed well-defined economic roles, both as regulators and entrepreneurs. In Guinea, pursuing a policy of "total decolonization," the PDG increased the state's economic role by expanding public ownership, exerting greater control over industrial and commercial activities, and promoting collective farms and cooperative organizations. In

Tanzania, by the mid-1970s government agencies or government-sponsored parastatals accounted for an estimated 80 percent of the medium- and large-scale economic activities and 44 percent of the monetary GDP.[25] In Ghana, Mali, Zambia, and Uganda in the 1960s, not dissimilar trends were identifiable. In party-mobilizing regimes, the public domain has been broadly defined.

These regimes have had a mixed history since independence. In some cases, especially where strong social (both primary and horizontal) organizations were present (Uganda, Ghana), it proved difficult to sustain a monopolistic ruling coalition. In Guinea, coercion was used as a substitute for acquiescence, and while Sekou Touré was alive this framework endured. With his death, however, his successors were unable to perpetuate the institutional arrangements that he had devised. Algeria underwent a process of bureaucratization, and the approval of its 1989 constitution signified the end of its one-party, socialist state. Tanzania in 1985 experienced a voluntary change in leadership as President Julius Nyerere retired in favor of then prime minister Ali Hassan Mwinyi (who was followed in 1995 by Benjamin Mkapa). The Tanzanian example has differed from the other cases, however, not only in the extent of competition afforded within the former one-party structure, but also in the flexibility demonstrated by the first-generation leadership.

The workability of mobilizing regimes has therefore been closely tied to the skills of a particular leader and to the absence of intermediary organizations, rather than to the viability of such regimes' institutional arrangements. This construct has exhibited virtually all of the difficulties associated with the crisis of African governance at the close of the third decade of independence: overextended administrative structures, institutional dualism, societal detachment, inefficiency, and poor performance. Perhaps for this reason, too, this regime form became virtually extinct in the 1990s in contrast to its prevalence in the early years of independence.

▉ Party-Centralist Regimes

A quite distinct regime type is of the party-centralist sort. Its proponents have insisted on extensive central control and direction and generally have been less tolerant of accommodation with local social forces or with most external actors. This category in the 1970s and 1980s included the Afro-Marxist states of Angola, Mozambique, Ethiopia, Guinea-Bissau, Congo-Brazzaville, and Benin. The institutional arrangements in this kind of regime put the unitary (and usually vanguard) party apparatus above the administrative structures, and in some countries (Ethiopia, Benin) the role of the military was also pronounced. Although the executive remained important, this pattern of institutionalization subordinated all other structures to the party mechanism.[26] Ethiopia, for example, in 1984 became Africa's first formal communist state. Over time, the ruling military clique, the *derg*, systematically suppressed all of the original movements that made up the joint civilian front established in 1977. What emerged from the struggle among these movements was the triumph of former President Mengistu Haile Mariam's view on the need for a centralized model of party organization. The outcome of Mengistu's approach was to confirm the *derg*'s control over the administrative apparatus by inserting a tightly organized monopolistic party structure, the Workers' Party of Ethiopia, at its helm.

In Angola, as in Ethiopia, Angolan President José Eduardo dos Santos confirmed the commitment of his predecessor, Agostinho Neto, both to Marxist-Leninist principles and to the construction of strong state institutions under firm party control. Influence over the bureaucracy by the MPLA's Politburo and Central Committee was enhanced. Moreover, dos Santos attempted, with Soviet-Cuban support, to establish an army powerful enough to insure regime stability and to resolve challenges to the party's position. Also in Angola, as in Mozambique and Ethiopia, the pattern of party-based organization relied most heavily on the support and control of the military. During the 1990s, however, dos Santos softened the official ideology (which is now closer to socialism than Marxism-Leninism) and agreed to the integration of UNITA officers and troops into the Angolan armed forces and to the assignment of UNITA cadres to high government positions (an arrangement that did not fully succeed).

The monopolistic party-rooted arrangements in this type of regime have encouraged a process of exclusion of those social groups calling for local autonomy or insistent on the maintenance of local cultural identities (usually organized by elites antagonistic to the rulers and supported by external forces). The MPLA government in Angola was severely challenged in the 1970s, '80s, and '90s by Jonas Savimbi's UNITA movement. Ethiopia, too, encountered resistance from such major regional and nationality groups as the Eritreans, Tigreans, and Oromo and, following Mengistu's fall in 1991, agreed to Eritrean independence and a decentralized political system in the rest of the country. One major basis for the linkage of various social groups to government in this type of regime, therefore, is ideological. The party-centralist type of regime in theory rejects state-society relations constructed on a pluralist foundation, although some accommodations, of necessity, have been entertained. Patronage systems have existed in these settings but have not been, as in administrative regimes, the mainstay of political exchange. Elite cohesion derives, in this instance, from solidarity among an ideological party vanguard, many of whom shared in long anticolonial struggles. In these cases, as in Mozambique, a relatively small group held sway over public affairs.

The guiding principles of interaction were formulated in terms of adherence to the basic premises of the binding ideology of the party. As a rule, compromise and bargaining were seen as evidence of weakness, even capitulation, going against the grain of the regime's centralizing thrust. These regimes consequently had to deal with violent rebellions, most often supported by inimical external forces. In Angola and Ethiopia, as in Mozambique's struggle against the South African–backed Mozambique National Resistance Movement (RENAMO), direct military confrontation between the formal government and dissident movements was the norm for well over a decade. And in Angola, where the laboriously negotiated Lusaka Protocal collapsed in 1999, a civil war has resumed, causing heavy casualties and extensive damage.[27] The use of the army to quell social discontent has further accentuated the military component of the centralized party structures. It is in these regimes that conflict often took on violent and generalized forms.

But protracted war sometimes gave way to political solutions. The bitter internal war in Ethiopia, involving the Mengistu government, the Ethiopian People's Revolutionary Democratic Front (EPRDF), the Eritrean Peoples Liberation Front (EPLF), and the Oromo Liberation Front, ended abruptly in May 1991, as the EPRDF won a decisive military victory in the Addis Ababa area and the EPLF gained control of Eritrea. U.S. Assistant Secretary of State for African Affairs Herman Cohen played an important mediatory role, recommending that the EPRDF move into Addis Ababa to prevent anarchy and destruction.[28] At the July 1991 National Conference of Ethiopian leaders on the management of the transition to elections, EPLF Secretary General Isaias Afwerki pledged that his organization would not disrupt the new transitional government, but firmly rejected participation in the new regime. The National Conference, on its part, agreed in principle to a UN-supervised referendum after two years to determine the political fate of Eritrea. The referendum was held in April 1993, resulting in independence for Eritrea on May 24, 1993. This separation did not prove tension free, however, because in 1999 bitter fighting broke out between Ethiopian and Eritrean forces over a contested border area.

Of course, the centralist inclination to resist entering into bargaining relations with opposing interests was frequently counterbalanced by expedient adaptations to reality. But these have never come together with a relinquishment of principles. Thus, the late President Samora Machel in Mozambique insisted that the Nkomati accords with South Africa did not signal the beginning of any sort of "ideological coexistence" with that country.[29] In Angola, too, the grave postindependence economic crisis required a tempering of the pledge to achieve collectivist goals and to nationalize private industries. Economic difficulties compelled dos Santos to negotiate a series of special arrangements with such multinational companies as Gulf Oil, Texaco, de Beers, and Fiat. In these and other instances, accommodations did take place, even if they were rationalized as temporary and necessary to the coalescence of strong public institutions.

As reconciliation between conflicting interests was resisted, and as bargaining with international capital took place reluctantly, party-centralist regimes initially engaged in establishing alternate, state-owned institutions, especially in the economic sphere. The public arena was perceived as the alternative to existing retrogressive social organizations (viewed as anathema because they were controlled by antagonistic classes), and emphasis was placed on the fortification of those bodies and organs that would support party domination. Ethiopia, Mozambique, and Angola, as well as Benin and Congo-Brazzaville, therefore sought in the 1980s to impose a uniformity on public institutions and to constrict the latitude allowed to social, cultural, religious, or economic associations that might threaten the hold of the central structures. The absence of a large group of indigenous entrepreneurs in these countries facilitated this task. Collective farms, party cells, or nationalized industries were given preference, at least initially, over other forms of social organization.

Until 1990 the persistence of party-centralist regimes was remarkably high in comparison with other forms. But if the party-centralist machinery was relatively stable, governability was not always enhanced during this period. Indeed, each of these countries has been noted for the volatility of its internal affairs, for civil wars, and for poor economic performance records. With Soviet support, the party-centralist regime form combined a perplexing mixture of regime durability and state fragility. After the collapse of the Soviet Union, however, this regime form disappeared for the time being from the African landscape.

■ Personal-Coercive Regimes

Idi Amin's Uganda, Jean-Bedel Bokassa's Central African Republic, and Macias Nguema's Equatorial Guinea provide the best examples of this type, although Liberia under Samuel Doe and Mobutu's Zaire (now Congo) in the 1980s also fall into this category. In these cases, the entrenchment of the regime has been predicated on the connection between a strong leader and the coercive apparatus. All other structures—the bureaucracy, the political machinery where it existed, the court system—have been subjugated to the whims of the leader backed by military force. Unlike the party-centralist countries, where a ruling clique dominates, in dictatorial regimes the predominance of the leader has precluded any firm pattern of regularized exchanges.

Personally based, coercive regimes have limited the ability to gain access to public institutions to those individuals or social groups loyal to the leader. Samuel Doe in Liberia, for example, systematically practiced a strategy of absolutist control, and in Uganda even Amin's cohorts were powerless in the face of the rapid changes in his personal likes and dislikes. The ruling clique in this situation is fundamentally variable and incohesive. Rules of political behavior consequently tended to be haphazard. Under these conditions, resistance to the regime, and outright repression of these efforts, has been marked.

The involvement of the executive in other spheres of activity was also unpredictable. In Uganda, at first Amin evinced a concern with the control of petty commerce and certain foreign holdings (Asian and British, most notably). Then he intruded into the domain of the judiciary; later he tampered with local institutions; and, in general, the areas of regime action changed with each change of mind. In Equatorial Guinea, similarly, idiosyncratic behavior became a substitute for any measured program of formal involvement in areas of economic and social activity. The underlying theme was not only one of personal variability but also of widespread exploitation and brutality. The rules of interaction in these cases were based on the threat of the use of force rather than on any visible principle of negotiation, reciprocity, or ideological preference.[30]

Contrary to conventional wisdom, personal-coercive regimes, unless routinized through the creation of a group of loyal followers (as in the patrimonial system established in Congo), have not fared well in postindependence Africa. Consistent abuse of public institutions has evoked vocal and organized dissent and, frequently, the armed ouster of brutally repressive leaders. This was the case with Bokassa in the Central African Republic, Amin in Uganda, Mobutu Sese Seko in Congo, and Samuel Doe in Liberia, all of whom personalized the public arena to such an extent that they threatened its very existence.

The transient nature of dictatorial regimes does not mean that they do not wreak considerable havoc or that elements of personalization and privatization of the public arena have not intruded in other countries as well. This pattern has proved costly and inefficient, and over the years it has provided perhaps the single most important indicator of civil discontent and repression. Personal-coercive rule, unlike other forms of authoritarian government, may be understood as a sign of the absence of any clear concept of institutionalization or of recognized norms of political behavior.

■ Populist Regimes

Populist regimes represented a form of regime that emerged in the 1980s and was in part a response to unpredictable dictatorial trends. Populist regimes in Ghana under Jerry Rawlings, Libya under Qaddafi, and Burkina Faso under Thomas Sankara marked a departure from previous patterns in that they sought to reconstruct public institutions by rearranging their interrelationship with social groups and with each other. The cornerstone of the populist mold, best exemplified by Ghana during the first phase (1982–1983) of the Provisional National Defense Council (PNDC), has been the subordination of the administrative apparatus to direct public scrutiny. In Ghana during the early 1980s senior civil servants and public employees were either dismissed or were monitored by people's defense committees or workers' defense committees (later called Committees for the Defense of the Revolution). Thus, although the civil service, certain public corporations, and the judiciary continued to function, their activities were circumscribed for a time by the establishment of an alternate set of institutions, including public tribunals, citizens' vetting committees, and national investigative commissions.

The effect of the reformulation of public organizations was twofold: to introduce a direct popular voice in policymaking; and to limit the independence of the sprawling bureaucracy, not by politicization or personalization, but by pressure to adhere to certain declared antiestablishment norms. Because this arrangement in 1981 and 1982 led to an institutional dualism and to the flight of trained personnel, after 1983 the PNDC proceeded to establish some safeguards against undue interference in the professional and technical roles of the administrative apparatus, while at the same time sustaining notions of public vigilance (thereby coming more to resemble administrative regime forms). Emphasis shifted to improving efficiency, to streamlining the public sector, and to downplaying direct participation through a promise to reexamine and rebuild the political machinery. Throughout this period, however, the crucial link was between the head of state, a small group of close advisers, and popular organizations in a combined effort to reorganize the administration and to curb its excesses.[31]

In Burkina Faso the administration of former president Thomas Sankara, looking closely at the Ghanaian experience, also altered the relationship between the executive, the administration, and its mass constituency with a view toward eliminating waste and undermining the bureaucracy as a bastion of privilege. The objective was to depart from the familiar modes of yesteryear in the hope of effecting a more thoroughgoing revision of the public arena.

An essential tenet of the populist regime form has been, therefore, a concept of social inclusion defined in nonelite terms. In the 1980s, there was a growing attempt to incorporate professionals and technocrats. Therefore, populist regimes questioned elite cohesion without evincing a capacity to entrench other social organizations at the political center. Indeed, rhetoric aside, prevailing patron-client networks and factional alliances persisted. Popular calls for greater accountability have been as vocal in these regimes as in many of their predecessors, as the ouster of Thomas Sankara in 1987 demonstrated. The principles underlying populist regimes have nevertheless differed from those guiding other types. Instead of highlighting either accommodation, compromise, or nationalist ideological rules, the main concern of these regimes has been with mobilizing a popular base of support and assailing pockets of elite privilege. However, by gaining control of the state apparatus, nonestablishment groups have not necessarily taken measures to change channels of political interaction.

The spheres of activity of the public arena in populist arrangements have been broadly defined. Although the key concern has been the regulation of state economic enterprises (and sometimes their dismantling), much activity has focused on marketing and distribution mechanisms as well. Legal, organizational, and administrative life has been closely controlled and autonomous political opportunities circumscribed.

The governments established along populist lines, as in the examples of Ghana and Burkina Faso, rapidly gave way to hegemonic-administrative forms. Durable political structures were not put in place, and the long-term workability of these experiments has not been demonstrated. Without significant resources to redistribute, these regimes have proven to be transitory.[32] It is not improbable that leaders of such governments may initiate regime changes to stay in power.

▓ Regime Breakdown

By the late 1970s and continuing through the 1990s, a handful of countries were in situations in which institutions at the political center had either collapsed or ceased to function in any familiar or identifiable manner. As I. William Zartman observes, "state collapse is marked by the loss of control over political and economic space."[33] Chad until 1987, Uganda from 1981 to 1986, and Congo, Liberia, Sierra Leone, and Somalia in the 1990s would fall into this category. Regime breakdown is the end result of the inability to meet and overcome the crisis that has afflicted public agencies and to establish a modicum of sociopolitical exchange. In these extreme cases, chaos, as opposed to order, prevails. "A fictitious state of armed men detaches itself from society and preys upon a dying economy. The picture is a grim one."[34] With no organized public arena, with little or no social links, without a recognizable governing elite, and hence with no rules of interaction and defined spheres of activity, it is difficult to speak of specific regime principles, let alone examine their activities. In this worst-case scenario, then, the challenge of power organization and consolidation has been posed anew some forty years after independence.

■ REGIME TYPES AND POLITICAL PROCESS

In brief, regimes, and the political processes they reflect, may be arranged along a continuum according to different degrees of structural autonomy and channels of political interchange. At one pole stand those regimes that have no clear organizing principles and hence possess highly erratic and conflictual relations with their constituent social groupings. At the other pole, it is possible to place those countries in which the practice of government and the management of conflict rest on some shared notions of obligation and in which mechanisms for the operationalization of such transactions do exist (pluralist and various administrative-hegemonic forms). In between these two extremes lie those regimes that have operated on monopolistic principles and where social tensions are high (party-mobilizing and party-centralist kinds); those in which participatory exchanges exist, but structures are weak (populist governments); and those regimes where competition is either pronounced or purposely circumscribed (administrative-competitive and patrimonial-administrative models). As time has progressed, the more administrative and pluralist modes have become more prevalent, achieving a modicum of salience in the 1990s.

The various regime types that have emerged on the continent have reflected both the many constraints and the variegated options open to African citizens and leaders since independence. Close analysis of regime forms and of their mutation assists in linking the practice of government with its purpose; the political process with the state and the dominant modes of social organization; and the theory of politics with the African setting in which it unfolds. Indeed, the study of political processes in Africa through the lens of these fluid regime forms requires not only the unraveling of the way decisions are made and implemented and what responses these actions evoke (although this is an essential part of such an undertaking); it also draws attention to the fundamentals of politics: to how centers are constructed and legitimated; how their political visions are crystallized and authority conceived; how civil societies form and break down; how transformations take root and why. It is to an examination of these facets of the political process that we now turn.

■ NOTES

1. This may be the most fundamental problem facing Third World leaders. See Christopher Clapham, *Third World Politics: An Introduction* (Madison: University of Wisconsin Press, 1985), pp. 43–44. Also see Joel Migdal, *Strong Societies and Weak States: State-Society Relations and State Capabilities in the Third World* (Princeton: Princeton University Press, 1988).

2. Robert H. Jackson and Carl G. Rosberg, *Personal Rule in Black Africa* (Berkeley: University of California Press, 1982).

3. Jean-François Bayart, "Civil Society in Africa," in Patrick Chabal, ed., *Political Domination in Africa: Reflections on the Limits of Power* (London: Cambridge University Press, 1986), p. 124.

4. Patrick Chabal, "Introduction: Thinking About Politics in Africa," in ibid., p. 12. See also Francis M. Deng et al., *Sovereignty as Responsibility: Conflict Management in Africa* (Washington, DC: Brookings Institution Press, 1996), pp. 53–60.

5. See the chapters by Olusegun Obasanjo, Ibrahim A. Gambari, and Solomon Gomes in Edmond J. Keller and Donald Rothchild, eds., *Africa in the New International Order: Rethinking State Sovereignty and Regional Security* (Boulder: Lynne Rienner, 1996). Also see Carnegie Commission on Preventing Deadly Conflict, *Preventing Deadly Conflict: Final Report* (Washington, DC: Carnegie Commission on Preventing Deadly Conflict, 1997), p. 136.

6. Roger Charlton, "Dehomogenising the Study of African Politics—The Case of Inter-State Influence on Regime Formation and Change," *Plural Societies* 14, no. 1/2 (1983): 32–48.

7. Roger Tangri, *Politics in Sub-Saharan Africa* (London: James Curry, 1985); Ruth Berins Collier, *Regimes in Tropical Africa* (Berkeley: University of California Press, 1982); and Dirk Berg-Schlosser, "African Political Systems: Typology and Performance," *Comparative Political Studies* 17, no. 1 (1984). 121 151, are some examples of these various approaches.

8. Richard Hodder-Williams, *An Introduction to the Politics of Tropical Africa* (London: George Allen and Unwin, 1984), pp. 113–146, suggests such a line of analysis.

9. *West Africa,* April 23, 1984, p. 865.

10. "Cameroon: Second CPDM Ordinary Congress Ends in Yaounde," Foreign Broadcast Information Service, *Sub-Saharan Africa* 96, 246 (December 20, 1996). http://wnc.fedworld.gov/cgi-bin/retrieve.

11. Robert H. Jackson, "Planning, Politics and Administration," in Goran Hyden, Robert Jackson, and John Okumu, eds., *Development Administration: The Kenyan Experience* (Nairobi: Oxford University Press, 1970), pp. 177–178.

12. Joel D. Barkan, "Kenya: Lessons from a Flawed Election," *Journal of Democracy* 4, no. 3 (July 1993): 85–99.

13. Victor T. Le Vine, "Cameroonian Politics: Scholarship and Partisanship," *Africa Today* 29, no. 4 (1982): 58. Also see Mordechai Tamarkin, "The Roots of Political Stability in Kenya," *African Affairs* 77, no. 308 (1978): 297–320.

14. Richard A. Joseph, "Class, State and Prebendal Politics in Nigeria," *Journal of Commonwealth and Comparative Politics,* no. 3 (1983): 21–38. Also see his chapter, "The Reconfiguration of Power in Late Twentieth-Century Africa," in Richard Joseph (ed.), *State, Conflict, and Democracy in Africa* (Boulder: Lynne Rienner, 1999), pp. 57–80.

15. Michael Bratton and Nicolas van de Walle, "Toward Governance in Africa: Popular Demand and State Responses," in Goran Hyden and Michael Bratton, eds., *Governance and Politics in Africa* (Boulder: Lynne Rienner, 1992), pp. 27–55.

16. Richard Sklar, "Democracy in Africa" (UCLA: Special Publication of the African Studies Center, 1982), and Ali A. Mazrui, "The Cultural Fate of African Legislatures: Rise, Decline and Prospects for Revival," *Présence Africaine* 112 (1979): 26–27.

17. Michael Bratton and Nicolas van de Walle, *Democratic Experiments in Africa: Regime Transitions in Comparative Perspective* (Cambridge: Cambridge University Press, 1997), p. 185.

18. See Tessy D. Bakary, "Political Polarization over Governance in Côte D'Ivoire," in I. William Zartman, ed., *Governance as Conflict Management: Potics and Violence in West Africa* (Washington, DC: Brookings Institution Press, 1997), pp. 88–93.

19. Bratton and van de Walle, *Democratic Experiments in Africa,* p. 185.

20. See Larry Diamond, Juan Linz, and Seymour Martin Lipset, eds., *Democracy in Developing Countries: Africa* (Boulder: Lynne Rienner, 1988), and John A. Wiseman, *Democracy in Black Africa: Survival and Revival* (New York: Paragon House Publishers, 1990).

21. Robert H. Jackson and Carl G. Rosberg, "Personal Rule: Theory and Practice in Africa," *Comparative Politics* 16, no. 4 (1984): 421–442.

22. John J. Okumu, "Party and Party-State Relations," in Joel D. Barkan with John J. Okumu, eds., *Politics and Public Policy in Kenya and Tanzania* (New York: Praeger, 1979), pp. 52–53.

23. Ekkart Zimmerman, "Macro-Comparative Research on Political Protest," in Ted Robert Gurr, ed., *Handbook of Political Conflict* (New York: Free Press, 1980), p. 210.

24. Lapido Adamolekun, *Sekou Touré's Guinea: An Experiment in Nation-Building* (London: Methuen, 1976), p. 77, and Isaa Shivji, "Tanzania—The Silent Class Struggle," in Lionel Cliffe and John Saul, eds., *Socialism in Tanzania II* (Nairobi: EAPH, 1973), p. 327.

25. Aguibou Y. Yansane, *Decolonization in West African States with French Colonial Legacy* (Cambridge, MA: Schenkman Publishing Co., 1984), pp. 140–141. These estimates were made by Reginald Green and referred to in Crawford Young, *Ideology and Development in Africa* (New Haven: Yale University Press, 1982), p. 106.

26. See David and Marina Ottaway, *Afrocommunism* (New York: Africana Publishing Co., 1981), and Edmond J. Keller and Donald Rothchild, eds., *Afro-Marxist Regimes* (Boulder: Lynne Rienner, 1987).

27. Paul Hare, *Angola's Last Best Chance for Peace* (Washington, DC: United States Institute of Peace Press, 1998); and Donald Rothchild, *Managing Ethnic Conflict in Africa: Pressures and Incentives for Cooperation* (Washington, DC: Brookings Institution Press, 1997), pp. 111–114.

28. See Donald Rothchild and Caroline Hartzell, "Great- and Medium-Power Mediations: Angola," *The Annals of the American Academy of Political and Social Science* 518 (November 1991): 39–57, and Terrence Lyons, "The Transition in Ethiopia," *CSIS Africa Notes,* no. 127 (August 27, 1991): 4–7.

29. *Africa Research Bulletin* 21, no. 3 (15 April 1984): 7167–7168.

30. See Samuel Decalo, *Psychoses of Power: African Personal Dictatorships* (Boulder: Westview Press, 1989).

31. Zaya Yeebo, "Ghana Defence Committees and the Class Struggle," *Review of African Political Economy* 32 (1985): 64–72; Adotey Bing, "Popular Participation Versus People's Power: Notes on Politics and Power Struggles in Ghana," *Review of African Political Economy* 31 (1984): 91–104.

32. Frank Holmquist pointed out these characteristics.

33. "Introduction: Posing the Problem of State Collapse," in I. William Zartman, ed., *Collapsed States: The Disintegration and Restoration of Legitimate Authority* (Boulder: Lynne Rienner, 1995), p. 9.

34. Richard Sandbrook, *The Politics of Africa's Economic Stagnation* (London: Cambridge University Press, 1985), p. 41. See also William Reno, *Warlord Politics and African States* (Boulder: Lynne Rienner, 1998).

6

High Politics:
The Procedures and
Practices of Government

The analysis of the political process commences with the study of high politics, with regime efforts to lay down procedures for decisionmaking and to create the mechanisms for their enforcement.[1] From the perspective of rulers, two core concerns guide this undertaking. First, how do rulers consolidate and entrench their position at the center: what rules do they establish and what patterns of decisionmaking do they encourage to increase their power? Second, how do they gain the compliance of their constituencies: what support bases do they construct and what means do they devise to maintain these alliances?

The various regimes that have emerged in Africa during the past three decades have provided different answers to these questions. Since independence, a wide variety of political centers, propelled by quite distinct principles and operating in diverse ways, have emerged. Despite the common constraints they faced, individual leaders have put their imprint on the manner in which politics is conducted. In some instances, their thoughts, rhetoric, and actions yielded uncertainty and in extreme cases even brought about the collapse of the political center (Uganda, Ethiopia, Liberia, Somalia, Chad). In other countries, rules and procedures survived their originators, furnishing presumptive principles of political behavior (Senegal, Cameroon, Tanzania). In many parts of the continent, however, experimentation and trial and error became the norm. As one leader succeeded another, different visions were expounded and diverse instruments devised to carry them out. Throughout, the connection between the rules of the political game and the institutions of government have been filtered through the ambitions, interests, limitations, and capabilities of the political elite. Nevertheless, the fact that in most cases state leadership is less salient at the end of the twentieth century than it was immediately after independence is in some cases indicative of the entrenchment of procedures and norms.

■ THE POLITICS OF THE CENTER: DECISIONMAKING AND THE RULES OF THE POLITICAL GAME

The consolidation and entrenchment of the political center—the source of political decisions—is the critical first step in the practice of politics. There are three main elements of this aspect of the political process: the articulation of a political vision, frequently an ideology, which sets forth the goals of the rulers and their plans for governing (principles for decisionmaking); the refinement of leadership styles and modes of operation (locus of decisionmaking); and the establishment of the rules of the political game (manner of decisionmaking). These facets are integrally linked: Together they define the essential features of the daily workings of various governments throughout the continent.

▦ The Ideologies of Independent Africa

The crystallization of political centers relies on, and inevitably mirrors, the premises outlined by their founders. The considerations guiding political action—whether explicitly stated or implicitly understood—constitute the political worldview within which decisions are made and initiatives launched. Political ideologies, as distinct from policies, are systems "of beliefs that serve as a standard of evaluation and a guide to action."[2] They give an indication of the preferences of rulers, of their reasons for acting. In a very real sense, ideologies attempt to grapple with tangible problems, describe and explain existing conditions, and prescribe desired courses of behavior. In this respect, they encompass the conceptual, and hence the subjective, principles of political action.

   In the aftermath of decolonization, most African regimes attempted to set out the framework of a political vision that would capture the exigencies of their circumstances and also provide a referent for policymaking. The transition to independence, in many cases, left a normative political vacuum. The ideas and propositions that upheld the colonial apparatus had been rejected, and substitute organizing notions had to be formulated. The ideologies of independent Africa have tried to offer answers to three interrelated problems: how to organize the psychological mobilization of identities around a concept of the new political entity; how to provide theoretical legitimation for the incoming regimes and their leaders; and how to design a blueprint for political and economic action in the future. The manner in which these issues have been addressed has varied markedly, both geographically and temporally. Regardless of precise contents, however, throughout the postcolonial phase the ideological component has set forth the charter of the rulers: the foundations for the rationalization and justi- fication of prevailing modes of government.

The first official wave of ideological construction occurred immedi- ately after independence and bore a self-proclaimed *African socialist* label.[3] Pioneered by the leaders of party mobilizing regimes (Kwame Nkrumah in Ghana, Ahmed Sekou Touré in Guinea, Modibo Keita in Mali, Gamal Abdel Nasser in Egypt, Ahmed Ben Bella in Algeria, and Julius Nyerere in Tanzania), African socialism had its origins in anticolonial movements and was propagated most forcefully by select members of the first generation of African leaders.[4] The founding fathers espousing no- tions of African socialism shared an aversion to colonialism and them- selves held a somewhat marginal position in the existing social order. They viewed independence as an opportunity to build a new society: to shed the intellectual and cultural as well as the material and political shackles of the colonial inheritance.[5]

The African socialism of the 1960s was nationalist in orientation and evolutionary in thrust. Although encompassing quite divergent strands, all early socialists, from Nyerere to Sekou Touré, proclaimed a commitment to the creation of an egalitarian, just, and self-sufficient polity. The mech- anism for the attainment of these goals was the state, which would furnish the pivot of critical identities, organize the economy, and supervise the second, societal, phase of decolonization. Although differing substantially in the degree to which they relied on precolonial values and traditional institutions to promote these goals, African socialist worldviews extolled political centralization and mobilization as the vehicles for real transfor- mation. Socialism at this juncture was hence both Afrocentric and non- aligned: It shunned the unselective transfer of socialist terminology (such as the class struggle) to Africa and at the same time laid claim to a uni- versality of political ideals.

The early socialist stirrings in Africa were, in many respects, the in- tellectual counterpart to the quest for political autonomy. They were avowedly all-encompassing, they contained a strong programmatic dimen- sion, they evinced a real preoccupation with defining the basis of a na- tional interest, they were concerned with retaining a populist aura, and they provided the justification for the imposition of political uniformity (via the single party) under the guise of forwarding national unity. In Mali and Guinea, Ghana and Tanzania, and to some extent in Zambia and Sene- gal, notions of socialism were carefully explicated to highlight the idea of the primacy of politics.

The orientation toward change implicit in the political thought of African socialist leaders was, therefore, accompanied by the firm belief that officials and party activists were best positioned to interpret the gen- eral will and hence to define the interests of the collectivity. Even when this stance was adopted with the best intentions in mind, it furnished a justification for authoritarian rule.

African socialism came to be regarded, as a consequence, as indelibly intertwined with the careers of its formulators. And, indeed, as a philosophy of rule it barely survived the first decade of independence. By the beginning of the 1970s Kwame Nkrumah, Ahmed Ben Bella, and Modibo Keita had been deposed, Nasser had died, and Nyerere and Sekou Touré had parted political paths.[6] Nevertheless, the impact of these first ideological experiments has outlasted their initiators. The sense of national pride and African dignity instilled by party mobilizing regimes via the principles of African socialism still has widespread appeal. The commitment to pan-Africanism may be traced back to these leaders. Most significant, because they were the first to attempt the exposition of a coherent (if also inconsistent) system of political ideas, their concepts have become a signpost against which subsequent political ideologies have been measured and evaluated.

While notions of African socialism gained currency during the course of the 1960s, another series of organizing principles were more quietly, though perhaps more firmly, implanted on the African scene. Dominant elites in the administrative-hegemonic regimes of Côte d'Ivoire, Nigeria, Gabon, Sierra Leone, Morocco, Cameroon, and Malawi opted for an ideology of *political pragmatism*. The first leaders who supported a more cautious approach to the articulation of binding values were also, like their socialist counterparts, part of the initial crop of African leaders. In contrast, however, to their peers, they tended to draw their support from more established groups in colonial society, to possess channels of access to nonstate resources within their countries, and to confine their anticolonialism to the elimination of the colonial political presence but hardly the colonial influence in other spheres.

The pragmatism of Felix Houphouët-Boigny, Abubakar Tafawa Balewa, Hastings Banda, and later Daniel arap Moi and Abdou Diouf set economic growth and prosperity squarely at the center of the preferred order. For this reason, emphasis was placed on continuity rather than change, on the emulation of the Western model of development, and on the nurturing of private initiative in the capitalist mode. Although declaring themselves nonideological (and in some instances, such as Ahidjo in Cameroon and Banda in Malawi, openly anti-ideological), these leaders did propound precepts that coalesced into an alternative to the more strident socialist ideologies of mobilizing regimes. Tolerance toward traditional and colonial institutions and practices was stressed, and the state was endowed with the task of facilitating entrepreneurship, attracting foreign investments, and establishing a climate conducive to material advancement. For the articulators of this approach, the meaning of independence was defined in economic terms; the refinement of the market economy to suit African conditions was encouraged.

Pragmatic worldviews were no less statist than the more populist-socialist theories; they were, however, advanced for different reasons and with other goals in mind (related, also, to the preservation of elite privilege). No pretense to a cohesive, holistic, political orientation exists in these notions of government. Neither, in most instances, is it possible to point to strong liberal underpinnings. Existing conditions rather than ideal values were deemed to dictate the range of options and choices, and economic concerns furnished the rationalization for the demand for political conformity. Centralization, therefore, was delineated not in a social or political but in an administrative sense; it nevertheless was as deeply ensconced in the political attitudes of pragmatists as in those of self-proclaimed socialists.[7]

African pragmatism has fared better over the years than African socialism, if only because the upholders of these views have exhibited a greater capacity for endurance. To be sure, Balewa in Nigeria, Sylvanus Olympio in Togo, and Foulbert Youlou in Congo-Brazzaville were among the first leaders to fall in military coups d'état. But Houphouët-Boigny, Ahidjo, Bourguiba, Banda, and Kenyatta combined ideological pragmatism with political skills to achieve remarkable longevity. And, as important, the orientations of these leaders were attractive to incoming military leaders, such as Nigeria's Yakubu Gowon and Ghana's A. A. Afrifa, who were impressed by notions of administrative order and organizational efficiency and were concerned with gaining the support of existing elites. African pragmatism and state capitalism, therefore, have furnished guidance to successive generations of African leaders. They thus constituted a second, more resilient, ideological pole devised during the first years of independence.

The late 1960s and early 1970s coincided with the rise of military leaders who had a notable dictatorial bent: Idi Amin in Uganda, Jean-Bedel Bokassa in the Central African Republic, Mobutu in Congo, and Gnassingbe Eyadema in Togo. These rulers were not central in the political struggle for independence. In these countries, political concepts were most evidently promulgated as rhetorical props for precarious heads of personal-coercive regimes who almost uniformly chose to forward crude *military-nationalist* precepts as a substitute for coherent political ideologies. They justified their actions as genuinely African and independent— as the first steps in the formation of a truly autonomous national existence.

Military-nationalist ideologies in Africa have in common a conscious xenophobia coupled with the glorification of African prowess (and by extension, of the warrior tradition in African history).[8] The emphasis in these thought patterns was most evident in purportedly cultural matters, especially the Africanization of names (Mobutu Sese Seko, Kutu Acheampong) and places (Congo, Ndjaména). National dress codes were designed, indigenous music was aired, and certain traditional practices were revived.

In economic terms, the idea of full control over national resources was underlined not only to deflect pressures from external creditors but also to account for statist monopolies. In the name of "authenticity" or "national redemption," all opposition was deemed treasonous and dissent forcibly quashed.[9]

Military nationalism in Africa developed a rhetorical terminology to exalt problematic leaders and to compel obedience. In many respects these notions lack even the minimal markings of ideologies: They are by and large bereft of intellectual content, they are replete with contradictions, they address key issues haphazardly. These orientations, at best, may be viewed as feeble attempts to legitimate their purveyors; in most instances, they have provided a cover for the exercise of brute force. Manifestations of this sort of military nationalism resurface periodically, as insecure leaders with dwindling support bases find refuge in cultural symbols in a desperate effort to gain some loyalty and legitimacy. In the last days of his rule in Chad, François Tombalbaye encouraged the revival of traditional cults. Acheampong in Ghana invoked culture and religion as an explanation for his unwillingness to leave office. Samuel Doe appealed to national pride. The resort to such devices has become one of the first (and quite accurate) signals of the breakdown of regularized patterns and hence of instability and ruler vulnerability.

In the mid-1970s, there was a concerted ideological regeneration in the form of *Afro-Marxism*. Pioneered by military leaders in Somalia, Congo-Brazzaville, Madagascar, and Benin, the place of Marxism-Leninism in Africa was accentuated with the independence of the lusophone states of Angola, Mozambique, and Guinea-Bissau and with the overthrow of the traditional monarchy of Emperor Haile Selassie in Ethiopia. The turn to a more scientific socialism, the mark of party-centralist regimes, was partly a result of protracted wars of national liberation; partly a reflection of the disillusionment of segments of the urban intelligentsia and rural dwellers with feeble and ineffective elites; partly an indication of the growth of Soviet influence on the continent; and partly a consequence of the appeal of a pure, universal, and change-bearing ideological framework heretofore untested on African soil.

Afro-Marxists negated the precolonial and colonial past in their quest for societal transformation. They uniformly attributed the maladies of the African experience to the lingering effects of imperialism and the ongoing perniciousness of neocolonial influences both within and outside Africa. In this approach, a totally new social order is required to abolish private ownership of the means of production and, with the help of a revolutionary vanguard, to alter drastically the distribution of power in society. Unlike African socialism, Afro-Marxism integrated class theory into domestic politics.[10] In this worldview, the Leninist principles of democratic centralism and state-directed economic institutions are seen as the crucial vehicles for the alteration of the social order. Scientific socialism as articulated in the 1980s in Angola, Mozambique, Ethiopia, and Congo-Brazzaville, therefore, set forth a revolutionary vision based on political unity, economic prosperity, and the elimination of a long legacy of inequality.

The introduction of Marxism-Leninism to Africa was, in many respects, a departure from the more eclectic ideological experiments of the preceding years. Professing a commitment to the application of universal truths to alter the African condition, scientific socialists transferred an entire, well-formulated, cohesive, and all-embracing political philosophy to the continent. They regarded the conceptual framework not only as a means of justifying their exercise of power but, and this is more telling, as a true guide to political action.[11] This second official wave of ideological construction sought theoretical understanding and practical direction in the philosophy and prescriptions of Marxism-Leninism. African Marxism has remained a conceptual force on the continent, although the regimes established on its foundations have floundered because of economic upheavals and internal wars. With the settlement of the civil wars in Ethiopia, Mozambique, and for a time in Angola, strategic ties with the Soviet Union (and later, Russia) declined in significance and economic links with the West were sustained or strengthened.

In the late 1970s, another ideological strain of the period of the transition to independence was revived as official dogma, albeit only temporarily. The ideas of *liberal democracy* were resurrected with the efforts of certain one-party states, such as Senegal, Côte d'Ivoire, and briefly Kenya, to open channels for greater competition and participation; these ideas were reinforced as tyrannies were abolished in the Central African Republic and Uganda and as military regimes were terminated in Nigeria, Ghana, and Burkina Faso (then Upper Volta). Indigenous educated elites concerned with civil liberties, human rights, and the protection of opportunities for free enterprise promoted liberal ideology.

Democratic precepts in Africa in the 1980s rested on the lifting of prohibitions on political competition, on the nurturing of private enterprise, and on the protection of personal freedoms. New constitutions were written to reflect the move away from the concentration of power in the hands of personal leaders and to expound on the need for greater representation. The guidelines for the reinstatement of democratic rule nevertheless highlighted nationalist orientations and generally evinced (Ghana, Nigeria, Senegal) a preference for presidential as opposed to parliamentary models.[12]

The appearance of liberalism in Africa was the political correlate of the more economic notions inherent in earlier pragmatic concepts. Despite conditions of economic recession and social inequality that continued to prevail, these ideas developed deeper roots in the 1990s as another democratic wave swept across the continent. Zambia's election, for one, led to a change of government, and military-led regimes in Ghana and Nigeria prepared the way for a return to constitutional government. Despite a variety of setbacks, including noncompetitive or managed elections (Ghana in 1992), the losers' refusal to accept election outcomes (Angola and Sierra Leone), and military coups (Burundi), democratic concepts were debated in a multiplicity of countries and were implemented in one form or another in two-thirds of the countries on the continent.

Prior to this resurgence, in the 1980s, the rise of a young, postindependence generation of military leaders (Jerry Rawlings in Ghana, Muammar Qaddafi in Libya, Thomas Sankara in Burkina Faso, Yoweri Museveni in Uganda) gave formal expression to the thoughts and aspirations of the have-nots of the continent. *Populism* in Africa, bred on resentment of the privileged establishment, arose in periods of sharp economic decline and growing scarcity and, at least at the outset, conveyed an African brand of radicalism aimed at restructuring the power apparatus to suit the needs of the common person.

Although Libya's Qaddafi set in motion the populist strain in Africa, Jerry Rawlings emerged as perhaps the most vocal exponent of African populism to date.[13] Unlike Afro-Marxists, Rawlings pressed for revolution from within through the reassertion of moral rectitude, probity, and accountability in ruling circles. The key element of the populist ideal in Africa is the need to restructure political institutions and to dismantle the elite establishment that has dominated public affairs since independence. This goal would be achieved through mass participation in decisionmaking, decentralization of economic control, and the creation of mechanisms for popular scrutiny of governmental affairs. The vehicles for this transformation, in populist thinking, are twofold: new inclusive organizations based on notions of direct mobilization; and the reformulation of values underlying behavior in the public domain. Corruption, exploitation, and abuse of office were proclaimed to be antisocial; industriousness, cooperation, and productivity were accentuated as virtues. The key, then, to economic recovery and social cohesion was to be found within Africa—in the mores, practices, and capabilities of its workers and farmers.

African populism contains strong moralistic and messianic overtones. It promises personal salvation and national redemption through hard work and cooperation. Populist thought is fiercely nationalist and anti-imperialist, and its basis is deeply entrenched in frustration, anguish, negation, and protest. In this worldview, the objects of change have shifted from the colonial legacy in general to the domestic purveyors of neocolonialism, from external exploiters to corrupt local elites. Although containing traces of socialist and Marxist terminology, African populism has advocated radical change from below. As such, it constitutes a set of ideas directly linked in time and place to local exigencies.

Populist notions proliferated during the course of the 1980s as an emotional antidote to economic dislocation and political disintegration. The psychological force of these ideas, as well as their future (sometimes millenarian) thrust, enhanced their appeal. Although frequently incohesive and unquestionably fraught with logical inconsistencies, populism proffers very simple and controllable solutions to complex problems. In this respect, its basic precepts can be sustained as long as poverty prevails and abuses of power are widespread.

The 1980s also proved to be a breeding ground for the insertion of *religious*, primarily Islamic, thought patterns into the realm of official African political discourse. Some of the prescriptions of Shari'a law were adopted by President Gaafar Nimeiri in Sudan in an attempt to redefine the foundations of his rule; the constitution of the Second Republic of Nigeria made provisions for Islamic courts of appeal. References to the Koran as justifications for policy have been cited repeatedly in Senegal and Somalia, Mauritania and Libya, even in Cameroon and Gabon.[14] This recourse to religious arguments is another manifestation of the retreat from secularism that has characterized this third wave of ideological experimentation in independent Africa.

African socialist, pragmatic, military-nationalist, Afro-Marxist, liberal, and populist ideological constructs have exhibited a broad range of ideas and a diversity of perceptions of reality and desired goals. Some regimes have enunciated fairly cohesive principles, whereas others have forwarded more haphazard political notions (military-nationalism, for one). Over the years, too, there have been sharp gyrations in the intensity of political rhetoric and in the relative significance of the ideological dimension of politics. Following independence, anticolonial ideologies were first adapted to local conditions and then universalized. The thought patterns of the 1980s were marked by the predominance of more parochial worldviews. And in the 1990s, there was a return to liberal ideas and a conscious effort to translate them into African terms.

During the course of the first four decades of African independence, nevertheless, the broad outlines of African political ideologies have been defined and some of their key features have been consolidated. Several themes transcend these different political thought frameworks. All official ideologies are avowedly nationalistic and seek to carve out an independent African position in the global arena. All contain the terminology, if not the conceptual tools, of anticolonialism and dependency theories.[15] They share a primary concern with overcoming poverty and underdevelopment. Until recently, in the political realm, the vindication of state power, with very few exceptions, was a major preoccupation.

Ideology is not always a sure guide to unraveling decisionmaking practices and procedures, especially in Africa where few regimes have been able to assert a symbolic distinctiveness; it does, however, provide irreplaceable clues to the motives, desires, penetrative capacities, and underlying principles of various regimes. By capturing the language of official political discussion and debate (although hardly of all political discourse), the ideologies of independent Africa are a significant part of the political process. They are as important for what they preclude as for what they encompass, for what they obfuscate as for what they illuminate. These notions, regardless of relative salience or logical coherence, do consequently have a direct bearing on the conduct of political life.

■ Leadership Styles and Modes of Operation

If ideologies establish some of the organizing principles of African political centers, the behavior of rulers furnishes the axis around which decisionmaking takes place. The prominence of political personalities in postcolonial Africa is largely an outgrowth of the fragility of many state structures. The emergent leaders of African countries on the eve of independence lacked many of the institutional bases of legitimate authority. Although a leader's standing rested to some extent on consensus or popular approval, his status resulted largely from his position within the new political structure. Not limited by constitutional restraints, and usually supported only by fragments of their diffuse societies, these elites initially gained salience as the embodiment of the nascent political center and subsequently as the personification of its modes of operation. In this situation latter-day forms of patrimonialism became commonplace.[16] Most African political centers have exhibited varying degrees of neopatrimonial rule.[17] Thus, although top leadership in all political systems tends to be highly individualized, in Africa political leaders, most notably in the early years of independence, were especially instrumental in defining the rules of the political game.

Center construction, therefore, bore the personal stamp of particular leaders. However, although in the first three decades of independence most such centers were by nature authoritarian, only some evolved into fullfledged networks of individual, or personal, rule.[18] Other leaders succeeded in laying down more regularized channels of access and decisionmaking. Under these circumstances, and most recently with the reintroduction of party politics, the salience of leaders has diminished. For this reason, the way that the role of leaders has been interpreted in different regimes has had a special impact on the nature of the political process in their polities.

The first distinctive style of leadership to surface in postindependence Africa was of a *charismatic* sort.[19] It has usually been associated with socialist leaders of the first generation of independence (Kwame Nkrumah, Julius Nyerere, Sekou Touré, Houari Boumedienne, Ahmed Ben Bella, and, to a lesser extent, Modibo Keita, Kenneth Kaunda, and Robert Mugabe;

Hastings Kamuzu Banda of Malawi, a distinctly nonsocialist leader, also falls into this category). Common to the background of these leaders was their schooling in the colonial system and their central role in the anti-colonial struggle. Some of these leaders did not enjoy a strong position either within their societies in general or specifically within the elite. Their support was based largely on the popular appeal of their message and their successes during decolonization. Their institutional backing was, as a result, frequently fragile. Inspirational personalities tended to emerge in situations of political uncertainty and social fluidity.

Charismatic leadership in Africa has been tied to a commitment to the implementation of ideological concepts. The political style it has fostered is consequently autocratic: Leaders of this sort chose to dominate rather than compromise, to dictate rather than to reconcile. Charismatic leadership in Africa therefore bore the external trappings, whether consciously or by attribution, of omnipotence. In the case of Kwame Nkrumah, it was exaggerated to the point of endowing the leader with godlike attributes. With the notable exception of Julius Nyerere, who subordinated personal ambitions to the prophecy of the political vision he sought to bring about, charismatic leaders nurtured an image of themselves as the embodiment of the nation, the state, power, and the future. They took on honorific titles, engaged in ostentatious practices, allowed (and even promoted) leadership cults, and methodically centralized political control.

The charismatic mode of operation was predicated on the creation of a coterie of followers with personal loyalty to the head of state and to the ideology he espoused. Rivals were systematically crushed, imprisoned, or exiled. Advisers were subordinated to the leaders and frequently dismissed or replaced when the need or the whim arose. In this mode of operation decisionmaking was politicized: The test of inclusion was fealty to the leader and his precepts. The single party became the repository of the faithful as well as the critical avenue to elite status. The politics of court intrigue flourished in such settings: Conspiracies, plots, purges, and reshufflings were the political order of the day.

The charismatic style, therefore, has invariably proven to be a high-risk one. "It tends to restrict choice, in the same way that it restricts the political groups actively involved in government, and it leads easily to the creation of an embittered opposition whose leaders are in prison or in exile."[20] It can therefore be effectively maintained only by those leaders who have sustained broad public support or who have not confronted organized groups with alternate worldviews. Although Nyerere, Kaunda, Banda, Nasser, and Sekou Touré stand out in this regard, Nkrumah, Ben Bella, and Modibo Keita were unable to perpetuate their position for a protracted period. Because charisma acted as a substitute for institutionalization, it was also susceptible to abuse: It could be misused to repress as well as to promote, as opponents in Guinea, Malawi, Ghana, and Egypt quickly discovered. The charismatic choice and the practices it engendered continued to possess some appeal because when it succeeded—as in the case of Nyerere—it could bring about far-reaching changes that could not otherwise have been achieved. Charismatic leadership, however, has been particularly vulnerable to crises of succession. Such leaders cannot afford to designate their inheritors, as such an act might tarnish their purported invincibility. When the leader was not overthrown by the military, charismatic leadership patterns inevitably underwent a process of routinization.

The second style of political leadership to appear on the African scene, the *patriarchal* one, has provided one prototype for such routinization, usually found in administrative-hegemonic regimes. Patriarchal leaders have best been represented by Jomo Kenyatta, Leopold Sedar Senghor, Habib Bourguiba, and Felix Houphouët-Boigny among the civilians or by Yakubu Gowon, Olusegun Obasanjo, Ibrahim Babangida, and J. A. Ankrah among military rulers. Some of these leaders, much like their charismatic counterparts, rose to the top of the educational ladder during the colonial period and usually led successful coalitions at the time of decolonization. They differed from charismatic leaders, however, in several important respects. Both civilian and military leaders of this sort sprung up from pre-existing elites, and, not surprisingly, they evinced a personal preference for pragmatism as a guiding conceptual framework.

The style developed by Africa's "princes"[21] has been manipulatory in essence. The role adopted by these leaders has been that of adjudicator and maneuverer, of instigator and peacemaker. By placing themselves above the conspiracies of daily political maneuvering, Houphouët, Kenyatta, Ahidjo, and Senghor, for example, were in a position to juggle vying factions, co-opt opposition groups, and to enhance dependence on their persons. Patriarchal leaders in Africa projected a carefully nurtured father image: Kenyatta liked to be called *Mzee* (the elder). Houphouët forwarded the image of a wise man and a chief, and Ahidjo held himself purposely aloof and reserved.[22] At the same time, aristocratic life-styles were practiced, monarchical residences constructed, and patriarchal leaders glorified as the "fathers of the nation." The most blatant example of such behavior in the 1980s was the construction of a basilica by Houphouët in his hometown of Yamoussoukro in Côte d'Ivoire.

The patriarchal mode of operation has rested on a mixture of clientelism between the head of state and powerful patrons, on the one hand, and the creation of similar bonds with bureaucratic elites, on the other. Rival groups in this type of pattern usually have been pitted against each other to enhance the position of the father figure. Although key decisions are still made by the leader and a handful of trusted advisers (who themselves may change from time to time), they are usually promulgated through subordinates. Decisionmaking is therefore centralized yet indirect. Personal relations have counted, but so have administrative skills and the political influence of mediators and brokers. Patriarchal modes of operation have thus rewarded favoritism and nepotism and fueled factionalism and corruption at the same time as they have generated a modicum of institutionalization, at least in an administrative sense.

Authoritarian rule of the patriarchal type has proven in Africa to be less fraught with dangers than charismatic-autocratic forms. Patriarchal leaders have options of when to intervene or not, of when to use the carrot and when to employ the stick. Mistakes can be more easily covered up and credit claimed for wise decisions of underlings. Felix Houphouët-Boigny exemplifies this pattern. In most instances he has allowed subordinates to manage daily political affairs. By purposely inducing competition between rival ministers, he succeeded in placing emphasis on tangible outcomes. Recalcitrant officials, on the other hand, were removed with alacrity. The astute manipulation of party members, opponents, and civil servants maintained Houphouët indisputably at the helm while at the same time laying the foundation for some measure of institutional growth.

Thus, this mode, because of the looser controls it imposes (frequently of necessity), does have the merit of greater elasticity. On the other hand, patriarchal rule has tended to be conservative: It propped up the existing order and did little to promote change. It required the exertion of a great deal of energy simply to maintain control; in many cases, it bred inequalities and consequently social resentment. The key to successful patriarchal rule in Africa, therefore, has been the skill of those who have adopted this style. Houphouët, Kenyatta, Kaunda, Banda, and Senghor, each in his own way, have proved with the benefit of hindsight to be master politicians, to the extent of introducing substantial political changes when circumstances demanded. When this style was adopted by less astute leaders, it tended to fail as its wielders (Balewa, Gowon) lost their autonomy or resorted to coercion (Omar Bongo, Acheampong, and, most recently, Daniel arap Moi and Togo's head of state, General Gnassingbe).

The practices generated by patriarchal leaders, nevertheless, often survived the demise of their originators. Patriarchal leaders were able to put in place a dominant administrative-bureaucratic elite whose interest lie in perpetuating this system. These leaders were also frequently able to appoint their successors. Whether they died in office (Kenyatta) or voluntarily retired (Senghor, Ahidjo, Nyerere), the network these successful patriarchal leaders established and manipulated assumed more institutional trappings.[23]

Successors to patriarchal leaders, because they could not lay claim to the birthright enjoyed by the founding fathers, and because they usually were selected from the ranks, adjusted their style, if not their mode, of operation. Paul Biya in Cameroon and Daniel arap Moi in Kenya evinced more autocratic tendencies, whereas Abdou Diouf in Senegal and Olusegun Obasanjo in Nigeria tended to stress more technocratic and conciliatory patterns of rule. This was also the disposition of the second wave of democratically elected leaders: Shehu Shagari in Nigeria, Hilla Limann in Ghana, David Dacko in the Central African Republic. Similar traits are also surfacing among the third wave of democratic leaders (including Chissano of Mozambique, Bakili Muluzi of Malawi, and Festus Mogae of Botswana). These men, usually highly educated administrators as well as successful politicians, amassed a great deal of professional experience since independence. They have preferred to view themselves as implementers rather than molders, as efficient rather than innovative. In this way, they have come to reflect the altered position of leaders in the more resilient pluralist and administrative-hegemonic regimes: their lower profile is in line with the changed relations between leadership and government institutions in these countries.

In the same vein, the 1980s version of the charismatic leader, the *populist prophetic* one, replicated many of the features of the early autocrats. Rawlings, Museveni, and Sankara, like Nkrumah and Sekou Touré, came to power amid great social unrest. They also had to confront severe poverty, having taken over the political mantle after years of economic mismanagement. These populist leaders were educated primarily within their own countries; they assumed office at a young age. Each exhibited a great deal of flair and developed his own unique style. Rawlings, for example, made it a point to travel freely in the country, deliver impromptu speeches, and dress in pilot fatigues during his early years in office. He tried, at that point, to embody the notion of a man of the people. Like their earlier models, populist leaders brought with them a set of political objectives that they propounded with messianic vigor.

The authority of these populist leaders was, indeed, autocratic, although they prided themselves on a down-to-earth life-style more attuned to their populist rhetoric. Rawlings and Sankara in many respects resurrected the mode of operation of their predecessors. The creation of participatory institutions (Committees for the Defense of the Revolution and public tribunals) did not change the location of decisionmaking, which still rested with the head of state and a small group of loyal advisers. Status and position depended on ideological purity and/or on total personal allegiance to the prophet. Expressions of opposition were quelled possibly more violently than in the past. Order was thus maintained through personal friendships and constant reshufflings in the composition of ruling organs. Populist leaders, being men with military experience who rejected traditional political parties, were unable to rely on party structures to regulate access, and as a result purges became more haphazard, and the turnover in auxiliary personnel became particularly noticeable.

Prophets, perhaps even more than charismatic leaders, were therefore especially aware of the absence of adequate decisionmaking structures. They attempted to overcome this weakness not only through decentralization and local-level mobilization and through the invitation of discussion on desired modes of government but also through the projection of religious images (in Ghana: the "second coming" of Jerry Rawlings, the reference to Rawlings as, J. J.—"Junior Jesus"). However, by the mid-1980s, both Rawlings and Sankara, although still personally popular, were finding it difficult to maintain their style because they were unable to consolidate their social support base. They condoned abuses by their cohorts, tended to retreat regularly from the public view, and were clearly aware of the tenuousness attendant upon their incapacity to routinize their charisma.

Autocratic and patriarchal styles of leadership (and their prophetic and technocratic variants) have evinced recognizable—if deeply problematic— modes of operation. *Tyrannical leadership*, the hallmark of personal coercive regimes, in contrast, has been noted for its capriciousness and unpredictability. The rule of Idi Amin Dada, Emperor Bokassa I, and Macias Nguema (of Equatorial Guinea) exemplifies the distortions that can accompany autocratic modes of government. Africa's tyrants—Ethiopia's Mengistu Haile Mariam and Liberia's former President Samuel Doe being examples in the 1980s and Nigeria's Sani Abacha and Sudan's Omar Hassan Ahmed al-Bashir in the 1990s—most frequently came to power via the barrel of a gun. Their backgrounds differed from those of most African leaders: possessing a rudimentary education, they joined the regular army and slowly rose through the ranks, often achieving officer status only after their rise to political power. Little in their childhood or early adulthood indicated particular leadership skills or organizational capacities. In many cases, they hailed from minority ethnic groups and had few, if any, connections with major social organizations in their countries.[24]

Africa's dictators chose a domineering, sometimes described as sultanic, style of rule. They saw the state as their private domain; its resources and people were to be exploited and used for personal gain. In this leadership type the distinction between private ambitions and public goods was completely erased. Potential sources of opposition were eliminated; repression and violence came to replace entreaties, cajolery, or emotional fervor. These leaders projected, and took pride in, a strongman image: warriorlike, defiant, and, supposedly, also invincible. Idi Amin, for example, highlighted his personal prowess and reveled in surrounding himself with sophisticated military hardware. He not only sported many uniforms and medals but tried to carve out a place for himself as a modern African military hero.

The dictatorial mode of operation in postcolonial Africa was characterized by its coercive, idiosyncratic, and whimsical nature. Leaders like Amin and Bokassa, and more recently Mobutu, Eyadema, and Abacha, sought to tower above other officials and bureaucrats. If the army itself could no longer be counted on, private mercenaries were hired to protect the leaders and partake in their spoils. It is difficult to exaggerate the severity of the abuses carried out within this framework: State coffers were emptied, human rights violated regularly, and fear instilled to maintain domination.

Autocracy gone bad in Africa led to the individualization of politics—to the disengagement of government from any normative or institutional constraints and, consequently, to the hinging of political procedures on a single person and his private economic activities.[25]

Sultanic traits have surfaced in patriarchal, charismatic, prophetic, and conciliatory leadership styles. Nevertheless, authority based purely on such forms of behavior has been much more confined than usually imagined. Africa's most grotesque dictators have, for the most part, been forcibly ousted from office, usually with the assistance of sympathetic external actors. Not one has been able to arrange for his own succession. In a very real sense, African personal patrimonialism has not been accompanied by the acceptance of tyrants or their methods.

Leadership patterns in centers of Afro-Marxist persuasion proved somewhat more resilient, especially where they adapted to domestic and international pressures. Samora Machel (and his successor Joaquim Chissano), Agostinho Neto, and, later, Eduardo dos Santos were all selected for their leadership positions from a pool of activists at the vanguard of movements, cliques, or militant groups. Prior to their accession to office they had taken part, in the case of the civilians in this group, in the struggle for national liberation or, in the case of the military men, in the preparations for the overthrow of the previous government. From the outset, therefore, they were bound by the rules of the structures that nurtured them and guided by the ideologies they sought to apply.[26] However, their ability to survive has depended on their willingness to accept change. Thus stalemates in the internal wars in Angola and Mozambique have led to acceptance in both countries of greater political liberalization—including acceptance of the principle of multiparty elections.

Several notable trends emerge from this discussion of leadership styles. First, since the early years of independence, during which the leader was for all intents and purposes synonymous with the political center, styles of rule have been refined and amplified, largely in light of institutional developments. Second, leadership trends evince a shift, however muted, from personalization to routinization, in some cases from individual to more collective modes of rule. This pattern is indicative of the emergence of some constraints on authority. In countries like Senegal and Côte d'Ivoire, Mozambique, Botswana, and perhaps Cameroon, these constraints are institutional. In other instances—Uganda, Ghana, and Nigeria in the 1980s—they are normative and popular.[27] In all cases, they have evolved on the basis of precedent and experience. If the first decade of African leadership was characterized by the appearance of salient and innovative leaders, the second was characterized by a mixture of unpredictability and reliability, and the third by the injection in some countries of managerial traits. The fourth decade largely reinforced the trend of the third, and its leaders reflected their environment more than they affected their surroundings. As a result, leadership is only one of many guides to the intricacies of political processes on the continent.

Although authoritarian modes of operation are still in evidence throughout sub-Saharan Africa, a shift toward greater openness and responsiveness is apparent. Through their behavior and conduct, varieties of regimes have formulated distinctive rules of the political game. Africa's first generation of rulers established procedures for policy formulation that, where not negated, have come (with all the problems they entail) to define the organizational distinctiveness of the centers they created. The weight of political processes has, therefore, slowly shifted from the leaders themselves to the procedures they have put in place. And, as shown by the elections in Cape Verde, São Tomé-Principe, Congo-Brazzaville, Benin, Namibia, South Africa, and Mauritius, such procedures allowed for an upsurge in multiparty competition in the 1990s, or even in the replacement of one set of governors by another.[28]

■ Decisionmaking Patterns

The conduct of daily political life in African capitals has derived from the diverse principles guiding ruling elites as well as from the patterns of interaction among their leaders. Each of these, in turn, has been molded in light of both external and domestic constraints. Variations in core political practices are noticeable, first, in the number of people involved in policy formulation. In highly personalized systems, Charles Taylor's Liberia for example, the head of state has a hand, directly or indirectly, in minute as well as fundamental policy choices. In administrative-hegemonic regimes, professional issues have been discussed by bureaucrats and experts; only basic political matters were handled regularly by, say, Houphouët-Boigny or Abdou Diouf. Alternatively, in places such as Ghana or Burkina Faso during their populist phase, the distribution of decisionmaking powers did not follow clear lines.[29]

The quantity of people involved in policy formulation and the spheres of their influence dictate, to a large extent, how decisions are made. In formerly Afro-Marxist Mozambique as in pluralist Botswana, consultation has been practiced on a regular basis. In most countries, leaders rely on the advice and ideas of friends and trusted lieutenants. The degree of discussion permitted also varies. In parliamentary systems, major issues are publicly aired; in many military governments, although debates are circumscribed at times, some controlled commentary is allowed.[30]

In these quite heterogeneous circumstances, the role of formal agencies does differ substantially from place to place. Administrative-hegemonic regimes rely heavily on the civil service both to design and carry out decisions. Party regimes use the party as an instrument to enforce, if not to suggest, preferred paths. Each of these centers does employ the armed forces, but hardly as consistently and as exclusively as do personal-coercive autocrats.

Avenues of approach to politicians and decisionmakers therefore differ. In most countries, understanding who makes decisions and what networks are activated is critical to gaining access and even, at times, attention. The durability of particular centers is a crucial guide in this regard: The longer certain arrangements have been in place, the easier it is to unravel personal and structural relationships, to know where pressure can be applied, and to use this knowledge as leverage to gain results. Foreign concerns engage in such analysis as much as local citizens. In more ambiguous regimes—Sudan or Togo in the 1990s—patterns were not always clear, and citizen involvement was more often shunned (foreign interests consequently usually sought direct access to the head of state). It is important to note that identification of decisionmaking procedures should not be confused with the power of any political center to make binding rules. The power of centers is closely connected to the resilience of the state apparatus and to its penetrative capacity. External agencies and local social groups may attenuate the decisionmaking powers of many African countries.[31]

The centers that have developed in Africa since independence, for all their variation, possess certain features in common: Their workings have been unduly influenced by the personalities and preferences of the elites who constructed them; the rules of the political game that these elites have devised usually attained a modicum of coherence, even if they generally diverged from rational-legal organizational precepts; and the decisionmaking procedures of these elites tended to be restrictive if not insular. Political centers in Africa have, therefore, coalesced around differently designed pacts of domination established by relatively small elite groups of people. The fact that they became the domestic sources of public policy does not, therefore, imply that they are necessarily strong foci of activity. Their record in this regard has depended on how they have managed social relations and dealt with protest and dissent. It is to these aspects of the political process that we now turn.

■ THE POLITICS OF SOCIAL RELATIONS

The maintenance of political centers is an outgrowth not just of the establishment of political procedures but also of the manner of their application. The practice of politics focuses on the exercise of power: on the mechanisms of decision enforcement and the means of social control. The crux of the political process relates to the structures and methods of interaction between leaders and followers. These interchanges revolve around channels of participation and control and forms of political exchange.

Regimes in independent Africa have experimented with a variety of techniques to ensure compliance and to maintain order. By a mixture of enticement and coercion, some have built up firm coalitions, whereas others have faltered in this task. The workability, and hence the viability, of regimes has rooted to no mean degree on the internal supports they have constructed and on the methods they have used to sustain their social bases. The attempt to achieve effective hegemony united the efforts of African rulers during the first four decades of independence, as it did political leaders in many other parts of the globe. The outcomes of these efforts have varied because the possibilities, dimensions, and dynamics of political transactions have differed.[32]

■ Strategies of Coalition Construction

Confronted with social diversity expressed in cultural, ethnic, linguistic, geographic, religious, and racial terms, and with growing social differentiation based on location, income, occupation, education, and life-styles, specific regimes have sought ways to mold and regulate social relations. This has involved making arrangements for the representation of key interests whose support was necessary to keep them in power, as well as deflecting demands for full participation from groups and forces either inimical to the government or too demanding of its resources. Most regimes sought to carry out this task through a variety of corporatist measures—the limitation of competition through the definition of permissible bases of social organization, the delineation of their functions and roles in the political and economic process, and the nurturing of their allegiance to the political center.[33]

These experiments in social ordering have been undertaken to consolidate the power of rulers, to promote their legitimacy, to enhance their penetrative capacity, and to assist in overcoming external constraints. Such endeavors proved to be most effective when alliances were cemented with a network of already existing social groups. In the many instances where social foundations were tampered with, new groups formed, and major interests excluded from ruling coalitions, social control was curtailed by the very forces it sought to dominate. Attempts to impose monolithic structures were usually greeted by the realignment of interests or the withdrawal of support, most notably in the beginning of the 1990s.[34]

The majority of African states achieved independence after a brief but intense period of party formation and electoral competition. Their first constitutions provided for multiparty structures, for political representation, and for participation via the ballot box. The liberal-democratic origins of these instruments presumed that existing social groups would be allowed to vie freely without undermining the power structure or its ability to implement decisions. The competitive option created at this time survived in only a limited number of pluralist African countries, including Mauritius, Morocco, and Botswana. It was revived in the 1980s in Senegal, and in the 1990s in the great majority of other African states as well. Participation, in these cases, is direct and instrumental: continuity stems from the belief of all groups that they can garner enough electoral support to gain office and that the existence of rival centers of power does not irrevocably threaten their own political prospects.[35] Most leaders of nationalist movements were neither secure enough in their position nor firm enough in their commitment to liberal ideologies to maintain these arrangements. Many rulers in newly liberalized regimes in the 1990s are evincing similar concerns. Each of the major regime types in the first decades of independence developed its own formula for the construction of social support.

The first, and perhaps one of the most problematic, attempts to reformulate the bases of representation and participation and to enhance social control was carried out by party-mobilizing regimes.[36] Traditional institutions were downgraded, ethnically based associations prohibited, and independent economic organizations and trade unions curbed. These were replaced, in most instances, by center-designed and functionally conceived monolithic interest groups closely tied to the ruling party: national associations of farmers, workers, students, women. The imposition of a uniform associational structure was intended to reshape social and economic relations, eradicate the competing coalitions that had begun to form during decolonization, and lay the foundation for other, broader channels of representation and mobilization.

This policy was justified by an appeal to notions of the common good, the national interest, and the new society. The focus of social ties in, for example, Guinea, Tanzania, and Ghana during the 1960s was shifted to the state and its leaders. This strategy was not, however, exclusionary. Participation was open to all those who accepted the government's ideology and identified with its goals. As these notions tended to appeal to young, mostly urban, partially educated, upwardly mobile, or ethnically peripheral segments of the population, the ruling coalitions constructed at this juncture possessed a progressive, usually change-oriented, aura.

The main instrument of participation and control was the single party. In Tanzania, Guinea, and Uganda, as well as Ghana and Mali, the ruling party was reconstructed to serve as an umbrella for the new organizations and as a funnel for the distribution of goods and services. Even though elections were held at regular intervals, they tended to be more symbolic than real. Elections provided ritual occasions for sanctioning the existing governing coalitions but allowed precious few opportunities for affecting the composition of ruling circles or policy outcomes. The Tanzanian innovation that permitted several candidates to compete for office within the single-party framework offered a partial solution to some of the problems of alienation in such systems.

Mobilizing-regime experiments at social control usually resulted in an institutional dualism (party versus bureaucracy), which permeated the public sector and extended to the lowest levels of government. Tensions between the party and the civil service were exacerbated and at times actually reduced the hold of the leadership on the state apparatus. More to the point, in these examples (Ghana stands out in this regard), the party itself was consequently enfeebled, and the political arena contracted.[37] These strategies, consequently, were neither particularly representative nor necessarily conducive to the effective management of social demands.

A second, more enduring, formula for social control was devised in administrative-hegemonic regimes. Introduced first by Houphouët-Boigny in Côte d'Ivoire, Kenyatta in Kenya, Banda in Malawi, and Ahidjo in Cameroon, it was also implemented by military leaders in Nigeria and Ghana and is still widely practiced in many parts of the continent. This strategy has generally been used by rulers who have a strong standing in the elite establishment, whose opposition is fairly weak or fragmented, and who are wary of popular movements.[38]

This scheme of social regulation is predicated on the idea of curbing or deflecting popular participation through the granting of a representational monopoly to powerful existing social formations and scrupulously monitoring their activities. Each of these groups is accorded limited autonomy to pursue its own interests within the parameters laid down by the rulers. The key bases of group definition in this method of social organization have been central ethnic units and elite professional and occupational associations. Chiefs, businesspeople, church leaders, large commercial interests, and religious communities were recognized; regional affiliations were accorded official sanction by governments in Cameroon, Gabon, Senegal, Nigeria, and Malawi.

This strategy was defended as efficient and hence beneficial for the fulfillment of development objectives. Competition was constricted and the superior knowledge of elites accentuated as the foundation for progress. This system was therefore, almost by definition, both statist and exclusionary. Departicipation and depoliticization of the bulk of the population were extolled. Administrative-hegemonic modes of social control unabashedly upheld elite interests and concerns. Needless to say, this approach appealed to middle-class groups and to major ethnic associations. Kenyatta, Houphouët, Balewa, and Banda, by espousing clear class and ethnic preferences, thus propped up existing institutions of social domination and sought to co-opt them for their own purposes. Those included in privileged categories were allowed to enjoy the benefits of their station; those not so privileged were clearly disadvantaged.[39] The ruling coalitions here conserved the interests of the already powerful in the cities and the countryside.

This type of social regulation relied heavily, although not exclusively, on fortifying the administrative apparatus at the expense of political institutions, most notably the party. In civilian regimes such as Kenya, Malawi, or Côte d'Ivoire, the significance of the party was downgraded and the bureaucracy reinforced. Elections were held, but as their outcomes were foregone conclusions, they became a perfunctory legitimation device except (as periodically in Kenya and in the 1980s in Côte d'Ivoire) when they could be used to bring about a circulation of elites.[40] Political participation, if it took place at all, was, in both civilian and military settings, far more indirect: It was routed through a complex network of patrons, or locally entrenched "big men," who became the main intermediaries between the citizen and the political center.

Administrative strategies have usually bred a good deal of political centralization, although still suggesting the possibility that diverse interests could be pursued as long as they did not impinge on the hold of the center. In the 1980s in Abidjan, for example, traders and businesspeople were given a measure of independence; attitudes toward the press, students, and intellectuals vacillated, depending on specific circumstances. In Côte d'Ivoire, after Houphouët-Boigny's death in 1993, Konan Bédié, his successor, had student demonstrators and highly critical media analysts arrested. Perhaps less overtly coercive than other forms of social control, these techniques were hardly indulgent of pluralism or individual liberties. Indeed, in most instances these practices led to (at times were openly permissive of) social inequalities.

Nevertheless, the administrative-hegemonic strategy has passed the test of durability (although hardly of equity) far better than its mobilizational counterpart. Ruling groups in Malawi, Togo, and Cameroon as well as in many other countries found this formula useful in consolidating their holds over the periphery. In these political centers, the ability to co-opt key opponents, to attract foreign support, and to maintain elite cohesion assisted in establishing an ongoing rhythm of interaction between rulers and subjects.[41] These techniques, however, relied heavily on the success of the center in generating resources to sustain its attractiveness to major social groups and their supporters. Where economic performance has faltered (as in Nigeria in the late 1970s and early 1980s, as well as in the 1990s, Burkina Faso and Zambia in the late 1980s and the 1990s, and Liberia and Somalia in the 1990s), not only has the specific government been undermined; so, too, has the basis of its system of control. What is more fundamental is that this approach has exhibited a tendency to evoke class as well as ethnic resentments: Social tensions are both more evident and more pronounced. As a result, leaders in some centers employing these measures have conceded the need to allow limited competition and to open up access to the center. This may help to explain the shift to multipartyism in several countries (Senegal, for one), the lifting of restrictions on the press in others (Nigeria), and measures for the civilianization of military governments in certain places (Ghana).

Neotraditional strategies of social control are a variant of these more hegemonic-administrative modes. They have been instituted mostly by military leaders ensconced in particularly weak centers (Niger) or by traditional elites in power in new states (Swaziland). The neotraditionalist form relies more heavily on attracting the support of already established leaders and, most especially, of chiefs, traders, civil servants, army officers, and sometimes even key foreign entrepreneurs. It is, in concept and implementation, far more decentralized than the administrative strategy. By channeling participation through these groups, leaders of the center entrench notions of political involvement by proxy. This system does have some attraction to local interests, especially when the center also has something to offer. The coalition on which neotraditional patterns rest is necessarily loose. Younger people, without traditional status and position, find difficulty in accommodating to these structures. In any event, direct participation is confined to the local level; it is rarely able to reach up to, let alone influence, national decisions.

Neotraditional strategies help the government maintain some networks of communication, although they do limit mobilization. If they are much less unequal than their exclusionary administrative counterparts, they are also less vigorous. These are more in the order of strategies of social separation or, at best, social transaction than of social control. They have proven useful in the few areas where they have been attempted, although they have not been put into widespread use as they offer few possibilities for social or economic change.[42]

Africa's tyrants have had to search for quite different mechanisms of establishing social order since they usually could rely only on a very narrow social support base and have headed political centers that are poorly institutionalized. They have generally turned to personal and coercive techniques.[43] This approach was employed by Bokassa in the Central African Republic, Amin in Uganda, Mobutu in Congo (Zaire), and Abacha in Nigeria. Personal modes of social control purposely deny the representational legitimacy of most existing groups and do not try in any systematic way to create new ones. Notions of national self-reliance, common objectives, and obedience are propagated in an effort to link citizens directly to the rulers. The dangers of politicization and competition have been used as excuses for the exercise of direct, and frequently arbitrary, control. The possibilities for access to the decisionmaking apparatus are severely circumscribed and require personal contact with the leader or his intimate circle (usually friends, family members, or army cohorts). The alliance of power in this type of regime has been purposefully narrow. What such a regime lacked in legitimate power it tried to achieve by force. In these situations, restrictions abounded: Curbs were placed on political activities, on public liberties, on middle-level interest groupings, on all forms of expression, on the judiciary, and eventually on the military as well. No critical monitoring of government policy was entertained, and few institutional brakes were in evidence.[44] In general, control was exercised through intimidation: tax raids, incarcerations, disappearances, public executions, forced labor. No meaningful participation in activities at the political center, however indirect, was possible in these conditions. Some individuals went into self-imposed exile; more often, withdrawal into informal organizations, passive resistance, and detachment from state-related activities became the norm.

Personal modes of control in independent Africa have been particularly destructive. They have generated protest, exacerbated violence, and, what is somewhat ironical, terminated in the constriction of the spheres of official control. These methods are more difficult to counteract than they are to avoid. They expand the distance between the political center and its social environment, restrict the capacity to govern, and most insidiously, violate human dignity.

The party-centralist approach to social ordering, although rooted in quite different ideas, has not fared much better than many personal-coercive schemes. This regime type, adopted in the 1970s and 1980s by Afro-Marxist countries such as Mozambique, Angola, and Ethiopia, was devised to deal with conditions of economic and social uncertainty and to promote a more fundamental societal reordering. The concept underlying party-centralist techniques of coalition construction in Africa was the reorganization of representation in line with ideological precepts. Existing class-based or ethnically defined associations were discredited (with the exception of the church in Ethiopia), and new institutions—farmer cooperatives, collective villages, worker-controlled enterprises—were put in their stead. The test of inclusion was ideological commitment, and the vanguard party—MPLA, FRELIMO, the Workers' Party of Ethiopia (WPE)—became the main instrument of societal monitoring.

The justification for the social control strategy of Afro-Marxist regimes was presented, as expected, in scientific socialist terms. But mass mobilization, as has already been pointed out, was not actively encouraged in either Angola or Congo-Brazzaville, let alone Ethiopia or Benin. This strategy, therefore, tended to be most attractive to precisely those elements who already benefited from the new system: party activists and portions of the urban population or the army who supported its rise to power. It was resisted, often vigorously, by existing social groups and especially by well-organized ethnic, regional, or professional organizations. The ruling coalitions in Afro-Marxist countries, therefore, tended to rely on a narrow social base and to be confined spatially to the capital cities and their immediate environs (with the exception, possibly, of Mozambique).[45] These governments, much like those led by dictators, were confronted by problems of penetration and therefore frequently had to resort to force to achieve compliance. They engaged not only in direct military operations but also, increasingly, in population relocation, resettlement schemes, and conscription. In these settings, the ability to influence government policy was the privilege of a select few; informal and insurrectionist modes of political activity were more commonplace.

The party-based centralist strategy of social control has not worked well either in sub-Saharan Africa or in the Maghreb. Although some of the regimes that tried to mold social relations in this way remained intact in the 1980s, they were not able to find a viable formula for interacting with their constituencies. In many cases, they exemplify the pitfalls of revolution from above, impeded as they are by poor networks of representation and mobilization. In Angola, the ruling coalition has had to admit the loss of control of some territories to the resistance movement, and the Ethiopian government was ultimately defeated by a coalition of regionally based insurgent movements.

In the 1980s, populist governments in Ghana and Burkina Faso, following the Libyan example, tried to design other means of gaining social backing. The basis of acceptable representation was defined by way of elimination: Those tainted by association with prior governments or with the establishment were excluded from the network. This approach enabled the formation, at least initially, of a ruling coalition composed mostly of the young, the disadvantaged in the rural areas, and the discontented. The task of societal reorganization was carried out not by dismantling existing structures but by establishing alternative ones, such as people's defense committees and citizens' vetting committees.[46] The PNDC in Ghana and the Sankara government in Burkina Faso used these groups both as foundations for the creation of support for the regime as well as organizations to monitor the population at large: Members were to report any evidence of opposition or expressions of disaffection. Individuals and groups that did not take part in these efforts at mass mobilization either voiced their dissatisfaction through informal group activity or simply opted out of the system.

Because this form of social organization proved less than efficient in maintaining social order, it has undergone considerable revisions in both Ghana and Burkina Faso. Representative possibilities were expanded within the organs established by the center (the defense committees in Ghana were no longer restricted to certain nonelite groups). At the same time, a variety of regime-sanctioned organizations were established (including women's and student groups), and the stress on direct participation in all decisionmaking was downplayed. In 1992, when the Rawlings regime became an elected one, its populist pronouncements sowed confusion and fomented discord, leaving room for haphazard actions and unpredictable (also repressive) behavior; with the 1996 elections, however, the rules of the political game appeared to have become more settled, and a transition to stable pluralism gained increasing acceptance.

African regimes have thus experimented widely with schemes aimed at realizing state control, social cooperation, and efficiency. The basis of representation proposed by each of these strategies has varied from total reliance on existing social structures or the manipulation of these social groups to various attempts to redefine the acceptable foundations of social organization. Most of these approaches, even those purportedly committed to mobilization, involved ways to limit participation. The size of coalitions has, therefore, varied from fairly broad networks of established interests to the most narrow alliances. The instruments of social control have also differed: besides the single party and the administration, various regimes in independent Africa have tried to supervise their populations through patrons, vanguard parties, committees, and tribunals, and most ubiquitously, via coercive mechanisms.

Each of these strategies, therefore, has revealed a particular Achilles heel. Mobilizational efforts have faltered in the face of resilient social constructions; administrative-hegemonic experiments have accentuated class cleavages; neotraditional schemes have proven exceptionally static; personal ventures have been brutal and exploitative; party-centralist attempts have hampered the exercise of control; populist measures have proven to be too diffuse, and in extreme instances, some centers have simply been unable to establish any meaningful ties with their constituencies. It has gradually become apparent that those social control strategies that attempted to undermine existing foundations of social organization were those that backfired most resoundingly.

In every instance, however, the coalition of groups with access to power in a particular country has found that other groups have coalesced into an elaborate faction in opposition to their alliance. Despite their ongoing quest for uniformity, official efforts at social control therefore succumbed by the 1990s, in one way or another, to the heterogeneous social reality of contemporary Africa. They could not find adequate means to allow for the representation and participation of diverse localities and interests in the political process.[47] There are several reasons for this pattern: Elites in most countries have been too fragmented to agree on rules of access and participation; political centers have not been sufficiently strong to exercise authority consistently in their territories; most rulers have not been willing to take into account the existence of alternative social institutions capable of disposing benefits and mobilizing support. These rulers have overestimated the willingness of social organizations to relinquish their autonomy, and ultimately all have fallen victim, in different degrees, to monopolistic fallacies. Nevertheless, the different networks of representation and participation they established became the pathways for policy implementation and political transactions.

■ Means of Maintaining the Political Center: Patrons, Clients, and Linkages

Regardless of the specific strategies used to construct a modicum of supervision over social relations, African regimes had to find ways to carry out their decisions, to extract resources, and to maintain their support bases, however fragile or incoherent. In a similar vein, citizens needed to devise means to obtain desired goods and services and to assure their security. Within the channels of participation and control designed by each regime, mechanisms of political interchange were put in operation and means of enforcement instituted. Throughout the postcolonial period in Africa, patron-client and patron-patron relations became the most common form of political exchange (as discussed in Chapter 4). Despite the tendency to view all political transactions in patronage terms, other instruments of interchange have evolved in the 1980s and 1990s to counteract the instability inherent in these kinds of political ties. The patronage method of postcolonial political interaction may be in the process of reformulation.

The initial foundation of political exchange in independent Africa was rooted in the symbols of nationalism. Support was garnered by successful anticolonial leaders, who in turn vowed to distribute the benefits of independence. Once delivery had to be made on these promises, it became apparent that more tangible means of exchange had to be designed. Ideological principles helped to define distributional preferences, but as class formations were too ambiguous to coalesce around common interests, and cultural symbols could not normally galvanize strong solidarity attachments, other forms of linkage had to be explored. In some countries, participatory mechanisms were cemented (Botswana and Mauritius are notable examples). Even in competitive party systems, however, these were of themselves inadequate to guarantee ongoing penetration and support.[48] What was palpably missing in most countries were organized structures of exchange backed by legally sanctioned rules for interaction between government officials and citizens. These structural linkages had not been developed during the colonial period and were given little time to solidify and become part of everyday practice during decolonization. When pressures on governments from different quarters mounted immediately after independence, other means of achieving support and responding to demands had to be established. The answer was found in most countries through the more personal mechanism of clientelistic ties.[49]

Specifically political modes of patronage were organized along several quite distinct lines.[50] The first to emerge, and perhaps the most resilient, sought to connect decisionmakers at the political center with many local communities through direct links with local leaders. During the anticolonial phase, organizers of nationalist movements identified local authority figures—frequently chiefs or prosperous farmers—who commanded respect in their communities. By giving these local leaders a role in the movement (as local representatives or functionaries), organizers garnered their support and that of their followers. "Big men" in various constituencies were courted with promises either of personal gain, public office, or local improvements; rival parties took advantage of local factionalism to wean electoral support away from these patrons.

National-local patronage ties have endured, especially in countries where elections take place, where parties have survived (Tanzania, Zambia, Botswana, Senegal), and where these networks have been used by successive military and civilian regimes (Nigeria). These geographically defined patrons have become *mediators* in the full sense of the word: They represent the locale to the government and the political center to the community.

A second, more administrative, form of clientelistic exchange has emerged in countries where party systems are either unimportant or no longer operative. It is in widespread use in administrative-hegemonic regimes. This type of patronage uses the various rungs of the civil service to bind officeholders in the central apparatus with lower echelons of the bureaucracy both in the capital city and in the rural areas. Patronage standing is, therefore, defined by position in the decisionmaking apparatus, by proximity to the head of state and his courtiers in more coercive centers. At the bottom of the administrative rung, appointed officials implement government directives at the local level and become the funnel for communication between the citizen and the administration. This kind of political clientage is more centrally controlled than its electorally rooted counterpart. Each patron in this hierarchy depends more on approval from above than on support from below. Patrons and clients range the vertical length of the administrative ladder.[51] Administrative patronage may, therefore, become highly personalized. These intermediaries are power *brokers* more than mediators: They represent the higher rungs vis-à-vis the lower ones; although they enforce decisions, they do not always transmit demands from their constituents.

A third way clientelistic ties have been organized has been on the basis of solidarity ties (ethnicity, religion, racial group). Such social modes of patronage have surfaced in areas where cultural forms of social organization and differentiation are particularly pronounced: Rwanda, Burundi, Sudan, South Africa, for example. In these countries, the ruling coalition depends heavily on the approval of the racial or ethnic group that brought it to office. Patrons at the political center direct funds and resources to members of their social constituency. In return, they hope to ensure these members' ongoing support. This type of patronage reverses the political weight apparent in administrative forms: In these instances, patrons are more beholden to their clients than the clients are to any individual patron.

If the ethnic or religious clientele is dissatisfied with the services rendered and with the way their interests are maintained, they can take steps to replace their patrons. These types of patrons are hence more in the order of *emissaries* than brokers or mediators.

A fourth type of patron-client linkage, associated mostly with populist regimes that have struck out against existing patronage structures, has been of an associational sort. Even though the leaders of these centers have consistently denounced the patronage system in its entirety, as Jerry Rawlings's proclamations exemplify, they have not dismantled its underlying structures so much as substituted one form of clientelism for another. The popular organizations established by these centers have become a key vehicle for the disbursement of benefits, just as membership in government-approved worker or village cooperatives has become one of the main means of access to government resources. Patronage position here, as in administrative patterns, derives from above. It is, however, far more haphazard than its bureaucratic counterpart.

The final kind of political patronage is of an individual sort. In situations of severe vulnerability and lack of institutionalization, as in Sierra Leone, Liberia, Somalia, and Chad during most of the last two decades, the state is weak and people have tied themselves to personal strongmen or warlords capable of providing some security. These highly personalistic forms of patronage delineate the role of this intermediary as that of *protector*. Protectionism also appears in urban settings—Lagos or Durban are cases in point—where migrants have few contacts and are vulnerable to the vicissitudes of unfamiliar surroundings. Individualized patron-client structures are thus reflective of situations where more formal and encompassing clientelistic networks have broken down.

The various types of political patronage that have developed in twentieth-century Africa form intricate networks of communication and enforcement. The view of politics generated by such ties is essentially extractive. The political arena is seen as a source of benefits with wealth, in the broadest sense, the reward for successful engagement.[52] This kind of thinking, in many places, encouraged a vicious cycle of competition for access to and control over national resources. It also frequently nurtured a zero-sum approach to politics. Winners take all to appease their backers and to make use of their position before other patrons take control and divert resources to their own ends. Patron-client modes of exchange do not draw sharp distinctions between the public and private domains.

Several problems are endemic to patron-client linkage arrangements. In the first place, because of their instrumental underpinnings, such arrangements are especially open to misuse through corruption. Political corruption encompasses a series of practices aimed at achieving personal gain from public office.[53] Bribery, embezzlement, and theft—sometimes on a grand scale—divert resources from public coffers to private hands.[54] Corruption is commonplace in Africa, as in many parts of the globe. Its degree and extensiveness have varied, however, from one setting to another.

In most African countries, petty corruption is a daily phenomenon: police extract bribes from hawkers and taxi drivers; clerks demand payment for issuing licenses, permits, and passports; chiefs receive presents from their communities; and politicians use official cars to go shopping and accept gratis trips on national airlines to relax on the Riviera. Institutionalized corruption is evident in places where geographical, ethnic, and administrative forms of clientage prevail. In these countries, corruption is systemic, and informal rules place limits on the amounts that may be skimmed by officials off public and private transactions. In Nigeria during the course of the 1970s, the expected kickback on contracts rose from 15 to 50 percent; in Ghana the figures fluctuated between 10 and 25 percent in the mid-1980s. Corrupt practices continued through the 1990s unabated. For example, President Ahmed Tejan Kabbah of Sierra Leone attributed a sharp fall in income tax and customs revenue in the first half of 1998/99 to "rampant corruption," and a leading Nigerian journalist charged Abacha and his family with "stealing" millions of dollars in public funds.[55] Because institutionalized corruption permeates every facet of public life, its effects are corrosive to the moral fiber of the society. By far the most pernicious form of corruption has been kleptocracy, a system in which the wealth of the state has been systematically plundered by a leader and his entourage (as Abacha was accussed of). The Swiss bank accounts of Mobutu Sese Seko, I. K. Acheampong, Jean-Bedel Bokassa, and Omaru Dikko (the wealthy Nigerian finance minister during the Second Republic) attest to the existence of such phenomena. Kleptocracy is usually propped up by officially sanctioned networks of smuggling, hoarding, and black-marketeering (*kalabule* in Ghana, *magendo* in Uganda and Congo).

In many instances, the norms of reciprocity inherent in patron-client ties control against excessive corruption. When the gap between the standard of living of patrons and clients has gone beyond acceptable limits, popular resentment has been aroused (Nigeria, Congo, Gabon) and demands made to hold politicians to account. Where public criticism is allowed, intellectuals have consistently decried corrupt practices.[56] By these methods, corruption has rarely been eliminated: it has, however, usually been contained within a predictable range.

A second common problem associated with clientelistic modes of exchange is inefficiency. As transactions based on patronage are concerned with garnering support, allocations are not always made according to considerations of cost efficiency or productivity. Patronage methods of political exchange are directly responsible for the rapid expansion of the public sector in many countries. Bureaucratic office is a valued prize for consistent support. Clientelistic alliances, although they may promote some integration, may also seriously hinder development.[57]

What is more profound, patronage linkages encourage passivity. They foster a concept of government that is based on the private consumption of purportedly public goods, but they do very little to suggest how these public goods may be expanded.[58] Nevertheless, patron-client ties have been a key method of political exchange in the postcolonial period. The norms underlying these linkages have exhibited a great deal of durability. This persistence is partly a result of the fact that, whatever their drawbacks, at least for the first two decades of independence these networks gave some assurances to both patrons and their clients. It is partly a result of the fact that patronage connections furnished many leaders with a measure of backing beyond the center, reducing demands for participation, offering some possibilities for representation, and guaranteeing some support.

These mechanisms could not, however, have been set in motion if African states had not monopolized so many desired resources and controlled so directly essential goods and services. These modes of exchange seemed to work better than other alternatives. If coercion and intimidation were employed instead of such personal links, the costs, both materially and politically, became too high. If force could not be used effectively and patronage was not in operation, no other means of exchange were readily available, with the result that decisions could not be enforced and relations between governments and their societies broke down (the situation in Congo in the late 1990s was symptomatic of this dilemma).

Several occurrences in the late 1970s and early 1980s, however, forced a reevaluation of the efficacy of these methods of maintaining support. The economic crisis of the 1980s and 1990s meant that government patrons had less and less to offer their constituents. The structural adjustment policies of the World Bank and IMF either froze government recruitment or streamlined the number of public-sector positions. Appointments to the bureaucracy—a key instrument of patronage—were consequently blocked. The appeal of many patrons waned. On the other hand, local leaders with control over nonstate resources offered alternative poles of allegiance. Informal systems of patronage continued in some locations, but these were not always connected with the state.[59] Where conditions deteriorated drastically and poverty became widespread, patrons were frequently blamed. More people were willing to take political risks in order to survive.

Above all, however, rulers themselves began to reassess the benefits of clientelistic exchanges. The experience accumulated since independence seemed to show that although patronage ties did help engender political support, they also increased competition within the elite, frequently creating internal divisions among patrons and eventually fomenting instability. Put simply, it appeared as if "with clientelism no stability, without it no support."[60] This realization led to a renewed quest for alternatives to patron-client ties. One direction has been to contain competition through decentralization and the funneling of resources to the local level. This option, however, has had limited effects, altering the form of patronage and enhancing the status of local administrators (Congo is one example). Another method has been to reinforce bureaucratic structures and redefine procedures in an attempt to promote rational-legal modes of exchange. And in some countries, more effort has been devoted to finding ways of reviving transactions based on participatory linkages, either through parties or through other structures of representation. In all of these instances, the thrust of this rethinking has focused on the need to replace the instrumental foundations and the extractive norms that have sustained patronage schemes in the past. Thus, although it is still too early to comment on the outcome of these experiments, the centrality of personalistic means of exchange may diminish as more organizational mechanisms of implementation and support maintenance are established.

■ CONSOLIDATION AND MAINTENANCE OF THE POLITICAL CENTER: SOME TRENDS

The multiple forms of center construction and political practice discussed in these pages capture only some of the variety of sociopolitical relations in Africa. Each regime possesses its own rhythm of interaction. In most cases, regularized patterns of decisionmaking and known methods of enforcement (via patrons more often than government agencies) have evolved. These have tended, with few exceptions, to be based on different combinations of ruling elite interests and personalized clientelistic ties. But in many countries hegemony and domination are giving way to various types of more sophisticated reciprocity and interdependence, to a quest for appropriate structures that would replace personal types of linkage.[61]

The transfer of political power from the center to the regional or local levels has taken place to varying degrees in Zimbabwe, Zambia, Botswana, Tanzania, Uganda, and Kenya, and represents an emerging trend in sub-Saharan Africa generally. Phillip Mawhood writes that, although there are many definitions of the term *decentralization*, the identifying characteristics include the control by regional or local governments over their own budgets, legal affairs, and allocative processes. Furthermore, the government must be comprised of representatives of the local population and must hold authority over a wide range of diverse arenas.[62] The move toward decentralization is described by some African writers as a framework for self-governance, one that enhances local responsibility and initiative.[63] For local governments to be effective, the state and regional governments must restrain their desire to control local politics and facilitate the ability of local leaders to mobilize resources. As Dele Oluwu writes: "It remains necessary to recognize [local governments] as *community governments* and to provide the legal, financial, and institutional mechanisms for them to take full responsibility for the overall economic, social, and political development of their respective communities."[64]

These trends highlight the complexities inherent in establishing rules of the political game and the means for their implementation. The ambitions, interests, and impulses of ruling elites (high politics) cannot be understood independently of the parallel concerns of social groups and local institutions (deep politics), The experience of the decades since independence has shown that although elites may establish decisionmaking procedures, define strategies of social control, and delimit the forms of political exchange—and in the process sometimes wreak considerable havoc and generate incredible human misery—they cannot always determine the outcomes of their designs. Some regimes in Africa have been cruel and suppressive and most have been not only inequitable but also fragile; nevertheless, several have become more efficient and/or forced to be more tolerant. Center consolidation and maintenance has depended more on the competence of leaders in forging alliances via adequate representation, participation, and regularized transactions than on their capacity to employ force indiscriminately. Effective power utilization has relied on subtle political practices. From the standpoint of the regimes that have emerged since independence, therefore, specific norms, procedures, and methods have been created and regularized; the results of these, however, have depended, to no mean degree, on the nature of social responses.

■ NOTES

1. The distinction between high politics and deep politics is based on John Lonsdale, "Political Accountability in African History," in Patrick Chabal, ed., *Political Domination in Africa: Reflections on the Limits of Power* (London: Cambridge University Press, 1986), p. 130.

2. Crawford Young, *Ideology and Development in Africa* (New Haven: Yale University Press, 1982), p. 184. The definition of ideology is a complex issue. This definition is used for working purposes, but implies neither the invalidity of other approaches nor the exclusion of possibilities for refinement and amplification.

3. For a good overview of the various ideological "waves" since independence, see Carl G. Rosberg and Thomas M. Callaghy, eds., *Socialism in Sub-Saharan Africa: A New Assessment* (Berkeley: University of California, Institute of International Studies, 1979).

4. Although Leopold Senghor and Jomo Kenyatta also labeled themselves socialists, in most respects they do not fall into this category. See William Friedland and Carl G. Rosberg, eds., *African Socialism* (Stanford: Stanford University Press, 1964).

5. For some examples, consult Kwame Nkrumah, *Africa Must Unite* (London: Heinemann, 1963), and Julius Nyerere, *Uhuru na Umoja: Freedom and Unity* (London: Oxford University Press, 1964).

6. Erich Leistner, "Socialism on the Wane in Africa," *Africa Insight* 14, no. 1 (1984): 2–3.

7. The best discussion of pragmatism as ideology may be found in Young, *Ideology and Development in Africa*.

8. See Ali A. Mazrui, "The Resurrection of the Warrior Tradition in African Political Culture," *Journal of Modern African Studies* 13, no. 1 (1975): 67–84.

9. For a good exposition, see Ladipo Adamolekun, "Mobutu's Authenticity: Rhetoric or Revolution?" *Afriscope* 5, no. 2 (1975): 29–30.

10. David Ottaway and Marina Ottaway, *Afrocommunism* (New York: Praeger, 1980), and Edmond J. Keller and Donald Rothchild, eds., *Afro-Marxist Regimes* (Boulder: Lynne Rienner, 1987).

11. Michael Radu, "Ideology, Parties and Foreign Policy in Sub-Saharan Africa," *Orbis* 15, no. 4 (1982): 967–992.

12. Ali A. Mazrui, "The Liberal Revival in Black Africa," *Africa Report* 25, no. 4 (1980): 45–47. The discussion of one case study may be found in Richard Sklar, "Democracy for the Second Republic," *Issue* 11, no. 1 (1981): 14–16.

13. Richard Jeffries, "Ghana: Jerry Rawlings ou un populisme a deux coups," *Politique africaine* 2, no. 8 (1982): 8–20. Also A. Adu Boahen, "Ghana: Conflict Reoriented," in I. William Zartman, ed., *Government as Conflict Management: Politics and Violence in West Africa* (Washington, DC: Brookings Institution Press, 1997).

14. Christian Coulon, "Le reseau islamique," *Politique africaine* 9 (1983): 68–83; Guy Nicholas, "Islam et 'constructions nationales' au sud du Sahara," *Revue française d'etudes politiques africaines* 165/166 (1979): 86–107.

15. Roger Charlton and Roy May, "African Politics and World System Theory" (Paper presented to the annual conference of the Political Studies Conference, University of Manchester, 16–18 April 1985).

16. Christopher Clapham, *Third World Politics: An Introduction* (Madison: University of Wisconsin Press, 1985), pp. 47–49.

17. S. N. Eisenstadt, *Traditionalism, Patrimonialism and Modern Neopatrimonialism* (Beverly Hills: Sage Publications, 1975).

18. Contrast with Robert H. Jackson and Carl G. Rosberg, *Personal Rule in Black Africa* (Berkeley: University of California Press, 1982), p. 19 and elsewhere, who view personal rule as any kind of patrimonial regime.

19. Ali A. Mazrui, "Leadership in Africa," *New Guinea* 5, no. 1 (1971): 33–50. Also see his "The Monarchical Tendency in African Political Culture," in Marion Doro and Newell E. Stultz, eds., *Governing in Black Africa* (Englewood Cliffs, NJ: Prentice Hall, 1970), pp. 18–38.

20. Clapham, *Third World Politics,* p. 74.

21. This term is used extensively in Jackson and Rosberg, *Personal Rule in Black Africa,* although the style of leadership suggested by this term dates back to Machiavelli.

22. Victor T. Le Vine, "Leadership Styles and Political Images: Some Preliminary Notes," *Journal of Modern African Studies* 15, no. 4 (1977): 631–638. For one example, see Brigitte Masquet, "Côte d'Ivoire: Pouvoir presidentiel, palabre et democratie," *Afrique contemporaine* 114 (1981): 10–12.

23. Lancine Sylla, "Succession of the Charismatic Leader: The Gordian Knot of African Politics," *Daedalus* 111, no. 2 (1982): 11–28.

24. For one example, see Peter Woodward, "Ambiguous Amin," *African Affairs* 77, no. 307 (1978): 153–164. For more details, consult Samuel Decalo, *Psychoses of Power: African Personal Dictatorships* (Boulder: Westview Press, 1989).

25. William Reno, *Warlord Politics and African States* (Boulder, Lynne Rienner, 1998); and Christopher Clapham, *Africa and the International System: The Politics of State Survival* (Cambridge: Cambridge University Press, 1996).

26. Richard Sandbrook, *The Politics of Africa's Economic Stagnation* (London: Cambridge University Press, 1986), p. 89, highlights this point.

27. See Thomas M. Callaghy, "State-Subject Communication in Zaire: Domination and the Concept of Domain Consensus," *Journal of Modern African Studies* 17, no. 3 (1980): 469–492.

28. Michael Bratton and Nicolas van de Walle, "Popular Protest and Political Reform in Africa," in Goran Hyden and Michael Bratton, ed., *Governance and Politics in Africa* (Boulder: Lynne Rienner 1991), chap. 2.

29. The entire issue of decisionmaking has been woefully neglected in studies of African politics. For one excellent case study, see Robert Price, *Society and Bureaucracy in Contemporary Ghana* (Berkeley: University of California Press, 1975).

30. Joel D. Barkan, ed., *Beyond Capitalism vs. Socialism in Kenya and Tanzania* (Boulder: Lynne Rienner, 1994).

31. Sara Berry of Boston University deserves credit for the distinction between decisionmaking procedures and decisionmaking power.

32. For an exposition of the need to map out the dimensions and features of state analysis in this respect, see Roger Charlton and Roy May, "The State of Africa: Evaluating Contemporary Challenges to Authority and Legitimacy" (Paper presented at the African Studies Association of the United Kingdom and the Centre of Commonwealth Studies Symposium on Legitimacy and Authority in Africa, University of Stirling, 23 May 1986).

33. These ideas are the basis for the analysis of corporatism. For background, see Phillippe Schmitter and Gerhard Lehmbruch, eds., *Trends Toward Corporatist Intermediation* (Beverly Hills: Sage Publications, 1979); Howard J. Wiarda, *Corporatism and National Development in Latin America* (Athens, Ohio: Center for International Studies, Ohio University, 1981); and Julius E. Nyang'oro, "On the Concept of Corporatism and the African State" *Studies in Comparative International Development* 21, no. 4 (Winter 1986): 50–51.

34. Kiflé Selassie Beseat, "Convaincre, controler ou contraindre? Systemes et mecanismes de controle du pouvoir en Afrique," *Présence africaine* 127/128 (1983): 79–113.

35. For background on regime types, see Ruth Berins Collier, *Regimes in Tropical Africa: Changing Forms of Supremacy, 1945–1975* (Berkeley: University of California Press, 1982).

36. Much of the following analysis is based on Naomi Chazan and Donald Rothchild, "Corporatism and Political Transactions: Some Ruminations on the Ghanaian Experience," in Julius E. Nyang'oro and Timothy M. Shaw, eds., *Corporatism in Africa* (Boulder: Westview Press, 1989), pp. 167–193.

37. See Nelson Kasfir, *The Shrinking Political Arena* (Berkeley: University of California Press, 1976), as well as his "Departicipation and Political Development in Black African Politics," *Studies in Comparative International Development* 9, no. 3 (1975): 3–26.

38. Samuel P. Huntington, *Political Order in Changing Societies* (New Haven: Yale University Press, 1968), p. 7.

39. See Richard L. Sklar, "Political Science and National Integration—A Radical Approach," *Journal of Modern African Studies* 6, no. 1 (1967): 1–11. Also Donald Rothchild, *Pressures and Incentives for Cooperation: The Management of Ethnic and Regional Conflicts in Africa* (Washington, DC: Brookings Institution Press, 1997), chaps. 1–3.

40. Dirk Berg-Schlosser, "Modes and Meaning of Political Participation in Kenya," *Comparative Politics* 14, no. 4 (1982): 397–416, gives one example.

41. On the possibilities for political engineering, see Timothy D.Sisk, *Power Sharing and International Mediation in Ethnic Conflict* (Washington, DC: U.S. Institute of Peace Press, 1996).

42. For one discussion, see Pearl Robinson, "Niger: Anatomy of a Neotraditional Corporatist State," *Comparative Politics* 24, no. 1 (October 1991): 1–20.

43. See the discussion of the Ghanaian government's use of "brutal repression" in the 1980s in Boahen, "Ghana: Conflict Reoriented," p. 135.

44. Some of these methods have been monitored by Amnesty International. For example, see the annual reports of Amnesty International during the course of the 1980s and 1990s.

45. Personal communication with Marina Ottaway. Also see Allen Isaacman and Barbara Isaacman, *Mozambique: From Colonialism to Revolution, 1980–1982* (Boulder: Westview Press, 1983).

46. A description of the PNDC policies in Ghana may be found in Boahen, "Ghana, Conflict Reoriented"; Donald I. Ray, *Ghana: Politics, Economics, Society* (Boulder: Lynne Rienner 1986); Deborah Pellow and Naomi Chazan, *Ghana: Coping with Uncertainty* (Boulder: Westview Press, 1986); and Donald Rothchild, ed., *Ghana: The Political Economy of Recovery* (Boulder: Lynne Rienner, 1991).

47. Naomi Chazan, "The New Politics of Participation in Tropical Africa," *Comparative Politics* 14, no. 2 (1982): 169–189.

48. Kay Lawson, ed., *Political Parties and Linkage: A Comparative Perspective* (New Haven: Yale University Press, 1980).

49. Clapham, *Third World Politics*. Also see: S. N. Eisenstadt and René Lemarchand, eds., *Political Clientelism, Patronage and Development* (Beverly Hills: Sage Publications, 1981), and J. C. Scott, *The Moral Economy of the Peasant: Rebellion and Subsistence in Southeast Asia* (New Haven: Yale University Press, 1976).

50. René Lemarchand, "Political Exchange, Clientelism and Development in Tropical Africa," *Cultures et developpement* 4, no. 3 (1972): 484–516.

51. The outlines of this type of patronage are discussed in Aristide Zolberg, *One-Party Government in the Ivory Coast* (Princeton: Princeton University Press, 1964).

52. Richard Hodder-Williams, *An Introduction to the Politics of Tropical Africa* (London: George Allen and Unwin, 1984), pp. 95–100.

53. Monday V. Ekpo, ed., *Bureaucratic Corruption in Sub-Saharan Africa: Toward a Search for Causes and Consequences* (Washington, DC: University Press of America, 1979). For an excellent case study, see Victor T. Le Vine, *Political Corruption: The Ghana Case* (Stanford: Hoover Institution Press, 1975).

54. Nathaniel H. Leff, "Economic Development Through Bureaucratic Corruption," *American Behavioural Scientist* 7 (1964): 8–14.

55. Sheku Saccoh, "Sierra Leone's War Against Corruption," *NewAfrican*, no. 370 (January 1999): 30; and Ogoh Alubo, "Year of Reckoning," *Newswatch* 28, no. 25 (December 28, 1998): 6.

56. For an excellent example, see Ayi Kwei Armah, *The Beautiful Ones Are Not Yet Born* (London: Heinemann, 1971).

57. Walter L. Barrows, "Comparative Grassroots Politics in Africa," *World Politics* 24, no. 2 (1974), esp. p. 232.

58. Thomas M. Callaghy, "Politics and Vision in Africa: The Interplay of Domination, Equality and Liberty," in Patrick Chabal, ed., *Political Domination in Africa: Reflections on the Limits of Power* (London: Cambridge University Press, 1986), pp. 30–51.

59. René Lemarchand, "The State, the Parallel Economy and the Changing Structure of Patronage Systems in Africa," in Donald Rothchild and Naomi Chazan, eds., *The Precarious Balance: State and Society in Africa* (Boulder: Westview Press, 1988), pp. 149–170.

60. Chris Allen, "Staying Put: Handy Hints for Heads of State" (Paper presented at the Symposium on Authority and Legitimacy in Africa organized by the African Studies Association of the United Kingdom and the Centre for Commonwealth Studies, University of Stirling, 23 May 1986).

61. Frank Holmquist, "Correspondent's Report: Tanzania's Retreat from Statism in the Countryside," *Africa Today* 30, no. 4 (1983): 35.

62. Phillip Mawhood, "Decentralization: The Concept and the Practice," *Local Government and the Third World: The Experience of Tropical Africa* (Chichester: John Wiley, 1983), pp. 9–10.

63. See, for example, Dele Olowu, "Beyond the Failure of the Centralized State in Africa," in Donald Rothchild ed., *Strengthening African Local Initiative: Local Self-Governance, Decentralisation and Accountability* (Hamburg. Institute for African Studies, 1994), p. 27; also see Mohamed Halfani, "Conclusion: Towards a New Paradigm of Self-Governance," in ibid., pp. 159–168.

64. Dele Oluwu, "Local Governance, Democracy, and Development," in Richard Joseph, ed., *State, Conflict, and Democracy in Africa* (Boulder: Lynne Rienner, 1999), p. 294.

7

Deep Politics:
Political Response,
Protest, and Conflict

Formal decisionmaking procedures and practices, high politics, are only one (albeit key) component of the political process. These formal procedures may be part of, subsist alongside, or stand in opposition to the deep politics of society. Deep politics are concerned not only with the way power is exercised but also with the purposes of governance; they may present challenges to policy, to the incumbents of public office, or to the dominant political vision.[1] At issue, therefore, are questions of authority and power as well as legitimacy. Participation, collaboration, cooperation, cynicism, dissatisfaction, protest, rebellion, insurrection, revolt, civil war, disengagement, and withdrawal are all ways of reacting to specific regimes; they may also be profound responses to reigning political doctrines.[2] As a consequence, patterns of political conflict have a direct bearing on policy decisions and on the dynamics of civil order and disorder in African countries. They also touch upon the fundamentals of political organization, on the creation of a civic public.

What do social groups complain about? How are their demands organized? How are they expressed? With what results? Societal responses to formal political actions in postcolonial Africa have varied in degree of organization, in scale of activities, in the amounts and types of resources utilized, in the reactions they have evoked, and invariably, in outcomes and implications. Five main types of domestic political conflict, which frequently take place concurrently in the same context, have developed during this period: elite, factional, communal, mass, and popular.[3]

Every government has had to deal with the effects of at least one of these forms of social response. Some countries have experienced prolonged cycles of instability and violence, whereas others have been more successful in maintaining order and establishing viable means to handle protest. The history of political conflict in most African countries has been punctuated by constant efforts to curtail unrest and refine the premises of political interaction. Gradually, though quite methodically, the focus of conflict has consequently shifted from disputes over political boundaries to disagreements over political values. As the center of political concern has shifted, however violent and dislocating this move, most countries in Africa have begun to develop coherent politics that have increasingly also displayed civic propensities.

■ ELITE CONFLICTS

Conflicts within the political center are the most common form of political strife in Africa. They have occurred in every African country throughout the postindependence period. Elites of different backgrounds, favoring diverging policy positions, and often pursuing a multiplicity of interests, have contended with each other to promote their separate concerns and to protest against measures perceived as detrimental to their well-being.

In Côte d'Ivoire, for example, during the past three decades, politicians of the old guard have competed with younger technocrats for party positions and for cabinet posts. In Tanzania, with its established party-mobilizing regime, one of the most persistent lines of division has been between ideologues and bureaucrats, between party functionaries and senior civil servants. Even in Jerry Rawlings's populist government, not to mention Kabila's Congo, machinations between individuals seeking the ear of the leader and between civil and military groups provide the fodder for the rumor mills of Harare and Kinshasa.

Elite conflict is, virtually by definition, extremely confined: it takes place in the capital cities and among the upper echelons of the government apparatus. It is prevalent precisely because it relates directly to the everyday activities of the political leadership regarding bureaucratic appointments, policy directions, governmental allocations. The aim of vying elites is to affect political decisions—to strengthen their position in the hierarchy, to have a say in the molding of policy, and, as a result, to increase their share of the political pie. The objective of these demands, often cast in class, ethnic, or ideological terms, is to alter the uses of state power.

The protagonists in these struggles are mostly urban elites whose social positions are defined by the political center and whose circumstances are most directly affected by government: civil servants, professionals, big businesspeople, students, intellectuals, and in some cases chiefs and religious leaders. Elite conflict, though small in scale and limited in scope, involves the actual or potentially powerful strata in African states. This form of conflict is frequently represented as espousing some concept of the way government should act and for what ends. It is usually, however, not terribly well organized: Sometimes individuals act alone or form temporary alliances with other people in order to bring about specific changes; sometimes such coalitions have endured for a long period of time as interests of key groups have coalesced (and, in these cases, elite conflicts have assumed factional dimensions as well).

Strategies and tactics in these kinds of conflict are indicative of the selective nature of demands and the narrow social bases of those articulating these claims. Many of the activities of competing groups take place behind the scenes: Allies are wooed through lavish entertainment, gifts, and promises of appointments or other benefits. Lobbying is commonplace as deals are struck between key personalities. Pork-barrel techniques, backroom manipulations, pacts, and negotiations are an important aspect of juggling for position and enhancing influence in African capitals. A good indication of the prevalence of these tactics is the degree of interest aroused in Yaoundé, Abidjan, Nairobi, Addis Ababa, Algiers, or Maputo by such issues as why the president's secretary was seen in the company of the party chairman; who was not invited to someone's reception; what a prominent intellectual was doing in deep conversation with a certain cabinet minister; the circumstances behind the cancellation of the director-general's trip to Washington; and the meaning of that all-night meeting at the castle.

In party systems, elite conflict also takes place in the parliament and the central organs of the party. In Senegal, Zambia, Angola, and Gabon, and more recently in Benin, Namibia, and Botswana, statements made in budget debates are indicative of political currents. The outcome of votes provides more tangible evidence of alliances as well as of agreements arrived at behind closed doors. These explicit and implicit modes of elite conflict are sometimes accompanied by more demonstrative manifestations as well: speeches criticizing government actions, grumblings in the market about particular decisions, and most notably, where the tradition of free journalism exists despite formal constraints (Ghana, Uganda, Senegal) or has been permitted (Nigeria), through newspaper editorials, the dissemination of pamphlets, and the development of information technology.[4]

Elite conflicts, especially where government performance has been unimpressive, have sometimes assumed more active expressions. In Ghana and Nigeria since independence, in Kenya and Namibia with increased regularity, and sometimes in Côte d'Ivoire, Congo, and Togo, when elites have not been able to gain concessions, they have resorted to petitions, demonstrations, and even strikes to press their claims. Some groups—usually students—have marched to voice their discontent, and these organizations (at the margins of the elite structure) have also taken strike action. Until recently, this kind of conflict (with the notable exception of some palace coups), remained within the bounds of the legal and the nonviolent; because the tactics of elite conflict were concerned with gaining benefits within the system rather than undermining its foundations, they evinced a great deal of self-restraint. This pattern shifted in the 1990s, however, when the unanswered demands of protesters in a majority of countries escalated into calls for a change of regime.

Elite strife is normally of a low intensity. It usually does evoke some official reaction, as leaders can rarely afford to alienate key elite groups. Felix Houphouët-Boigny and Jomo Kenyatta proved to be masters in the management of elite discontent. Both used a mixture of co-optation and repression, compromise and contempt, to mollify competing factions and to maintain control. When students in Côte d'Ivoire denounced government orientations and criticized what they considered to be inequitable practices, some of their leaders were dispatched abroad on government grants, some were incarcerated, and others given high positions in the administration. In 1990, when these same groups again raised similar issues, multiparty accommodations were made.

The key means of dealing with elite demands, however, has been through the manipulation of appointments and policy shifts. The careful disposition of bureaucratic posts is used as a means of appeasement (and partly accounts for the rapid growth of the state machinery). In relatively stable administrative regimes, such as those of Kenya, Cameroon, and Côte d'Ivoire, where issues of succession are a pivot of intra-elite strife, cabinet reshuffling and constitutional changes were used until recently to keep pretenders in check. When discontent was rife in elite circles in these countries at the end of the 1970s, some policy concessions were made: salaries were raised in the public service, certain state corporations were closed down, and steps were taken to offer new opportunities for the accumulation of wealth. The same response was evident in Ghana in 1992, when civil service salaries increased by more than 50 percent just prior to the elections.

Leaders confronted by elite demands have, when all else fails, a final, most effective, tool at their disposal: political excommunication. This measure has been employed when the position of the leader was seriously threatened by elite machinations. Kwame Nkrumah imprisoned J. B. Danquah and forced Kofi Busia into exile; Houphouët-Boigny regularly sacrificed the careers of some of his most trusted lieutenants to hold other politicians at bay; Daniel arap Moi engineered the political demise of Charles Njonjo and other opponents; Mengistu Haile Mariam physically eliminated major portions of the urban intelligentsia; and Sani Abacha imprisoned retired head of state Olusegun Obasanjo and others on the basis of an alleged coup plot (though ultimately to no avail—Obasanjo won the 1999 election held after Abacha's death).

It is inevitable that accommodation of elite demands has also involved some overtures toward the external partners of domestic elites. Leaders have periodically met the claims of local business interests (and by extension their foreign counterparts) by lowering taxes, giving preferred access to foreign exchange, providing credit facilities, or granting immigration permits. However costly such actions are, every government has had to make some gestures to elite groups in order to insure its own survival.

The dynamic of elite conflicts has subsequently tended to fluctuate: the more personalized the elite demands, the lower the level of confrontation; the more generalized and contradictory, the higher the level of tension and the more varied the techniques employed to stem them. Most governments have gone to great lengths to avoid the consolidation of permanent elite factions, either through purposely narrowing the size of elite groups (Côte d'Ivoire, Malawi) or through engineering the constant circulation of elites (Congo, Ghana under Rawlings). The outcomes of these efforts have a direct bearing on government stability. Where elites were successfully manipulated, leaders enjoyed relative continuity (Sekou Touré, Kenneth Kaunda, Mathieu Kerekou, Sam Nujoma, Joaquim Chissano). Where elite conflicts were continuously mishandled and internal factions coalesced (Uganda, Nigeria, Burkina Faso), the conflicts resulted in palace coups or spread beyond the confines of the center and constituted a more serious challenge to its stability. The meaning of elite conflicts, therefore, lies in their implications for the resilience of officeholders and, at times, of their governments.

■ FACTIONAL CONFLICTS

Factional conflicts, in many respects elite conflicts writ large, are nevertheless distinct: They assume different dimensions, possess their own unique dynamic, and carry quite separate implications. Factional strife, organized by elites, nevertheless reaches out to a variety of social groups and down to the local level. This mobilization takes place to further access to the center, increase participation and even control of the government, and influence political outlooks as well as specific policies.

Factional conflict, unlike elite competition, has not appeared in all African states. It has been most noticeable in those pluralist and administrative-hegemonic regimes where either intermediate social organizations have flourished and/or where elaborate patronage networks have thrived (Nigeria, Ghana, Senegal, Zambia, Sierra Leone, Kenya).[5] Factionalism has become the most visible and consistent kind of formal confrontation in countries that experienced a great deal of party competition on the eve of independence and in which elite cohesion has been relatively low.

Factional disputes tend to be wider in scope than their counterparts among the elite. The purpose of factional politics is to influence the composition of the official power apparatus, to determine who rules in a given political center. The minimum demand raised is for a place in the decisionmaking apparatus—for a say in the direction of government affairs and in the disbursement of government benefits. At times, factions aim at gaining control, at possibly bringing about a more basic change in regime. Factional strife, therefore, is a dispute over access to and/or control over the reins of government, and is propelled by rent-seeking behavior.

Factional conflicts in contemporary Africa have commenced as contending elites mobilized their constituents to vie with other groups for scarce state-controlled resources. This competition was sharpened by the makeup of the political coalition controlling the offices of state, the different access that urban and rural patrons had to decisionmaking elites at the center, and the varying rates of subregional development. In Nigeria, Cameroon, Sudan, Congo, and elsewhere, ethnoregional inequalities have intensified competition and conflict among various interests. It is precisely because socioeconomic change differentially affects ethnoregional interests that it raises the consciousness of the people living in the less-advantaged areas about their relative lack of services, amenities, and economic opportunities.[6]

Where leaders of the relatively disadvantaged regions have had reason to hope that demands for proportional or extraproportional (redistributive) treatment will lead to more balanced development policies, they mobilized constituent support for a change of priorities. However, such a call for proportional, and especially extraproportional, allocations was never put forward in a political vacuum. The relatively advantaged, who often have had better access to state decisionmakers, were expected to respond vigorously, basing their counterdemands upon what they contend is a common imperative for rapid economic growth. These appeals have frequently been received positively by bureaucratic officials at the political center, who shrink from the heavy expenditures involved in meaningful social transformation and who are protective of their own interests. In Zambia, for example, the former governor of the Bank of Zambia, raising questions about President Kenneth Kaunda's call for a decisive effort to reverse colonially determined rural-urban disparities, asserted bluntly that "the rural areas have the human material neither to [pursue] nor sustain a development effort, and such development as is created has only temporary effect as it depends largely on urban manpower and materials."[7]

Factional conflicts have been organized by elite groups and, therefore, have a decidedly elitist flavor. In Ghana, chiefs, lawyers, and businesspeople have banded together against progressive intellectuals, trade union leaders, middle-level clerks, and independent farmers. In Senegal, Muslim marabouts have competed with bureaucrats; in Nigeria, ethnoregional leaders have struggled against each other for political power. But factionalism requires mobilization of support beyond the confines of the urban areas: it breeds on local conflicts and strikes deep roots in the countryside. Limited in political scope, it is quite broad in scale.

Mobilization takes place through conscious appeals on the basis of ethnicity and class (as discussed in Chapter 4). In Nigeria, political elites have unabashedly played on ethnic, religious, and sectional identities and tensions. In Ghana, Congo, Sierra Leone, and Liberia, similar calls have been made. At the level of the village, too, local leaders have been co-opted. The particularistic basis of recruitment concluded by factional leaders feeds on the competition and inequality wrought by processes of social and economic change and takes advantage of cultural cleavages to advance the goals and ambitions of big patrons.[8] Factional alliances (however elitist in derivation) are therefore represented as cutting across different class distinctions.

The recruitment of factional support, however, has generally also been conducted along interest lines, resting on the backing of key horizontal groups (professional organizations, women's associations, trade unions, students, religious communities, youth, and farmers). Leaders have tried to delineate common concerns: free enterprise or equality, competition or justice, equitable distribution or increased opportunities. The maintenance of viable factions relies heavily on ideological rhetoric, if not on deep ideological conviction. The differences among parties in Nigeria or in South Africa in 1998–1999 are cases in point. Factional networks thus have a vertical structure (they divide the society from the top down) but are heavily weighted in favor of elite interest.

As the social bases of factions may cut across ethnic and class distinctions (while still drawing on these cleavages), factional strength depends on the capacity of elite leaders to meet the demands of constituent units, through successful rent-seeking operations. Factional demands, in most instances, are low in intensity and negotiable: access to jobs for supporters, expanded educational opportunities, funds for local development, salary hikes, higher producer prices, and improved roads, clinics, marketing facilities, and sanitation. Stress is placed on benefits; efforts are therefore directed, at least in the first instance, to attaining distributional gains. Factional leaders have consequently employed a variety of political tactics. They devote a great deal of time and energy to establishing close ties with decisionmakers. In the best patronage tradition, marabouts in Senegal and trade unionists in Nigeria have offered political support in exchange for goods and services. Negotiations, backslapping, and trade-offs are the stuff of factional politics: Such activities can still be seen in the streets of Lagos and the government complexes of Dakar. Lobbying, rallying public opinion (especially in the urban areas), petitions, strikes, and demonstrations are also commonplace.

Factional conflict has galvanized especially at the time of elections, which in many places have come to embody and accentuate factional disputes. At these times, gains are assessed, scores settled, and alliances reformed. Factionalism does not require regular electoral opportunities to function; but this mode of political confrontation has thrived in countries where elections have been held periodically or where some circulation of elites is possible via the ballot box (Kenya to some extent, Senegal in the 1980s and 1990s, Ghana in 1996).[9] These findings have important implications today, when competitive elections are being conducted throughout the continent.

Government responses to initial factional demands have generally consisted of well-placed handouts to factional leaders and their constituencies, hence the class bias of so many policies. Allocations are the main instrument of conflict management at this level and consequently depend on the availability of resources as well as adherence to some distributional principles. In a number of situations where the state apparatus has been controlled by a particular ethnic group or cluster of groups (white domination in apartheid South Africa, Amharic leadership in Ethiopia until 1991, northern/Arab influence in the government of Omar Hassan Ahmed al-Bashir's National Islamic Front in Sudan), the allocation of public resources was likely to be skewed in favor of those groups in control of the center. In many cases, however, leaders have utilized some measure of proportionality to guide disbursements. In Nigeria and Kenya in the 1970s, for example, attempts were made to distribute resources as equitably as possible.[10] When the resource supply diminishes or is in any event scarce (as happened in Nigeria in the early 1980s or Ghana during the same time period and since then in most of the continent), government leaders may attempt to ignore factional demands, increase their requests for foreign aid, justify their actions by appeals for understanding, devise and publicize new criteria for disbursement, or conduct an all-out campaign to discredit their opponents.[11] These techniques are familiar to politicians and citizens in all countries where factional politics prevail.

If initial requests are not satisfied, a second set of demands may be raised by dissatisfied factional leaders: for greater participation or for the displacement of existing officeholders. Calls for a change in government—inevitably forwarded most emphatically by those who benefit the least from the current system—require different strategies. Assemblies, strikes, and demonstrations, the fundamentals of protest politics, have been used regularly in factionalized countries throughout the period of independence. These techniques frequently cross the frontiers of the legal and the nonviolent; calls are made for civil disobedience and noncooperation. Direct clashes between government supporters (especially when these belong to one particular faction) and opponents take place; at times, sporadic violence occurs. The opposition to Acheampong in Ghana during the mid-1970s and to Shehu Shagari in Nigeria several years later illustrates the multiplicity of methods used by spurned factional leaders and their allies. However, the protests in Zimbabwe in 1999 highlight the limited ability of these methods to effect change.

As these higher-intensity pressures directly affect the position and the influence of those in power, governments can ignore them only at their peril. Several sorts of responses have been used. First, many governments have attempted to reduce such demands by incorporating vocal opposition leaders into their ranks and by negotiating with them within the cabinet or party executive committee (a process sometimes referred to as hegemonic exchange). In Kenya, Zambia, Uganda, and Niger, in very different ways, factional leaders were brought into the policymaking process. If these gestures did not suffice, or if a government ignored demands for inclusion (on ideological or other grounds), the conflict might escalate even further.

Second, political changes have been launched to alleviate demands. These have often involved opportunities for greater participation. Military governments have sometimes capitulated to demands by agreeing to transfer power to civilians, as happened in Nigeria in 1979 and 1999 and in Ghana in 1969 and in 1979, and most governments employed this technique in the 1990s by initiating political reforms.

Third, and usually in tandem, governments cracked down on their main detractors: opposition or potential opposition leaders (such as Obasanjo in Nigeria) were imprisoned, or in some cases driven into exile, and their supporters were hounded; election results were manipulated when the opportunity arose. If pressures continued to mount, emergency measures were brought to bear: competition was circumscribed, channels for the articulation of criticism foreclosed, and in the case of Nigeria in 1995, Ogoni leader Ken Saro-Wiwa and several other key members of the Movement for the Survival of the Ogoni people were hung. At times, more administrative methods have also been employed: Governments faced with acute factional demands have tried to decentralize the bureaucratic apparatus and place certain allocational decisions in local hands. These methods, when effectively implemented, may buy time and set in motion factional realignments that maintain center stability; they do not actually provide long-term solutions. When they fail, military interventions may occur, secessionist movements may form, or pressures for a change in government may mount.

Factional conflicts have had a distinctive rhythm and dynamic. They proceed in several waves of action and response, receding if demands are met or proceeding either to the overthrow of the incumbents and their replacement by competing factional leaders or to the intensification of strife. When they are prolonged and unresolved, they may embrace broader segments of the population and involve greater amounts of violence. Because they bind (albeit in conflict) different levels of social organization and heterogeneous groups, they play, not inconsequentially, an important role in consolidating national identities and norms.

The outcomes of factional disputes are, nevertheless, consistently skewed in favor of segments of the elite. For this reason, it is difficult to contain factionalism without major modifications. The skills required are subtle, the resources needed are great, and as factions also have external allies and backers, the techniques demanded are intricate. Moreover, even if individual leaders and governments succumb to their rivals, this form of conflict may endure as long as there is reason to believe that power may be regained by similar means. The displacement of one faction by another perpetuates this sort of competition and the patronage networks that prop them up. Factionalism may induce regime changes; it also delineates a pattern of political engagement over time. This kind of conflict may consequently foster protracted instability. It can, as has happened in certain countries, be controlled, although at great cost to state coffers. But if regime changes are frequent and living conditions decline, this kind of conflict can deteriorate into more severe, and violent, conflagrations.

■ COMMUNAL CONFLICTS

Communal and mass conflicts, in contrast to elite and factional disputes, call into question, in quite different ways, not only the legitimacy of specific regimes but also the essentials of state power. Communal conflicts challenge the state's territorial integrity, and mass confrontations protest the existing distribution of power. Communal demands, by far the more prevalent in postcolonial Africa, seek to forward the political expression of subnational identities. This goal can be achieved either through adequate representation (including the protection of minority rights), the granting of autonomy, or through secession, the creation of an independent political entity. Communal conflicts, therefore, pose a threat by a portion of the state to its territorial sovereignty.

Ostensibly, most African countries should be subject to communal disturbances, because, with the rare exceptions of Swaziland, Somalia, Lesotho, and some of the Maghreb countries (most notably Tunisia), all of them have internal subdivisions and do not qualify as nation-states. The fact that only a handful of serious secessionist movements have emerged on the continent, and that only Eritrea's movement for self-determination has been successful, is an important measure of the durability of colonial frontiers, if not of the independent political entities that came into being within their boundaries.

Nevertheless, several important communal confrontations have taken place: the Katanga secession in Congo (1960–1963); the Biafran secession from Nigeria (1967–1970); the Sudanese civil wars (1955, 1962–1972, 1983–present); the South African confrontation; and the ongoing ethnic conflicts in eastern Congo, Burundi, and Rwanda.[12] In several places, serious ethnic or subethnic tensions persist: Liberia, Somalia, Congo-Brazzaville, Zimbabwe, Ethiopia, and Uganda. Unlike most African countries, which either encompass many small and disparate ethnic groups or contain a dominant configuration and many smaller agglomerations, the national structure in communally unstable cases has been characterized by the existence of several large, geographically distinct ethnoregional groups (Nigeria, Sudan, Angola, Congo) or by a dominant group and an extremely cohesive, culturally distinct, and usually economically more advanced minority (Mengistu's Ethiopia, Uganda).

The basis for the organization of sectional demands and secessionist movements is the ethnic community located in a regional stronghold, usually at some distance from the capital. The definition of the group (the potential nation) rests on a combination of several criteria: a territorial base, history, language, religion, kinship, cultural norms, traditional institutions, colonial experience, race, economic circumstances, and/or a history of shared problems since independence. The more these aspects of ethnicity overlap in any instance, the greater the likelihood of political organization along sectional lines.

The evolution of ethnic conflict also has a strong subjective component. The differential diffusion of economic change during the colonial period and the administrative divisions of the colonial state activated local identities and underlined the differences between major groups (the Tutsi and Hutu in Rwanda and Burundi; the Yoruba, the Igbo, and the Hausa-Fulani in Nigeria; the Sara and the Toubou in Chad). Electoral competition during the transition to independence politicized these distinctions. Because democratic competition gives an undue advantage to numerically superior ethnoregional units, the underrepresentation of smaller, although frequently more educationally and economically advanced groups, exacerbated a feeling of inequality.[13]

The sense of exploitation, discrimination, and neglect (for example, of the Ndebele by the Shona in Zimbabwe, or the Ovimbundu by the Mbundu in Angola), intensified after independence, when factional leaders of rival groups in power pursued policies that were perceived as favoring other ethnic communities and their elites. Interethnic animosity grew, especially when religion and custom clearly distinguished between groups. As inimical or ostensibly inequitable decisions were implemented, ethnoregional leaders began to reassess the profitability of continued participation in the center. In all these cases, leaders first demanded greater representation; only when these demands were not met to their satisfaction did they proceed to conceive of autonomy or separate independence as a way of assuring their survival and development (or, in the late 1980s and 1990s, of the conquest of the capital by force). As tensions escalated, ruling coalitions took specific actions that served to fuel the crystallization of a full-fledged secessionist movement. In Nigeria, the overthrow of the Johnson Aguiyi Ironsi regime, pogroms against Igbo in the north, conflicts over representation at the political center, the discovery of oil in commercial quantities in the east, and the resulting confrontation over revenue allocation provided the necessary catalysts. The evidence of Belgian neocolonial control over the mining industry in Congo and the annexation of Eritrea in 1960 by Ethiopia caused deep resentments in these two countries. Moreover, the ability of communal interests to resist state authority was evidence of the fragility of the political center. Indeed, "only the extraordinary conjuncture of a virtual decomposition of the state really opens the way for successful separation."[14]

Demands for territory or for guarantees of group identity and survival are not easily negotiable. The call for ethnic autonomy is usually presented in zero-sum terms: The intentions of those claiming autonomy or the right to secede cannot but be viewed as irredeemably detrimental to those in power at the center. This was particularly noticeable in vertically stratified countries such as Rwanda, Burundi, and Zanzibar before their revolutions. It is also evident, however, in horizontally stratified countries (Nigeria, Ethiopia, Liberia, and Somalia) where cohesive social linkages did not develop adequately and the claims of rulers to central political control clashed with the demands of strong ethnoregional groups for power. Seen in this light, Biafra's and southern Sudan's secessionist actions and Eritrea's claim of separate status were not surprising. Recognizing the central state's general fragility and receiving what they considered to be inadequate responses to their claims for self-determination, these sectional interests took matters into their own hands and resorted to violence. These acts, invariably, were justified in terms of a higher law of collective survival.

Communal conflicts in their secessionist form are broad in scale. Their organization has rested, first, on the careful preparation of the community, the mobilization of political support, and the methodical accumulation of resources through contributions from the countryside and appeals for outside assistance. In Katanga this meant the coalescence of popular support behind Moise Tshombe and the procurement of the financial backing of the Union Minière du Haute Katanga (and some sections of the Belgian government). In Biafra, C. Odumegwu Ojukwu and his peers capitalized on Igbo fears and aspirations, consolidating local opinion behind their movement. Goukouni Oueddei in northern Chad engaged in a mobilization effort based on appeals to kin and locale in the early 1970s, simultaneously garnering Libyan backing for his undertaking. The early Eritrean stirrings involved discussions with Muslim countries as well as calls for the revival of Eritrean nationalism. In southern Sudan, black African (often Christian) leaders sought the support of ethnic cohorts in Uganda and Ethiopia. At the outset, therefore, separatist leaders utilized political strategies to build up their movements. They also publicized their demands and attempted to negotiate for their realization. When these techniques did not yield desired results, proclamations of independence were promulgated and violent strategies were brought into play.

Communal conflicts, at their zenith, are expressed in the form of civil war and direct military confrontations.[15] Leaders demanding autonomy, power, or secession created armed branches of their movements, usually led by former officers and soldiers in the national army. These militias recruited local conscripts, organized logistical support in the villages, and externalized their conflict by acquiring arms (and sometimes training and mercenaries) from abroad. They generally employed the tactics of guerrilla warfare, mixing attacks on government installations with limited skirmishes with government forces. Where the military confrontation was protracted, as has been the case in Eritrea, Chad, and Sudan, tactics of people's war (based on the Chinese and Latin American examples) have also been utilized. Despite these measures, however, the military balance of power has rarely been in favor of the secessionist groups.

Consistently, the organization of communally based autonomy or secessionist claims has evoked an immediate, and aggressive, military response on the part of governments. Nigeria, Congo, Ethiopia, Sudan, Angola, and Chad expanded their armies and imported military hardware from abroad. For African leaders, resistance to autonomy or secession was axiomatic: These demands threatened the basis of the postcolonial state system in Africa, they set a totally unacceptable precedent for communal claims in neighboring countries, and they constituted a direct challenge to leaders' authority. This official position has found widespread support in African capitals and, more significant, in the international community. Armed with superior might, therefore, governments set out to quell communal uprisings forcibly.

The outcome of these efforts has often, but not always, resulted in the coercive reduction, if not the termination, of violent ethnic insurrections. The Katangan and Biafran independence movements were militarily defeated. Sudan negotiated an accord with the southern-based insurgent movement in 1972 that lasted for a decade before a new upsurge in fighting occurred. In Ethiopia and Rwanda, however, the central government lacked the capacity to put down the insurrections; and in Angola the regime negotiated (and then renegotiated) a peace agreement with the National Union for the Total Independence of Angola (UNITA) insurgents, only to see UNITA leader Jonas Savimbi escalate the war in 1999.

Three dynamic patterns of violent communal conflicts have consequently emerged. The first, evident in the Nigerian civil war and the Katanga crisis in Congo, is one of escalation and military resolution. The second, one of protracted conflict, has a vacillating rhythm: periods of political negotiation are followed by short violent spurts, which subside and then are revived at periodic intervals. The civil wars in Angola and Sudan fall into this latter category. The third, and most recent, relates to the conquest of regimes by ethnically based insurgents (Liberia, Ethiopia, and

Rwanda). The discrepancies between these types may be attributed partly to the different ethnic structures prevailing in these countries (prolonged communal conflicts are usually conducted by disaffected minorities); partly to the continued involvement of competing external actors (usually both on the side of the government and of the rebels based in neighboring countries); and partly to the relative strength of the political center. In Nigeria, military engagement served to fortify the state and augment its apparatus of control. In Sudan, initial military successes temporarily had the same effect, but these gains were not cemented for other reasons. Thus, the containment of continued communal violence has also depended on the measures introduced immediately after the end of the military phase of the conflict.

Virtually all governments in Africa have had to contend with the possibility of communal disorder. They have, therefore, enacted policies to deal with ethnic strife.[16] Three main strategies have been devised and applied. The first is essentially structural: the reorganization of the federal system in Nigeria after the civil war and the granting of administrative autonomy to southern Sudan in the 1970s are two cases in point. The second is normative: the introduction of national symbols, values, and cultural orientations through education, indoctrination, and language policies, in the hope of implanting national identities to replace or coexist with ethnic ones (Tanzania provides a good example). The third technique has been political: the application of provisions for carefully balanced representation of all ethnic groups in high-level party, government, or legislative positions, or conversely, the replacement of ethnic with other (usually class) bases of representation.

The careful ethnic arithmetic practiced in Côte d'Ivoire under Houphouët-Boigny is an instance of the third political method. The attempted redefinition of criteria for participation in Angola is an example of the second political strategy: the MPLA, after its rise to power, expressed its "longstanding . . . disdain for racial and ethnic loyalties" by banning all organizations established on that basis and encouraging a sense of national loyalty.[17] This method of dealing with ethnic friction has not, however, been particularly successful. Ignoring ethnic divisions has not helped them disappear, as the Angolan government's protracted but unsuccessful effort to eliminate Jonas Savimbi's largely Ovimbundu-based UNITA movement has so aptly demonstrated. Social foundations of political action do not necessarily have to be ethnically conceived; it is doubtful, however, whether ethnic affinities can be achieved by government fiat.

Although the motivation behind these approaches to the containment of communal conflict may vary (in some countries the aim of integration policies is to displace existing ties through the amalgamation of a new set of identities; in others it is to assimilate smaller ethnic groups into the culture of the dominant people; in still others it is to aggregate existing links in a pluralistic community), African leaders have generally exhibited a great deal of sensitivity in analyzing the roots of communal conflicts and an equal sophistication in designing policies to handle such disputes.

The record of African governments in the management of communal conflicts has been, on the whole, quite impressive. Violent insurrections have generally been firmly put down (with rare exceptions that may spill over international boundaries),[18] and communal confrontations have either been diverted through provisions for adequate representation or channeled along more familiar associational lines. Militant Hutu genocide in Rwanda was followed by a successful overthrow of the regime by a Tutsi-led insurgent force; a Tutsi-led military coup in Burundi in 1996 quickly encountered Hutu-inspired guerrilla attacks, as well as an embargo imposed by the eastern African countries. The fact that, with the exception of Ethiopia (Eritrea) and possibly Somalia and eastern Congo, the territorial integrity of the African state has not been assailed through successful separation does not mean that its viability has not been questioned in other ways. These challenges, however, have been of a different order.

■ MASS CONFLICTS

Political movements with the purpose of inducing a rapid, complete, and permanent alteration of the power structure have been a rarity in independent Africa. By definition, revolutionary conflicts of this sort pose a basic threat to the validity of state power as currently constituted and offer an alternative political vision guided by a clearly defined set of organizing principles. The continent has known only a single transformation of the social order, the Ethiopian revolution (which brought about the irreversible demise of the feudal structures that had existed in that country for centuries). Ethiopia was one of the few African states not subjected to colonial rule. The 1974 revolution, even though it did not achieve its proclaimed Marxist-Leninist objectives, nevertheless did induce a fundamental shift in social structures and in the distribution of power in society. Africa has also witnessed two revolutionary experiments, in Mozambique and Angola. The stirring of mass discontent, however, is evident in several countries and deserve some, albeit abbreviated, attention.

The social basis of mass conflict of a revolutionary sort is the crystallization of class distinctions and class consciousness and, consequently, the creation of a class foundation for political action. In most independent African countries, politics intensified social differentiation and underscored inequalities, instead of generating political organization along class lines. The entrenchment of factional alliances acted as a brake to the emergence of such ties. Links between farmers and their local or national patrons have provided a substitute for class action in most instances. The absence of an indigenous and independent middle class has also impeded class consciousness. Revolutionary ideologues, usually comfortably ensconced in capital cities, have not been able to capitalize on peasant or worker discontent, as in many parts of Latin America.[19] Where mass protest does occur, it is usually a result of the development of a gap between factional leaders as a group and their followers.

Radical political change has taken place in Africa only in the very specific circumstances of the decaying traditional monarchy of Ethiopia and the prolonged struggles for national liberation in lusophone countries. In the first case, an oligarchic regime failed to maintain strong links with the rural areas, to furnish opportunities for urban intellectuals, to protect an apparatus of control even with the assistance of an external power, and to begin to confront the effects of the drought and subsequent widespread famine of the early 1970s. The strong sense of Ethiopian nationalism and the equally embedded tradition of central government, coupled with the absence of viable alternative social institutions to those of the state, combined to focus dissent on the imperial authority structure. In Ethiopia, the revolution was carried out by the Mengistu regime from above. In the second set of examples, the lusophone countries, violent and protracted anti-colonial wars provided opportunities for the forging of strong bonds between nationalist leaders and the population at the local level. Although such links were established in Guinea-Bissau as well as in Angola and Mozambique, only the latter two chose to follow a revolutionary course. Subsequently, as leaders there proved unable to consolidate their authority (challenged by UNITA and RENAMO, respectively), they liberalized their political processes, opening the way for multiparty electoral competition. In 1997, plans were in place in Angola to form a government of national unity and to include nine UNITA generals in leadership positions in the national army. But as the intermittant fighting between UNITA and the government army escalated into a major war in 1999, the Lusaka Protocol collapsed and UN peacekeeping forces withdrew.

Despite the absence of revolutionary situations in most parts of Africa, some indications of mass (although not revolutionary) forms of conflict have surfaced from time to time, most notably in Ghana and Burkina Faso. Behind these appearances of mass-based political protest is the distinction between the establishment and the loosely defined "have-nots," those who did not benefit from existing patterns of distribution. As vertical patronage networks were weakened and their leaders discredited, some alliances were formed between the cities and the rural areas (a shadow, perhaps, of established factional coalitions), thereby creating urban-based movements with some claim to a nationwide constituency. The aim of mass conflicts in these settings was defined essentially in negative terms as the displacement of the dominant elites and the institution of direct popular supervision over public officials; no firm alternative political doctrine was proffered or elaborated.

The quasi-mass political movements in Ghana and Burkina Faso, although initially embracing large segments of the population, possessed only a rudimentary ideology and organization. They relied heavily on the emergence of a leader (usually in uniform) who would give voice to the movement's sentiments and act upon them. The tactics employed by groups organized along these lines have been purposefully confrontational: not only in these two cases, but also in Nigeria, Kenya, Zambia, and Congo in the 1980s and 1990s, these movements have openly condemned regime policies and denounced the corruption and insensitivity of public officials. They have advocated noncompliance with official policies and engaged in illegal practices. They have not usually, however, been able to carry out the more violent strategies that they so vociferously espouse. Indeed, governments have generally responded to these outbursts by jailing movement leaders and by closing opportunities for the expression of such forms of dissent.

What many governments have been unable to accomplish—unless they could engineer a massive internal reform and bring about rapid improvements in living conditions—is the suppression of mass rumblings. Potentially, if not in actuality, mass conflicts contain the ingredients of intense, widespread, and particularly violent conflict. Thus, although the possibility of revolutionary change may be greater in the stronger states on the continent (Nigeria, Kenya, Côte d'Ivoire), where center consolidation has taken place and class distinctions have begun to appear as a consequence of factional disputes, implicit in the history of mass conflicts in Africa is the possibility of another, fifth and most recent, form of political confrontation.

■ POPULAR CONFLICTS

Popular political protest chips away at the foundations of state power from below, thereby undermining its viability without altering its form. It constitutes a quiet rebellion against state authority, a way of responding to exclusion and lack of access by limiting the reach of existing central institutions. Popular conflict of this kind emerges most emphatically in conditions where state structures are especially weak and leaders capricious, where patronage networks have broken down, where alternate avenues for power accumulation exist, and where economic conditions have wrought widespread misery.[20] Popular conflict came to the surface in most parts of the continent in the third decade of independence.

Incidences of popular protest reflect a desire to minimize vulnerability to official interventions and to reduce exposure to the vicissitudes of government actions, regardless of regime type. They are expressions, on a micro level, of a quest by the officially disempowered for protection from uncertainty and economic hardship through some form of self-encapsulation. Popular protest is thus a series of attempts to assert autonomy in a multiplicity of locations and ways. It differs from all the previous forms of conflict in that it need not be directly concerned with gaining access to the center (elite or factional disputes) or with changing the political center or altering its forms (communal and mass conflicts) but is often concerned with creating a distance between the formal domain and individual citizens, local communities, and specific social groups.[21]

Popular modes of political confrontation have emerged in countries where certain social groups, such as women, have been systematically excluded from the center and have been unable to partake in its benefits. The growing divergence between the life-styles of patrons and their clients created fissures in patronage structures and intensified the gnawing resentment that had been brewing within factional alliances. The exploitation felt by individuals and groups had come to outweigh the gains they gleaned from such associations.

The social basis of these activities, therefore, rests on formations not inextricably bound with the construction of the formal power structures. Ethnicity and class in Africa have been shaped and defined in important ways by the state, which has served as the primary arena for their articulation (as demonstrated not only in mass and communal conflicts but, most significantly, in factional cleavages).[22] Popular protest commences, then, with the disorganization of ethnicity and with class fragility.[23] The most obvious framework for such activities has been the rural collectivity. Territorially defined and physically removed from official power centers, local communities do control some resources and usually have evolved their own political institutions based on shared norms. Although they cannot exercise a full exit option, they carve out their own independent niches in certain spheres. In urban areas, local neighborhood groups have sometimes been able to fulfill similar roles.

In many countries, however, as evidence from the 1980s and 1990s in Ghana, Nigeria, Somalia, Congo, Kenya, Angola, and Ethiopia corroborates, new bases of social organization have surfaced. Islamic networks throughout western Sudan, trading alliances around domestic and transnational markets, craft guilds, women's associations at the interstices of local and state power, credit unions, and mafia-type bands are all cases in point. In many respects, kin groups possess several crucial features of these new forms of affiliation: They are based on strong personal bonds, advocate clearly defined joint interests, revolve around shared symbolic schemes, and may have a broad geographic scope.[24] Whatever the precise social foundation of specific manifestations of popular resistance, popular conflict in general is characterized by a variety of activities conducted by separate, sometimes overlapping, small-scale groups and social agglomerations that maintain lateral ties with each other and that, although not cohering in any umbrella-like frameworks, do comprise identifiable components in the African social web.[25]

Popular acts of protest are thus defined emphatically by their lack of overarching organization, although they carry concrete meaning mostly for the particular individuals involved. They remain sporadic and informal but together yield a general pattern of disengagement.[26] Techniques of dissent vary. In economic terms, local microeconomies have been fortified and elaborated, self-help schemes initiated, new commercial ventures launched, artisan collectives formed, black markets expanded, and smuggling techniques refined. Job absenteeism, petty theft, industrial sabotage, embezzlements, work stoppages, and periodic strikes are some illegal (although not always criminal) tactics used to whittle away at manufacturing capacity. The informal economy, in its many manifestations, has proliferated. On the cultural plane, "songs and anecdotes may be the principal channel of communication for people who are denied access to the official media."[27] Popular arts— music, film, dance, theater, street performances, market literature, underground presses, graphic art, sculpture, painting—are freed from the constraints of the official traditions of the state and indigenous political institutions. They act as cultural brokers of an informal sort. Religious revivals, antiwitchcraft movements, and messianic sects may serve as expressions of popular protest as well, as do migrations on a more individual level.

Popular strategies all contain a political dimension, but some are more distinctly political in fact. Antisocial political acts have spread in recent years. Armed robbers, bandits, and thugs roam the highways of Nigeria and the streets of Johannesburg. Small acts of sabotage (cutting of phone wires to obtain copper) may wreak havoc in communication systems. Gangs threaten social order in the cities of Congo and have taken over the rural areas in Uganda. These activities, felt in many African countries, have had the effect of undermining security, as have activities such as distributing anonymous political circulars and spontaneous rioting in the workplace and the countryside (in quite different ways). Most political acts of popular protest are more nuanced: engagement in constant and acrimonious political debates, cynicism, indifference to government dictates, regular noncompliance with laws, systematic tax evasion, avoidance of participation in elections and plebiscites, and at times, political withdrawal through the revitalization of traditional, or the creation of alternate, decisionmaking institutions and networks of adjudication.

Popular protest, then, is in the first place about coping mechanisms. It is expressed not only through confrontation but also through quiet alienation and passivity. These seemingly disparate undertakings have tended to gravitate increasingly around the unofficial and the informal: They are clear indications of the prevalence of straddling (between state and society, between the formal economy and the unofficial market) in everyday life on the continent.[28]

African governments have found it difficult to control, let alone curtail, popular political protest measures, as these are disorganized, at times latent, and their eruption is usually unpredictable. Because these actions undermine the existing political fabric by limiting its reach, even promises of better economic management and large-scale political reforms have only gone a short way toward reducing the threat to central authority inherent in this form of conflict. Unlike factional demands, it is difficult to appease popular complaints by buying off local leaders and thereby mitigating calls for greater accountability. Unable to govern exclusively through coercion precisely because of the weaknesses that engendered this kind of protest, some governments have consciously reconciled themselves to their reduced circumstances, divesting themselves of responsibility in critical spheres or regions of the country (the policies of Ghana and Guinea in the mid-1980s pointed in this direction). Others have combined such approaches with the intensification of repression and officially sanctioned violence (Nigeria, Sudan, Congo).

In the short term, therefore, popular protest has underscored disintegrative and autocratic trends in many African political environments. But its deeper political meaning may lie elsewhere. When taken together, acts of popular confrontation may reveal the outlines of a hidden deep politics in situations where official political organization is not endowed with a vision based on an integrative set of values other than a commitment to domination. Implicit in many of the strategies adopted in this mode of conflict are "customary notions of political obligation such as trusteeship, probity and public accountability in the public institutions of the state."[29] Thus, some essential tenets have been formulated; they cohere around a notion of a civic public. What they lacked until recently was a more precise institutional expression, a concrete formula for power sharing. But with the closure of exit options, popular conflict has given way to demands for changes in broader political arrangements. Whether these will take the shape of a rehabilitation of existing authoritarian state structures or of a broader process of democratization is unclear. In the meantime, popular types of political expression continue to highlight civil unrest and magnify the predicament of governance on the continent.

■ THE INTERPLAY OF POLITICAL CONFLICTS

The five main kinds of political conflict in independent Africa reflect an absence of consensus on questions of policy, participation, representation, equality, justice, and accountability. In distinct ways, they have challenged either the decisions or composition of the particular regimes or the integrity, validity, or viability of state authority. None of these categories is mutually exclusive: Different forms of conflict appear in different combinations in sub-Saharan Africa. Each African country and each regime type has invited its own structure of political conflict.

If issues of elite competition or communal strife preoccupied leaders at the outset of independence, in the third decade leaders were forced to confront the consequences of their rule. The role and position of patrons provide a fairly accurate guide to the nature of conflict in any given setting. A cohesive set of patrons points to elite conflict; divided leadership indicates factionalism; strong local patrons excluded from state power circles suggest communal conflict; the breakdown of communication in clientelistic networks may yield mass conflict when control of state resources is desired and appears feasible. When it is not, popular protest might ensue under similar circumstances, and eventually yield to more thoroughgoing reform.

Political instability and civilian insurrection have been the order of the day in quite a few African countries. Although no single political entity has collapsed entirely (Liberia and Somalia have come closest), neither has any one country totally escaped periods of militant or subversive strife. "At a minimum we have seen that the threat of anarchy is [for the most part] unfounded."[30] Political cohesion has been equally elusive. Violence, however, need not be politically dysfunctional, just as fundamental political change does not have to be contingent on an organized opposition.[31] Out of some of these confrontations, new types of elite pacts (Liberia) and coalitions (South Africa) are forming and new rules for the management of conflict may be emerging. In due course these might yet compel the formulation of some principles of power sharing and their translation into more workable political practices. The ways in which such changes have been carried out and what patterns they may yield is the subject of the final chapter in this section on political processes.

■ NOTES

1. John Lonsdale, "Political Accountability in African History," in Patrick Chabal, ed., *Political Domination in Africa: Reflections on the Limits of Power* (London: Cambridge University Press, 1986), p. 130. See also Goran Hyden and Michael Bratton, eds., *Governance and Politics in Africa* (Boulder: Lynne Rienner, 1991).

2. See also Robert H. Jackson and Carl G. Rosberg, "Popular Legitimacy in African Multi-Ethnic States," *Journal of Modern African Studies* 22, no. 2 (1984): 177–198.

3. This classification expands substantially on a scheme originally presented in Donald G. Morrison and Hugh Michael Stevenson, "Integration and Instability: Patterns of African Political Development," *American Political Science Review* 76, no. 2 (1972): 902–927.

4. Maureen Chigbo, "Nigeria Not Ready," *Newswatch* 28, no. 24 (December 21, 1998): 26–28.

5. Many works recognize the significance of factional conflicts but do not analyze them in detail. For one notable exception, see Jonathan S. Barker, "Political Factionalism in Senegal," *Canadian Journal of African Studies* 7, no. 2 (1975): 287–315.

6. Karl W. Deutsch, "Social Mobilization and Political Development," *American Political Science Review* 55, no. 3 (September 1961): 493–514; Robert Melson and Howard Wolpe, "Modernization and the Politics of Communalism," *American Political Science Review* 64, no. 4 (December 1970): 1114–1117; and James R. Scarritt and William Safran, "The Relationship of Ethnicity to Modernization and Democracy," *International Studies Notes* 10, no. 2 (Summer 1983): 17.

7. Quoted in Donald Rothchild, "Rural-Urban Inequities and Resource Allocation in Zambia," *Journal of Commonwealth Political Studies* 10, no. 3 (1972): 233.

8. Robert H. Bates, "Ethnic Competition and Modernization in Contemporary Africa," *Comparative Political Studies* 6, no. 4 (1974): 457–484. Also see Nelson Kasfir, "Explaining Ethnic Political Participation," *World Politics* 31, no. 3 (1979): 365–388.

9. Timothy D. Sisk and Andrew Reynolds, eds., *Elections and Conflict Management in Africa* (Washington, DC: U.S. Institute of Peace Press, 1998).

10. Donald Rothchild, *Managing Ethnic Conflict in Africa: Pressures and Incentives for Cooperation* (Washington, DC: Brookings Institution Press, 1997), pp. 78–82.

11. Donald Rothchild, "Comparative Public Demand and Expectation Patterns: The Ghana Experience," *African Studies Review* 22, no. 1 (1979): 127–149. See also Donald Rothchild and Victor Olorunsola, "Managing Competing State and Ethnic Claims," in Donald Rothchild and Victor Olorunsola, eds., *State Versus Ethnic Claims: African Policy Dilemmas* (Boulder: Westview Press, 1983), pp. 1–25.

12. Not included are irredentist schemes, which spill across boundaries. For a superb analysis of these ethnic conflicts, see Benyamin Neuberger, *National Self-Determination in Postcolonial Africa* (Boulder: Lynne Rienner, 1986). See also Naomi Chazan, ed., *Irredentism and International Politics* (Boulder: Lynne Rienner, 1991).

13. Crawford Young, *The Politics of Cultural Pluralism* (New Haven: Yale University Press, 1978).

14. Crawford Young, "Comparative Claims to Political Sovereignty: Biafra, Katanga and Eritrea," in Rothchild and Olorunsola, *State Versus Ethnic Claims,* pp. 199–232.

15. Samuel Decalo, "Chad: The Roots of Centre-Periphery Strife," *African Affairs* 79, no. 317 (1980): 491–509; Samuel Decalo, "Regionalism, Political Decay and Civil Strife in Chad," *Journal of Modern African Studies* 18, no. 1 (1980): 23–56.

16. David A. Lake and Donald Rothchild, "Containing Fear: The Origins and Management of Ethnic Conflict," *International Security* 21, no. 2 (Fall 1996): 41–75; and Timothy D. Sisk, *Power Sharing and International Mediation in Ethnic Conflicts* (Washington, DC: U.S. Institute of Peace Press, 1996).

17. John A. Marcum, "Angola: A Quarter Century of War," *CSIS Africa Notes,* no. 1, 37 (21 December 1984): 3.

18. John Ravenhill, "Redrawing the Map of Africa," in Donald Rothchild and Naomi Chazan, eds., *The Precarious Balance: State and Society in Africa* (Boulder: Westview Press, 1988).

19. Much of the following discussion is based on Christopher Clapham, *Third World Politics: An Introduction* (Madison: University of Wisconsin Press, 1985), pp. 160–168.

20. Jean-François Bayart, "Civil Society in Africa," in Chabal, *Political Domination in Africa,* pp. 114–115.

21. This type of conflict is not limited to Africa. See D. L. Steth, "Grassroots Stirrings and the Future of Politics," *Alternatives* 9 (1983): 1–24.

22. Crawford Young, "Patterns of Social Conflict: State, Class, and Ethnicity," *Daedalus* 111, no. 2 (1982): 71–99. This sentence is a paraphrase of p. 72.

23. Nelson Kasfir, "Class, Political Domination and the African State," in Zaki Ergas, ed., *The African State in Transition* (London: Macmillan, 1987).

24. This notion was suggested by Sara Berry in a series of discussions: Thanks are due to her for her assistance in clarifying this matter.

25. Bayart, "Civil Society in Africa," p. 118.

26. This analysis is based on Naomi Chazan, "Patterns of State-Society Incorporation and Disengagement," in Rothchild and Chazan, *The Precarious Balance,* and on Victor Azarya and Naomi Chazan, "Disengagement from the State in Africa: Reflections on the Experience of Ghana and Guinea," *Comparative Studies in Society and History,* no. 1 (1987). For a more general discussion, see Albert O. Hirschman, *Exit, Voice, and Loyalty* (London: Oxford University Press, 1970), pp. 106–131.

27. Karin Barber, 'The Popular Arts in Africa," (ACLS/SSRC Paper presented at the Twenty-ninth Annual Meeting of the African Studies Association in Madison, Wisconsin, 29 October–2 November 1986), p. 6. This is a superb discussion of politics and popular arts in Africa.

28. See Irving Leonard Markovitz, ed., *Studies in Power and Class in Africa* (London: Oxford University Press, 1987), esp. pp. 27–66. Also see Sara Berry, *Fathers Work for Their Sons: Accumulation, Mobility and Class Formation in an Extended Yoruba Community* (Berkeley: University of California Press, 1985).

29. Maxwell Owusu, "Custom and Coups: A Juridical Interpretation of Civil Order and Disorder in Ghana," *Journal of Modern African Studies,* no. 1 (1986): 72.

30. Irving Leonard Markovitz, *Power and Class in Africa* (Englewood Cliffs, NJ: Prentice Hall, 1977), p. 346.

31. Roger Charlton and Roy May, "The State of Africa: Evaluating Contemporary Challenges to Authority and Legitimacy" (Paper presented at the African Studies Association of the United Kingdom and the Centre of Commonwealth Studies Symposium on Legitimacy and Authority in Africa, University of Stirling, 23 May 1986). Also see, for one example, Thomas M. Callaghy, "State-Subject Communication in Zaire: Domination and the Concept of Domain Consensus," *Journal of Modern African Studies* 18, no. 3 (1980): 469–492.

8

Political Transitions
and Patterns of Change

The political history of Africa since independence, so diverse in its details, has been marked not only by the establishment of identifiable norms and procedures but also by its fluidity and movement. No one set of rules, practices, or processes has remained unaltered—as the concept of politics infers—by the dynamics of state action and social response. The question of political change is therefore central to understanding the course of political processes over time. Political transitions have been set in motion either from within, through the initiative of incumbents themselves, or by individuals and groups outside the circle of officeholders, frequently employing violent political means. Each of these methods has involved some dislocation and at times major upheavals with grave human consequences. Whether they have also brought about more significant changes in the organization of the public arena or in its practices is still open to question.

In this chapter, we examine how political changes have taken place and what effects these shifts have had on the course of contemporary African politics. At issue are the nature of representation and participation and the mechanics of political accountability. The study of regime dynamics makes it possible to analyze emerging patterns of state-society interactions and to determine their significance for policy formulation and effective implementation.

Although preemptive actions by civilian leaders and military coups continue to determine the manner in which formal transitions take place, the impetus for change as well as its direction, as the events of the 1990s demonstrated, are an outgrowth of the many interactions between governments and social groups, between rulers and citizens. Periodic reevaluations, negotiations, confrontations, and internal wars have yielded different formulas for

221

political conduct. The nature of political processes has had a direct impact on the extent and nature of state-society exchanges and, therefore, on the capacity of formal institutions to carry out their programs. As political relations have solidified and more Africanized patterns have begun to emerge, attention has shifted from the outward forms of governments to a greater preoccupation with defining governments' underlying norms and creating structures to monitor their behavior.

■ MODES OF POLITICAL CHANGE

▓ Managed Political Transitions

Some of the shifting currents of politics in Africa may be attributed to measures introduced by those in power. Three main methods of supervised transition, excluding decolonization, have been in constant use over the years; reform, succession, and change through elections. The purpose of *reform* by fiat is to alter the procedures or the practices of the political center. Most changes of this sort have been of a substantive order: the launching of a new economic program, expanding external alliances, drawing up or modifying an official ideology, designing new techniques of social control, or clamping down on dissent. These decisions are made by the head of state or select advisers, frequently under pressure from international financial agencies and donor institutions, and may require different allocations of resources or even institutional adjustments on a broad scale. In almost all instances, such shifts herald a self-imposed policy reorientation.

Policy reform may stand alone or come together with changes in personnel. Reshuffles and purges may be used to apportion blame for failure, justify a change in policy direction, eradicate corruption, improve efficiency, allow some rejuvenation of leadership, or, as is most common, assure continued control over key operations. When major policy changes are instituted, as in accordance with World Bank and IMF proposals, these generally involve more massive changes in the size of the public sector and in its capabilities.

Guided shifts of this kind have been most significant when they have involved a restructuring of government agencies. The decision to create new states in Nigeria or to decentralize decisionmaking in Ghana are two examples of important modifications in the frameworks of political action. The reorganization of political institutions has been of particular significance. The transition to a one-party system was usually implemented on the initiative of the leaders of the day, as was the so-called process of civilianization of military coalitions in Togo, Mali, Niger, and Congo in the 1970s, or, for that matter, many of the liberalization measures of the early 1990s. Indeed, in retrospect, many changes in the delineation of political centers or in the structures of political interchange have been the result of executive command. The meaning of these moves lies, therefore, in their implications for the conduct of the political center. Usually, they do not influence the composition of its leadership and, therefore, even when progressive in orientation and design, tend to entrench the positions of its ruling elite.

Succession and inheritance, in contrast, are mechanisms for bringing about a change in the top leadership without also causing a subsequent alteration in regime.[1] Inheritance entails the designation of an heir apparent (usually by the president himself) and the formalization of this choice through proclamation or appropriate constitutional amendment. Provisions of this sort have been made in almost every African capital, although they are of particular interest in countries where the founding father remained in office for a protracted period of time, until his death. Such provisions assured continuity after the death of William Tubman in Liberia, Seretse Khama in Botswana, Houari Boumedienne in Algeria, Abdel Nasser in Egypt, Jomo Kenyatta in Kenya, Felix Houphouët-Boigny in Côte d'Ivoire, Agostinho Neto in Angola, and Samora Machel in Mozambique (they faltered after the passing away of Sekou Touré in Guinea). Succession involves not only the appointment of a new head of state but also the voluntary abdication of the incumbent. Peaceful succession took place in Senegal, Tanzania, Cameroon, and Sierra Leone in the 1980s. Despite ongoing strains between ex-leaders and present incumbents, the importance of such transitions through succession cannot be exaggerated: What has been shattered is the axiom prevalent during the first two decades of independence that no rotation of civilian leaders could occur without a concomitant regime change.

Managed political change has also been launched through the ballot box. Myths aside, *elections* in most parts of the continent have been neither infrequent nor totally manipulated. Five main types of postcolonial elections may be identified.[2] The first are symbolic elections—mostly the hallmark of rigid one-party governments—in which a single slate of candidates for parliament and the presidency is presented to the voters and receives a near unanimous (engineered) mandate. In symbolic elections no significant change of any sort transpires. The second kind of elections permits competition for office within a single-party system. Tanzania and Kenya pioneered this form of elections.[3] In this way, it was possible to allow for some monitoring of politicians (indeed, frequently cabinet members did not secure reelection and the composition of national assemblies was altered) and to tie parliamentarians to local constituencies. A third form of elections, held regularly in the more pluralist regimes of Botswana, Mauritius, and Senegal in the 1970s and 1980s, entertains limited multiparty competition. In these countries, the scope of political debate was expanded, although with the exception of Mauritius the position of the dominant party was not called into question before 1990. These three electoral modes are essentially minimalist: they allow for some political activity, but do not constitute a means of altering either the top leadership, the administration, or the regime.

The remaining two types of elections are maximalist in thrust. Plebiscites seek popular approval for constitutional changes or proposed adjustments in the organization of the political center. In Ghana, the 1960 plebiscite on the republican constitution and the Union government referendum of 1976 are two examples of the widespread practice of seeking to bring about a regime change without a shift in the composition of the government.

A fifth kind of elections, however, has provided a mechanism for the simultaneous turnover of both leaders and regimes. These elections are a concomitant of a military withdrawal from the political arena or of the movement from authoritarian to multiparty government. The 1978 elections in Burkina Faso (then called Upper Volta), the 1979 elections in Ghana and Nigeria, and the 1999 Nigerian elections are cases of transition from military rule.[4] The pattern of these elections is fairly clear. Following the drafting of a new civilian constitution and its approval by a constituent assembly, the ban on party politics is lifted and open elections are held. The military then hands over the reins of government and returns (if only temporarily) to the barracks. The newly installed leaders, at the head of pluralist and often factionalized systems, usually pursue many of the policies of their military predecessors. Although decisionmaking procedures, modes of operation, and practices may change dramatically after transfer elections, such elections have proven to be a critical instrument for the maintenance of the continuity of ruling elites. This pattern of military handover through the ballot box recurred in Ghana in 1992 (with the civilian election of Jerry Rawlings); it was attempted and failed in Nigeria in 1993, but appears to have succeeded in 1999.

The widespread political reforms in the 1990s, the so-called democratization wave, usually involved open elections of this sort, where both leader and regime forms can be changed via the polls. By the end of 1996, elections of the maximalist kind either had taken place or were planned in most African countries, including Angola, Benin, Burkina Faso, Cameroon, Cape Verde, Congo-Brazzaville, Côte d'Ivoire, Ethiopia, Gabon, Kenya, Mali, Mauritania, Mozambique, Namibia, Niger, São Tomé and Principe, Sierra Leone, Togo, Zambia, and Zimbabwe (for details see Appendix 2). Perhaps most significantly, South Africa underwent a successful transition via the ballot box in 1994 (see Chapter 13).

Elections in Africa have offered greater scope for political change than other modes of supervised transition. Although some have merely endorsed decisions already made in policymaking circles, most elections have been a mechanism for some political movement. They differ from other managed transition measures in that they institutionalize means of supervising change and shift part of the responsibility of determining future directions from the top leadership to the electorate. In very few instances, however, have they implied, to date, a fundamental alteration in the organization or distribution of power in society (although the recent spate of elections may be pointing in this direction).

Supervised methods of political change, including elections, all insert a certain dynamism into the public domain without necessarily undermining the continuity of the political order. The common thread underlying these techniques in the past has been the preservation of the position of already dominant groups in the society. Nevertheless, transitions initiated from above, especially when institutionalized through regularized procedures, may prove to be an important tool not only for the self-regulation of the political center (even under duress) and for compelling periodic reevaluations, but also for more far-reaching changes. Indeed, these guided mechanisms, where firmly in place, have frequently nurtured a climate of openness vital to the constructive formulation and realization of tangible goals.

■ Forced Political Transitions

Political changes in Africa have come as often in a violent as in a peaceful wrapping. The *military coup d'état* has been the most prevalent way of inducing change against the will of those in office. The incidence of coup attempts and successful military takeovers in Africa is exceedingly high: most countries on the continent have experienced at least one threat of a military intervention, and in 1999 almost half were still governed by soldiers or by soldiers turned civilians.

The recurrence of military coups highlights the pervasiveness of conditions supportive of armed incursions into the political realm. Certainly, theories on the underlying causes of military intervention differ in the relative weight they place on environmental, external, organizational, idiosyncratic, and systemic factors.[5] Although this is not the place to delve into the vast literature on the subject, the militarization of politics in Africa may be explained by reference to a combination of several variables.

First, economic stagnation, and especially rapid decreases in standards of living, foster political uncertainty and intensify demands for change.[6] Second, military takeovers are, therefore, frequently tied to the loss of political legitimacy of the incumbent government, to the shrinkage of its ruling coalition. In these circumstances, there are few popular constraints to prevent armed intervention. Third, military coups are integrally linked to low levels of institutionalization and relatively high levels of factional competition.[7] Direct military action is probable under these conditions.

Fourth, access to most African regimes (and the rewards they offer) is circumscribed. Military intervention is one way of allowing factions excluded from the governing alliance to gain control of the state and its resources. Fifth, then, there must be some military predisposition to articulate its corporate interest and to act on these perceptions.[8] Sixth, personal ambitions of individual soldiers also play a role. Many studies seeking to uncover why a specific coup took place fall back on idiosyncratic explications.[9] Seventh, precedents do matter. Successful coups in neighboring countries may have a contagion effect, spurring a rash of attempted takeovers.

Over time, African armies in most countries have been integrated into the political arena.[10] Thus, in many respects, military coups are an outgrowth of and have contributed to the ineffectiveness, inefficiency, and, most significant, the fragility of the power apparatus in many of those countries.

It is, perhaps, as important to point to reasons why coups have not taken place as to analyze the elements conducive to their occurrence. Malawi, Zambia, Tanzania, Kenya, Angola, Mozambique, Zimbabwe, Gabon, Côte d'Ivoire, Cameroon, Botswana, Swaziland, Senegal, and Morocco did not experience successful military takeovers in the first four decades of African independence. In some of these countries, external military support was instrumental in putting down attempted coups (Kenya, Gabon, Gambia); the location of foreign military bases there has served as an ongoing deterrent. Other countries (Angola, Mozambique) were involved in civil wars. Some countries simply did not establish an army at independence. In a few places the lack of a military takeover may be attributable to sheer luck. Usually, however, the skillful management of civil-military relations and the gradual legitimation of civilian institutions provide the key for the successful deflection of military takeovers.[11] Political skill, in the sense of astute responsiveness to demands and the initiation of reforms, plays an important role. Indeed, the subordination of the military to civilian institutions through the use of a variety of techniques, such as indigenization, reorganization, professionalization, adequate finance, and appropriate training, has gone a long way toward averting coups. When these measures have been accompanied by the implantation of acceptable methods for changes in government within existing regimes, takeovers have perhaps been attempted but have rarely succeeded.

The proliferation of coups in Africa does not, however, imply that all military takeovers have been similar or that the immediate motivations underlying them have always been identical.[12] The history of military interventions reveals important shifts in the objectives of soldiers turned politicians and in the types of political changes their actions have generated. Initial uprisings in the armed forces, dating back to the 1963 mutinies in Kenya, Tanzania, and Uganda, were spurred by internal military concerns: low salaries, slow rates of Africanization in the officer corps, poor service conditions. Though primarily in the mode of a trade union dispute, these first stirrings were a precursor of broader army political action.

The early 1960s also furnished evidence of a more abrupt type of transition brought about by violent means: *political assassination*. The murder of Togo's Sylvanus Olympio in 1963 was the first instance of such an occurrence; the death of Colonel E. K. Kotoka in Ghana in 1967, and of Murtala Mohammed in Nigeria in 1976 at the hands of army officers are other examples of this phenomenon. More recently, the killing of Samuel Doe in Liberia, Thomas Sankara in Burkina Faso, and successive leaders in Rwanda and Burundi in the early 1990s are cases in point. In these instances, the effective head of state or a key political personality was eliminated, and his regime collapsed with him.

By the end of the 1960s, quite a few civilian regimes had been ousted by the armed forces in full-scale military takeovers. The common purpose of all these interventions was to depose ruling coalitions and their leaders and to establish other dominant alliances in their stead. First coups, therefore, in the 1980s as well as in the preceding decades, have always signaled a regime change, in the sense that the principles, rules, and behavioral patterns of incoming rulers differed from those of their predecessors. Other than that, however, initial coups did not indicate a shift in political orientations or in decisionmaking procedures or practices in any one common direction. The only certainty was that the new leaders would adopt approaches that differed from those of their discredited precursors. The Ghanaian and Nigerian coups of 1966 and the Mobutu takeover in Congo in 1965 provided ample substantiation for the observation that the meaning of initial military interventions (and many subsequent ones as well) lay mostly in the circulation of ruling elites (the Guinea coup in 1985 offers a more recent example).

Frequently, countercoups (the Gowon intervention in Nigeria in 1966, a series of military takeovers in Dahomey—now Benin—in the 1960s) revealed deep divisions within the military hierarchy. Although first coups were carried out either by senior, middle-level, or junior officers (in some cases by noncommissioned officers, such as Samuel Doe in Liberia), countercoups have often been initiated by soldiers of a rank lower than the initial military incumbents.

By the end of the 1970s, repeated military interventions in some countries (Benin, Ghana, Nigeria, Uganda) exposed a more complex pattern of military-induced political change. First, the putsch technique had come into use: the impeachment of the ruling military leader to protect the interests of the military clique in power. The forced abdication of Acheampong in Ghana and of Gowon and later Mohammed Buhari in Nigeria highlighted a growing tendency of senior military officers to preempt more radical change by regulating what they perceived to be unacceptable behavior by incumbents. The putsch, therefore, has become a method for bringing about a change in leadership without a change in government.

Second, some coups had become instruments of political reform, as in the populist-inspired interventions of Jerry Rawlings and Thomas Sankara. In these cases, fragments of the military, usually led by young officers joined by rank-and-file soldiers, challenged not only the previous ruling coalition but also, more fundamentally, the hegemony of dominant elites in general.[13] The possible degree of change wrought by such coups has been more extensive than in most managed modes of political transition until the 1990s.

This trend, third, was particularly apparent in the handful of instances where military leaders sought, through recurrent coups or internal reordering within the army, to lay the foundation for a more comprehensive redistribution of power in the society. The second or third coups in Ethiopia, Congo-Brazzaville, Madagascar, Mali, Chad, Benin, and Burundi pointed to the fact that the possibility of significant change in postcolonial situations, however rare, has usually been set in motion by military men. Fourth, at least in two cases—the ouster of Idi Amin in Uganda and of Jean-Bedel Bokassa in the Central African Republic—a countercoup has involved the direct intervention of external forces. In these instances, the political center was weakened for a considerable time. Finally, in 1986, Yoweri Museveni, at the head of an armed movement, defeated the military in power in Uganda. This latest Ugandan takeover was an example of a privately organized army assuming control of the center, and it paved the way for a reconstruction of the social order in Uganda. In 1991, the regimes in Liberia, Somalia, and Ethiopia were toppled in a similar manner and a similar pattern recurred in Sierra Leone and Congo in the late 1990s.

The political implications of the involvement of the military in African politics have, therefore, appeared to diverge over the years. Although, in general, transition by coercion has implied little more than the rotation of factions in the political center, during the past decade the coup has been a tool, on the one hand, to obviate any political change or, on the other hand, to set the stage for a more basic political transformation. These latter patterns are especially significant as, with the exceptions of Guinea and Tunisia in the 1980s and Gambia in 1994, no first military takeovers have occurred since 1980. These variations may be more a reflection of the diversification of political and social conditions on the continent in the 1980s and 1990s than of drastic changes in the impact of military interventions on political change. "As society changes, so does the role of the military. In the world of the oligarchy, the soldier is a radical; in the middle-class world he is a participant and arbiter; as the mass society looms on the horizon, he becomes the conservative guardian of the existing order."[14]

Military regimes, once in power, have generally not diverged markedly from their civilian counterparts. Some have been more efficient, others more corrupt; in some countries their rulers have been technocrats, in others they have developed into tyrants; some have constructed viable social alliances, others have failed.[15] Any attempt to go beyond the specific case in drawing conclusions on the performance of soldiers as governors would be missing the central point that in the vast majority of African countries, the means by which formal power has been achieved, whether violent or not, are less significant than how that power has been used and for what ends. Thus, although later military interventions may have opened the door for widening the opportunities for political participation, it is the conduct of the new regime and its leadership that has been the key to such political transformations.

This is especially true of military governments, as they confront, more directly than civilian regimes, continuous problems of legitimation. Within a few years of their rise to power, they face a choice between attempting to routinize their rule or handing over power to civilians.[16] Military governments are consequently inherently transitory: if they do not reform themselves, they will be replaced. Many leaders have opted for a process of civilianization: the general becomes a president, a party is formed, symbolic elections are held (Congo [Zaire], Togo, Mali in the 1970s and 1980s, Benin, Ghana, Uganda in the 1990s). In the late 1970s and early 1980s more subtle techniques were employed. Acheampong in Ghana suggested a representative no-party Union government with ongoing military involvement as a way of staying in power (an idea resurrected by Jerry Rawlings a decade later). The merits of a military-civilian dyarchy have been debated in Nigeria since the beginning of the 1980s. The most stable governments actually retaining a military label in Africa—and several have consolidated their positions in the past decade—co-opted civilians into decisionmaking circles or engaged in mass mobilization (Ghana, for one). In some cases, the military has disengaged from politics, usually to return within several years either because the successor civilian government duplicates problems of previous administrations or because civil-military relations in such circumstances are severely strained.[17] In many instances, therefore, one military regime is replaced with another, and, unless halted, a cycle of unplanned and unstable transition ensues.

The military has not proven to be essential to the conduct of politics in Africa, even though it has gradually become an integral part of that process. Military engagements in political affairs have led to political fluctuation, although not necessarily to political movement. In some cases, military coups have been the only way to depose oppressive regimes; these acts have not, however, provided any guarantee that the incoming military leaders would behave any differently (Uganda in the late 1970s and early and mid-1980s, Liberia, Rwanda, Burundi in the 1990s). Most of Africa's tyrants have been military men; so have some of its more enlightened rulers. The African experience with the military coup as a mechanism of political change has been, at best, equivocal; the fascination with military politics has all too often diverted analyses away from the careful scrutiny of political process and obfuscated the centrality of other instruments of transition and change.

Violence, nevertheless, potentially if not actually, may be a central catalyst for political transformation. Countries that have undergone civil wars have frequently emerged from these confrontations not only intact but also with well-defined political centers. The possibility of revolutionary change, which inevitably involves violence, cannot be summarily dismissed. Localized rebellions and disturbances may be transforming African politics from below: the war against the Mengistu regime led to the creation of Eritrea in 1993; Rwanda, Burundi, and segments of Congo have been in turmoil since the genocides of 1994. Even if external powers impose change from outside, this may involve some recourse to force, as in the attempts to intervene in Somalia in the early 1990s.

In the meantime, however, violent transitions have generally constituted more of a manifestation of chronic political uncertainty than an instrument for its elimination. Like their nonviolent counterparts, they may be conceived of as different attempts by those in the political center to alter aspects of its operations.

■ The Course of Postcolonial Political Change

How political transitions have been effected in Africa in the past provides only a crude guide to the degree and direction of political change on the continent. Managed political transitions do not generally offer opportunities for the radical redefinition of the political process; violent mechanisms may slightly enlarge the options in this regard, but usually prevent the regularization of political practices and foster a climate of unpredictability. What these methods do not reflect is the possibility of the existence of other sources of transformation outside the dominant power constellation. It is not inconceivable that as the state cannot change itself, society, through its interaction with government agencies over time, might impose its wishes on the state, as it has begun to do more systematically in recent years. For the most part, therefore, these formal mechanisms reveal the methods in which change will take place. Supervised modes are usually evolutionary and continuous; violent ones may be disruptive and disjointed. The regime map of Africa at the end of the century (as Appendix 3 demonstrates) is totally different from the one seen at independence. Political processes have shifted, largely as a result of varying patterns of interchange set in motion by global economic trends, material circumstances, and the exercise of choice by actors at all levels of social organization.

■ PATTERNS OF POLITICAL INTERACTION

The political experiences of African countries since independence have yielded differing modes of interchange between specific regimes and their local constituencies. The frequency and the nature of these relationships are reflective not only of the relative success or failure of governmental efforts to penetrate the dense social matrix in their countries; they also mirror the willingness of individuals and groups to collaborate with official agencies and to involve themselves in their activities. The resilience of indigenous social institutions and practices has meant that the effectiveness of official designs has been filtered through local interests, needs, values, and concerns. The exercise of political power has, therefore, been a function both of the resources, capacities, objectives, techniques, and political conduct of ruling elites and of the vulnerability, organization, and priorities of specific communities.[18]

Forms of political interaction have varied substantially in different countries since independence. In some instances, center domination has been achieved; in others, increasingly larger portions of the population have sought to detach themselves from the reach of government agents. In most instances, however, intricate combinations of autonomy and reciprocity have prevailed. South Africa until the rise of de Klerk, Rhodesia until the independence of Zimbabwe, and Burundi during the 1960s lie at one extreme on this continuum. In these countries the regime was particularly repressive and possessed few structural linkages with the bulk of the population. Local communities had very limited autonomous resources at their disposal and were extremely vulnerable to outside interference. The other extreme on the continuum is best illustrated by the recurrent cases of Chad and Uganda during the 1970s and early 1980s and Liberia, Sudan, Congo, Rwanda, and Somalia in the 1990s. In these countries the political center, for much of the postcolonial period, could barely muster control of the capital city. Local communities devised ways of disengaging from the center and its vagaries: They mobilized their own resources, established autonomous systems of justice, sought protection behind warlords, and reduced their exposure (although not always their vulnerability) to the center. Political life was unpredictable and haphazard.

In between these two extremes, various dynamic patterns of political interaction emerged, including those of individual domination (as in Mobutu's Zaire and Equatorial Guinea), state-society confrontation (the mark of many former Afro-Marxist countries), and subtle forms of vertical interchange (Malawi, Côte d'Ivoire, Cameroon, and Gabon).[19] In Nigeria, Kenya, and Zambia, competition, often of an unproductive sort, intruded.[20] On the other hand, Senegal and Botswana have permitted relatively participatory patterns to evolve, and reciprocity (albeit unequal) is in evidence in these and a growing number of second- and third-wave competitive regimes.[21] Ghana and Sierra Leone have exhibited intermittent rhythms of state-society transactions, whereas in Tanzania local communities have been able to detach themselves from the formal arena.[22]

By the late 1990s, it had become clear that certain countries, as presently constituted, could hardly expect more than continued unrest, decline, or stagnation. In others, the severity of the crisis of the 1980s and 1990s evoked certain adjustments: more responsible financial management, cutbacks in the public sector, a relaxation of repression, decentralization, and even competitive elections. Most significantly, the realization that the monopolization of official power by authoritarian means had limited utility and hence that political problems required political solutions had been grimly drawn to the attention of many of the continent's leaders. Through a process of forced reckoning, introspection, and consultation, some have not only assumed fuller responsibility for their predicament, but have also begun to seek ways to break away from the deleterious consequences of authoritarian rule.

The quest for a stable and more effective form of government has elicited a growing distaste for military interventions and a search, even in centers led by soldiers, for the establishment or institutionalization of political procedures and practices based not on patrimonial principles but on some constitutional notions of power sharing and reciprocity between rulers and ruled. Although these efforts have generally yielded only limited results, they do indicate a willingness to deal with issues that had heretofore been considered taboo. And indeed, a growing number of countries are opting for this course (though political despair reigns in others). Intrinsic to these processes is an understanding that if the political center is to be consolidated, the method for its entrenchment may have to commence with the creation of organized mechanisms of interchange between it and its social environments, especially in light of shifts in social organization and in the direction of social and economic transactions. Such a process involves the localization of political change—in all probability, an even greater diversity in political practices and dynamics. In some, although surely not all, countries these initiatives may signify the beginning phase of African constitutional processes. Whatever their outcome, the scope of choice has been expanded and with it the range of change mechanisms and the possible directions of political transformation.[23]

The outlines of African political dynamics—despite their vagaries and marked fluctuations—have coalesced substantially during the few short years since independence. Political centers have established themselves and devised means to extend their reach, not always resourcefully, to the countryside. Although dependence on government has become inescapable, lateral transactions among formerly separate individuals and groups have increased and been given expression through new social networks pressing for a modicum of reciprocity in the conduct of political life. These demands are not the preserve of any one ideal regime type; they do, however, require the normalization of effective, and stable, checks on power. Indeed, workable government structures buttressed by norms of regime conduct may be a precondition for fortifying state capacities. The political challenge, therefore, in the years ahead as African countries move from the postcolonial to the independence phase of their development, focuses squarely on the delineation of firm criteria for accountability and the construction of structures to guarantee their enforcement.[24]

Good government is inextricably tied to economic prospects. Probity curbs the dissipation of resources; obligations and responsibilities may engender greater efficiency. Stability is surely a precondition for development. Economic policies cannot be effective if their political prerequisites are not in place.

Political processes have to do with modes of decisionmaking, not with their substance. "The problem is not where you should be trying to go, but how you should get there."[25] The procedures, practices, and underlying premises of political conduct have had a direct bearing on the selection of domestic and foreign policies and on the manner in which they have been carried out. Indeed, the content of African politics cannot usefully be separated from the ways politics work on the continent.

■ NOTES

1. Victor T. Le Vine, "The Politics of Presidential succession," *Africa Report* 28, no. 3 (1983): 22–26.

2. Naomi Chazan, "African Voters at the Polls: A Reexamination of the Role of Elections in African Politics," *Journal of Commonwealth and Comparative Politics* 17, no. 2 (1979): 135–158. Also see Dennis L. Cohen, "Elections and Election Studies in Africa," in Yolamu Barongo, ed., *Political Science in Africa: A Critical Review* (London: Zed Press, 1983), pp. 72–93, and Fred M. Hayward, ed., *Elections in Independent Africa* (Boulder: Westview Press, 1986).

3. It is interesting that such limited competition was being considered by former President Mikhail Gorbachev in the Soviet Union in 1987, prior to the more massive changes that took place in 1991.

4. For a good discussion of these issues and of the Nigerian case, see Richard A. Joseph, "Democratization Under Military Tutelage: Crisis and Consensus in the Nigerian 1979 Elections," *Comparative Politics* 14, no. 1 (1981): 75–100.

5. These debates are summarized well in Roger Charlton, "Plus Ça Change? A Review of Two Decades of Theoretical Analyses of African Coups d'Etat," *Cultures et Développement* 13, no. 1/2 (1981): 26–62. Also see L. Adele Jinadu, "Why the Guns Are Never Silent: Military Coups in Africa," *Afriscope* (July 1979): 13–19.

6. Pat McGowan and Thomas H. Johnson, "African Military Coups d'Etat and Underdevelopment: A Quantitative Historical Analysis," *Journal of Modern African Studies* 22, no. 4 (1984): 633–666.

7. Robert Jackman, "The Predictability of Coups d'Etat: A Model with African Data," *American Political Science Review* 72, no. 4 (1978): 1262–1275.

8. William Gutteridge, *The Military in African Politics* (London: Methuen, 1968).

9. Samuel Decalo, *Coups and Army Rule in Africa* (New Haven: Yale University Press, 1975). Also see his "Praetorianism, Corporate Grievances and Idiosyncratic Factors in African Military Hierarchies," *Journal of African Studies* 2, no. 2 (1975): 247–273, and "The Colonel in the Command Car: Towards a Reexamina-

tion of Motives for Military Intervention in Africa," *Cultures et Développement* 5, no. 4 (1973): 765–778.

10. David L. Huff and James M. Lutz, "The Contagion of Political Unrest in Independent Africa," *Economic Geography* 50 (1974): 352–367; J. I. Elagwu, "Military Intervention in Politics: An African Perspective," *Geneve-Afrique* 19, no. 1 (1981): 17–38.

11. David Goldsworthy, "Civilian Control of the Military in Black Africa," *African Affairs* 318 (1981): 49–71; Elise Forbes Pachter, "Contra-Coup: Civilian Control of the Military in Guinea, Tanzania and Mozambique," *Journal of Modern African Studies* 20, no. 4 (1982): 595–612; and Agola Auma-Osolo, "Objective African Military Control: A New Paradigm in Civil Military Relations," *Journal of Peace Research* 17, no. 1 (1980): 29–46.

12. Roger Charlton, "Predicting African Military Coups," *Futures* (August 1983): 281–291.

13. Maxwell Owusu, "Custom and Coups: A Juridical Interpretation of Civil Order and Disorder," *Journal of Modern African Studies* 24, no. 1 (1986): 72.

14. Samuel Huntington, *Political Order in Changing Societies* (New Haven: Yale University Press, 1968), p. 221.

15. Isaac James Mowoe, ed., *The Performance of Soldiers as Governors: African Politics and the African Military* (Washington, DC.: University Press of America, 1980); William Gutteridge, *Military Regimes in Africa* (London: Methuen, 1975); R. D. McKinlay and D. D. Cohan, "A Comparative Analysis of the Political and Economic Performance of Military and Civilian Regimes," *Comparative Politics* 8, no. 1 (1975): 1–30; Eric A. Nordlinger, "Soldiers in Mufti: The Impact of Military Rule Upon Economic and Social Change in Non-Western Society," *American Political Science Review* 64, no. 4 (1970): 1131–1149; and John Ravenhill, "Comparing Regime Performance in Africa: The Limits of Cross-National Aggregate Analysis," *Journal of Modern African Studies* 18, no. 1 (1980): 99–126.

16. Claude E. Welch, "Military Disengagement from Politics," *Armed Forces and Society* 9, no. 4 (1983): esp. 539–540. Also see William Gutteridge, "Undoing Military Coups in Africa," *Third World Quarterly* 7, no. 1 (1985): 78–89.

17. Christopher Clapham, *Third World Politics: An Introduction* (Madison: University of Wisconsin Press, 1985), p. 156.

18. Jonathan Barker, "Local-Central Relations: A Perspective on the Politics of Development in Africa," *Canadian Journal of African Studies* 4, no. 1 (1970): 3–16.

19. Michael Cohen, "The Myth of the Expanding Center: Politics in the Ivory Coast," *Journal of Modern African Studies* 11, no. 2 (1973): 227–246; and Martin Staniland, "The Rhetoric of Centre-Periphery Relations," *Journal of Modern African Studies* 8, no. 4 (1970): 617–636.

20. Frank Holmquist, "Toward a Political Theory of Rural Self-Help Development in Africa," *Rural Africana* 18 (1972): 60–80 and esp. 76. For a superb case study, see Sara Berry, *Fathers Work for Their Sons: Accumulation, Mobility and Class Formation in an Extended Yoruba Community* (Berkeley: University of California Press, 1985).

21. Donal Cruise O'Brien, "Des bienfaits de l'inégalité: L'état et l'économie rurale au Sénégal," *Politique africaine* 14 (1984): 34–38; Jonathan Barker, ed., *The Politics of Agriculture in Tropical Africa* (Beverly Hills: Sage Publications, 1984).

22. Walter Barrows, *Grassroots Politics in an African State: Integration and Development in Sierra Leone* (New York: Africana Publishing Co., 1976). Also see Roger Tangri, *Politics in Sub-Saharan Africa* (London: James Currey, 1985), pp.

39–42. On Tanzania, see Zaki Ergas, "Why Did the Ujamaa Village Policy Fail? Towards a Global Analysis," *Journal of Modern African Studies* 18, no. 3 (1980): 387–410, and Goran Hyden, *Beyond Ujamaa in Tanzania: Underdevelopment and an Uncaptured Peasantry* (Berkeley: University of California Press, 1980).

23. There is much more discussion around the idea of democracy, partly motivated by Richard L. Sklar's challenging African Studies Association presidential address, "Democracy in Africa," published in the *African Studies Review* 26, no. 3/4 (1983). Also see Robert H. Jackson and Carl G. Rosberg's more sober analysis, "Democracy in Tropical Africa: Democracy Versus Autocracy in African Politics," *Journal of International Affairs* 38, no. 2 (1985): 293–305.

24. John Dunn, "The Politics of Representation and Good Government in Post-Colonial Africa," in Patrick Chabal, ed., *Political Domination in Africa: Reflections on the Limits of Power* (London: Cambridge University Press, 1986), p. 177.

25. Clapham, *Third World Politics*, p. 186.

Part 3

POLITICAL ECONOMY

9

Coping with Transformation:
Approaches
to Development

The travails of economic development have played a defining role in African states and societies. Economic growth and transition are clearly important as sources of popular welfare, material output, and public revenues. Economic change also affects the composition of social groups, as well as their relative opportunities and constraints. Material conditions affect the resources available to key political actors. At the same time, political regimes and the balance of societal interests are often crucial for economic outcomes. The reciprocal interactions of economic and political factors are evident in the fortunes of state-building and social mobilization in Africa, as well as in the more obvious aspects of economic performance. This section considers the structures, attributes, and prevailing patterns of economic development in Africa, with special attention to the political context of economic policy.

African countries, regardless of regime type or ideology, have confronted three general challenges of economic development in the postcolonial era: poverty, structural transformation, and dependence. The dilemma of poverty is the most glaring and fundamental of these issues. The region has reflected predominantly low-income economies, with a high incidence of mass impoverishment and generally inadequate standards of living. The difficult tasks of raising average incomes and improving levels of welfare have preoccupied myriad leaders and organizations.

The second challenge, that of structural transformation, concerns efforts toward economic diversification and higher productivity. Historically, African economies have been predominantly agrarian, embodying labor-intensive forms of production, low levels of industrialization, and a narrow foundation of trade. The goals of structural transformation include efforts to expand manufacturing, to broaden the range of tradable products in various sectors, and to shift labor toward more productive areas of the economy. This also calls for a more intensive application of capital and technology to raise levels of efficiency and output. The process is complex and entails an array of changes in investment, production, labor, and institutions.

The third challenge, that of managing or reducing economic dependence, is perhaps the most imposing goal of African countries and certainly the most acutely felt. As we have noted, Africans have broadly affirmed the objectives of self-sustaining growth and a more autonomous footing in the international economy. African states emerging from colonialism confronted a host of problems arising from a disadvantageous position in global markets. Trade patterns constituted one important source of dependence. African economies, formed in the colonial mold, were generally outward-oriented, reliant on external trade for crucial goods and revenues. Most countries exported a few primary commodities for essential hard currency, and virtually all economies in the region were highly dependent on imported manufactures. Alongside the vulnerabilities of trade dependence African economies also exhibited substantial reliance upon external capital, technology, and expertise to provide basic functions. Aspirations for greater economic independence and dynamism have been expressed through distinctive national development strategies and regional and global initiatives.

■ THE RANGE OF CHOICE

A crucial question woven through debates over African development concerns the relative latitude for choice available to states in the region. Although there has been wide agreement on the problems of economic dependence and underdevelopment, analysts differ over possibilities for managing or overcoming the historical impediments to economic change. The theoretical approaches discussed in Chapter 1 provide different answers to this fundamental question. Classic modernization theory was guardedly optimistic about the prospects for African countries, asserting that forward-looking governments assisted by the necessary inputs of external capital could generate transformation and growth. The key policies for change included the expansion of infrastructure and educational programs, as well as the maintenance of a hospitable setting for foreign investment. From the modernization perspective, governments were essentially benign (or at least neutral), whereas foreign aid and investment provided important resources for development.

The modernization view was repudiated by underdevelopment theorists, who argued that African economies were sharply constrained by domestic structural arrangements and by their position in the world economy. From this perspective the range of choice for African leaders was extremely narrow and the possibilities for autonomous development were rather limited. By virtue of their historical inheritance and the continuing inequalities in global markets, African economies were relegated largely to slow growth and chronic impoverishment, or at best a distorted, insecure form of "dependent development."[1] Moreover, theorists of underdevelopment—especially adherents of the dependency school—challenged the assumption of the benign state, arguing instead that African elites were active collaborators in the inertia and immiseration of their own economies. They advocated radical solutions for this developmental impasse, including socialist strategies and selective withdrawal from international markets. State control, autarky, and collective self-reliance were the watchwords of this approach.

Theories of underdevelopment usefully emphasize the international setting of development, and they draw attention to the role of economic and political structures rather than focusing simply on sociocultural endowments and short-term policy issues. These writers also challenge the presumption that state leaders are necessarily concerned with economic advancement. In recognizing that local elites are often self-interested or predatory, underdevelopment theorists have elucidated important features of the region's political economy.

Despite these contributions, the scope and assumptions of the underdevelopment perspective remain too restrictive to gain a comprehensive view of the problems of African development. By assuming that development is mainly a function of external forces, these theorists discount the significance of domestic factors in economic change, commonly overlooking the importance of national political institutions and policy choices. Yet the importance of internal factors in growth and change is evident in the distinctive economic strategies pursued by African regimes and the variations in performance throughout the region. Underdevelopment theory also tends to reduce diverse countries to uniform structures and problems, overlooking significant disparities among regions of the world. The fact that developing regions such as Southeast Asia and Latin America have achieved more substantial levels of economic development despite similar external constraints casts doubt on the pessimistic homogenizing premises of underdevelopment theory.

The approach taken here, in keeping with the political interaction framework elaborated in Chapter 1, emphasizes the political context of economic change and the mutual relationship of economic and political factors in development. We assume that elites have significant choice and that domestic political arrangements and policies are consequential for economic change. Decisions made by political leaders are important for developmental outcomes, even if nominal policies are not the only factor shaping performance. The latitude for policy selection and structural change is limited by physical endowments, historical legacies, and the influence of

external forces. But African policymakers and interest groups have voli-
tion, however constrained, and this suggests the possibility of different
paths to achieve economic growth and development. Consequently, any inquiry into the developmental challenges of African countries must account
for the influence of internal forces and public policies. Political leaders,
state institutions, and social coalitions are dynamic elements in the general
setting for economic growth.

The historical evolution of African economies has reflected diverse
factors. Ecology and demography have played important roles in shaping
the contours of the region's economic systems. Despite the great variety of
climates and types of geography on the continent, a general ecological
constraint has restricted settlement patterns and agricultural productivity.
Outside the more favorable zones of the Mediterranean and southern
Africa, soils in the region tend to be thin and nutrient-poor and thus difficult to work intensively. Rainfall is generally insufficient in semi-arid and
savanna areas. In the forest zones precipitation is erratic, veering between
drought and downpour. The inundation of the rainy season often leaches
nutrients from the soil and fosters erosion. Also, as mentioned earlier, the
African continent is host to a daunting array of tropical diseases and parasites, including malaria, bilharzia (schistosomiasis), river blindness (onchocerciasis), and sleeping sickness (trypanosomiasis, transmitted by the
tsetse fly). Mosquito and tsetse infestations have prevented settlement and
husbandry, in some areas, and the populations of even the more hospitable
regions are commonly subject to debilitating maladies. More recently, the
devastating impact of AIDS has also taken a toll on development, particularly in central and southern Africa.

Demographic factors have been equally consequential for economic
change in Africa. In this realm we observe that colonialism prompted fundamental change. Historically, most of the continent reflected low population densities and slow growth rates. The combination of labor shortage,
land abundance, and limited competition for resources gave rise to
economies that were relatively secure and ecologically sustainable yet that
had modest propensities for productivity increases. With the advent of
colonialism, these factors shifted decisively. Changes in public health, settlement, and production patterns fostered a demographic transition leading
to vigorous and sustained population growth. Population pressures placed
new demands on production and distributive systems, a process aggravated
in many instances by colonial policies. The transitions from land abundance
to land scarcity and from labor shortage to labor surplus have been important features of regional economies throughout much of the past century.

These inherent features provide only one set of influences on economic
change in the region. The conditions of Africa's integration into the international economy have been highly consequential for patterns of production,

trade, migration, and adaptation. Africa was not historically an isolated region, and many peoples on the continent reflected long interactions with other civilizations and markets. The advent of European engagement altered the scope and character of external linkages, and the imposition of colonial rule created fundamental changes that have conditioned the economies of independent African states. Colonial regimes shaped the structures of most African economies, including the sectoral distribution of activities, key products in the economy, the extent of physical infrastructure, and the development of human capital. The metropolitan state also defined the terms of investment, taxation, commerce, and external trade. Despite the considerable changes in African political economies since independence, many of these features and relationships have persisted. The partial integration of African economies into the global economy, on generally unequal and disadvantageous terms, reflects a legacy extending back to precolonial and colonial times.

Aside from resource factors and the influence of the global economy, African economic development has also been determined by domestic political factors. The forms of political control, the configuration of interest groups, and the character of institutions have all shaped economic policy and performance in independent African states. Modes of leadership, economic doctrine, and policy choice are especially important for development. Political regimes influence social mobilization and the representation of societal interests. The incorporation of such key sectors as agricultural producers, urban workers, and manufacturers commonly has important economic effects. Finally, the development of state institutions shapes a number of important functions that condition the economy—the public bureaucracy and regulatory agencies, transportation and communications, and services including education, health, and housing. The nature of regimes and the qualities of state-building have had a significant impact on the course of economic change in independent Africa.

It is also essential to recognize the ways economic structure and performance have influenced politics in the region. Conditions of economic scarcity hold far-reaching consequences for the needs of society, the legitimacy of governments, and the basis of state resources. Moreover, patterns of growth influence social inequalities and the relative mobilization of different groups. As governments have concentrated their political dominance over African economies, they have relied on statist economic strategies. This interventionist pattern tends to restrict autonomous economic activity and to limit the dispersal of social power. Economic centralization focuses competition over the state as a central source of wealth and accentuates the economic spoils of political office.[2] Finally, as we shall see in the next chapter, the poor performance of African economies over time has been highly consequential for regional patterns of political reform.

■ AFRICA IN THE WORLD ECONOMY

Contemporary problems of African development inevitably cast a shadow over any assessment of the historical evolution of the region's economies. The depredations of the slave trade and the modes of exploitation under colonialism have inspired a widespread view that global economic interactions with Africa have been entirely adverse, a view often linked to the argument that African economies were both shaped and impeded mainly by forces from outside the region. In the least sophisticated version put forth by dependency theorists, Africa's indigenous systems have been progressively subordinated by foreign powers during the past three centuries, resulting in the purposeful "underdevelopment" of the region. From this vantage, integration into the international economy is the principal source of economic backwardness.[3]

This argument does much injustice to the breadth and nuance of African experience, not least because it reduces Africans to mere objects of external domination rather than treating them as subjects and agents of their own history. Moreover, the dependency perspective obscures the range of economic and political systems in the region and the diverse responses to the challenges of external commerce and control. Although the colonial episode was definitive for contemporary African economies, the developmental problems of the postcolonial era cannot be attributed simply to the effects of external control. Underdevelopment theorists often presume that African countries, if unburdened by foreign intervention, would have followed an autonomous transition toward capitalist forms of production and exchange or possibly indigenous forms of socialism. Although imperial control undoubtedly disrupted local processes of accumulation in most of Africa, the historical and structural features of African economies were not necessarily conducive to independent capitalist (or industrial) transformation. A full assessment of the region's development should consider the attributes and limitations of economic change in comparative perspective.

Economic historians have observed that Africa's position in the world economy has been characterized by dependence and marginality.[4] For at least two centuries African economies have reflected a lopsided reliance on external markets and inputs. Somewhat paradoxically, however, the region has generally held a peripheral role in global trade and capital flows. Africa has been a perennial source of goods and resources for foreign markets, yet the extent of global integration has been inhibited by a variety of factors, including adverse geography, fragmented political organization, and limitations of local technology and production. Although one must recognize the constraints created by the imperial powers, it is equally important to note that inherent constraints on growth and innovation have contributed to many contemporary developmental problems. In particular, limited productivity in agriculture, weak infrastructure, and the difficulties of late industrialization have created substantial challenges for economic advancement. African development reflects the combined influences of external and endogenous factors, and both elements must be weighed to understand economic transition in the region.

■ Precolonial Economies

The preceding debates are important for assessing Africa's economies in historical perspective. On the one hand, some analysts have implied that precolonial economies were static, often "irrational" in their choices of technique and organization, and generally incapable of flexibility and adaptation. Underdevelopment theorists, on the other hand, have insisted that African economies displayed a historical succession of change, growth, and dynamism; yet these processes were truncated or distorted by the imposition of colonial rule. To put the debate somewhat more starkly, African economies have been caught between images of primitive stasis or of deliberate suppression. Neither of these vivid depictions provides an accurate view of Africa's complex economic profile prior to colonial rule. Many societies displayed substantial capacities for adaptation and progress, yet endogenous limits on growth and innovation inevitably curbed the extent of economic dynamism.

If we consider global economic change over time, it is possible to identify several factors that have been especially influential in fostering transformations of organization and productivity. Such elements can be witnessed, for example, in the evolution of Mediterranean and northern European economies, as well as in phases of economic change in Asia. One important element has been the pressure of demographic expansion, which compels greater surpluses from existing land and resources.[5] The scope and degree of human migration have also been critical, as intensive contact among peoples fostered opportunities and inducements for commerce. In addition, the dispersal of ideas and technology has frequently disseminated innovation. The demands or disruptions of strategic rivalry and war have exerted multiple effects on economic change. The challenge of an external threat often motivates states to become more efficient and productive to generate resources for military defense.[6] The social upheavals of conflict may force people into new modes of living or make them available for different economic roles.

With these elements in mind, the distinctive historical experience of sub-Saharan Africa is noteworthy. Precolonial Africa exhibited few of the demographic stresses or market outlets mentioned earlier, and these circumstances yielded different patterns of economic evolution. Most of the African region reflected low population pressures, sufficient land, and adequate resources relative to habitation. Contact with other regions, although regular, was also peripheral, a situation offering limited inducements for trade. Dispersed inhabitants, difficulties of transport and communications, and the formidable barriers posed by the Sahara Desert and interior forest zones impeded commerce and contact between neighboring civilizations, especially those of the Mediterranean fringe and central Africa. These limitations probably had beneficial effects in reducing potential conflict between regions, but they also hampered the distribution of technology and commerce, along with broader cultural interactions. The impetus of war and state-building was also relatively limited. African societies reflected conflict and rivalry, and the need for defense spurred the creation of centralized states prior to the nineteenth century. But the limited scale of conflict, combined with constraints on available resources and technology, generally conspired to inhibit large-scale innovations in production and exchange. States were not generally constructed through the intensive mobilization and extraction of resources.

The economic setting. As today, precolonial Africa encompassed a wide array of societies, cultures, and economic patterns. Forest, savanna, and desert peoples exhibited distinct livelihoods and social structures. Settled agriculturalists and nomadic pastoralists coexisted, often uneasily, in many parts of the continent. The region was home to expansive heirarchical states including Axum, Songhai, Borno, and Sokoto, as well as an array of kingdoms or chieftancies such as Ashanti, Benin, Yoruba, and Buganda. Many small-scale, decentralized communities prevailed throughout much of Africa, probably encompassing the majority of the population prior to the colonial era. Most of these "stateless" societies, including the Igbo of West Africa and the Kikuyu in the east, were organized through kinship structures, with few distinct political institutions. Nomadic hunter-gatherer communities were also evident in many areas and in a few instances, notably the !Kung of southern Africa, have survived to the present day.

A few general factors affected economic variation and change throughout precolonial Africa. Ecological conditions, distinctions in settlement and subsistence, and different forms of social and political organization shaped the patterns of economic activity in assorted settings. Some broad parameters of climate and ecology should be kept in mind. The African continent has a comparatively limited percentage of arable land. Because of environmental conditions, the areas available for cultivation generally have low carrying capacities relative to population. Thin laterite soils, uneven rainfall, erosion, and leaching of nutrients are especially prevalent in tropical zones. In savanna and Sahelian zones, erratic and insufficient precipitation has been a general constraint on productivity. The prevalence of tropical diseases and parasites has limited both human settlement and animal range. As observed earlier, the ecological constraint in Africa was historically an obstacle to economic growth, especially in agriculture. Until the late nineteenth century, such conditions also constrained population expansion and the bounds of migration.

Settlement and subsistence. Another source of diversity was the range of settlement patterns and types of economic organization. The agricultural revolution likely began in the Middle East around 10,000 years ago, spreading fairly soon to the African continent. This transition signaled an epochal change in the development of human society. The beginnings of settled agriculture and organized pastoralism signaled a shift from small-scale, nomadic hunter-gatherer societies to larger sedentary communities embodying greater specialization and scale. Agricultural settlement not only made possible larger population concentrations, but the surplus from agriculture was also the basis for broader social, political, and economic organization. In areas such as the Nile valley, where agriculture was the most advanced, substantial societies grew—including the first large-scale urban civilization, that of ancient Egypt, from about the third millennium B.C.[7]

By the time of the Greek and Roman civilizations in Europe (about 500 B.C.–300 A.D.), several trading and administrative kingdoms had emerged in northern and eastern Africa. In the centuries following the emergence of Egyptian civilization, the centers of Carthage and Axum developed in northern and northeastern Africa, respectively. By the ninth and tenth centuries, a period corresponding to the Middle Ages in Europe, similar kingdoms embodying centralized rule and administration were established in western and central Africa. These precolonial societies were not highly urbanized, although commercial and administrative concentrations developed throughout the region from the eleventh through the nineteenth centuries. Prominent centers of commerce and production included Timbuktu, Kano, Benin, and Ashanti in West Africa, as well as Mombasa, Zanzibar, and Great Zimbabwe in eastern and southern Africa.

Despite the presence of commercial and administrative centers, population concentrations were generally sparse and settlement diffuse south of the Nile Valley. A few communities derived a livelihood from trading activities or crafts production, but the great majority of Africans were occupied in subsistence farming and herding, with limited engagement in mercantile networks. Two dominant practices, shifting agriculture and pastoralism, were resilient modes of livelihood that have persisted in many parts of Africa through the present era.

Shifting agriculture was widely employed in the forest and savanna zones of precolonial Africa. This farming system uses land continuously for a limited time, followed by a long period of dormancy. The forms of shifting cultivation vary according to planting techniques, fallow periods, and land tenure patterns.[8] As a generic practice the system has proved well suited to the different soils, rainfall patterns, and crop varieties of the continent. Among the more common forms of shifting cultivation was swidden agriculture, also known as slash-and-burn cultivation, although many households utilized mixed techniques according to plots and ecological zones.

Swidden agriculture is practiced mainly in tropical zones, notably in the forest belts of coastal West Africa and the central African interior. Plots are prepared by cutting down brush and trees and burning the waste on the spot. The ashes and residual materials fertilize the soils, compensating for meager nutrients. Several different plants are intercropped in seemingly haphazard fashion on the plot. The cropping patterns actually mimic the canopy of the forest, providing shade and symbiosis among different flora. Despite these measures, a plot is commonly exhausted after a few years of use and is left to lie fallow for periods ranging from five to twenty-five years as cultivators move on to a new section. Swidden agriculture is a low-technology affair, needing little more than an ax or a machete for felling bush and a digging stick for planting. Obviously, this system requires an abundance of land and a frontier for expansion. If such conditions are met, this technique can yield a durable livelihood for limited populations in poor climatic and agricultural conditions.

Pastoralism, a pattern of subsistence based on the domestication of animals, was commonly practiced in fringe areas of the Sahelian region and other semiarid zones. Relatively small groups of people moved regularly with their grazing herds to take advantage of diverse climatic zones and resources. The community lived from the by-products of animals, occasionally supplementing its needs through hunting, foraging, or trade.

Pastoralism required an extensive range, and nomadic bands often came into contact with other groups and settlements. This precarious livelihood fostered tensions with settled agricultural communities, which resented pastoralists' infringement and their frequent raiding to supplement herds and supplies. The pastoralists' relative mobility and adaptation to a harsh environment afforded them relative advantages in the competition for resources, and in several instances in precolonial Africa pastoralist societies encroached upon or conquered settled agrarian societies. Among the most prominent examples were the dominance of Fulani groups over Hausa communities in West Africa and the hegemony of the Tutsi over the numerically greater Hutu agriculturalists in central Africa. More commonly, agrarian and pastoralist communities coexisted through a mixture of trade and conflict.

By and large, these subsistence activities were based on methods that responded well to adverse conditions but embodied low productivity. They employed extensive rather than intensive utilization of land, as output relied on the availability of a wide territorial domain instead of eliciting increased production from fixed assets.[9] The prevailing techniques and economic organizations were clearly "rational" in the sense of being pragmatic adaptations to existing resources and ecological pressures. Moreover, many traditional economies were sustainable in that they carried relatively stable populations for long periods of time. The great merit of these systems was that they preserved consistent average yields amid uncertain conditions. They were not dynamic, however, in terms of producing dramatic increases in output or quickly improving technology and production methods. The comparative isolation of African societies served to maintain relative economic stability and stasis. Lacking powerful incentives for economic expansion, for centuries most of the region experienced few essential changes in subsistence, technology, and exchange.

Aside from the predominance of agriculture and pastoralism, other economic activities throughout the continent included crafts production, mining, and commerce. In many parts of Africa during the first millennium A.D., metallurgy was well established. The smelting and working of iron, bronze, copper, and gold became widespread in many areas between the ninth and sixteenth centuries. Iron and bronze work was most common, yielding a few utilitarian objects such as cutting blades but more often devoted to the production of objects of ritual and prestige commissioned by rulers and elders. Metallurgical work was frequently the domain of specified lineages or castes, and in some areas guild formations governed the craft. In addition, skills such as textile production, carpentry, and other specialized occupations were practiced at community levels. Overall, these trades provided products for local use rather than for large-scale commercial output. Mining was practiced by indigenous peoples with low technology and on a modest scale. These activities provided basic goods such as ore and salt for community needs and some trade.

In several entrepôt settlements throughout Africa, commerce provided an important source of livelihood. Long-distance trade had to contend with formidable transport and communication barriers. Deserts and forests were largely inimical to the use of wheeled transport, and camel caravans were the central means of traversing the Sahara. For centuries the limited range and capacity of animal carriage, as well as prevailing maritime routes to Asia, confined the volume of interregional trade. Long-distance commerce nonetheless developed around gold, salt, and slaves, as well as other goods such as palm oil. This trade was conducted principally with the Mediterranean fringe of north Africa and the Middle East, as well as Red Sea networks and the ports of Oman and Yemen. There were also intermittent maritime contacts as distant as India, Indonesia, and China. After the fifteenth century ocean-borne trade with Europe was an important feature of economic life in the region. Entrepôts thrived in the Sahelian region, the Atlantic and Indian Ocean coasts, and interior settlements in present-day Mali, Zimbabwe, and Sudan.

Social and political influences. Social and political organization throughout Africa carried distinctive implications for economic organization. A number of centralized empires and kingdoms embodied administrative principles, governing through a set of officials whose authority was delegated by a central ruler. Some of these systems, such as Dahomey, were fairly sophisticated in monitoring and regulating land distribution, production, and commercial relations.[10] Although several centralized forest kingdoms encompassed substantial areas and populations, few traditional political structures governed large-scale societies or managed complex economies. Segmentary lineage societies were generally characterized by dispersed household production and limited market integration.

African societies embraced different forms of social differentiation. In the central highlands of Ethiopia and the emirate system under Sokoto, a form of feudal relations emerged in which aristocratic elites controlled the lands and fealty of cultivators. Social divisions varied in the forest kingdoms. Rulers typically exacted tribute from their subjects and held sway over the circulation of wealth, according privileged status to a set of royal kinsmen, retainers, and warriors. A number of communities contained domestic slaves and subordinate castes, and gender roles were commonly unequal. In some centralized states and most "stateless" societies, the large body of commoners enjoyed relative equality in the distribution of assets and status.

The normative and social setting of African economic relations is also significant. The definition of property rights and the division of labor are reinforced by social relationships and rationalized by cultural norms. Family and kinship structures, authority relations, and prevailing views of morality commonly define economic practices. Economies are "embedded" in society to a significant degree, and the social setting creates an environment for persistence or change.[11] Social relations in precolonial Africa embodied features that engendered continuity but also produced rigidities that inhibited domestic transformation. Rulers' personal discretion over allocation of wealth restricted the distribution of resources. The use of social or kinship networks to facilitate exchange often hampered market expansion. Practices of social reciprocity and mutual aid fostered community welfare yet frequently constituted barriers to transactions beyond the local level.[12] Inflexible social roles limited labor mobility. Many of these aspects of African societies and economies survived the colonial era.

Although traditional polities and economic institutions were capable of managing dispersed agrarian systems, few could accommodate the challenges of political organization and economic transition that confronted them after the seventeenth century. During the centuries prior to colonial partition Africa was profoundly influenced by external contact, reflecting an expansion of domestic commerce and significant incorporation into external commodity markets. African rulers, producers, and entrepreneurs responded to incentives for greater trade and output, and they were flexible in their production and investment decisions. Through the late nineteenth century, however, growth depended on increased utilization of land and labor within existing methods of production. There were significant but limited innovations in productivity and scant evidence of a local impetus toward industrialization. Major catalysts of change in the region came mostly from without, and Africa was recast by the successive influences of trade, military challenges, cultural encounters, and foreign domination.

Contact and Colonization

European involvement in Africa spanned around 500 years. The Portuguese were the first Europeans to establish regular contact with the continent, as the "voyages of discovery" ranged down the western African coast in the late fifteenth century. In the decades that followed, Portugal established a series of fortified coastal settlements and trading entrepôts that were eventually followed by British, French, Dutch, German, Belgian, Spanish, and Italian ventures. For nearly three centuries the European presence in Africa was confined largely to coastal enclaves, as outsiders were deterred by the formidable barriers of forest and desert and the hazards of dealing with peoples in the interior zones. European commercial undertakings were commonly supported by armed force, although merchants and adventurers generally relied on diplomacy or commercial incentives to secure relationships with indigenous rulers. The colonial impulse was not fully apparent until the mid–nineteenth century.

Along with the activities of Arab and Indian traders in East Africa, Europeans expanded the long-distance commerce in gold, ivory, salt, and other commodities, including human slaves. The European slave trade wrought extensive, often devastating changes in local economies, power relations, and demography. Viewed in historical perspective, these developments also paved the way for later imperial expansion.

The slave trade.   Although Europeans did not introduce slavery to Africa, they transformed the scale and context of the institution. Slavery was a long-standing indigenous convention in Africa. In many societies war captives, subject castes, and some producer groups were enslaved, as their labor was not compensated and they were bound to a given master or chief. In areas of northern Nigeria, significant plantation economies were sustained by bound labor.[13] In many other settings slaves filled more limited and occasional roles as artisans, domestic help, or military forces. Many of these people were regarded as chattel, and for centuries preceding the European trade Arab and South Asian entrepreneurs and middlemen organized a steady commerce of African slaves—principally from East Africa—to the Middle East and India. This traffic was limited by the constraints of the trans-Sahara route and dhow transport, as well as by the demands of recipient markets. Over time the non-European slave trade nearly equaled the magnitude of the Atlantic traffic, but the latter was far more intensive and unsettling to African societies.

When Europeans established a permanent trading presence on the African coast, trade in humans became part of their diverse market for commodities. The demand for slaves was stimulated by the labor needs of the emerging colonial plantation economies in the New World. Contemporary European shipping greatly expanded the capacity to supply this burgeoning market, and Africa became a crucial point in the trans-Atlantic "triangular trade" of slaves, sugar, and rum. European agents sometimes organized raiding parties, but they typically procured captives through African and Arab middlemen. The local intermediaries were generally traditional rulers in the region, although some were entrepreneurs who responded to the new commercial opportunities. The commercialization of slavery was linked to the expansion of firearms and other trade goods, along with the spread of a money economy, and these factors impelled the growth of slave raiding for purely economic motives. The European presence enormously increased the scope and range of slavery by organizing it as a commodity market and introducing new means of exchange and coercion. Thus a localized and fairly modest domestic institution was altered and expanded into a sizable international trade.

Although many questions have been asked about the precise demographics of the slave trade, figures compiled by Philip Curtin and Paul Lovejoy provide a useful benchmark. In the trans-Atlantic trade from the mid–fifteenth century through the late nineteenth century, approximately 9 and a half million enslaved persons reached foreign ports.[14] This figure does not include the horrendous casualties of the Atlantic "middle passage," totaling perhaps 2 million souls. In addition, as Curtin notes, the associated losses from raiding, land transit in Africa, and disease in the New World are virtually incalculable. The European commerce was paralleled by trans-Saharan and Indian Ocean routes—beginning in the seventh century A.D. and lasting until the early twentieth century—through which an estimated 11 and a half million persons were exported.[15]

The slave trade, along with other forms of foreign diplomatic, commercial, and military relations, had uneven effects on African societies. Spanning centuries, the average population losses to slave commerce were often moderate, although unevenly distributed. In many regions trade was sufficiently gradual and dispersed that it did not seriously disrupt the social and economic fabric. In some areas such as Angola, however, intensive slave traffic resulted in depopulation that devastated local communities and undermined subsequent growth. In addition, the growth of slave raiding prompted substantial population migrations from the vulnerable coastal regions to the more remote and inhospitable interior zones, with adverse effects on economic activity. Relationships between local rulers and foreign agents influenced the balance of power in many parts of the continent, frequently upsetting the authority and cohesion of centralized states.

Imperialism and colonialism. However pernicious the nature of these activities, European powers held a limited and intermittent presence on the continent for hundreds of years. The central exception was the expansion of settlement in southern Africa described in Chapter 13. By the mid-nineteenth century, however, a combination of economic and political factors impelled a more aggressive quest for territorial control. The age of imperialism created a new epoch in Africa's history.

The origins and motives of European imperialism have prompted a good deal of controversy. Without reprising these debates at length, we can identify economic and political conceptions of imperialism. Economic arguments owe much of their inspiration to Marxist theory, but there have also been non-Marxist analyses in this vein.[16] This perspective has generally stressed the need of Europe's emerging industrial economies for raw materials, cheap labor, and new markets for industrial goods. The quest for empire was prompted by the need to extract a surplus from non-European territories or to establish a hegemonic position in the international trading system.

This view has been supplemented, and often challenged, by analyses stressing political and military motives for imperialism.[17] Intensifying strategic competition among European powers in the late nineteenth century was the cardinal incentive for imperial expansion. Although contending European countries sought the potential wealth afforded by colonial rule, they were also concerned with garnering prestige and denying resources to their competitors. Colonial expansion owed as much to the power politics of Europe as to the imperatives of capitalism.

Both sets of motives can be witnessed in the encroachment of European rule throughout Africa. Foreign dominion was inspired by mercantile and strategic pressures from the home countries, as well as by the exhortations of venturesome European "men on the spot" throughout Africa. After the 1840s a wave of explorers, missionaries, and military officials began to chart the interior of Africa, establishing alliances or supremacy in different areas and conducting military campaigns against hostile groups. The "scramble for Africa" was in full flood after 1870, as various countries marked their spheres of influence and delineated territorial boundaries.[18]

The competing claims of the colonial powers were reconciled at the Berlin Conference of 1884–1885. In this forum rival European governments agreed on spheres of influence, thus establishing the era of modern colonialism in Africa. The conference essentially regularized the partition of Africa, and in the decades following the convocation European powers established a permanent military and administrative presence in the colonies. Economic activities including mining, commerce, and commercial agriculture extended into the interior. The expansion of infrastructure accompanied this process. Social agencies and missionary activities also grew in scope.

Some broad policy and strategic considerations affected the development of African economies under colonial rule. Colonies were to be self-financing, as the proceeds from colonial exports and the taxation of trade were intended to cover the costs of rule. Ironically, colonies were expected to pay for their own subordination and development.[19] The returns of the colonial enterprise were highly uneven, as periods of rapid accumulation alternated with substantial deficit. The European powers often calculated the worth of their territories less in current terms than in view of a long-run competitive advantage. Many colonial regimes and firms incurred large initial losses, as the costs of administration, security, and infrastructure exceeded early returns on investment. Some historians have estimated that colonialism actually yielded net financial deficits for some European countries, although the overall gains of empire are often difficult to quantify.

The economic impact of colonialism varied across Africa. In general, indigenous forms of economic organization proved fairly resilient, and the introduction of capitalist forms of production and exchange challenged but did not supplant precapitalist patterns. In some areas traditional economic systems and subsistence patterns were substantially disrupted, whereas in others the effects of foreign rule were less intrusive. Indigenous economies, previously engaged in independent processes of adaptation and change, responded in diverse fashion to the commanding challenges of colonial rule. Many populations sought to evade colonial encumbrances and innovations, whereas a number managed to combine traditional subsistence with new activities and still others were thoroughly transformed by foreign intervention. These dynamics were influenced by the political and economic forms of colonial rule, the resource bases in various colonies, and the social and cultural features of different territories.

The economics of colonialism. European colonialism reflected three general economic forms. Most colonies in West Africa, along with several in East and central Africa, reflected an agricultural export pattern under administrative direction. Ralph Austen has characterized such colonies as "peasant-statist" regimes.[20] In eastern and southern Africa the establishment of settler rule created a "labor reserve" system, as described by Samir Amin.[21] These colonies were shaped by the presence of substantial communities of European immigrants and the creation of distinctive labor markets to support the settler economy. The emergence of "company rule," also indicated by Amin, established a third economic pattern in central and southern Africa. In these areas the colonial authority granted monopoly powers to chartered companies that carried out economic and quasi-governmental functions.

A number of colonies throughout the continent reflected "peasant-statist" systems. These territories were centrally governed by European regimes, although the metropolitan powers had a limited presence in the hinterland and maintained comparatively few of their citizens on the ground. They included Nigeria, the Gold Coast (Ghana), and the French territories of western and central Africa, as well as such colonies as Northern Rhodesia (Zambia) and Nyasaland (Malawi). Their economies were characterized by the commercialization of peasant agriculture in tandem with substantial state intervention in rural markets.

These colonies were built on export agriculture, often supplemented by mineral production. Peasant economies—composed of self-provisioning smallholders with limited market involvement—were substantially preserved, but agrarian activities were altered toward exports. Colonial policies induced peasants to supplement or replace food crops with cash crops, as they shifted cultivators toward such commodities as palm oil, cocoa, rubber, coffee, cotton, and groundnuts. Producers were often impelled to enter the market through imposition by colonial authorities of arbitrary "poll" or "hut" taxes, which created an immediate demand for monetary income. The incentives of new consumer markets and the rapid monetization of rural economies created further inducements to engage in commercial activities. In a number of colonies such as Senegal and the Ivory Coast (Côte d'Ivoire), smallholder activities were augmented by plantation agriculture, initiated by private European investors and a few African entrepreneurs. Forced labor was also used in some instances to increase export capacity. In addition to agricultural commodities, mineral exports were prominent in several economies, as foreign mining concerns exploited copper, gold, iron ore, phosphate, and bauxite reserves in various countries.

Another leading feature of these economies was the extensive role of the state in shaping production and exchange. European rule was mercantilist in character, and colonial states were instrumental in developing infrastructure, defining markets, setting prices, determining rules on land ownership and use, selecting products, shaping factor choices, and dictating areas of investment. Although these interventions were rarely comprehensive or efficient, they were widespread and influential. State intervention in colonial markets intensified significantly after World War II, and the newly independent governments inherited extensive mechanisms of control.

In the early decades of colonial rule a variety of public and private enterprises structured agricultural markets, and in the late 1930s government commodity boards that held a legal monopsony on the procurement and export of selected food or cash crops were established in the British colonies. As the sole legal buyer, the boards obtained produce from farmers at prices below open market rates and retained the surplus realized upon export or local sale. The rate of implicit taxation in these pricing policies ranged as high as 60 percent on some commodities.[22] These proceeds, along with the excise on imports, provided the major proportion of colonial revenues. Although these funds were supposedly intended to stabilize rural incomes and the development of producer regions, they were commonly diverted to general administration or urban infrastructure. Commodity boards became increasingly important as patronage resources for nationalist administrations in the 1950s.

A different economic pattern emerged in eastern and southern Africa, where many territories had lower population densities and more temperate climates. These conditions gave rise to several settler societies, including the British colonies of Kenya, Southern Rhodesia, and South Africa; the Portuguese territories of Mozambique and Angola; and the French possession of Algeria in north Africa. These colonies were settled by large numbers of immigrants from the metropolitan country who established permanent communities in the colonies. Settler regimes commonly imposed restrictions on African landholding and economic activities to preserve European commercial monopolies and maintain privileged access to agricultural markets. In these territories the wholesale alienation of Africans from fertile land created a rural proletariat and a population of urban migrants who were integrated into the settler economies. These reserves of displaced labor were employed in the mining sector, commercial farms, and service activities. Botswana, Lesotho, and Swaziland were also included in the migrant labor complex in southern Africa.[23] The settler colonies carried out substantial export activities in such products as gold, diamonds, coal, copper, tea, and coffee. The presence of large European populations engendered greater urbanization and more concentrated infrastructural development, although the benefits of such growth centered mainly on settler communities.

In a third set of territories, chiefly in central Africa, large-scale metropolitan firms gained exclusive rights (or concessions) in particular zones where they carried out central roles in investment, infrastructure development, administration, and security. The main example was the notorious regime in the Belgian Congo, ruled as a personal fiefdom by King Leopold in the decades before World War I. The French Congo (Congo-Brazzaville) and other central African holdings were also sites of large company activities. Most of these concessions were ended in the early twentieth century, as their financial and political costs became insupportable. The concessions were generally unprofitable, and home governments balked at company directors' continued demands for subsidies. The pattern of labor exploitation in these territories was often distinctive in its brutality, provoking resistance by indigenous peoples and criticism from some members of the European public. Company rule rarely persisted beyond World War II, and these colonies shifted toward statist forms of administration.

Despite these variations in production, trade, and labor markets, significant likenesses existed among colonial economies. As Paul Kennedy has observed, in the course of the colonial era a three-tiered structure emerged in much of Africa as different social groups dominated particular sectors and activities.[24] The apex of most economies was held by a small number of major enterprises in international trade, mining, and manufacturing controlled by metropolitan firms or settler interests. The dominance of Europeans in the large-scale "modern" sector was not simply a consequence of colonial policies, although these policies were instrumental in the settler regimes and territorial concessions. Equally important were the competitive advantages Europeans enjoyed as a result of their comparative business expertise, control over technology, and privileged access to financing and markets.

A middle tier of commerce, import-export trade, medium-size manufacturing, and services was occupied by resident groups from the Middle East and South Asia, many of which were encouraged to immigrate by the colonial powers. These groups, especially the Lebanese in West Africa and the Indians in East Africa, fulfilled important economic roles in colonies where Europeans were either too sparse or indifferent to invest. A strong immigrant commercial class had little potential to develop into a nationalist constituency and was broadly tolerated by the colonial regimes, especially after the 1930s. Members of these communities often served as adjuncts of imperial rule, occupying roles as clerks and commercial agents in the colonial system.[25]

Within the colonial economies Africans were engaged mainly in peasant production, agricultural wage labor, and a limited industrial employment. Local entrepreneurs established positions in retail trade, produce buying, real estate, transport, small-scale industry, and nominally "informal" activities. These activities commonly reflected the areas in which African business groups had relative aptitudes or particular competitive advantages. The economic roles were also influenced, especially in the settler colonies, by colonial restrictions on African landholding, enterprise, and access to capital.

Colonial-era reform. The period from the end of World War II until the advent of independence around 1960 signaled a new stage in the evolution of colonial economies. Following the war, the principal colonial powers made substantial commitments to promote economic development in their dependencies. This new developmentalism was motivated in part by a more enlightened attitude toward colonial stewardship and in part by a desire to realize greater returns from economic activities. The colonies were regarded as an important outlet of surplus capital for rebuilding the war-damaged economies of Europe.[26] In addition, some colonial officials reasoned that economic growth and expanding opportunities would provide an effective bulwark against rising nationalist pressures in the colonies, possibly forestalling demands for autonomy and independence. From the late 1940s the metropolitan powers made dramatic increases in transfers, credit, and investment. The total value of British aid to the colonies (in dollar equivalents) was about $572 million from 1880 to 1945, and $1.25 billion from 1945 to 1960; French allocations for these periods were $676 million and $3.45 billion, respectively.[27]

Development efforts during the late colonial period were dominated by the state and covered a wide array of activities. Among the leading areas of expenditure were infrastructure, agriculture, and industrial production. The colonial regimes created large numbers of government enterprises. Rail and road networks, electricity, and telecommunications expanded significantly in British and French possessions, although they were still confined to urban areas and central economic zones. The output of major cash crops increased substantially, and African trade generally rebounded from the Depression and war years. The value of exports from the British colonies increased fivefold in the fifteen years after the war, and French colonial exports rose by 40 percent between 1948 and 1953.[28] Investment in industry flourished, and the continent witnessed rapid growth rates, although they increased from a meager base. Colonial governments also directed expenditures, however belatedly and inadequately, toward human capital. Education and health services expanded significantly in many colonies, along with various training and support schemes for farmers and entrepreneurs.

These uneven, sporadic efforts failed to assuage local popular demands for autonomy or development, although they substantially advanced the transformation of African economies. Most colonies experienced significant expansion of productive capacities, increases in incomes and consumption, and growth of indigenous groups in business, the professions, and urban wage labor. In addition, an extensive state sector was established, along with broad government prerogatives for planning and regulation. During the late period of colonialism, Africa was more thoroughly integrated into global markets, and many contemporary patterns of trade and investment evolved. As a consequence, Africa's relationship with the world economy changed from a prewar model of simple extraction to a more complex structure of interaction and exchange.

■ The Economic Legacy of Colonialism

Colonialism left a diverse and far-reaching inheritance throughout Africa. Complementary changes can be seen in production, exchange, inequality, and international interactions. The scope and scale of production grew significantly in much of the region, although the forms of production were not always transformed. As noted earlier, agricultural yields increased markedly under colonial rule. By the time of independence sub-Saharan Africa accounted for a significant proportion of world exports of cocoa, palm kernels and oil, groundnuts, sisal, cotton, tobacco, coffee, tea, and several other crops. Production of domestic food crops, which by the 1950s still occupied 70 percent of cultivated land, also grew during the colonial era.[29] Most of this output was based on the expansion of peasant agriculture, entailing minimal changes in farming systems or technology. A number of ill-considered colonial plantation schemes foundered, and later efforts at research and extension provided few benefits for the rural sector.

The development of industrial enterprise was a more basic innovation in the productive sphere. Factory production was a significant colonial introduction in virtually all African economies, and mining activities were recast through modern techniques and organization. Despite the rapid growth of these sectors during the late colonial era, African countries were still not substantially industrialized at independence. In 1960 the industrial share of gross domestic product (GDP) in sub-Saharan Africa was slightly below the average proportion for all low-income developing countries.[30] Few countries had a manufacturing share greater than 10 percent, and the imprint of industry was generally scant. The structure of industry was typically haphazard, embodying few linkages or complementaries among domestic activities. Manufacturing was concentrated in light consumer products with little development of intermediate or capital goods.

Exchange relations were substantially altered by European rule. A nearly universal change was the extension of commerce and the money economy to the interior of the colonial territories. Dispersed agriculturalists and artisans, previously engaged in subsistence, barter, or small-scale trade, were now integrated into a wider array of transactions under a common monetary framework. The expansion of monetary exchange led to widespread commercialization of land, labor, and produce. Specific prices became attached to activities that previously had not been monetized but had been mediated mainly by status, kinship, and other social criteria. The growth of wage labor was among the central effects of commercialization. Also, the development of the market led to the expansion of commodity production, as cultivators and artisans provided specifically for trade. The modification of exchange relations fostered greater economic integration both domestically and externally. Much of the hinterland in parts of English- and French-speaking Africa was linked to export markets, imported manufactures were consumed widely, and intraterritorial commerce spread considerably.

A third dimension could be seen in patterns of economic and social inequality. The uneven effects of economic change influenced social stratification and competition for resources. As cities burgeoned and greater disparities opened with the countryside, an increasing divide between rural and urban sectors became evident. Despite the limited industrialization in most countries, urbanization attained great momentum under colonial rule. The comparative earnings and amenities available to a small segment of urban workers fostered a growing stream of migration from the country-side to the cities. The concentration of infrastructure and social services in urban areas served as a catalyst of this process.

The urban-rural divide was paralleled by ethnic and regional dispari-ties. Colonial economic development was typically centered in coastal re-gions or around the capital city. Ethnic groups closest to these areas of de-velopment often gained disproportionate access to employment, education, skills, and opportunities in the modern economy. Ethnic and regional in-equalities were accentuated (and sometimes created) by these variations. Among the many aspects of colonial rule, economic change and state allo-cations formed a crucible for the ethnic competition discussed in Chapter 4.

New forms of class differentiation also emerged within colonial econ-omies. Peasant smallholders continued to predominate, and at indepen-dence close to 90 percent of the region's labor force was active in agricul-ture.[31] Urban workers and agricultural proletarians emerged as significant groups in most countries, and a distinct "informal" sector could be dis-cerned, particularly in urban economies. These changes also reflected an increasing mobility and variety of economic roles, as many Africans com-bined or rotated their activities.

Colonial investments in human capital, as we have observed, were to-tally inadequate. By the time of independence it is estimated that only 16 percent of Africans were literate, and merely 3 percent of eligible sec-ondary students were enrolled in school.[32] Many countries had only a few dozen college graduates, and several, like Congo and the territories of French Central Africa, had almost none—an inauspicious base for future development. A narrow window of opportunity nonetheless fostered a small educated middle class throughout much of colonial Africa. In addi-tion, new commercial openings gave rise to nascent African business classes. These strata could be significant, as in Kenya, Ghana, Nigeria, and the Ivory Coast, or negligible as in Congo, Mali, Mozambique, and the Central African Republic.

Another crucial dimension of change in colonial economies was the new degree of integration into global markets. The classic model of the "open economy," elaborated by Dudley Seers and Anthony Hopkins, cap-tures the pattern of colonial development throughout Africa.[33] Open economies were organized around external trade and managed by industri-alized countries on terms that favored their own needs. The colonies sup-plied commodities to the metropolitan economies and relied mainly on im-ported manufactures from the industrialized West. Exports were highly concentrated in a few primary products, whereas imports tended to favor consumption goods. Economic administration and monetary affairs were generally dictated by external powers with the central objective of expe-diting these preferred flows of trade.

The outward orientation of colonial economies was reflected in high degrees of trade concentration, as well as patterns of infrastructural development. For sub-Saharan Africa as a whole, the three leading commodities in each country comprised over 60 percent of export values at independence. In nearly half of these countries the principal exports accounted for more than three-fourths of earnings from trade. The design of transport and communications throughout the region served to expedite commodity flows while providing little basis for internal development. The sparse networks of roads, rail lines, and telecommunications tended to run from central mining or agricultural zones to the coastal areas with few lateral connections within countries or linkages among colonial territories.

Returning to the dual themes of dependence and marginality, the unbalanced character of Africa's trade with the industrialized North should be stressed. By independence about half of the trade of anglophone countries was conducted with Britain, and nearly three-quarters of the total trade of French-speaking Africa was linked to the metropolitan power.[34] Yet the colonies were not nearly as consequential for "Northern" trade as for Africa; trade with Africa accounted for only about 6 percent of the total for the European powers.[35] This was also reflected in patterns of foreign investment, as external capital was broadly instrumental in mining, large-scale industry, and some infrastructural ventures. At the same time, investment in late colonial Africa was dominated by the public sector, and few private firms ventured beyond large-scale trade or mineral development. Africa attracted modest amounts of foreign capital, and investments in the region were of minimal importance to most European private sectors.

▦ Postcolonial Economies: Promise and Challenge

The leaders of independent African states faced a host of demands for development and redistribution. Animated by the high expectations of the nationalist struggle, African societies clamored for employment; access to public infrastructure, education, and health services; investment in regional and local development; agricultural progress; and the foundations of modern industry. The new regimes also had pressing needs to deliver benefits to their constituencies in the ruling party, the military, civic associations, particular ethnic communities or regions, and strategic social groups. In confronting these multiple and often competing pressures, African states were impaired by limited capacities and resources. The fledgling governments generally had sparse administrative reach and suffered from a shortage of experienced personnel. Public organizations were hardly equal to the tasks of planning and regulation entailed by statist policies. Moreover, African countries had few options for enhancing their meager resources. There were slim margins for extracting greater revenues from indigent, low-growth economies, few opportunities for rapidly increasing export revenues, and limited outlets for attracting foreign aid and investment. Against the urgent economic challenges of independence, African regimes often had a narrow room for maneuver.

During the first decade of independence, Africa was generally regarded within the mainstream of developing countries in terms of its central problems and prospects for development. Basic measures of performance placed Africa in the sphere of low-income economies, but many concerned with Africa's economic progress believed the region's abundant resources and human energies, supported by external aid and investment, would be sufficient for advancement within a reasonable period. In retrospect, we can see that Africa was at lower levels of development even in the 1960s; during that decade the average increase in gross domestic product for sub-Saharan countries was 3.9 percent, significantly less than the 4.5 percent growth for all low-income countries.[36] The growth of GDP per capita was only 1.3 percent, compared with 3.5 percent for developing countries in general. School enrollments were about half the average for low-income countries, and literacy rates were well below the mean for the developing world. Formidable problems of change were evident.

Frustrated by slow progress and eager to chart an independent economic course, postindependent African regimes embarked on a wave of policy experimentation. During the first two decades following independence, ideological distinctions were consequential in shaping the goals, policies, and institutions pursued by various governments. African states employed a variety of economic strategies and doctrines, from the relatively market-oriented approaches of Ivory Coast and Kenya to eclectic socialist experiments in Tanzania, Ghana, and Guinea to more orthodox Marxist strategies in Ethiopia, Angola, and Mozambique. An apparent relationship existed between ideological differences and comparative economic performance through the early 1980s, but a growing convergence was evident as fiscal crisis gripped the region. After the middle of the decade, economic strategy clearly became more homogeneous in Africa, as traditional populist and Marxist regimes dropped their ideological mantles and adopted liberalization programs, largely sponsored by multilateral financial institutions. Historical legacies have nonetheless continued to frame development in reforming countries.

The general patterns of development were often related to the regime variations we discussed in Chapter 5. African governments differed in their approaches to economic management and in their sectoral policies, even when they shared general institutional features such as military rule or professed common doctrines such as socialism. The differences were influenced by the structure of the national economy, relations with the former colonial power and other northern states, the relative influence of local social groups, and the bent of individual leaders. Nonetheless, a range of fairly consistent and coherent economic approaches was associated with specific leadership doctrines. Drawing on a scheme elaborated by Crawford Young, three central economic strategies can be identified as capitalist, populist, and Afro-Marxist.[37] While distinguishing these approaches, we will also call attention to the substantial continuities in economic policy among diverse African states.

■ REGIMES, IDEOLOGY, AND DEVELOPMENT STRATEGIES

▓ Capitalist Strategies

Capitalist strategies were favored mainly by pluralist and administrative-hegemonic regimes. Leading capitalist states included Côte d'Ivoire, Kenya, Nigeria, Cameroon, Malawi, Botswana, Gambia, and Mauritius. These governments were often pragmatic and ostensibly "nonideological" in their approach to economic strategy, even though some, like Kenya, professed an official commitment to "African socialism."[38] They emphasized growth over redistributive goals and were broadly tolerant of social inequalities in the course of development. Within the spectrum of African countries, this group accorded greater importance to market forces and the private sector. They also made nominal efforts to promote local entrepreneurs and encourage the rise of domestic business classes.

Capitalist regimes recognized the general parameters of the open economy and sought to promote growth mainly through expansion of primary commodity exports. They emphasized the use of selective market incentives for producers and invited private sector involvement in export activities. To a significant degree these countries accepted the prevailing terms of integration into global markets; at the same time, their governments sought to restructure by developing import-substituting industries and were generally hospitable toward private foreign investment. As we will see, however, they usually maintained protectionist and interventionist policies in many areas and did not adopt a liberal approach to economic management.

Although many African states reflected generically similar attitudes regarding trade and private sector activity, capitalist strategies differed in structure and emphasis. The early exemplars of this approach, Côte d'Ivoire and Kenya, relied principally on the development of agricultural exports. At independence both countries had strong inducements for building market-led economies and emphasizing the agricultural sector. President Houphouët-Boigny of Côte d'Ivoire was a commercial farmer, and much of the base for his ruling Parti Democratique du Côte d'Ivoire (PDCI) was found among the nation's emergent African planter class. The postindependence regime charted a conservative strategy that maintained close ties with the former colonial power and relied principally on traditional cash crops as a basis for growth. The leading exports were coffee, cocoa, and timber, and the government stressed indigenous smallholder activities in the first two crops. The country diversified into palm oil, cotton, rubber, fruits, and vegetables, principally through smallholder production supplemented by large-scale plantation schemes under foreign or government ownership.

Côte d'Ivoire also encouraged import-substitution manufacturing, concentrated in agro-processing and consumer goods. These ventures were dominated by external (especially French) capital, often in partnership with the state. Through the late 1970s, private Ivorian investors held a small fraction of equity in manufacturing. In the sphere of foreign economic relations Houphouët pursued an unabashedly "neocolonial" policy, preserving a collaborative association with France and inviting broad foreign participation in the economy. A member of the CFA (Communaute Financiere Africaine) franc zone, Côte d'Ivoire was a leading beneficiary of French aid, investment, and trade preferences. Several thousand French managers and technocrats staffed the Ivorian public and private sectors, and the number of resident expatriates multiplied fivefold after independence. The government embarked only gradually on an "Ivoirianization" campaign to indigenize management in the 1970s. Still, by 1984 foreigners held nearly half of senior management positions in major Ivorian manufacturing enterprises.[39]

The fortunes of the Ivorian economy were firmly joined to external markets, and during the first two decades after independence this approach yielded impressive growth rates averaging over 7 percent annually. In structural terms the economy experienced significant diversification, as industry grew to 23 percent of GDP by 1979 (from 14 percent at independence) while agriculture contracted proportionally from 43 to 26 percent during that period. Export concentration decreased significantly, and Côte d'Ivoire's trade patterns shifted away from France, although they remained centered on the European market.[40]

The Kenyan experience varied from that of Côte d'Ivoire. As a former settler colony, Kenya faced substantial problems of rural inequality and land allocation. Jomo Kenyatta, president during the first fifteen years of independence, fashioned an economic strategy stressing the growth of commercial agriculture in tandem with substantial land reform. These policies also bolstered Kenyatta's base among the Kikuyu ethnic group, which had suffered acutely from colonial land appropriation. In Kenya as in Côte d'Ivoire, political leaders regulated access to the benefits of a growing economy, and market-driven strategies advanced important political constituencies.

The ascendance of agricultural interests in Kenya was influenced by the departing colonialists. In the final decade of colonial rule the British sought to address the enormous racial imbalances in land ownership and the problem of African landlessness, notably in the "white highlands" of the central region. The 1955 Swynnerton Plan alloted land to Africans and sought to encourage a class of "progressive" commercial farmers as a source of social and economic moderation. Colonial-era land reform, and subsequent redistribution schemes by the Kenyatta government, stratified the agrarian sector among a minority of affluent commercial farmers, a large number of poorer smallholders, and a significant pool of landless agricultural laborers.[41] After independence, favorable pricing policies and government extension facilities promoted output in coffee, tea, maize, and several other cash and food crops.

Kenyan industrial policy provided substantial incentives and special protection for foreign investors. Manufacturing consisted mainly of import substitution activities, concentrating on final consumption goods. External capital dominated this sector, especially in medium- and large-scale enterprises, and multinational firms were widely engaged in the market.[42] In contrast to Côte d'Ivoire, however, an aggressive "Africanization" program fostered an earlier shift toward Kenyan management in foreign-owned firms.[43] In addition, state finance and training programs promoted a relatively larger role for indigenous Kenyan investors in manufacturing. During the first fifteen years of independence, Kenya achieved impressive industrial growth rates averaging more than 9 percent, although industry increased only marginally as a proportion of gross domestic product.

Nigeria embodied a stark departure from this pattern. The former British colony resembled Côte d'Ivoire and Kenya in many respects during the decade after independence. The economy was dominated by agricultural exports including cocoa, palm oil, groundnuts, cotton, and rubber, along with a few minerals such as limestone and tin. Smallholder production constituted the foundation of agriculture, whereas foreign capital predominated in the industrial sector. Manufacturing comprised less than 7 percent of total domestic product at independence and was centered in a few urban nodes. The first postcolonial government worked through the open economy, seeking to expand output in traditional cash crops and to attract external industrial investment.[44] Political leaders also introduced policies to encourage local business through loan programs and development assistance.

The dimensions of the Nigerian economy changed completely after 1970, as the country shifted abruptly from agricultural exports to a reliance on crude oil.[45] In the wake of the civil war, petroleum extraction activities by foreign firms grew rapidly. Nigeria joined the Organization of Petroleum Exporting Countries (OPEC) in 1971, and the government soon took a majority interest in the energy sector. By 1973 rising production and OPEC price hikes stimulated a ten-year petroleum "boom" that peaked in the mid-1970s and again in 1980. The economy ballooned as the oil windfall prompted enormous growth in both the public and private sectors. Gross domestic product expanded by a yearly average of 7.5 percent in the 1970s, and public consumption grew by 12.4 percent.[46] At the peak of the oil market in 1980, Nigeria garnered around $25 billion in export revenues. State-sponsored development programs expanded in infrastructure, manufacturing, agriculture, and human capital as public enterprises multiplied. Foreign firms scrambled for a foothold in the large and seemingly affluent market. The Nigerian government, reflecting an increasingly nationalist direction in public policy, instituted a comprehensive indigenization program to transfer companies from foreign to private domestic ownership, with corresponding changes in management.[47]

The oil boom also carried substantial liabilities. The appearance of sudden wealth inspired reckless spending, rampant corruption, and widespread speculative activity. Adverse policies created a number of distortions in the economy. The exchange rate appreciated, and the influx of foreign exchange encouraged an import spree of consumer goods and food items. As a consequence domestic agriculture and manufacturing were neglected, and production of nonoil exports plummeted. Rapid economic expansion also prompted inflation, urban sprawl, and congestion. The boom brought highly unequal benefits, with unimaginable prosperity for a few alongside continuing poverty and frustration for the bulk of the population.

The petroleum boom was inherently unstable. By the mid-1970s oil provided 80 percent of government revenues and over 90 percent of foreign exchange, making the economy highly vulnerable to fluctuations in global markets. Even in the midst of the windfall the energy sector proved volatile, and the government borrowed heavily from external lenders to sustain expenditures in lean years. When prices and demand in energy markets fell in the early 1980s the boom turned to bust, and the vulnerabilities of the preceding decade were exposed. The economy was dependent upon an export monoculture, the country was heavily indebted, and the state and the private sector were corrupt and inefficient. These circumstances yielded a chronic economic malaise.

Mauritius is the principal exception to the classic open economy model, as it achieved high growth through the expansion of manufactured exports.[48] This small island nation emerged from colonialism in the late 1960s with a sugar plantation economy. Against the background of a stable democratic political climate, the government promoted export processing zones (EPZs) and generally sound macroeconomic policies, fostering impressive growth in manufacturing including substantial (although not majority) foreign investment. Manufactures grew from less than a quarter of total exports in the late 1970s to more than two-thirds of exports in the mid-1990s. Although small and politically marginal, Mauritius stands (along with Botswana) as a distinctive African success, with sustained GDP growth rates of over 5 percent in the two decades after independence.

Until the late 1970s, capitalist states generally reflected some of the strongest growth records in sub-Saharan Africa. The average growth rate of GDP among a set of six countries (Kenya, Côte d'Ivoire, Botswana, Gambia, Cameroon, and Mauritius) from 1960 to 1979 was 7.2 percent, or 3.6 percent in gross national product (GNP) per capita.[49] This group omits Nigeria, whose dramatic petroleum-led growth in the 1970s was idiosyncratic. Many critics of capitalist strategies in Africa have discounted this record, observing a number of distortions and adverse features of these economies. Because much of this growth was fueled by foreign investment and external markets, some analysts have emphasized the dependent nature of development in the capitalist states. They have asserted that structural distortions undermine self-sustaining growth and that the reliance on external trade and capital has rendered these economies vulnerable to sudden decline. Many of the same critics also point to the persistent inequalities in these countries and to the general failure to alleviate mass poverty despite high growth.

■ Populist Strategies

Populist strategies were more clearly animated by assertive ideological concerns than were capitalist approaches. Several unorthodox strands of African socialism were articulated by African leaders after independence. Although avoiding the notions of class analysis and class struggle of conventional Marxism, African socialists emphasized egalitarianism, social welfare, economic autonomy, and planned development. These programs were commonly adopted by party-mobilizing and populist regimes. Among the notable proponents of populist approaches were Tanzania, Guinea (under Sekou Touré), Ghana (under Kwame Nkrumah and later Jerry Rawlings), Mali, Niger, Burkina Faso (under Thomas Sankara), and the north African states of Algeria and Libya. Many of their leaders were seriously committed to economic and social transformation, and they accorded the state sector a leading role in administering such changes.

Populist strategies rested on three central orientations. First, these governments contested the terms of the open economy and sought to achieve relative self-reliance in production and trade relations. They adopted nationalist rhetoric and policy orientations, calling for local ownership of key enterprises, as well as regulation of financial movements, import and export flows, and external investment. The governments typically controlled exchange rates, limited capital mobility, and restricted the activities of foreign firms.[50] They promoted import-substituting manufacturing through direct state ownership, along with protection and assistance to some domestic entrepreneurs. In agriculture many of these governments established rural collectivization schemes or large-scale government farms.

Second, populists were committed to reducing social inequalities and promoting economic redistribution. They discouraged the formation of large indigenous capitalist classes and in some instances attempted to restrain corrupt or self-interested behavior within the bureaucracy. Reforms in the agrarian sector were also designed to foster relative equity and to avoid the emergence of powerful rural elites. These regimes also committed themselves, at least rhetorically, to spending on health, education, and infrastructure to aid rural areas and the urban poor. They commonly provided extensive subsidies for public services and basic commodities.

Finally, populist regimes embodied a fundamental distrust of market mechanisms and sought direct control over many domestic and external transactions. These governments created large state sectors and pursued an array of administrative interventions in domestic markets. They fostered bureaucratic expansion along with a proliferation of public enterprises. In addition, populist governments often created state monopolies in agricultural markets, import-export trade, and domestic wholesale and retail activity. As described earlier, these institutions were accompanied by price controls on agricultural produce, staple foods, fertilizer, fuel, electricity, and communications, as well as the broad provision of health and education services.

As was the case among capitalist states, African populist regimes also followed diverse policies. Two leading variations in populist strategy were found in Ghana and Tanzania. In Ghana, Kwame Nkrumah implemented an ambitious developmental agenda in the first decade after independence. His economic program, especially during the "socialist" phase from 1961 to 1966, was oriented toward rapid industrialization, mainly through the expansion of a large state-owned manufacturing sector.[51] Nkrumah regarded industrial development as the key to economic independence, yet he wished to avoid the twin pitfalls of foreign domination and bourgeois class formation. These concerns prompted the regime to rely on public investment and ownership, which would presumably allow greater control of the industrialization process. His government embarked on schemes such as the Volta Dam hydroelectric project, in addition to forming many new state firms and joint manufacturing enterprises with foreign capital. Official approval was also given for collaborative ventures between transnational firms and local private investors. Manufacturing growth was concentrated in import-substitution activities, mainly in consumption goods, supported by high levels of protection and subsidies.

The obverse side of Nkrumah's enthusiasm for industry was his disdain for agriculture, especially the strategic cocoa sector. He regarded cash crop activities as a vestige of colonial dependence and cocoa production as the bastion of backward rural elites, an attitude that resulted in policies that discriminated against cash crop producers. The most conspicuous practice involved pricing policies of the state cocoa marketing board, which paid producers only 37 percent of the realized FOB price in 1965.[52] This discriminatory rate of taxation, combined with decreasing world market prices in the early 1960s, squeezed farmers and sharply reduced marketed output. The revenues accrued by the marketing board were siphoned from the producing areas, as the government neglected investment in infrastructure, inputs, and extension services for the cocoa regions. Instead, many of these resources were channeled into a burgeoning sector of state farms, which the regime saw as an important counterweight to peasant agriculture. By the mid-1960s government farming schemes garnered most of the agricultural development budget, including major allocations for inputs, equipment, and extension. Public credit programs also favored a few large-scale farmers.[53]

These sectoral approaches were accompanied by a set of macroeconomic policies designed to protect domestic markets and confer subsidies to favored groups.[54] The government maintained a fixed exchange rate, and amid rising domestic inflation and trade deficits, the national currency became steadily overvalued. Although affording relatively cheaper imports of finished goods and industrial inputs, overvaluation also discouraged exports and gave rise to a large parallel market. These distortions prompted compensatory measures, as the government tried to defend the balance of payments by extending import licensing and placing controls on prices and financial flows. The regime also embarked on a spree of public borrowing to finance its projects and cover public deficits.

The cumulative effects of these policies were grievous. Inefficient state production, rising public spending and debt, and disincentives to private production and investment had negative effects on performance. Growth rates sagged by the mid-1960s, as industrial output bogged down and export revenues declined. In the vital cocoa sector, farmers moved into food crops or covertly marketed their produce through neighboring countries where they could obtain better prices. Exports declined steadily, and Ghana's world market share in cocoa dropped by half between the mid-1960s and the mid-1980s. By the end of Nkrumah's tenure government finances were in disarray, and escalating inflation quickly eroded popular gains from subsidies and public sector employment. Although some elements of populist strategy were discarded after Nkrumah's ouster in 1966, many policies persisted. Populism was briefly (and ardently) revived in the early 1980s under Jerry Rawlings's regime, much to the detriment of the Ghanaian economy.

Tanzania's version of populism contrasted substantially with that of Ghana. Whereas Nkrumah looked askance at peasant agriculture, Tanzanian president Julius Nyerere actively embraced the rural sector as a linchpin of the country's development. Compared with the corruption and authoritarian bent of Ghana's populist regimes, the Tanzanian government, at least in its public pronouncements, sought to maintain a modicum of integrity within the public sector and to incorporate popular participation and public accountability. Populism in Tanzania scarcely registered greater economic success, and it was saddled with elements of authoritarianism and corruption, but the character of politics and that of policy were arguably distinct.

Tanzania embarked on a populist course beginning in 1967. In the early years after independence Nyerere became uneasy over growing inequalities in his society, as well as over impending problems of corruption and arrogance within the bureaucracy and the ruling party. He was also disappointed with prevailing levels of aid and investment and sought new options for growth. These concerns prompted a new direction in development, signaled by the 1967 Arusha Declaration.

The new policies focused on two areas. First, Nyerere wanted to build a dynamic socialist agricultural economy. He argued that industrialization was an inappropriate emphasis for a poor agrarian country since an urban-centered strategy would exclude much of the population. He invoked the virtues of traditional "socialist" elements in the African village, including mutual aid, community self-help, strong moral codes, and social equality.[55] Developmental renewal could be achieved through the creation of collective settlements, or *ujamaa* villages (from the Swahili word for family-hood), throughout the country. These villages would entail moving people from the dispersed private homesteads then prevalent in the Tanzanian countryside to communal settlements organized around collective farming. Villagization would combine traditional social practice with modern technology. The second important feature of Nyerere's program was the development of a leadership code for the party and the government, prohibiting officials from pursuing private interests. This policy had some early effect in setting a standard for public life and in limiting corruption, at least relative to other African countries.

The *ujamaa* program, however, proved more difficult to implement. Initially, Nyerere envisioned a voluntary movement to the new *ujamaa* villages, based on persuasion by the party. Two years after the program was launched, however, response was minuscule, and the government switched to a policy of material inducements. Officials and party cadres promised people better land, water, schools, and clinics to entice them into the settlements. When this plan increased participation only slightly, Nyerere grew impatient and declared that all peasants would be compelled to resettle. During a two-year period after 1974, about 80 percent of the peasant population was forcibly relocated into *ujamaa* villages.[56] Although the government's coercive measures were not excessively brutal, the program disrupted many rural communities and much of the agricultural economy.

Throughout much of the country villagers in the new settlements had to adapt to unfamiliar rainfall, soil conditions, and terrain, upsetting established farming patterns. The response to the collective farming activities that were the core of the *ujamaa* experiment was apathetic. In most villages peasants simply established new private plots for individual households while maintaining a marginal (and commonly neglected) communal plot, the output from which was generally negligible. These problems were compounded by a serious drought that peaked in 1974, seriously reducing agricultural yields. In the years immediately following villagization, marketed output dropped severely. Although food production recovered within a few years, the costs of the villagization program contributed to a general economic decline.[57]

The Tanzanian government also pursued far-reaching intervention in other areas of the economy. In the early years following the Arusha Declaration, the state nationalized financial institutions and major portions of import-export trade, domestic commerce, and urban real estate, as well as a host of industrial firms. The number of public enterprises (or parastatals) more than doubled after 1967, reaching 139 by 1974.[58] The government also took a majority of equity in ventures established by foreign investors. This was accompanied by extensive wage and price controls, including most public services, food, and export crops. Trade and investment regulations were intended to reduce dependence on northern industrial economies and to increase interactions with developing and socialist countries.[59]

Tanzania's economic performance in the wake of the Arusha Declaration was not propitious. By the late 1970s the country was mired in an economic downturn. Agricultural growth in the second half of the 1970s averaged only 0.3 percent annually, and GDP grew at a little more than 2 percent. Food imports increased nearly twenty times (by value) between 1973 and 1980.[60] Tanzania became one of the highest per capita recipients of foreign aid in the region, a development that thwarted aspirations to self-reliance. Industrial growth averaged an anemic 1.9 percent in the 1970s and showed absolute declines in the early years of the next decade.[61] Production lagged far behind population growth. As the economy weakened, corruption and demoralization set in throughout the political system. The main achievements of Nyerere's government seemed to reside in a significant expansion of health and education, along with some success in reducing social inequalities and aiding poorer segments of the population. Nonetheless, a deteriorating economy sullied the populist endeavor.

The francophone populist regimes displayed some variations in policy but little distinction in performance. The landlocked savanna states of Mali, Niger, and Burkina Faso faced daunting prospects regardless of the economic strategy employed, although policy errors nonetheless contributed to these basic problems. Despite Guinea's comparative abundance of minerals and agriculture, its growth was scarcely more robust. The general policy motif in these countries and in states such as Madagascar and Congo-Brazzaville emphasized centralized planning, state trading monopolies, parastatal industrial enterprise, exacting restrictions on private capital, and agricultural cooperatives or state production schemes. The results were universally disappointing in the areas of output, structural change, and poverty alleviation.

The African countries attempting populist experiments eventually arrived at a common impasse: the goals of economic autonomy and redistribution, however laudable, were illusory without a vigorous foundation of economic expansion. The average combined per capita growth rate for Ghana, Tanzania, Guinea, and Mali from 1960 through 1979 was a meager 0.7 percent, which could hardly provide for a significant expansion of popular welfare. Slow growth was commonly paralleled by increasing debt burdens and aid requisites, which impeded investment and deepened external dependence. In the throes of economic crisis, most populist regimes quietly abandoned their more radical policies by the mid-1980s.

◼ Afro-Marxist Strategies

A more orthodox expression of socialist ideology could be found in the Afro-Marxist states, which included the party-centralist regimes of Angola, Mozambique, Ethiopia, Benin, and Congo-Brazzaville. Some analysts have also included Somalia, Madagascar, and Guinea-Bissau in this circle. As with politics, a gap often existed between formal doctrine and actual practice in Afro-Marxist economic strategies.[62] Many of these countries, particularly the military governments that were latter-day devotees of "scientific socialism," fashioned economic policies that varied marginally from those of the populist states. Nonetheless, Afro-Marxism formed a separate trajectory in the spectrum of regional economic change.

The strategic focus of Afro-Marxist regimes differed from populism in important ways. First, these states emphasized class struggle and the organization of a vanguard party, as they sought to mobilize important producer groups, notably peasants and workers.[63] Second, these regimes adopted the facade of the command economy, emphasizing a high degree of centralization and detailed planning in economic affairs. As part of this approach the Afro-Marxist states generally extended public control over leading financial and industrial enterprises, and they typically created large-scale state farms and production schemes. Third, at least in terms of official policy, these governments sought to constrain private economic activity. They often intervened in domestic commerce, sometimes penetrating to the level of retail activity, while displaying little overt tolerance for the independent entrepreneurial classes. Finally, Afro-Marxist regimes sought to manage their relations with the international economy by regulating direct foreign investment, controlling external trade with industrial capitalist states, and expanding aid and commercial relations with socialist bloc countries.

Afro-Marxist experiments faced obstacles and flaws that severely limited their prospects. The most prominent states—Angola, Mozambique, and Ethiopia—were embroiled in military strife that prevented economic progress. These conflicts emanated from internal political and ethnic rivalries, as well as external aggression. Civil wars, chronic insurgencies, and clashes with regional neighbors placed a virtual brake on development. In these circumstances substantial public funds were diverted to military spending, infrastructure and productive assets were ruined, large areas of the country were unsettled by war, and refugee flows upset production and distribution systems while further burdening state resources.

Although military insecurity affected some Afro-Marxist countries, broader constraints were evident in these regimes, which had extremely limited institutional capacities and were unsuited for the demands of elaborate, centralized economic management.[64] Angola and Mozambique inherited public institutions that had been plundered and vandalized by the departing settler governments, and they possessed few skilled people to revitalize these structures. The Ethiopian public sector was significantly disrupted by political unrest in the mid-1970s, and the low-income economies of Benin, Madagascar, and Somalia lacked basic resources for development. Given the fundamental dearth of bureaucratic capabilities and the limits of political organization, the notion of "command" economies in these settings was essentially a fiction. Despite the pretense of planning and direction, the central state had little effective control over major aspects of production, distribution, or exchange, although governments often pursued disruptive interventions in these areas.[65]

Afro-Marxist regimes developed a considerable reliance on external support from the socialist world, especially the Soviet sphere. The Soviet Union, Cuba, and several Eastern European states provided economic and security assistance to many regimes. Whereas military support was often crucial for governments such as Angola and Ethiopia, economic aid was generally less fruitful. The Soviets sponsored some large-scale industrial projects and agricultural schemes, and other countries—notably Cuba—offered training and technical assistance. These resources were uneven, however, and external assistance was clearly insufficient for economic transition in the aspiring Afro-Marxist regimes. There were also significant opportunity costs for these countries in reduced access to Western export markets, private capital, and multilateral resources. In 1976 U.S. trade with Africa was about $17.8 billion, more than eleven times greater than Soviet exchange with the region.[66]

Ethiopia pursued one of the most comprehensive Afro-Marxist experiments. In the aftermath of the 1974 military revolt that ousted Emperor Haile Selassie, radical officers constituted a Marxist regime under the *derg* (or "committee" in Amharic), which elaborated a program of radical social and economic change. The new government, under Mengistu Haile Mariam, nationalized banks, insurance companies, and the major industrial and mercantile firms. The state established control over urban and rural land, as it expropriated landlords and banned private employment of agricultural labor.

The leading thrust of the *derg*'s program was in the rural areas, where 90 percent of Ethiopians worked. The regime sought a comprehensive land reform to dismantle the feudal system prevalent under the imperial order. With the nationalization of property the landed elite was largely dispossessed, and strict limits were placed on the size of cultivators' plots. The state took several other steps to restructure the agrarian sector. A network of official peasant associations was created to back the land reform, and the government sent 50,000 urban students into the countryside to help mobilize the peasantry. Through the associations, peasants were encouraged to form service cooperatives for the dispersal of inputs and producer cooperatives to organize collective production. The producer schemes proved contentious, as Ethiopian peasants were generally unwilling to cede their use rights on individual plots to enter into communal farming.[67] Such concerns over property rights created a lukewarm response to the villagization program launched in 1985. This was paralleled by a large rural resettlement campaign that created severe, often brutal dislocations in many areas.

In addition, state marketing firms were created to handle food and cash crops. These measures had negative effects on export income and food security. Low official producer prices and uncertain land tenure diminished farmers' incentives, and output fell in many parts of the country. Haphazard distribution by public agencies led to serious imbalances in local food supplies. The government attempted to boost agricultural production by establishing large-scale state farms. These centralized, capital-intensive ventures suffered from inefficiency and mismanagement, leading to mediocre performance and financial losses.

The problems in the agricultural sector had important consequences for urban areas. Supply bottlenecks from the countryside led to significant food deficits in the cities, prompting a dramatic increase in imports of staple crops. Spending on imported cereals soared seventy-five-fold between 1973 and 1985.[68] These expenditures, which equaled 28 percent of export revenues in 1985, squeezed the resources available for other imports, especially industrial inputs. The regime's sweeping nationalizations and restrictive laws generally deterred investment in manufacturing and commercial activities. Government efforts to construct large public sector industrial projects, many with funding from the Soviet bloc, proved costly and inefficient. In the 1984 Ten-Year Guiding Plan, half of the planned spending on industries was allocated to only thirteen projects. In addition, the enterprises nationalized by the regime were often mismanaged and inadequately financed. Industrial production grew at a rate of less than 2 percent (in absolute terms) throughout the 1980s.[69]

The problems of Ethiopian socialism were evident in other Afro-Marxist states. Agrarian collectivization schemes were resisted by peasants who were anxious to preserve household property rights. State intervention in agricultural markets depressed production and disrupted allocation mechanisms, and government farms generally proved wasteful and unproductive. Industrial ventures also fared poorly under public ownership and management. Private lenders and investors were discouraged by stringent regulations on foreign capital, and Afro-Marxist countries drew scant new investment aside from mining activities in Angola and Congo-Brazzaville. Overextended state sectors were commonly undermined by bureaucratic disarray and deepening corruption. These shortcomings, in addition to the dislocations of violent conflict in several countries, yielded a dismal economic performance. Between 1980 and 1987, among a group of five Afro-Marxist states (Angola, Mozambique, Ethiopia, Congo-Brazzaville, and Benin), GNP per capita *declined* by an average of 3 percent annually.[70]

By the late 1980s Afro-Marxist experiments were being curtailed throughout Africa. Angola and Mozambique relaxed their adherence to Leninist models, as Soviet sponsorship receded and both regimes strengthened their ties to Western countries. The guise of ideology weakened in other "scientific socialist" countries, as they sought resources from multilateral financial institutions and entered into structural adjustment programs. The Soviets, in fact, encouraged Mozambique to look outward during the late 1980s. In Ethiopia, Mengistu began to liberalize in the late 1980s, and a decisive turn was evident after armed rebels overthrew his regime in 1991. The new government under President Meles Zenawi adopted a more liberal course of economic policy.

■ SECTORAL POLICIES

The distinction among ideologies and development strategies in Africa, although important, should not be overdrawn. There have been substantial continuities in economic policy throughout the region, often transcending the labels adopted by different governments. In practice, the range of policies in most sectors has been limited. African capitalist states, regardless of their rhetorical stance, have used protectionist measures to shield domestic industries, and nearly all have established large numbers of public enterprises. Socialist regimes, despite their professed ideals, have commonly admitted some foreign investment, and many have tolerated private markets in significant portions of their economies. A focus on key sectors and trends will highlight the important features of African economic policy through the early 1980s, providing a background for the discussion of economic crisis and reform in the next chapter. The following sections examine industry, agriculture, and human resources.

■ Industrial Policies

Many African leaders have considered industrialization to be the essence of economic development. In the era following World War II, this view has been prevalent in much of the developing world, and it has been supported by diverse strands of development theory. Modernization theorists virtually equate industrialization with modernization. They view the growth of industry as a hub of social and economic change, integrally linked to the expansion of education and infrastructure, the spread of technology, the process of urbanization, and the shift toward more complex class-based societies.

Among mainstream development economists, the importance of industrial activities for developing economies has been widely acknowledged. Industrial development is a vehicle for establishing higher value-added activities, increasing productivity, and gaining a more advantageous position in international trade. In predominantly agrarian economies, the expansion of industry may allow for greater flexibility and faster growth. The industrial sector absorbs labor and raises average incomes (although this is driven by a small group of higher-income wage earners), which in turn increases total purchasing power. The export of manufactures allows countries to realize economies of scope and scale while strengthening outlets of foreign exchange and diversifying trade.

Economists are not unanimous on the relative place of industry in economic development. Many neoclassical analysts, invoking arguments based on comparative advantage, admonish African countries to give priority to agricultural development while tempering ambitions for rapid industrial growth. Others, notably from the structuralist perspective, envision a more prominent role for industrial development. Underdevelopment theorists and orthodox Marxists have stressed the importance of industry as the leading sector in economic transformation. Dependency analysts regard manufacturing activity as a catalyst for self-sustaining growth since it lessens reliance on hard currency, foreign goods, and imported technology while helping to stimulate domestic economic activities and to supply local markets. A strong domestic industrial base helps to weaken the exploitive ties between the core northern economies and the peripheral countries of the south.

Industrialization is also viewed as a key to reversing the unfavorable terms of trade confronted by commodity exporters. Underdevelopment theorists maintain that exporters of primary products (unprocessed agricultural produce and minerals) face an inherent disadvantage in trade with advanced industrialized states.[71] The relative purchasing power of primary producers tends to decline since their export incomes cannot keep pace with the rising cost of imported manufactures. Commodity exports embody low value-added and are abundant in world markets; hence, their prices remain stagnant over the long term. Manufactured goods, by contrast, are specialized and embody higher added value, and their prices appreciate. This disparity in market position is seen as a basic inequity in global exchange and as a source of economic malaise among peripheral economies. Developing countries, by increasing their proportion of manufacturing and reducing the significance of primary commodity production, can presumably improve their terms of trade.

Further, orthodox Marxists stress the importance of industrialization as integral to control the "commanding heights" of the economy, which embodies the greatest concentration of capital and provides critical goods. Industry is also regarded as the crucible of the proletariat, a pivotal social class in the construction of socialism. Industrialization is also a prestigious symbol of modernity and national attainment.

Consequently, African regimes of many persuasions have aspired to develop their industrial potential. This aim, however, has been especially difficult in Africa. We have remarked on the limited extent of industrialization under colonial rule. In 1960 industry provided 16 percent of total gross domestic product in the region. Even this low figure, however, inflates the contribution of productive activities since national accounting statistics group manufacturing along with mining, utilities and construction under the heading of "industry." Manufacturing comprised 9 percent of Africa's GDP in 1965, and roughly 5 percent of the labor force was engaged in the sector at independence. Twelve countries reflected an industrial share of GDP greater than 20 percent, but most of these (including Mauritania, Togo, Liberia, Sierra Leone, Gabon, Congo, Zambia, Zimbabwe, and Botswana) were economies dominated by mining.[72] Overall, more than half of value-added in African manufacturing came from consumer goods, especially food processing and textiles. The picture that emerges is one of a comparatively small, restricted manufacturing base, limited mainly to lower-technology final consumption goods and substantially under foreign ownership.

Industrial strategies in postindependence Africa pursued several objectives. Beyond the simple expansion of output, governments sought to diversify manufacturing activities and to promote complementarities throughout the economy. Numerous development plans focused on the need to deepen the industrial sector by augmenting consumer goods with the production of intermediate goods (industrial inputs such as chemicals and metals) and capital goods (machinery and transport equipment). In addition to linkages within the manufacturing sector, some planners emphasized the value of ties to other sectors, especially agriculture. Many policymakers stated the importance of achieving a geographic balance of industrial activities among different regions of their countries, and nearly all stated a commitment to reduce the degree of foreign ownership and enhance local control of production.

Import-substituting industrialization (ISI) became the chosen model for manufacturing policy in Africa. The strategic focus of ISI is to replace imported goods by developing local manufacturing production for the domestic market. For many industrializing states the logic of this policy is compelling, and virtually all "late industrializing" countries have initially relied on ISI.[73] By reducing the need for imported manufactures, especially nondurable consumer goods, countries can improve their balance of payments position and save foreign exchange. The expansion of local production presumably also allows developing economies to capture greater benefits from industry. An initial emphasis on simple technologies and labor-intensive production can permit the acquisition of industrial know-how while expanding employment. Greater density of industrial enterprise fosters backward and forward linkages among firms, as complementary activities are established. The growth of manufacturing may spur the development of indigenous business, as local entrepreneurs (some with initial experience in foreign-owned companies) establish new ventures to compete with or complement major industries. Public investment and regulation can play a leading role in fostering these processes.

The package of industrial policies has been fairly consistent throughout Africa.[74] First, governments have provided an array of incentives for domestic and foreign corporations to invest in manufacturing. These include tax relief, dispensation on customs duties for imported industrial inputs, cheap land and utilities, liberal policies for hiring expatriate staff, government-provided credit or equity capital, and guarantees against nationalization. Second, protectionist policies have been used to nurture the manufacturing sector. By raising the cost of imports or restricting them altogether, policymakers hoped to shield domestic "infant industries" from harmful foreign competition until they could become sufficiently efficient to compete in open markets. Consequently, governments have imposed high tariffs, quotas, or bans on selected imports and regulations on entry into domestic markets. They have also maintained overvalued exchange rates, which reduced the local cost of imports while making exports relatively expensive. An implicit rationale behind this policy was to make imported machinery and raw materials, as well as other essential goods such as medicine and food, more affordable. Foreign exchange was rationed through import licensing, and manufacturers ostensibly had priority allocations.

Conditions for industrial growth were not favorable in most of the region. Investment in manufacturing was hampered by deficits in entrepreneurship, labor markets, finance, and infrastructure. As we have noted, African entrepreneurs had little exposure to manufacturing in the segmented colonial economies. The private sector in most independent African states had insufficient experience or resources to enter into manufacturing, preferring more familiar investments in areas such as trade, real estate, or transportation. The labor force embodied low levels of education and skills, which limited the pool of industrial workers and managers, especially for more sophisticated enterprises. Access to capital was extremely limited in most countries, as financial systems were weak and many private bankers were conservative in their lending practices. Fiscal constraints and patronage pressures often limited government capacity to deliver effective financial support for industry. Inadequate infrastructure also hindered investment and raised the cost of industrial activities. In Nigeria, for instance, virtually all large-scale firms generate their own electricity, and two-thirds provide their own water.[75] Bottlenecks at the ports, bad road networks, and sparse railway systems create major obstacles to industrial expansion.

African policymakers had various outlets for boosting investment in manufacturing activities. They could encourage entrepreneurship by the domestic private sector, attract investment by foreign corporations, or directly provide capital and production through state enterprises. The first option, promoting indigenous entrepreneurs, was pursued by some African capitalist states, although it was not a central component of growth. Kenya and Nigeria, for instance, set up development assistance agencies to train, aid, and finance African enterprise.[76] Populist states rarely provided direct support to local capitalists, although the government of Ghana under Nkrumah did approve a number of joint ventures between foreign and domestic investors.

Generally, however, government initiatives toward indigenous business failed to advance industrial growth, and such efforts played a minor role in the development of the sector. One reason for this situation was simply that the supply of entrepreneurs was insufficient, and most domestic investors could not easily respond to incentives in this area. The diseconomies of scale presented by Africa's small markets further constrained growth. Equally important, however, was the political context. Most African governments held reservations about support for the private sector. In capitalist states such as Côte d'Ivoire, Nigeria, and Kenya, senior officials were concerned about the spread of economic and social power, particularly among ethnic and regional groups viewed as competing with governing elites. In populist and Afro-Marxist regimes the emergence of a domestic bourgeoisie was anathema, and local private enterprise was discouraged except for small-scale activities in trade and services. Additionally, governments typically employed development assistance programs as a tool of patronage, and resources generally went to political loyalists and cronies rather than to economically worthwhile ventures.

Foreign investors, possessing skills, technology, and capital, were the crucial source of manufacturing growth for most African countries. Much of this investment came from large-scale international firms, commonly known as transnational corporations (TNCs). African countries have long maintained an ambivalent relationship with TNCs. Although these corporations provide needed resources and production, they are often regarded as exploitative interlopers in African economies. Regardless of these concerns, African governments have generally welcomed some degree of foreign investment. In the wake of independence, most countries actively sought external capital, and foreign companies established core industrial activities throughout the region. African capitalist states have been the most broadly hospitable to foreign firms and have attracted investment in a variety of industrial activities. In Marxist Angola major oil production companies, including Gulf, dominated the critical petroleum sector. In Sekou Touré's Guinea, a populist state, U.S. mining firms developed the extensive bauxite reserves that provided a lifeline of foreign exchange for the regime. Populist regimes in Tanzania and Ghana welcomed a variety of investors, notably in the latter's Volta Dam project.

Many Africans feel that TNCs, by virtue of their size, mobility, and control of specialized assets, have overwhelming leverage in their dealings with the governments of African host countries. Consequently, the effects of foreign involvement are often detrimental. The critique of TNC activities comes from many quarters, although underdevelopment theorists have been the most trenchant. First, such ventures are said to foster the "disarticulation" of African economies. The arbitrary nature of foreign investment gives rise to a haphazard array of industries with little relation to one another. Because foreign subsidiaries deal mainly with their own home offices, they rarely establish linkages with local firms.

Moreover, TNCs often employ capital-intensive production methods, thus limiting the need for labor and the potential for employment generation. In addition to "inappropriate" technologies, foreign companies may provide goods that are unnecessary or ill suited to local economies. Liquor, cigarettes, soft drinks, infant formula, automobiles, and consumer electronics are among the wares critics cite in this regard. Finally, it is argued that TNCs are a central medium for the transfer of resources from peripheral to core economies. Through vertical integration—segmented production methods that take place in multiple countries—TNCs realize greater value-added that accrues to the corporation's home country rather than to the various host countries. Many subsidiaries of transnational corporations repatriate their profits without reinvesting in the local economy; some firms also borrow in local capital markets, further draining national resources. In addition, foreign firms have often been culpable of evading local regulations and laws through bribery, legal manipulation, or other tacit arrangements. A prominent example is the use of transfer pricing to evade taxes or other rules. By manipulating prices for transactions among the international branches of a TNC, the home office can produce losses in one subsidiary (to escape taxes, for example), and the gains will appear in another. The firm can therefore maintain a profitable balance sheet at the expense of particular host countries.

Although a critical view of TNC activities is warranted, some of these problems have been misconstrued, and many are not attributable to the designs of foreign firms. Misguided public policies and inadequate regulation by host country governments have also created a number of problems. The vagaries of market forces—including relative factor prices, market size, and competitive pressures—equally influence the scope and content of foreign investment. Sovereign states have considerable leverage in dealing with foreign firms, and TNCs rarely behave as the leviathans portrayed in the dependency literature.[77] Even the smaller and weaker African regimes have been able to impose some constraints on external investors, although admittedly these constraints are often inadequate and costly.

African states have sought to control foreign capital through a variety of measures. Many countries have required that overseas investors accept a minority share (usually 49 percent) of equity in local ventures, with the majority share held by the host government. In other instances, foreign firms have faced stipulations for a minimum share of local private equity or participation in management. Nigeria's indigenization program in the mid-1970s was the most extensive in this respect, and Kenya's Africanization policy had similar aims.[78] These programs targeted local immigrant groups as well as TNCs, requiring them to divest controlling shares of their ventures to "indigenous" investors. Foreign firms are commonly barred from many activities, not only in sensitive areas such as infrastructure and arms production but also in products that might compete with local entrepreneurs or state enterprise. In view of overriding concerns for import substitution, many TNC subsidiaries have been restricted in their ability to export products. High rates of taxation and limits on repatriation of profits are frequently applied to foreign companies.

African governments have also entered directly into manufacturing operations, either as partners with foreign capital or through wholly owned state enterprise. State officials have perceived market failures in instances where industries could not attract sufficient private capital or expertise, commonly large-scale, technologically advanced ventures where high start up costs and long gestation periods may deter private investors. The limited domestic markets in many African countries—as a result of small populations and low purchasing power—also restrict economies of scale. In other cases, governments wish to retain control of particular industries for reasons of national security or prestige.

Public utilities, air and rail transport, and mining ventures have typically been controlled by African states. Other large enterprises such as vehicle assembly, tires, cement, chemicals, paper, and machinery have also come under some degree of public ownership. Nigeria—West Africa's most ambitious industrial power—attempted (without success) to create an integrated steel complex, a petrochemical sector, and an automotive industry. In Cameroon, Côte d'Ivoire, Kenya, and several other countries, governments held shares in food processing and textile operations. Generally, public ownership extended to diverse industries, and in most African economies a substantial portion of manufacturing output was derived from parastatals or joint ventures. Public enterprises were often high-cost, inefficient ventures, as they suffered from faulty planning, overstaffing, insufficient funding, and frequent political meddling. Few countries were able to raise industrial productivity through government firms.

The results of ISI strategies were discouraging. Although these policies have produced acceptable results in other regions, they were clearly less fruitful in Africa. In many respects it can be said that African governments adopted the ideas of ISI without providing the necessary enabling factors for industrial growth. Industrialization schemes in most countries proved economically inefficient, and they were ineffective in developing sustainable domestic production. High levels of protection and subsidies created a number of distortions in the manufacturing sector. Many firms, operating behind tariff barriers or import bans, were generally uncompetitive in terms of costs, quality, or output. A number of ostensibly import-substitution industries were actually net losers of foreign exchange, as they required substantial inputs of imported machinery and raw materials. Unprofitable public enterprises created a substantial fiscal drain for many governments. Large ventures sometimes crowded out smaller producers (for example, in shoes, clothing, or leather goods), and state enterprises and foreign firms often dominated capital markets at the expense of local entrepreneurs. Private investors—both foreign and domestic—were deterred by stringent regulations, weak infrastructure, and bureaucratic obstruction. In addition, many countries encountered an "ISI wall," as their small domestic markets restricted the scope of production. Most large firms used only a limited portion of their capacity, and economies of scale were difficult to achieve.

The record of industrial development reflected many of these liabilities. By 1987 for sub-Saharan Africa as a whole, manufacturing provided 10 percent of gross domestic product, a share virtually unchanged since independence. Manufacturing activities were clustered narrowly, and fully 66 percent of the region's manufacturing value-added (MVA) came from seven countries—Cameroon, Côte d'Ivoire, Ghana, Kenya, Nigeria, Zambia, and Zimbabwe.[79] Manufacturing still comprised less than 10 percent of GDP in countries such as Benin, Burkina Faso, Liberia, Mali, Niger, Sierra Leone, Somalia, Uganda, Tanzania, Congo (Zaire), and Congo-Brazzaville. The composition of manufacturing throughout the region also reflected minimal change, as final consumption goods remained the principal output and intermediate and capital goods increased only slightly.

Trade figures underscore the limited extent of import substitution and diversification. In 1965 three-quarters of Africa's imports were manufactured goods; and two decades later that proportion was still 73 percent. Policies emphasizing import substitution naturally gave little impetus to the development of manufactured exports, which is also reflected in regional trade. Merely 7 percent of African exports in 1965 were manufactured goods, and this figure actually decreased to 6 percent by 1980. The region provided about 10 percent of developing countries' manufactured exports in 1965, dropping to less than 0.4 percent in 1984; in that year Africa's share of global manufactured exports was virtually nil.

From the 1970s forward the trends in African manufacturing steadily worsened. In the first ten years of independence Africa's manufacturing expansion, at about 8 percent, outpaced the average for developing countries. Thereafter, Africa's growth lagged considerably, reaching only 5 percent in the 1970s. The sector virtually collapsed in the following decade.[80] During the ten-year period after 1976, thirty-three countries registered manufacturing growth rates under 5 percent, and in fourteen economies these rates were negative. For the region as a whole, from 1980 to 1986 the growth of value-added in manufacturing was 0.3 percent.

The decline in African manufacturing is attributable to both domestic and international factors. Aside from problems of infrastructure, entrepreneurship, and policy-induced distortions, global economic developments were unfavorable for African industrialization. In the 1970s rising energy costs and stagnant prices for commodity exports aggravated balance of payments deficits in most countries. Many states borrowed internationally to stanch these shortfalls, and the accumulation of external debt worsened the squeeze on hard currency. The far-reaching international recession beginning in the late 1970s also subdued demand for many African exports while raising the prices of manufactured imports. As a result, African economies were often starved of vital imports (such as raw materials and spare parts) necessary for manufacturing.

A further cause of Africa's industrial decline was the region's growing marginality in global markets. After the 1960s many international investors were discouraged by perceptions of instability and difficult operating conditions in Africa. Foreign firms were drawn to more promising markets in Asia or Latin America, and direct foreign investment slowed in most of Africa. By the 1980s many traditional investors were divesting their African operations, contributing to the process of "deindustrialization" throughout much of the region. Net foreign direct investment in Africa was $823 million in 1973 and $878 million in 1990, showing virtually no growth. In 1990 direct foreign investment in Indonesia exceeded the total for all of sub-Saharan Africa. Mining activities were the only segment of industry in which investors sustained a commitment, although here again investment declined in the 1980s, and activities were highly concentrated in a few countries. Foreign direct investment in Nigeria, where external capital is centered in the petroleum sector, accounted for 47 percent of all investment in sub-Saharan Africa by 1985.[81]

In most countries the industrial malaise lasted well into the 1990s, and prospects for the development of African manufacturing were somber. African policymakers, often under pressure from external donors, abandoned ISI-inspired strategies, yet there was no effective new package to supplant the discredited policies. Many governments adopted economic reforms intended to revive investment and production, but the general environment for manufacturing remained weak. The region's isolation in the global economy also slowed investor response. Moreover, as we shall see in the next chapter, some elements of the orthodox adjustment package proved inimical to industrial growth.

▩ Strategies and Policies in Agriculture

Agricultural development in Africa has been marked by a basic paradox. Agriculture holds a major role in African economies, as the sector provides a substantial portion of national output and occupies the majority of the labor force. Yet governments in the region have often neglected the rural sector in their economic policies and more often than not have actively discriminated against agricultural producers. There are various reasons for this discrepancy. Ideologically, elites have regarded agriculture as a source of tradition and dependency, a vestige of the colonial past. Governments have also had an economic motive in seeking to extract surpluses from agriculture, whether for industrialization or simply to shore up general revenues. Politically, rural residents have not constituted a powerful interest group in most countries, and they have often been eclipsed by pressures from urban-based constituencies. The prevailing official strategies have yielded extremely poor agricultural performance, with negative consequences for popular welfare and economic growth.

Newly independent Africa was dominated by agrarian economies. In 1965, 43 percent of the region's gross domestic product was derived from agriculture. At one end of the spectrum, the contribution of agriculture in mining economies such as Congo, Congo-Brazzaville, and Zambia constituted 20 percent or less of GDP. At the other end, in such low-income economies as Burkina Faso, Mali, Niger, Benin, Nigeria, Ethiopia, Sudan, Uganda, and Malawi, agriculture exceeded 50 percent of national output. In most instances official statistics underestimate the importance of agriculture, since a large share of subsistence production is not recorded and the output passing through government marketing channels is commonly undervalued by inflated exchange rates. The labor-intensive character of agriculture is reflected in the large proportion of people occupied in the sector. In 1965, 77 percent of the regional labor force was employed in agriculture; the figure exceeded 90 percent in such economies as Lesotho, Botswana, Rwanda, Burundi, Uganda, and many of the Sahelian states. Food and other agricultural commodities provided 62 percent of Africa's exports in 1962. The region provided more than a quarter of world exports of coffee, over half of global trade in groundnut oil, palm oil, sesame seeds, and sisal; and at least 80 percent of cocoa, groundnuts (peanuts), and palm kernels.

Economic theory and experience point to the crucial role of agriculture in developing countries. The growth of the rural economy, including farming and related marketing activities, increases incomes and enlarges the domestic market. Whereas self-sufficiency in food is not always attainable or necessary, food security is a foundation of development. Food security is ensured when household incomes, public revenues, agricultural output, and distribution systems are adequate to provision all segments of the population. Agrarian expansion can benefit the trade balance, as food security may reduce imports while cash crops increase exports. Internationally, the historical record—from nineteenth-century Europe to the newly industrializing countries (NICs) of Asia—indicates that an agricultural foundation is usually essential for industrial expansion. The agricultural sector can furnish raw materials for manufacturing processes, and it serves as a market for inputs such as fertilizer and machinery. The fiscal surplus realized from agriculture may provide revenues for the development of industry.

The lessons from successfully developing regions demonstrate the need for a productive transformation of agriculture through changes in organization and technology. Within the first decade after independence, African agriculture largely reached the limits of expansion under prevailing techniques. Only 30 percent of Africa's land area is arable, and many soils and climates provide limited yields under rain-fed cultivation. Population increases and land tenure patterns (often inherited from colonial economies) have created significant land constraints in a number of areas, including the Sahelian states and much of southern Africa. Agricultural output grew significantly under colonial regimes and in the early years of independence, but this growth mainly reflected the expansion of land under cultivation and the absorption of more labor. By the 1960s a number of countries were experiencing some degree of land scarcity, as rising populations increased demands for greater productivity in the rural sector. Advancements in farming practices, inputs, and rural institutions were necessary to increase the efficient use of land and labor.

Amid the variations in ecology and farming patterns, some common defining features of African agriculture can be identified. Rain-fed agriculture is prevalent throughout the region, as irrigation is used sparsely. Even in countries such as Zimbabwe, Kenya, and South Africa, where the commercial farming sector is substantially irrigated, the bulk of peasant households depend on rainfall for their yields. Peasants comprise the great majority of rural producers in Africa, and most are smallholders, farming on modest plots with family labor. Peasants are engaged primarily in subsistence agriculture, although they are also commonly involved in markets through the sale of surplus food or cash crops, as well as through supplementary activities such as petty trade. Because they are usually self-provisioning, peasant households have a degree of flexibility in their economic strategies. The possibility of retreating to subsistence production or of turning to parallel markets offers many rural households an "exit option" in their engagement with the market and the state. When official producer prices are too low, inputs and infrastructure are inadequate, or government officials too intrusive and corrupt, peasants often withdraw from official markets to pursue more autonomous production and marketing.

The modernization of agriculture involves several components. One of the most important innovations is the introduction of improved crop varieties, which provide higher yields and greater resistance to pests and diseases. This entails research efforts to develop the relevant crops, as well as extension services to disseminate knowledge of new farming techniques. Distribution of other agricultural inputs—including fertilizer, pesticides, and equipment—usually accompanies the application of new seed varieties. The expansion of rural infrastructure—including storage facilities, feeder roads, and irrigation networks—is another important factor. In many areas land tenure patterns, credit, or labor markets constrain productivity, and reforms are necessary in the laws and institutions affecting the agricultural economy. Finally, it is essential to offer producers incentives to foster innovation and increase output.

Most African states have lacked essential features of this generic package of agricultural development. Rather than emphasize incentives and investments in the rural sector, most governments have followed policies that have dampened inducements for producers, and numerous regimes have favored large segments of the urban economy at the expense of agriculture. Pricing policy is the most commonly mentioned distortion. Independent African regimes (like their colonial predecessors) have typically controlled producer prices for major food and export crops, setting levels well below prevailing market rates. Price controls have been enforced through government marketing boards, which proliferated in the region from the 1950s onward. Official interventions in rural markets and food distribution networks have usually been inefficient. The overvaluation of exchange rates has also had adverse effects on agriculture by lowering returns to export producers, encouraging food imports, and raising costs for external investors.

In the majority of African states, governments have dominated the procurement and distribution of farm inputs. Fertilizers and chemicals are often provided at controlled prices, ostensibly to support the majority of poor farmers. In practice, state management of these activities has generally missed its mark. Fiscal lapses and administrative problems have fostered chronic irregularities in the supply of inputs. These programs often become patronage outlets for officials, agents, and transporters; and in many instances distribution is heavily skewed toward more affluent commercial farmers. Similar problems can be witnessed in state-sponsored agricultural credit programs, which also claim to compensate for market failure.

Investments in rural infrastructure have been seriously deficient in most countries. Inadequate roads, rail networks, and communications hinder the development of markets, the operation of extension services, and the distribution of inputs. Storage facilities, typically under the control of government marketing agencies, are poorly administered and maintained, and administrative problems have impeded the delivery of inputs and extension services to farmers.[82] This situation discourages farmers from dealing with the parastatals and results in substantial losses of produce. Irrigation is underutilized in much of Africa. A few countries—notably Nigeria, Senegal, Sudan, and Madagascar—have made major investments in irrigation facilities. Most governments have been drawn to large-scale, capital-intensive schemes, which have failed to provide the desired yields. Financial problems and a dearth of qualified personnel often create major problems of upkeep in these projects.

Governments have also allocated insufficient resources to social services in the countryside. Substandard education and health benefits undermine productivity and living standards. A particular failing is seen in the relatively low achievements in female education and health, especially since women form the majority of farm laborers in many countries. Poorly educated populations are less adept at assimilating new technologies and, especially where health services are also lacking, are less likely to respond to family planning initiatives. Africa's rural populations have sparse access to safe drinking water, sanitation, and medical facilities. Pervasive health problems handicap many farmers, placing inherent limits on labor and output. In addition, the relatively greater amenities in urban areas often prompt migration from the villages, which burdens urban infrastructure while sometimes disrupting rural communities.

Two key elements in agricultural modernization—research and extension services—have not met the needs of most African economies. For many years research efforts focused mainly on export rather than food crops or on staple crops, such as wheat and rice, not widely cultivated in many parts of the region. The one exception in food crops was the introduction of high-yielding maize varieties in southern Africa. Research efforts were also funded mainly by international institutions, with little connection to local capabilities. More recently it has been recognized that greater attention should be given to root crops (e.g., cassava and yams) and local cereals (e.g., millet and sorghum), and there has been a shift in this direction. Efforts to link international research to local-level applications and farming systems have been less successful, mainly because domestic capacities remain weak in most African countries.

Extension services, the main channel for spreading innovations among rural producers, have also suffered from inadequate funding and misplaced priorities. In many countries extension services are poorly staffed and equipped, and they are greatly hampered by the poor state of infrastructure. Moreover, extension services frequently cluster around the larger commercial farms and more affluent households, which are more receptive to new technologies and practices. Peasant smallholders, especially those in more precarious ecological zones, are quite rationally risk-averse and less likely to adopt untested innovations. These cultivators, however, form the bulk of African producers, and they are greatly in need of productivity-enhancing changes.

The institutional setting has been equally troublesome in fostering growth. In many countries farmers have possessed uncertain rights to land, wheras in others government land reforms or collectivization efforts have denied free title to cultivators. Consequently, farmers have been unwilling to invest in improvements to the land, such as irrigation and antierosion measures. Formal credit markets have generally been inaccessible to or risky for smallholders because of discriminatory lending practices and high charges. Rural organizations, including cooperatives and farmers' unions, have often suffered from poor resources and organizational weakness. Many peasants, especially women, are marginalized from these associations and are therefore placed at a competitive disadvantage.

These factors have led to deficient agricultural performance in most of Africa since the late 1960s. From 1975 through 1984, the region's recorded agricultural production grew at an average of only 0.6 percent a year. Agricultural malaise has persisted, with at least fourteen countries showing negative growth from 1988 to 1992.[83] These trends were reflected throughout the rural sector, although export agriculture probably suffered the most drastic decline. In the 1970s sixteen of sub-Saharan Africa's top twenty agricultural exports dropped in volume. Moreover, many African economies lost substantial global market share, as trade shifted to neighboring countries or to other regions such as Southeast Asia. For example, Ghana's share of world cocoa exports dropped from 30 percent in 1972 to 15 percent in 1991, largely to the benefit of Côte d'Ivoire, which tripled its world market share from 12 percent to 35 percent in the same period. Nigeria's market share in cocoa went from 23 percent to 8 percent during this interval. Uganda's share of coffee exports dropped by half in that period, and Sudan's share of cotton trade declined by two-thirds.[84]

Food production also suffered. Because much of Africa's food output is consumed on the farm or sold in local markets, national statistics do not accurately reflect supply conditions. With this caveat in mind, however, there are several indications of unfavorable circumstances. An overall index of food production compiled by World Bank analysts showed regional growth of only 1 percent from 1975 through 1984, well below the population growth rate of 2.7 percent. Average yields for key cereals were also lower in Africa than in the rest of the world. At the end of the 1970s, maize yields (in output per hectare) for the region were only 32 percent of the world average, rice yields 54 percent, and those for sorghum and wheat 53 percent and 61 percent, respectively.[85] Low productivity and inefficient distribution systems have necessitated increasing food imports, especially to supply urban areas. These imports have been encouraged by overvalued exchange rates and by a shift in tastes, especially in urban areas, toward grains such as rice and wheat. Between 1973 and 1980, the value of staple food imports grew by 440 percent. External food aid to Africa increased by 18 percent annually from 1975 to 1984.[86]

Of course, not all problems of agricultural development can be attributed to a coherent design on the part of African governments. Drought is a common hardship in agrarian economies, affecting at least twenty-five countries in the 1980s alone. Wars and political upheavals have also been unsettling to rural communities, creating varying degrees of food shortage. The dislocation of people and distribution networks has induced famines in Ethiopia, Somalia, Sudan, and Mozambique since the 1970s. Numerous challenges of agricultural development emerge from limited state capacities, weak market structures, prevailing social inequalities, and ecological constraints. Economic policy throughout the region has nonetheless reflected a consistent bias against the rural sector, manifest in heavy taxation of cash crops; attempts to control markets for inputs and subsistence food crops; relative underinvestment in rural infrastructure, support services, and social amenities; and a preference for large-scale agrarian projects rather than dispersed assistance to smallholders.

As Robert Bates has explained, these policies reflect the political priorities of governing elites and the relative salience of domestic interest groups.[87] African regimes have typically been concerned with maintaining stability in urban areas, where influential groups such as civil servants, industrial workers, and students have close proximity to officials. Consequently, leaders fearful of food riots or other unrest have pursued "cheap food" policies since food is a wage good that comprises a major share of household expenditures for low-income urban groups. Urban food costs have been contained by controlling producer prices, regulating distribution, and maintaining overvalued exchange rates to subsidize imports of food and agricultural inputs. Governments have also been lured by the appeals of "modern" production from state farms, plantations, and irrigation schemes, and they have emphasized such projects over market inducements for smallholders. Another reason for the emphasis on projects and the use of parastatals to regulate markets is that officials can control patronage more effectively through these mechanisms.

Rural producers have few political resources to defend against discriminatory measures. Because they are dispersed and often marginal, farmers (especially smallholders) face collective action problems that limit their ability to lobby for better policies. Farmers are difficult to organize and therefore tend to be less effective than urban-based interest groups. They do, however, possess some latitude in their production and marketing decisions. As Goran Hyden has emphasized, many peasants, facing adverse prices and market conditions, have varying options for withdrawing from the formal marketing system.[88] They may reduce production of cash crops, sell their produce through parallel markets, switch to locally marketed food crops, or retreat to subsistence farming. Although these strategies can preserve household security, they commonly lead farmers to reduce their cash crop output or to divert produce from officially regulated markets. Consequently, governments lose revenue, and they are often saddled with high food import bills to provision the cities. Antiagricultural bias is politically sustainable in many instances; however, it is economically costly. A few countries have steered away from these policy distortions, including Kenya, Côte d'Ivoire, and Zimbabwe; in all of these states agricultural interest groups have had a higher political profile.

Having discussed rural policies in the previous section on development strategies, we will note some broad outlines here. There have been significant ideological differences in approaches to agriculture. Populist and Afro-Marxist regimes have frequently opted for expansive state farms, as in Ghana, Mozambique, and Ethiopia. Some of these governments, notably Ethiopia and Tanzania, have also been attracted to collectivization schemes, often linked to rural resettlement or villagization programs. State ventures held out promise of applying mechanized farming techniques on a considerable scale, yielding large marketable surpluses of food or export crops. The employment of agricultural workers also presumably breaks down traditional attachments to land and household labor. Collectivization presents a more direct assault on rural property relations, as governments have tried to engage peasants in communal farming, thereby reducing their involvement in individual household production.

These policy approaches have reflected flaws in both conception and practice. As was the case with the large plantation schemes previously attempted by some colonial governments, state farms in postindependent Africa have been expensive and unproductive. Many schemes have been ruined by poor management, insufficient financing, and widespread problems with procuring or maintaining equipment. Labor markets have not always proven responsive, and shortages of workers have often hindered operations. Inappropriate farming systems have frequently yielded poor results. Many African soils are not conducive to sustained mechanical cultivation, and crops such as wheat have generally been poorly suited to local climatic conditions. Collectivization has been equally disappointing. African small-holders have an inveterate reliance on household access to land, and peasants have resisted surrendering their property rights to communal agriculture. In Tanzania, although 90 percent of the peasantry was in *ujamaa* villages by the late 1970s, merely 5 percent of agricultural output came from communal plots. In Mozambique, of the peasants who lived in collective settlements, only an eighth actually farmed communally.[89]

African capitalist states placed greater emphasis on private investment in the agricultural sector, but they were also attracted to large-scale ventures and mechanized farming. A significant portion of Côte d'Ivoire's exports came from sizable farms and plantations, many under foreign ownership. Nigeria made large investments in river basin development, with the expansion of wheat cultivation a major objective. Much of Kenya's coffee and tea production also developed on large private tracts. Although many of these enterprises were productive, they created enclaves that did not generally enhance the productivity of the rural sector, and they sometimes contributed to land scarcity.

Some states gave smallholders significant attention. Kenya encouraged smallholder cultivation of tea and coffee, whereas Côte d'Ivoire promoted peasant activities in both export and food crops. The large-scale agricultural development programs (ADPs) established by Nigeria in the 1970s with support from the World Bank were integrated programs intended to bolster smallholder production in particular districts or regions. Critics have faulted some of the governments for emphasizing the advancement of "progressive" farmers, generally the upper stratum of the peasantry, instead of promoting broadly dispersed efforts among poorer or more marginal rural communities. Moreover, endeavors such as the ADPs, although often producing impressive short-term gains in output, sometimes proved costly and unsustainable. Nigeria in particular has overextended the scope of its ADPs, and many projects were moribund in the 1980s.

The critical challenge for African agriculture has been to improve incomes and output among the mass of peasant smallholders. These peasants will comprise the bulk of the rural economy in most countries for the foreseeable future, and they are the key to enhancing growth and living standards in the region. Promoting smallholder agriculture entails a series of changes in institutions, pricing policies, inputs to agriculture, social services, and economic distribution in rural areas. In the 1980s and 1990s African governments began to take steps toward some of the necessary changes, but progress was impeded by the fiscal crises of many governments, the constraints of economic adjustment, and other factors such as political instability. In addition, as we discuss in the next chapter, protectionist measures by the governments of the industrialized states hindered the expansion of African exports, further dampening recovery.

■ The Environment

Growing population pressures and economic needs have aggravated a host of environmental problems in sub-Saharan Africa. In much of coastal and central Africa, deforestation has been an accelerating phenomenon. Côte d'Ivoire's forests were decimated at a rate of more than 5 percent a year in the 1980s, and in such countries as Malawi, Nigeria, Gambia, Burundi, and Liberia, rising populations and the demands of commercial agriculture have accentuated these problems. The reduction of forest cover often creates serious problems of soil erosion, which in several countries on the Sahelian fringe is synonymous with desertification. The encroachment of the Sahara has been evident, for instance, in Mauritania, Mali, Niger, and Burkina Faso.

Given the acute pressures for land and fuelwood in many low-income African communities, it is virtually impossible to subordinate these needs to concerns for environmental preservation, and there is often scant economic basis for dissuading people from existing patterns of land use. Government interests in securing revenues for timber and other exports, along with a lack of comprehensive policies or adequate enforcement, have commonly deepened these problems. In a few areas of eastern and southern Africa, where wildlife conservation is a leading issue, efforts to offer incentives for environmental regulation have not resolved the tension between agriculturalists and animals. International sanctions on the sale of ivory have sometimes had perverse effects in this area. Governments such as Zimbabwe, which have been relatively responsible in husbanding their wildlife resources, have been unable to garner revenues from the sale of officially culled ivory. This makes it difficult to provide returns for communities in the reserve areas or to subsidize their conservation efforts.

■ Human Resources

The development of human resources constitutes a foundation of economic growth. Educational endowments are among the most basic determinants of economic performance worldwide, and health services are integral to both popular well-being and productivity. Population policies offer a further challenge, especially in low-income countries. Excessive population growth undermines gains from economic expansion, and in many areas the pressures of rising populations also contribute to social and political tensions. These issues have placed formidable demands on policy and resources in postindependence Africa.

In our discussion of the colonial legacy, we described the inadequacy of social provisions. Education and health services were often concentrated in major urban areas and were commonly skewed toward European and immigrant communities. In 1960 little more than a third of eligible

Africans were enrolled in primary school, and the region counted one physician per 50,000 inhabitants—levels well below the averages for all low-income developing countries at the time. Not only was the distribution of social services unequal, but the models adopted by the colonial powers were not matched to local needs. In education the interests of the colonial powers were paramount, and many programs carried strong European cultural biases. The provision of different levels of schooling, the content of instruction, and criteria for advancement were largely borrowed from metropolitan patterns. Health systems emphasized curative medicine, mainly for urban elites. Reproductive health services were extremely limited, and family planning was virtually nonexistent.

In addressing the widespread clamor for social services, Africa's newly independent governments were constrained by scarce resources and shortages of skilled personnel. Most regimes struggled to balance competing objectives, as they sought to expand basic facilities and improve access while ensuring the quality of services and meeting the fiscal demands of social programs. These goals were not always well served. The overall commitment to social services among African regimes was relatively consistent across ideological lines, but significant differences existed between countries in the design and scope of programs.

For African states and societies alike, education has been a leading developmental issue. Governments have viewed education as a principal means of breaking the confines of underdevelopment by enhancing the productivity of labor and building a complement of skilled bureaucrats and managers. For the average household or community, education provides a crucial medium for strengthening access to resources and ensuring social mobility across generations. Under colonialism the connection between education and status was widely recognized. The families of chiefs and other notables in particular sought to preserve their social position by providing their children with skills and credentials, often at great financial cost. For many Africans the desire for access to missionary education was an important motive for religious conversion. In the decades since independence, extended families and community organizations in many societies continue to make sacrifices to subsidize the education of promising young people.

Primary schooling has been a pervasive concern of African governments; indeed, one of the most widely shared policy goals has been to achieve universal primary education. Although few countries have approached this ideal, the proportional enrollment of primary-age students doubled in the two decades after independence, and by 1980 about 79 percent of eligible students received primary schooling. In several countries including Gabon, Togo, Cameroon, Botswana, Lesotho, Swaziland, Zimbabwe, and Mauritius, enrollment rates exceeded 100 percent, as older pupils were included at the primary level. Still, by the end of the 1970s a substantial number of countries had enrollment rates below 50 percent, including Senegal, Guinea, Mali, Niger, Burkina Faso, Chad, Ethiopia, Somalia and Burundi. Also, a persistent (although narrowing) gender gap was found in education, as primary enrollments were 87 percent for males compared with 67 percent for females.[90]

The development of secondary and tertiary education has created basic tensions for most African countries. On the one hand, secondary education is essential for raising national capacities and is an avenue of social mobility. Tertiary education is even more important in this regard, and universities are a crucial source of specialized skills and training. With just a handful of university graduates at independence, most countries established or augmented institutions of higher education, and a few—such as Nigeria—created extensive postsecondary systems.

Governments face substantial pressure from citizens for access to these educational outlets, and competition for admission is intense. At the same time, postprimary education is often costly, and many low- or middle-income African economies have too few jobs to absorb the supply of advanced graduates. Unemployed graduates have created social tensions in a number of countries, and these concerns, in addition to the fiscal demands of higher education, have left many governments ambivalent about the design and scope of postprimary education. Few low-income countries have registered strong achievements in this area. In 1980, secondary enrollments in Africa constituted only 16 percent of the eligible population, and university enrollments represented merely 1 percent.[91] These levels were about half of the average for all low-income developing countries.

Some distinctions along ideological lines have been evident in educational policies. Many of the region's capitalist states—including Nigeria, Côte d'Ivoire, Cameroon, Kenya, and Malawi—have generally adhered to Western educational patterns. They have relied on traditional curricula, made substantial commitments to postprimary institutions, and used examination-based systems of advancement. A few populist and Afro-Marxist regimes have sought departures from this model, emphasizing mass education in basic skills. In Tanzania and Mozambique only about a third of primary-age students were enrolled at independence, but by 1980 both countries had achieved primary enrollments greater than 90 percent. Tanzania's president, Julius Nyerere, articulated an alternative model that emphasized practical education, especially for rural households, and he sought to create a primary curriculum that could stand on its own merits without necessarily being seen as a conduit to higher education.

Socialist governments have also conducted mass literacy campaigns, sometimes with impressive results. Ethiopia's literacy drive in the late 1970s mobilized tens of thousands of soldiers, students, teachers, and civil servants to reach around 7 million people, the majority of whom were women. Tanzania reached about 5 million adults in its campaign, and countries such as Mozambique and Somalia made similar efforts.[92] These campaigns have often had considerable impact, notably in Tanzania where adult literacy jumped from 10 percent at independence to 66 percent by 1976.

African governments have generally made large fiscal commitments in this area, and by the late 1970s nearly 16 percent of budgeted spending went to education, slightly above the average for all developing countries. Yet progress has been slower than desired. By the mid-1970s the literacy rate for the region was still about half the general level for low-income developing countries, and general adult literacy in Africa did not exceed 50 percent until the early 1990s. Again, these achievements varied among countries and were unequal by gender and region. Whereas two-thirds of African males were literate in 1995, the ratio for females was 48 percent.[93]

As in other sectors, some education problems were beyond the immediate control of African governments. The challenges of developing educational foundations in low-income rural societies are forbidding, given the scarce resources available to most African states. It is also important to recall that the region began from a lower base than other developing areas. In 1965 Africa's primary enrollment rates were less than half those in Asia, and secondary enrollments were as low as one-sixth the Asian average.[94] By 1995 overall adult literacy in Africa was beginning to approach the 1960 Asian level.

Nevertheless, there have been a number of difficulties in the planning and delivery of educational services in the region. The laudable rhetoric of universal primary education often has led to rapid growth of formal enrollments, but services are unevenly distributed. Most countries reflect persistent disparities among regions, ethnic groups, and gender groups. The continuing lag in the schooling of girls and women is a particularly acute problem, as education is a crucial factor affecting household incomes, family planning, and child and maternal health. More generally, the nominal expansion of enrollments in many countries has not been matched by commensurate training or administration, yielding serious deficiencies in the quality of education. Poor teacher preparation, inadequate textbooks and supplies, rudimentary buildings, and overcrowded classes are the norm in many countries, particularly in rural areas.

Especially in postsecondary education, large start-up costs and heavy subsidization have created substantial fiscal burdens for many governments. The average cost of educating an African secondary school student in the late 1970s could be as much as six times greater than comparable costs in Asia or Latin America; for a university education African costs were five to nine times greater, reflecting in part problems of infrastructure, buildings, teacher training, and administrative inefficiency.[95] The returns for these expenditures were often disappointing, as curricula and incentives did not always foster the necessary skills for these developing economies. There has generally been insufficient output of students with specialized technical and scientific training, and many talented graduates have been attracted to opportunities abroad. In addition, few countries have established networks of technical education or in-service training, and practical abilities in such areas as industry, management, and public administration remain weak.

The economic crisis of the 1980s had a severe impact on education throughout Africa. Budgetary and administrative constraints seriously curtailed educational services, as schools were neglected, materials were wanting, and teachers' salaries were often not paid. Growing unemployment and deepening poverty forced many children and young people into subsistence activities. The donor-assisted economic reforms many governments initiated in the 1980s seem generally to have aggravated these problems. Faced with the necessity of budget cuts, few leaders were able to preserve social spending rates. The imposition of school fees also restricted access for many segments of African populations. In the course of the decade, average primary enrollments declined.

Similar trade-offs in funding and distribution have been evident in the health sector. As we have noted, public health is one of the foundations of long-term economic growth. The many hazards of tropical disease and parasites constitute a significant constraint on welfare and productivity in the region. At independence public health systems in most countries were concentrated in urban centers, whereas rural populations were erratically served by missionary groups or private voluntary organizations. Many people had no access to modern health facilities, relying instead on household care or indigenous healers. Existing health services were oriented largely toward curative medicine, and inadequate attention was frequently paid to prevalent tropical diseases. Although colonial regimes often made some improvements in public sanitation and disease control, systems of primary care—including immunization and maternal health—were poorly developed. Infant mortality rates were the world's highest, and 38 percent of African children did not survive to age four. In addition, there were few programs for limiting parasitic infections or contagious diseases.

African governments faced demands for expanded of health services, along with pressing needs to restructure the sector. One urgent priority was the area of preventive medicine, including immunizations and basic health education. This required delivery networks that could reach large segments of the rural population, as well as the urban poor. The scope of hospitals and clinics was limited, in large part because of shortages of doctors and nursing staff. In addition, the control of pests and parasites, requiring extensive spraying or treatment programs, was essential to contain such maladies as bilharzia, malaria, and river blindness.

The resources devoted to health by African governments have not been equivalent to those in education; by the late 1970s health expenditures averaged 6 percent of total government spending in the region, slightly above the average for all developing countries but substantially less than the 10.5 percent spent on defense. Considerable variation was found among countries, but differences in spending did not correspond to ideological distinctions. Most countries attempted to train or recruit more physicians and nurses, often with considerable success. The overall ratio of population per doctor dropped significantly in the decades after independence, although the relative availability of doctors in the mid-1980s was still four times lower than that in other low-income developing countries.[96] The pool of nurses grew more dramatically, and access to nurses in Africa was on a par with developing country standards.

In most states the inherited health systems were retained and expanded after independence, although several countries experimented with new models. Tanzania was again a pioneer in this area, adopting a strategy in the mid-1970s that emphasized rural health centers and dispensaries. Despite the severe economic downturn the following decade, the Tanzanian system was able to provide broad services. The government fostered general access to health care and child immunization at levels well above the average for Africa.

International influences have been important in the health sector, with decidedly mixed impact. Donors have often reinforced the concentration of health services by providing hospital facilities in towns and cities and by focusing on curative medicine. International pharmaceutical firms have aggressively pursued the African market, and they have sometimes promoted inappropriate or obsolete drugs. The sale of infant formula and milk powder by foreign firms attracted international notoriety in the early 1980s. In a number of countries, these products were promoted among poorer women who could not secure clean water or sterilized bottles and were unable to afford sufficient milk powder to nourish their babies. An international campaign eventually compelled the firms to curtail their marketing activities and adopt a code of conduct regulating their activities.

On the positive side, private voluntary organizations (PVOs) and aid agencies have contributed to the expansion of basic services, especially in traditionally neglected areas. Additionally, the efforts of international organizations have been instrumental in controlling or eliminating some hazards. The World Health Organization successfully presided over the eradication of smallpox in the early 1980s, and efforts have been made to limit other diseases and parasites, including Guinea worm and onchocerciasis (river blindness).

Food security is integrally related to public health. Insufficient nutrition is obviously a serious affliction in itself, and it is also an important disposing factor for a variety of other diseases and conditions. The problems of domestic food production and distribution, noted earlier, have had negative impacts on nutrition levels throughout much of Africa. This has been aggravated by depressed incomes in the midst of economic crisis. The 1980s witnessed declining average caloric intake in the region, with a number of countries—including Guinea, Sierra Leone, Ghana, Nigeria, Cameroon, Chad, Central African Republic, Sudan, Ethiopia, Somalia, Kenya, Tanzania, Rwanda, Mozambique, and Angola—showing significant nutritional deficits in the course of the decade. Some of these areas improved in the 1990s as a result of better weather, the resolution of civil conflicts, or policy reforms.

In the 1980s HIV and AIDS reached devastating proportions in much of sub-Saharan Africa, and the overall incidence of HIV-1 among adults was over 4 percent in 1994. Southern and eastern Africa have been particularly afflicted, and in Botswana, Namibia, Zambia, and Zimbabwe adult seroprevalence has been estimated to exceed 15 percent. In other countries including Togo, Côte d'Ivoire, Kenya, Tanzania, Uganda, Congo, Mozambique, and South Africa, the infection rate is above 10 percent.[97] By the early 1990s an estimated 1 million Africans were developing AIDS each year, and cumulative deaths exceeded 10 million by 1997. The human toll of HIV/AIDS has been ruinous, and the high costs of prevention, treatment, and care have placed acute burdens on national health budgets. As people with AIDS turn to their families and communities for care, the social and economic fabric of many countries has been acutely strained, especially in rural areas.

Family planning and reproductive health programs are important for several reasons including maternal and infant well-being, limitation of sexually transmitted diseases, and population control. The costs and logistical problems of such programs have often been prohibitive, and few governments have made substantial progress in these areas. Many countries lack a traditional concern with population growth, and governments have been slow to respond to these problems. Cultural pressures have also frequently impeded the spread of family planning practices. The significant effort required in public education, distribution of materials, and behavior monitoring has commonly exceeded the capacities of African governments. In consequence, population programs have been weak or absent in most countries, and family health services have remained limited. In the early 1990s only five countries—Mauritius, Zimbabwe, Namibia, Botswana, and Kenya—had rates of contraceptive use above 25 percent, and most countries were well below 10 percent.[98] In light of these figures and the generally low levels of female education in the region, it is not surprising that population growth rates have moved upward in Africa in the decades since independence, from an average of 2.7 percent in 1965 to 3.1 percent annually in the early 1990s.

The regional economic crisis took a severe toll on African health systems, as spending dropped, medical staff went unpaid, and shortages of drugs and equipment caused care to degenerate in many countries. As in education, the introduction of structural adjustment measures was often inimical to the health sector, as governments could not switch expenditures to basic services and user fees restricted access for much of the population. Little reliable longitudinal data are available on levels of health spending or access to services in Africa, but anecdotal evidence strongly suggests that health standards deteriorated throughout much of the region during the 1980s.

■ NOTES

1. For example, see Immanuel Wallerstein, "Dependence in an Interdependent World," *African Studies Review* 17, no. 1 (1974); Colin Leys, *Underdevelopment in Kenya* (Berkeley: University of California Press, 1975); and Fernando Henrique Cardoso and Enzo Faletto, *Dependency and Development in Latin America* (Berkeley: University of California Press, 1979).

2. These dynamics are elaborated in Robert Price, "Neo-Colonialism and Ghana's Economic Decline: A Critical Assessment," *Canadian Journal of African Studies* 18, no. 1 (1984); Larry Diamond, "Class Formation in the Swollen African State," *Journal of Modern African Studies* 25, no. 4 (1987); and Richard Joseph, *Democracy and Prebendal Politics in Nigeria* (Cambridge: Cambridge University Press, 1987).

3. Paul Baran, *The Political Economy of Growth* (New York: Marzani and Munsell, 1957); Walter Rodney, *How Europe Underdeveloped Africa* (Washington, DC: Howard University Press, 1974).

4. This is emphasized in Frederick Cooper, "Africa and the World Economy," *African Studies Review* 24, nos. 2–3 (June–September 1981): 1–86; and Ralph Austen, *African Economic History* (London: James Currey, 1987).

5. Carlo M. Cipolla has elaborated this factor in *The Economic History of World Population* (Harmondsworth: Penguin, 1978) and *Before the Industrial Revolution: European Society and Economy 1000–1700* (New York: Norton, 1980).

6. Charles Tilly, *Coercion, Capital, and European States 990–1992* (Oxford: Blackwell, 1992).

7. Robert July, *A History of the African People* (New York: Charles Scribner's, 1980) p. 19.

8. Anthony Hopkins, *An Economic History of West Africa* (New York: Columbia University Press, 1973), p. 32.

9. Security and risk are discussed in James C. Scott, *The Moral Economy of the Peasant* (New Haven: Yale University Press, 1976). See also Clifford Geertz, *Agricultural Involution* (Berkeley: University of California Press, 1963) for a discussion of cultivation systems.

10. Peter Duignan and L. H. Gann, "The Pre-Colonial Economies of Sub-Saharan Africa," in Duignan and Gann, eds., *Colonialism in Africa* (Cambridge: Cambridge University Press, 1975), vol. 4, p. 33.

11. Mark Granovetter, "Economic Action and Social Structure: The Problem of Embeddedness," *American Sociological Review* 91 (November 1985): 481–510.

12. Goran Hyden, *Beyond Ujamaa in Tanzania: Underdevelopment and an Uncaptured Peasantry* (Berkeley: University of California Press, 1980); Scott, *The Moral Economy of the Peasant*.

13. Austen, *African Economic History*, p. 47.

14. Philip Curtin, *The Atlantic Slave Trade: A Census* (Madison: University of Wisconsin Press, 1969); John Iliffe, *Africans: The History of a Continent* (Cambridge: Cambridge University Press, 1995), p. 131; and Paul Lovejoy, *Transformations in Slavery: A History of Slavery in Africa* (Cambridge: Cambridge University Press, 1983), p. 19.

15. Different estimates are provided in Austen, *African Economic History,* p. 275; and Lovejoy, *Transformations in Slavery,* pp. 25, 60, 137.

16. For a cogent summary see Anthony Brewer, *Marxist Theories of Imperialism: A Critical Survey* (London: Routledge and Kegan Paul, 1980); and Roger Owen and Bob Sutcliffe, *Studies in the Theory of Imperialism* (London: Longman, 1972).

17. Paul Kennedy, *The Rise and Fall of the Great Powers* (New York: Random House, 1987), pp. 219–220; R. E. Robinson and J. Gallagher, *Africa and the Victorians: The Official Mind of Imperialism* (London: Macmillan, 1965).

18. Thomas Pakenham, *The Scramble for Africa* (New York: Avon, 1992).

19. Crawford Young, "The African Colonial State and Its Political Legacy," in Donald Rothchild and Naomi Chazan, *The Precarious Balance: State and Society in Africa* (Boulder: Westview Press, 1988), p. 45. For a fuller elaboration, see Young, *The African Colonial State in Comparative Perspective* (New Haven: Yale University Press, 1994).

20. Austen, *African Economic History,* Chapter 6.

21. Samir Amin, "Underdevelopment and Dependence in Black Africa: Origins and Contemporary Forms," *Journal of Modern African Studies* 10, no. 4 (1972): 503–524.

22. Gerald K. Helleiner, *Peasant Agriculture, Government, and Economic Growth in Nigeria* (Homewood, IL: Richard D. Irwin, 1966).

23. Ronald T. Libby, *The Politics of Economic Power in Southern Africa* (Princeton: Princeton University Press, 1987), pp. 35–36.

24. Paul Kennedy, *African Capitalism: The Struggle for Ascendancy* (Cambridge: Cambridge University Press, 1988).

25. See Donald Rothchild, *Racial Bargaining in Independent Kenya* (Oxford: Oxford University Press), 1973.

26. D.K. Fieldhouse, *Black Africa 1945–1980: Economic Decolonization and Arrested Development* (London: Unwin Hyman, 1986).

27. Austen, *African Economic History,* pp. 200–201.

28. Fieldhouse, *Black Africa,* p. 32.

29. World Bank, *Accelerated Development in Sub-Saharan Africa* (Washington, DC: World Bank, 1981), p. 12.

30. Ibid., p. 145. The share of industry for African economies was 16 percent, compared with 17 percent for all low-income economies and 30 percent for middle-income developing countries.

31. Ibid. p. 178.

32. Fieldhouse, *Black Africa,* p. 34.

33. Dudley Seers, "The Stages of Economic Development of a Primary Producer in the Middle of the Twentieth Century," *Economic Bulletin of Ghana* 7 (1963): 57–69, cited in Hopkins, *An Economic History of West Africa,* pp. 168–169.

34. Hopkins, *An Economic History of West Africa,* p. 176.

35. Austen, *African Economic History,* pp. 277–278.

36. World Bank, *Accelerated Development in Sub-Saharan Africa,* p. 3; Samir Amin, "Development and Structural Change: The African Experience, 1950–1970," *Journal of International Affairs* 24, no. 2 (1971): 209.

37. Crawford Young, *Ideology and Development in Africa* (New Haven: Yale University Press, 1982).

38. Ibid.

39. Roger Riddell et al., *Manufacturing Africa: Performance and Prospects of Seven Countries in Sub-Saharan Africa* (London: James Currey, 1990), p. 203.

40. Fieldhouse, *Black Africa*, p. 194.

41. Leys, *Underdevelopment in Kenya;* Young, *Ideology and Development*, pp. 206–207.

42. Nicola Swainson, *The Development of Corporate Capitalism in Kenya, 1918–1977* (Berkeley: University of California Press, 1980).

43. David Himbara, *Kenyan Capitalists, the State, and Development* (Boulder: Lynne Rienner, 1994). See also Rothchild, *Racial Bargaining in Independent Kenya.*

44. Peter Kilby, *Industrialization in an Open Economy: Nigeria, 1945–1966* (Cambridge: Cambridge University Press, 1969).

45. Anthony Kirk-Greene and Douglas Rimmer, *Nigeria Since 1970: A Political and Economic Outline* (London: Hodder and Stoughton, 1981); Gavin Williams and Terisa Turner, "Nigeria," in John Dunn, ed., *West African States: Failure and Promise* (Cambridge: Cambridge University Press, 1978).

46. World Bank, *Accelerated Development in Sub-Saharan Africa*, pp. 144, 146.

47. Thomas Biersteker, *Multinationals, the State, and Control of the Nigerian Economy* (Princeton: Princeton University Press, 1987); Ernest J. Wilson III, "Strategies of State Control of the Economy: Nationalization and Indigenization in Africa," *Comparative Politics* (July 1990).

48. Deborah Brautigam, "Institutions, Economic Reform and Democratic Consolidation in Mauritius," *Comparative Politics* 30, no. 1 (October 1997).

49. Data derived from World Bank, *Accelerated Development in Sub-Saharan Africa*, pp. 143–144.

50. Thomas Biersteker, "Self-Reliance in Theory and Practice in Tanzanian Trade Relations, " in John Ravenhill, ed., *Africa in Economic Crisis* (New York: Columbia University Press, 1986).

51. Tony Killick, *Development Economics in Action: A Study of Economic Policies in Ghana* (London: Heinemann, 1978).

52. Fieldhouse, *Black Africa*, p. 145.

53. Ibid., p. 146.

54. Killick, *Development Economics in Action.*

55. This rendering of rural society was considerably idealized, and Tanzanian peasants proved far less responsive to agrarian socialism than Nyerere 's conception implied. See Young, *Ideology and Development in Africa*, pp. 115–118. One of the key problems in Tanzanian socialism, as in similar experiments elsewhere, was the leadership's misperception of land ownership and use rights. Although traditional African societies did not recognize "private" property in the sense of legal freehold, virtually all rural communities maintained the principle of individual *usufruct* (use rights) to land. Collectivization policies required peasants to surrender individual rights of access to land, which inevitably provoked resistance.

56. A comprehensive account of the villagization program is provided in Dean McHenry, *Tanzania's Ujamaa Villages* (Berkeley: University of California, Institute of International Studies, 1979).

57. Michael Lofchie, "Agrarian Crisis and Economic Liberalisation in Tanzania, " *Journal of Modern African Studies* 16, no. 3 (1978): 451–475.

58. Fieldhouse, *Black Africa*, p. 175.

59. Biersteker, "Self-Reliance," pp. 214–215.

60. Global Coalition for Africa (GCA), *1993 Annual Report* (Washington, DC: Global Coalition for Africa, December 1993), p. 68 (hereafter cited as GCA, *Annual Report*).

61. World Bank, *Accelerated Development in Sub-Saharan Africa,* p. 144; ibid. p. 56.

62. Edmond J. Keller, "Afro-Marxist Regimes," in Edmond J. Keller and Donald Rothchild, eds., *Afro-Marxist States* (Boulder: Lynne Rienner, 1987).

63. Kenneth Jowitt, "Scientific Socialist Regimes in Africa: Political Differentiation, Avoidance, and Unawareness," in Thomas M. Callaghy and Carl G. Rosberg, eds., *Socialism in Sub-Saharan Africa: A New Assessment* (Berkeley: University of California, Institute of International Studies, 1979).

64. Thomas M. Callaghy, "The Difficulties of Implementing Socialist Strategies of Development in Africa: The First Wave," in ibid.

65. Ibid.

66. Young, *Ideology and Development in Africa,* p. 283.

67. Christopher Clapham, *Transformation and Continuity in Revolutionary Ethiopia* (Cambridge: Cambridge University Press, 1988), p. 160; David Ottaway and Marina Ottaway, *Afrocommunism* (New York: Africana, 1981), p. 131.

68. Data provided by the Food and Agriculture Organization, presented in GCA, *Annual Report,* pp. 68–69,

69. World Bank, *World Development Report 1997* (Washington, DC: World Bank, 1997), p. 234.

70. World Bank, *Sub-Saharan Africa: From Crisis to Sustainable Growth* (Washington, DC: World Bank, 1989), p. 221; ibid., p. 214.

71. Joan Robinson, "Trade in Primary Commodities," in Jeffry Frieden and David A. Lake, eds., *International Political Economy,* 2d Edition (New York: St. Martin's, 1991).

72. World Bank, *Sub-Saharan Africa,* pp. 123, 224.

73. See, for example, Stephan Haggard, *Pathways from the Periphery* (Ithaca: Cornell University Press, 1990); and Gary Gereffi and Donald Wyman, eds., *Manufacturing Miracles: Paths of Industrialization in Latin America and East Asia* (Princeton: Princeton University Press, 1991).

74. R. F. Steel and J. W. Evans, *Industrialization in Sub-Saharan Africa: Strategies and Performance* (Washington, DC: World Bank, Technical Paper no. 25, 1984); Riddell et al., *Manufacturing Africa.*

75. World Bank, *Sub-Saharan Africa,* p. 28.

76. See Himbara, *Kenyan Capitalists;* and Sayre Schatz, *Nigerian Capitalism* (Berkeley: University of California Press, 1977).

77. This point is emphasized in Robert Gilpin, *U.S. Power and the Multinational Corporation* (New York: Basic Books, 1975).

78. Biersteker, *Multinationals;* and Himbara, *Kenyan Capitalists.*

79. Riddell et al., *Manufacturing Africa,* p. 26. South Africa was not included in this study.

80. Ibid., p. 13.

81. GCA, *Annual Report,* p. 72.

82. Gunilla Andrae and Bjorn Beckman, *The Wheat Trap: Bread and Underdevelopment in Nigeria* (London: Zed, 1985).

83. GCA, *Annual Report,* p. 55. The figures exclude Angola, Liberia, Somalia, and Congo (Zaire), for which no data were available. These countries also likely registered declines in agriculture.

84. Ibid., pp. 61–63.

85. World Bank, *Accelerated Development in Sub-Saharan Africa,* p. 169.

86. World Bank, *Sub-Saharan Africa,* p. 232.

87. Robert Bates, *Markets and States in Tropical Africa: The Political Basis of Agricultural Policies* (Berkeley: University of California Press, 1981), and

Essays on the Political Economy of Rural Africa (Cambridge: Cambridge University Press, 1983).

88. Hyden, *Beyond Ujamaa in Tanzania.*

89. Figures provided in Naomi Chazan, Robert Mortimer, John Ravenhill, and Donald Rothchild, *Politics and Society in Contemporary Africa,* 2d ed. (Boulder: Lynne Rienner, 1992), p. 262.

90. World Bank, *Sub-Saharan Africa,* p. 274.

91. Ibid., pp. 274–275.

92. Chazan et al., *Politics and Society,* p. 240.

93. World Bank, *African Development Indicators 1997* (Washington, DC: World Bank, 1997), p. 341.

94. David L. Lindauer and Michael Roemer, *Asia and Africa: Legacies and Opportunities for Development* (San Francisco: Institute for Contemporary Studies, 1994), pp. 34–35.

95. World Bank, *Accelerated Development in Sub-Saharan Africa,* p. 82.

96. World Bank, *Sub-Saharan Africa,* p. 276.

97. Figures are from the World Health Organization, quoted in the *New York Times,* August 6, 1998, p. A6; see also World Bank, *African Development Indicators 1997,* p. 334.

98. GCA, *Annual Report,* p. 85.

10

Coping with Change: Crisis and Attempted Reform

The preceding chapter described the historical evolution of African economies and the range of strategies and policies that guided African regimes
in the decades following independence. Economic performance weakened
considerably throughout sub-Saharan Africa in the course of the 1970s,
and a number of countries displayed serious problems. As leaders experimented with domestic economic policies, they also sought to reduce dependence through changes in regional and global economies. These concerns were evident in negotiations with foreign capital, changing trade
relationships, regional integration schemes, and collective efforts to
change economic relations between the North and the South. The first part
of this chapter will discuss these approaches to altering Africa's international economic relations.

In the 1980s, Africa entered a deep and sustained economic crisis.
Throughout the region growth and production stagnated, poverty spread,
living standards declined, and basic services deteriorated. Africa became
increasingly marginal in the international economy as trade and investment dwindled. There were multiple reasons for the continent-wide downturn, including unfavorable global economic trends, domestic policy errors, institutional weaknesses, civil wars, and the corrosive effects of
patronage politics. African leaders, in the throes of fiscal crises, turned to
the multilateral financial institutions (chiefly the International Monetary
Fund and the World Bank) for supplementary financing and access to
world markets. These institutions gained greater influence in economic
policymaking, and they promoted stabilization and structural adjustment
programs throughout the region. The meandering path of economic reform
and the discouraging performance of economies in Africa have intensified
debates about the necessary conditions for African recovery. The second

305

part of this chapter discusses the genesis of crisis and the course of attempted reform.

■ MANAGING DEPENDENCE: NATIONAL STRATEGIES

As we described in the previous chapter, African states have faced a disadvantageous position in the global economy. Most countries rely on a narrow range of primary commodity exports for their foreign exchange earnings. World prices for these commodities are often unstable, leading to considerable fluctuation in the incomes of exporting states. Hard currency provides the means for importing essential manufactured goods, and the volatile basis of foreign earnings often has adverse effects on growth. Moreover, patterns of external investment and lending have not been conducive to productive transformation. In the view of underdevelopment theorists, African states are permanently relegated to a subordinate position in the international economy. This is an overstatement, and considerable evidence indicates that African countries have some latitude in managing their external economic relations. Nonetheless, the current structure of international markets creates undeniable constraints on progress.

A common response to the problems of dependence and underdevelopment has been the pursuit of self-reliance, or inward-oriented development. African countries have rarely attempted autarky, or total withdrawal from external economic relations. Indeed, apart from the communist regimes in North Korea, Albania under Enver Hoxha, and China under Mao Zedong, there are few international examples of such insular strategies. In line with many other developing countries, however, a number of African states have attempted to uncouple selectively from Northern trade and investment, especially from linkages with former colonial powers. In the 1970s countries following populist and Afro-Marxist paths sought to increase self-sufficiency through agrarian reform and import-substituting industrialization. They also took steps to limit foreign investment (although most remained heavily reliant on external aid) and to reorient their trade toward other developing economies or socialist states, especially those in the Eastern-bloc Comecon.

The most concerted efforts at self-reliance could be found in such populist countries as Guinea, Algeria, and Tanzania. Afro-Marxist regimes in Mozambique, Angola, and Ethiopia also sought to lessen their ties with Northern economies in favor of the socialist world. As we have noted, these experiments were generally unsuccessful. Rural collectivization, manifest in Tanzania's experiment with *ujamaa,* proved a general failure, and state-run agricultural and industrial ventures yielded poor returns. Consequently, these countries developed severe deficits in production and revenues that could be bridged only through external assistance or trade. Tanzania and Mozambique ultimately became two of the most aid-dependent countries in the developing world.

A number of market-oriented regimes in Africa also introduced regulations on investment and trade in an effort to promote local entrepreneurship and the utilization of domestic resources. Kenya, Nigeria, and Côte d'Ivoire sought to assist local business in the 1970s. Many of these policies, having failed to yield the desired results, were eased in the following decade during the course of economic liberalization. Confronted with severe balance of payments problems in the early 1980s, Nigeria opened barter (or countertrade) arrangements with several countries, including Brazil and Romania. This effort to circumvent conventional trade flows proved ineffectual, as countertrade included a limited range of goods that were considerably overvalued by the exporting countries. In sum, African countries, regardless of ideological orientation, have not developed effective alternatives for engagement in the world economy. Efforts at national self-reliance have receded over time in favor of more open trade and investment policies.

■ STRATEGIES TOWARD FOREIGN CAPITAL

International corporations (also referred to as transnational or multinational firms) have had a prominent and often contentious role in African economies. As a result of the low levels of economic development in the region and the legacy of colonial investments, foreign firms have established monopolistic or oligopolistic positions in many sectors. These corporations also account for a significant share of formal private sector employment in numerous countries, and they frequently dominate product markets. In 1967, the countries of the Organization of Economic Cooperation and Development (OECD) had some $4 billion invested in sub-Saharan Africa, half of which was in the mining sector. These investments were highly concentrated, with mining economies such as Zambia, Congo, and Nigeria reflecting large stakes, along with the market-oriented economies of Kenya and Côte d'Ivoire. Others, including the Sahelian states of Burkina Faso and Mali and smaller economies such as Togo and Malawi, had manufacturing investments of less than $5 million each. Although foreign companies often held an important position in African economies, the region's marginality was reflected in its low proportion of global investment. Only 1.3 percent of Northern investments in developing countries went to Africa in 1967.[1]

Foreign investment has been a source of controversy throughout the postindependence era. In the view of orthodox development economists and the international business community, international corporations are important catalysts of growth. These firms bring essential capital, technology, managerial skills, employment, marketing capacity, goods, and services to African economies. In the first decade of independence, when African entrepreneurship was comparatively weak and there were few other sources of external finance, direct foreign investment was especially crucial. In the 1990s, as the region faces narrow access to global financial markets and local entrepreneurs have limited capacities for engaging in activities such as mining, infrastructure development, and high-tech manufacturing, international investors still play a leading role.

Many observers, including exponents of dependency theory and critics in the host countries where transnational firms operate, have a less sanguine perspective. They maintain that foreign capital is a source of underdevelopment, as these firms encroach on the sovereignty of African states, foment distortions in their economies, and divert resources from domestic growth. Transnational corporations (TNCs) often appear to possess disproportionate bargaining power with respect to host country governments. In many instances these firms control assets much larger than the gross national product of most African countries, and the enormous resources at their disposal permit them to eclipse the governments with which they do business. These firms' mobility allows them to search out the most hospitable markets, and their superior bargaining acumen affords greater leverage in negotiating with African states. As a result, TNCs are able to wring concessions from host countries, such as protected markets, tax breaks, and relaxed labor and environmental regulations. They may also engage in corrupt business practices, which fuels the climate of corruption in much of Africa. Other liabilities of foreign investment can be recalled from the discussion in Chapter 9: TNCs do not provide balanced investment, they often introduce unsuitable technologies and products, and they frequently draw resources from local economies rather than provide net benefits.

In light of these problems, critics of TNCs advocate assertive strategies to control or limit the operations of foreign capital. This view accords with the nationalist sentiments of African leaders and their desire to affirm sovereignty over economic affairs. Although African states have provided varying incentives to foreign investors, most have also sought to control TNCs through four general approaches: exclusion, nationalization, indigenization, and regulation.[2] These policies are not mututally exclusive, and they have been used in combination by many countries. In the first instance, governments may adopt a straightforward policy of prohibiting foreign investment in certain activities and sectors. Socialist governments have been the most restrictive in this regard, and TNCs are often barred from investments outside of mining and other large-scale ventures. Even in Nigeria, however, foreign firms (including those owned by local Lebanese residents) were excluded in the 1970s from investing in many smaller manufacturing and service ventures, and they could not hold a majority share in most medium-sized companies. In countries such as Kenya and Nigeria, limits on foreign investment have been linked to programs to encourage local enterprise in protected sectors.

Nationalization is another common response to foreign capital. In the 1960s and 1970s most governments had recourse to these policies. Nationalization involved the takeover of full ownership or majority shareholding (51 percent or more) in a firm by a host country government. Nationalization typically entails compensating the foreign investor for these assets, although in rare instances governments may pursue expropriation, confiscating assets without recompense. Because expropriation has a chilling effect on further investment, it is used sparingly and has appeared only in rigidly ideological regimes or in acrimonious breaks with colonial firms. Angola (after 1975) and Guinea (after 1958) provide examples.

The more common form of nationalization, compulsory purchase of equity, has been adopted by a wide variety of African governments. Tanzania pursued an extensive program of nationalization following the 1967 Arusha Declaration, as did Zambia, the Nkrumah and Acheampong regimes in Ghana, and Afro-Marxist regimes in Mozambique and Ethiopia. A study of worldwide nationalizations from 1960 through 1977 found that nearly half took place in sub-Saharan Africa, indicating the popularity of this policy.[3] Mining operations, the energy sector, banking, and large manufacturing ventures were particularly susceptible because of their strategic nature. Although nationalization was initially resisted by TNCs, by the 1970s many international firms had acquiesced to this arrangement. Companies discovered advantages from accepting the capital and protection of host country governments, and by the late 1970s most new foreign investment was embodied in joint ventures between foreign firms and African states. The number of wholly owned foreign operations diminished substantially.

Indigenization refers to the transfer of ownership or managerial control from foreign to domestic hands. Such policies have been adopted mainly by African capitalist states, notably Nigeria, Kenya, and Côte d'Ivoire, although Ghana also introduced a program in the 1970s. Indigenization policies typically compel foreign firms to relinquish equity (often a majority shareholding) to local private owners by admitting indigenous partners or divesting shares through the market. Some activities may be barred altogether to foreign investors, whereas other new ventures are required to include national participation. These policies are usually supplemented by quotas for increasing local management. Nigeria's indigenization program was probably the most extensive in the region.[4] Two decrees, in 1972 and 1977, specified dozens of categories for manufacturing, commercial, and service enterprises—reserving the smaller and least capital-intensive ventures exclusively for Nigerians and allowing foreign ownership of 40 percent or more of a variety of larger, more complex activities. Thousands of enterprises were ultimately affected by the decrees.

Finally, African countries have introduced an array of regulations to govern the activities of international corporations. Aside from policies covering ownership and employment, rules on "local content" often require that a certain proportion of domestic materials or manufactured inputs be used by TNCs. Governments commonly set the range of products or the scope of marketing for TNCs to protect local firms from competition. Policies governing technology transfer can oblige foreign investors to train local technicians, convey machinery, or license techniques and formulas to domestic producers. The finances of foreign subsidiaries are frequently regulated through rules on profit repatriation, taxation, banking, and foreign transactions. Most countries also impose legal restrictions on ownership of land by foreign investors and on their proprietary rights over natural resources.

Attempts by African states to regulate TNCs have had limited effectiveness. Many foreign corporations have resisted or evaded the stipulations of host country governments. They may use transfer pricing to avoid taxation or circumvent limits on the repatriation of profits. Companies often employ "fronting" tactics—the use of token personnel or passive shareholders—to skirt indigenization laws and retain control of their operations. By retaining essential managerial or technical skills, many TNCs are able to maintain de facto control over a subsidiary even when the parent firm has a minority share of equity. Moreover, bribery and other collusive relations can often provide insulation from unwanted laws and regulations. Many TNCs are able to engage substantial legal and technical resources to prevail in disputes with host country governments.

Although African countries have had weak leverage in shaping the behavior of TNCs, their regulatory efforts have had the unfortunate effect of deterring investment. External investment in the region has been largely stagnant since the mid-1970s with the principal exception of petroleum exploitation. Capital outflows also increased relative to new commitments, and in the early 1980s net direct foreign investment (DFI) in Africa was actually negative. In 1995 the region recorded around $2 billion in net DFI, about half the level of twenty years earlier. Steps toward economic liberalization in the 1980s prompted many governments to amend or remove excessive restrictions on foreign investment, including the repeal of indigenization laws and divestiture of state ownership. Despite the introduction of a more hospitable policy setting in many countries, international firms have remained diffident toward sub-Saharan Africa.

■ COLLECTIVE STRATEGIES: REGIONAL INTEGRATION

Regional cooperation provides another strategic approach to reducing dependence. The idea of "collective self-reliance" has an enduring appeal for African countries, and the Organization of African Unity's 1980 Lagos

Plan of Action articulated this idea as a central part of the continental agenda. Regional integration, a goal for many Africans since the late colonial era, has been seen as an answer to some of the more troubling legacies of colonial rule. The imposition of arbitrary state boundaries gave rise to political, social, and economic fragmentation, which has continued to impede development in many areas. A related problem is the prevalence of small internal markets throughout the continent: seven countries in sub-Saharan Africa have populations under 1 million, and another fourteen have fewer than 5 million people. Even in larger countries low average incomes limit purchasing power and constrain the scope of domestic markets. In addition, fourteen African countries are landlocked, creating another need for cooperation. Colonial infrastructure was designed to facilitate external administration and commodity exports, offering scant basis for transactions within or between territories. Disparities in monetary systems and trade regulations also create barriers to commerce. The international marginality of African economies and difficulties attracting outside investment and trade on favorable terms have additionally spurred efforts toward integration.

Given these challenges, the appeal of regional integration would seem evident. The creation of larger markets allows for the realization of economies of scale and scope. By focusing on specialization and encouraging economic complementarities, countries can take advantage of variances in production, infrastructure, and trade. The opening of regional markets and harmonization of monetary policies should foster intraregional transactions, enabling African states to move away from their traditional dependence on Northern economies. Import-substituting industrialization, often constrained by small domestic markets, could be more viable within a larger regional community. Linking markets offers a further possibility of enhancing the attractiveness of regional economies to external investors and increasing the bargaining leverage of member states. The coordination of industrial policies in particular holds out the prospect of distributing productive facilities more equitably, avoiding redundancy and needless competition among states. The adoption of common tariffs and investment regulations can also enhance protection for local producers.[5]

Regional solidarity provides other potential benefits, often mingling political and economic goals. At the most general level cooperation can offset the traditional weakness of African states, bolstering their efforts to negotiate reforms in global markets and institutions. The objectives of free trade among African countries have been enshrined in the Lagos Plan of Action and in numerous programs put forward by the UN Economic Commission for Africa (ECA). Collaborative arrangements may have more targeted objectives, such as efforts of southern African states in the 1980s to disengage from the South African economy and confront the apartheid regime. The experience of the Economic Community of West African States (ECOWAS) in the 1990s reflects a shift from economic roles to diplomatic and security functions. Regional integration has been pursued for all of these reasons, and it has equally been inspired by the appeal of unifying kindred societies, reflected in the doctrine of pan-Africanism.

Regional integration schemes have met with little success in postindependent Africa. Although dozens of regional and subregional organizations have been formed on paper, relatively few have become viable entities. A number of regional organizations have dissolved or fallen into inactivity. Several of the more ambitious integration schemes, notably ECOWAS, have failed to move beyond initial stages of planning and implementation. In spite of the meager accomplishments of regionalism in Africa, efforts at cooperation retain an attraction for African leaders, intellectuals, policymakers, and some external donors. The continuing appeal of regional cooperation can be explained by the strong economic rationale mentioned earlier, along with ideological commitments and latent functions in diplomacy and security. In the 1990s the realization of economic unification in Europe and the burgeoning of regional cooperation through the North American Free Trade Agreement (NAFTA), the Asian-Pacific Economic Cooperation (APEC) forum, and the Mercosur pact in South America also spurred African efforts.

Regional economic organizations range in scope and objectives. Broader subregional groupings include ECOWAS, the Economic Community of Central African States (ECCAS), the Southern African Development Community (SADC), and the Preferential Trade Area (PTA) for eastern and southern Africa, each with ten or more members. There have been many smaller associations, such as the Mano River Union and the East African Community with three members each. These organizations embrace a range of goals. ECOWAS aims at a West African common market and full economic integration of its member states. The SADC, by contrast, is a development coordination organization that seeks cooperation on some aspects of regional planning and policy while rationalizing the allocation of external aid to the subregion. A third type of organization is represented by the Southern African Customs Union (SACU), which harmonizes tariffs and trade regulations among its constituents. The Mano River Union envisioned a customs union and a series of collaborative development projects among its members.

The origins of regional integration can be traced to some institutions of the colonial era. Many colonial territories, especially in the zones of French West Africa and French Central Africa, were incorporated into larger subregional entities with shared services and administration. Colonial governors, however, dominated the separate territories, and the African nationalist elites who succeeded them were anxious to consolidate their newly won sovereignty.[6] At independence the francophone countries emerged as distinct states with disparate levels of development. Strategies for regional integration were encouraged by an emerging pan-African sensibility, as well as by the developmental aspirations of many leaders.

■ The East African Community

An explicit effort toward integration could be found in the British territories of East Africa, where colonial authorities established cooperative institutions among Kenya, Tanganyika, and Uganda beginning in 1948. These arrangements included a common railway, port service, and an airline, in addition to posts and telecommunications, a meteorological service, tourist promotion, and medical and veterinary research. Eventually, an East African Currency Board, a Development Bank, and a Court of Appeals were formed. The three countries were linked in a common market, which provided for a unified external tariff and virtually free trade within the community. Intraregional commerce accounted for a significant proportion of trade for each of the territories. In the later years of colonial rule, these arrangements were embodied in the East African Common Services Organization. An East African Federation was proposed soon after independence, but it never came to fruition.

In 1967, three years after Kenyan independence and Tanganyika's union with Zanzibar (forming Tanzania), the East African Community (EAC) was formally established. The organization was intended to build on the existing common market and joint services framework to promote integration and development among these anglophone countries. The EAC had a troubled history, weathering a series of economic conflicts and tensions among political leaders until its collapse in 1977. Central organs such as the Currency Board gave way to separate national monetary authorities, and the member states were embroiled in disputes over the relative benefits from regional services and investment. Provisions to compensate the less developed countries for some of these inequalities were largely unfulfilled.

Ultimately, the EAC fell victim to "backwash effects" arising from the uneven gains of regional trade and development.[7] Kenya boasted superior infrastructure, a benign climate, a vigorous agricultural export economy, and a more developed industrial sector than its neighbors. The government of Jomo Kenyatta also pursued more lenient policies toward foreign capital. Consequently, external investment and trade flowed toward the most attractive economy, and Kenya was in a better position than its neighbors to take advantage of many regional services. Tanzania and Uganda feared that integration, offering the lure of a larger regional market, would only reinforce these imbalances: foreign firms would locate in Kenya to service the EAC. In addition to the tensions of regional inequality, growing political rifts thwarted cooperation. Ideological divisions were prominent between populist Tanzania and market-oriented Kenya, and after 1971 Idi Amin's capricious rule in Uganda aggravated these strains. The failure of Africa's most advanced integration scheme illustrates some prominent economic and political liabilities.

■ The Economic Community of West African States

In the 1970s discussions in the Organization of African Unity (OAU) and the UN Economic Commission for Africa encouraged regional cooperation. Among the most ambitious programs was the Economic Community of West African States, whose creation owed much to the initiative and inducement of Nigeria. The organization, established in May 1975 with the Treaty of Lagos, has sixteen members: Benin, Burkina Faso, Cape Verde, Côte d'Ivoire, Gambia, Ghana, Guinea, Guinea-Bissau, Liberia, Mali, Mauritania, Niger, Nigeria, Senegal, Sierra Leone, and Togo. ECOWAS encompasses the region's largest economy, that of Nigeria, with about half the population and 70 percent of total gross domestic product among the member states. The organization also includes seven countries with populations under 5 million. The grouping brings together anglophone, francophone, and lusophone countries, as well as diverse ideologies and economies.[8]

The ECOWAS charter outlines a fifteen-year process of gradual integration in three stages. In the first stage member states freeze tariffs on key commodities and manufactured goods to encourage trade among community members. The second phase calls for broader trade liberalization, eliminating tariffs and nontariff barriers among member states. Finally, the members of the community should move toward a common market by creating a joint external tariff and removing obstacles to the mobility of labor, services, and capital.[9] The coordination of macroeconomic and sectoral policies (especially in industry and agriculture) forms another important component of integration, along with the introduction of a regional currency. Seeking to avoid some of the pitfalls evident in the EAC, ECOWAS introduced a Fund for Cooperation, Compensation, and Development to offset uneven benefits among participating states. The fund, supported by proportional subscriptions from community members, would compensate some members for losses from trade liberalization and would provide resources for industrial development.

More than two decades after its creation, the community has barely moved beyond general agreement on the first stage of integration.[10] Although members have made formal commitments to liberalize regional trade, commerce within the community has not grown appreciably. In part, this reflects the persistence of restrictive regulations and inflexible behavior by some member states. Considerable mistrust has endured among francophone and anglophone countries. In the 1980s efforts to advance cooperation under ECOWAS faced competition from the francophone grouping in the Economic Community of West Africa (CEAO), whose six members were also part of the French-governed African Financial Community (CFA). Fears of Nigerian domination have fostered reluctance on the part of several countries to push ahead with integration, and Nigeria's unilateral expulsion of alien workers in 1983 and 1985 discouraged cooperation. The small size of most regional economies, the shortage of effective demand, and the lack of complementary activities among the economies reduce the potential gains from integration. The economically troubled members of the community have been chronically delinquent in paying due, leaving the organization severely underfunded. Political friction among regional leaders and numerous domestic and interstate conflicts have also deterred regional progress.

The most significant activity of ECOWAS in the 1990s was the regional intervention in Liberia and Sierra Leone. Invoking a collective security provision in the ECOWAS charter, member states sent a peacekeeping force, the ECOWAS Monitoring Group (ECOMOG), to Liberia in August 1990 at the height of the civil war. The joint force was dominated by Nigerian troops, and the Nigerians soon took command of ECOMOG and became embroiled in the fighting. The travails of ECOMOG are elaborated in Chapter 11, but in light of the present discussion, the intervention is meaningful as an initiative that expands ECOWAS's role from economic integration to regional security. As the economic dimension of ECOWAS has grown moribund, the political elements of the organization have risen in salience.

■ The Southern African Development Community (SADC)

In April 1980, nine states in southern Africa (Angola, Botswana, Lesotho, Malawi, Mozambique, Swaziland, Tanzania, Zambia, and Zimbabwe) formed the Southern African Development Coordination Conference (SADCC). The creation of SADCC countered Prime Minister P. W. Botha's proposal for a South Africa–led "constellation of states" in the region. SADCC aimed to unite the key Frontline States with other countries to disengage from the South African economy, thereby reducing members' dependence and isolating the apartheid regime. In addition, the organization sought to coordinate development planning and assistance to promote growth and reconstruction among the relatively poor, frequently war-torn countries of the region.

The members of SADCC were primarily concerned not with market integration, but rather with cooperation on regional development projects and the allocation of international aid. Each country was assigned responsibility for coordinating a different sector or activity. Angola hosted the committee on energy, whereas mining was delegated to Zambia, trade and industry to Tanzania, transportation and infrastructure to Mozambique, food security to Zimbabwe, and so forth. This led to a dispersed, less formal structure, in contrast to the bureaucratic centralization of other regional schemes.[11] Another distinctive feature of SADCC was its functional organization, which focused on interministerial coordination instead of the traditional convocation of heads of state.

SADCC registered some positive achievements during the 1980s. The organization garnered aid for regional infrastructure, and trade grew among several members. Through the mid-1990s, moreover, there were few noticeable political tensions among member states. To a large degree, the complementarity of activities and the possibility of balanced gains from cooperation bolstered the organization's stability. Nonetheless, SADCC's efforts yielded only modest results. As an aid-coordinating body, SADCC remained dependent on external donors, often with disappointing returns. By 1990 the community had realized only about a third of the $6 billion needed for regional programs.[12] Donors were generally more amenable to infrastructural projects than to industrial or agricultural schemes. In general, it is unclear whether SADCC fostered a net increase in foreign assistance or merely rearranged allotments.

SADCC's central problems during the apartheid era emanated from South Africa's efforts at regional destabilization. Under P. W. Botha, South Africa launched a multifaceted strategy to subvert the key Frontline States and reinforce regional dependence on the apartheid state. South African troops staged attacks on a number of neighboring countries and provided assistance to antigovernment guerrillas in Angola, Mozambique, and Zimbabwe. The rebel UNITA (National Union for the Total Independence of Angola) forces in Angola and RENAMO (Mozambique National Resistance Movement) in Mozambique caused widespread havoc, displacing populations, destroying production, and sabotaging infrastructure. Angola's western Benguela Railway and Mozambique's eastern Beira corridor were SADCC's key outlets to the sea, but both rail links were incapacitated by guerrillas for much of the 1980s. At one point, Zimbabwe stationed several thousand troops from its elite Fifth Brigade to protect the Beira corridor from RENAMO attacks.

In addition to military aggression, South Africa employed economic leverage to undermine regional cooperation. Botswana, Swaziland, and Lesotho were members of the Southern African Customs Union, and South Africa frequently withheld payments from trade levies as a means of coercion. As the hub of much of the region's infrastructure, South Africa could also disrupt power, communication, and transportation links with neighboring countries. Several hundred thousand workers migrated annually to the South African mining and industrial sector, and the obstruction of these labor flows placed significant hardship on neighboring economies.[13] In the early 1980s a hundred thousand Mozambicans were prevented from entering South Africa, adding another source of privation to a devastated economy. Analysts have estimated that the region suffered losses of $10 billion in the early 1980s as a result of South African aggression and subversion.

In the 1990s, the character of SADCC changed considerably. Upon attaining independence in 1990, Namibia joined the organization. In 1992 the grouping was renamed the Southern African Development Community (SADC), retaining its general focus but adopting a broader regional identity in anticipation of South African membership. President F. W. de Klerk's succession in South Africa prompted the demise of apartheid rule. The country's aggressive efforts in the region largely subsided after 1990, and following the 1994 transition to democracy South Africa became a member of SADC. With the addition of Mauritius, Seychelles, and Congo, the community's membership increased to fourteen. The resolution of conflict throughout much of the region (apart from Angola) has created new opportunities for SADC, as member states contemplate greater benefits from cooperation. At the same time, perennial concerns about South African dominance and uneven gains among the region's disparate economies raise questions about the prospects for regional harmonization.

Several factors account for the generally discouraging history of regionalism in Africa. First, political and ideological diversity has worked against cooperation. Personal rivalries among African leaders, differences in economic and political doctrines, and more specific disagreements over trade, investment, and monetary policies have polarized the members of many regional organizations. This is illustrated by the tension between Kenya and Tanzania in the EAC, as well as the personal rancor between Ugandan and Tanzanian leaders. The early ideological contrasts in ECOWAS between Benin, Burkina Faso, and Guinea-Bissau on the one hand and Côte d'Ivoire, Nigeria, and Gambia on the other are also noteworthy. Francophone and anglophone countries have also sustained a mutual distrust. Apart from personal and political disparities, few African leaders have been willing to relinquish state sovereignty to supranational organizations, especially since the gains from integration may be indeterminate.

A second hindrance can be found in the nature of African economies. Small markets, low incomes, and a narrow range of production severely constrain the immediate gains from trade among African countries. Most African economies produce a similar array of primary commodities; consequently, they are more likely to be competitive than complementary. Relatively limited opportunities exist for specialization in production and trade. Indeed, many countries confront the "fallacy of composition" in expanding trade: the growth of traditional exports (such as cocoa, coffee, and palm oil) among neighboring economies may encroach on market share, or create a glut that depresses prices.

In addition, deficiencies in the infrastructure of most countries pose serious obstacles to integration. Throughout West Africa the colonial bias of infrastructure—linking the hinterland with the coast and the capital with the former colonial power in Europe—has persisted. There are few lateral links by air, rail, road, or telecommunications. Financial markets as well tend to be segmented by different monetary systems and poor communications networks. These factors are even more rudimentary and fragmented in central Africa. In southern Africa South Africa's historical dominance of markets and facilities inhibits broader cooperation. The poor condition of infrastructure in many parts of Africa, especially in the wake of the region's economic crisis, compounds the problem.

Despite the weak linkages among formal economies in Africa, there are numerous informal markets throughout the region. Substantial activities are undertaken by transregional ethnic networks such as Fulani livestock traders and Hausa merchants in West Africa. Labor migration, cross-border trade among ethnic communities, informal credit markets, and large-scale smuggling (often by profiteer and warlord interests) create broad webs of commerce in many parts of the continent. These endeavors are frequently at odds with governments seeking to control transactions within their borders, not to mention the desire of bureaucrats to tax or extract tribute from such activities. Since informal trade faces a tenuous legal position and many markets are relatively limited in scale, it is difficult for this realm of activity to contribute significantly to economic regionalism.

The uneven benefits of economic integration have frequently deterred cooperation. The dominant role of Nigeria in ECOWAS, Kenya's preeminence in the EAC, and South African primacy in SADC have fostered apprehension among the weaker states and economies in each community. Neighboring governments have been concerned that the leading country would capture disproportionate benefits from integration by siphoning off investment and trade. A further problem is the disparity between risk and reward: countries engaging in integration schemes are asked to open their economies to potentially damaging competition, while the dividends from this are often distant and uncertain.[14] In these circumstances the temptation to maintain protection can be great.

Africa has been host to an unusually large number of cooperative arrangements, and efforts at regional integration have been undermined by tensions among competing institutions. In West Africa, for instance, many countries have overlapping memberships in ECOWAS, the francophone CEAO, and the French-led CFA monetary zone, with smaller groupings such as the Mano River Union also in place. The nineteen-member Preferential Trade Area of East and Southern Africa (PTA), established in 1981, includes ten members of SADC. The Economic Community of Central African States (ECCAS) also includes three PTA members and some CFA countries. Many African countries are simultaneously engaged in parallel integration schemes, often with divergent goals or competing markets. In addition, African economies remain firmly linked to Northern markets through the CFA, the Lomé Convention, the Commonwealth, and other arrangements. These ties often overshadow efforts toward regional collaboration.

International experience suggests that successful integration schemes are typically supported and subsidized by a dominant, or hegemonic, power. A regional hegemon can provide resources for organizational development, foster trade, assist with monetary stability, and provide compensatory financing to weaker members of the community. Regional leadership of this caliber has generally been lacking in Africa. To be sure, a dominant country can be found in each subregion, but these countries have not provided the types of public goods necessary to promote successful cooperation. Nigeria's declining economy and its occasional self-interested behavior (evident in the expulsion of alien workers in the early 1980s) have rendered it ineffectual as a regional economic leader, although it did lead the ECOMOG interventions of the 1990s. Similarly, South Africa's preoccupation with internal questions of growth and redistribution has muted its regional impact. In the absence of effective regional or external sponsors for integration, African endeavors are likely to be constrained in the foreseeable future.

■ AFRICA AND NORTH-SOUTH RELATIONS

As the countries of Africa explored possibilities for regional solidarity and self-reliance, they also sought a more forceful voice in negotiating the terms of economic relations with Northern states. The success of the OPEC petroleum cartel in the early 1970s encouraged developing countries to press for major reforms in global markets and institutions. Some leaders discerned possibilities for using OPEC's leverage to advance broader Southern demands, while others, inspired by the cartel's example, pursued additional forms of collective action. The UN system and other international organizations provided a platform for the developing countries to more readily exercise their voting weight. The Nonaligned Movement (NAM) provided a further outlet for Southern demands. In addition, the emerging perspective of structuralism, articulated by the UN Economic Commissions for Latin America and Africa, provided a common economic doctrine for the South.[15]

These political and market factors gave rise to the campaign for a New International Economic Order (NIEO). In the wake of the 1974 OPEC-inspired oil price hikes, the Sixth Special Session of the UN General Assembly adopted a Declaration and Action Programme on the Establishment of a New International Economic Order, followed shortly by a Charter of Economic Rights and Duties of States. The NIEO was backed by the Group of 77 developing countries, with Algeria and a few others as leading proponents. Over the next several years this agenda was pursued through the General Assembly, the UN Conference on Trade and Development (UNCTAD), and other international organizations. The Nonaligned Movement echoed many of these demands.

The NIEO encompassed a number of issues and themes. Developing countries pressed for greater sovereignty over their economic affairs, including control over natural resources (such as a 200-mile limit for fisheries) and prerogatives for nationalization or expropriation of foreign firms. They also urged a binding international code of conduct to regulate the operations of TNCs. Addressing the problem of unequal terms of trade, the NIEO contained provisions for indexing commodity prices (linking the price of commodities to the average cost of manufactured goods), as well as for creating buffer stocks and a stabilization fund to smooth international commodity earnings. The right to form producers' cartels was asserted, and Northern governments were admonished to open their markets to a greater scope of Southern exports.

In addition, the NIEO outlined measures to redress the flow of resources between North and South. The framework called for significant increases in Northern aid, specifying that a minimum percentage of industrialized states' gross national product be devoted to foreign assistance. The multilateral financial institutions were directed to increase resources available to Southern countries, and increased Southern decisionmaking authority in the International Monetary Fund (IMF), the World Bank, and the United Nations was proposed. The program advocated generalized debt relief, especially for the poorest indebted countries. It was also recommended that Northern technology and skills should be made more accessible to developing economies on reasonable terms.

For several years demands for a New International Economic Order were debated in UN forums as well as in meetings of the Nonaligned Movement, the OECD, the multilateral financial institutions, and the Conference on International Economic Cooperation (CIEC). The main NIEO proposals made little headway, and by the early 1980s the program was largely dormant. The limited impact of the NIEO reflected several factors—the most important being resistance from Northern states and corporations, which were generally unwilling to consider Southern proposals despite nominal interest among certain OECD countries. The advent of conservative administrations in Britain, the United States, and Germany also had a chilling effect on reform efforts since these governments regarded the NIEO as incompatible with the expansion of free markets.[16]

For their part, the Group of 77 had scant leverage to advance its agenda. Despite their rhetorical stance the developing countries did not embody a common set of interests, as reflected in the dissension within the Nonaligned Movement between activist states such as Algeria and more moderate governments. Large industrializing countries—including Brazil,

Mexico, and India—embodied different priorities and concerns than the smaller, low-income countries of Africa; they often sought disparate policies with regard to technology transfer, debt settlement, and trade. The Southern negotiating bloc was often divided on or ambivalent toward key issues.

Ironically the developing countries' demands were undermined by OPEC's success. Hopes for linking the NIEO platform to the negotiating strength of the oil cartel proved illusory. OPEC members focused on controlling petroleum supplies and prices and resisted the idea of diluting their leverage with extraneous demands. The effectiveness of OPEC as a cartel weakened Southern economies by raising energy costs, fueling external debt, and fostering global recession.[17] The bargaining weight of African countries declined along with their economies. Whereas the oil-producing countries offered modest lending and development assistance to African states, there was little transfer of abundant petrodollar surpluses to their beleaguered economies. The bulk of these resources were invested in OPEC states or recycled into Northern financial institutions.

Although efforts to enact a comprehensive New International Economic Order were largely unsuccessful, the program articulated by the Group of 77 did affect North-South economic relations over the longer term. By tabling a common set of demands, developing countries were able to press reforms across a wide range of issues. Through bargaining on a bilateral or regional basis, African states secured a number of incremental changes. Many countries took a more assertive stance toward transnational corporations, and several governments attempted to strengthen their sovereign rights over local resources. The dialogue over aid and debt elicited some new resources from bilateral donors and international financial institutions. Beginning in the 1980s, creditor countries outlined a series of plans for reorganizing or reducing developing country debt, most of which included the low-income economies of Africa. The Lomé Convention and other interregional arrangements sought to improve average terms of trade for African exporters. These piecemeal changes in North-South interactions often fell short of Southern expectations, and they did not upset the prevailing international regimes governing the global economy.

By the 1980s, as discussed later, the modest gains from the NIEO agenda had been overshadowed by the consequences of global recession, rising debt, and domestic austerity in developing countries. Commodity producers had little influence in shaping international economic relations. Over the following decade North-South issues were decided largely on a bilateral basis, with concerns such as immigration, narcotics trafficking, the AIDS pandemic, and regional security topping the list. Monetary and trade matters were addressed primarily through multilateral organizations such as the IMF and the World Trade Organization (WTO), although some regional initiatives were also proposed.

African countries have looked to additional collective strategies to alter their position in international markets. The impressive attainments of the OPEC cartel led other commodity producers to attempt similar arrangements. Exporters of copper (notably Zambia and Congo), bauxite (Guinea), cocoa (Ghana and Côte d'Ivoire), and coffee (Kenya, Tanzania, and Ethiopia) could potentially benefit from cooperation, and many of these countries sought to develop producers' groups with African and non-African states. The oil cartel proved unique, however, and other commodities did not lend themselves to effective market organization.

The achievements of OPEC rested on several distinctive conditions.[18] Petroleum was essential to world energy needs, especially for the industrialized countries of the North, and there was no ready substitute for this commodity. This meant oil was price inelastic: consumers could not roll back demand (at least in the short term) in response to price increases. Supply was controlled by a relatively small number of Southern producers with substantial common interests. The 1973 oil embargo, prompted by the Arab-Israeli conflict, demonstrated strong cultural and political identity among Middle Eastern producers.

Cartels typically face problems of cheating, as individual members may increase supply or reduce prices to gain short-term advantage even if doing so erodes market leverage for the group. In the case of OPEC a few countries (notably Saudi Arabia) had excess capacity, and as "swing" producers they could potentially flood the market and depress prices. This sanction helped to sustain discipline among cartel members, thus reducing the problem of defection. Against the unity of producers, consumers were unable to provide a common response. Europe and Japan were heavily dependent on Middle Eastern suppliers, and they had little choice but to accede to OPEC requisites.

When these circumstances changed in the 1980s, the leverage of the oil cartel waned. The development of new oil and gas production in the North Sea, Mexico, and other areas diversified sources of supply. Demand was correspondingly reduced by global recession and by efforts at energy conservation in industrialized economies. Divisions among OPEC members, notably the rift between Iran and Iraq, loosened solidarity within the organization. In addition, the growing economic problems of countries such as Nigeria and Venezuela intensified pressures for cheating. These "capital-scarce" exporters needed revenues to meet the demands of their comparatively large populations, and they increasingly skirted production quotas to supplement revenues.[19] Oil prices dropped from a high of around thirty-five dollars in 1981 to an average of eighteen to twenty dollars over the next decade, dipping as low as nine dollars at some intervals.

For African countries no other commodity has reflected the features of the energy markets of the 1970s. The main exports for the region—cocoa, coffee, tea, sugar, cotton, timber, fisheries, copper, iron ore, bauxite, and phosphates—have significant price elasticities. Few of these items are essential to consumers, and most can be readily substituted by alternate goods or suppliers. The main international producers are scattered among different regions, and there is little inherent unity among them. Moreover, production is more evenly dispersed, providing less opportunity for a swing producer to enforce discipline within a cartel. Consequently, African commodity exporters have generally been unable to combine to improve their returns or stabilize revenues. Also, some items such as diamonds and gold are derived from countries such as Angola, Congo, Sierra Leone, and Liberia that are wracked by political instability. In these instances the weakness of sovereign states and the influence of foreign business groups have vitiated the possibility of creating effective producers' organizations. The dominance of the international diamond market in particular by a private cartel (the South African company DeBeers) has largely eclipsed the prerogatives of national exporters.

Regional trade agreements offer an alternative path to enhance or stabilize incomes. The Northern states have endorsed in principle arrangements to reduce the volatility of revenues for Southern commodity exporters and to create a more favorable trading environment for African states. This was the spirit behind the Lomé Convention, a multilateral trade agreement concluded in 1975 between the countries of the European Economic Community (EEC) and forty-six African, Caribbean, and Pacific (ACP) nations. The Lomé Convention was built on an existing compact, the Yaoundé Convention, signed in 1963 between the EEC and eighteen francophone African states. This convention offered African exports better access to the European market, with the stipulation that African countries offer reciprocal concessions to European states. The pact also created a European Development Fund (EDF) to aid participating African countries.

The Yaoundé pact was a source of tension between anglophone and francophone countries in Africa. France had already provoked criticism of its "neocolonial" policies by sponsoring monetary unification through the African Financial Community (CFA) and maintaining special trade arrangements with its former colonies. The anglophone states viewed the preferential treatment of the EEC as a further indication of this tendency. The Lomé Convention assuaged some of these concerns by including members of the English-speaking Commonwealth in the agreement. As the convention was revised during the course of the 1980s, participation grew to sixty-nine ACP states, including all of sub-Saharan Africa.

The Lomé Convention offered several provisions. First, the EEC reduced tariffs and other barriers to exports from the ACP countries. These concessions were provided on a nonreciprocal basis—that is, the Southern states did not have to furnish comparable access to their markets. Second, the European countries formed the Stabilization of Export Earnings Scheme (STABEX), a reserve fund that would compensate commodity exporters for variations in their revenues. Third, the European community furnished special terms for sugar exports, offering higher returns on the commodity. The community also expanded development assistance by increasing the European Development Fund and introducing a new Center for Industrial Development.

The Lomé Convention was greeted with considerable enthusiasm, but over the course of twenty-five years it has yielded disappointing results. The trade allowances in the agreement proved less permissive than they appeared, as European states maintained protection against many African agricultural commodities and manufactured goods such as textiles and clothing. Thus some of the more promising export outlets for African economies were largely precluded by Northern trade barriers. Also, as Africa lost market share in certain essential commodities, there were no provisions to arrest this trend. At the same time, African states found that Northern exporters preserved their share of regional trade.[20] There has also been dissatisfaction with development assistance and financial compensation. Although the EDF received substantial nominal funding, during the 1980s aid from Europe diminished in real per capita terms, and the industrial assistance scheme was slow to materialize. The STABEX program has been disparaged for its limited coverage, erratic disbursements, and funding problems.[21]

On balance, many ACP countries have concluded that the Lomé Convention is an expedient for preserving traditional North-South trade relations and is hardly the foundation for the "New International Economic Order" proclaimed in the original document. In the 1990s the acceleration of European integration and the shift in trade and investment toward Central Europe and Asia have clearly overshadowed the relationship with other developing regions.

In 1998 a comparable trade opening was suggested by the United States. The Clinton administration's proposed African Growth and Opportunity Act would enhance Africa's access to U.S. markets and provide additional incentives for trade and investment. The initiative also promised modest financial assistance to encourage U.S. private investment and to develop African infrastructure. The act drew criticism from some Africans, including South African President Nelson Mandela, for its apparent emphasis on private investment at the expense of bilateral aid. Detractors also noted that the trade concessions were selectively targeted at countries pursuing market-oriented economic reforms and political liberalization, rather than applying to the region as a whole. In the United States, the act faced some resistance from agricultural interests, textile producers, and other groups fearing competition from African exports. Although Clinton's package appeared likely to be passed by Congress, it seemed unlikely to create significant new opportunities for most African economies.

In the first two decades of independence, endeavors by Africans to promote growth and self-reliance often proved frustrating. Domestic policy experiments, especially by populist and Afro-Marxist states, yielded discouraging results, and collective strategies also failed to improve the global economic architecture for African countries. By the mid-1970s a series of unfavorable developments in international markets pushed Africa over the boundary from malaise to crisis. The region continues to grapple with this legacy.

■ AFRICA'S ECONOMIC CRISIS

Economic growth slowed substantially throughout Africa during the course of the 1970s, and by decade's end many countries were afflicted by declining output, fiscal shortfalls, and rising debt. These problems peaked over the next several years, especially in the wake of the 1982 debt crisis. The 1980s are commonly referred to as Africa's "lost decade" since the region's sagging economies caused a drop in incomes, social services, and investment. These difficulties touched most African countries regardless of official ideology, location, size, or economic structure. After years of decline and slow recovery, in the 1990s many countries were just getting back to levels of output and consumption reached twenty years earlier.

The African crisis embodied several features. Perhaps foremost was the prevalence of stagnant or declining growth rates. From 1980 to 1987 gross domestic product grew by only 0.5 percent on average for all of sub-Saharan Africa. Merely eight countries in the region displayed growth rates above 5 percent, including Botswana, Mauritius, Congo-Brazzaville, and Cameroon; twenty were below 3 percent, including Benin, Togo, Côte d'Ivoire, Ghana, Ethiopia, Kenya, Tanzania, Malawi, Zimbabwe, and Lesotho; and another nine showed negative growth, including Liberia, Nigeria, Niger, Zambia, and Mozambique.[22] Given the high rates of population expansion, average incomes declined in many countries. For the region as a whole, GNP per capita dropped an average of 2.8 percent a year, with at least twenty-eight countries showing negative trends.

The deteriorating performance of productive sectors was a leading component of this decline. The region's industrial output dropped by a yearly average of 1.7 percent during the first seven years of the 1980s. The downfall of Nigeria's oil economy accounts for much of the picture, but removing Nigeria from the figures still leaves an anemic (although positive) growth rate of 3.4 percent—far below the late 1960s when Africa's industry was expanding in excess of 10 percent a year.[23] A trend toward deindustrialization was evident in many economies as investment waned, facilities deteriorated, and manufacturing output diminished as a share of national product.

During this period, according to World Bank data, African agricultural growth averaged only 1.8 percent annually. As we noted in the preceding chapter, these figures should be viewed with caution since much of the rural economy does not show up in official statistics. But the numbers do indicate a dwindling of officially marketed output in most countries, and they suggest that production lagged behind population growth in many areas. These general figures are consistent with the regional picture of declining GDP, shrinking exports, and greater dependence on food imports and aid.

Africa's position in international trade worsened in the 1980s, as the relative scope of foreign commerce shrank considerably. The value of the region's merchandise exports, at current prices, declined by more than a third between 1980 and 1987.[24] For at least five of Africa's leading exports (cocoa, coffee, cotton, iron ore, and timber), the region's global market share slipped during the 1980s. We have also noted that manufactured exports, never a large part of regional trade, diminished to the point of invisibility at this time. Pressed by shortages of hard currency, many countries had less capacity for purchases abroad, and imports contracted by at least 25 percent during this period.

Sub-Saharan Africa was enmeshed in the international debt crisis, one of the most visible aspects of economic malaise. The region's external debt rose from about $16 billion in 1975 to $58 billion in 1980 and $144 billion seven years later.[25] By 1985 foreign debt equaled 43 percent of Africa's GDP and 218 percent of total exports, as the ratio of debt service to export revenues climbed to 35 percent. In consequence, the balance of payments worsened for most countries. The deficit in the current account nearly tripled from 2.2 percent of regional GDP in 1980 to 6.5 percent in 1987.[26] The rising levels of debt contributed not only to import strangulation but also to declining savings, investment, and public expenditures.

During the 1980s poverty expanded markedly, and living standards deteriorated for the broad mass of Africans. There were many sources of popular hardship. In rural areas peasants were squeezed by low producer prices, rising inflation, and tattered infrastructure. For urban wage earners too inflation steadily eroded incomes, and in countries such as Zambia, Congo, Nigeria, Ghana, Liberia, and Sierra Leone fixed salaries depreciated rapidly—when they were paid at all. As a direct consequence of budget problems and mismanagement, many governments were delinquent in paying wages for their employees. As fiscal constraints tightened, austerity measures often required cutbacks that removed many from the public sector payroll altogether. In the private sector as well, decreasing profits and a growing tide of business failures put many employees out of work. For all segments of society the declining availability and quality of basic services, such as health and education, created further hardships.

The effects were far-reaching. Large segments of the middle class were driven toward penury. Many urban wage earners were pushed into the informal economy or back to rural areas. For much of the peasantry, already on the margins of public services and the market economy, the

shocks from economic decline were perhaps less abrupt, but they too suffered from the deterioration of facilities and social provisions.

With the failure of formal economies in so much of the region, many
Africans moved to informal activities or parallel markets for survival.[27] In
the cities this often meant a turn to petty trade or services, whereas in the
countryside it implied a shift to subsistence activities, localized commerce,
or cross-border trade. In a reversal of historical patterns, some urban residents migrated to rural areas to obtain subsistence in the rural economy.
Smuggling, parallel currency markets, and other semilegal activities
formed important segments of many African economies, and it has been
estimated that the "second" economy of a few countries, such as Congo,
actually exceeded the official economy.[28] Regardless of the relative scale,
it is evident that parallel economies provided a livelihood, however tenuous, for large portions of African societies. These coping mechanisms,
however, exacted costs on government revenues, national savings and investment, and institutions of the formal economy.

The rise of parallel economies was entwined with another important
feature of the African crisis: the decline of the state. As public resources
waned and fiscal pressures grew, many governments were unable to sustain basic functions or services. Government deficits in Africa grew from
an average of about 2 percent of GDP in 1980 to more than 6 percent in
1989. The primary deficit, which includes debt service, rose from less than
2 percent to more than 10 percent of GDP.[29] Most governments were unable to raise additional internal revenues from their dwindling economies,
and they could not adequately compensate for fiscal shortfalls through external borrowing or aid. In consequence, spending on such basics as infrastructure, administration, and social services often declined noticeably.
The failure of public institutions aggravated the course of economic decline and undermined the legitimacy of numerous regimes. In countries
such as Ghana, Liberia, Sierra Leone, Uganda, Zambia, and Congo, the
downward spiral was especially striking. Leaders throughout the region
took recourse to patronage or repression, which tended to worsen the
malaise. Africa's economic crisis spilled over into the political arena and
fueled a crisis of governance.

■ Explaining the Crisis

There has been much disagreement over the causes of the African crisis
and the prospects for recovery. Many commentators, especially analysts in
the leading African regional organizations, have attributed the downturn
mainly to the effects of the international economy. They cite adverse terms
of trade, exogenous price shocks, restricted access to markets of the industrialized economies, and unforgiving terms of indebtedness to Northern
creditors. Drought and other arbitrary factors have contributed as well.

From this perspective, the origins of the crisis are to be found in Africa's subordinate position in the global economy, and the proximate sources of decline have been viewed as being largely beyond the control of African leaders.[30] In addition, many observers hold that the policy reforms introduced by multilateral financial institutions have done little to spur recovery and have often aggravated poverty and political instability.

Analysts from the multilateral institutions and major donor countries have traced the region's declining fortunes to domestic policy errors and, to a lesser degree, institutional failures. This critique of policies is most closely identified with the World Bank, beginning with the controversial Berg Report,[31] which generally downplays the role of external factors as the basis of economic decline. Problems of dependence, price instability, and drought have been continuous features of African economic development and cannot adequately explain the timing of the region's downswing. Other developing regions adjusted more successfully to adverse trends in the 1970s and 1980s, suggesting that policy choices play a significant role in economic performance.

The policy critique points to the general set of statist and nationalist measures detailed in Chapter 9. The key problems include maintenance of overvalued exchange rates, restrictions on capital flows and financial markets, constraints on foreign trade and protection of inefficient domestic producers, and excessive regulation of private investors, both foreign and domestic. In addition, states in the region have provided costly, often indiscriminate subsidies to consumers and enterprises; they have funneled large amounts of public funds to bloated administrations and loss-making state firms; and policymakers have discriminated against the large rural sector. These policies, often pursued for reasons of political expediency, have created numerous distortions and rigidities in African economies. Policy failures have reduced productivity and increased vulnerability to external shocks. Pervasive state intervention in markets encourages rent seeking—the pursuit of "special" gains in politically regulated markets.[32] This is often accompanied by corruption, which further undermines investor confidence.

Somewhat belatedly, donors have also recognized that institutional problems contribute to economic stagnation. Feeble states and weak markets have equally hindered growth. Dysfunctional administration, ubiquitous corruption, decaying infrastructure, fragmented markets, indistinct property rights, and the lack of stable legal systems all pose obstacles to economic progress. Donors have generally maintained their primary concern for pruning the role of the state in African economies, but many have added the language of "capacity building" to acknowledge the need to promote more effective public functions. They also note the importance of a broad "enabling environment," including conducive institutions, to inspire private sector development.

These concerns have been encouraged by a distinct school of political analysis. A number of observers emphasize the political foundations of economic decline, pointing to the prevalence of weak authoritarian states, predatory rulers, patronage politics, and warlord activities throughout much of the region.[33] From this perspective policy choices and styles of economic management are related to the interests of African leaders and the coalitions of support that provide the foundations for regimes.

The model of neopatrimonial rule captures many of these elements. Neopatrimonial regimes outwardly reflect the features of formalized bureaucratic states while working essentially along patrimonial lines.[34] Beneath the layers of administration, legal procedure, and constitutional order inherited from the colonial state, neopatrimonial states have been organized through an array of personal linkages and patron-client networks. In these regimes, power is concentrated and personalized, and rulers have broad discretion over most aspects of public life. The personal prerogatives of leaders typically override the rule of laws and organizations, giving rise to weak and unstable institutions.[35] Because clientelist systems rely largely on material rewards, these regimes are under pressure to provide a regular flow of benefits to elite loyalists and core constituencies.

Some common aspects of economic oversight are found in these regimes, reflecting a consistent political logic. Public finances, under the discretion of the ruler and a few senior officials, are poorly monitored and administered. Bureaucratic corruption is endemic, as citizens seek benefits from state personnel and the distinction between public and private resources is commonly blurred. Economic policies fall at the whim of the executive and are subject to arbitrary, unexpected change. As a leading consequence of corruption and political uncertainty, public agencies provide inadequate or irregular services. State elites, motivated by the need to maintain influence over resources, pursue intervention in markets and regulatory control over firms. Clientelist politics foster alliances between government officials and cronies in the private sector, who benefit from rent-seeking opportunities and public patronage.[36] The reliance of business on government favor has curbed the emergence of autonomous domestic capitalist classes. The dominant coalitions in many states have also created biases toward urban sectors and particular ethnic groups.

The patterns of state-building and political leadership in the region, detailed in Chapters 2 and 6, have important consequences for economic development. Neopatrimonial regimes rarely assert the political autonomy needed to chart a long-term path of economic accumulation, and they possess limited institutional capacities for managing complex economies. The immediate demands of patronage exert greater claims on policies and resources, whereas personal rule has commonly frustrated the development of key institutions including bureaucracies, judiciaries, and central banks. Without these institutional foundations governments cannot adequately ensure property rights, enforce contracts, or maintain a general rule of law. African leaders, lacking accountability to voters and restraint from strong institutions, have often pursued self-interest and economic predation rather than the goals of development. These political dilemmas have undermined socialist as well as capitalist regimes.[37]

Each of the contending views on the African crisis contains some validity. The region's economic decline had myriad causes, as international and domestic elements produced the degeneration of many economies. External factors such as price shocks, changes in the terms of trade, shifts in world markets, and the global debt regime created detrimental conditions for most countries. These factors aggravated the inherent weaknesses created by inappropriate policies, and in some instances the domestic effects were worsened by bad weather or civil strife. Also, the political imperatives of various regimes tended to work against effective reform, and the failure to pursue economic adjustment deepened the crisis.

■ The Genesis of Decline

Africa's economic distress emerged in the 1970s, with major changes in the international economy playing a prominent role. A central and much debated issue has involved trends in the region's terms of trade, or the relative purchasing power of exports. Terms of trade are not uniform, varying among countries by the nature and volume of exports. For mineral exporters, particularly oil-producing economies, the terms of trade have been particularly volatile. Many agricultural exporters have experienced minor fluctuations since the mid-1970s.

African countries generally enjoyed appreciating terms of trade during the 1960s, but they saw a significant reversal in the following decade. For sub-Saharan Africa as a whole, the net barter terms of trade declined by 20 percent from 1970 to 1979.[38] With depressed world prices for such commodities as copper and iron, mineral exporters experienced an especially steep deterioration, amounting to 55 percent for Congo and Zambia and 33 percent for Liberia. For the Sahelian states, the average depreciation was 20 percent, and for middle-income economies, 12 percent. The exception to these trends was the windfall enjoyed by a few oil exporters in the 1970s—including Nigeria, Gabon, Congo-Brazzaville, and Angola—whose terms of trade appreciated by nearly 100 percent.

In the following decade, the net barter terms of trade for the region declined sharply, by an average of 52 percent. This mainly reflects losses for oil exporters, which were deprived of more than half of their relative purchasing power.[39] Exporters of beverage crops (mainly coffee, tea, and cocoa) lost about 28 percent in their terms of trade, whereas other agricultural producers saw virtually no change, and mineral exporters generally gained slightly. Broadly speaking, it is fair to say that the countries of the region did not benefit from significant improvements in their terms of trade after the late 1970s, and many experienced steep declines.

Africa's downturn cannot be closely linked to changes in relative trade values, which were unstable and diverse whereas the general economic slope was more consistent and uniform. Additional factors come into play. The most significant developments included the oil price shocks of the 1970s and the related growth of Africa's external debt. The effective cartel power of the Organization of Petroleum Exporting Countries (OPEC) in the wake of the 1973 Arab-Israeli war led to major increases in global fuel prices. Crude oil prices increased from about $3 per barrel at the beginning of 1973 to more than $12 in 1974, and by 1981 oil prices topped $35 a barrel. For the economies of sub-Saharan Africa, even though their relative consumption of fossil fuels was substantially lower than that of other regions, the rise in costs created significant economic strains. Purchases of fuels jumped from 6 percent of the region's total imports in the mid-1960s to 18 percent at the end of the 1970s.[40] Growing energy costs also tended to increase the prices of many manufactured goods imported by African countries.

Confronted with these financial pressures, African governments sought to borrow abroad in a bid to sustain expenditures and growth rather than to adopt austerity measures that might slow their economies. The preference for financing over adjustment echoed practices in many developing countries at the time.[41] These choices reflected the ambitious development strategies charted by African governments and the opportunities created by changing global financial markets. The enormous surpluses of petrodollars accumulated by many OPEC producers were recycled into Western financial institutions, and this inflow of capital increased liquidity in the burgeoning international money market known as the Euromarket. Private bankers were eager to lend to developing countries since there was a perception that export receipts would permit future debt repayment and an assumption that sovereign states could not declare bankruptcy or default on their obligations. In many instances lending was aggressively promoted by Northern banks. In addition, traditional sources of bilateral and multilateral finance were available to African states.

The result was a rapid accumulation of sub-Saharan Africa's external debt. The region's total outstanding obligations grew from about $6 billion in 1970 to $42 billion—a sevenfold increase—in 1979. Four years later Africa's debt had doubled, reaching $86 billion. The composition of the debt was perhaps more important than the absolute magnitude. Prior to the mid-1970s the bulk of Africa's finance came from bilateral or multilateral lenders, many of which provided concessional terms including lower interest rates and longer maturities. Over the next several years more of the region's borrowing was done through private sources, mainly Western banks and credits from suppliers. A greater share of the borrowing from bilateral sources was also done on a nonconcessional basis. In sum, an increasing proportion of Africa's debt existed on harder terms.

A few figures illustrate these trends. In 1970, a little more than 70 percent of Africa's debt was with official sources, whereas only about 5 percent of the region's total debt was owed to private banks. The mix of borrowing quickly shifted, and in 1978 private banks held more than a quarter of the region's debt. By 1983, nearly a third of African debt was from private banks, and the proportion from official sources had slipped to about 58 percent. Moreover, terms became more exacting, and nonconcessional debt grew from 16 percent of bilateral lending in 1975 to more than 40 percent eight years later.[42]

Following the initial energy price shock in 1973, another sharp price hike in 1979 provided the catalyst for the debt crisis. Changes in global markets significantly increased Africa's debt burden, and the countries of the region had a reduced ability to meet their commitments. The 1979 shock aggravated recession in the Northern economies, with several consequences for Africa. Purchases of key commodities went down, prompting a reduction in export volumes and prices for many African states. The region's terms of trade consistently declined during the six years after 1977. The industrialized countries, especially in Europe, also maintained significant barriers to entry in their markets, making it difficult for Africa to expand or diversify exports. All of these factors compressed Africa's export earnings.

Against the reduction of incomes, African states suddenly faced stiffer obligations. Economic stabilization measures by the Northern economies caused an appreciation of the dollar against local currencies and a rise in global interest rates, changes rapidly transmitted to debtor governments. Borrowers saw increases in both the nominal dollar amounts of debt and prevailing interest rates. The average interest rate for new commitments was 5.5 percent in 1977 and climbed to 9.3 percent by 1981.

As debtor states were increasingly pressed, they improvised different means to meet their immediate financing needs. First, many governments drew down their external stocks of foreign currency, and regional reserves dropped from over $2 billion in 1977 to an outflow of $600 million in 1984. Second, numerous countries resorted to short-term finance, often on tough terms, to meet current commitments. Such credits totaled only $100 million in 1975 but grew to over $5 billion in 1983.[43] As long-term and short-term borrowing came due, a bunching of debt service occurred. This soon created insupportable demands for many economies, causing governments to fall delinquent on some of their obligations. Arrears on Africa's foreign debt soared, reaching almost $10 billion by 1982. For some governments the accumulation of arrears provided an additional tactic to manage external financing needs.

However important these external factors, the region's economic descent cannot be explained solely by trends in the international economy. The prevailing policy regime in most countries aggravated the effects of external shocks, and the failure of African governments to adopt necessary adjustment measures in the early stages of distress hastened the crisis. The combination of inflexible exchange rates and restrictive trade practices hampered the expansion of exports, and rigorous terms for foreign investors impeded other capital inflows. These problems tended to worsen the balance of payments. In addition, much of the borrowing undertaken by governments was directed toward loss-making public enterprises, invested in unproductive projects, channeled into costly subsidies, or dissipated by corruption. Consequently, many states incurred liabilities without generating additional income or productive capacity.

Furthermore, as we discuss later, few governments in Africa began serious stabilization measures before the 1980s. In contrast with Asian regimes such as South Korea and Indonesia, which took relatively prompt measures in the late 1970s to devalue their currencies and balance spending, most African governments continued to defer adjustment. A number of countries, including Ghana and Nigeria, experimented with "homegrown" austerity programs in the early years of economic difficulty. These measures proved ineffective, and the countries soon turned to multilateral institutions for assistance. By the time reform began, in the early to mid-1980s (and even later for a few), the economic rut was already deep.

The reluctance to adjust was related to the political character of African regimes. State elites were loath to curtail spending or to relinquish control over key areas of the economy, which provided their central levers of patronage. Ideology also played a role, and the statist outlook of the 1970s was averse to economic liberalization. Also, governments faced considerable pressure from traditional constituencies—such as labor, business elites, regional groups, and elites of the ruling party—for continued entitlements. Interests for short-term political survival worked against disruptions of the status quo, however necessary they might be to arrest long-term economic decline. The neopatrimonial state in Africa resisted economic reform.

■ STRUCTURAL ADJUSTMENT AND THE INTERNATIONAL FINANCIAL INSTITUTIONS

The stopgap efforts introduced by various governments proved ineffectual at stabilizing their economies and prompting growth. By the early 1980s it was impossible to avoid some form of adjustment to restore external balances and correct deep-seated distortions in African economies. The availability of diverse sources of external finance had allowed African governments to avoid or defer adjustment through much of the 1970s, but those outlets dried up in the early 1980s. Africa's balance with private creditors changed from a net inflow of $3.4 billion in 1982 to an outflow of $2 billion in 1984, as new lending halted and old obligations came due.[44] With the buildup of arrears, sources of official credit were also curbed. African states faced urgent needs to secure new external finance and to reschedule their debts to ease current pressures for repayment.

These circumstances invited a more prominent role for the multilateral financial institutions, including the International Monetary Fund (IMF), the World Bank, and the African Development Bank (ADB). The IMF and the World Bank—the Bretton Woods institutions—have been the leading organizations in terms of resources and policy leverage. They serve as international "lenders of last resort" for countries experiencing acute problems in their balance of payments or bottlenecks in economic growth. With different mandates and funding, these institutions serve complementary functions of addressing financial needs and promoting policy change in African countries. They have been pivotal to the course of African economies since the 1980s.

Few issues in contemporary African development have been as contentious as the role of these international financial institutions (IFIs) over the past two decades. To their critics the IFIs are domineering representatives of the Northern economies, bent on enforcing the rules of international capital, to the detriment of Africa's people. For their proponents, these institutions provide the global architecture for ensuring international stability and financial assistance to poor and marginal economies, and they are the advocates of necessary, if painful, economic reforms. Much confusion has surrounded the activities of these institutions, the policies they advance, and their relation to the processes of economic reform and recovery in Africa.

Emerging from the Bretton Woods conference toward the end of World War II, the International Monetary Fund was created to help assure global stability in finance and trade. In recent decades the central role of the IMF has been to assist governments (mainly in the developing world) that experience severe problems in their balance of payments, usually accompanied by general macroeconomic instability. The forms of assistance are twofold. First, the IMF can provide temporary financing to help countries meet their external commitments; the bridge loans provided directly by the fund are often modest in size, are quickly disbursed, and extend over short periods of one to three years. Second and often far more important, the IMF can serve to ratify a country's eligibility for debt relief and new resources.[45] Two international consortia, the Paris Club of bilateral creditors and the London Club of commercial creditors, coordinate the management of developing country debt. When debtor countries are in distress, these groups can take vital decisions to reschedule obligations, cancel some debt, or provide new lending. This is crucial to relieve the acute resource constraints faced by many African governments. The actions of the creditors' clubs, however, are contingent on approval from the IMF, which serves as the implicit gatekeeper for debt restructuring. Debtor governments have had little success negotiating directly with these lenders in the absence of an IMF agreement.

IMF assistance is predicated on a series of policy reforms by debtor governments. Loans from the fund are disbursed in stages (or "tranches"), and countries' performance on key policies is regularly monitored as a condition for continued support. The requirement of reform as the basis for aid is known as "conditionality." The standard IMF package is concerned with broad macroeconomic stability, targeting essentials such as inflation, fiscal balances, and the external current account. The central focus is on demand management, which entails reducing aggregate demand in the economy to decrease inflation and bring spending in line with income.

Several key policy changes, with assorted rationales, are included in IMF conditionality. First, currency devaluation is urged. By making imports relatively more costly and exports more competitive, devaluation should redress trade imbalances. Second, trade liberalization (including tariff reductions and the removal of other barriers) can introduce competitive pressures to the local economy, and it opens possibilities for importation of needed inputs to enhance productivity. Third, governments must balance their budgets to improve their overall fiscal health, reduce the need for external finance, and contain inflation. Fourth, monetary restraint is aligned with conservative fiscal policies as a means of limiting inflation. Fifth, the reduction or removal of subsidies can reduce a major burden on government spending; it also permits realistic pricing for such items as food, fuel, agricultural inputs, utilities, and social services. Subsidy reduction is usually accompanied by broader deregulation of prices. Sixth, cutbacks in government personnel are another budget-cutting measure. Wage controls can assist in achieving this goal. Reduction of excess staff can also improve the efficiency of the public sector. Seventh, governments are urged to privatize or liquidate public enterprises as a further step in decreasing fiscal burdens, reducing debt, and improving general efficiency.

The World Bank's charter and activities are distinct, although the bank cooperates closely with the IMF. In its role as a development finance institution, the World Bank provides long-term funding for specific development activities, traditionally for discrete projects in infrastructure, industry, agriculture, social sectors, and administration. In 1980 the bank also began to provide program lending to assist broader policy reforms such as price liberalization, state enterprise divestiture, and currency devaluation.[46] Although the World Bank directs some resources to commercial enterprises through its private sector lending arm, the International

Finance Corporation, the bulk of its loans has been channeled through governments in developing countries.

The World Bank provides much of its finance on a conditional basis. Program lending is explicitly tied to specific policy reforms, whereas new financing for projects is often contingent on timely debt service and the existence of an agreement with the IMF. Although echoing the key elements of IMF conditionality, the World Bank has also urged changes in sectoral policies and sundry institutional reforms. These commonly address such areas as restructuring and divesting state enterprise; liberalizing financial systems; reforming regulatory arrangements; increasing producer prices; fostering competitive markets for labor, land, and industrial and agricultural inputs; encouraging competition in public infrastructure and other large-scale enterprise; and improving public sector financial management. Some agreements between the Bank and African governments have contained forty separate targets or conditions.[47]

The IFIs have been counterpart organizations in the process of policy reform in Africa. The main concern of the IMF is current economic stability, whereas the World Bank focuses on issues of protracted growth and transformation in developing economies. The priorities of the World Bank imply a broader focus on sectoral problems, economic distribution and welfare, and economic institutions, while the IMF has been more narrowly interested in macroeconomic management.

These differing orientations are reflected in the reforms emphasized by each institution. In Africa the standard package of IMF conditionality has emphasized *stabilization,* or rapid improvement of macroeconomic balances. As we have noted, this implies a set of demand-management policies. The IMF programs have lengthened over time, but arrangements with African countries in the early 1980s averaged eighteen months. The World Bank, for its part, has stressed the process of *structural adjustment,* which involves shifts in relative prices and the reallocation of resources to more efficient or productive activities. This is a supply-side strategy, primarily concerned with revitalizing production and restoring growth over time.[48] Structural adjustment encompasses sectoral changes as well as macroeconomic stability, and it is expected to take several years to realize effective change. In fact, the nominal span of adjustment has lengthened over time, from early assessments of three to five years to current estimates of ten to fifteen years.

It is important, however, not to exaggerate these distinctions. Both of the leading IFIs operate within a common framework of neoclassical economic theory, and they share a consensus on market-oriented approaches to development and reform. Their respective packages are often regarded as phases in a sequence of recovery. Short-term stabilization is a prerequisite for effective structural adjustment, whereas structural change necessarily carries through the process of reform. Despite this accord over goals and methods, the IFIs have sometimes held different views on priorities of reform. There have been tensions and disagreements between the World Bank and the IMF over such issues as the speed of reform, the sequencing of different policy changes, and the urgency of debt relief for African states.

In the course of the 1980s a growing number of African governments turned to the IFIs for assistance; at least thirty-six countries in the region entered into stabilization agreements with the IMF or structural adjustment programs with the World Bank. In all, the IFIs cooperated in 243 separate agreements, of which 153 were various IMF facilities and standby arrangements. The World Bank participated in 90 assorted program loans.[49] Most countries began these programs in the early 1980s, although several—including Benin, Cameroon, Congo-Brazzaville, Lesotho, Nigeria, and Mozambique—did not initiate reform until later in the decade. Nearly all of the countries that drew on resources from the IFIs entered into multiple agreements; Senegal, Côte d'Ivoire, Ghana, Togo, Central African Republic, Congo, Mauritius, Madagascar, Malawi, and Kenya each had ten or more programs during this period.

The needs of debtor countries gave the IFIs unprecedented leverage over the region's economic policies. During the 1980s multilateral institutions substantially influenced major aspects of macroeconomic management in the region, and in many instances they shaped sectoral policies as well. For non-CFA countries, which previously had imposed few external restrictions on monetary or fiscal policy, the spread of conditionality was especially significant. There is little question that these new requirements constrained many governments. Although some African leaders and policy advisers embraced the logic of orthodox economic reform, most remained skeptical or diffident. In pressing these changes on reluctant policymakers, the multilaterals were often seen as arrogant and heavy-handed.

The IFIs, however, were hardly all-powerful, and their influence varied over different periods, locales, and issues. Conditionality was intensely contested by governments and social constituencies in many countries. However rigorous the provisions in formal lending agreements, actual monitoring and enforcement were extremely uneven. The numerous conditions were difficult to measure, and it was frequently impossible to gauge compliance on programs.[50] Furthermore, many of the promised benefits of structural adjustment failed to materialize, including renewed growth, debt relief, and foreign investment. African governments eventually grew tired of austerity without results, and a frequent reaction to such "adjustment fatigue" was to relax or abandon their commitment to the IFIs' programs. Ultimately, political factors determined the course of economic change in Africa.

■ The Politics of Economic Reform

In most instances, the governments charged with implementing structural adjustment were the same ones that had fomented the initial economic crisis.[51] This contradiction frequently stymied the process of reform. Apart from their immediate fiscal emergencies, political leaders had little motivation for undertaking broad revisions in policy. Many remained committed to nationalist tenets that called for state control of key resources and enterprises. The few government officials and professional economists who argued for liberalization were an isolated minority in much of the region. Ideology aside, the interests of state elites also militated against reform. As noted earlier, officials did not want to relinquish their traditional prerogatives or their control of patronage resources. In addition, policymakers perceived genuine political hazards in removing consumer subsidies, retrenching workers, selling off government firms, and lifting protection for local business. Austerity measures provoked demonstrations and riots in many countries, including Zambia, Nigeria, Kenya, and Sudan. The weakness of key institutions that caused the failure of statist economic strategies also undermined the management of market economies.

There was also limited support for adjustment within African societies during the 1980s. A central problem in countries undergoing reform was the difficulty of mobilizing constituencies in favor of liberalization.[52] Adjustment measures had uneven effects on different segments of the population, and those groups fearing losses from reform often vigorously opposed these policies. They included civil servants and public enterprise employees concerned about unemployment, manufacturers in protected industries worried about competition, business elites anxious about the loss of government contracts, students restive over the imposition of school fees, and urban consumers angered over rising prices. On the other hand, the potential beneficiaries who might be expected to back liberalization were often unsure of their prospective gains or were difficult to organize. Such groups included farmers of export crops, manufacturers with export potential, segments of private business that could enter activities dominated by state firms, and consumers who were poorly served by public enterprise. In consequence, African governments could not count on a political base for reform, and they commonly confronted the prospect of moving ahead with adjustment in the face of popular antagonism or opposition.

These factors help to explain the patterns of reform in Africa. The implementation of structural adjustment programs was often incomplete. Most governments fulfilled a few conspicuous reforms that could be enacted by a single executive order and were easily measured by the IFIs; these included currency devaluation, increased producer prices, trade liberalization, budget cutbacks, subsidy reduction, and debt service. Another class of reforms focused on key institutions, such as the civil service, public enterprises, and the financial sector. These reforms were slower and more politically complex, as they involved many organizations and affected diverse interests. They also required prolonged efforts from various elements of the state administration, and it was difficult for the IFIs to measure implementation and results. Institutional reforms, particularly privatization and financial liberalization, were often stalled or abandoned by African governments.[53]

The determination of African governments to implement programs of structural adjustment also wavered over time. Many regimes relaxed their commitment to reform when opposition became too pronounced or results were slow to appear. Following violent protests against the removal of food subsidies, Zambia's government dropped its structural adjustment program in 1987. Nigeria, after sustaining key policies for a few years, also slackened reform after 1990 in response to growing political pressure and a brief reappearance of the oil windfall. Côte d'Ivoire and Zimbabwe each went through different episodes of adjustment in the 1980s. Even Ghana, which preserved an orthodox adjustment program for more than a decade, began to waver after 1992 when electoral politics were introduced. Budget deficits inched upward, and the government hesitated in introducing tax reform and privatization.

The course of structural adjustment was shaped by a process of bargaining among debtor governments and the IFIs.[54] African leaders sought the benefits of debt relief and new resources while moving cautiously on risky policy changes or avoiding them altogether. They also tried to balance the policy requirements of creditors and the contrary pressures from their own domestic constituencies in an effort to preserve the political status quo. The IFIs and creditors' groups, on the other hand, tried to extract as many reforms as possible in return for their assistance. In numerous instances the multilaterals pushed for quicker progress or further conditions as countries proceeded with adjustment. A number of governments, weary of the aggressive stance of the IFIs or unwilling to sustain the political risks, retreated from reform.

Consistent and successful adjustment has been rare in Africa. In a 1994 report surveying the course of reform throughout the region, World Bank analysts found only six countries that had sustained a basic package of adjustment for a reasonable period; even within this group, some countries had broken off reform because of regime change or political upheaval.[55] The study also confirmed the uneven degree of policy shifts. Among the countries engaged in agreements with the IFIs, price reforms were almost universally implemented, whereas institutional reforms were relatively infrequent. These observations underscore the political challenges of structural adjustment.

The countries that have sustained reform have embodied changes of leadership and shifts in the coalitions surrounding economic policy. New leaders with a strong commitment to change are the most effective in sustaining adjustment measures. Also, countries experiencing deeper, more enduring economic crises often show greater receptivity to reform, as the groups supporting the old clientelist system have been weakened by economic decline.[56] Ghana and Uganda provide the best illustrations of these circumstances. Zambia, Benin, and Nigeria displayed similar patterns at various times, although in those instances adjustment was eventually undermined by political uncertainty.

However ambivalent Africans have been toward structural adjustment, fiscal realities have compelled most countries to accept some degree of orthodox economic reform. Leaders and citizens in the region have contended with the IFIs over the design of programs, the degree of compliance, and the flow of external resources, but the basic agenda of policy change has not been in question. Whether these programs have achieved a measure of economic recovery or have merely compounded Africa's troubles is a further controversy to which we now turn.

■ The Effects of Adjustment

Structural adjustment has been an important factor in Africa's economic policies for nearly two decades. Although many governments have undertaken tough reforms, the region has been slow to recover from its economic mire. Gross domestic product in sub-Saharan Africa grew by only 2.2 percent on average between 1990 and 1995, actually subsiding from the late 1980s, when growth averaged 3 percent. Not until 1995 did regional growth rates exceed 4 percent, outpacing birth rates and therefore high enough to allow for a net increase in per capita incomes.[57]

Other signs of economic performance have been equally lackluster. Trade has rebounded modestly, but the productive sectors of most economies have remained sluggish. Overall, the region's exports expanded by almost 3 percent a year in the first half of the 1990s, and imports began to recover from the decline of the preceding decade, rising a little more than 1 percent annually. The growth of industrial output diminished considerably, however, from 3 percent in the late 1980s to only 1 percent in the early 1990s. During this period agricultural growth also slowed, from 3.2 percent to 2.2 percent on average.[58]

Despite the gradual expansion of trade, the region's balance of payments has continued to slide, showing the effects of mounting debt service and trade imbalances. The deficit in the regional current account was 5 percent of regional GDP in 1990 and over 8 percent in 1993. Government deficits have also risen, from an average of nearly 5 percent of GDP at the end of the 1980s to almost 7 percent over the next five years. A stifling debt overhang has hindered growth, as total external obligations exceeded $226 billion by 1995, and debt service generally claimed 15 percent of export revenues.[59] During the era of structural adjustment, a number of countries reversed their downward slide or significantly increased their growth rates. But even after a decade or more of these reforms, growth in Africa lags behind that of most other developing regions, and few economies have surpassed the levels of development that were evident before the onset of crisis. These are hardly signs of revitalization.

For critics of structural adjustment, Africa's disappointing performance comes as little surprise. They regard the IFIs' programs as an inappropriate response to Africa's economic problems, designed to safeguard the economic needs of the North rather than to advance African development. In this view, conditionality imposes draconian cuts on domestic spending and investment while ensuring that governments service their external debts and open their economies to foreign capital and trade. Adjustment measures also impose severe social costs through the erosion of incomes, the withdrawal of subsidies, increased joblessness, and the displacement of local production by imports. These analysts argue that the IFIs have actually slowed African recovery and in many instances have worsened conditions for the region's people.

Proponents of structural adjustment reply that these reforms are necessary to restore stability, remove long-standing distortions from these economies, and improve Africa's position in global markets. Although some policies in the reform package may cause distress or difficulty in the short term, over the long term they provide a foundation for sustained growth and improved welfare. Advocates of this perspective draw from a substantial body of economic theory, and they cite the comparative experience of countries in other regions—including Asia and Latin America—that have successfully pursued adjustment.

A fair assessment of structural adjustment in Africa is complicated by several factors. First, it is often difficult to separate the effects of the initial economic crisis from those of adjustment. Slow growth, poverty, unemployment, and oppressive debt afflicted most African economies prior to the introduction of externally sponsored reforms. Independent of the IFIs, many governments adopted austerity measures in the early 1980s as a response to urgent fiscal pressures, and these measures often entailed cuts in public spending and employment. It is true that austerity measures continued or even intensified during reform, but some degree of contraction was inevitable given the region's economic plight. The economies of many countries were in virtual free fall before the adoption of IFI programs, and local, ad hoc measures showed meager results in arresting decline. Many ills attributed to structural adjustment can be traced to problems of low investment, weak institutions, and continued fiscal pressures that did not result directly from orthodox policies.

The modest implementation of adjustment measures raises further questions. Although formal agreements with the IFIs have abounded, the actual fulfillment of policy reform has been relatively limited. Consequently, there is some debate about whether the region's economic lassitude is a consequence of structural adjustment or of insufficient reform. In general, it can be said that African economies have considerably stabilized, in the sense of improving external balances and restoring a degree of macroeconomic equilibrium. There has been relatively little structural adjustment, however, in the sense of enduring changes in prices, markets, and institutions. Only a few countries, including Ghana and Uganda, have sustained an adjustment package for more than a few years. The incomplete character of reform makes it difficult to link economic performance in most countries to the effects of orthodox policies.

The World Bank, in a series of reports, has tried to demonstrate that orthodox programs are effective when fully implemented. The Bank has produced figures suggesting that economic performance in the 1980s and 1990s was closely correlated to the degree of policy reform, with the more conscientious reformers doing better. These reports have been widely criticized for inadequate or distorted data, and they provide little conclusive evidence on the effects of adjustment.[60] Although there is no confirmation that structural adjustment produces recovery, there is an equally weak basis for alleging that the programs of the IFIs are wholly responsible for Africa's continued economic ills, especially when those programs have scarcely been fulfilled.

One way to sort out these problems is to consider the *counterfactual*: what would have happened to these economies under different circumstances? By constructing such an alternative scenario, we can place existing conditions in perspective. Some analysts have offered depictions showing that African economies, in the absence of structural adjustment, would have continued to deteriorate or perhaps moved downhill faster.[61] This would seem to indicate that orthodox reform has been necessary to curb the region's downward trend. While this exercise may be suggestive, it cannot confirm the effects of specific policies. Given the large role of unrecorded parallel markets in Africa and the poor economic information for most countries, modeling cannot provide reliable speculation about the effects of policy change. Moreover, economic performance is often influenced by exogenous factors such as climatic changes and the resolution of civil conflict. For instance, drought severely depressed output in much of southern Africa in the early 1990s, and the advent of peace in Mozambique briefly prompted double-digit growth rates. These elements can obscure the impact of policy reform, making firm generalizations difficult.

Although we recognize that Africa's economic performance has multiple causes, it is still possible to venture conclusions about the efficacy of structural adjustment in the region. Many of the basic elements in the IFIs' programs were prudent and necessary. African governments evidently needed to contain budget deficits, raise prices for agricultural producers, trim bloated bureaucracies and state enterprises, establish more realistic exchange rates, and bring their balance of payments into equilibrium. These macroeconomic fundamentals are scarcely contested today, and abundant evidence from around the world affirms the value of such policy reforms.

The process of adjustment, however, can be faulted in at least two dimensions. First, the design and pace of many programs create liabilities that are inimical to economic recovery. The rapid introduction of multiple reforms has fostered economic dislocations and often elicited perverse effects. Currency devaluation, pursued in tandem with trade liberalization, frequently devastates domestic manufacturers who cannot afford imported inputs and are unable to compete with a new influx of foreign goods. Financial reforms commonly hike interest rates, making credit inaccessible for many firms. The high costs of credit and foreign exchange also hurt many farmers who cannot afford agricultural inputs, especially as subsidies are eased. Privatization has often been captured by political insiders who acquire cheap state assets but fail to enhance service delivery or production. The rapid divestiture of government firms, along with other cutbacks in state payrolls, creates substantial pools of unemployed workers. The multilateral institutions, eager to see quick results, have been insufficiently attentive to these problems, especially in the early years of reform.

Adjustment measures often had the effect of curtailing access to social services. Officially, the IFIs have admonished debtor governments to adjust through a combination of expenditure *reduction* and expenditure *switching*, which entails shifting funds to the most essential uses.[62] In theory, switching priorities should allow governments to lessen spending while preserving social programs and critical investments. In practice, however, many leaders have tightened budgets across the board rather than reallocating funds. Governments have introduced user fees for health and education and reduced funding to many programs and regions. In consequence, many citizens find these basic services inaccessible. Evidence from Ghana and Tanzania, for instance, shows significant losses in the coverage of social services, particularly in urban areas and marginal regions.[63]

Another dimension in which economic reform has fallen short is the enabling context for production and investment. Many of the fiscal and price reforms in structural adjustment may be necessary for economic improvement, but they are clearly insufficient to foster a broad regeneration of African economies. In retrospect, expectations about the adaptability of African economies to policy change were unrealistic. The leading institutional impediments to growth were not addressed by most adjustment packages in the 1980s. Deficient infrastructure, feeble or corrupt administrations, inappropriate regulatory regimes, and weak human capital are among the most intractable sources of economic stagnation. Political uncertainty has also hampered investment from domestic as well as foreign sources. The reform process has done little to enhance basic state capabilities, and rigorous cuts in public spending have arguably worsened some of these problems. In the 1990s, donors showed a greater appreciation for institutional development, and various "capacity-building" initiatives were undertaken to bolster civil service, legal, and regulatory systems and key economic management agencies. In most instances, these fragmentary efforts have yet to produce substantial results.

The inherited structural problems of African economies, along with uncertainty about the credibility of policy reform, have resulted in a limited supply response to adjustment programs. Agrarian producers and manufacturers have not reacted to nominal price incentives with substantial growth of output. The majority of countries have only marginally improved their export performance, and few have developed nontraditional exports.[64] The problem of long-term capital accumulation is also reflected in depressed levels of savings and investment. The rate of gross domestic savings for the region, about 14 percent of GDP in the mid-1980s, has been low by international standards and has remained virtually unchanged for a decade. Similarly, gross domestic investment was 17 percent of GDP in the late 1980s and 18 percent in the early 1990s, considerably below the rates of most countries in Southeast Asia and lower than those of many countries in South Asia and Latin America.

Furthermore, the international response to African reform has been discouraging. Despite the adoption of many fundamental policy changes, trading partners, investors, and lenders have been slow to engage with African markets. Africa's dwindling share of international commodity markets has not rebounded substantially in the past decade. Commercial lending has been depressed since the early 1980s, and direct foreign investment remains modest, with little entry of capital outside the petroleum and mineral sectors. By the late 1990s Africa was receiving only about 2 percent of total direct investment in developing countries. The region had attracted growing interest as a destination for portfolio investment, as many countries opened their economies and developed local equity or financial markets. But portfolio equity flows to Africa totaled about $3.6 billion in 1996, a pittance by international standards.[65] These flows were concentrated in a few countries, including South Africa (which claimed 89 percent), Mauritius, Zimbabwe, Kenya, Ivory Coast, and Ghana. Hopes for Africa's emerging markets had dimmed considerably by the late 1990s, as the Asian financial crisis caused a retreat of global portfolio investment.

The sluggishness of private capital flows has accentuated the importance of official aid. Official development assistance constituted less than 4 percent of Africa's overall GDP in 1980, but at decade's end it had grown to nearly 10 percent, and it reached 12 percent in 1994. For sixteen countries in sub-Saharan Africa—Rwanda, Burundi, Malawi, Tanzania,

Comoros, Djibouti, Mozambique, Zambia, Guinea-Bissau, Cape Verde, Mali, Niger, Burkina Faso, Chad, Mauritania, and Sierra Leone—aid exceeded 10 percent of GDP in the mid-1990s. External assistance also comprised 61 percent of Africa's gross domestic investment in 1995, three times its share in the early 1980s.[66]

Although the relative weight of external aid increased for many African economies, the absolute magnitude of assistance did not rise commensurately. Foreign aid, measured in real terms, doubled during the 1980s, growing from $7.6 billion to $15.1 billion in the course of the decade. These flows then leveled off, remaining virtually unchanged in the first half of the 1990s. In part, this reflected the frustrations of "donor fatigue," as African economies continued to founder. After 1990 assistance from the multilateral institutions grew modestly, but aid from the Western industrialized countries was flat, and assistance from other sources such as OPEC states and the former communist bloc countries virtually disappeared.

A further external constraint on growth has been the oppressive debt burden throughout the region. We have noted that Africa's debt continued to grow throughout the 1980s, as rescheduling and new lending compounded existing commitments. By the mid-1990s, the ratio of debt to GNP in sub-Saharan Africa was 81 percent, and the ratio of debt to exports exceeded 270 percent—the highest among the developing regions. The composition of debt continued to work against most African countries. Obligations to private creditors diminished considerably as a proportion of total debt, but nonconcessional official debt expanded from 15 percent in 1980 to more than 26 percent by 1995. Even more consequential was the increased reliance on lending from multilateral institutions, whose share nearly tripled from 9 percent to 24 percent of total debt in this period.[67] About three-quarters of multilateral lending has been on nonconcessional terms, and these organizations do not permit rescheduling of their loans. In fact, net transfers (disbursals minus repayments) from the IMF to Africa turned negative by the mid-1980s, producing outflows of several hundred million dollars annually. As African debt has increased, the region has faced harsher terms and less flexibility in restructuring obligations.

Creditors have been diffident about easing the region's debt burden. The prevailing regime for international debt emphasizes full repayment of existing obligations, at least for private and multilateral creditors, which currently hold about 45 percent of overall African debt. Among many of Africa's poorer economies a substantial share of debt is owed to bilateral creditors that could potentially forgive some commitments. Nonetheless, the process of restructuring has been slow and halting. Several proposals for debt relief have emerged since the onset of the crisis. Successive U.S. administrations put forth the 1985 Baker Plan and the 1989 Brady Plan, which called for a mix of new money and debt rescheduling for countries that adopted austerity measures and liberalized their economies. These plans, however, mainly addressed commercial and multilateral lending, and the chief beneficiaries were the larger debtors of Latin America.

Not until 1988 did official creditors begin to resolve some of the problems of bilateral debt. Annual reschedulings under the Paris Club jumped from only a few each year before 1982 to an average of seventeen annually over the next decade, most of which were in Africa. In a series of international meetings, the principal creditor countries introduced arrangements known as the Toronto Terms (1988), Trinidad Terms (1990), Houston Terms (1990), "Enhanced" Toronto Terms (1991), and Naples Terms (1995), covering the rescheduling of Paris Club debt. These arrangements provided different procedures for low-income and lower-middle-income countries experiencing severe debt problems. Although they allowed for longer maturities and lower interest, these plans simply rolled over existing obligations without reducing the magnitude of debt. Repeated reschedulings, increased borrowing from multilateral institutions, and the practice of using bilateral lending to cover payments due on multilateral debt all served to increase the total debt stock.

Following on the 1995 Naples Terms, the Paris Club and the multilateral institutions began to contemplate plans for actually decreasing of debt stock, rather than simply reducing current payments (or net present value). In 1996, the Highly Indebted Poor Country (HIPC) initiative was announced by the IFIs. This arrangement provides for a substantial abatement of debt for low-income countries showing sustained commitment to economic reform. This plan could signal a new direction in the management of African debt, but the effects are not yet evident. The HIPC initiative has been criticized for being excessively rigorous and complex, since it requires a six-year process of policy reform and certification before debt relief comes into effect. By the end of the 1990s, only two African countries, Uganda and Mozambique, were set to benefit from the HIPC provisions.

Structural adjustment has registered mixed results throughout Africa, but there is consensus that existing efforts toward orthodox reform have not generally succeeded. There are several reasons for this disappointing performance, including flaws in the design of adjustment policies, deficient implementation by African governments, prevailing structural problems in the region's economies, and ineffective response from international donors and markets. In view of the shortcomings of the programs advanced by the IFIs, many analysts have suggested alternatives to adjustment.

■ Alternatives to Adjustment?

The search for alternatives to orthodox reform has engaged a wide variety of scholars and practitioners. A number of academic critics (within Africa and outside the region), occasionally joined by local policymakers, have criticized conventional adjustment programs. A scattering of national research institutions and regional consortia have addressed the problems of economic recovery. International nongovernmental organizations (NGOs) concerned with development have also contributed critical assessments of orthodox reform. For the most part, these efforts have produced no coherent set of alternative policy options. International organizations, especially groupings within the UN system, have offered the most comprehensive proposals. African countries nonetheless lack sufficient resources and leverage to effectively challenge the programs of the IFIs. The dialogue over structural adjustment has yielded some ad hoc modifications of economic reform but few changes in the regional priorities of multilateral institutions.

Critics of orthodox policies have staked out a range of positions. Partisans of dependency theory challenge the foundations of market-oriented adjustment, insisting on the virtues of Africa's selective disengagement from the world economy. They advocate strategies of self-reliance and state-led development as the key to the region's economic revival. Analysts closer to the mainstream have accepted many of the price and fiscal reforms of structural adjustment, but they encourage better sequencing of policies, continued protection for some sectors, greater debt relief, and increased attention to social welfare and distributional issues.

The structuralist perspective is probably the most prevalent throughout the region. Structuralists focus on domestic institutional problems and the region's disadvantageous position in the international economy. Although acknowledging the value of some economic liberalization, structuralists generally emphasize the importance of more favorable terms for African economies in global markets and enhanced government supervision of domestic economies.

By the mid-1980s concern was growing over the adverse distributive impact of orthodox policies. The emphases on fiscal stabilization and improved trade balances carried a number of consequences for African societies. Unemployment grew, at least in the formal sector, as civil servants and parastatal employees were retrenched. In many countries private employment also declined, as domestic businesses were squeezed by competition from imports, rising prices from devaluation, and the high cost of credit. Moreover, structural adjustment was intended to shift rural-urban terms of trade, which commonly meant higher food prices and declining real incomes for urban wage earners. The reduction of subsidies, as we have noted, frequently limited access to social services. The net effect was widespread privation, notably among the urban poor and nominally middle-class groups such as civil servants, teachers, and small entrepreneurs. Critics have also charged that structural adjustment programs markedly increased inequality in Africa since the costs of austerity were borne disproportionately by certain segments of the population.

Much of this analysis was driven by a group of researchers sponsored by UNICEF (the United Nations International Children's Emergency

Fund), who emphasized the social costs of adjustment, urging greater concern for the basic needs of vulnerable groups—especially women and children.[68] Following this direction in 1988, the government of Ghana, after several years of orthodox reform, initiated the Program to Mitigate the Social Costs of Adjustment (PAMSCAD) in a bid to offset some of the worst effects of austerity. This received limited funding, and the effects were modest. Compensatory policies were also attempted in Mauritania, Senegal, Gambia, Guinea, Côte d'Ivoire, Nigeria, and Zambia.

The most cogent expression of the structuralist alternative is contained in a 1989 analysis by the United Nations Economic Commission for Africa (UNECA). The African Alternative Framework to Structural Adjustment Programmes (commonly known as AAF-SAP) presents a broad critique of orthodox adjustment and a set of proposed measures for economic revitalization.[69] Similar to an earlier statement, the Lagos Plan of Action, the AAF-SAP attributes the African crisis largely to external factors—notably adverse terms of trade and the burden of external debt.[70] The document gives greater recognition to domestic governance, however, stressing the capacities of African states to effectively manage development; it also devotes considerable attention to social welfare and equity. Although recognizing the need for fiscal restraint and greater efficiency, the AAF-SAP's recommendations point toward a state-centered strategy of economic recovery. The authors admonish African governments to streamline their planning and regulatory capabilities while urging concerted external debt relief and greater flexibility from the IFIs.

Critics of adjustment confront a twofold challenge: identifying the resources for economic recovery and specifying the political agency of reform. Without the assistance of the IFIs, Africa's states face an acute shortage of external finance, especially in view of the retreat of foreign companies and financial markets. The failure of homegrown stabilization attempts by several countries in the early 1980s demonstrated the impracticality of attempting to conserve funds solely through domestic austerity. There has been no compelling solution to these resource problems outside the framework of orthodox programs. In the political realm, statements such as the AAF-SAP appeal for more effective governance without explaining how it can be achieved. Experience has amply shown the difficulty of trying to achieve reform by working through the political status quo. Structuralists argue for more efficient regulation and planning of development, yet they have not traced a political process for transforming Africa's traditionally weak and predatory regimes into more development-oriented ones. In fairness, the IFIs have manifestly failed in this area as well, but critics of adjustment have yet to outline an alternative politics of reform.

Despite these shortcomings, the critique of structural adjustment has not been entirely fruitless. The IFIs, especially the World Bank, have reexamined their programs with respect to the sequence and design of policy reforms and have sought to address calls for social safety nets, the need to revive or build institutional capacity, and the imperative of debt relief for the poorest countries. Some donor organizations and multilateral lenders have also changed their operations to allow for greater dialogue and participation by Africans. Although these changes do not involve the foundations of orthodox reform, they do represent an incremental response to myriad critics.

■ ECONOMIC REFORM AND DEMOCRATIZATION

The dramatic political changes overtaking Africa in the 1990s raise further questions about the region's economic prospects. A wave of political reform yielded fourteen new electoral governments by 1994, and a host of countries significantly opened their politics to greater participation and competition. These innovations draw attention to the contentious relationship between political and economic change. Analysts of Africa and other developing regions have asked whether political liberalization will necessarily produce better economic governance. Many have also asked how economic performance might affect the consolidation of new democracies.

One view, rooted in the modernization perspective, sees political and economic liberalization as mutually reinforcing. Political freedoms should allow for a more liberal and flexible economy, and the resulting growth bolsters the legitimacy of democratic governance. Market economies also disperse social power, which tends to reinforce pluralist politics. In the African context, observers have noted that the most stable democracies, Botswana and Mauritius, have also been among the most economically successful countries in the region. These examples provide a stark contrast to the general continental record of authoritarian decline.

Some political analysts have offered a more skeptical view, suggesting a potential contradiction between political and economic reform.[71] Democratic regimes, which are accountable to diverse interests and pressure groups, often lack consistency or effectiveness in managing their economies. Poor economic performance will tend to undermine confidence in democratic rule, and the regimes may break down. This school of thought points to a more appropriate sequence of reform, beginning with economic adjustment and proceeding to political liberalization. The successful experiences of the newly industrializing countries (NICs) of East Asia and the economic reform efforts of authoritarian governments in Uganda and Ghana provide support for this view.

International experience over the past two decades suggests that the relationships are not as clear as these theories propose. Democracy offers benefits (such as improved human rights, political choice, and government accountability) that are valued in themselves, and citizens do not necessarily

judge the democratic system on the basis of economic performance.[72] As
we have discussed in Chapter 8, the consolidation of democratic regimes
in Africa depends on many factors other than economic performance, although such performance is certainly a major element in democratic stability. Furthermore, many elected leaders around the world have been able
to provide competent economic management, and in view of the generally
shoddy economic record of Africa's authoritarian regimes, there is little
reason to suppose they have an inherent advantage in this area.

Regardless of conjecture about an ideal sequence of change, many
African countries face a situation of concurrent political and economic reform. If political liberalization enables a departure from the practices and
institutions associated with neopatrimonial rule, then democratizing
African states can begin to shift the terms of economic governance. There
is also a possibility, however, that traditional politics may persist, although
perhaps in a different guise. Reform is influenced by the nature of leadership, the composition of social coalitions, and the capacities of public
institutions.

Africa's political transitions have not always produced dramatic
changes in these dimensions of public life. Although democracy offers the
possibility of transferring elites, there has been considerable continuity
among African leaders in the past decade. In most countries the movement
for political reform was driven by seasoned politicians, and many familiar
notables and parties shaped the new democratic governments.[73] The opposition coalition in Zambia included veteran labor leader Frederick Chiluba,
along with many supporters who defected from the ruling party. With the
electoral successes of Mathieu Kerekou in Benin and Didier Ratsiraka in
Madagascar, the previous autocrats returned in the second posttransition
elections. In Ghana former military ruler Jerry Rawlings retained power
through competitive elections, and in Mozambique Joaquim Chissano continued after the transition. In short, most political shifts have not introduced leaders with drastically new approaches to economic management.

The constituencies supporting democratic regimes also have a significant influence on the nature of economic governance. Liberalization provides new opportunities for political participation, although that does not
inevitably yield stronger coalitions for reform. Business associations, labor
unions, agricultural organizations, regional and ethnic movements, women's
groups, and a host of other interests have greater outlets for expressing
their concerns. Emergent party organizations can also influence the conduct of economic policy, and an independent media is an important agent
for increased transparency and accountability.

These factors have had varying effects in new democracies. In some
countries, political opening has encouraged forces lobbying for economic
liberalization and better governance. Business groups, professionals, journalists, and international organizations have gained a greater voice in policy

debates. In other instances, however, populist groupings and traditional patronage networks have asserted themselves, providing a brake on change. Civil servants, urban workers, students, and import-competing manufacturers are often opposed to structural adjustment, and they commonly press for expansionary fiscal policy along with continued subsidies, services, and protection. Considerable evidence reveals that traditional patronage politics have been preserved or resurrected in many of the region's new democracies. Cronies of the regime, reluctant to accept more competitive markets, frequently resist economic opening. Political insiders have often discredited adjustment efforts by narrowly appropriating the benefits of privatization, trade liberalization, and financial reform.

Many interest groups with a potential stake in economic reform have remained politically marginal under democratic regimes. Rural constituencies, which are commonly dispersed and fragmented, face collective action problems that limit their ability to organize.[74] Agricultural interest associations generally have not had prominent roles in the region's new democracies. Business groups are better organized, but they are frequently co-opted through patronage or distanced by their association with opposition parties. In Ghana, for instance, business associations have complained of governmental bias because of their links to the political opposition. Where the organized private sector is politically contained, these groups have not been effective advocates of economic reform.

Institutional development presents a further challenge to transitional regimes. Most of the region's nascent democracies have inherited weak administrations, moribund economies, and estranged societies from their autocratic forerunners. These problems stem largely from the predatory actions of authoritarian rulers, and additional problems have emerged from orthodox adjustment programs. Elected governments are typically caught between the budget constraints of donor conditionality and the pressures of popular constituencies for expedient spending. They have little scope for directing resources to administration, infrastructure, or regulatory reform. Democratization does not necessarily provide advantages in grappling with the challenges of institutional growth, and the legacy of state weakness undermines economic recovery.

Apart from these theoretical concerns, the general record of economic policy and performance in Africa's new democracies has failed to reveal a substantial progression. The evidence is tentative given the short period since these political transitions and the problem of assembling reliable comparative data; several trends are nonetheless clear. Nearly all governments have sustained relations with the multilateral financial institutions, which commonly entails engaging in policy dialogue, conditional lending, and adherence to basic orthodox policies. In countries such as Benin, Zambia, Ethiopia, and Mozambique, the first posttransition governments renewed or accelerated economic liberalization; in most other instances existing programs and donor affiliations were preserved. A commitment to economic liberalization by the executive has often been sufficient to maintain reform under democratic auspices.

Macroeconomic management has lapsed in some instances. In a few countries fiscal policy has displayed the effects of electoral competition, with public sector deficits and monetary expansion increasing during election years. Both Ghana and Zambia have reflected politically induced spending cycles. Some governments have responded to popular pressure with stalling measures such as tax reform, subsidy cuts, and privatization. Along with unstable macroeconomic policies, several democratizing countries have shown signs of malfeasance and illicit activities. These problems are exemplifed by the charges of corruption surrounding Frederick Chiluba's administration in Zambia and the spread of drug trafficking in that country.

Leaders in the nascent democratic regimes are cross-pressured by domestic and external forces. While confronting electoral competition and popular demands, politicians are also constrained by the requisites of donors and international markets. A significant loss of foreign exchange, debt relief, or foreign investment can be as damaging to political stability as dissension from local constituencies. Most African states have few alternatives to economic adjustment, however reluctant and uneven it may be. The international political and economic environment induces an orthodox course of reform.

Statistics on the region's economies also show mixed results. Regimes that have emerged from civil conflicts or political turmoil—including Mozambique, Namibia, and Ethiopia—have shown significant improvements in growth immediately after political transition, although the initial surge usually subsides after a few years, as the benefits of peace recede. Other countries have reflected ambiguous trends. Benin, Malawi, and Congo-Brazzaville increased their growth under democratic regimes (although growth in the latter was modest and temporary), whereas Madagascar, Niger, and Zambia moved slightly downward. A more sophisticated assessment would include such indicators as fiscal deficits, money supply, inflation, and investment, but here too the data do not offer a clear picture.[75] An assessment of the early posttransition period offers little evidence that democracy has had a systematic effect on economic performance in Africa.

Amid the general obstacles to democratic consolidation in Africa, the region's sluggish economies constitute a leading dilemma. Economic stagnation holds the potential to erode public confidence in the new regimes. By heightening the stakes of political power, conditions of scarcity sustain the pathologies of ethnic contention, electoral misconduct, and patronage politics that have historically corroded African democracies. Economic stasis, however, does not inescapably threaten the survival of democracies, and indeed there are signs that many African voters are willing to reject incumbents at the polls rather than challenge entire regimes. On the other side of the ledger, the collapse of Niger's democratic government, the genocidal eruption in Rwanda, and Nigeria's downward spiral in the 1990s show that economic malaise and failed reform can be liabilities for democratic change.

These problems and tensions suggest different potential trajectories for the region's new democracies. The first is the consolidation of democratic capitalism: in some countries economic and political reform may prove compatible, and these elements of liberalization will move in tandem. A second direction is that of populism, in which the political strains of economic reform lead governments to abandon adjustment and increase state intervention. This is likely to produce further stagnation, which leads to a third possibility—that of democratic failure and the resurgence of authoritarian rule. Democratization has opened a window of opportunity to meet the challenges of economic restructuring, although the opening is narrow and perhaps fleeting. The viability of democratic rule and market economies will be an important question for African development in the years to come.

■ NOTES

1. These figures are from Leslie L. Rood, "Foreign Investment in African Manufacturing," *Journal of Modern African Studies* 13, no. 1 (January 1975): 23, cited in Naomi Chazan, Robert Mortimer, John Ravenhill, and Donald Rothchild, *Politics and Society in Contemporary Africa,* 2d ed. (Boulder: Lynne Rienner, 1992). This section and subsequent discussions of regionalism and North-South relations draw substantially on material in the second edition; special acknowledgment is made to John Ravenhill.

2. See Thomas J. Biersteker, *Multinationals, the State, and Control of the Nigerian Economy* (Princeton: Princeton University Press, 1987); and Ernest J. Wilson, "Indigenization and Nationalization in Africa," *Comparative Politics* 22, no. 3 (1990).

3. F. N. Burton and Hisashi Inoue, "Expropriations of Foreign-Owned Firms in Developing Countries: A Cross-National Analysis," *Journal of World Trade Law* 18, no. 5 (September–October 1984): 396–414; cited in Chazan et al., *Politics and Society in Contemporary Africa,* p. 291.

4. Biersteker, *Multinationals.*

5. Robert Gilpin, *The Political Economy of International Relations* (Princeton: Princeton University Press, 1987), p. 294.

6. Chazan et al., *Politics and Society in Contemporary Africa,* p. 277.

7. This topic is discussed in John Ravenhill, "Regional Integration and Development in Africa: Lessons from the East African Community," *Journal of Commonwealth and Comparative Politics* 17, no. 3 (November 1979); see also Christian P. Potholm and Richard Fredland, eds., *Integration and Disintegration in East Africa* (Lanham, MD: University Press of America, 1980).

8. Mark W. DeLancey and Terry M. Mays, *Historical Dictionary of International Organizations in Sub-Saharan Africa* (London: Scarecrow Press, 1994), p. 123.

9. See the discussion in Carol Lancaster, "The Lagos Three: Economic Regionalism in Sub-Saharan Africa," in John W. Harbeson and Donald Rothchild, eds., *Africa in World Politics* (Boulder: Westview Press, 1991), p. 255.

10. Ibid. See also Makhtar Diouf, "Evaluation of West African Experiments in Economic Integration," in World Bank, *The Long-Term Perspective Study of Sub-Saharan Africa*, Volume 4: *Proceedings of a Workshop on Regional Integration and Cooperation* (Washington, DC: World Bank, 1990).

11. Dominic C. Mulaisho, "SADCC: A New Approach to Integration," in World Bank, *The Long-Term Perspective Study*, p. 41.

12. DeLancey and Mays, *Historical Dictionary*, p. 244.

13. South African destabilization is detailed in Joseph Hanlon, *Beggar Your Neighbors* (London: James Currey, 1986). See also Hanlon, "Political Economies in Conflict: SADCC, South Africa, and Sanctions," in David Martin and Phyllis Johnson, eds., *Destructive Engagement: Southern Africa at War* (Harare: Zimbabwe Publishing House, 1986).

14. Lancaster, "The Lagos Three," p. 261. See also Omotunde E. G. Johnson, "Economic Integration in Africa: Enhancing Prospects for Success," *Journal of Modern African Studies* 29, no. 1 (1991): 8–9.

15. These factors are elaborated in Stephen D. Krasner, *Structural Conflict: The Third World Against Global Liberalism* (Berkeley: University of California Press, 1985), Chapter 1.

16. Chazan et al., *Politics and Society in Contemporary Africa*, p. 300.

17. Gilpin, *Political Economy*, p. 300.

18. Ibid., pp. 297–298.

19. The comparative political economy of oil states is discussed in Terry Lynn Karl, *The Paradox of Plenty: Oil Booms and Petro-States* (Berkeley: University of California Press, 1997).

20. Joanna Moss and John Ravenhill, "Trade Developments During the First Lomé Convention," *World Development* 10, no. 10 (1982).

21. John Ravenhill, "What Is to Be Done for Third World Commodity Exporters? An Evaluation of the STABEX Scheme," *International Organization* 38, no. 3 (Summer 1984).

22. World Bank, *Sub-Saharan Africa: From Crisis to Sustainable Growth* (Washington, DC: World Bank, 1989), p. 222.

23. Ibid.

24. World Bank, *African Development Indicators 1997* (Washington, DC: World Bank, 1997), pp. 73–74. These figures exclude South Africa but include Nigeria, which accounts for a major proportion of the decline.

25. These figures are drawn from Carol Lancaster and John Williamson, eds., *African Debt and Financing* (Washington, DC: Institute for International Economics, 1986) pp. 31, 34–35, 40; and World Bank, *African Development Indicators 1997*, p. 176.

26. World Bank, *African Development Indicators 1997*, p. 80. These figures exclude South Africa.

27. Janet MacGaffey, *Entrepreneurs and Parasites* (Cambridge: Cambridge University Press, 1987), and "Initiatives from Below: Zaire's Other Path to Social and Economic Restructuring," in Goran Hyden and Michael Bratton, eds., *Governance and Politics in Africa* (Boulder: Lynne Rienner, 1992); and Aili Mari Tripp, *Changing the Rules: The Politics of Liberalization and the Urban Informal Economy in Tanzania* (Berkeley: University of California Press, 1997).

28. Janet MacGaffey, *The Second Economy of Zaire* (Philadelphia: University of Pennsylvania Press, 1991).

29. World Bank, *African Development Indicators 1997,* p. 191.

30. See Organization of African Unity, *Lagos Plan of Action for the Economic Development of Africa, 1980–2000* (Geneva: International Institute for Labour Studies); and UN Economic Commission for Africa, *African Alternative Framework to Structural Adjustment Programmes for Socio-Economic Recovery and Transformation (AAF-SAP),* [E/ECA/CM.15/6/Rev.3] (Addis Ababa, June 1989).

31. World Bank, *Accelerated Development in Sub-Saharan Africa* (Washington, DC: World Bank, 1981).

32. Anne Krueger, "The Political Economy of the Rent-Seeking Society," *American Economic Review* 64 (June 1974): 291–303. See also Catherine Boone, "The Making of a Rentier Class: Wealth Accumulation and Political Control in Senegal," *Journal of Development Studies* 26, no. 3 (April 1990): 425–449.

33. Richard Sandbrook, *The Politics of Africa's Economic Stagnation* (Cambridge: Cambridge University Press, 1985); Thomas M. Callaghy, "The State and the Development of Capitalism in Africa: Theoretical, Historical, and Comparative Reflections," in Donald Rothchild and Naomi Chazan, eds., *The Precarious Balance: State and Society in Africa* (Boulder: Westview Press, 1988), and "Lost Between State and Market: The Politics of Economic Adjustment in Ghana, Zambia, and Nigeria," in Joan Nelson, ed., *Economic Crisis and Policy Choice: The Politics of Adjustment in the Third World* (Princeton: Princeton University Press, 1990); and Peter M. Lewis, "Economic Reform and Political Transition in Africa: The Quest for a Politics of Development," *World Politics* 48, no. 3 (October 1996).

34. See Max Weber, *Economy and Society,* 2 vols. (Berkeley: University of California Press, 1978); Christopher Clapham, ed., *Patronage and Public Power* (London: Frances Pinter, 1982); Michael Bratton and Nicolas van de Walle, "Neopatrimonial Regimes and Political Transition in Africa," *World Politics* 46 (July 1994); and Peter M. Lewis, "Economic Statism, Private Capital, and the Dilemmas of Accumulation in Nigeria," *World Development* 22, no. 3 (March 1994).

35. Robert Jackson and Carl Rosberg, *Personal Rule in Black Africa* (Berkeley: University of California Press, 1982).

36. Richard Joseph, *Democracy and Prebendal Politics in Nigeria* (Cambridge: Cambridge University Press, 1987); and Boone, "The Making of a Rentier Class."

37. Richard Sandbrook, *The Politics of Africa's Economic Recovery* (Cambridge: Cambridge University Press, 1993).

38. World Bank, *Accelerated Development in Sub-Saharan Africa,* p. 155. The net barter terms of trade reflect the ratio of export unit values over import unit values.

39. Global Coalition for Africa, *1993 Annual Report* (Washington, DC: Global Coalition for Africa, 1993), p. 67. Basic data are provided by the World Bank.

40. World Bank, *Sub-Saharan Africa,* p. 242. These figures exclude Nigeria.

41. This observation is attributed to Philip Ndegwa, governor of the Central Bank of Kenya, quoted in Carol Lancaster and John Williamson, "Africa's Economic Predicament," in Lancaster and Williamson, eds., *African Debt,* p. 2.

42. Edward Brau, "African Debt: Facts and Figures on the Current Situation," in Lancaster and Williamson, eds., *African Debt,* p. 34.

43. Ibid., pp. 34–35.

44. Ibid., pp. 32–33.

45. David Gordon, "Debt, Conditionality, and Reform: The International Relations of Economic Policy Restructuring in Sub-Saharan Africa," in Thomas M. Callaghy and John Ravenhill, eds., *Hemmed In: Responses to Africa's Economic Decline* (New York: Columbia University Press, 1993), p. 111.

46. Paul Mosley, Jane Harrigan, and John Toye, *Aid and Power: The World Bank and Policy-Based Lending,* Vol. 1 (London: Routledge, 1991).

47. Matthew Martin, "Neither Phoenix Nor Icarus: Negotiating Economic Reform in Ghana and Zambia, 1983–92," in Callaghy and Ravenhil, eds., *Hemmed In,* p. 144.

48. John Ravenhill, "A Second Decade of Adjustment: Greater Complexity, Greater Uncertainty," in Callaghy and Ravenhill, eds., *Hemmed In,* p. 31.

49. Eva Jesperson, "External Shocks, Adjustment Policies, and Economic and Social Performance," in Giovanni Cornia, Rolph van der Hoeven, and Thandika Mkandawire, eds., *Africa's Recovery in the 1990s* (New York: St. Martin's Press, 1992), p. 12.

50. Gordon, "Debt, Conditionality, and Reform," p. 113.

51. Miles Kahler describes this "orthodox paradox" in "International Financial Institutions and the Politics of Adjustment," in Joan Nelson, ed., *Fragile Coalitions* (New Brunswick, NJ: Transaction and Overseas Development Council, 1989).

52. Jeffrey Herbst, "The Structural Adjustment of Politics in Africa," *World Development* 18, no. 7 (1990).

53. A World Bank study of twenty-nine countries in sub-Saharan Africa found that price reforms were far more prevalent than institutional reforms such as privatization and financial liberalization. See World Bank, *Adjustment in Africa: Reforms, Results and the Road Ahead* (New York: Oxford University Press for the World Bank, 1994).

54. See Nicolas van de Walle, "The Politics of Nonreform in Cameroon," in Jennifer Widner, ed., *Economic Change and Political Liberalization in Sub-Saharan Africa* (Baltimore: Johns Hopkins University Press, 1994); and Callaghy, "Lost Between State and Market."

55. World Bank, *Adjustment in Africa.*

56. Barbara Grosh, "Through the Structural Adjustment Minefield," in Widner, ed., *Economic Change and Political Liberalization.*

57. World Bank, *African Development Indicators 1997,* p. 34.

58. Ibid., pp. 19–20.

59. World Bank, *World Debt Tables 1996* (Washington, DC: World Bank, 1996), p. 202.

60. The key reports by the World Bank are *Africa's Adjustment and Growth in the 1980s* (Washington, DC: World Bank, 1989), and *Adjustment in Africa.* Responses include Ravenhill, "A Second Decade of Adjustment"; Paul Mosley and John Weeks, "Has Recovery Begun? 'Africa's Adjustment in the 1980s' Revisited," *World Development* 21, no. 10 (1993); and Sayre Schatz, "Structural Adjustment in Africa: A Failing Grade So Far," *Journal of Modern African Studies* 32, no. 4 (1994).

61. David E. Sahn, Stephen D. Younger, and Paul Dorosh, *Structural Adjustment Reconsidered: Economic Policy and Poverty in Africa* (Cambridge: Cambridge University Press, 1997).

62. This tactic is discussed in Paul Streeten, "Structural Adjustment: A Survey of the Issues and Options," in Simon Commander, ed., *Structural Adjustment and Agriculture: Theory and Practice in Africa and Latin America* (London: James Currey for the Overseas Development Institute, 1989), p. 10. For a more critical view, see Howard Stein and E. Wayne Nafziger, "Structural Adjustment, Human Needs, and the World Bank Agenda," *Journal of Modern African Studies* 29, no. 1 (1991): 178-179.

63. Stein and Nafziger, "Structural Adjustment"; and Jon Kraus, "The Political Economy of Stabilization and Structural Adjustment in Ghana," in Donald

Rothchild, ed., *Ghana: The Political Economy of Recovery* (Boulder: Lynne Rienner, 1991).

64. See, for instance, Kwasi Anyemedu, "Export Diversification Under the Structural Adjustment Program," in Rothchild, ed., *Ghana*.

65. Deborah Brautigam, "Economic Takeoff in Africa?" *Current History* (May 1998): 205.

66. World Bank, *African Development Indicators 1997*, p. 316.

67. Ibid., p. 177.

68. Giovanni Cornia, Richard Jolly, and Frances Stewart, eds., *Adjustment with a Human Face* (Oxford: Clarendon Press, 1987).

69. See the UN Economic Commission for Africa, *African Alternative Framework to Structural Adjustment Programmes*.

70. See John Ravenhill, "Collective Self-Reliance or Collective Self-Delusion: Is the Lagos Plan a Viable Alternative?" in John Ravenhill, ed., *Africa in Economic Crisis* (New York: Columbia University Press, 1986).

71. Adam Przeworski, *Democracy and the Market* (Cambridge: Cambridge University Press, 1990). Alternative views are discussed in Leslie Armijo, Thomas Biersteker, and Abraham Lowenthal, "The Problems of Simultaneous Transitions," in Larry Diamond and Marc F. Plattner, eds., *Economic Reform and Democracy* (Baltimore: Johns Hopkins University Press, 1995).

72. Raymond Duch, "Economic Chaos and the Fragility of Democratic Transition in Former Communist Regimes," *Journal of Politics* 57, no. 1 (February 1995).

73. Robert Bates, "The Impulse to Reform in Africa," in Widner, ed., *Economic Change and Political Liberalization*.

74. Robert Bates, *Markets and States in Tropical Africa* (Berkeley: University of California Press, 1982); and Jennifer Widner, "The Discovery of Politics: Smallholder Reactions to the Cocoa Crisis of 1988–90 in Côte d'Ivoire," in Callaghy and Ravenhill, eds., *Hemmed In*.

75. These conclusions are based on a preliminary assessment of macroeconomic indicators for Benin, Congo-Brazzaville, Ethiopia, Madagascar, Malawi, Mali, Mozambique, Namibia, and Zambia for the period 1987–1996. Figures are from World Bank, *African Development Indicators 1997*.

Part 4

INTERNATIONAL RELATIONS

11

Inter-African Relations

Africa has been prolific in the production of states. Home to 10 percent of the world's population and occupying about 20 percent of its landmass, the continent contains roughly 30 percent of the world's states. More than fifty territorial units have been carved out of the deserts, highlands, forests, and savannas of the continent and its neighboring islands. From the Mediterranean to the Cape, Africa presents an intriguing mosaic of states whose relations are complex and diverse.

Africa would thus appear to be the expression par excellence of the state system in which modern international relations take place. Like the rest of the world's states, those of Africa compete with one another to defend their national interests. Tensions among governments and frictions across borders abound in this environment of multiple sovereignties. Alliances and counteralliances have been forged and dissolved here as elsewhere in the state system. Yet, if the inter-African system has reproduced many of the familiar features of international politics, it has distinctive and unique attributes as well.

One striking feature of inter-African politics has been the attempt to manage African diplomacy on a continental scale. A vision of African unity, historically rooted in the concept of "pan-Africanism" and institutionalized in the Organization of African Unity (OAU), has influenced the course of inter-African relations. Founded in 1963 after the first wave of accessions to independence, the OAU has experienced more failures than successes, but it remains a focal point for collective initiatives and for conflict management. The attempt to construct solidarity at the continental level is not a sentimental illusion but rather a reasoned response to Africa's dependent position in the global economic system. African leaders are conscious of the utility of cooperation at the same time that they have found cooperation difficult to achieve in practice.

African states—like others—are jealous of their national sovereignty. One of the founding precepts of the OAU, as of the UN, was noninterference in the domestic affairs of the member-states. Increasingly during the 1990s, however, civil wars and state collapse (as in Liberia, Sierra Leone, Rwanda, and Somalia) have weakened the norm of nonintervention. In fact, during the Cold War period as well, African governments often perceived their own national interests to be at stake in the outcome of struggles for power elsewhere on the continent. In this chapter, we examine international relations among the states of Africa, analyzing how local conflicts and regional disputes often escalated into continental-scale issues. Conversely, we shall see that continental cleavages have sometimes exacerbated local frictions.

The heterogeneity of African regimes has contributed to inter-African rivalry. Because they are susceptible to external influence, African governments have accorded high priority to foreign policy. Most have focused on their proximate geopolitical environment, but a few states such as Algeria, Libya, and Nigeria have pursued more ambitious diplomacies. During the 1960s, Egypt, Ghana, and Ethiopia played particularly active roles in African affairs. These activist states have generally taken the lead in promoting continental-scale conceptions of African politics. In defining their own interests in continental terms, they have contributed to the "continentalization" of African affairs.

For analytic purposes, we shall initially identify three geopolitical subsystems that have emerged as distinct arenas of inter-African relations. These three systems cut across the older subunits that divided Africa according to colonial administrations. They have been demarcated more by political interactions—both competitive and cooperative—since independence than by patterns of trade or cultural orientation. The first subsystem is trans-Saharan Africa, a large northerly bloc that is joined (rather than divided) by the Sahara Desert. Trans-Saharan Africa includes the Mediterranean states of predominantly Arab culture from Morocco to Egypt, the largely Muslim states that stretch from Mauritania to Sudan and on to the Horn, and the West African coastal states from Senegal to Nigeria. Under colonial rule, these states were divided among French North Africa (or the Maghreb), French West Africa, part of French Equatorial Africa (Chad), numerous British dependencies, a Portuguese colony, a Spanish colony, areas under Italian control, and the independent states of Liberia and Ethiopia. Libyan adventurism, the prolonged conflicts in Western Sahara and the Horn, the civil war in Liberia, and the breakup of Ethiopia have made the northern tier into a geopolitical unit of intricate calculations and maneuvers.

The second band, central Africa, extends from Cameroon and Gabon in the west to Kenya on the east coast. It also embraces a body of states that were parts of diverse colonial domains—French, Belgian, British, and

Spanish. This central belt is physically dominated by Congo, whose internal troubles have made it the site of numerous interventions, both inter- and extra-African. Turmoil in Uganda and Rwanda has also sparked intervention. This zone astride the equator is of considerable geopolitical significance to both the states to its north and to its south. African diplomacy has time and again focused on this central region, especially its Congolese heartland.

Third, we can designate southern Africa as the area south of Congo and Kenya to Cape Town, a region long overshadowed by the military might of the minority government of South Africa. International politics in this subsystem centered around the issues of liberation from Portuguese rule (until 1975), white settler rule in Rhodesia/Zimbabwe (until 1980), South African rule in Namibia (until 1990), and (until 1994) the question of majority rule in South Africa itself. Thus, the independent states of the southern tier dubbed themselves Front Line States in their confrontation with the minority regime that governed South Africa until 1994. Tanzania was an important actor in the Front Line group, which is why we place it in this third subdivision.

As active as Tanzania has been in the southern subsystem, it has also been much involved with its northern neighbors, Burundi, Kenya, and Uganda. Located at a juncture connecting the central and southern regions, Tanzania is geopolitically engaged with both. Its involvement in both zones exemplifies that these subsystems are the component parts of an ever-evolving continental system. Although each geopolitical zone has its distinctive strategic character, the stronger or more ambitious states in each zone seek to influence events wherever they see their interests at stake.

The distance from north to south across Africa exceeds 5,000 miles (8,000 km); from east to west at the widest point is almost as great (about 4,700 miles or 7,500 km). The continent is 20 percent larger than North and Central America combined. What is surprising, therefore, is not that unity has been difficult to achieve, but rather that the fifty-four states of this vast expanse have concerned themselves with one another as much as they have. Our intention is to examine these interactions as expressions of the policy goals of the numerous state actors on the continent, analyzing inter-African politics as foreign policy choices. For most African governments, foreign policy, like other policy, must be conducted under constraints of scarcity: a shortage of skilled personnel, limited resources to establish embassies or to gather information about external events. These factors impel African states to concentrate their diplomatic activity on continental affairs, contributing to the intensity of inter-African relations.

One may discern five rough periods in inter-African relations since 1960, the "year of independence"(pre-1960 events serving as a suggestive prelude). The first was a turbulent phase of multiple rivalries. Diplomatic coalitions, often designated by the cities in which they held conferences—the Casablanca bloc, the Brazzaville group, the Monrovia group—came together to form competing camps. This period came to an end with the formation of the OAU in May 1963. During the second period, which ran from mid-1963 until 1970, states nominally acknowledged the continental authority of the new OAU, but there persisted considerable jockeying to define the direction of the continental system. A series of crises over Congo, the Unilateral Declaration of Independence by Rhodesia's white minority, and the secession of Biafra from Nigeria continued to divide states; potential rivals to the OAU, such as the francophone Afro-Malagasy Common Organization (OCAM), took form but never gained real substance.

The third period, 1970 to 1975, saw the upsurge of a spirit of solidarity and militance behind the idea of a New International Economic Order; conferences of the Nonaligned Movement in Lusaka (1970), Algiers (1973), and Dakar (1975) punctuated this period, which was marked by strong identification with OPEC and a widespread break of diplomatic ties with Israel. This phase of relative solidarity gave way to a resurgence of divisive conflicts by late 1975 or early 1976. Angola's civil war and the Moroccan-Algerian tensions over Western Sahara ushered in the fourth period, which was further marked by violence in Chad, the Horn, Congo (during the 1971–1997 period, called Zaire), and much of southern Africa. This period lasted more than a decade, until the waning of the Cold War in the late 1980s. The fifth, or post–Cold War, period has been marked by a rash of internal breakdowns and the need for all African states to adjust to the new global distribution of power. The next three sections of this chapter delineate relations within the three major zones during the years of the Cold War.

■ TRANS-SAHARAN AFRICA

The Sahara is a vast, forbidding environment sparsely populated by nomadic peoples. It appears to constitute a formidable barrier between the peoples of its northern and southern "shores." Throughout history, however, traders have traversed the Sahara in caravans, and today its expanses are shared by almost a dozen sovereign states. The conflicts and issues that have arisen in parcels of this enormous territory, notably concerning Chad and Western Sahara, have had significant repercussions upon international relations throughout the continent. Arab North Africa and black West Africa have been drawn into a set of issues that delineate a single geopolitical theater.[1]

Yet, the civil war in Chad and the clash between Morocco and the Algerian-supported Polisario Front (Frente Popular para la Liberación de Saguia el-Hamra y Rio de Oro) over what was once called Spanish Sahara would not have engaged so many other states had it not been for the ambitious diplomacy of certain key states. Algeria and Libya have both undertaken unusually active foreign policies in Africa. Morocco has become deeply involved in continental politics, largely in response to Algeria's reaction to its irredentist policies. Other major trans-Saharan actors include Nigeria, Africa's most populous state, and Egypt, which aspired to a broad Third World leadership role under Gamal Abdel Nasser. During limited periods the leaders of Ghana, Côte d'Ivoire, Senegal, and Ethiopia have exercised wide influence on regional and continental affairs. We shall begin our study of international relations in trans-Saharan Africa by examining the foreign policy objectives of these activist states.

▪ Algeria

Algeria was deeply immersed in inter-African politics long before it became independent in 1962. Indeed, it was the long war for independence that plunged the Algerian nationalists of the 1950s into intense relations with the "fraternal" states of Arab and black Africa. The diplomatic demands of the struggle against France obliged the Algerians to solicit every possible source of support for their cause, and they saw anticolonial solidarity as a crucial potential force. Having turned first to the Arab world and Asia, Algeria next sought the opportunity to participate in the early Conferences of Independent African States. Algeria's policy goal was to win further Third World backing for its own cause of independence. Its bid for support in turn posed policy issues for other African states.

The first Conference of Independent African States was organized by Kwame Nkrumah in 1958, only a year after Ghana's independence. The Accra conference may be viewed as the point of departure for modern inter-African relations. It brought together three sub-Saharan states—Ghana, Liberia, and Ethiopia—four North African states—Morocco, Tunisia, Libya, and Egypt—and Arab/African Sudan. The guiding force behind the meeting was Nkrumah's commitment to pan-Africanism. He saw the conference as a platform for his notions of African unity rooted in what he called the "African personality." These ideas accordingly found their way into the conference's final declaration alongside resolutions condemning "racialism" in South Africa and colonialism in any form. In these, one sees early formulations of the anticolonial and antiapartheid themes that for some thirty years were major sources of consensus in collective African diplomacy.

For Algeria, the Accra conference and a follow-up meeting in Addis Ababa in 1960 were precious opportunities to censure France and to win international recognition. The National Liberation Front (FLN) thus devoted major attention to these early African forums. It expected the African states to rally to its cause once they entered the United Nations, where Algeria's informal representatives were seeking a resolution demanding a referendum on Algerian self-determination.

The 1960 General Assembly session was the first for more than a dozen former French colonies. Both Algeria and France severely pressured these new states to support their respective positions, France being steadfastly opposed to any UN-mandated referendum. The newly independent francophone states were caught in a squeeze, reluctant to oppose their French patron, President Charles de Gaulle, but embarrassed to vote against Algeria's position. After deliberating in Abidjan, the francophones decided to vote against the call for a referendum and merely in favor of negotiations between France and the FLN. The Algerians were bitterly disappointed by the failure of these African governments to grant them unqualified support. They became all the more determined to play a forceful role in inter-African affairs on behalf of their vision of what independence ought to mean.

Another major event in 1960 likewise contributed to Algeria's engagement in continental politics—namely, the "Congo crisis." Within days of the independence of the Belgian Congo, army mutiny, Belgian intervention, the secession of the mineral-rich Katanga Province, and generalized instability brought the new state to its knees. Prime Minister Patrice Lumumba, the leader of the major nationalist party, called on the United Nations to prop up his reeling country, and the Security Council duly dispatched a force known as ONUC (after the French acronym for United Nations Operation in the Congo). The UN force played a controversial role in a series of events that led to the overthrow of Lumumba in September 1960. Algeria reacted with outrage to what it called "a conspiracy of the western powers to implant neo-colonialism in Africa."[2]

The rupture of Congo into warring factions was a major factor in stirring a series of inter-African meetings that divided Africa into two camps. The first of these assembled most of the francophone states in Brazzaville in December 1960. The Brazzaville group, having given faint support to the FLN, now urged a Round Table Conference to negotiate a political settlement to the strife across the river in Congo. This position tacitly supported the Congolese factions that had overthrown Lumumba, a stance that further dismayed the Algerians. The meeting also decided to create a more permanent grouping under the title Union of African States and Madagascar (UAM), a group composed solely of former French colonies.

This arrangement provoked a counterreaction from seven other states that met in Casablanca, Morocco, in January 1961. The expression "Casablanca bloc" was coined to designate this association of Algeria, Morocco, Egypt, Ghana, Guinea, Mali, and (somewhat mysteriously in light of its conservative orientation under King Idris) Libya. In fact, the Casablanca conferees were far from being a "bloc," but their meeting highlighted an early cleavage between more conservative and more radical orientations toward world politics. The Casablanca states backed the FLN and supported Lumumba. The Algerian war and the Congo crisis both raised questions about African policy toward continuing European influence on the continent. The Casablanca and Brazzaville groupings as such proved short-lived, but the policy issues proved to be perennial matters in inter-African debate.

At independence in mid-1962, Algeria promptly adopted a policy of prominent support to liberation movements around the continent. Its first president, Ahmed Ben Bella, initially also took an interest in opposition movements in states such as Niger, Cameroon, and Chad, whose governments had been tepid in their support of the FLN. Soon, however, Ben Bella ventured that a continental organization might be the most promising means by which to reshape African affairs.

The Organization of African Unity was to be the prime instrument of this strategy. Algeria became one of the most active promoters of the founding conference of the OAU in 1963. As Immanuel Wallerstein points out, the creation of the OAU transformed the concept of African unity (or pan-Africanism) from the mobilizational theme of a social movement into an alliance of governing elites or, to put it slightly differently, into the foundation for a state system in Africa.[3] Algeria, however, did not immediately recognize this, seeking instead to use the new organization to effect radical change in 1964 when a struggle for power again flared in Congo.

Conflict erupted in Congo when Moise Tshombe was named prime minister. Tshombe had been the leader of the Katanga secession that had contributed to Lumumba's downfall. Tshombe, in turn, had been defeated in 1962 and banished from Congo. His sudden return at a moment when the centrist Congolese government was facing serious armed resistance from Lumumba's political heirs prompted Algeria to mount a diplomatic campaign in the OAU to isolate and undermine Tshombe. The first phase of this campaign succeeded as Tshombe was barred from the July 1964 OAU summit. In August, when Tshombe resorted to South African mercenaries and Western military aid to quell the insurgents, Algeria, acting in concert with Mali, called for a special session of the OAU's Council of Ministers to condemn this maneuver. Algeria sought OAU intervention to depose Tshombe and aid potential allies to come to power. Yet, there was no continent-wide consensus to oust Tshombe, and the Algerian initiative was thwarted.

Algeria's attempt to utilize the OAU in this manner nevertheless revealed a dynamic approach to inter-African politics. Declaring that "it is no longer Katanga that threatens Congolese unity, it is the whole Congo that has become the Katanga of Africa,"[4] Ben Bella defended a broad conception of Algeria's African interests. Algeria sought through its African policy to encourage the emergence of like-minded forces committed to a genuinely independent Africa. The conception of continental solidarity implicit in Algeria's support of liberation movements and the Congolese rebels continued to mark Algerian policy, making Algiers an important actor in a host of disputes that erupted between Afro-Marxist or socialist states and others around the continent.

This Algerian impact will be evident as we examine some of these cases in the rest of this chapter. Suffice it to say here that Algeria generally sought to promote the emergence of more leftist regimes. As an oil and natural gas producer, Algeria has the material resources to conduct an ambitious diplomacy. It quickly signed economic agreements with Benin and with Madagascar when radical officers came to power in these states that had formerly maintained very close ties with France. Similarly, Algeria was among the first to offer aid and technical assistance to Guinea-Bissau, Angola, and Mozambique when these states gained independence from Portugal. It has, moreover, maintained close lines of communication with the geographically distant Front Line States (as illustrated, for example, by the extensive southern Africa tour of President Chadli Benjedid in 1981). These material bonds and ideological commitments were the expression of an Algerian outlook that represented a major presence in inter-African relations.

■ Libya

Like Algeria, Libya has the resource base to exercise influence beyond its borders. Unlike Algeria, it did not have an extended period of diplomatic struggle for independence; rather it entered the state system in 1951 as a traditional monarchy. Only with the overthrow of the monarchy by Colonel Muammar Qaddafi in 1969 did Libya emerge as a prominent actor in inter-African affairs. But Qaddafi has made up for lost time.

The military officers who seized power as the Revolutionary Command Council (RCC) saw themselves primarily as Arab nationalists. Their model was Nasserist Egypt, and their early foreign policy was oriented toward the Arab world, particularly the cause of the Palestinians. Qaddafi's African policy began largely as an effort to counter Israeli influence in black Africa. Later as Egyptian-Libyan relations deteriorated after the death of Nasser, counterbalancing Egypt also became a policy goal. Moreover, as the Sanusi brotherhood (a Muslim religious order) of southern Libya had proselytized widely throughout the Sahara, Qaddafi readily perceived states to the south, such as Chad and Niger, as belonging to a Libyan sphere of influence.

Qaddafi first wooed Niger by generous grants of aid (some $100 million) during the early 1970s. He succeeded in establishing quite cordial relations with Niger's first president, Hamani Diori, culminating in a state visit in March 1974. Only a month later, the military overthrew the Diori government, souring relations between the two states. Libya then resorted to subversive tactics by encouraging Niger's northern Toubou and Tuareg populations to oppose the central government.

Coercion through intervention was central to Libya's Chad policy from the outset. Of all Libya's African initiatives, the engagement in Chad had the most impact upon the inter-African system as a whole. Shortly after coming to power, the RCC began to aid Frolinat (Front pour la Libération Nationale du Tchad), a northern-based oppositional movement that was waging a civil war against the southern-based government of François Tombalbaye in N'djaména. Like many of the francophone states, the Tombalbaye government had good relations with Israel. Libya's primary goal in aiding the rebels was to exert pressure upon Tombalbaye to sever relations with Israel. In 1972 a deal was struck: Libya agreed to suspend its aid to Frolinat, and Tombalbaye broke diplomatic relations with Tel Aviv. Libya sweetened the deal by extending financial aid to the Tombalbaye government—although Chad apparently paid a further price in the form of acquiescence in another matter, Libya's occupation of the uranium-rich Aouzou strip, a contested area along Chad's northern border.[5] Libya could count this early venture into trans-Saharan politics a policy success.

Qaddafi perceived another opportunity to pursue his anti-Israel campaign when Idi Amin seized power in Uganda, a state with which Israel had developed especially close relations. When Israel refused Amin's exorbitant requests for new military aid, the dictator expelled the Israeli diplomats and advisers. In return, Libya dispatched a small military detachment a few months later when rebel forces backed by Tanzania sought to overthrow Amin. Qaddafi's gesture sealed a close relationship that lasted until 1979, when once again Libya sent troops in an attempt, this time unsuccessful, to rescue Amin from a second clash with Tanzania.

Qaddafi's early anti-Zionism evolved into a broader anti-imperialism directed at governments that he perceived as pro-Western. This view incited the Libyan leader to support opposition forces in numerous states—Mali, Senegal, Gambia, Liberia—across the entire trans-Saharan region. Libya's attempts to exert influence extended well beyond the official national map that it issued showing Libya incorporating some 7,000 square miles (18,000 square km) of Niger, a like-sized chunk of Algeria, and the entire 27,000-square-mile (70,000-square-km) Aouzou strip.[6] Magnified by its aid to the Polisario Front in Western Sahara, Libya's far-reaching Saharan policy raised anxiety in such distant capitals as Abidjan, which had friendly ties with most of the target states.

To the east as well, Libya had tense relations with Egypt and Sudan. There were frontier incidents after the reopening of the Suez Canal in 1975 and a brief border flare-up in July 1977, presumably attributable to Egypt's rapprochement with the United States for the sake of the recovery of Sinai. As Nimeiri of Sudan followed Anwar Sadat's lead, Qaddafi took an interest in toppling him. This objective, in turn, encouraged Libya to enhance its ties with Ethiopia and Uganda, Sudan's eastern and southern neighbors.

Qaddafi's Uganda policy was one of the connecting links between the trans-Saharan and the central zones.

At the heart of this vast network of Libyan inter-African relations lay crippled Chad, a victim of its own internal divisions as well as Libya's ambitions. In 1975, the army deposed Tombalbaye, while the opposition Frolinat split into several factions led by such warlords as Hissene Habré and Goukouni Oueddei. The latter turned primarily toward Tripoli for support. Although the government of Nigeria and the OAU sought to mediate a settlement among some dozen factions, the situation remained unstable. In December 1980 at Goukouni's request, Libya sent 6,500 troops into Chad that momentarily allowed him to prevail against his rivals.

The success (though short-lived) of the Libyan operation in Chad set off alarm signals from one end of trans-Saharan Africa to the other. Libya's African revisionism and overall orientation (Soviet arms, support of the Iranian revolution, militance on Middle East issues) unsettled a host of moderate governments from Senegal to Togo and Nigeria along the western shoulder of the continent. Libya's 1980 intervention did not bring an end to Chad's civil strife, but it epitomized a decade of activism that had a tumultuous impact on the trans-Saharan subsystem.

■ Nigeria

Nigeria is Africa's most populous country. It also has substantial quantities of oil. Like Algeria and Libya, it is a member of OPEC and like them it has sought to influence and shape its regional and continental environment. Although not a Saharan state, Nigerian interests have led it to develop an important role in the northern tier as well as beyond it. Yet, Nigeria was slow to assume the role that its power resources appeared to hold out to it. Despite the grandiose statement of its first Foreign Minister, who declared in 1960 "Our country is the largest single unit in Africa . . . we are not going to abdicate the position in which God Almighty has placed us. . . . The whole black continent is looking up to this country to liberate it from thralldom,"[7] Nigeria pursued a rather modest foreign policy until the mid-1970s. Although it did send a military contingent to Congo as part of the UN operation, otherwise the country's early leaders were sufficiently absorbed by domestic politics to steer clear of continental initiatives. Prime Minister Tafawa Balewa limited his efforts through 1965 to debunking the unity proposals of Ghana's Nkrumah. Then military coups and the Biafra secession stunned the country, obliging Nigeria to limit its diplomacy to the requirements of the civil war.

Only after containing the secession did Nigeria begin to exert itself as an African power—in part to settle some scores from the civil war period. Although most African states had abstained from recognizing the Biafra rebels, a few states—Tanzania, Zambia, Côte d'Ivoire, Dahomey (now

Benin), and Gabon—gave diplomatic or military support to the secessionist cause. Nigeria came to view French influence in West Africa as a threat to its national integrity; accordingly, it devised a long-term strategy to reduce France's role in the region. With oil revenues gushing into the treasury, Nigeria could readily imagine itself as the economic core of a huge West African hinterland. Nigerian economic integrationists like Adebayo Adedeji, then serving as commissioner for economic development, pressed the idea of a West African common market as a lever to pry French neocolonial influence out of Nigeria's potential hinterland.

Nigeria thus embarked upon a sustained diplomatic offensive to create the Economic Community of West African States. According to Olatunde Ojo, "It took Nigerian leadership, extensive efforts in national coalition formation, and even more intensive and difficult regional negotiations and coalition formation to get ECOWAS inaugurated."[8] The decision to work for a regional common market was an important step in redefining West African geopolitical space, for it implicated Lagos in matters beyond economic cooperation.

In assuming a leadership posture in the region, Nigeria had to respond to security concerns as well. As Niger, Mali, Senegal, and Côte d'Ivoire all were uneasy about Libyan policies and feared the broad destabilizing effects from the collapse of Chad, Nigeria projected itself into the various efforts to mediate a Chadian settlement. It sponsored a series of meetings in Kano and Lagos designed to work out a compromise. Moreover, as part of the first Kano accord, Nigeria dispatched a peacekeeping force to Chad that became more involved than the Chadians wanted; later, it briefly imposed an oil embargo to bring pressure upon the local parties. These interventions were signs of a more activist diplomacy, of which ECOWAS leadership was but one component.

The broad policy of diplomatic activism had become more pronounced after the overthrow of General Yakubu Gowon in 1975, which brought to power Murtala Mohammed. When Mohammed was killed in an abortive coup, General Olusegun Obasanjo succeeded him. The Mohammed/Obasanjo government (1975–1979) generally expanded the conception of Nigeria's interests in Africa, most notably in southern Africa. An early expression of this "Afrocentric activism," as Timothy Shaw calls it,[9] was Lagos's decision to recognize the leftist MPLA government in Angola. We have already noted that the struggle for power in Angola was one of the major polarizing issues in inter-African affairs. In associating itself with the more radical states on the Angolan question, the post-Gowon leaders sought to give Nigerian foreign policy a more militant orientation.

Under Obasanjo, Nigeria assumed a place as virtually a sixth member of the southern group of Front Line States (originally comprising Tanzania, Zambia, Mozambique, Angola, and Botswana). The southern African policy was a logical extension of the drive to build a structure of influence in western Africa. At the core of both initiatives was a nationalist "Africa-for-the-Africans" impulse rooted in the notion that Nigeria was potentially Africa's greatest power. Afrocentrism implied the expulsion of non-African influence from the continent: that of France from its immediate regional environment; that of Portugal, Great Britain, and European settlers from the unliberated south. In a continent purged of the vestiges of the colonial era, Nigeria's human and petrochemical resources would have room for their full development. The continent as a whole would assume its rightful place in global affairs and Nigeria's voice would be extremely important in representing Africa. Regional leadership accorded Nigeria continental (and global) credibility, whereas continental activism reinforced its legitimacy at the regional level. The two subsystems, trans-Saharan and southern, were linked in a praxis that went beyond an abstract pan-Africanism.

As we deal later with southern Africa as a subsystem, this is not the place to examine in detail Nigeria's specific Front Line initiatives. Suffice it to note here that the Obasanjo government put its weight behind pressure on Western governments, notably those of the United States and Great Britain, to assist in the decolonization of Rhodesia and Namibia. It exerted power most directly by nationalizing British Petroleum assets on the eve of the 1979 Commonwealth conference in Lusaka that was to formulate a policy on Rhodesia. In these initiatives, Nigeria spurred the process that brought Robert Mugabe's Patriotic Front to power. Nigeria insisted on its right to be consulted as a Front Line State despite its geographical distance from the "front line." The cultivation of national prestige was an integral component of this southern strategy.

When the 1979 election brought the Shehu Shagari government to power, the new administration, although less militant in tone, sought to continue along essentially the same lines of regional and continental prestige. The new president's first trip abroad was to Monrovia to participate in the OAU's ad hoc committee seeking a settlement in Western Sahara. He announced his government's willingness to participate if necessary in a Saharan peacekeeping force. Nigeria also proposed to take the lead in establishing an ECOWAS defense force. These gestures implied an intent to act as the regional hegemon. In a similar vein, Shagari acted to exclude the new Liberian leader, Sergeant Samuel Doe, who had just seized power in a particularly bloody coup, from OAU and ECOWAS sessions in the spring of 1980, just as the Obasanjo government had cut off oil deliveries to Ghana the year before in order to coerce the new Rawlings government. In all these instances, successive Nigerian leaders sought to control events in the regional environment, which it increasingly perceived as its sphere of influence.

Nigeria thus emerged as the third major actor in the trans-Saharan system. It backed its claim to regional leadership with financial commitments, such as contributions to the completion of the trans-Saharan highway (this route, which will one day connect Algiers and Lagos, is itself a manifestation of the development of a trans-Saharan system) and the road from Lagos to Cotonou in Benin. These contributions to regional infrastructure are part of a drive to enhance trade so as to translate the ECOWAS concept into economic reality. The convening in Lagos of the OAU's economic summit in 1980 applied this regional aspiration to the continent as a whole. It was appropriate that Nigeria should host this occasion, for the ambitious Nigerian diplomacy of the late 1970s and early 1980s was premised on its emergent economic strength. The subsequent collapse of oil prices and the return of political instability derailed Lagos's drive for continental leadership, but Africa's most populous country remains a consequential actor, especially in the trans-Saharan subsystem, as its role in the Liberian civil war, discussed below, reconfirmed.

■ Other Trans-Saharan Actors

If Algeria, Libya, and Nigeria most actively triggered developments in trans-Sahara, other states have also figured prominently in the emergence of this regional system. In many cases dominant leaders like Nasser, Nkrumah, Houphouët-Boigny, Senghor, Bourguiba, and Hassan II projected their states into major roles.

During the mid-1950s, Cairo became one of the havens for African nationalists from both Arab and black Africa. Egypt had a geopolitical stake in the Nile Valley. The British, after all, had gone into East Africa in the nineteenth century in the name of protecting the headwaters of the Nile. But Nasser's motivation was actually more ideological than geopolitical. As a progressive nationalist, he wanted to see other nationalist movements come to power. Toward this end, Nasser created a Supreme Committee to Supervise African Affairs and established the headquarters of the Afro-Asian Peoples' Solidarity Organization (AAPSO) in Cairo. These organs served to channel aid to nationalist movements across the continent.

For Egypt as for Algeria, events in Congo assumed great significance. Like Ben Bella, Nasser interpreted the crisis as an attempt by the West to wrest control of the newly independent state from Prime Minister Lumumba. Egypt promptly sent technicians and medical personnel to aid the faltering Lumumba government and subsequently committed troops to the UN force, only to be dismayed by its failure to protect Lumumba. Upon the ouster of Lumumba, Egypt took the lead in channeling aid to the pro-Lumumba faction holding out in Stanleyville in the east. In 1964 when the second round of turbulence broke out, Nasser again tried unsuccessfully to shore up the rebels.

Twice thwarted, in about 1965 Nasser drew back from deep involvement in Africa. The means that Egypt could bring to bear in distant places were in the final analysis rather limited compared to those of the Western powers that were competing with Egypt in Congo. Nasser was sufficiently pragmatic to acknowledge limitations on his capabilities; moreover, Middle Eastern politics reclaimed almost all his diplomatic attention. As one of Africa's largest states and as a crossroads, Egypt is necessarily involved in continental affairs, but it has not exercised the active role that Nasser once envisaged.

Throughout the period during which Nasser was particularly oriented toward Africa, he had a major rival for the mantle of continental leadership. This was Kwame Nkrumah, whose prestige as the head of the first sub-Saharan state to negotiate independence was enormous. Steeped in the pan-Africanist tradition, Nkrumah promptly set about to organize inter-African relations. "I am necessarily as much concerned with the problems of all the different countries which make up our great continent as I am with those of Ghana," wrote Nkrumah in his *Africa Must Unite,* and he acted upon this presumption from the earliest days of independence.[10]

His first initiative was to convene the Conference of Independent African States (CIAS), for which he meticulously laid the diplomatic groundwork from August 1957 through April 1958. He sent personal envoys in advance to all seven of the invited states in order to "anticipate difficult issues on the agenda."[11] Nonetheless, the conference had a tough time coming to agreement on some of these "difficult issues," notably the conflicting policy priorities of Ghana and Egypt. Egypt wanted a militant stand on the Algerian question, whereas Ghana did not want North Africa to be the focus of the proceedings; Ghana proposed a liberation fund for black Africa, whereas Egypt was content with an existing AAPSO fund. Most important, Ghana wanted support for creation of a permanent secretariat to assure continued coordination on matters of common interest to the independent African states. Egypt, backed by Liberia, which was already suspicious of Ghanaian activism, downplayed the idea, proposing instead that consultations at the United Nations would suffice. To Nkrumah's disappointment, no secretariat was established, but the CIAS did serve to launch Ghana on its ambitious pan-African diplomacy.

Nkrumah recognized quickly that independent African states were neither his only nor his best policy framework. He thus poured funds into a second gathering known as the All African Peoples Conference (AAPC), a meeting of parties and nationalist movements, not of independent governments. Convening in December 1958, "the conference was ideally timed to meet the needs and mood of a rebellious continent." To this conference, W. Scott Thompson attributes

> much of the strength on which Nkrumah was able to draw in later years.
> He remained within the castle (seat of government in Accra) throughout
> most of the proceedings—consulting, reconciling, advising delegates; he

was never too conspicuous. He dominated the conference all the more by such tactics. Thereafter he had a network of admirers throughout the continent, some of whom, like Kenneth Kaunda, were to remain loyal even after being assailed by Ghanaian organizations.[12]

The AAPC did serve briefly as a vehicle of Nkrumah's vision of uniting Africa. Yet, as Thompson suggests, Nkrumah had admirers rather than followers, essentially because his vision of a federated Africa clashed with the very country-focused nationalism that he inspired. In the final analysis, Nkrumah was slower than Nasser to recognize that each new state's national identity must be respected. In his own drive to move beyond nationalism to continental union, Nkrumah ultimately alienated the goodwill that his support for independence had won him.

When Guinea broke abruptly from France in September 1958, Nkrumah moved swiftly to embrace Sekou Touré as an ally. In November, the two states announced an agreement to constitute "the nucleus of a Union of West African States."[13] Two years later, Mali briefly associated itself with the "union." In fact, however, independence was rapidly undermining Nkrumah's dream, as newly sovereign states, intent to consolidate national power, expressed their disdain for anyone who "makes the mistake of feeling that he is a Messiah who has got a mission to lead Africa."[14] The impact of the Congo crisis was a further major blow to the Ghanaian leader's crusade for unity.

Ghana began to follow developments in Congo closely as early as 1958, when Patrice Lumumba attended the AAPC conference in Accra. Nkrumah urged Lumumba to demand independence and offered technical assistance to smooth the transition. Even though the two countries were over 1,000 miles (1,600 km) distant from one another, Nkrumah harbored hopes of an eventual Ghana-Congo union. When the disorder began, Ghana was the first country to send military forces. These promptly became embroiled in a controversy over their action in disarming some Congolese units. The Ghanaian contingent walked a tightrope between the wishes of the Lumumba government and the need of UN Secretary General Dag Hammarskjöld to maintain broad international backing for ONUC. Lumumba lost trust in the Ghanaians, and Nkrumah, in turn, lost any real leverage over the course of events. Like Egypt, Ghana did not have adequate resources to control the course of events in Congo. Although Nkrumah maintained an extremely innovative and unconventional inter-African policy until his overthrow in 1966, the events of 1960 largely revealed that it was a diplomacy beyond his means.

Activism in pursuit of unity often took the form of subversion. Thompson has suggested that Nkrumah "equated obstinate heads of state, who would not surrender their 'petty national sovereignty' (as he called it), with Ashanti chiefs, and thus as candidates for destoolment."[15] Nkrumah's neighbors to the east and west were understandably wary of such designs. To the east, Togo warded off Ghanaian efforts to exploit the idea of Ewe reunification, but the frontier between the countries was a site of frequent incidents and perpetual tension for several years. On the western border, Nkrumah toyed with a group of Sanwi separatists at odds with the government of Côte d'Ivoire. Here he faced a covert counteroffensive of destabilization from a major rival, Felix Houphouët-Boigny, who had no intention of being "destooled."[16]

Côte d'Ivoire assumed leadership of a more conservative group of states that feared the hegemony of Nkrumah's Ghana and later of Nigeria. Houphouët made a famous wager with Nkrumah in 1957, betting that Côte d'Ivoire, by maintaining ties with France, would be economically better off in ten years than its newly independent neighbor. Within the framework of his close relationship with Paris, he was extremely careful to create a zone of security around his country as a safeguard to winning his bet. Thus, Côte d'Ivoire took the lead in creating a politico-economic organization called the Conseil de l'Entente, which brought three other French colonies into its orbit: Upper Volta (now Burkina Faso), Niger, and Dahomey (now Benin). Although the Conseil was originally conceived to counter a Senegalese project of regional federation, it served through the 1960s essentially as a barrier to contain Ghana as well as to assure the Ivorian cocoa and coffee plantations a supply of cheap labor from Upper Volta.

Houphouët's foreign policy has been preeminently oriented toward maintaining ties among the francophone states. In 1960 he took the lead in creating the UAM. When this was disbanded after the founding of the OAU, he laid the groundwork for a new regrouping, the Afro-Malagasy Common Organization. Founded in 1965 in the aftermath of the second Congo crisis, OCAM resketched the lines of division between moderates and radicals as well as reaffirmed the notion of a francophone alliance (all the original members were francophone states). The formal organization sputtered along for several years without ever acquiring much diplomatic force, but its presence reflected an orientation that has weighed heavily in inter-African relations under the impulse of states like the Côte d'Ivoire. As OCAM declined, Houphouët backed yet another francophone regrouping, the Economic Community of West Africa (see Chapter 10).

Senegal's influence in inter-African relations has stemmed from the eminence of its leaders: Leopold Sedar Senghor, an internationally acclaimed poet, who governed from 1960 to 1980, and Abdou Diouf, a brilliant manager, who succeeded him. Because Dakar had served as the capital of the entire colonial federation of French West Africa (AOF), Senghor sought to retain a West African federal structure after independence. The best that he could achieve was a federal union with Mali, which disintegrated almost immediately. But Senghor persisted, eventually succeeding in regrouping four of the former AOF territories in the Organization of

Senegal River States (later refashioned as the Senegal River Development Organization, or OMVS). In addition to Mali, Mauritania and Guinea are members of the OMVS. Senegal's historical affiliation with Mauritania in the AOF has stamped Senegalese diplomacy with a northward orientation that took on renewed saliency when Mauritania became embroiled in the Western Sahara dispute.

Senegal has also been closely involved in the affairs of tiny Gambia, the fingerlike entity poking into Senegal's midsection. Senghor mildly encouraged the integration of British Gambia into Senegal, but did not oppose eventual Gambian independence in 1965, opting instead for a policy of close Senegambian cooperation. In 1981 Senegal dispatched troops to Gambia to thwart an attempted coup that the Gambian authorities attributed to Libyan subversion. Senghor's efforts to construct these regional cooperative arrangements coexisted with his most ambitious commitment to *la francophonie* (the French-speaking world), which he understood as an association for technical and economic cooperation among all French-speaking peoples (in Europe, Asia, and the Americas as well as in Africa). Although a francophone agency was created in 1970, it never achieved Senghor's far-reaching ideal, but it did serve to establish Senegal as an actor of note in global and inter-African affairs.

One of Senghor's closest associates and, indeed, actually the initiator in the francophone project was Tunisia's Habib Bourguiba. Tunisia was the first of the Maghreb states to pursue an active policy in sub-Saharan Africa. Although subsequently overshadowed by the initiatives of Libya, Algeria, and Morocco, Tunisia's early attraction southward is another component of the trans-Saharan system. Bourguiba attended the ceremonies marking the independence of Ghana in 1957 and declared that "the trip to Ghana was for me truly a discovery, that of the great African continent from which we were long cut off and with which we hope to reestablish our historical ties of exchange. . . . It is important that Tunisians . . . pay attention to the huge act of gestation of the African continent. We can not let ourselves be overwhelmed by the pace of events."[17]

Bourguiba understood that Tunisia was caught up in the processes of political change that were beginning to sweep across the continent. He saw his own country as a relay station between Mediterranean (Western) civilization and the emergent regimes to the south. As the Tunisian scholar Mohsen Toumi astutely observes: "Fundamentally [Bourguiba's] attitude toward black Africa derives from a larger set of assumptions: solidarity with the western world."[18] Tunisia pursued a policy of support to moderate African governments as a way of protecting its own pro-Western orientation. Tunisia and Senegal ("heirs of the same legacies,"[19] as Bourguiba put it during his state visit to Senegal in 1965) have closely coordinated their policies on African questions. The Tunis-Dakar axis is another manifestation of durable trans-Saharan ties.

At the other end of the Maghreb, Morocco's African policy has been driven by its goal of recovering precolonial lands. In laying claim to Mauritania, Morocco bucked a widely prevailing consensus—namely, to recognize colonial borders as the framework for transferring sovereignty to Africans. So long as Morocco seriously pursued the goal of reclaiming Mauritania, it found itself virtually isolated. King Hassan refused to attend the founding conference of the OAU because Mauritania's president was present; then Morocco hesitated four months before signing the charter.

A brief border war with Algeria in October 1963 obliged Morocco to cultivate some alliances. Morocco's general pro-Western orientation was akin to that of Tunisia, Senegal, and Côte d'Ivoire, all three of which were firmly committed to Mauritania's right to exist. Thus, King Hassan moved away from his Mauritanian claim in order to solidify his standing with Bourguiba, Senghor, and Houphouët. Even so, as Mohammed Bouzidi observes, Morocco maintained only a limited number of embassies in black Africa and could count upon only "a limited number of African friends" when once again it became embroiled in a serious dispute.[20] A few years after officially recognizing Mauritania in 1970, Morocco set about to gain control over Western Sahara, an ambition that hurled it to the very center of inter-African politics.

The Western Sahara dispute is one of several divisive issues (the Congo crisis, civil wars in Angola and Nigeria, the hostilities in Chad and the Horn) that have had continent-wide repercussions. It has contributed to the forging of a trans-Saharan subsystem because states have been obliged to become involved with one another over the matter. However ironic it may seem, the struggle over this arid and inhospitable stretch of land, one of the last remnants of the colonial order, has greatly intensified the network of interconnections across the northern third of the continent.

■ Trans-Saharan Conflicts and Connections

The Western Saharan issue has involved virtually every African state via its impact upon the OAU. At the regional level, the interconnections are especially intricate because each of the principal adversaries has its own set of networks. Fundamentally, the conflict has involved Morocco and the Saharawi rebels, but Mauritania, Algeria, and Libya have all been significantly involved as well. Each direct participant called upon its allies for diplomatic support, embroiling most trans-Saharan states in the conflict in one manner or another.

The dispute had its origins in the same historical interpretation that had earlier prompted Morocco to claim Mauritania. Some of the nomadic clans of Western Sahara had paid fealty to Moroccan sultans in the eighteenth and nineteenth centuries. Rabat thus concluded that the territory colonized by Spain since 1884 was historically Moroccan. King Hassan, shaky on his throne after two attempted coups in 1971 and 1972, staked his regime upon recovering these Saharan "provinces." Yet, by the 1970s, indigenous leaders had called for independence and established a liberation movement called the Polisario Front. Algeria, which had long championed the cause of liberation movements throughout Africa, gave support to Polisario. On geopolitical grounds, Algeria had no desire to see extension of Moroccan sovereignty another 500 miles (800 km) down the Atlantic coast. Algiers invoked the principle of self-determination, confident that the Saharawi people would elect independence rather than integration into Morocco—if given the chance. Libya's initial goal in supporting the Polisario guerrillas was essentially to thwart King Hassan, whose Western orientation Libya deplored: Having overthrown one monarch, Qaddafi had no inhibitions about dethroning another. (Although supporting its war effort, Qaddafi, the confirmed Arab unionist, advised Polisario to form a confederation with Mauritania.)

These conflicting notions came into sharp clash in 1975, when King Hassan organized the "Green March," a massive mobilization of some 350,000 unarmed Moroccan citizens who crossed the border brandishing flags and the Koran. The Spanish were dumbfounded by this maneuver and capitulated in the Madrid Tripartite Agreement, by which they turned over their colonial administration to Morocco and Mauritania (the latter getting the impoverished southern third of the Spanish holdings). Polisario for its part organized a large-scale exodus from the territory into Algeria, where the Saharawis set up camps around Tindouf. Since then the Polisario guerrillas have been resisting the Moroccan-Mauritanian takeover both militarily and diplomatically.

On the military front, Polisario succeeded in knocking Mauritania from the battlefield (the military overthrew President Mokhtar Ould Daddah in July 1978 and signed a peace treaty in 1979). Morocco, a more determined adversary, deployed some 140,000 soldiers and constructed hundreds of miles of fortifications in order to hold on to the territory. On the diplomatic front, Algeria and Polisario steadily gained ground behind the principle of self-determination, creating strains within the OAU after 1976. Both sides have exerted strong pressure on the other African states to support their cause, making the matter a continental as well as regional issue.

The dispute has been before the OAU since 1976. After proposals to convene a special summit meeting devoted to the problem failed to materialize, the OAU turned the problem over to a Committee of Wisemen in 1978. The "sages" were the heads of state of Mali, Guinea, Côte d'Ivoire, Nigeria, Tanzania, and Sudan. A year later, at the Monrovia summit, this committee proposed a cease-fire and a referendum to determine the will of the Saharawis. Upon approval of this recommendation, the Moroccan delegation walked out of the conference in protest and set about to dissuade the OAU from persisting in this path.

Morocco's tactic was to call in some IOUs from a number of friends, such as Congo (for military assistance during the Shaba uprisings), Guinea (for aiding the Guinean-French rapprochement), and Egypt (tacit support of the Camp David Accords). Hassan also appealed to Senghor of Senegal, who was disposed to worry about an Algerian bid for hegemony in the Sahel, and to Tunisia, with its interest in balancing Algeria. Consistently conservative states like Côte d'Ivoire and Gabon could also be relied on. In this manner, Morocco was able to line up some dozen states willing to threaten a walkout from the OAU if Moroccan interests were not respected. Although more than half of the OAU membership had recognized what Polisario called the Saharan Arab Democratic Republic (SADR) by 1980, Morocco had enough supporters to head off proposals that year to admit the SADR to the OAU.

These developments from 1976 to 1980 well illustrate how a local conflict in northwestern Africa gradually engaged a large number of African governments. This "continentalization" of the issue reflected again the perennial split between radicals and moderates. By and large, francophone and Arab moderates supported Morocco, whereas the radicals rallied to Polisario's cause alongside Algeria. That Morocco was dependent upon French and U.S. weaponry (and Saudi financing) to wage the war increased the radicals' devotion to the cause of self-determination. The issue took on continental significance, not only because the OAU was obliged to deal with it, but also because of global alignments that it implied. Continental and global implications in turn enhanced the saliency of the issue for the regional governments.

The Committee of Wisemen dutifully continued its efforts but could not persuade Morocco to sit down at the bargaining table with Polisario. As more and more states became irked at Moroccan obstructionism, the support for admitting the SADR grew. Moreover, riots over food prices and unemployment in the war-torn economy rocked Casablanca in June 1981. Hassan was obliged to make a conciliatory gesture at the 1981 Nairobi summit. In a rare move, the king personally led his delegation to Nairobi to announce his readiness to permit a "controlled referendum" in ˙the former Spanish colony. Algeria welcomed the Moroccan offer as a "first step in the search for peace"[21] and proposed that Morocco withdraw its troops and administration as a second step. The heads of state voted down the latter proposal, restricting themselves to the creation of a new implementation committee to work out the arrangements for a cease-fire and referendum. The new committee had the same membership as the Committee of Wisemen plus Kenya's President arap Moi, incoming chairman of the OAU.

Kenya then set to work organizing two sessions of the new committee in August 1981 and February 1982. No progress was made at these sessions, the main stumbling point being Morocco's refusal to negotiate directly with the Polisario Front. Frustrated by the deadlock, Algeria brought pressure upon OAU Secretary General Edem Kodjo to try something new. Kodjo obligingly issued credentials to the SADR delegation to attend the annual administrative meeting of the organization. Via this diplomatic coup, Polisario hoped to strengthen its hand by occupying a seat at the OAU. Morocco, however, stormed out of the meeting, sweeping eighteen other members along with it,[20] and the OAU faced a major crisis because it no longer had the two-thirds quorum necessary to conduct business.

The paralysis of the OAU over the Western Saharan question reproduced the major cleavage that marked inter-African relations from 1960 to 1990. States that generally relied on the West for support stuck by Morocco, whereas those that looked toward the socialist world backed the Polisario Front. Morocco's coalition had its roots in the old Brazzaville group, augmented by further Cold War–related alliances. Most of these states had no immediate stake in the outcome in Western Sahara; even less were they persuaded of Morocco's historical sovereignty over the land. Their motivation in joining Morocco was their consciousness of a network of like-minded governments with a mutual interest in supporting one another. The solidarity of the conservative states was a form of collective security. Their walkout demonstrated that almost twenty years of OAU activity had not transcended the radical-moderate cleavage; by the same token, it showed that the OAU could function only by accommodating the viewpoint of the moderate camp.

The states that had recognized the SADR were themselves a relatively heterogeneous group.[23] Although its core consisted of socialist or Afro-Marxist regimes, it included numerous other states that simply supported a process of self-determination. Like the Congo crisis of the early 1960s, a local matter assumed continental proportions that generally reflected the larger structure of international politics.

The Western Saharan case is not the only trans-Saharan conflict to affect the larger continental system. The civil war in Chad has likewise hobbled the OAU. We have already seen that Libya sent troops into Chad in 1980. Under French pressure, Libya withdrew them in 1981. For Goukouni Oueddei, the Libyan withdrawal was to be compensated by a contingent of OAU troops to protect his government from his rival, Hissene Habré, who had reconstituted his own forces with Western help during his exile in the Sudan. OAU "peacekeepers" (from Nigeria, Senegal, and Congo) were duly deployed, but their mandate was unclear. Goukouni sought an active military role that was, in fact, beyond the means of the OAU force. For its part, the OAU urged Goukouni to negotiate a new political settlement with Habré. Goukouni refused, and Habré's men stormed back into power in June 1982. Goukouni then fled the capital to regroup again in the north. The inability of the OAU to impose or police a settlement on the ground in Chad was apparent. Moreover, the Chadian strife compounded the disarray in an organization already rocked by the Western Sahara crisis. An attempt to convene the OAU in Tripoli in November failed when host government Libya refused admission to the Habré government. This exclusion prompted another boycott that reinforced the cleavage in inter-African affairs.

In a more direct bid to remove Habré, Libya again sent troops into Chad in mid-1983. In this second round, France intervened directly by positioning 3,000 French troops across the country at the fifteenth (and later the sixteenth) parallel. The French involvement, urged by the United States but also by Senegal and Côte d'Ivoire, was a move to reassure the francophone moderates by foiling Libya's objectives in Chad. The French intervention did stabilize the military situation but at the cost of a virtual de facto partition of the country. Although OAU mediators sought periodically to bring the competing factions to the bargaining table, the stalemate held firm until December 1986, when fighting erupted again. By March 1987, Habré's army drove the Libyans out of Chad except for the disputed Aouzou strip.

The Habré regime was overturned in 1990 by General Idris Déby, who had received limited support from both Libya and Sudan after breaking with Habré in 1989. Libya subsequently agreed to submit the dispute over the Aouzou strip to the International Court of Justice, which found in Chad's favor in 1994. Qaddafi agreed to withdraw his forces from the strip under UN auspices. Subjected to international sanctions since 1992 for its alleged involvement in two instances of terrorism against civilian aircraft, Libya was obliged to draw back from its long-standing involvement in Chad.

Like Western Sahara, Chad would hardly appear to be worth all the commotion that it has caused. The country is poor and sparsely populated, but it borders on six other countries and constitutes a door into black Africa for Libya. Geopolitics, like nature, abhors a vacuum; thus, states as distant from Chad as Senegal and Congo were willing to join Nigeria (which has a short northeastern border with Chad) in seeking to reconcile the competing factions in order to contain Libyan expansion. The vacuum in Chad has, therefore, had the effect of stimulating a stronger regional consciousness throughout trans-Sahara.

Likewise, the dispatch of troops from Congo to the short-lived OAU force illustrates that central African states have also felt the repercussions of Chad's civil war. Cameroon has seen refugees crossing its border, and Kenya became involved during its tenure in the OAU chairmanship. Thus, the Chadian imbroglio also has effected linkages between trans-Saharan and central Africa.

■ Ethiopia and the Politics of the Horn

Much the same is true about the final foyer of conflict in the northern zone. The Horn of Africa, the great bulge of the continent projecting into the Indian Ocean, contains the hostile pair of Ethiopia and Somalia, as well as Africa's largest territory, Sudan, and one of its tiniest, the Republic of Djibouti. Ethiopia, the most densely populated of those four countries, is an indigenous imperial state that for decades incorporated the province of Eritrea, which achieved independence in 1993 after a long struggle, and that continues to incorporate the Ogaden, also claimed by Somalia. These two fierce disputes in this strategic area on the Red Sea and the Indian Ocean have made the Horn the site of explosive tensions and frequent external intervention.

Sudan is the hinterland of the Horn, stretching from the Red Sea to the Sahara across the upper Nile. Bordering Egypt, Libya, Chad, Congo, and Ethiopia, among others, it has been buffeted by a host of conflicts surrounding it, and drought and civil strife have periodically driven large numbers of refugees into the country. These external strains have exacerbated its own severe domestic problems marked by the resumption of civil war between the dominant Muslim regime in the north and the largely Christian population in the south. Since 1989, when the National Islamic Front came to power, the government has pursued a policy of active support to Islamist movements, which has placed it in conflict with numerous other states.

As an imperial state, Ethiopia's central policy concern has been to preserve the integrity of its borders. As Christopher Clapham puts it, "For as far back as records reach—at least 500 years—control of the local periphery has been, in its own view, the historic mission or manifest destiny of the Ethiopian state."[24] In recent times, under Emperor Haile Selassie, Ethiopia expanded to absorb the territory of Eritrea, which had fallen under Italian control in 1890. As Eritrea had twice been the pathway for Italian campaigns against Ethiopia, control of this outlet to the Red Sea was of great value to Addis Ababa. Proceeding by stages, Ethiopia succeeded in attaching Eritrea, first under a federal arrangement from 1952 to 1962 and then by outright annexation. The Eritreans, however, rejected incorporation into the Ethiopian state and began a struggle for independence in 1961 under the banner of the Eritrean Liberation Front (ELF). Thirty years later, Eritrean rebels would play a leading role in the overthrow of the central government.

Likewise, Ethiopia has historically sought control of the Ogaden, roughly speaking the eastern spearhead of territory that thrusts into Somalia. Ethiopian Emperor Menelik conquered this territory in the last decade of the nineteenth century; it was then taken by Italy in the 1930s and subsequently occupied by Great Britain during World War II (when Italy's colonies on the Horn fell). In 1948 Britain withdrew, allowing Ethiopia to reassert its rule over the Somali population that lived there. The Somalis along the coast bitterly resented the British move, and the seeds of future conflict were sown.

Haile Selassie thus had two dissident groups to worry about. He conceived a diplomatic response to this situation that was tactically brilliant. His greatest asset, he realized, was symbolic, for he was heir to a dynasty that had been the only African elite successfully to resist the imposition of colonialism. Having ascended to the throne in 1930 (after a fourteen-year regency), Selassie had made a famous speech at the League of Nations in 1936 defending Ethiopia's right to independence. His kingdom was the symbol of resistance to colonialism, and he was indisputably the elder statesman of African leaders. Selassie astutely exploited this image as the rest of Africa acceded to independence.

When the UN Economic Commission for Africa was formed in 1958, Ethiopia welcomed its headquarters to Addis Ababa. In 1960 Selassie was host to the second Conference of Independent African States, laying the groundwork for his greatest diplomatic coup: the founding of the OAU at Addis Ababa in 1963. The emperor was well placed to promote the ideal of African unity, for he had the advantage of neutrality between formerly British and formerly French Africa and between Arab and black Africa, and he had not been prominently involved in the split between moderates and radicals. Although other leaders, like Kwame Nkrumah, had taken the lead in promoting African unity, Selassie seized the opportunity to host the founding conference and to offer the Ethiopian capital as its site. Of particular utility to Ethiopia was the key charter provision calling for respect of the existing African boundaries.[25] Virtually every African government had some fear of ethnic or regional dissidence. The charter adopted by the thirty-two independent states in May 1963 reinforced the Ethiopian position and enhanced the prestige of Haile Selassie.

Once the OAU headquarters were located in Addis Ababa, the Ethiopian ruler was well placed to preside benevolently over continental matters. When fighting flared along the Algerian-Moroccan border in October 1963, for example, Selassie was called upon to serve as a mediator. In turn, Ethiopia called upon the OAU to uphold the status quo during clashes in the Ogaden border region in 1964 and 1965. Haile Selassie's role of senior statesman and the frequent sessions of OAU council meetings in Addis Ababa provided the Ethiopians a kind of diplomatic moral stature that neutralized Somali and Eritrean claims against the empire. Coupled with a long-standing reliance upon U.S. military supplies and economic assistance, Ethiopia had the means to assure its territorial integrity up to the end of Haile Selassie's reign. Internal tensions arising out of domestic misrule were more important in the overthrow of the emperor in 1974 than were issues of foreign policy.

The period following the fall of Haile Selassie was marked by a fascinating mix of inter-African policy continuity combined with a dramatic reversal of extra-African alliances. The military committee (the *derg*) that took power was as determined as the emperor to hold on to Eritrea and the Ogaden. But it was also committed to a policy of land reform that disrupted the countryside; the crumbling of the old order unleashed new expressions of ethnic and national separatism. The revolutionary officers cracked down on various dissident groups, causing the United States to protest human rights violations and to grow wary of the overall course of the revolution. In these circumstances, the United States was not eager to continue to arm the Ethiopians, who began to look elsewhere.

Conversely, so did the Somalis. From 1969, when Mohammed Siad Barre had seized power in Somalia, until the mid-1970s, Somalia had relied upon the Soviet Union for support in its domestic development and foreign policy. By 1974, when the two governments signed a twenty-year treaty of friendship and cooperation, Somalia appeared to have become the Soviets' favored client in black Africa. Somali policy was in good measure the mirror image of Ethiopia's; when conditions changed, it reversed itself. So long as Ethiopia was supported by the United States, strains in the Soviet-Somali relationship could be glossed over. But, in fact, the Soviets had never been willing to unleash the irredentist Somalis; thus, as Robert Gorman observed, once "it became obvious that Ethiopia, at least in name, had embraced socialist dogma, it became increasingly difficult for both Somalia and the USSR to hide their differences."[26] Somalia denounced its treaty with the Soviets and veered westward in 1977, ever in search of its primary objective, the recovery of the Ogaden.

The reversal of alliances was effected, moreover, in the heat of battle, as Somali forces entered the Ogaden in July 1977. The Somali move was opportunistic, relying upon a perception that Ethiopia was crumbling under the weight of a new Eritrean offensive in the north and domestic turmoil elsewhere. Somalia took note as well of the fact that Sudan, which had previously practiced a policy of neutrality toward the Eritrean conflict, was now aiding the nationalists and other opponents of the *derg*. (Sudan's switch was part of the overall pattern of shifting alliances: As Ethiopia moved left, Addis Ababa became friendlier with Qaddafi—Nimeiri's nemesis. Suspecting Libyan and Ethiopian complicity in a foiled coup attempt in 1976, Nimeiri countered on the Eritrean front.) Somalia did not actually declare war or even admit the presence of its own troops in the Ogaden; its official version was that the hostilities were between the Western Somali Liberation Front (WSLF), a movement of the indigenous Somali population of the Ogaden, and the Ethiopian military. By October 1977, the combined Somali/WSLF offensive controlled over 90 percent of the Ogaden. Somalia's short-term calculation of Ethiopian disarray was accurate, but Siad Barre miscalculated Ethiopian determination and the Soviets' willingness to rebuild Ethiopia's military strength. For their part, the Soviets decided that Ethiopia was worth more than Somalia; and although

the West was content to take back Somalia, it was not ready to endorse Somali irredentism (for much the same reasons that had motivated Soviet
caution on this matter).

Thus, Soviet aid, bolstered by Cuban troops, eventually restored the
territorial status quo ante in the Horn. The student of inter-African relations cannot help but be struck by the paradox of the Horn. On the one
hand, we see the unswerving determination of the local actors to pursue
their goals by whatever means are available. On the other hand, we see
how dependent the local actors are upon foreign support. In order to pursue its primary goal of territorial integrity, Ethiopia devised a new military
supply relationship when the old one faltered. Somalia, in turn, was
obliged to swap patrons. The Soviet Union, we might add, did make a
valiant attempt to reconcile the adversaries in the name of common socialist values, but neither side would compromise, obliging the Soviets to
choose their partner. The African states had the freedom to realign rather
than the resources to deal autonomously with their problem.

Soviet support likewise provided the central government of Mengistu
Haile Mariam with the means to prosecute the war against the Eritrean
rebels. By the early 1990s, however, the Soviet commitment waned, and
other regional/ethnic/nationality groups (Tigre, Oromo) also entered into
dissidence, producing the collapse of the Mengistu government in May
1991. Once Ethiopia lost the capacity to manipulate Cold War patronage,
it also lost Eritrea.

Sudan has not been directly involved in the Ogaden conflict, but it
was intermittently involved in the Eritrean secession, or the struggle for
the Red Sea. Upon the establishment of the Ethiopian-Eritrean federation
in 1952, Sudan became a natural haven for nationalist exiles from neighboring Eritrea. Throughout the 1960s, as fighting intensified in the province, Sudanese support for the Eritreans waxed and waned; Muslim sym-
pathizers pressed the government to aid their Eritrean counterparts, but
this exposed the Sudanese to counterintervention by Ethiopia in the southern Sudan, where Khartoum likewise faced a secessionist movement. In
1972 both parties agreed to desist from interference in one another's se-
cessions. This agreement held until 1976, when the emergent Libyan-
Ethiopian alignment prompted Nimeiri to reopen the Sudanese-Eritrean
connection. Once again Libyan policy prompted far-flung reactions.

Common antagonism with Ethiopia provided grounds for Sudan and
Somalia to cultivate friendly relations. During the late 1970s and 1980s,
after their respective flirtations with the East, both states, accompanied
also by Egypt, moved into the camp of the African moderates. It was during this period that Sudan helped Hissene Habré. From a different perspective, one can see that Nimeiri had to choose between Egypt and Libya
and opted for Sudan's traditional partner on the Nile, thereby creating tensions along the Libyan-Ethiopian axis. After the coup against Nimeiri in

1985 (and faced with a renewal of dissidence in the southern sector of the country), the new leadership in Sudan sought to improve relations with Libya and Ethiopia in order to reduce their propensity to intervene in Sudanese affairs. Thus, the flow and counterflow of pressure entered a new stage that included Sudanese aid to Habré's opponents.

The Horn, therefore, is not at all a self-contained system. Rather, the unresolved conflicts there have repercussions throughout the continent and continually invite extracontinental intervention. Such intervention is not reserved to the great powers, but has included several Middle Eastern states as well (most notably Saudi Arabia, Syria, and Iraq). In the mid-1980s, these geopolitical instabilities were further complicated by a devastating drought that crippled already feeble economies. The dual disasters of starvation and refugee flows did nothing to resolve the underlying conflicts that have made the Horn a perennial trouble spot.

The vast trans-Saharan region with its activist states and its unresolved conflicts has been, therefore, a major theater of inter-African relations.[27] Its issues and actors have generated camps and countercamps within and beyond the zone. From the Horn to Western Sahara, from Chad to Liberia, interstate and intrastate competition have knit a fabric of interactions and multiple linkages that have embraced all states in the region. And, in numerous ways, the activism of the trans-Saharan states has also impinged upon central Africa.

■ CENTRAL AFRICA

The band that we call central Africa is geographically dominated by Congo. Around Congo is deployed a semicircle of relatively lightly populated states including Congo-Brazzaville, Gabon, Cameroon, Central African Republic, Uganda, Rwanda, and Burundi. With the exception of Uganda, this area was subject to French and Belgian colonial rule, and these states have been associated in the various francophone groupings that we have already discussed—*la francophonie* is thus one form of linkage between central and trans-Saharan Africa. The other major actor in this central band is Kenya, the most prosperous of the East African economies. Under the leadership of Jomo Kenyatta until 1978, Kenya pursued a basically pro-Western foreign policy as an inducement to foreign investment. Kenya's economic policies caused some tensions with Tanzania and Uganda, but otherwise it maintained a rather low profile in inter-African affairs. Like Ethiopia, Kenya also had to worry about Somali nationalism, for Somalia laid claim to Kenya's North Eastern Province, which like Ogaden contained a large number of ethnic Somalis. Kenyatta addressed this matter right after independence by a classic move, a treaty with Ethiopia against Somali irredentism. The treaty handily survived the change of government in Ethiopia in the mid-1970s. Although Kenya largely ignored the shifting alignments of its neighbors in the Horn, Western strategic concerns during the 1980s drew Kenyatta's successor, Daniel arap Moi, more tightly into the Western camp.

With the partial exception of Congo, none of the states of the central zone has assumed a major role in inter-African relations. Although this equatorial band might appear to be a buffer zone between the wars of trans-Sahara and the liberation politics of southern Africa, it is perhaps even more a buffeted zone that registers the political shock waves from the adjacent subsystems. We know already that its Congolese heartland has been the object of multiple rivalries. But these states have not failed to use what means they have to influence their external environments.

■ Congo's Protracted Malaise

The Congo crises of the early 1960s had their prolongations in the Shaba crises of the latter 1970s; external debt, internal corruption, and a host of foreign dependencies have extended Congo's malaise through the 1990s. Even more than Chad, Congo has had a turbulent postindependence history that has polarized the rest of Africa. Despite its unsettled situation, it plunged into the struggle for power among Angola's competing liberation movements in 1975, compounding its domestic difficulties. In the midst of this turmoil, Mobutu Sese Seko managed to navigate a foreign policy course that helped to maintain him in power by utilizing "the very bonds of economic dependency . . . with virtuosity."[28]

Mobutu took power in 1965 at the end of the first round of crises that we have already discussed as inter-African issues. The complex tripartite struggle for power between Lumumba, Joseph Kasavubu, and the Katanga secessionists opened the country to multiple interventions and ceaseless controversy. Throughout this five-year period, the competing Congolese factions sought external support from fellow Africans and from extra-African patrons. The West and the African moderates ultimately succeeded in keeping pro-Western elements in power. Mobutu inherited this situation and never significantly departed from this general orientation. He shored up his ties to the West, nevertheless playing Belgium, France, and the United States off against one another to gain a modicum of maneuvering room. He maintained participation in OCAM, the vehicle of the pro-Western francophones, for several years. In the early 1970s, Mobutu initiated a brief venture in the direction of a more radical policy, visiting Romania and China, signing a military training agreement with North Korea, breaking with Israel and Taiwan, and nationalizing some foreign companies. He also traveled widely throughout Africa, visiting many African states in pursuit of a continental-scale diplomacy; in 1973, for example, he paid calls in no less than fourteen African countries. These gestures did not signify any real break with the past, however. Motubu's ambitions for a more independent image were short-lived, as pressures emanating from events in Angola pushed him back into the embrace of the moderates and the West.

Congo shares some 1,500 (2,400 km) miles of border with Angola. Moreover, northern Angola is populated by Bakongo people, the dominant ethnic group in lower Congo. Congo had had a role in the Angolan liberation movement from the outset of armed resistance to Portuguese rule in 1961. Congo favored the National Front for the Liberation of Angola (FNLA) under Holden Roberto over the Marxist-oriented MPLA led by Agostinho Neto. This preference "paralleled that held by the United States and China, which were, for somewhat different reasons, convinced that the MPLA was under Soviet influence. As Angola moved toward civil war, both governments collaborated with Congo, though not with each other, in reinforcing the FNLA's military capabilities."[29] Mobutu's policy goal was to assure Roberto at least a foothold in a coalition government after Portuguese withdrawal. Congo's rather modest ability to achieve this goal was quite overwhelmed by the flood of other interventions that the last round of the struggle for power in Angola released.

In mid-1975, Mobutu made the fateful decision to intervene directly in Angola alongside the FNLA. Presumably encouraged by the CIA, which had long financed Holden Roberto and which had just received the go-ahead for covert military action, Congo sent a company of commandos and armored cars into combat in Angola.[30] Over the next two months, Mobutu committed another four battalions of paratroopers to the FNLA cause. At the same time, South African forces moved across Angola's southern border in support of the FNLA and of another contender, UNITA, led by Jonas Savimbi. Had the MPLA stood alone against these forces, Mobutu's venture might have succeeded. But the MPLA had allies as well. Once Cuban troops and Soviet arms joined the fray, the military situation was reversed. The Cubans helped the MPLA to drive out the FNLA-Zairian force, and Mobutu had to come to terms with a Marxist government in Luanda.

For Congo, the episode was even more humiliating politically than militarily. Mobutu's effort to establish an independent and progressive image was shattered by the apparent alliance with South Africa (not to speak of the CIA). His pretension to influence the course of events even in the contiguous environment proved a fiasco. He was obliged to disengage and to "normalize" relations with the MPLA government by declaring that he had merely been fighting against "Portuguese colonialism." Worst of all, however, the episode left the Angolans ill disposed to Congo's leader and not unsympathetic to his opponents, certain of whom were camped in northeastern Angola near the border with Shaba (formerly Katanga) Province. Rather than shoring up his regional environment, Mobutu had in fact weakened it. The result was even greater dependence upon external protectors.

The Shaba front deteriorated in March 1977 when opponents of the Mobutu regime infiltrated from Angola and took control of several localities. Congo claimed that it was being invaded by five thousand Cuban-led Katangese mercenaries from Angola and sent out an alarm to Washington and Paris. In reality, although the incursion enjoyed the tacit support of the Angolan government (which was still being harassed by the FNLA), it was more indicative of a regime crisis than of a foreign threat. Yet, whatever the mix of causes, the crisis was real and Mobutu needed help. The new Carter administration was not eager to get involved, but the French government saw an opportunity to improve its position in the former Belgian sphere in conjunction with another ally-in-need, Morocco. King Hassan, in turn, was willing to supply troops to shore up an African government that had backed Morocco on the Western Sahara issue. French planes transported Moroccan soldiers and materiel to the front, and the rebel forces slipped back into the countryside or across the border. The threat "appeared to have come and gone as quickly as the afternoon showers common to Shaba province,"[31] but in fact a more violent storm lay ahead in Shaba II.

The second round began in May 1978 much as the first with rebel forces reentering the copper zone. This time, however, they succeeded in seizing the important mining town of Kolwezi, where some twenty-five hundred Europeans worked. Once again, the Mobutu government had to appeal to external sources to redress a situation that the Zairian army could not handle. With European lives presumed in danger, France and Belgium dispatched their own forces into the contested zone. French Foreign Legionnaires engaged in a bloody battle over Kolwezi that took some eight hundred lives. The rebels were beaten back, but once again Congo became the site of bitter controversy over Western intervention and the character of Mobutu's dependent regime. Congo could only reinforce its ties with the francophone moderates and meekly work out a modus vivendi on noninterference with Angola.

The French were reluctant to withdraw without establishing more durable security arrangements. Once again, they mobilized the Moroccans, who provided the bulk of an inter-African peacekeeping force that also included smaller contingents from Senegal, Togo, Gabon, the Central African Republic, and Egypt. The reinsertion of Congo into the francophone family was clear. Although outspoken leaders like Tanzania's Nyerere deplored the rescue of Mobutu, his allies acquiesced in the salvage operation. Shaba II was remarkably reminiscent of Stanleyville 1964; the Congo (Zaire) of 1978 was as porous as the Congo of 1964, and the African alignments surrounding the issues were remarkably stable.

The inter-African force remained in Shaba for about a year, but Mobutu remained conscious of his political debt to the participant states for several years thereafter. Most prominently, Congo became Morocco's most fervent defender on the Western Sahara question. Elsewhere, Congo reciprocated the support of the Central African Republic by sending troops to crush student demonstrations there. It supplied a contingent to the OAU force that was deployed in Chad in an effort to reduce Libyan influence in that country, an undertaking earnestly desired by Mobutu's African allies in Senegal and Togo. Congo consistently supported Egypt on the Camp David Accords and eventually renewed diplomatic ties with Israel, a project that many of the black African moderates tacitly supported. In this manner, Congo gradually refurbished its standing in moderate Africa even if the political foundation of the regime remained fragile.

Earlier, we saw how the Western Sahara dispute broke the OAU apart in February 1982. Congo stood fast by Morocco through 1982 as two attempts to overcome the boycott by Morocco's supporters failed. By 1983 a compromise (voluntary withdrawal from the meetings by the Western Saharans) allowed the OAU to resume its sessions. In 1984, the compromise broke down in the face of Moroccan intransigence and growing support for the Polisario's SADR. When the November 1984 summit formally seated the SADR, Congo alone joined Morocco in leaving the organization (Morocco withdrew from the OAU, whereas Congo officially "suspended" its participation). Thus, the Rabat-Kinshasa axis remained firm while the rest of Africa elected to carry on without them. Congo's fidelity to Morocco was impressive, although its willingness to leave the OAU was consistent with a different project that appealed to Mobutu.

This project was the proposal to abandon the OAU and found a new "League of Black Africa," which Mobutu advanced in 1984. Nobody paid much attention to Mobutu's appeal to dissociate black Africa from Arab Africa. Despite the fact that disputes in the northern tier had caused major divisions within the OAU, there remained a broad consensus that the organization was needed. Nor were the cleavages in the OAU a function of differences between Arab and black states; on the contrary, as Mobutu in particular had good reason to appreciate, inter-African coalitions and linkages reflected alignments that extended beyond Africa. By the same token, they reflected Africa's dependency in world politics. However limited its means, the OAU symbolized a strategy for overcoming this dependent status. Thus, whatever dream Mobutu may have cherished to lead a League of Black Africa was not to be realized. His gesture to King Hassan in November simply underlined his previous dependence on Moroccan aid.

In June 1989, Mobutu again sought the diplomatic limelight by inviting eighteen African heads-of-state to his remote hometown of Gbadolite, ostensibly to witness a reconciliation between the warring parties in Angola. Although a vague agreement on a cease-fire and national reconciliation was worked out under Congo's auspices, it was never implemented.[32] Congo had little influence upon the peace agreement that was finally reached between UNITA and the MPLA in 1991—by which time Mobutu had pushed his country to the brink of anarchy.

Virtual isolation at the continental level, vulnerability to insurrection at the regional level, financial dependency at the global level—in all these ways, Congo was revealed as a giant with feet of clay. This sprawling land lying in the center of Africa might well have seemed the logical core of a central African common market. Indeed, Congo had sought to build a customs union encompassing such states as Central African Republic, Chad, Gabon, and Congo-Brazzaville. This scheme never achieved much substance, as Congo inspired little confidence and each of the smaller states of the region sought other, more reassuring partners. For states like Central African Republic and Gabon, France remained the major patron long after independence. The Central African Republic, especially during the days when the tyrannical Jean-Bedel Bokassa pursued Napoleonic fantasies, was a grim case of external dependency and internal misrule (much like Uganda under Idi Amin). Gabon had more attractive options by virtue of its oil resources, which led it into OPEC membership. But the sparsely populated equatorial country had little infrastructure other than the offshore rigs, and it was content to follow the lead of more prominent francophone states (Côte d'Ivoire, Senegal, Cameroon) on most matters.

Of Congo's northern neighbors, only Congo-Brazzaville broke out of the moderate francophone pattern toward an orientation closer to that of the progressive states. Recriminations occasionally arose between Brazzaville, which lies just across the Congo River from Kinshasa, and the Kinshasa government over the former's toleration of oppositional activity against Congo. Yet, the frontier never gave rise to incidents comparable to the Shaba episodes, and the two states' relations remained strained but not prone to violence. The tensions between Congo-Brazzaville and its larger namesake were symptomatic of the fragmented nature of what might have become a Congo-dominated subsystem under other circumstances. Instead, the single most influential political actor throughout the region remained France until the 1990s, when Museveni's Uganda began to project its power in the Great Lakes region (this is discussed further, below).

▪ Cameroon and Kenya

Only two states across central Africa have had relatively successful development experiences, but neither has mounted a very active inter-African policy. Cameroon and Kenya may be seen as the "peripheral powers" on the western and eastern coasts of the zone. Cameroon has a modest oil-exporting capability, and its agricultural development programs have done well; as a result, it has one of the higher per capita incomes on the continent. It has not ventured much beyond the confines of the francophone group, however, despite the fact that part of the country was once under British rule. Under the rather conservative leadership of Ahmadou Ahidjo for two decades, the government was initially wary of radical opposition forces that enjoyed some external support in Ghana and Guinea. Thus, Cameroon elected to emphasize its ties with the moderate states in organizations like OCAM. The French connection was likewise reassuring with regard to occasional tensions along the border with Nigeria. Here as well, prudence has prevailed, Cameroon cautiously maintaining a policy of support to the Nigerian federal government during the Biafran secession, from 1967 to 1970. To do otherwise would have invited Nigerian countermeasures to be sure; but more fundamentally, it would have violated Cameroon's traditional practice of maintaining a low profile in inter-African affairs.

Likewise, Cameroon's counterpart on the east coast, Kenya, has followed a policy that has been "cautious from the day that she gained her independence."[33] Aside from the issue of Somali irredentism, Kenyan foreign policy has been principally directed to its economic relations with Uganda and Tanzania, its partners in the East African Community (as discussed in Chapter 10). Kenya's strong encouragement of foreign investment in fact placed higher priority upon national development than upon regional integration. In choosing heavy reliance on external capital, Kenya adopted an orientation that discounted the importance of inter-African relations.

Kenya, nonetheless, could not ignore Somalia as the Somali ethnic claims extended across the length of their common border. Britain had decided in 1963 to attach what was called the Northern Frontier District (where some 240,000 Somalis lived) to Kenya. Kenya thus inherited a disputed frontier and local hostilities (known as the *shifta* war), to which it responded by means of a pact with Ethiopia. This treaty was not affected by the coup in Ethiopia, as "the threat posed to Kenya by Somalia's territorial claim was far more serious than the ideological orientation of the Ethiopian regime."[34] Yet, the main thrust of Somali irredentism has always been directed against "Greater Ethiopia," and as Somalia recognized that the *shifta* war was unwinnable and that Kenya was a desirable economic partner, Kenyan-Somali relations gradually improved. This rapprochement was especially pronounced during the 1980s, as both countries moved into a closer relationship with the United States—in part because of Ethiopia's growing ties with the Soviet Union and in part because of larger geopolitical pressures (notably the U.S. scheme for a Rapid Deployment Force, which we discuss more fully in Chapter 12).

Circumstances briefly thrust Kenya into a more visible continental role in 1981–1983 following the OAU summit meeting in Nairobi. As chairman of the organization, Daniel arap Moi found himself at the center of two major disputes—concerning Western Sahara and Chad. He was designated to chair the implementation committee, which the Nairobi summit set up to work out procedures for the mandated referendum on Western Sahara. Likewise, he was called upon to oversee arrangements for the short-lived OAU force in Chad, and he undertook mediation efforts in the civil conflicts in Uganda and Mozambique. Kenya's good offices proved inadequate to settle these intractable conflicts, however, and arap Moi, moreover, had to confront an attempted coup at home. Kenya turned back upon its immediate regional environment and local security needs, matters on which the United States was willing to help. An external patron, in other words, appeared the surest guarantor against domestic and regional upheavals.

The Kenyan case confirms the most striking attribute of central Africa as a whole—namely, the resort to external supporters. In contrast to trans-Saharan Africa, where several states mounted quite active independent diplomacies at one or another period, the states of central Africa at best can maneuver among alternative patrons. With the temporary exception of Congo, these states have not aspired to leadership roles in continental affairs. The reasons are obvious: None of them has power resources comparable to Algeria, Libya, or Nigeria. Even the best endowed, Congo, is a fragile construct. Given their limited resources, these states have attended to their local environments far more than to the continental environment. As a general rule, this has meant integrating their respective economies into the global economy rather than seeking to challenge their position by organizing Africa into a coherent unit.

But if the governments of central Africa have rarely sought the mantle of continental leadership, they are no less obliged than others to formulate a foreign policy, no matter how constrained. As relatively weak states, the external environment impinges upon them in substantial ways. Their strategy has been to call upon external patrons—France, the United States, the former Soviet Union, Great Britain—for protection rather than to pursue some version of the model of continental self-reliance proffered by one or another of the activist states. To the extent that the inter-African system had broken into two camps, most of these states entered the moderate camp. The struggle in and over Congo epitomized the victory of pro-Western social forces across the central zone. As Congolese-Angolan relations suggest, however, the liberation politics of the southern zone produced a rather different pattern in the third subdivision of the continent.

■ SOUTHERN AFRICA

Inter-African relations in the southern subsystem have been primarily concerned with the agenda of liberation from colonial and minority rule. Of the southern states, only the island of Madagascar belonged to the 1960 generation of independence. At the founding conference in 1963, the OAU established a Liberation Committee to channel support to the peoples of southern Africa. The headquarters of this body was placed in Dar es Salaam, capital of Tanzania, the only independent mainland state in the region at the time. By 1965, when the white settlers of Rhodesia (now Zimbabwe) issued their Unilateral Declaration of Independence (UDI), only Zambia and Malawi had joined the ranks of African self-rule. Whereas Malawi opted for a policy of accommodation with white power, Tanzania and Zambia became significantly involved with the liberation movements of Zimbabwe, Angola, Mozambique, Namibia, and South Africa.

The entire southern African subsystem was dominated by the military might of South Africa, until 1994 the bastion of minority rule on the continent. Through 1975, South Africa was aligned with Portugal as it clung futilely to Angola and Mozambique. The withdrawal of Portugal substantially altered the regional environment, but Angola and Mozambique, in turn, had to confront the reality of Pretoria's economic and military capability. Even the independence of Zimbabwe in 1980 did not overturn the pattern of South African hegemony, which weighed especially on the former British protectorates of Botswana, Lesotho, and Swaziland.

The common adversary of apartheid gave the southern subsystem a rather different character from those of central and trans-Saharan Africa. Policymaking was dominated by issues of decolonization and security to a much greater degree than elsewhere. The black-governed states formed such collective arrangements as the Front Line States and the Southern African Development Coordination Conference (SADCC). But these associations could not obscure the fact that the different members often pursued dissimilar policies in dealing with South Africa and with competing national liberation movements. Although issues of liberation politics were a constant in regional decisionmaking, the governments of southern Africa faced a constantly evolving policy environment after 1975. Portugal's decolonization, the termination of UDI, the steady pressure culminating in Namibian independence in 1990, and the turbulence that marked the P. W. Botha years and sparked the reforms of F. W. de Klerk made the southern subsystem extremely intense.

■ Tanzania and Zambia: The First Front Line

Because of its central location and its borders with four territories engaged in anticolonial struggles (Angola, Namibia, Zimbabwe, Mozambique), Zambia was at the heart of regional politics. On geopolitical grounds, Zambia had no choice other than to deal with a host of security issues thrust upon it by its embattled environment. Tanzania, on the other hand, had a broader range of options and might have been expected to orient its diplomacy primarily toward an East African community. One of the most interesting features of Tanzanian foreign policy has been its choice of a southern orientation. Many factors contribute to explain this choice, including disillusionment with developments in Kenya and Uganda, but none was more important than Nyerere's belief that ideologically sympathetic regimes coming to power in Mozambique and elsewhere across the south would enhance Tanzania's ability to pursue socialism and self-reliance. Because differing rationales lay behind the two countries' policies, the Tanzania-Zambia relationship was not always free of disagreement, but they generally viewed one another as partners in the enterprise of confronting minority power.

In its overall posture, Tanzania has been a maverick in inter-African relations. Two episodes especially illustrate Nyerere's willingness to buck the tide: his recognition of Biafra during the Nigerian civil war and his refusal to recognize the Idi Amin government in Uganda. In both cases, Tanzania violated OAU norms of noninterference or respect for colonial borders. In the former case, Tanzania's support for the principle of Biafran self-determination had little practical impact. In the latter case, however, Nyerere backed Ugandan exiles loyal to his friend, Milton Obote, in efforts to overthrow Amin; although a first attempt failed in 1972, a later campaign (brought on by Amin's ill-considered sortie into northern Tanzania in 1978) succeeded when Nyerere committed his own troops alongside the exiles. With Uganda in a shambles from the despotic Amin's policies, Tanzania continued to exert influence until Obote was eventually restored to power. This rare instance of a successful inter-African military intervention was exceptional also in its northward thrust, for the most prominent characteristic of Tanzanian foreign policy until the 1990s was its southern orientation.

The border with Mozambique was the immediate source of Tanzanian involvement in liberation politics. Tanzania welcomed the creation of the Front for the Liberation of Mozambique in the early 1960s and offered it headquarters in Dar es Salaam. This offer was a practical commitment to a movement pledged to socialism as well as anticolonialism, and Tanzania consistently backed the primacy of the FRELIMO leadership against other contenders when splits in the nationalist movement occurred. Tanzania did what it could, in other words, to assure the triumph of an ideologically sympathetic movement on its southern flank.

A primary component of Tanzania's policy was partnership with Zambia upon its independence in 1964. Zambia was especially exposed to the many pressures in the region. Its landlocked Copper Belt was dependent upon rail lines through Portuguese and South African territory for access to the sea. Rhodesia supplied virtually all its industrial energy. In these circumstances, it was little wonder that Zambia had an "obsessive preoccupation" with the liberation of southern Africa.[35] President Kenneth Kaunda fully shared Nyerere's moral indignation over minority rule, and the two leaders formed an extraordinary working relationship, meeting no less than seventy-one times over the years 1964–1974.[36] They collaborated in the construction of road, rail, and pipeline links in order to extricate Zambia from the stranglehold upon its transport options. The TanZam partnership constituted a significant new axis in inter-African relations, but the immediate pressures upon the two governments remained unequal as illustrated in their differing responses to the crisis created by UDI in November 1965.

Zambia's original policy dilemma was how to persuade the British government to prevent a seizure of power by the white settlers of Southern Rhodesia. Kaunda went so far as to offer the British military bases in Zambia to deter a breakaway by the settler government under Ian Smith. Lacking adequate military resources of his own, Kaunda felt obliged to seek his goal through collaboration with London, which ignored his offers and his advice.

Once deterrence failed, Zambia took the lead in an African/Third World campaign to pressure Great Britain to end the rebellion. Although Britain accepted its formal responsibility to do so, it insisted that economic sanctions were the correct means. Other African governments, notably Tanzania, disagreed with Zambia over diplomatic tactics. The OAU met shortly after UDI and passed a resolution calling upon all African governments to break diplomatic relations with London if Prime Minister Harold Wilson did not promptly use military force against the breakaway regime; likewise, it requested governments to make military advisers available to study the feasibility of a joint African force. But Zambia was opposed to both these approaches for compelling reasons. A multilateral OAU force would be cumbersome and expensive, and the logistics of the operation would make Zambia vulnerable to retaliation. Kaunda was convinced that only British troops could move quickly enough while avoiding a racial confrontation. Thus, he opposed breaking with Britain at the same time that he attacked Wilson's reluctance to employ force. Tanzania, on the other hand, did sever diplomatic relations.[37] This divergence in policy was an early indication of tactical differences that would from time to time separate the two states in their liberation policies.

Why have these two relatively like-minded states behaved differently? Geopolitics explains some of the discrepancy, but the nature of domestic elites is also pertinent. The Zambian policymaking elite contained competing factions of "national politicians" and "technocrats."[38] The former espoused thoroughgoing support of liberation causes, whereas the latter advocated cooperative relations with South Africa and with foreign investors in the mining industry. Zambian foreign policy has fluctuated as one or the other group held sway or as Kaunda tried to compromise between their competing preferences. Regarding UDI but more generally as well, Kaunda sought a middle ground between these two policy groups. The Tanzanian elite (which to be sure had less to risk) was somewhat more homogeneous in its ideological commitments—both on economic and liberation issues. Its foreign policy was more systematically "liberationist."

Kaunda was also influenced by a belief that South Africa might be persuaded not to assist the Smith secessionist government. Over the years, Kaunda fluctuated between outspoken denunciation of apartheid and quiet overtures toward accommodation with South African leaders. In dealing with UDI, as in dealing with South Africa, Zambia paid a high price. Kaunda asserted in 1978 that twelve years of redirected trade, transport, and military preparedness cost the country $6 billion, the equivalent of two years of GNP.[39]

As it became obvious that Great Britain would not employ military force and that economic sanctions would not suffice, the focus shifted to guerrilla warfare conducted by the Zimbabweans. Once again Zambia and Tanzania had to make policy decisions about whom to support between two principal contenders, the Zimbabwe African National Union (ZANU) led by Robert Mugabe and the Zimbabwe African People's Union (ZAPU) led by Joshua Nkomo. The split in the Rhodesian nationalist movement predated UDI and reflected both ethnic and ideological divisions and differing international linkages. Zambia decided in 1964 that ZAPU had the greater internal support and generally remained faithful to Nkomo. Meanwhile, ZANU won the favor of a collection of more radical states including Tanzania. Although both states encouraged the two movements to come together—and eventually succeeded in creating the coalition Patriotic Front, in 1976—they nevertheless disagreed in their approach to Zimbabwean nationalism.

Both states, it should be stressed, offered facilities to most of the movements combating minority rule in southern Africa. Lusaka's Liberation Center had a generally open door policy, and Dar es Salaam harbored all those recognized by the OAU Liberation Committee. Still, each state was inclined to support most vigorously the group or leadership that it saw as most congenial to its long-term interests. Tanzania particularly desired to see leftist movements accede to power, whereas Zambia preferred moderate nationalists. More exposed to South African power and more fully integrated into the southern African mineral production economy, Zambia walked a tightrope, seeking decolonization with minimal destabilization. Both sought to channel the process of change in accordance with their own security concerns in a volatile environment, all the more so as the violence expanded in the Portuguese colonies.

■ Liberation Movement Politics

Nowhere was the rivalry for African recognition and control over liberation politics so intense as in Angola. The question of whom to support in Angola plagued other governments through the 1960s and burst into a profoundly divisive inter-African disagreement in 1975 as Portugal withdrew. More than any other case, the Angolan revolution illustrates how the future orientation of a state may become a stake for other states.

No sooner had the guerrilla war against Portugal begun in 1961 than a "salient pattern of . . . intrarevolutionary rivalry" was established.[40] Two parties with distinctive social bases had organized in the 1950s to oppose colonial rule. The MPLA was an urban movement, Marxist in intellectual orientation, multiracial but mainly Mbundu in its ethnic base. The UPA (Union of Angolan Peoples, which would subsequently reconstitute itself as the FNLA) by contrast was rural, ethnopopulist, uniracial, and ethnically Bakongo and Ovimbundu [41] Even before the insurrection, the leaders of both groups were well known outside Angola, having attended the various anticolonial gatherings, such as the All-African People's Conference. From the very outset, the Angolan revolution was an international affair, as Angolan guerillas received training elsewhere in Africa. Algerians, for example, began training the FNLA recruits in Tunisia in 1961 even before the end of the Algerian war. But this was only half the story: Other Algerian military based in Morocco were giving comparable training to MPLA personnel. Although it was possible to have a foot in both camps at this early stage, over the years African governments would be pressed to choose between the Angolan contenders.

It was Holden Roberto's FNLA that initiated hostilities in 1961 in northern Angola, taking advantage of an operational base in Congo. The MPLA hastened to open up its own theater of operations, but it faced greater logistical difficulties. Not until 1963, when a sympathetic regime came to power in Brazzaville, did the MPLA have comparable access to Angolan territory—namely, the Cabinda enclave (which is separated from the rest of Angola by part of Congo, but which also borders Congo-Brazzaville to the north). Both anti-Portuguese movements, however, threw themselves equally into the battle for African recognition. For example, Mario de Andrade, a founder of the MPLA, traveled to Algiers in November 1962 to seek continuing support for his organization, which Ben Bella granted. Two months later, Holden Roberto likewise won a pledge of support from the Algerian leader. By the summer of 1963, both movements were invited to present their cases for support before the newly formed OAU Liberation Committee. The FNLA was better organized at the time and was duly recognized. But the internecine battle continued, and the FNLA, which had formed a government-in-exile (called the Angolan Revolutionary Government in Exile or GRAE), suffered defections. At its 1964 meeting, the OAU reaffirmed its support of Roberto's movement but also recognized the MPLA as an authentic anticolonial force. The OAU tried to reconcile the two to no avail.

Over the succeeding decade, therefore, both movements maintained their own external relations.The MPLA, now under the leadership of Agostinho Neto, cultivated friendly relations primarily with Marxist and other leftist governments, notably including Cuba. The FNLA enjoyed support mainly from the West and pro-Western governments. By the mid-1960s, a third actor appeared on the scene, mainly in southern and east-central Angola. The

National Union for the Total Independence of Angola, or UNITA, was the creation of Jonas Savimbi, a "spellbinding orator" who had represented the southern Ovimbundu in the FNLA/GRAE.[42] Although UNITA's impact was relatively limited until 1974, it then suddenly emerged as a significant contender for power. There is some evidence that UNITA had established a working relationship with the Portuguese authorities against the MPLA in the later years of the war.[43] UNITA did not receive aid or recognition from the OAU, which channeled its aid preferentially to the MPLA after 1966. The FNLA received modest aid from the OAU and bilaterally from Tunisia, Morocco, and Côte d'Ivoire—that is, governments friendly to its principal supporter, Congo.

The strain of the colonial war (being waged concurrently in Mozambique and Guinea-Bissau) took its political toll in Lisbon. The turning point for all three colonies came when a dissident faction in the Portuguese military toppled Portugal's right-wing government in April 1974. The officers' decision to negotiate with the African nationalists provoked a bitter struggle for power in Angola that once again brought to the fore the old cleavage between moderates and radicals in the inter-African system. These divisions were much exacerbated by extra-African intervention, which overwhelmed an OAU effort to reconcile the Angolan antagonists.

The civil war in Angola was much like the earlier Congo crises in its impact on inter-African politics. The question of who would govern Angola fitted into the larger structure of continental alliances and ideological affinities. Each government had its preference in the event that a nationalist coalition should prove impossible; but the OAU sought first to achieve Angolan unity. Thus the OAU brought together Neto, Roberto, and Savimbi to negotiate a common front in January 1975. They indeed signed a trilateral accord and then proceeded to negotiate an agreement with Portugal that fixed the date of independence for November 11, 1975. In the meantime, elections were to determine the shape of the government. The OAU's good intentions went for naught, however, as the intrarevolutionary fratricide burst forth again with a little help from the United States and the Soviet Union. The former approved a covert grant of funds to the FNLA that emboldened it to attack MPLA offices in Luanda. The Soviets dispatched arms to the MPLA to help defend its stronghold in the politically crucial capital city. Savimbi, who had been the first to negotiate a cease-fire with the Portuguese in 1974, presented UNITA as an alternative to the Marxist MPLA, thereby engaging the aid of such odd partners as China and South Africa.

In June, the OAU once again tried to avert the looming civil war by bringing the three parties to the bargaining table. This temporary detente was shattered in July when the FNLA, assisted by Congo, began an offensive. An OAU summit meeting at the end of that month appointed a commission to work for a coalition government. All African governments adhered to this posture right up to the appointed independence day in November. In October, however, a new element was injected into the struggle for power. South Africa, which had long held an operational sector in southeast Angola (under agreement with the Portuguese), began an offensive of its own. By mid-November the South African march penetrated some 500 miles northward, and the MPLA was squeezed between two hostile forces. At this point the MPLA launched an urgent appeal to Cuba, which had already sent military advisers, for further assistance.

Although the Cuban intervention was controversial, South Africa's offensive was the kiss of death for the MPLA's rivals. The aggression provided the grounds for several states sympathetic to the MPLA to break ranks with the OAU policy by promptly recognizing the MPLA government.[44] These same states also encouraged Havana to respond to the MPLA call for help. States friendly to the FNLA meanwhile called for an extraordinary OAU summit that revealed an Africa evenly divided into two camps.

Twenty-two states sponsored a resolution calling for withdrawal of all African and non-African states, a cease-fire among the Angolan combatants, and an agreement to set up a National Union Government. The other twenty-two submitted a counterresolution calling for military aid to the MPLA in the face of what they called "incontrovertible evidence about the blatant interference of imperialist forces seeking to dictate to Africa."[45] The groupings behind each resolution reflected almost perfectly the configurations that we have previously observed.

Backing the FNLA were most of the francophone states—Senegal, Côte d'Ivoire, Burkina Faso, Togo, Cameroon, Gabon, Central African Republic, Congo, Rwanda, and their northerly associates Tunisia, Morocco, Mauritania, and Egypt; the smaller West African states—Gambia, Sierra Leone, and Liberia; the southern African dependencies—Botswana, Lesotho, Swaziland, and Malawi; and perhaps less predictably, Kenya and Zambia (Kaunda having previously backed the MPLA). By and large, these were states closely tied to one or another Western power.

The coalition behind the second resolution was somewhat more heterogeneous. Its most consistent leaders were Algeria and Tanzania, both active promoters of socialism and aid to liberation movements. Libya (since Qaddafi), Mali, Guinea, and Ghana were generally to be found at their sides. Benin, Congo-Brazzaville, Burundi, and Madagascar formed a category of sorts, all francophone states in which leftist military regimes had come to power. The four other ex-Portuguese territories (Mozambique, Guinea-Bissau, Cape Verde, and Sao Tome and Principe) were the newest recruits to this grouping, and the small ex–Spanish colony of Equatorial Guinea voted with them. So did the Indian Ocean mini-states of Mauritius and the Comoro Islands, then under mildly leftist governments. Likewise Sudan, Somalia, and Chad were all in leftist phases. One can see that these states tended to be more dispersed, and many of them had little geopolitical weight. This group was bolstered, however, by Nigeria, which had reacted furiously to the South African invasion—more than any other government, Nigeria reversed an earlier suspicion of the MPLA in response to Pretoria's intervention.[46]

The summit met for three days without breaking the twenty-two/twenty-two stalemate. More than a decade after its creation and with half again as many members, the organization still reproduced the rough pattern of radicals versus moderates that it had been founded to transcend. Not only did the deadlock preclude any action by the OAU, but it revealed graphically the limitations of the organization when squarely confronted by the radical-moderate cleavage. The division over Angola exemplified the dominant feature of the inter-African system during the Cold War years. So long as the global system had a pronounced bipolar character, African states tended to divide into two competing camps.

The even split at the OAU left the way open for the matter to be settled on the ground in Angola. The military tide turned toward the Cuban forces, allowing the MPLA to secure its hold on Luanda and to win widespread diplomatic recognition. Within a month of the deadlocked special summit, the next regular OAU session admitted Angola to the organization.

Independent Angola generally identified itself with the radical camp, but its foreign policy concerns centered on its immediate environment, where initially it felt isolated, surrounded by Congo, Zambia, and, via Namibia, South Africa. Zambia was the first to improve relations by backing away from UNITA. After two rounds of fighting in Shaba Province, Congo also moved to a rapprochement with Angola in agreeing to close down FNLA offices in return for Angola's pledge to keep the anti-Mobutu ex-Katanga gendarmes under wraps. On the southern front, however, South Africa continued to sustain UNITA, and even periodically occupied southern Angolan territory, ostensibly to counter SWAPO but also to destabilize the MPLA government. With its southern provinces essentially a war zone, Angola clung to its Cuban alliance and focused its diplomacy on the Front Line issues of Namibia and apartheid.

These issues equally confronted Mozambique and Zimbabwe, the other new actors in the subcontinent. Mozambique acceded to independence shortly before Angola, under less divisive circumstances. Armed resistance to Portugal began in Mozambique in 1964, aided notably by Tanzania, Zambia, and Algeria. The former pair provided crucial logistic support by permitting bases in their territory that allowed FRELIMO to establish fronts in the north and northwest. Algeria (and to a lesser extent Nasser's Egypt) provided military training to the early guerrilla leaders, including Samora Machel, who became Mozambique's first president twelve years later, in 1975. Consistent with these alliances, FRELIMO developed a socialist ideology similar to that of the MPLA, but contrary to the MPLA it also managed to monopolize the anticolonial movement. Thus in 1974, the new Portuguese government faced a relatively coherent nationalist movement ready to assume power.

No sooner was a transitional government set up than FRELIMO participated in the founding of the Front Line States organization in November 1974. As an original member along with Tanzania, Zambia and Botswana, Mozambique gave the highest priority to assisting the struggle in Zimbabwe. By transferring weapons and opening its 750-mile border to the guerrillas, it transformed the logistics of the Rhodesian war. Like Zambia before it, Mozambique paid a heavy price economically and militarily for this solidarity.

In committing Mozambique to the overthrow of Ian Smith's Rhodesian Front, the Machel government chose to channel its aid primarily to ZANU rather than to ZAPU. Mozambique entered the network of inter-African relations with a set of historically determined preferences that extended beyond the southern theater. A sentiment of solidarity with Algeria, grounded in comparable national liberation experiences and concretized by Algeria's early assistance, created similar policy preferences among these partners at opposite ends of the continent. An Algiers-Maputo common approach became evident during the OAU's Angola debate and in subsequent alignments over Western Sahara, Shaba, and other matters. More broadly, the entry of the liberation movements of Portuguese Africa into the inter-African system created new linkages from North to South.

All the more so did the independence of Mozambique and Angola strengthen the Front Line States on the Rhodesian question—now it was the Smith regime that was virtually encircled. Moreover, the departure of Portugal made the United States and Britain much more interested in achieving a settlement. Backed by a strong African consensus, the Front Line States maintained diplomatic pressure on the West and likewise pressed the Zimbabweans to form a single bargaining agent, the Patriotic Front. This contributed to the independence of Zimbabwe in 1980 under a coalition government led by Mugabe's ZANU. Echoing an insight familiar to Zambia, Zimbabwe's foreign minister observed that "while nations are free to choose their friends, they cannot, however, choose their neighbors."[47] Zimbabwe's friends were largely in the progressive camp, and its impact at the OAU has been along those lines; its most prominent neighbor, of course, was South Africa.

Much like Zambia fifteen years earlier, Zimbabwe felt exposed to South African power. The Mugabe government has steered a narrow course between principle and practical constraints. It denied the use of its territory for incursions across the border and maintained South Africa as its number one trading partner. Still, Zimbabwe's independence made the

Front Line grouping one country stronger. The period of 1975–1980 re-defined the geopolitics of the southern tier without eliminating its residual focus on liberation politics.

■ The Final Bastion

The release of Nelson Mandela in 1990 and his subsequent election as president of South Africa in 1994 marked the end of an era in southern African international relations. In this section, we briefly review South Africa's role in the regional system during the period of white minority rule.

The apartheid regime was a formidable adversary to the Front Line States. Elaborately integrated into the global capitalist economy, it harbored the most powerful military establishment on the continent, enabling it to hold on to South West Africa, or Namibia, and to carry out operations against neighboring states with virtual impunity. The white government alternately pursued policies of accommodation and confrontation in its relations with black Africa in seeking to deter them from assisting the African National Congress (ANC) and the South-West African People's Organization (SWAPO).

We have seen that South Africa's external environment changed significantly after 1974. Even prior to that, the geopolitical pattern evolved as Botswana, Lesotho, and Swaziland acquired formal sovereignty. These three states, High Commission Territories under British protection during the colonial period, were severely constrained geopolitically. Nonetheless, Botswana became a "pipeline for escaping refugees and political militants"[48] and a founding member of the Front Line States. Lesotho and Swaziland likewise harbored antiapartheid organizers, policies that exposed them to punitive military strikes and economic coercion. All three joined SADCC, the regional organization designed to deprive South Africa of its economic hinterland. SADCC exposed a vulnerability in South Africa's situation: what the South African economy needed was the regional market that it enjoyed so long as Portugal and Rhodesia were present in the subcontinent, but by the 1980s that market was increasingly denied to it.

Although South Africa made occasional overtures to assist the neighboring black governments in economic development (such as its ill-starred 1979 "constellation" proposal for regional cooperation), its main instruments of influence were subversion and coercion. We have seen that South Africa invaded Angola during the civil war. Until the late 1980s, it carried out periodic incursions while channeling a steady flow of arms to Savimbi's opposition movement, UNITA. Likewise, it underwrote the Mozambique National Resistance Movement (RENAMO), whose sabotage operations wrought havoc on the Mozambican economy. Indeed, the Machel government felt constrained to sign in 1984 the Nkomati Accord, by which it agreed to cut back its support to the ANC in return for Pretoria's pledge of noninterference. Likewise, Angola negotiated a similar agreement, the Lusaka Accord. Nonetheless, South Africa continued clandestine support of RENAMO and UNITA while initiating direct military strikes on ANC offices in Lesotho, Botswana, and Zambia.[49] Violent confrontation between South African military power and the Front Line was the distinguishing feature of the southern subsystem until 1988, when the U.S-brokered South Africa–Angola-Namibia accord ushered in a new phase in inter-African relations discussed in greater detail below.

South Africa clung to Namibia for as long as it could, because the colony allowed it to extend its military power to the borders of Angola and Zambia. SWAPO's broad international support created strong pressure during the 1970s for withdrawal from the territory. But the Reagan administration's 1981 decision to link the Namibian question to the withdrawal of Cuban troops from Angola provided several years of respite, until changes in global politics, a Cuban military offensive, and the weight of international military and economic sanctions forced South Africa to negotiate a settlement that produced independence for Namibia in March 1990. By that time, moreover, South Africa itself was moving toward domestic negotiations over power sharing. (See Chapter 13 for further discussion of politics in South Africa.)

■ INTER-AFRICAN POLITICS IN THE WANING COLD WAR ERA

The international confrontation in Angola remained the most acute inter-African problem until the late 1980s when a confluence of African and extra-African determinants combined to bring about some major changes. The decade-long pattern of South African versus Cuban-Angolan thrusts and counterthrusts reached a climax during 1987–1988. In August 1987, the Angolan army launched a major offensive against UNITA forces in southeastern Angola; after initial gains by the MPLA expedition, the South African Defense Force (SADF) rushed in reinforcements to rescue its protégés, forcing the government troops to retreat to the town of Cuito Cuanavale. At this point, UNITA and the SADF mounted a counteroffensive, which the government forces resisted with Cuban assistance. Unable to capture Cuito Cuanavale, the joint UNITA–South African force withdrew in April 1988, but Fidel Castro ordered his crack 50th Division to engage the South Africans along the Namibian border in June. When Cuban pilots bombed the Calueque Dam, which provides water and electricity to northern Namibia, South African officers recognized that the "presence of the heavily-armed Cuban troops has altered the balance of power in the area."[50]

This series of military engagements, costly to all the combatants, increased the interest of all parties in a negotiated settlement. On the one hand, South Africa, financially strained by the impact of economic sanctions and by unrest at home, reevaluated its commitment to hold on to Namibia; on the other hand, Angola, which had been striving to achieve more pragmatic relations with the West, recognized that the new balance was sufficiently stable to contemplate the departure of its Cuban allies. The latter in turn could withdraw honorably, having challenged and faced down the SADF along the Namibian border. On top of this, the external conditions were favorable, for both the United States and the former Soviet Union wanted a regional settlement.

The great powers, which, as discussed more thoroughly in Chapter 12, had played a significant role in exacerbating the Angolan crisis in 1975, were by 1988 prepared to mediate a solution. In particular, U.S. Assistant Secretary of State for African Affairs Chester Crocker tirelessly labored to bring off a deal based upon a linked withdrawal of Cubans from Angola and South Africans from Namibia. Throughout 1988, as the parties wearied of their military exertions, Crocker engaged in a diplomatic marathon: (1) in January, he met with a joint Angolan-Cuban delegation in Luanda to establish that they would contemplate a phased but total Cuban withdrawal; (2) in March in Geneva, he conferred with South African Foreign Minister R. F. Botha about withdrawal from Namibia while holding parallel talks with the former Soviet Union to ensure their cooperation; (3) in May, he gathered Angolan, Cuban, and South African negotiators in London, associating the Soviets in the enterprise as counselors, and secured the principle of South African implementation of Namibian independence in accordance with U.N. resolutions; (4) during the summer, the parties initialed a statement of principles in New York defining a linked withdrawal—and began to disengage along the Namibian border; (5) during the fall, he conducted a series of meetings that produced a draft treaty and the Protocol of Brazzaville, which created a Joint Commission (that included the United States and former Soviet Union as "observers") to oversee the agreement; (6) his efforts culminated at the United Nations on December 22, 1988, with the signing of the Tripartite Agreement, according to which South Africa withdrew its troops from Angola and established a timetable for Namibian independence while Cuba began a phased withdrawal from Angola.[51]

Crocker's diplomacy, coupled with Mikhail Gorbachev's "new thinking," facilitated the process by which one of Africa's most damaging international conflicts was resolved (the civil war between UNITA and the MPLA did not end, but negotiations on this front carried on throughout the 1990s). In March 1989, a United Nations Transition Assistance Group (UNTAG) began deployment in Namibia; despite many tensions during the run-up to U.N. supervised elections in November, the agreement held and

Namibia became independent under a SWAPO government in March 1990. The arrival of Namibia as a sovereign actor in the southern African sub-system was (like Eritrean independence in the Horn) the end of a very long process, but its significance was dwarfed by the process of change by then under way in South Africa itself. As discussed in detail in Chapter 13, the transition from minority to majority rule that took place in South Africa from 1990 to 1994 transformed the nature of inter-African relations not only in southern Africa but indeed throughout the entire continent. The end of decolonization and minority rule as mobilization issues and the emergence of Mandela's South Africa as a legitimate actor in the continental system transformed the landscape of inter-African affairs.

In northern Africa, too, states faced challenges that pushed them to redefine the regional environment. Algeria and Morocco, long engaged in building counteralliances, began to perceive advantages in regional economic integration in the late 1980s, especially as the European Community advanced toward fuller integration. In May 1988, the two governments restored diplomatic relations after a break of twelve years. That summer, as a consequence of the Algerian-Moroccan rapprochement, the Polisario Front and the Moroccan government accepted the broad outlines of a U.N.-sponsored peace plan for Western Sahara. Settlement appeared even closer when King Hassan agreed to meet personally with representatives of the Polisario Front early in 1989. These signs of an impending settlement opened the door to the creation of a new regional economic organization called the Arab Maghreb Union (UMA), composed of Mauritania, Morocco, Algeria, Tunisia, and Libya. Yet since its formation in February 1989, the UMA has made very little progress toward implementing a common market in the Maghreb. Moreover, the new spirit of regional cooperation did not lead to prompt resolution of the Western Saharan question, despite a major effort by UN Secretary General Javier Perez de Cuellar to organize a self-determination referendum. In April 1991, the Security Council approved deployment of a UN mission (MINURSO) to supervise such a referendum. After the successful service of UNTAG in Namibia, hopes initially ran high that the United Nations could facilitate resolution of the Saharan dispute as well, but disagreements over the voting lists prevented implementation of the UN plan.

Deescalation of the two major trans-Saharan conflicts (Western Sahara and Libya-Chad) moderated tensions, although an ugly incident inflamed the border area between Senegal and Mauritania in 1989. Even more disruptive was the Liberian civil war that began when rebel forces led by Charles Taylor invaded from bases in Côte d'Ivoire in December 1989 and engulfed the country in violence that sent some 400,000 refugees into Côte d'Ivoire, Guinea, and Sierra Leone. The Liberian tragedy sparked a major inter-African peacemaking effort under the auspices of ECOWAS. In August 1990, five member-states—Nigeria, Ghana, Guinea, Sierra Leone, and

Gambia—dispatched 2,000 ECOWAS ground and naval to Monrovia to impose a cease-fire on the warring factions. Under the command of a Nigerian major-general, the multinational force (known as ECOMOG, for ECOWAS Cease-Fire Monitoring Group) quickly grew to 12,000 soldiers and played a major role both militarily and politically. It installed Amos Sawyer, a longtime opponent of the Doe regime, as head of an interim government and brought all the combatants together for negotiations in Bamako, Mali, in November 1990. Although ECOMOG restored calm for a time to Monrovia and the southern part of the country, it did not succeed in reconciling all the factions; Charles Taylor, enjoying tacit support from Côte d'Ivoire and Burkina Faso, continued to hold on to the northern provinces and extended his influence into neighboring Sierra Leone. Relying predominantly on Nigerian forces and without the full support of key francophone states, ECOMOG soon found itself bogged down in a protracted conflict in Liberia.

The civil war in Liberia divided ECOWAS, but it did not divide the entire continent as Congo and Angola had. The fact that intervention was left to a regional coalition was another sign of the decline of bipolar competition in Africa. We have already seen that détente, manifested in Soviet-U.S. collaboration, smoothed the way for the Angola-Namibia accord. More broadly, the continental cleavages between moderates and radicals lost much of their saliency as the ideological divide between East and West narrowed in the late 1980s. For all its specific characteristics, the inter-African system operates within the context of the global system. As rapprochement between the superpowers brought the Cold War to its end, new problems and issues arose in the inter-African system.

■ INTER-AFRICAN POLITICS IN THE POST–COLD WAR ENVIRONMENT

The end of communist rule in Eastern Europe affected Africa in the form of challenges to one-party rule and military regimes across the continent. Likewise, the ebbing of bipolar rivalry reduced strategic competition over Africa. The consequence of these two transformations was the collapse of states such as Somalia and Liberia and the intensification of internal strife in numerous others, including Rwanda, Burundi, Sudan, Congo, Algeria, and Nigeria. Coping with state breakdown became the major challenge to the inter-African system in the 1990s.

Somalia provided the most striking example of collapse under the changing international environment. We have seen how the military regime of Siad Barre exploited the external environment to garner first Soviet military support, then U.S. backing, as well as aid from other sources—what one observer called an "aid avalanche."[52] In the process,

Somalia became both an oppressive clan-based dictatorship and a highly armed society. So long as external resources did not dry up, explains Hussein Adam, Siad "was able to hold on to power."[53] In the late 1980s, however, the aid flow did begin to dwindle in response to severe human rights abuses accompanying the repression of a revolt in northern Somalia. The rise of domestic opposition coupled with the decline of foreign aid toppled the dictatorship in January 1991, leaving a host of contenders for power in the stricken state.

As Somalia slipped into anarchy, the government of Djibouti attempted to bring the competing factions around a bargaining table in July 1991. Likewise the new president of Ethiopia, Meles Zenawi, sought to organize a regional conference in 1992 to deal with the chaos next door. The scale of the crisis was far beyond their means, however. The regional governments and even the OAU had little choice but to turn the problem over to the UN. Nor indeed did the United Nations—or the United States in carrying out Operation Restore Hope in 1992–1993—have much success in coping with the collapse of the Somali state. While UN, US, and NGO interventions did much to alleviate the humanitarian catastrophe that befell Somalia, the political crisis defied resolution into the late 1990s.

The dissolution of Somalia into clan warfare had negative repercussions, primarily in the form of refugees, for neighboring states. It also projected abroad an image of violence, disorder, and incapacity to govern that harmed all African states in their efforts to gain development assistance. Local, regional, and continental institutions all failed to find a mechanism capable of restoring authority in Somalia; after having successfully developed techniques for dealing with the power relations of the bipolar world, the inter-African system was adrift in the post–Cold War structure.

Similar post–Cold War processes played themselves out in Ethiopia, as Mengistu fled his country about the same time that Siad Barre left Somalia. Although a well-organized movement took power in Addis Ababa, it had to yield authority over Eritrea to the EPLF, which had been a major force in the insurgency. Thus three decades of violence and intervention produced a new state in the Horn, while leaving the regional system "awash in arms."[54] The Horn remained a foyer of great insecurity as the civil war persisted in Sudan, war broke out between Eritrea and Ethiopia in 1998 over contested areas along their border, and other dissident movements were present in Ethiopia and Djibouti. Although forums like the Inter-Governmental Authority on Drought and Development (IGADD) and various NGOs worked to address the humanitarian crisis in this splintered region, the Horn was symptomatic of the huge difficulties that states were experiencing in adjusting to the post–Cold War environment.

Central Africa was also severely afflicted by the worldwide rise of ethnonationalism in the aftermath of the Cold War. The most shocking case of ethnonationalist violence erupted in Rwanda in a context of long-simmering frictions between Hutu and Tutsi populations. The origins of Rwanda's 1994 crisis reach back at least to the intercommunal hostilities of 1959–1962, when large numbers of Tutsis left the country for exile in Congo and especially Uganda. These exiles assisted Yoweri Museveni to come to power in 1986 and subsequently enjoyed his backing in forming the Rwandan Patriotic Front (RPF), a Tutsi force that began incursions into Rwanda in 1990. France immediately came to the aid of the Habyarimana government, providing a huge flow of weaponry that allowed the Rwandan army (Forces Armées Rwandaises, or FAR) to expand tenfold—from 5,200 to 50,000—in two years.[55] Coupled with other forms of opposition to the Habyarimana military regime, the conflict simmered along Rwanda's northern border until peace talks were arranged in Arusha (Tanzania) in summer 1992.

Punctuated by continuing hostilities between the RPF and the FAR, the Arusha talks dragged on for more than a year until an agreement was finally signed there on August 4, 1993, in the presence of the presidents of Tanzania, Uganda, and Burundi and the prime minister of Congo. The agreement created a broad-based government and called for a UN monitoring force (UNAMIR, for UN Assistance Mission in Rwanda) to oversee its implementation. Hutu extremists, however, managed to block implementation of the agreement in an atmosphere greatly clouded by the assassination of the newly elected Hutu president of Burundi, Melchior Ndadaye, in October 1993. Regional leaders gathered again in Dar es Salaam in April 1994 to bring pressure upon President Habyarimana to implement the Arusha agreements; it was as Habyarimana was returning from this meeting that his plane was shot down as it was landing in Kigali. The fanatical Hutu elements that murdered the president then unleashed their gruesome genocide against the Tutsis, slaughtering moderate Hutus as well in their orgy of terror.

The massacre in Rwanda was the horrendous outcome of a struggle for power in a small country with porous borders. The Hutu generals and propagandists who devised this terrible plan feared for their power in the face of an externally supported rebel group. Likewise they were vulnerable to external pressures for political change that favored moderate Hutu opposition leaders and accommodation with the RPF. The extremists looked abroad for support to France and to Congo, both of which were loath to see the "English-speaking Tutsis" from Uganda gain control in Rwanda.[56] Events in Burundi (whose interim president was also killed in the plane crash) exacerbated the political crisis that tore apart Rwanda. Once the violence began, Rwandans fell victim to a mood of reluctance to intervene on the part of Europe, the U.S., and the UN after the fiascoes of Somalia. And while regional and global geopolitics contributed to the struggle for power in Kigali, regional states and the OAU lacked the means to intervene to stop the bloodshed.

Once unleashed, the genocide ran its terrible course, claiming hundreds of thousands of lives. At the same time, it of course stirred the RPF back into action. The Tutsi exile force immediately laid siege to Kigali and quickly captured several other cities, taking control of most of the eastern part of the country. Even while it was slaughtering innocent people, the FAR was being forced to withdraw toward the west and the border with Congo. By July 1994, Kigali fell to the RPF, which set up a new government led by guerrilla leader Paul Kagame under the formal presidency of Pasteur Bizimungu, a Hutu who had opposed the fallen government. Meanwhile millions of Hutu, including much of the FAR leadership, fled into exile, primarily in Congo.

A paradoxical consequence of the large-scale refugee flows out of tormented Rwanda was the diplomatic rehabilitation of the Mobutu regime, whose assistance was needed to deal with the ensuing humanitarian crisis as Hutus and the collapsing FAR fled the RPF takeover of the country. Not only did Congo reemerge as a key actor for the UNHCR and the NGOs, but it gained further leverage as a haven for the unrepentant Hutu extremists. (President Mobutu later paid dearly for harboring the Hutu militants, as Uganda and Rwanda backed the insurrection that led to the downfall of his regime in 1997.) The states of central Africa continued to cope with the refugee problems and the political repercussions of the Rwanda crisis into the mid-1990s, all the more so as Burundi tottered on the same brink.

By no means could Burundi remain unaffected by the turmoil in Rwanda. Its ethnic composition was virtually identical; the major difference was that the Tutsi-dominated army had held on to power. A major Hutu uprising against the regime of President Pierre Buyoya (who seized power in 1987) occurred in August 1988. Although Buyoya later allowed national elections in 1993, his elected successor was assassinated six months later, provoking another wave of killings; by September 1994 a Hutu rebellion was under way. The idea of a "preventive intervention" to head off Rwanda-scale violence was put forward in early 1996 by UN Secretary General Boutros-Ghali. The Burundian government, however, resisted the idea, and no one stepped forward to implement the secretary general's proposal.

The situation remained explosive as Hutus seeking to avenge the deaths of Ndadaye and his successor Cyprien Ntariamira (in the 1994 plane crash) clashed with the Tutsi-dominated army. In June 1996, senior statesman Julius Nyerere undertook a mediation effort in the town of Arusha. Spurred on by Nyerere and the surrounding governments, the Hutu president and the Tutsi prime minister of Burundi appeared to accept the deployment of an inter-African preventive interventionary force to be composed of troops from Tanzania, Uganda, and Kenya. In the month following, however, no progress was made in implementing the African peacekeeping unit as leaders of both the Hutu rebels and the Tutsi military denounced the idea. Meanwhile, massacres and reprisals multiplied inside Burundi in the absence of any multilateral intervention. On July 25, 1996, former president and military officer Buyoya carried out another coup, claiming that his leadership was necessary to end the communal violence.

During the Cold War era, such a coup would have been considered essentially an internal matter by the OAU. In the new international climate, however, the OAU encouraged the concerned regional states to meet again regarding the situation in Burundi. They gathered in Arusha to condemn the coup and invoke economic sanctions against the new Buyoya regime. Tanzania and Congo closed their borders with Burundi, and even the RPF government in Rwanda agreed to enforce the sanctions. The Arusha regional summit called on Burundi's new rulers to reinstate Parliament and resume talks with all parties to the national crisis, and the idea of sending a multilateral force into the country continued to be discussed. On balance, however, it remained unclear to many observers whether such a force was any more likely than Major Buyoya to restore some semblance of order to troubled Burundi.

While central African states wrestled with the twin crises of Rwanda and Burundi, west African states sought to bring an end to Liberia's strife. ECOMOG encountered many of the difficulties already familiar to peacekeepers around the world: ECOWAS's regional force ran into an intractable local situation, as well as a lack of genuine international consensus. Nigeria's leadership in launching ECOMOG in fact rang alarm bells in some of the francophone capitals, requiring Lagos to enlist several other regional states—notably Côte d'Ivoire, Senegal, and Benin—in the search for a diplomatic resolution of the Liberian civil war.

Houphouët-Boigny initiated the process of expanding the diplomatic consensus by convening a meeting in Yamoussoukro at the end of June 1991. This initiative prompted ECOWAS to create a new Committee of Five chaired by Houphouët at its July annual summit meeting. In effect this committee, which also included Senegal, Togo, Gambia, and Guinea-Bissau, replaced the Standing Mediation Committee as the primary diplomatic actor addressing the Liberian conflict. At the same time, Senegal agreed to commit troops to the ECOMOG force, thereby diluting somewhat the group's previous heavily anglophone composition. Abdou Diouf, who assumed the chairmanship of ECOWAS at this moment, engaged the Senegalese forces on the premise that Charles Taylor would be more willing to cooperate with ECOMOG if Nigeria's role in the force were diminished. Despite the arrival of the Senegalese soldiers, however, the situation on the ground in Liberia deteriorated as a new faction, the United Liberation Movement for Democracy in Liberia (ULIMO)—backed by and operating along the border of Sierra Leone—emerged as another rival to Taylor's NPFL.

Clashes between ULIMO and the NPFL obliged the peacekeeping force to withdraw from some of the regions in which ECOMOG was supposed to be disarming the factional armies. Diouf concluded that ECOWAS needed to strengthen its mandate by enlisting the full support of the OAU behind a tougher strategy that would entail an embargo against the warring factions. As Diouf began to implement this strategy (in his new capacity as chair of the OAU for 1992–1993), full-scale fighting erupted between ECOMOG and the NPFL, leading the regional organization to appeal to both the OAU and the UN to back its policy of sanctions against the warlords. Thus a process that began in ECOWAS's Standing Mediation Committee in the summer of 1990 evolved into Security Council Resolution 788 in November 1992, declaring a general arms embargo against Liberia. Indeed, the expansion of the diplomatic process entailed nomination of a UN special representative, an OAU liaison person, the subsequent inclusion of additional peacekeepers from Tanzania and Uganda, and a small UN Observer Mission (UNOMIL) whose role was to monitor implementation of the peace agreement that was finally signed in July 1993 in Cotonou.

Nor did the laboriously negotiated Cotonou Agreement bring a definitive end to the struggle for power in Liberia. Almost three years and many factional clashes later, ECOMOG still was embroiled in violence in the very streets of Monrovia in April 1996. Although it seems fair to conclude, as Margaret Vogt did, that without ECOMOG "the situation in Liberia would have degenerated into a major regional crisis,"[57] one can observe at the same time that ECOMOG was sometimes drawn into the very disorder that it was supposed to bring to an end.[58] Rather than ushering in a brave new era of regional peacekeeping, it ran into residual notions of regional rivalry and stubborn local interests that rendered its mission extremely arduous.

ECOWAS did finally achieve peaceful elections in Liberia, which brought Charles Taylor to power in 1997, but not before the spillover of the war into Sierra Leone. ECOMOG withdrew from Liberia only to redeploy in Freetown, where it intervened in 1998 to restore the government of President Kabbah (elected in 1996, deposed in 1997) under controversial conditions.

While the Liberian imbroglio was occupying most of the member-states of ECOWAS, many of them were also concerned with the repercussions of Islamist politics across the northern tier of trans-Saharan Africa. The emergence of an Islamist regime in Sudan created a haven for Islamist movements in other states, and the insurgency mounted by Islamist forces in Algeria raised questions about the stability of that regime across the entire region. Despite its domestic woes, Algeria attempted to maintain diplomatic pressure on Morocco with regard to Western Sahara.

On this matter, however, Morocco was able to hold on to its de facto control of the bulk of the territory while prolonging the debate over eligibility to vote in the UN-mandated self-determination referendum. The

MINURSO peacekeepers dispatched in 1991 found themselves condemned to a dreary watch in the desert as the voter registration process bogged down under Moroccan attempts to add additional voters to the rolls. The dispute remained on the Security Council agenda into 1999, and Polisario threatened to resume hostilities in the absence of a referendum. After two decades of Moroccan determination to absorb the territory, however, the issue had lost salience in inter-African affairs, much as had the radical-moderate split that surrounded it during the Cold War era.

Indeed, throughout the 1990s, the two states whose foreign policies had done the most to create trans-Saharan linkages were confronting major constraints. In the case of Libya, international sanctions and Chad's relative return to domestic stability significantly reduced its opportunities for intervention. In Algeria's case, a severe domestic political crisis turned the country inward—other than to forge alliances with other states threatened by violent Islamist oppositions. The socialist/pan-Africanist logic that drove Algeria's African policy throughout the Cold War period no longer provided clear guidelines in the turbulence that marked Africa in the 1990s. Nigeria, which (like Algeria in 1992) annulled the results of elections in 1993, also lost much of its capacity for effective regional leadership. Plagued by domestic crises, ethnonationalism, and state collapse, and deprived of the ability to exploit superpower rivalry, the inter-African system reverted to local efforts at crisis management.

Only in southern Africa did the regional environment evolve toward greater security. The post–Cold War attenuation of ideology eased tensions in Mozambique and Angola, and the transfer of power in South Africa raised hopes for the emergence of a stable security community in the region. The transformation in August 1992 of the Southern African Development Coordination Conference into the Southern African Development Community (SADC) with full South African participation symbolized the new role of the subcontinent's major power. Having created SADCC to confront apartheid, the redefined SADC represented an attempt to build a strong regional economic community around the core South African economy. Although South Africa has the potential to act as a benevolent hegemon in the region, its leaders are well aware of the numerous possibilities for political and economic insecurity; thus, the ANC government can be expected to maintain the weapons industry and strong military that made the country a dominant regional power under the minority National Party government.

■ CONCLUSION

The inter-African system reveals a mix of competition and cooperation, of conflict and consensus. African governments have pursued their national interests much as others have in the state system. They have been attentive to the distribution of power on the continent and its implications for their security and welfare. Although wars have broken out between African states in numerous instances, direct military threats to security have not been the foremost feature of inter-African politics. The most intense conflicts have revolved around civil wars, or the struggle for power within states. The question "Who shall rule?" (such as in Congo or Angola or Chad or Liberia) has been the most persistent inter-African issue, because states (inside and outside Africa) have viewed these struggles in terms of the overall distribution of power on the continent. African governments have sought to shape the flow of events, sometimes by direct intervention, more often by forming diplomatic coalitions and by utilizing the instrument of the OAU.

Although there has been no continental consensus on who shall rule, there has nonetheless been an underlying notion that all African governments should collaborate in addressing common problems. From this sentiment, the OAU was created in 1963. The decision to transcend the rivalries of the earliest phase of inter-African relations produced an institution that has somehow survived a host of battles. Its formal organization is unexceptional: headquarters in Addis Ababa operated by a modest secretariat led by a secretary general; a set of standing commissions on various economic, social, political, and administrative matters, of which the Liberation Committee was long considered the most important; regular intergovernmental sessions at the ministerial level; and, as its principal organ, an annual meeting of heads of state. Each year a state is selected to chair the organization, thereby thrusting its leader to the forefront of continental politics. In 1998, for example, President Blaise Compaoré of Burkina Faso served in this capacity; as such, he participated in mediatory efforts to deal with the insurrection in Congo and the war between Eritrea and Ethiopia.

We have seen that the OAU has had limited success in solving Africa's most salient conflicts. Its peacekeeping force failed to keep the peace in Chad; its implementation committee failed to implement anything in Western Sahara; its special session on Angola only dramatized an even split among Africa's governments. Yet, from 1963 through 1981, the organization did succeed in convening an annual summit conference. Even after the crises of 1982 broke this pattern, the member states discovered the means to resume the summitry in 1983.

The OAU has endured because it does serve a diplomatic need of the African states. It has successfully mediated some lesser disputes, and it has articulated a common position to the external world on apartheid and economic development issues. It has provided a framework for the generation of common economic strategies, such as the Lagos Plan of Action. Most important, however, it serves to keep lines of communication open on a continental scale.

The OAU has exemplified both the divisions of the inter-African system and the expressed will to act collectively for the welfare of Africa as a whole. The dominant pattern of inter-African politics has been for like-minded coalitions to form around competing notions of who shall rule. Each of the three regional zones has had specific issues that have primarily concerned the proximate states, but allegiances that cut across these zones have produced a continental network of interactions as well.

From 1960 to 1990, two loose inter-African coalitions roughly paralleled the global bipolar structure. Issues erupted in each of the three major zones, the most salient of which had a continent-wide impact. While the system evolved across several periods, a major transition occurred with the breakdown of bipolarity in the 1990s. The relative withdrawal of the superpowers (whose role has been left primarily to Chapter 12) left African states much more vulnerable to internal breakdown, and coping with the transnational repercussions of civil war and state collapse have become the dominant security issues since 1990. These security matters have been compounded by the economic marginalization of the continent.

Africa's post–Cold War crisis has spurred new thinking about the linkage between security and economic development. As early as 1991 a group of independent leaders, constituted as the Africa Leadership Forum, came together in Kampala for a Conference on Security, Stability, Development, and Cooperation in Africa. This was an effort to "renew the search for endogenous solutions to the continent's crises of insecurity, instability, and underdevelopment" by strengthening civil society, promoting self-reliance, and fashioning a more effective conflict management mechanism via the OAU.[59] Two years later, Africa's heads-of-state formally approved the proposed conflict management mechanism at their annual summit meeting. Thus, on the thirtieth anniversary of the founding of the OAU, they renewed the commitment to cooperatively manage continental affairs. Yet, in the rather ill-defined post–Cold War distribution of power, amidst the wreckage of several collapsed states, the path to a more secure inter-African system was not well marked.

■ NOTES

1. For an early analysis of the emergence of trans-Saharan geopolitics, see Robert A. Mortimer, "Politics in Trans-Saharan Africa," *Africa Report* 26, no. 3 (May–June 1981).

2. The quote is from the official nationalist newspaper, *El Moudjahid,* in its issue of 5 August 1960 (even before the actual fall of Lumumba).

3. Immanuel Wallerstein, *Africa: The Politics of Unity* (New York: Random House, 1967).

4. *Le peuple* (Algiers), 26 November 1964.

5. René Otayek, "La Libye révolutionnaire au sud du Sahara," *Maghreb Machrek* 94 (October–December 1981): 27.

6. Hervé Bleuchot, "La politique africaine de la Libye," in *Annuaire de l'Afrique du nord*, 1978 (Paris: Conseil National de la Recherche Scientifique 1979), p. 76.

7. Cited in Timothy Shaw and Orobola Fasehun, "Nigeria in the World System: Alternative Approaches, Explanations, and Projections," in Timothy Shaw and Olajide Aluko, eds., *Nigerian Foreign Policy: Alternative Perceptions and Projections* (New York: St. Martin's Press, 1983), p. 205.

8. Olatunde Ojo, "Nigeria and the Formation of ECOWAS," *International Organization* 34, no. 4 (Autumn 1980). See also his chapter, "Nigeria," in Timothy Shaw and Olajide Aluko, eds., *The Political Economy of African Foreign Policy* (New York: St. Martin's Press, 1984).

9. Timothy Shaw, "Nigeria in the International System," in I. William Zartman, ed., *The Political Economy of Nigeria* (New York: Praeger 1983), p. 213.

10. Kwame Nkrumah, *Africa Must Unite* (New York: International Publishers, 1970), p. xii.

11. The phrase is from Ako Adjei, one of the envoys along with George Padmore, the Jamaican pan-Africanist who advised Nkrumah in this period, as cited in W. Scott Thompson, *Ghana's Foreign Policy, 1957–1966* (Princeton: Princeton University Press, 1969), p. 33.

12. Ibid., p. 61.

13. Ibid., p. 57. In May 1959 a more elaborate declaration used the language "Union of Independent African States" opening the arrangement to "all independent African States or Federations." See the text in Legum, *Pan-Africanism* (New York: Praeger, 1962), p. 160.

14. Y. M. Sule, leader of the Nigerian delegation at the Second Conference of Independent African States, as cited in Colin Legum, *Pan-Africanism*, p. 174.

15. Thompson, *Ghana's Foreign Policy*, p. 5.

16. Jacques Baulin, a French aide to Houphouët, has revealed that Houphouët carried out his own destabilization campaign against Ghana and Guinea. See his *La politique africaine d'Houphouët-Boigny* (Paris: Editions Eurofor, 1980).

17. Mohsen Toumi, "La politique africaine de la Tunisie," in *Annuaire de l'Afrique du nord*, 1978, p. 115.

18. Ibid., p. 118.

19. Ibid., p. 126.

20. Mohammed Bouzidi, "Le Maroc et l'Afrique sub-saharienne," in *Annuaire de l'Afrique du nord*, 1978, p. 109.

21. *New York Times*, 27 June 1981.

22. The protesters were Cameroon, the Central African Republic, Comoros, Djibouti, Equatorial Guinea, Gabon, Gambia, Guinea, Côte d'Ivoire, Liberia, Mauritius, Morocco, Niger, Senegal, Somalia, Sudan, Tunisia, Upper Volta, and Congo. See John Damis, "The OAU and the Sahara," in Yassin el-Ayouty and I. William Zartman, eds., *The OAU After Twenty Years* (New York: Praeger, 1984), for a thorough account of the OAU's handling of this issue.

23. The twenty-six states that recognized the SADR in February 1982 were Algeria, Angola, Benin, Botswana, Burundi, Cape Verde, Chad, Congo-Brazzaville, Ethiopia, Ghana, Guinea-Bissau, Lesotho, Libya, Madagascar, Mali, Mozambique, Rwanda, Sao Tomé and Principe, Seychelles, Sierra Leone, Swaziland, Tanzania, Togo, Uganda, Zambia, and Zimbabwe.

24. Christopher Clapham, "Ethiopia," in Shaw and Aluko, *The Political Economy of African Foreign Policy*, p. 80.

25. Article III, provision 3, calls for "respect for the sovereignty and territorial integrity of each State."

26. Robert E Gorman, *Political Conflict on the Horn of Africa* (New York: Praeger, 1981), p. 55.

27. Our account has focused on the most far-reaching and prolonged clashes. Other problem areas could be added, such as the tensions among Senegal, Côte d'Ivoire, and Guinea throughout the 1960s; the strains between Nigeria and Ghana over the expulsion of Ghanaian workers; sporadic border closings; or the frontier dispute between Mali and Burkina Faso that erupted into war in December 1985. The latter dispute was resolved by a ruling of the International Court of Justice in December 1986.

28. Crawford Young, "Zaire: The Unending Crisis," *Foreign Affairs* 57, no. 1 (Fall 1978): 177.

29. Crawford Young, "The Portuguese Coup and Zaire's Southern Africa Policy," in John Seiler, ed., *Southern Africa Since the Portuguese Coup* (Boulder: Westview Press, 1980), p. 204.

30. An authoritative account of U.S. policy is Nathaniel Davis, "The Angola Decision of 1975: A Personal Memoir," *Foreign Affairs* 57, no. 1 (Fall 1978). Davis was assistant secretary of state for African affairs in 1975 until he resigned over the decision to intervene militarily.

31. Galen Hull, "Zaire: Internationalizing the Shaba Conflict," *Africa Report* (July–August 1977): 9.

32. Donald Rothchild and Caroline Hartzell, "Great- and Medium-Power Mediations: Angola," *Annals of the American Academy of Political and Social Science* 518 (November 1991): 46–53.

33. John Okumu, "Kenya's Foreign Policy," in Olajide Aluko, *The Foreign Policies of African States* (London: Hodder and Stoughton, 1977), p. 138.

34. Vincent B. Khapoya, "Kenya," in Shaw and Aluko, *The Political Economy of African Foreign Policy*, p. 155.

35. Douglas G. Anglin and Timothy Shaw, *Zambia's Foreign Policy* (Boulder: Westview Press, 1979), p. 16.

36. Ibid., p. 189.

37. Only nine governments actually ever implemented the OAU resolution. They were Algeria, Egypt, Sudan, Mauritania, Ghana, Guinea, Mali, Congo-Brazzaville, and Tanzania.

38. Marcia Burdette, "Zambia," in Shaw and Aluko, *The Political Economy of African Foreign Policy*, pp. 325–326.

39. Anglin and Shaw, *Zambia's Foreign Policy*, p. 35.

40. John A. Marcum, *The Angolan Revolution*, vol. 2, *Exile Politics and Guerrilla Warfare* (1962–1976) (Cambridge, MA: MIT Press, 1978), p. 9.

41. Ibid., p. 50. Marcum notes as well that the ethnic divisions were reinforced by different religious sectarian affiliations.

42. Ibid., p. 247.

43. See Michal Wolfers and Jane Bergerol, *Angola in the Storm* (London: Zed Press, 1983), for an attempt to document this.

44. They were Algeria, Congo-Brazzaville, Guinea, Somalia, and four former Portuguese colonies whose independence preceded that of Angola: Mozambique, Guinea-Bissau, Cape Verde, and Sao Tomé and Principe.

45. *Africa Contemporary Record*, vol. 8 (1975–1976), p. A73.

46. Nigeria's position (and Algeria's) no doubt influenced that of Niger, which provided the final pro-MPLA vote, departing from its customary affiliation with the francophones. (Uganda and Ethiopia abstained.)

47. Cited in Ken Good, "Zimbabwe," in Shaw and Aluko, *The Political Economy of African Foreign Policy*, p. 364.

48. Bernard Magubane, "Botswana, Lesotho, and Swaziland: South Africa's Hostages in Revolt," in Thomas M. Callaghy, ed., *South Africa in Southern Africa* (New York: Praeger, 1983), p. 357.

49. In this regard, Pretoria even advanced its own version of the Monroe Doctrine, claiming a "special responsibility" to police southern Africa. See Callaghy, *South Africa in Southern Africa,* pp. 4–5.

50. Cited in Michael McFaul, "Rethinking the 'Reagan Doctrine' in Angola," *International Security* 14, no. 3 (Winter 1989/90): 126.

51. See Chas. W. Freeman, Jr., "The Angola/Namibia Accords," *Foreign Affairs* 68, no. 3 (Summer 1989): 126–141. The texts of the agreements may be found in Selected Documents, No. 32, United States Department of State, Bureau of Public Affairs, December 1988, or in Owen E. Kahn, ed., *Disengagement from Southwest Africa* (New Brunswick, NJ: Transaction Publishers, 1991), pp. 223–235.

52. Anna Simmons, "Somalia: A Regional Security Dilemma," in Edmond T. Keller and Donald Rothchild, eds., *Africa in the New International Order* (Boulder: Lynne Rienner, 1996), p. 76.

53. Hussein Adam, "Somalia: A Terrible Beauty Being Born?" in I. William Zartman, ed., *Collapsed States: The Disintegration and Restoration of Legitimate Authority* (Boulder: Lynne Rienner, 1995), p. 75.

54. Terrence Lyons, "The International Context of Internal War: Ethiopia/Eritrea," in Keller and Rothchild, eds., *Africa in the New International Order*, p. 87.

55. Gérard Prunier, *The Rwanda Crisis: History of a Genocide* (New York: Columbia University Press, 1995), p. 113.

56. On this point see Prunier, who quotes an interview in which Bruno Delaye (Mitterrand's special counsellor for African affairs) told him: "We cannot let anglophone countries decide on the future of a francophone one" (*The Rwanda Crisis,* p. 279).

57. Margaret Aderinsola Vogt, "The Involvement of ECOWAS in Liberia's Peacekeeping," in Keller and Rothchild, *Africa in the New International Order,* p. 167.

58. For evidence of the involvement of peacekeepers in pillaging the Liberian economy, see William Reno, "The Business of War in Liberia," *Current History,* May 1996: 211–215.

59. Denis Venter, "Regional Security in Southern Africa in the Post–Cold War Era," in Keller and Rothchild, *Africa in the New International Order,* p. 141.

12

Africa in World Politics

Like other regions of the South in world politics, Africa has been greatly affected by the interests and ambitions of external powers. During the sixteenth century, the slave trade began to integrate black Africa into the global division of labor, but most of the continent was not incorporated into the global political system until the latter part of the nineteenth century. As Ronald Robinson and John Gallagher show in their classic *Africa and the Victorians*, Africa acquired new strategic significance after the opening of the Suez Canal made control of Egypt critical to British imperial policy; the scramble for Africa was triggered by Britain's response to Egyptian nationalism. With the demise of colonialism, Africa became a geopolitical stake in the rivalries of the Cold War era. Today, Africa's place in the new distribution of power is being redefined.

France and Great Britain were, of course, the continent's most intrepid colonizers, while other European states claimed lesser shares. France remains a very influential actor in African affairs and has taken the lead in fashioning a close economic relationship between Africa and the entire European Union. After World War II, the two global superpowers gradually increased their involvement in Africa. (On a more modest scale, so did China.) For the Soviet Union, decolonization represented an opportunity to forge friendly ties with the new states, especially where strong anti-imperialist movements emerged. For the United States, African independence posed the challenge of keeping the former European colonies inside the Western orbit of influence. Just as the Congo crisis of 1960 was one of the major issues in inter-African relations, it also marked a considerable intensification of East-West rivalry on the continent. U.S. policy was often dominated by the fear of Soviet gains; whether these fears were well founded became a source of much debate among policy analysts.

Soviet-U.S. competition was long the most significant determinant in the external environment facing African states. Changes in the Third

World, however, also had an impact on African foreign policies. The emergence of such organizations as the Nonaligned Movement and the Group of 77 provided a framework for Third World collective diplomacy in which African states have actively participated.

While African governments have sought to develop more extensive relations with Latin American and Asia, ties with the Arab world have been particularly intricate for geographic, cultural, and economic reasons. The North African states are, of course, part of the Arab world, and many black African states have significant Muslim populations. Especially after OPEC, with its strong Arab contingent, asserted itself as a force in the global economy, the notion of an Afro-Arab partnership received considerable attention. Together, the states of Africa and the Middle East constitute the geographic and political core of the Third World coalition that has tried to reshape the North-South relationship.

Thus, African states, which individually can wield little power in international politics, have been particularly attracted to the strategy of acting collectively with other developing states. Yet, there is abundant evidence of the difficulty of Africa, Asia, and Latin America coordinating their policies toward the North when regional and national interests vary. African states must balance individual and collective interests as best they can in coping with an external environment containing stronger actors than themselves.

The end of the Cold War transformed the environment of global politics and raised fears of Africa's marginalization. Strategic competition over Africa declined considerably, depriving African governments of a significant source of bargaining power. Yet, external powers continue to pursue interests and zones of influence on the continent, and African states individually and collectively face the need to promote their development in a competitive global economy. During the Cold War, the great powers intervened according to their own agendas, while African elites drew what advantages (in foreign aid and arms deliveries) they could from the strategic rivalries. As in inter-African politics, periods of crisis—over Congo in the 1960s, Angola and the Horn in the 1970s, Libya and southern Africa in the 1980s—tended to exacerbate great power rivalry. In the dialectic between Africa's quest for greater autonomy and its vulnerability to external intervention, moreover, the economic crisis of the 1980s provided additional leverage for Western pressure on African governments. Arresting Africa's economic decline is a precondition for reasserting African political autonomy.

■ AFRICA AND EUROPE

▦ France

Plus ça change, plus c'est la même chose: time and again, observers have been struck by the extraordinary continuity of French policy in Africa. The reasons for this continuity are quite straightforward. The African empire was one of the great exploits of French history. Especially since 1830, when an expeditionary force set foot in Algeria, Africa has loomed very large in the French imagination and worldview. By the end of the nineteenth century, France claimed control of vast expanses of the Sahara, the Sahel, and posts along the Atlantic coast stretching to the Congo River in the south. Over the next twenty years, France gained a protectorate over much of Morocco and mandates over Togo and most of Cameroon. This extensive overseas domain was crucial to the fortunes of the Free French under General Charles de Gaulle during World War II. When President de Gaulle subsequently presided over the decolonization of this empire, he took great care to preserve a close relationship with *l'Afrique française*.

France fought two terrible colonial wars, in Indochina and then in Algeria. De Gaulle, who came to power in 1958 in a country ravaged by the war in Algeria, chose not to resist decolonization in black Africa. Rather, he turned over local political power to a generation of African leaders who had represented their territories in the French National Assembly. With the exception of Guinea-Conakry, whose leader Sekou Touré broke with France in 1958, all the colonies of French West and Equatorial Africa plus Madagascar acceded to independence in 1960 under leaders like Leopold Senghor and Felix Houphouët-Boigny who had strong attachments to France. Culturally, economically, militarily, and thus politically, the newly independent francophone states remained bound to the metropole, and successive French presidents since de Gaulle have cultivated and even extended this sphere of influence.

All the French colonies were relatively small in population. The largest by far were Algeria and Morocco in the Maghreb; the sub-Saharan territories, therefore, were generally quite economically dependent. France's strategy was to maintain maximal influence in these states via financial and technical aid combined with highly personalized relations with the leaders. As Tamar Golan puts it (in her well-titled piece "How Can France Do Everything That It Does in Africa—and Get Away with It?"), de Gaulle and his successors have nurtured an atmosphere of "club" and "family" that has offered prestige to the elites of the francophone states.[1] Landlocked countries like Chad and Central African Republic, countries in need of infrastructure like Gabon and Côte d'Ivoire, sparsely populated countries like Mauritania and Niger, very small countries like Togo and Djibouti all have relied on the link for technology, education, communications, internal security, and even administrative personnel. These were the perquisites of membership in the club, however paternalistic the family has appeared to stronger states like Nigeria and Algeria.

De Gaulle's cult of national dignity and presidential authority appealed to many of the leaders of fragile newly independent states. Gaullist France cultivated this affinity by supplying the technical advisers and teachers that these new governments needed to build a state apparatus and provide basic services. The French astutely named this dependent relationship "*la coopération*"; it assured the flow of French goods into these markets and protected the environment for French capital investment. By supporting a common currency—the CFA franc—Paris assured tight financial links and a measure of monetary stability throughout the entire francophone community (only Guinea and Mali tried to establish their own money, and both eventually sought readmission to the franc zone). Likewise, France maintained military bases, supplied arms, and trained the military and the police; military coups have rarely yielded any significant change in relations with France. Not only has France been a major military supplier to the francophone club, but its weapons sales to other states (Libya, Nigeria, Kenya, Somalia, South Africa) have ranked it the foremost Western arms merchant (second only to the former Soviet Union) on the continent.

Under de Gaulle, all these arrangements were overseen by his special adviser on African affairs, Jacques Foccart, a rather shadowy figure from the intelligence services. Foccart's position, discretely sheltered in the president's office, was typical of the highly personalized relationship between the francophone leaders and the French government. When de Gaulle stepped down in 1969, Georges Pompidou kept Foccart in office to manifest his intention for continuity in Franco-African affairs. Only when Valéry Giscard d'Estaing became president in 1974 was Foccart removed, only to be replaced by a new aide (René Journiac) who continued the practice of special attention to the African leaders. Nor did the socialist government of François Mitterrand see fit to change this special relationship. Mitterrand's choice of a trusted associate, Guy Penne, as his personal emissary to Africa revealed how deeply ingrained this approach to the former empire had become. Indeed, when the Gaullist Jacques Chirac became French prime minister in 1986, for African expertise he called upon none other than—Jacques Foccart.[2] Africa is important to France's claim to be a global power. The francophone elites, in turn, have become accustomed to this privileged treatment at the highest level of the French government. Such treatment accords them a visibility and international recognition that would be difficult to acquire otherwise. In return for France's flattering attention, they have reserved an open door for French influence.

What looks like cooperation to some appears as neocolonialism to others. What France has managed to "get away with" has been a series of interventions in the weaker states and a record of propping up conservative regimes.[3] In 1964, French troops reversed a coup d'état against the government of Gabon's Leon M'Ba. Gabon, now a relatively wealthy country thanks to minerals and offshore oil, epitomizes what critics call the *chasse gardée* (or private hunting preserve); France has stood by Omar Bongo, the autocratic successor of M'Ba, in spite of violations of democratic rights and dubious expenditures of oil revenues. President Giscard d'Estaing developed particularly close ties with the Central African Republic's dictator, Jean-Bedel Bokassa, who spent millions on French goods when he crowned himself "emperor" in a grim parody of Napoleonic rule; but eventually, Bokassa's excesses led the French to encourage the Central African Republic army to remove him. Paris dispatched troops to Chad on several occasions during its prolonged civil war. The most audacious intervention, however, no doubt occurred in Congo (Zaire) in 1978. Here Giscard's apparent affinity for pro-Western autocrats and his determination to spread French influence carried him beyond the frontiers of the old empire. During the second Shaba incursion, Giscard sent in the Foreign Legion to quell the disturbance and shore up the Mobutu government. These various operations were only the most overt expressions of France's proclivity to exercise power in Africa.

The moderate francophones have welcomed this French role. Many of them have security agreements with France, and French troops remain permanently based in Senegal, Côte d'Ivoire, Gabon, the Central African Republic, and Djibouti (the francophone outpost on the Horn). The role of these troops essentially has been to assure internal security, as when French soldiers squashed a mutiny in Bangui in 1996. Giscard, however, used the base in Dakar to attack Polisario forces in Mauritania during the early part of the Western Sahara war. This operation, carried out about the same time as the parachute drop into Shaba, revealed how extensive French interests in Africa were. An axis of strong French influence extended from Paris to Rabat to Dakar to Abidjan to Libreville to Kinshasa. Another rougher line could be sketched from Corsica (whence the Legionnaires departed) to Tunis, Ndjamena, Bangui, and Kolwezi (where they landed). The Shaba campaign was the crowning episode in an effort to extend the French presence deeply into an area once dominated by Belgium, thereby to rival the growing U.S. influence in Congo. President Mobutu, for his part, gratefully accepted his recruitment into the club.

Although largely an extension of de Gaulle's conception of France's African vocation, Giscard's Africa policies did draw considerable criticism in France. Whereas de Gaulle and Pompidou had projected a dignified relationship with partners of stature such as Senghor and Houphouët (Pompidou and Senghor had actually been classmates in Paris in the 1920s), Giscard hobnobbed with petty dictators like Bokassa and Bongo. Gaullists criticized the style more than the substance of Giscard's policies. However, the socialists offered a more fundamental critique of interventionism, support for autocrats, indifference to human rights, and arms sales to South Africa—in short, of French alignment with the most conservative governments in Africa. The 1981 Socialist Party platform stressed support for self-sustaining development and implied a new progressive orientation for France's Africa policy. Thus, when Mitterrand was elected in 1981 after twenty-three years of rightist government, observers in France and Africa wondered what might lie ahead.

In practice, little changed under Mitterrand, who himself had long been involved in the Franco-African network. Indeed, he had served as minister of overseas colonies during the Fourth Republic and had been instrumental in forging an important parliamentary alliance with Houphouët-Boigny in those days of shifting governmental coalitions. Although Mitterrand talked of innovation, he took care to reassure France's long-standing African partners. His principal gesture toward a new relationship with Africa was the nomination of Jean-Pierre Cot as minister of cooperation. Cot was known for his "distrust of the old guard," and emphasized building relations with the Front Line States, the former Portuguese colonies, and Ethiopia—all beyond the traditional francophone club.[4] Meanwhile, however, Mitterrand's special adviser, Guy Penne, was assigned to cultivate the old guard.

Before the end of 1982, Cot was ousted from the government, but Penne was still in place (moreover, with Mitterrand's son Jean-Christophe working in his office, the family ties had most assuredly won out). Most of the familiar patron-client relationships reasserted themselves as the socialists responded to the political needs of France's traditional partners in the Central African Republic, Gabon, Chad, Morocco, and elsewhere. As the editor of the weekly *West Africa* observed in 1983, it quickly became evident that Mitterrand's government shared "the idea that France's high profile in Africa should be maintained."[5]

One of the intriguing forums of this remarkable relationship has been the Franco-African summit. Inaugurated in 1973 by Georges Pompidou, these meetings were converted into an annual institution under Giscard d'Estaing. Alternating between sites in France and in Africa, the summits grew in participation from an original francophone core of ten states (plus France) in 1973 to thirty-eight participants (including some "observers") a decade later. Giscard enlarged the circle to include Congo in 1975 and such lusophone states as Guinea-Bissau and Cape Verde in 1976. He used the 1977 conference in Dakar to rehabilitate Senghor's old notion of Eurafrica and the 1978 session to call for an inter-African force to serve in crises such as Shaba. Mitterrand settled very comfortably into the summit institution while expanding it to even greater dimensions and utilizing it principally to orchestrate his Chad policy.[6] The November 1982 summit was particularly noteworthy in assembling thirty-six African delegations together with the president of France at a moment when the OAU was itself incapable of mustering a quorum. That France should be able to mount such a gathering each year—with participation continuing to grow during the 1990s—is indicative not only of its special relationship with Africa but of the importance that its leaders, regardless of political complexion, accord to perpetuating the linkage.[7]

Many factors contribute to explaining the francophone elites' tolerance of the French presence, but they are most simply summed up by the concept of dependency. The states where French aid and influence loom largest are among the least developed on the continent. They are predominantly commodity exporters with relatively poor terms of trade. This weak economy supports an often bloated bureaucracy of privileged wage earners whose position largely results from their command of the French language and technical skills acquired in francophone institutions. Cultural assimilation, ultimately the greatest triumph of French imperialism (even if limited to an elite), constitutes a durable bond between the ruling class and the former metropole. This link is reinforced by the political fragility of many of the francophone states, where ethnic divisions, sometimes reinforced by religious differences and regional fragmentation, render national unity precarious. Rising class tensions and splits between urban and rural interests increasingly challenge the ruling parties. Beleaguered rulers readily turn to external support systems for internal security, provision of technical skills, and financial bailouts. Chad, where French forces have come and gone over decades of unrest and civil war, is perhaps the most extreme manifestation of dependency. Côte d'Ivoire, which lies at the other end of the spectrum economically and in terms of political stability, likewise has encouraged French private investors and technical personnel to stay in the country as guarantors of the regime.

For these states, France remains the most accessible and the most willing external partner. Even those governments that shifted briefly to the left under military regimes, such as Benin, Congo-Brazzaville, and Madagascar, retained military technical assistance agreements and did not leave the franc zone. Even rebel Guinea ultimately returned to the fold, because France was more willing than any other country to provide needed assistance. Although a few deeply assimilated leaders, most notably Senghor and Bourguiba, romantically extolled the notion of *la francophonie* as a distinctive cultural framework, most have simply found the French connection a practical necessity. In a world of scarce resources, France has offered the best arrangement to ruling elites facing a multitude of problems. Furthermore, the deal has looked attractive to newcomers like Congo and the other former Belgian protectorates, Rwanda and Burundi, both of which, for example, have security agreements with France. Several other small dependent states, such as Guinea-Bissau, Cape Verde, Mauritius, Sierra Leone, and Liberia, have likewise sought to enter the "family."

There have, of course, been a few holdouts from this club of Franco-African *fraternité*. The most serious challengers, as previously suggested, have been Algeria, Libya, and Nigeria. Algeria has tried with variable success at different periods to woo such states as Mali, Niger, and Mauritania into its own sphere of influence. Libya challenged France in Chad, and has tried to exploit the Islamic connection in other French preserves as well. Nigeria has been most suspicious of France, as the French aided the Biafran secession, and is acutely aware of its encirclement by francophones.

But even these competitors have had an ambivalent relationship with Paris, for as de Gaulle perceived from the beginning, France offered an alternative of sorts to the superpowers. Algeria continues to trade extensively with and export labor to France, and the rise of an Islamist movement in the 1990s has forced it to rely increasingly on French security and financial assistance. Libya has seen France as less hostile to its interests than the United States, and Nigeria has viewed business deals with French investors as a useful bargaining chip in regional affairs.

Hence France, whether under Gaullist, liberal, or socialist government, has been committed to an active role in Africa. Jean-Pierre Cot's brief fling in the Ministry of Cooperation revealed both the special assets that France enjoys and the constraints within which it must operate. In seeking to extend French influence to new horizons—Nigeria and Ethiopia, Kenya and Tanzania, Angola and Zimbabwe—Cot exploited the notion of a progressive, "Third Worldist" France standing up for Southern development in Northern circles. He wished to project France less as the patron of a group of francophone clients than as the champion of a new conception of North-South relations. This was, in effect, Mitterrand's version of the older Gaullist notion of French aid as an alternative to superpower hegemony.

The francophone core, nevertheless, reasserted itself as the foundation of French influence in Africa. Cot had to give way to Guy Penne lest the core group fragment and undermine the whole edifice. In this manner, Mitterrand remained well within the framework of his predecessors. Jean-François Bayart puts it best in explaining the residual continuity in French policy. It is not so much that Mitterrand returned to an earlier scheme of things, but rather that

> [Mitterrand's predecessors took] the road that Mr. Mitterrand opened in 1951 in managing the split between [Houphouët-Boigny's] African Democratic Rally and the French Communist Party. . . . The real continuity is older than claim the rightist parties, it flows from Mitterrand to General de Gaulle and his successors.[8]

The waning of the Cold War prompted a wave of political change that took the form of "national conferences" in many francophone states. Mitterrand appeared to associate France with this movement toward democratization during the sixteenth Franco-African summit held at La Baule in 1990. While declaring that "we shall continue to be present in Africa and to aid our African friends who are our companions in History," he also announced that henceforth France would link its aid programs to progress in democratization.[9] In fact, however, the French government exerted little pressure on the old guard of francophone leaders to conduct genuinely free elections.

In 1995 the Gaullists returned to power with the election of Jacques Chirac as president. Over his many years in government, Chirac had cultivated plenty of ties with francophone leaders, and he devoted his first major trip abroad to Africa in order, as he put it, to "listen to" France's friends in Africa. Officially committed to the support of democratization across Africa, Chirac's France, like that of Mitterrand, comfortably accommodated a wide range of regimes old and new in the post–Cold War environment. Despite speculation in the early 1990s about a declining French role in Africa—and despite occasional disagreements among the Ministry of Foreign Affairs, the Ministry of Cooperation, and the presidential African bureau over specific policies—France has retained a broad political consensus that its role as a major power in world affairs is rooted in Africa.

■ The Idea of Eurafrica

No other European state has maintained an African policy comparable to that of France. Despite its extensive involvement in colonial Africa, Great Britain has played a declining role in African affairs since independence. Certainly London has remained an influential partner for such states as Nigeria, Kenya, and Zambia, and it has been a central player in southern African affairs, most notably regarding Rhodesia. Indeed, Britain has been embroiled in a series of crises, including the civil war in Nigeria and the expulsion of its Asian citizens from Uganda, that have required delicate policy decisions. Moreover, African issues have been crucial ones for the Commonwealth, Britain's favored instrument for the management of post-colonial relations. Yet, in fashioning the Commonwealth as their primary forum for Third World relations, both Labour and Conservative governments have elected to treat Africa as but one component of a larger scheme.

British policy was initially to channel change in ways that would least undermine its own investments and trade. Thus, for example, Britain joined with the other Western powers to undermine Lumumba and encourage the Katanga secession in 1960. By the end of the decade, however, British policymakers saw their interests aligned with Nigeria's Federal Military Government against the Biafran secession. Despite an active lobby for Biafra in England, the British government supplied large quantities of arms to Lagos in order not to jeopardize its commercial preeminence there. The overall thrust of British policy, however, was away from Africa and toward Europe as it sought entry to the Common Market.

For fifteen years, from 1965 to 1980, British policy was burdensomely shackled to the Rhodesian issue. Several African governments broke diplomatic relations with London in 1966 over its unwillingness to apply force to unseat the minority government of Ian Smith. African governments turned their efforts to supporting a guerrilla resistance movement. By the late 1970s, Britain faced two hardy adversaries, black and white, contending for control over Rhodesia. Moreover, it confronted growing international pressure, notably from Nigeria, which had by then passed South Africa as Britain's foremost market in Africa, and from the United States, which under President Carter was eager to see majority rule. In these circumstances, a youthful Labour foreign secretary, David Owen, undertook a major negotiating effort between the Patriotic Front and the Smith forces. Spurred onward by a Commonwealth conference in Lusaka, Owen's successor, Lord Carrington, presided over the Lancaster House Conference (September–December 1979), which painstakingly produced a constitution and a cease-fire agreement. Ultimately, therefore, British diplomacy achieved a rare feat—negotiated settlement of a guerrilla war before either side was clearly defeated.

Britain's colonial legacy likewise entailed a significant stake in the economy of South Africa. These commercial interests required a diplomatic balancing act between Commonwealth pressures for sanctions against Pretoria and pressures from British investors and exporters intent upon maintaining a strong economic presence in that country. Great Britain is first and foremost a trading nation, and its overall approach to Africa has been to do what is necessary to maintain markets. London has had its hands full reacting to political turmoil in Nigeria, Uganda, Zimbabwe, and South Africa, leaving it little opportunity to challenge Paris as the preeminent European actor in Africa. More like Belgium than France, it has accepted the European Union (supplemented by the Commonwealth) as the framework for its evolving relations with Africa.

The other states of Europe also have generally chosen to multilateralize their relations with Africa under the auspices of European institutions. Not surprisingly, France has taken the leading role in defining the European Union's Africa policy, of which the Lomé Convention, which we examined in Chapter 10, has been the principal instrument. Although Lomé IV extends well beyond the continent, Africa remains the core area of an enduring geopolitical conception—namely, that Europe must preserve a sphere of influence to its south if it is to compete in global politics and markets.

This conception has not been limited to European strategists, as might be expected. African leaders have sometimes been more fervent Eurafricanists than have the Europeans themselves. No doubt, the best example is Leopold Senghor, the poet and theoretician of "negritude" who was president of Senegal from 1960 to 1980. Senghor had unusually deep personal roots in Europe. He had arrived in France as a student in 1928, earned the prestigious agrégation degree, taught school, and served in World War II before entering the French National Assembly in 1945 as a deputy from Senegal. By the late 1940s, he was a committed federalist, actively supporting unity in Europe, large federations in Africa, and ultimately a transcontinental federation. Senghor held an idealized vision of Eurafrican cooperation, but underlying it was essentially the same rationale that appealed to the Europeans: it was a way of creating a third force in world politics capable of resisting the hegemony of the superpowers.

During the 1960s, Senghor's Eurafricanism was eclipsed by the decade of independence; instead of federating, Africa and Europe negotiated the terms of their economic relations in the two Yaoundé Conventions of 1963 and 1969. The idea resurfaced in the 1970s in the context of the energy crisis, the fear of raw materials shortages, and general economic insecurity. As the European Community became more inclusive (incorporating all of the former colonial powers in Africa), the Brussels institutions assumed increasing responsibility for negotiation of the accords by which Europe has maintained its economic presence in Africa. Each Lomé Convention has involved strenuous bargaining over the precise terms of the evolving economic relationship, but the grand lines of these relations still reflect the pattern imposed during the colonial period.

Decolonization, however, meant that European states were no longer the sole external actors on the continent. The Cold War led the United States and the former Soviet Union to become increasingly involved, especially where political breakdowns opened the door to superpower rivalry.

■ SOVIET-U.S. COMPETITION IN AFRICA

The United States and the former Soviet Union shared an important attribute in common in African affairs. They were both relative newcomers to the continent. Their lack of experience and genuine knowledge led both to make blunders in their African policies, but their military and economic capabilities sufficed to make them actors to be reckoned with. Each approached the continent in the light of their mutual rivalry: neither was particularly attentive to African realities, and both interpreted African interests in terms of containing the other.

There was also an asymmetry in their respective stances in that the United States was allied with the former colonial metropoles, whereas the former Soviet Union had neither the advantages nor the drawbacks of partners. The Soviets enjoyed the rhetorical advantage of approaching the continent with a clear anti-imperialist ideology. The United States, although laying claim to an anticolonial tradition, was generally content to defer to its European allies so long as the latter could maintain a stable presence in their spheres of influence. When they failed, as, for example, most dramatically in Congo, the United States became much more visibly involved. Whether the United States was seconding or displacing its European ally, the concern was the same: to prevent Soviet influence, just as the Soviets strove to diminish Western influence.

Both superpowers tended to become involved in those states where the transition from colonialism to independence was most turbulent. Yet, it would be misleading to suggest that the great powers took all the initiatives. On the contrary, competing African leaders often looked abroad for support against internal factions or external enemies. The exigencies of domestic and regional struggles for power often opened the door to intervention. Sometimes, as the local context evolved, this door turned out to be a revolving one. The fact remains that from the late 1950s to the late 1980s, the newcomers were poised on the threshold, ready to enter a new arena in their global competition.

■ Soviet Anti-imperialism

Tsarist Russia pretty much lost out in the scramble for Africa. After Great Britain closed the Suez Canal to Russian ships during the Russo-Turkish War of 1877, Tsar Alexander III dreamed of revenge on the Nile. His plan was to secure a Russian presence on the Red Sea that would "thwart Britain's ambition to control a swath of imperial territory from the Cape of Good Hope to Cairo" and give Russia access to the headwaters of the Nile.[10] Although they never succeeded in their scheme for an Eritrean colony, the Russians did end up assisting Emperor Menelik II in defeating Britain's ally, Italy, at Adowa in 1896. This alliance of Coptic and Orthodox Christendom lasted until World War I and may even have won the tsar some trade-offs from the British in the Far East, but it left the Bolsheviks with a clean slate regarding Africa when they came to power. Indeed, the new Soviet regime's strongest asset in dealing with Africa was its ideological opposition to imperialism. From the outset, the revolutionary Soviet government championed the cause of national liberation in the colonial world. Africa was distant, however, and Lenin focused his early sympathies on nationalists in the immediate environment who could challenge British influence around the borders of the Soviet state. As Robert Legvold puts it, "for the first forty years of Soviet history . . . [Africa] stood on the outermost edge of Soviet consciousness."[11]

Only as the post–World War II wave of nationalism reached African shores did the Soviets begin to pay serious attention. The war in Algeria and its repercussions in Morocco, Tunisia, and Egypt; Nkrumah's push for independence in Ghana; Sekou Touré's sudden breakaway from France— all alerted Moscow to the opportunity to establish the presence that had eluded the tsars. The Soviets were attracted by targets of opportunity much more than by any coherent design. First Nasser appeared to be interested in Soviet support, then Sekou Touré looked eastward. The Soviets did their best to respond, but their early moves tended to be clumsy in an environment about which they knew little.

Egypt became the point of entry when Nasser sought weapons that a West protective of Israel denied him. Nasser's procurement of arms (from

Czechoslovakia) led U.S. Secretary of State John Foster Dulles to renege on an earlier commitment to finance the Aswan Dam. Soviet Premier Nikita Khrushchev quickly offered to build the high dam and then backed Egypt during the Suez crisis of 1956. Western antipathy opened the first door for Soviet sympathy; the Egyptians in turn promised the Soviets further access to anticolonial leaders through a forum like the Afro-Asian People's Solidarity Organization. The Soviet presence in Cairo proved to be a slippery foothold as Nasser himself maneuvered about (before Sadat eventually totally reversed camps); despite Soviet arms and technical assistance, Nasser suppressed the small Egyptian Communist Party and largely pursued his own aims. To a considerable extent, this pattern has been repeated time and again.

Guinea provided the first black African example of a target of opportunity. At first, the prospects looked even more propitious, because unlike the officer Nasser, Sekou Touré was a trade union leader who had had some contact with French communist cadres in "study groups" organized by the party in the colony. Moreover, the abrupt expulsion of Guinea from the French fold in 1958 rendered it particularly needy of external support. The Soviets were prompt to supply arms and economic credits and to invite Sekou Touré to Moscow, where he declared that "we are fighting imperialism and are therefore allies of the world that has chosen freedom and a place for all nations."[12] To the Soviets, Guinea appeared to be a vanguard country ushering in an era of revolutionary change. For a brief period, it became even more than Cairo a center for black African militants from such colonies as Cameroon, Congo-Brazzaville, Angola, Niger, and Côte d'Ivoire. But most of these radical nationalists never came to power (as moderate elements prevailed in most colonies), and Guinean-Soviet relations soured after a brief honeymoon. The Guineans became disillusioned with the quality of Soviet aid and trade (one notorious incident involved the shipment of snowplows to tropical Conakry) and intervention in domestic affairs by an overly zealous ambassador. Sekou Touré brusquely expelled the Soviet diplomat, leaving the Soviet policymakers "gun-shy and suspicious" and henceforth wary of the "unpredictability of African personalities and events."[13]

The rapid pace of African events nevertheless opened up other opportunities for Soviet diplomacy. The assassination of Lumumba and the ideological cleavage over Congo led other governments to seek Soviet support. New candidates for socialist honors appeared on the scene, such as Modibo Keita of Mali and Kwame Nkrumah, as he began to pursue a more radical vision. Similarly, when Algeria acquired independence under Ahmed Ben Bella, Soviet optimism rekindled. Yet, what became increasingly evident was that the former Soviet Union's highest priority was simply to establish a diplomatic presence on the widest scale possible. Although the Soviets had their African favorites, they desired satisfactory working relations with such states as Senegal, Nigeria, Côte d'Ivoire, and Liberia. Their goal was more to be recognized as a great power in dialogue with African states than to subvert the conservative governments in power.

Indeed, China took the Soviet leadership to task for its alleged betrayal of the national liberation revolution in Africa. The Soviets, in fact, were engaged in a dual rivalry for influence on the continent with both China and the United States. China, for example, succeeded in establishing a substantial role in Tanzania and close ties with the Mugabe wing of the Zimbabwean resistance. Chinese Premier Chou En-lai conducted a triumphal tour of progressive African states in 1964, presenting China as a revolutionary model. At the same time, the United States was succeeding in thwarting the radicals from achieving power in Congo. In this context, the Soviets had little choice but to back leaders who professed socialism in order to establish their own credibility as an actor in African affairs.

Throughout the 1960s, however, the Soviet Union had relatively little to show for its efforts. Ben Bella was overthrown in 1965, Nkrumah in 1966, and Modibo Keita in 1968; Sekou Touré, largely discredited by oppressive policies at home, drifted back toward France. Conservative leaders like Senghor and Houphouët-Boigny proved to have more staying power. Looking for whatever partners they might find, the Soviets responded readily to the Nigerian military government's appeal for weapons during the Biafran secession. By the end of the decade, in other words, the Soviet Union's most active ally in West Africa was not a revolutionary regime but a centrist government in need of arms. The relationship revealed two major facets of Soviet policy: pragmatism in the choice of governmental partners and a reliance upon arms deliveries as its principal instrument of influence in Africa.

Over the next decade, the Soviet Union established itself as the world's leading arms dealer in sub-Saharan Africa. From 1975 to 1979 alone, Soviet arms sales to Africa rocketed to about $3.4 billion, a fifteenfold increase over the period from 1965 to 1974; and during 1980–1983, a like amount ($3.87 billion) was again transferred. The bulk of this supply, however, went to only two states, Ethiopia and Angola, new targets of opportunity made available by local conflicts. Beleaguered governments, subject to internal rebellion and external attack, turned to the Soviet Union (and its allies) in order to survive. To be sure, the MPLA had long considered itself a Marxist party and the Ethiopian *derg* eventually convinced itself of the same, but in both cases Soviet access was largely attributable to dire straits and a lack of alternatives.

The collapse of Portuguese colonialism ushered in this new era of Soviet involvement in continental affairs. Although leftist regimes had come to power periodically (in Congo-Brazzaville, Benin, and Madagascar, for example) the abrupt emergence of three new governments professing Marxism (Guinea-Bissau and Mozambique as well as Angola) was unprecedented. The situation in Angola, moreover, took on the dimensions of an obligation—if the Soviets could not defend the MPLA, their reputation as a power in Africa would be dashed. The Soviet Union had long-standing ties to the MPLA as a liberation movement reaching back to the early 1960s. But even in these circumstances, the Soviet government proceeded very cautiously, for it was divided in its assessment of the stakes and the risks of intervention. Its initial policy objective was essentially to secure a place for the MPLA in a coalition government with UNITA and the FNLA.

Jiri Valenta, an expert on Soviet decisionmaking, concludes that Moscow decided to "go for broke" in Angola only after the U.S.-Chinese interventions.[14] Until then, policymakers in both the Ministry of Foreign Affairs and the Ministry of Defense opposed intervention, arguing that it would endanger detente and could prove to be very expensive, as they harbored doubts about the MPLA's ability to prevail. The U.S. involvement, however, unleashed the critics of detente on the eve of the Twenty-fifth Communist Party Congress, placing Leonid Brezhnev in a difficult position. Valenta argues that irresolution on Angola made Brezhnev politically vulnerable at home. He continues: "A tough stand, on the other hand, afforded Brezhnev and his supporters a convenient demonstration to critics at home and abroad that détente was not a 'one-way street,' that the USSR did not 'betray' the revolutionary forces in the Third World, and that Angola would not become another Chile."[15]

A second major factor that reinforced Soviet resolve was Cuban policy. Castro's support for the MPLA was more intense than the Soviet Union's. Agostinho Neto had visited Havana on numerous occasions over the years of the liberation struggle, and he and Castro shared a common ideological outlook. Castro perceived Angola as a test of Cuban revolutionary commitment and believed that he could enhance Cuban prestige in Third World affairs by rallying to the MPLA cause. Although the Cubans, of course, relied on Soviet material and logistical support, Cuba was not so much the proxy as the prod of the Soviet Union. For Cuba the stakes were clear-cut: a gain or a defeat of progressive forces in the Third World.

Valenta's analysis of the Angolan intervention led him to conclude that there was no Soviet "master plan vis-à-vis Africa."[16] On the contrary, as David Albright put it, Soviet policy was reactive and opportunistic: "Key Soviet initiatives have come in response to developments and trends in the African countries themselves and to the behavior of other major outside powers."[17] The scale of the Soviet commitment to Angola went well beyond its previous engagements because Soviet prestige was at stake in a way that it never had been in Guinea or Congo. The pattern was essentially the same, however—namely, to capitalize on changing conditions as the old colonial order crumbled. By the same token, the longer-term outcome was quite similar. The Angolan leaders became wary of the Soviet presence. Economically, the Soviet Union had little to offer, and the Angolans continued to rely on Western oil companies to exploit their major resource. Meddling in domestic affairs in Angola got the Soviet embassy in trouble as it did in Guinea; and even in foreign policy, the Angolans recognized that they had to deal with the United States in order to achieve their goals regarding Namibia and South Africa. Soviet influence was eventually reduced to its role as a counterweight to South Africa.

Mozambique was the East African counterpart of Angola. FRELIMO declared itself a Marxist-Leninist party in 1977, the outcome of a process of ideological evolution during the anticolonial war. The government concluded a Treaty of Friendship and Cooperation with the Soviet Union at about the same time. Engaged in active support of the Patriotic Front in Zimbabwe and the African National Congress in South Africa, it needed military aid, which the Soviets could supply. Embattled even after its independence, it appeared a primary candidate for client status. Called upon by the Mozambicans to support their development, the Soviets responded as best they could, dispatching Bulgarian agronomists, East German engineers, Cuban sugar specialists, and Soviet factory managers to provide technical assistance. For their efforts, the Soviets requested a naval base on the Indian Ocean. Mozambique refused. In this instance, one might have wondered whether it was not the Soviet Union that was the "target of opportunity."

Certainly the Soviet government could only have welcomed the emergence of an ideologically friendly government in Maputo. The Soviets viewed the entire southern African theater as an area ripe for change. When South Africa struck across its borders, as it did against Mozambique early in 1981, the Soviets had to show the flag; when Pretoria armed RENAMO, the Soviets were virtually obliged to provide weapons to FRELIMO. Thus, Mozambique received some $250 million worth of armaments over the period 1978–1982 (significantly less than such states as Libya, Ethiopia, and Angola). Likewise, official exchanges between the two Marxist-Leninist parties were frequent, yet none of this prevented Mozambique from widening its range of diplomatic and economic relations.

In Mozambique, as elsewhere, the Soviets ran afoul of their relatively limited capacity to provide aid and investment beyond the military sector. President Machel traveled to France and Great Britain in 1983 and to the United States in 1985 in search of new trade and finance; in between, he suffered the ignominy of signing a nonaggression pact, the Nkomati Accord, with South Africa. Soviet assistance, in other words, proved inadequate to control RENAMO destabilization. At the same time, Soviet support was crucial to the Front Line States' efforts to effect change in Namibia and South Africa. In the circumstances, the Soviets had to play a role in southern Africa.

The Horn of Africa was perhaps the only part of sub-Saharan Africa in which the Soviets had an active strategic interest. Lying on the Red Sea route from the Mediterranean to the Indian Ocean, the Horn constitutes the southern periphery of the Middle East. From the Soviet perspective, it was desirable that the Red Sea not become a conservative Arab lake; hence, they consistently sought a diplomatic presence in the region. Even while feudalism reigned in Ethiopia, the Soviet Union sought to improve relations with Emperor Haile Selassie through the 1960s. It hopped on the bandwagons of Nimeiri in Sudan and Siad Barre in Somalia when these military men seized power. Somalia appeared well on its way to becoming the major Soviet client in black Africa (it received some $180 million in arms deliveries and a major buildup of naval installations at Berbera) until the coup in Ethiopia. Then, as the leftward-drifting *derg* made overtures to them, the Soviets changed camps, perceiving Ethiopia as the better prize.

To be sure, the Soviet government, assisted by Fidel Castro, first made a valiant effort to reconcile Ethiopia and Somalia. From Moscow, the logic of a solution appeared straightforward: since both states (as well as the Eritrean nationalists, who were to be part of the deal) embraced a socialist ideology, secessionist and irredentist sentiments ought to give way to a federation in the name of the overriding goal of socialism. The logic, moreover, coincided admirably with Soviet interests. Castro managed to bring Siad and Mengistu together at a meeting in Aden (likewise a candidate for the federation in the grand design), but Somalia argued that self-determination for the Ogaden (and Eritrea) should precede federation. Ethiopia preferred just the opposite. The logic of socialism failed to prevail over that of nationalism, forcing the Soviets to choose between partners.

Even then the Soviet policymakers still tried optimistically to keep a foot in both camps, offering Ethiopia arms and Somalia spare parts. They left it to Siad Barre to denounce the Treaty of Friendship and Cooperation in November 1977 before finally undertaking a massive airlift of weaponry and Cuban troops into Addis Ababa. The Soviet shift was really faute de mieux; having alienated Somalia, the Soviets could not allow the dismemberment of Ethiopia. As Marina Ottaway observes, the "new alliance with Mengistu was of little use if it only meant presiding over the disintegration of Ethiopia."[18]

Ethiopia's military needs far outstripped those of earlier clients. From 1977 to 1980, the Soviets supplied nearly $2 billion worth of arms, almost quadruple what Angola purchased and more than ten times what they had supplied to Somalia over the previous decade. This military support, backed by Cuban soldiers, turned the tide in the Ogaden and much of Eritrea. There were in the mid-1980s an estimated four thousand Soviet military and technical advisers, one thousand East German security and intelligence personnel, and a thirteen-thousand-strong Cuban troop contingent still in the country. This commitment to the maintenance of the Ethiopian state and regime became the major Soviet engagement in black Africa.

Yet, the foothold in the Horn ultimately yielded little benefit to the Soviet Union. In exchange for their aid, the Soviets were allowed to establish a major naval-servicing facility in the Dahlak Islands that in effect replaced an earlier base at Berbera in Somalia; this modestly enhanced Soviet naval capability in the Indian Ocean. The Soviets pressed the *derg* to form a workers' party, but the officers never really yielded power to socialist cadres. Despite Ethiopia's apparent dependency, in practice the Soviets were serving Ethiopian national purposes more than vice versa. Eventually, under Gorbachev, the Soviet government came to question the utility of satisfying Mengistu's voracious appetite for armaments, but for a decade the Soviets practiced the classic great power maneuver of inserting military capability into a strife-ridden area.

What was true of the Indian Ocean was likewise true of the Mediterranean. The area was obviously of strategic interest to the former Soviet Union, and North Africa was the site of the earliest Soviet initiatives on the continent. In North Africa as elsewhere, nonetheless, the record shows the Soviet Union reacting to local leaders' appeals. As an early practitioner of the art of playing East against West, Nasser turned to the communist world for arms. Fifteen years later, as Egypt veered back toward the West under Sadat, Libya's Qaddafi sought Nasser's mantle as pan-Arab leader and similarly armed his military with Soviet equipment. In each instance, the Soviet Union had a complicated relationship with its North African partner. What Moscow provided, in effect, were the means by which these states pursued relatively independent foreign policies.

Khrushchev considered Nasser to be one of the major Third World leaders. Thus, he backed him at Suez in 1956, as later Brezhnev would agree to rearm him after the disastrous Six-Day War in 1967. Until Sadat's reversal of alliances after the 1973 war, Egypt was by far the major recipient of Soviet arms—in fact, it received more arms than all the rest of Africa combined. To be sure, Soviet aid to Egypt was more a function of its Middle Eastern than its African policy. Most important of all, however, was Nasser's desire to free himself of dependency upon the West. Thus, despite Nasser's harsh treatment of the Egyptian communists and despite his more markedly nationalist than socialist orientation, the Soviets judged his regime to be worthy of support. The relationship did entail access to submarine-servicing facilities in Alexandria (which Sadat closed in 1976); while this was of considerable utility to the Soviet navy, it was not the rationale for the relationship. It was a side-payment in the larger deal by which the Soviets underwrote Egyptian anti-imperialism.

Libya later replaced Egypt in this regard. Long before Qaddafi appeared on the scene, the Soviet Union somewhat halfheartedly proposed that it assume trusteeship responsibility over Libya after World War II. Instead, Libya was rather quickly granted independence under a conservative monarchy that accepted the United States and Great Britain as protectors.

The discovery of oil subsequently gave the country potential influence, but King Idris had few international ambitions. The United States enjoyed the use of Wheelus Air Force Base, but otherwise nobody paid much attention to the country. Colonel Qaddafi's 1969 coup abruptly changed the givens of the situation; he ejected the Americans from Wheelus and embarked upon a foreign policy hostile to U.S. influence in both the Middle East and Africa. Especially after the death of Nasser in 1970, the Soviets took interest in this new revolutionary regime. Qaddafi did not have the stature of Nasser, but he did have plenty of petrodollars. Libyan activism not only disconcerted the West, but it poured hard currency into the Soviet treasury. The Soviets never hesitated to sell Qaddafi what he ordered.

Thus, by the mid-1980s, Libya's 55,000-person army, the largest per capita force in Africa, had no less than 2,900 tanks (Egypt by comparison had 2,100 tanks for its army of 340,000, which was Africa's largest in absolute terms). Overall, Libya built up the highest ratio of armaments to soldiers in the world, a very costly arsenal valued at about $12 billion, roughly two-thirds of which was purchased from the Soviet arms industry. Libya thus displaced Egypt as the major African recipient of Soviet weaponry, far outstripping Ethiopia and Angola as well. Libya's maverick status is distinctive, yet the same pattern of policy may be discerned in all these "client" relationships. In each case, a regime that has broken with the past has called upon the Soviet Union for assistance. In each instance, the Soviet government has responded to the call in the name of anti-imperialist solidarity. What was primarily at stake from the Soviet perspective was its own reputation as a great power capable of assisting radical forces.

The Soviet-Libyan relationship was an "alliance at arm's length" in which the Soviets saw Libya "more as a wealthy trading partner than as a reliable political ally."[19] Qaddafi refused Soviet requests for bases on Libyan soil; only in 1981, when relations heated up with the Reagan administration, did he grant naval visiting rights. The Libyan leader is ideologically a pan-Muslim activist, certainly not a Marxist. The Soviets, in turn, gave only the faintest endorsement to Libyan involvement in the Chadian civil war, and they were aware that Qaddafi's destabilization activities elsewhere were largely counterproductive. Even at arm's length, the alliance for some time courted the risk of a serious clash with the United States, which adopted strong anti-Libyan policies in the 1980s.

The Soviet role in North Africa has been essentially as an arms merchant and a political guarantor. This has been as true of Soviet relations with Algeria as with Egypt and Libya. In the Maghreb, however, the Soviets never became involved on the same scale. During the Algerian war, Khrushchev was extremely cautious in his contacts with the FLN. The reasons for Soviet restraint stemmed from European, not African concerns. Khrushchev saw in President de Gaulle a potential challenger to U.S. hegemony in Western Europe. For fear of alienating de Gaulle, the Soviets maintained a low profile on the Algerian question. Only when de Gaulle himself had come to terms with Algerian nationalism did the Soviets venture closer ties.

Algeria encouraged technical assistance, and the Soviets aided them to set up an oil engineering institute and a steel plant, but here as elsewhere the major bond became arms sales. Recognizing Algeria as an influential leader in Third World affairs, they maintained a cordial relationship but never acquired any leverage over Algerian decisionmaking. If anything, Boumedienne challenged the Soviet Union to prove itself the balancer of U.S. power, especially in the Middle East. Algeria increased its arms purchases substantially once the conflict with Morocco over Western Sahara began, but the Soviets refrained from fully endorsing the Algerian position. They preferred a more ambiguous policy that allowed them to maintain a profitable economic arrangement with Morocco in the phosphate industry. Despite the fact that Algeria ranks third among African states (behind Libya and Egypt) in overall arms deliveries from Soviet stockpiles, the Soviet Union never acquired any significant foothold in the country.

Soviet policy in Africa, it is apparent, focused on the Mediterranean states. The bulk of Soviet arms transfers went to the northern tier of Algeria, Libya, and Egypt. After 1955, Soviet influence waxed and waned in this region intimately connected to the Middle East. The Soviet presence in sub-Saharan Africa was modest. Even during the period of severe strife in Angola and Ethiopia, only 10 percent of total Soviet arms transfers went to black Africa and 90 percent of that was concentrated in five states. The Soviets became engaged south of the Sahara principally on behalf of Afro-Marxist governments. Engaged in a global geopolitical competition with the West, the Soviets were compelled, as Robert Grey argued, "to help defend the threatened 'states of socialist orientation.'"[20]

Finally, with regard to southernmost Africa, the Soviet Union became the foremost arms supplier to SWAPO and the ANC. These policies prompted the South African government to proclaim that they were under assault from global communism. In fact the actual outlay of weapons was not very great, just enough to keep the ANC going; indeed, some observers conjectured that the Soviets were content simply to watch the situation fester as an example of the evils of capitalism. In the late 1980s, however, as discussed in greater detail below, the Soviets adopted a much more pragmatic attitude based on negotiated reform in South Africa. This shift in Soviet policy no doubt reflected a belief that the era of revolutionary opportunity was waning. Over three decades, the Soviets responded to anti-imperialist initiatives arising in Africa. In the process, they demonstrated the capacity to project power—essentially military capability—onto distant shores. In the turmoil of the postcolonial era, the Soviet Union acted like other historic great powers, becoming entangled here, overextended there, and suffering its share of setbacks, because it dared not leave the field to other competitors.

■ U.S. Anticommunism

Like the former Soviet Union, the United States knew little of Africa when decolonization began. Through normal channels of diplomatic and commercial relations and through aid programs, it acquired a minimal foothold on the continent. Perhaps the most original feature of the U.S. approach to Africa has been the Peace Corps, which has provided a distinctive brand of grassroots people-to-people technical assistance. Indeed, service in the Peace Corps has probably produced the largest body of U.S. citizens with a sound understanding of Africa's development problems. Top policymakers, on the other hand, have rarely had direct contact with Africa. Visits by U.S. presidents or secretaries of state, especially to black Africa, have been few and far between. Although President Bill Clinton's twelve-day visit to the continent in 1998 broke this pattern, Africa has been a low priority historically, and U.S. policy has suffered as a result.

The United States observed the passing of colonialism in Africa with a mix of approval and apprehension. On the one hand, the U.S. heritage was anticolonial; the national instinct was to applaud the advance from European rule to self-government. On the other hand, African nationalism emerged during the Cold War and challenged the hegemony of the West on the continent. As European control receded, some U.S. policymakers worried about the political evolution of the continent. Vice President Richard Nixon was present to celebrate Ghana's independence in 1957—after all, Kwame Nkrumah had studied in the United States before emerging as the leader of Ghanaian nationalism. Yet, anticolonialism was an unpredictable force, as the Ghanaian pan-Africanist himself turned out to be; rather than wholehearted support of independence across Africa, U.S. policy leaned toward damage limitation. When Congo erupted in disorder in 1960, the Eisenhower administration feared major damage to Western interests. Much of U.S. policy during the Cold War era was influenced by what Henry Jackson called the "Congo syndrome."[21]

We have seen, in Chapter 11, how the Congo crisis catalyzed divisions within Africa. By the same token, East and West differed sharply over who should govern the rich but unstable ex-Belgian preserve. At the center of this controversy was the passionate and charismatic Patrice Lumumba,[22] fervently committed to the territorial integrity of his country, which was immediately threatened by Belgian intervention and the secession of Katanga Province. Although his government turned first to the United States for aid in quelling the secession (aid that was refused), Lumumba was deeply mistrusted in Washington, notably by the CIA, which promptly established a station in Leopoldville that hatched a plot to assassinate him.

The Eisenhower administration elected to deal with the Congo crisis through the United Nations, an approach initially supported by the Soviet Union and most Third World governments as well. Moscow assumed that ONUC would assist Premier Lumumba in restoring control over the country; Washington hoped that the UN presence would allow pro-Western factions to assert themselves (and, by the same token, render unilateral Soviet intervention difficult). The outcome bore out U.S. hopes. First President Kasavubu and next Colonel Mobutu challenged Lumumba's authority; the UN force abetted Mobutu's coup; Lumumba was cut off from his power base, subsequently taken into custody by Mobutu's army, and then transferred to Katanga, where he was murdered. With the help of Lumumba's internal enemies, the CIA got what it wanted; this grim episode marked the U.S. entry into significant involvement in postcolonial Africa. The Congo syndrome, the fear of radical nationalism in Africa, had already taken hold.

The perception of Africa as part of a "global East-West chessboard"[23] largely governed U.S. policy after the Congo crisis. Although there were always critics of this globalist approach, they rarely prevailed in policy debate. Democratic administrations sometimes cautiously challenged this orthodoxy, but the anticommunist impulse remained strong. The Carter administration made the most determined effort to deal with Africa in regional rather than globalist terms, but it was seriously divided within; when Carter's national security adviser, Zbigniew Brzezinski, declared that "SALT lies buried in the sands of Ogaden," he revealed the irrepressible propensity to situate African issues on the Soviet-U.S. chessboard. As a result, the United States was often supportive of reactionary and repressive regimes so long as they appeared staunchly anticommunist.

U.S. policy toward Congo is a primary example of this. Even after the death of Lumumba, the United States remained concerned that his followers would seize power. The State Department and the CIA remained actively involved in Leopoldville in support of pro-Western centrists like Cyrille Adoula, whom the Kennedy administration deemed better suited than Kasavubu or Mobutu to contain the leftists. In order to strengthen the Adoula government, Kennedy collaborated with the UN operation to end the Katanga secession. By mid-1964, however, with the departure of ONUC, civil war flared again, and the United States flew to the support of the central government now led by the ex-secessionist Moise Tshombe. Authorizing mercenary forces and a Belgian paratroop drop into Stanleyville, U.S. officials rescued the Tshombe government in 1964; when it appeared in 1965 that Tshombe was losing political control, the CIA encouraged Mobutu to carry out his second coup.[24] Congo became a major recipient of economic aid and the second-largest U.S. arms client in black Africa. Despite incontrovertible evidence of human rights abuses and economic mismanagement, the U.S. supported Mobutu's regime until his overthrow by Laurent Kabila, hailing him as a "good friend" and wise leader for whom U.S. officials professed "a warm spot in our hearts."[25]

Such warmth was fueled by cobalt, copper, and other mineral resources, but especially by Congo's sprawling strategic dimensions. The corruption of the Mobutu regime was deemed tolerable so long as it kept Congo in the Western camp. Under Carter, the United States distanced itself somewhat from Mobutu but supported France in its Shaba rescue operations—the critical objective was not so much direct U.S. influence as securing the government's Western orientation. Belgium failed in this task, and the United States reacted accordingly.

Otherwise, until 1975, the United States refrained from substantial involvement elsewhere in black Africa so long as French or British influence appeared adequate. When the Nigerian civil war erupted, Secretary of State Dean Rusk frankly declared that this was Britain's sphere of influence; likewise, the United States largely deferred to British policy regarding Rhodesia. Thus, the only major U.S. involvement during the 1960s was in Ethiopia, bereft of a European guarantor. Despite Haile Selassie's autocratic regime, Ethiopia became a major recipient of U.S. economic and military aid; indeed, before it became the number one Soviet arms client in black Africa, it had the distinction of being the number one U.S. client. The United States set up a major communications station at Kagnew (in Eritrea) that was useful in monitoring the Middle East, Africa, and the Indian Ocean. U.S. policy was to support the regime for its virtue of being anticommunist. The deposing of Haile Selassie was a rude blow, but the United States initially hoped to retain influence with the new military leadership. Arms flowed unabated during the postcoup transitional period until it became apparent that the left wing of the army was in control. When Mengistu reversed alliances, the United States discovered Somalia. U.S. policy in the Horn was generally comparable to that in Congo, its objective to contain Soviet influence by aiding friendly autocrats.

The changes in the Horn occurred in the midst of other major events that pushed Africa much higher among U.S. foreign policy concerns. Just as the withdrawal of Portugal changed Soviet opportunities, so too did it jolt U.S. policymakers into heightened awareness of the instabilities of southern Africa. If SALT was eventually to decay in Ogaden, Soviet-U.S. détente was first shaken by the conflict over Angola. Secretary of State Henry Kissinger interpreted the struggle for power there as a Soviet-U.S. confrontation; declaring détente "indivisible," Kissinger warned the Soviet Union against any response to his decision to release CIA funds to the FNLA. He thereby transformed an intra-Angolan battle into a Cold War proxy battleground.

Earlier U.S. policy toward Angola typified U.S. ambivalence toward African nationalism. Under President Kennedy, the government initiated modest and discrete assistance to Holden Roberto, at the time widely perceived as the most authoritative Angolan leader. Kennedy, who in 1957 had distinguished himself on the Senate floor by a speech in favor of Algerian independence, sought to distance U.S. policy from Portugal's colonial wars. The Johnson administration cut back on this aid in deference to Portugal (whose Azore Islands provided a mid-Atlantic link on military flights to the Middle East), and the Nixon administration terminated it altogether. Arguing that "the whites are here to stay" throughout southern Africa, Kissinger advised Nixon to "relax political isolation and economic restrictions on the white states."[26] From Kennedy's to Kissinger's analysis lay a considerable gulf, but neither saw Angola as a major theater until Kissinger rediscovered the FNLA.

Kissinger's intervention in Angola was a huge fiasco. He miscalculated the capability of the FNLA, misjudged the local situation, and gravely underestimated the reaction of Cuba and the Soviet Union. Kissinger professed disbelief that his authorization of $300,000 of covert aid ("to buy bicycles [and] paper clips") could have sparked the Soviet aid that subsequently alarmed him. Yet, as Gerald Bender argues, "the aid indicated that the United States had decided to meddle in Angolan affairs even before the transitional government had an opportunity to prove whether or not it could work" and reinforced "the large amounts of support which China [and Congo] had been giving to the FNLA at the same time."[27] Once the fighting escalated, Kissinger overruled the objections of the State Department's Africa Bureau and pushed through a major increase in (still covert) aid to the FNLA and, at this point, to UNITA as well. Bender demonstrates that there was no significant difference in the overall amount of the combined external assistance—Soviet and Cuban, on the one hand; U.S., French, British, Belgian, Chinese, and South African, on the other—to the warring parties between July and October 1975. As we have seen, the difference on the external scale ultimately turned upon the willingness of Cuba to send troops. Kissinger's proxy failed him; his globalist analysis merely succeeded in creating a military solution to a situation that probably could have been resolved diplomatically.

The U.S. decision to intervene, however futilely, in Angola stemmed from the same fear of communism capturing African nationalism that had motivated Eisenhower's policy in Congo. Kissinger had little genuine knowledge of Africa and overrode those who had more. He subsequently ran into a congressional roadblock in the form of the Clark Amendment, which officially prohibited aid to the warring parties from 1976 through 1985. The debacle in Angola, however, alerted Kissinger to the fact that southern Africa was not the stable bastion of white supremacy that he had imagined.

U.S. policy toward Rhodesia/Zimbabwe began to shift as a result. Until 1976 the United States had given little attention to the conflict there, limiting itself to a posture of generally backing British policy toward the breakaway Smith regime. Even this policy was severely compromised by the 1971 passage of the Byrd Amendment, which had the dubious effect of setting the United States in violation of United Nations sanctions against

Rhodesia. Ostensibly a measure to avert U.S. dependence on the Soviet Union for strategic minerals, the real intent of the Byrd Amendment (sponsored by an old-guard conservative senator from Virginia) was to help Ian Smith by importing Rhodesian chrome. Anthony Lake has shown that the Nixon administration did nothing to deter this legislation despite its harmful impact on U.S. relations with Africa.[28]

Kissinger traveled to Zambia in 1976 to usher in, as he put it, "a new era in American policy" devoted to "self-determination, majority rule, equal rights, and human dignity." Racial justice, Kissinger now stated, was "not simply a matter of foreign policy but an imperative of our own moral heritage."[29] This newfound sensitivity was, in fact, a tribute to the changing balance of power in southern Africa; the secretary of state undertook one of his patented exercises in shuttle diplomacy in September. The package that he negotiated with Ian Smith unraveled quickly, and Kissinger was denied a final diplomatic coup; nor was he entitled to one on the basis of his African policy. On the contrary, the shift revealed how ill chosen the Nixon-Ford southern Africa policy had been. By counting on Portuguese and Rhodesian colonialism as bulwarks against communism, U.S. policy misread both power and principle.

More genuinely than Henry Kissinger, it was the Carter administration that ushered in a new era of southern African policy. UN Ambassador Andrew Young gave Africa high priority. Leaving a Rhodesian settlement primarily to British responsibility, he zeroed in on the Namibia issue. Both Vice President Walter Mondale and Secretary of State Cyrus Vance exerted pressure on Pretoria to accept Namibian independence; Young worked at the United Nations to secure Resolution 435, which called for a UN presence to monitor a transition to self-government there. This was the most sustained U.S. engagement on behalf of majority rule in southern Africa; it came from an administration that shelved the global chessboard in favor of a regional analysis. This policy eventually succeeded in moving the South African government to a negotiating conference in January 1981. Here, however, the process stopped, for the November 1980 election had relieved the pressure on South Africa.

Instead, the old era returned in the retailored garb of "constructive engagement," a policy proposal that earned Chester Crocker the job of assistant secretary of state for African affairs in the Reagan administration. Crocker offered an amended version of "the whites are here to stay" argument. According to Crocker, the Afrikaners faced an "awesome political dilemma" in the face of which it was not the place of the United States to choose between black and white.[30] In theory, constructive engagement was to encourage South Africa gradually toward racial equality and self-rule in Namibia; in practice, Crocker linked the withdrawal of South Africa from Namibia to the withdrawal of Cuban troops from Angola. Once again, U.S. priorities reverted to the specter of communism in Africa. In its sympathy for the awesome plight of the Afrikaners and its antipathy for the harassed Angolans (subject both to direct South African attack and indirect South African subversion via UNITA), the Reagan administration turned back the clock to the vintage Kissinger era.

Crocker's solicitude for South Africa, in fact, had even deeper roots in U.S. policy. As early as 1950, a State Department official observing southern Africa declared it "gratifying to single out a region of ten million square miles in which no significant inroads have been made by communism, and to be able to characterize the area as relatively stable and secure."[31] This relative stability was perceived as a valuable strategic asset, protecting the Cape route and assuring access to harbors, communications bases, and minerals. South African administration of Namibia was an integral component of this apparent oasis of Western security. Through the 1950s, the United States was reluctant to disturb the status quo, even abstaining on General Assembly resolutions condemning apartheid. The Kennedy administration changed the rhetoric and voted for a voluntary arms embargo in 1963, but only after negotiating a weapons sale in return for a space-tracking station in 1962. Backsliding occurred under the Johnson administration, which was loath to jeopardize the Cape passage for "ships en route to and from Viet-Nam waters."[32] Although apartheid was a considerable embarrassment to U.S. policymakers, the realpolitik of anticommunism often overwhelmed moral qualms.

The Carter administration's emphasis on human rights was the first serious attempt to dissociate the United States from South Africa. Carter's policy focused particularly upon Namibia as the most likely issue on which to make progress. Since 1966, the United States had formally endorsed Namibia's right to independence under UN stewardship, but in practice Namibian rights remained hostage to the larger concern to accommodate Pretoria. A mild case of the Congo syndrome afflicted Washington insofar as the South West African People's Organization was concerned. Like other liberation movements, SWAPO received some aid from the Soviet Union. During the Carter years, SWAPO was treated as a legitimate representative of Namibian opinion, and it in turn cooperated with the Western effort to implement Resolution 435. The Carter interlude demonstrated that U.S. pressure could have some impact upon South African policy. The return of globalist thinking to the White House in 1981, however, once again checked Namibian independence on the strategic chessboard. The Cuba-Namibia linkage realigned Washington with Pretoria in the view of Africans.

U.S. willingness to accommodate South Africa was in part attributable to economic interests. Many U.S. corporations had invested in the country: the nearly $3 billion in direct capital investment by 1983 constituted by far the largest U.S. holdings anywhere on the continent. There was also some $4 billion worth of annual trade. Investment and trade certainly served to shore up the white government, but they did not suffice to explain U.S. policy. Rather, from the 1950s into the 1980s, the United States was soft on apartheid because the South African regime was hard on communism. However abhorrent the racial legislation of the Afrikaners, white rule was perceived as a lesser evil than the prospect of Soviet influence. The fear of communist gains—the Congo syndrome—shaped U.S. policy on southern Africa for decades, constructive engagement being merely one prominent expression of this outlook. Violence in South Africa (see Chapter 13) ultimately discredited constructive engagement and prompted Congress to pass stiff economic sanctions against apartheid in 1986. This shift in U.S. policy (enacted over a presidential veto) was a factor, among the several others discussed below, that eventually led to major changes in southern Africa.

Although the United States was relatively less involved in trans-Saharan Africa, where French influence remained strong, it nevertheless treated the area as another Cold War battleground. The crucial arena for the United States was the northern tier of Arab states from Morocco to Egypt; here, as elsewhere, it worried about radical regimes—initially that of Nasser, then that of Ben Bella, but especially that of Qaddafi. The corollary has been to assist friendly regimes: the heftiest aid has gone to Nasser's successors, Sadat and Hosni Mubarak, and to King Hassan of Morocco, especially once he became embroiled in the war over Western Sahara.

U.S. relations with Nasser's Egypt were often stormy, more as a consequence of Nasser's Middle Eastern than his African policies. But the United States acknowledged Nasser as an independent leader, comparable in stature to Nehru of India and Tito of Yugoslavia. However exasperating Nasser's policies, however extensive Soviet aid became, U.S. policymakers did not see him as primarily a Soviet puppet; over the Nasser years, the United States watched warily from a respectful distance. The relationship changed dramatically under Sadat, not immediately in 1970 nor even in 1972 when Sadat expelled the Soviet military advisers; on the contrary, Sadat had to go to war in 1973 to seize Kissinger's attention. Once Kissinger embarked upon shuttle diplomacy in the Middle East, however, the United States became extremely solicitous of Egypt's welfare. Sadat became convinced that he needed the United States to achieve his aims in the Sinai, and the United States poured military and economic aid into Cairo so that he would not change his mind. Sadat's spectacular journey to Jerusalem in 1977 and the Camp David Agreement of 1978 made the U.S. commitment even stronger.

Egypt's reversal of alliances was akin to and roughly contemporaneous with that of Ethiopia. The United States responded to Egypt's wants much as the Soviet Union did to Ethiopia's. In each case, the superpower disbursed aid for the sake of influence; in each instance, the African state sought to secure vital goals through external support. Sadat's shift to a pro-Western orientation was especially welcome in light of other events that reduced Western influence in the large Middle Eastern–Mediterranean region. Of paramount concern to U.S. policymakers were the fall of the shah of Iran, the Soviet intervention in Afghanistan, the possible vulnerability of oil sources, and the growing activism of Qaddafi's Libya. Sadat's willingness to cooperate with the U.S. Rapid Deployment Force was a strategic windfall in these circumstances.

Whereas the United States had grudgingly respected Nasser, it viewed his would-be political successor, Qaddafi, as a serious threat to U.S. interests. Libya and the United States clashed violently on a number of occasions during the 1980s. The United States charged Libya with responsibility for the 1988 destruction of a U.S. civilian airliner over Lockerbie, Scotland, and subsequently convinced the UN Security Council to impose sanctions and an arms embargo on Libya for its refusal to hand over two suspects. These sanctions, as suggested in Chapter 11, severely limited Libya's influence in the 1990s.

Although somewhat perturbed by Morocco's takeover of Western Sahara, the United States generally has regarded King Hassan as a valuable and reliable ally in both Arab and African affairs. Like South Africa, Morocco has been considered strategically important to Western interests, leading successive U.S. administrations to maintain friendly ties with the monarchy. While officially favoring a self-determination referendum in the desert territory, the United States has been reluctant to do anything that might destabilize the king. Throughout the Cold War era, Washington's tilt toward Morocco took its toll on U.S. relations with Algeria.

Policy toward Algeria illustrates well some of the shortcomings of the globalist approach to Africa. When inserted onto the global chessboard, Algeria looked like a Soviet gain: for a long time, it acquired most of its armaments from Moscow, and it pursued a vigorous anti-imperialist foreign policy, loudly criticizing U.S. policy in Vietnam, in Central America, in the Middle East, and in Congo, Angola, and South Africa. Yet, as we have seen, Soviet interests did not determine Algerian policy, nor did the former Soviet Union ever acquire significant strategic advantages there. Moreover, Algeria's trade has been predominantly with the West, and for a period in the late 1970s the United States was its major trading partner (for exports of oil and natural gas). The globalist model could make little sense of these data. The regionalist model readily attributed Algerian support of national liberation movements to its own historical experience, its backing of Polisario to the immediate geopolitical environment, and its trade pattern to economic pragmatism. Throughout the period of the Cold War, U.S. policy was handicapped by the globalist approach in dealing with nationalist states like Algeria.

As we saw in Chapter 11, the wars in Western Sahara and Chad became major issues in African international relations. The instabilities triggered by these conflicts affected many states in trans-Saharan Africa and beyond. The U.S. government did not bring much fresh thought to these problems in trans-Saharan Africa. Just as earlier it approached difficult transitions in Congo/Zaire and Angola with simple models of East-West competition, so too did U.S. policy toward the Maghreb settle for simplified categories of friends and enemies. The elevation of King Hassan to the status of guardian of Western interests in northern Africa actually constrained U.S. options. The policy was perfectly representative, however, of the anticommunist guideline that long governed the U.S. approach to Africa.

Throughout the Cold War, therefore, Soviet and U.S. strategic policies were mirror images. The United States tried to contain Soviet influence, whereas the Soviet Union sought to establish a presence in the wake of colonial rule. Both states sought to channel the changes of the postcolonial era in directions favorable to their own interests. The Soviets capitalized on anti-imperialist sentiment when they could, and the United States all too often invested in conservative regimes. Both states largely respected France's residual sphere of influence. All three exercised the classic role of great powers toward weak states, intervening in an environment highly susceptible to external influence, sometimes directly and sometimes through proxies. African governments in turn exploited the bipolar power structure to gain what advantages they could. Thus, the decline of the Cold War in the late 1980s introduced major changes in Africa.

■ DÉTENTE IN AFRICA

At the Moscow summit in June 1988, President Reagan announced that "Mr. Gorbachev and I agreed that there must be peaceful solutions to [regional] conflicts."[33] The Angola/Namibia accords were one of the first fruits of the rapprochement between the former Soviet Union and the United States that began as Gorbachev fashioned perestroika at home and what he called the "new political thinking" abroad. As a specialist on Soviet foreign policy observed:

> One cannot appreciate the evolving Soviet position in southern Africa outside of the overall context of Gorbachev's new political priorities and foreign policy agenda. Highest on that agenda is the revitalization of Soviet society and the reform of its economic structures. Next is a regularization of relations with the United States. . . . The agreements . . . on Angola and Namibia must be seen as part of an overall package designed to lay the foundations for a long period of Soviet-American and Soviet-Western cooperation.[34]

The Soviet leader knew that an earlier round of détente had begun to founder in Angola. He was keenly aware of the importance that the Reagan Administration attached to the issue of Cuban troops in Angola. The shift in Soviet policy, coupled with military developments on the ground in southern Africa, enabled U.S. Assistant Secretary of State for African Affairs Crocker finally to effect the linkage that he had long sought.

The military offensives of 1987–1988 (discussed in Chapter 11) were costly for all concerned. Herman Cohen, who was Crocker's successor and his associate in the Angola/Namibia negotiations, observed that the hostilities provoked "growing domestic opposition within the South African white community to what appeared to be an unbending and increasingly expensive military commitment in southern Angola and northern Namibia."[35] Once Pretoria indicated that it was willing to pull out of Angola and to implement UN Resolution 435, Crocker appealed to the Soviets to convince the Angolans and the Cubans to cooperate. For a while, negotiations bogged down over the timetable for Cuban redeployment and eventual withdrawal. The Soviets pressed their allies to make concessions on the timing; they did, and Crocker commended the Soviet Union for its "important and constructive role" in the negotiations.[36]

The disaffection of South African public opinion was all the more significant because of a host of domestic woes there: "a collapsed currency, sustained capital export and private capital flight, no fresh money from abroad, reduced access to imported technology, growing black unemployment, higher inflation and interest rates, and declining white living standards."[37] These problems were attributable to internal unrest and external financial sanctions, the latter of which were imposed by numerous foreign governments (in the U.S. case, as we saw, imposed by Congress over a presidential veto). Yet if pressure on South Africa was a necessary condition, the evolution in Soviet policy was also critical in achieving the Tripartite Accord. Change in the Soviet approach to the struggle in South Africa itself was a further key variable. After years of rhetorical support for armed revolution in South Africa, Moscow began in the latter 1980s to emphasize peaceful negotiations as the appropriate policy, expressing the need "to behave more realistically, more flexibly, with every side participating in the [resolution] of the conflicts."[38] Anatoly Adamishin, deputy foreign minister and Crocker's counterpart in the Namibia negotiations, declared that "we have common interests with Americans in stabilization in the region."[39] In 1989 Soviet diplomats began to visit South Africa amidst intimations of the establishment of diplomatic relations. By 1991 there was little discernible difference in the broad lines of Soviet and U.S. policy regarding South Africa: both favored reform through negotiation.

Having pursued a policy of "targets of opportunity" in Africa, Soviet analysts appeared to have concluded by the end of the 1980s that the targets were moving and the opportunities were missed. They made no real effort to dissuade the Mozambicans when they began to turn to the West in the early 1980s. Whether it was a lack of resources or fear of a damaging clash with South Africa or both, the Soviets rather meekly surrendered their earlier preeminence in Maputo, leading one observer to comment on "Soviet ambivalence toward Africa" as early as 1985.[40] Similarly, Soviet policymakers appeared anxious to reduce their role in the Ethiopian quagmire: military and technical assistance to the Mengistu government declined in the latter 1980s, and Moscow sent signals to the Ethiopians of the desirability of a political solution to the Eritrean war. When exploratory talks subsequently began with the Eritrean People's Liberation Front, they took place not in Leningrad but in Atlanta, Georgia, under the auspices of former President Carter. Africa did not loom large in the "new political thinking" of Gorbachev. The optimism concerning the continent's, and especially the southern region's, potential for revolution had dissipated. By the end of the 1980s, Soviet aspirations were largely limited to participation in multilateral diplomatic undertakings to resolve conflict.

The withdrawal of Cuban troops, completed in July 1991, achieved a long-standing U.S. policy objective, but the Tripartite Agreement did not entirely resolve the Angolan question so far as the United States was concerned. There remained the issue of national reconciliation between the MPLA government and the UNITA forces under Jonas Savimbi. Having armed UNITA under the Reagan Doctrine (a policy of assisting anticommunist guerrillas in the Third World), the United States continued to press for an accommodation between Savimbi's movement and the MPLA government. The civil war continued in Angola until a cease-fire was achieved in 1991—only to break down again after September 1992 elections, the results of which Savimbi refused to accept. A sustained UN mediatory effort approached a more stable settlement in 1994, but this ultimately broke down in 1998. Savimbi, largely deprived of external support, remained a spoiler in Angolan politics.

Despite the long epilogue in Angola, the Tripartite Agreement marked the end of an era in U.S. policy, as in Soviet policy. Largely freed of serious concerns about Soviet expansionism in Africa, the Bush administration pledged itself to promote a negotiated political settlement in South Africa and democratization elsewhere on the continent. Détente thus had concrete consequences in Africa as elsewhere—but it proved to be a transitional period. With the stunning disintegration of the Soviet Union in 1991, the parameters of the state system were substantially redefined.

■ AFRICA IN THE NEW MULTIPOLAR SYSTEM

The end of the bipolar era had many consequences for Africa's place in world politics. With no East-West strategic chessboard left on the table, external powers reevaluated their interests on the continent. Many observers agreed with John Harbeson that "Africa became . . . even more peripheral to the international political and economic order."[41] Certainly the 1990s represented a period of relative disengagement from Africa by the major powers—with the exception of France. Yet, while Africa's perceived importance in the global balance of power declined during this period, numerous theaters of violence erupted on the continent that could not be ignored by other states. African states affected by the refugee flows, market disruptions, and general instability occasioned by a series of crises—in Somalia, Rwanda, Congo, Liberia, Sierra Leone, Burundi—appealed to international institutions to intervene in order to stem the rash of state breakdowns that threatened the stability of various regional balances.

Probably the paradigmatic case of post–Cold War state collapse occurred in Somalia. No government moved rapidly to address the breakdown of the Somali state, but the United Nations was summoned to offer assistance. Secretary General Boutros Boutros-Ghali named an experienced Algerian diplomat, Mohamed Sahnoun, as his special representative to Somalia, and Sahnoun in turn won agreement from the competing warlords for a small UN peacekeeping presence.[42] Yet, the modest UN force did not have the means to stem a burgeoning humanitarian crisis in the war-torn country. Scenes of suffering and starvation beamed by the U.S. media pushed President Bush into authorizing a U.S.-sponsored operation to protect the NGOs whose efforts to distribute food were being harassed by the warring factions. Dubbed "Operation Restore Hope" by Bush and known officially as the United Task Force (UNITAF), this international coalition numbered some 38,000 at its peak in January 1993.[43] The operation achieved its immediate humanitarian goals effectively, but was less successful in laying the groundwork for an amplified UN peacekeeping force (UNOSOM II) that took over from UNITAF in May 1993.

Neither the U.S. government nor the United Nations gave adequate attention to the fundamental issues confronting Somalis: "the nature, prospects, and timing of reconciliation [among the factions], what would be needed to rebuild Somalia's institutions, how to disarm and demobilize the militias, the best approach to the faction leaders, and a definition of success and the 'endgame.'"[44] The consequences of this omission took the form of a murderous clash in which the forces of warlord Mohamed Farah Aideed killed twenty-four Pakistani peacekeepers in June 1993. Later that year, eighteen U.S. soldiers serving in UNOSOM II (although under U.S. command) died in an operation intended to arrest Aideed. The U.S. casualties caused extreme political embarrassment to President Bill Clinton, who ordered the U.S. contingent in UNOSOM II withdrawn by the end of March 1994. Over the next year, the other national contingents were progressively withdrawn on the recommendation of a UN envoy who concluded that "UNOSOM had, in effect, achieved all that it could achieve in Somalia."[45]

The various UN-sponsored interventions saved innocent lives in Somalia, but never succeeded in restoring stable political institutions. Moreover, the murderous debacles of June and October 1993 dampened the early post–Cold War enthusiasm about a new world order of international peacekeeping and humanitarian intervention. The very collapse of Somalia reduced the incentive to devote sustained international resources to reconstructing the divided country. Thus, the U.S. and the UN did intervene to deal with extreme crises, but did not stay the course in the face of local resistance to their presence.

The situation in Liberia revealed a similar disposition to limit extracontinental commitments to resolving civil strife—despite appeals by ECOWAS for larger-scale international support for its own effort there via ECOMOG. When the multilateral force was drawn into a second round of armed confrontation with Charles Taylor's NPFL in October 1992, ECOWAS appealed to both the OAU and the UN to back its operations in Liberia. A UN mediator, Trevor Gordon-Somers, played a helpful role in negotiating the 1993 Cotonou Accord, which restored a semblance of order to the country. What struck many observers, however, was the relative absence of the United States in addressing Liberia's civil war. As Liberia had long been considered a kind of U.S. "protectorate," the unwillingness of both the Bush and Clinton administrations to provide major relief to the country (after years of relatively generous aid to the dictator Samuel Doe) was another sign of disengagement. In fact, Liberia's plight was made worse by a rather discreet French effort to fill the vacuum created by the retreat of the United States. While the United States did give moderate financial and diplomatic support to ECOMOG, France did not. Such French client states as Burkina Faso and Côte d' Ivoire sided with the NPFL, supplying Taylor's movement with arms and business opportunities across the Ivoirian border. Although France maintained a low profile in this matter, the lack of cooperation between Paris, which was not averse to Taylor's coming to power, and Washington, which did not trust the Liberian dissident, did not facilitate the task of the ECOWAS peacekeeping force (itself perceived by France as an instrument of Nigerian hegemonic ambitions in the region).

The French distrust of ECOMOG was part of a muted rivalry between France and the United States in the post–Cold War African environment. As civil society challenged entrenched elites throughout the continent in the 1990s, both the United States and France professed a commitment to democratization. But the latter was not at all eager to see pro-French leaders ousted by a wave of free elections. In several long-standing preserves of French influence such as the Central African Republic, Cameroon, Togo,

Congo-Brazzaville, and Mauritania, U.S. diplomats annoyed their French counterparts by the interest that they took in opposition candidates. According to a member of the French embassy in Lomé, the U.S. ambassador was deeply involved in the Togolese political process: "it's part of a political campaign," he asserted, "that's been going on for several months in West Africa."[46] The fact that the United States pressured Senegal into contributing about 1,500 soldiers to ECOMOG in Liberia further exacerbated the rivalry, as did the efforts of African Americans like Reverend Leon Sullivan and Secretary of Commerce Ron Brown to promote U.S. business investment in the francophone preserves. What these frictions primarily revealed was the enduring importance to France of its status and reputation in Africa.[47]

The same concern was manifest in French involvement in the central African crises surrounding Rwanda, Burundi, and Congo. As noted in Chapter 11, France was significantly involved in building up the Rwandan army against the Ugandan-backed Rwandan Patriotic Front. As evidence of the army-sponsored genocide began to emerge during spring 1994, the French government found itself in an embarrassing position. At the same time, it was loath to see the RPF gaining control out of the very chaos unleashed by its military clients. Thus, in mid-June, Foreign Minister Alain Juppé announced that France would send an interventionary force, dubbed Operation Turquoise, to Rwanda; ostensibly a humanitarian mission to end the massacres, the intervention served in part to provide an exit route for the Hutu armed forces out of southwest Rwanda to Congo. The humanitarian impact of Operation Turquoise was relatively limited, but it gave France an opportunity to limit the political damage as the RPF took over from its erstwhile clients in the Rwandan army. In carrying out their operation from eastern Congo, the French also contributed to the diplomatic rehabilitation of another client who had fallen on hard times in the 1990s, President Mobutu.

The appalling events that unfolded in Rwanda after April 1994 confirmed one form of marginalization of African peoples. Despite clear signs of crimes against humanity, major powers and international institutions reacted slowly and cautiously to the genocide. In his thorough study of the international response to the Rwandan crisis, Jean-Claude Willame concluded:

> No [UN] member-state nor regional organization could or would become genuinely engaged in the conflict: contrary to other crises, there were no stakes deemed sufficiently important or urgent for an 'international community' which failed to see any way in which the inter-state security system was threatened.[48]

Yet, if Rwanda was largely abandoned—until France felt compelled to act—to its paroxysm of violence, one can see that the Hutu-Tutsi antagonism was much exacerbated by the interests and alliances of external actors. French attempts to balance the "anglo-supported" Tutsi rebels contributed to polarization rather than reconciliation in Rwandan politics.

Africa's rash of civil wars in the 1990s stemmed from internal frictions to be sure, but these were exacerbated by the changes in the global balance of power. Clan warfare in Somalia and warlordism in Liberia were in part domestic reactions to the strategic withdrawal of the superpowers, ethnofascism in Rwanda and Burundi was stoked by post–Cold War pressures for democratization that threatened established regimes. Bipolarity created incentives to shore up client regimes; multipolarity considerably reduced such incentives. Even in the face of severe collapse, the major powers demonstrated their reluctance by the mid-1990s to commit sustained resources to the reconstruction of failed states.

While the flow of arms to Africa was reduced in the 1990s, the flow of development assistance did not increase. More than any other power, Russia disengaged from the continent, closing nine embassies in 1992 after the dissolution of the Soviet Union. It restored full diplomatic relations with South Africa, however, reflecting a more general worldwide trend to orient trade and diplomacy toward the southern subregion. The emergence of Mandela's South Africa redefined the parameters of Africa's place in world politics by establishing a potential new pole in the African subsystem.

In assessing the changes of the 1990s, former Nigerian president Olusegun Obasanjo concluded, "whatever dividends are available in the post–Cold War global system seem to be passing Africa by."[49] Representing a widespread African view, he deplored that the processes of reconstruction, rehabilitation, reconciliation, and redevelopment that are called for after war, whether hot or cold, are not being significantly implemented in Africa. As one of the conveners of the 1991 Kampala Forum on security and development, Obasanjo strongly emphasized Africans' own responsibilities to strengthen endogenous institutions and construct a framework for collective action on a regional and continental basis. At the same time, he warned of the possible emergence of another bipolar world, North versus South, if post–Cold War reconstruction is neglected.[50]

■ CONCLUSION:
AFRICA AMONG THE LESSER POWERS

In this chapter, we have focused on unequal relationships between African states and various great powers. The Europeans and the superpowers are not, of course, the only external actors to pursue interests in Africa. We have looked very briefly at Chinese policy in Africa. China has wooed African leaders assiduously and has been a significant donor of economic aid. During the 1970s, for example, China committed $1.8 billion in assistance to Africa, nearly twice what the Soviet Union extended over the same period (arms transfers excluded). The largest portion of this aid went to Tanzania and Zambia to build the TanZam railroad. Long active in southern Africa, during the 1980s China increased its profile in West Africa. China has been involved in Africa primarily to counter the Soviet Union, which it has characterized as the "tiger" entering Africa at the very moment that the Western "wolf" was being repelled.[51] Chinese activity, for example in Angola, has occasionally served to trigger Soviet countermoves, but its overall impact upon African affairs has been relatively limited.

Much the same generalization applies to other external actors such as Japan, Canada, the Scandinavians, and Israel. As elsewhere in the world, Japan has profitably extended its markets in Africa while also steadily increasing its aid. Canada has developed a constructive and respected aid program, relying largely on Quebecois citizens to win friends in francophone Africa. Sweden has given particular attention to development projects in Botswana and Tanzania. Politically, Israel has been the most deeply involved of these secondary powers. It established substantial aid programs in more than thirty black African countries, exporting Israeli expertise in agriculture, cooperatives, water management, engineering, and security training. As Michael Curtis observed, "For Israel this set of relationships meant enlarging its circle of international contacts with the hope that African countries would support—or at least not oppose—Israel's struggle for existence."[52] Israel was quite successful in cultivating such contacts until the Six-Day War; after 1967, Arab pressure focusing on the issue of Israeli occupation of Egyptian territory began to erode Israel's ties. The Yom Kippur war and its repercussions upon oil politics gravely weakened Israel's diplomatic network, largely nullifying its investment in African solidarity at the United Nations. The aid and trade relationship did not entirely disappear, however, and over the course of the 1980s several African governments reestablished diplomatic relations with Israel.

Just as Israel sought to win friends in Africa, so have the Arab states of the Middle East, and in many ways, their task has been much easier. With nine African states actually members of the Arab League, Afro-Arab solidarity is an obvious notion. Moreover, many other African societies have large Muslim populations, and over the past decade, the number of black Africans making the religious pilgrimage to Mecca has grown steadily. The establishment of the Islamic Conference has provided a further forum for contacts. These cultural ties create affinities that states like Saudi Arabia have exploited since the 1960s. OPEC diplomacy after 1973 added a new dimension to the Afro-Arab relationship, as both sets of parties adjusted to new economic conditions. Brimming coffers in Saudi Arabia, Kuwait, and the Emirates created opportunities for and expectations of enhanced Afro-Arab solidarity.

Such expectations were only partly met. New financial institutions, such as the Arab Bank for Economic Development in Africa, the Arab-African Technical Assistance Fund, the Islamic Development Bank, and the OPEC Special Fund, were established. So too were bilateral Saudi and Kuwaiti aid programs. But the bulk of the disbursements went to a small number of Arabo-Muslim states (Egypt receiving the lion's share).[53] An Afro-Arab summit was convened in March 1977 in recognition of the dissatisfaction of many African governments, and new pledges of assistance were extended. Nevertheless, the aid flow never achieved proportions adequate to sustain a major new Afro-Arab connection; for the African scholar Dunstan Wai, African hopes of Arab largesse proved to be "misplaced optimism."[54]

Of the Middle Eastern governments, only Saudi Arabia has become a significant actor in African affairs, pursuing specific national interests in the Horn and in northwest Africa. In the Horn, the Saudis adopted Somalia after its break with the Soviet Union; Saudi Arabia purchases most of Somalia's livestock exports and during the 1980s gave large amounts of aid for military and other needs. Likewise, the Saudi government became involved in Eritrea, supporting Muslim elements hostile to the *derg*. Its largest commitment has been to Morocco, for which it picked up much of the bill for the Saharan war (though this did not prevent it from trying to mediate the settlement in the late 1980s). In 1991, the Saudis provided massive aid to Senegal in order to underwrite a summit meeting of the Islamic Conference in Dakar. Via these various efforts, Saudi Arabia has sought to accentuate the place of Islam in Africa.

Though on a lesser scale, the Saudis became involved in Africa for much the same reasons as France, the Soviet Union, and the United States. They committed resources to help people whom they viewed as friendly to their own interests. In the latter 1980s, this policy increasingly took the form of covert aid to Muslim fundamentalist movements. Such is the overall pattern of Africa's place in world politics. Africa has been an arena of competition in which stronger powers have intervened militarily and economically with relative ease. Although the incentives for intervention shifted in the 1990s, the structural pattern remains the same.

Economic scarcity and political fragility have made Africa vulnerable to foreign influence. Because the external powers act competitively, however, African actors have been able to retain some margin for maneuver. The distribution of power is sufficiently different from what it was in the heyday of imperialism to permit Africa greater freedom than it had then. In the new multipolar environment, African states now seek fresh approaches to exerting influence on the external environment.

One continuing means to this end is collective action. This was one of the main reasons that African states created the OAU in 1963. The OAU has served to articulate common African positions, notably on decolonization and apartheid, that have influenced the policies of external powers. On many issues, however, the OAU has been divided and its influence accordingly neutralized. In any case, the OAU has been a necessary but not a sufficient instrument to promote collective African interests. The charter of the OAU (Article III, section 7) explicitly commits the member states to a policy of nonalignment. Active participation in the Nonaligned Movement (NAM) and the related Group of 77 has become the principal means by which African states have sought to achieve a voice in international decisionmaking.

Africa's role in the evolution of the NAM has been substantial. Twenty-five states formed the NAM in Belgrade in 1961; of these, eleven were African. By the time the second summit convened, in Cairo in 1964, nineteen more African governments participated; thus, well over half the membership (which had climbed to a total of forty-seven) was African, and the conference resolutions focused less on Cold War mediation (major topics in Belgrade) than on the evils of superpower intervention in the Third World and the need to promote Third World economic development.

Tanzania and Zambia hosted the next two meetings, which firmly established the NAM as the principal vehicle of Third World collective diplomacy. President Nyerere urged the nonaligned states to return to the practice of regular meetings by calling a preparatory meeting in Dar es Salaam in April 1970. This conference led to the third summit meeting, held in Lusaka five months later. Here President Kaunda placed southern African issues (Angola, Mozambique, Rhodesia, Namibia, South Africa) at the center of the nonaligned agenda. The Lusaka meeting also issued a Declaration on Nonalignment and Economic Progress, which identified the structural constraints upon development that hampered African and other Third World economies. Economic issues, in turn, occupied an important place at the subsequent summit meeting held in Algiers in 1973 (which gave rise, as we saw in Chapter 10, to the NIEO resolutions). African states thus seized upon the organizational framework of the larger NAM to bring their policy concerns to the attention of the more powerful governments of the industrial North.

The NAM was also instrumental in creating the other major vehicle of collective southern diplomacy, the Group of 77; the nonaligned sponsored the initiative that gave rise to the 1964 conference at which the Group of 77 took form. African governments have played a key role in sustaining Group of 77 activities. African diplomats, like Kenneth Dadzie of Ghana, who later became secretary general of UNCTAD, provided leadership within the Group. Key meetings took place in Algiers and Arusha, which in Arusha aptly were devoted to the strategy of Third World collective self-reliance.

In 1986, the NAM returned to Africa to hold its eighth summit. This time the site was Harare in independent Zimbabwe; coupled with a prior foreign ministers' session in Luanda, the Harare summit symbolized the progress that Africa had made in the overthrow of colonialism. The organization created an Africa Fund to assist the Front Line States in their continuing campaign for majority rule in South Africa and Namibia. For Robert Mugabe (Zimbabwe), who assumed the presidency of the movement, the NAM was a unique instrument of Third World collective diplomacy on behalf of such causes. Although the East-West structure that gave birth to the concept of nonalignment has dissolved, African states have played a key role in preserving the organization as a voice for their concerns.

The United Nations is also a forum to which African policymakers have given much attention. At its inception, the UN had but four African members (Egypt, Ethiopia, Liberia, and South Africa), but since 1960 Africa has been an integral part of a Third World majority in the General Assembly. Africa now controls, by informal agreement, three nonpermanent seats on the Security Council. Concerting their positions in the United Nations, generally with the support of Asian and Latin American states, Africans have used UN resolutions to bring sanctions against Southern Rhodesia, an arms embargo against South Africa, and recognition to SWAPO as the legitimate representative of the Namibian people as well as to mobilize support on a host of other political and economic issues. As small states with limited means for diplomatic representation, Africans have found the United Nations system an indispensable framework for diplomacy.

Nevertheless, the United Nations mirrors a distribution of world power that has never been favorable to Africa. Colonies in the first half of the twentieth century and spheres of influence during much of the second half, African states fear economic marginalization as much as political intervention at the century's end. All states were obliged to respond to a more complex multipolar distribution of power during the 1990s. Some African states have the potential to consolidate themselves as subregional poles in the emergent balance of power; all of them have an interest as well in finding the means to a revitalized collective diplomacy capable of establishing the continent as one of the poles in the new multipolar world.

■ NOTES

1. Tamar Golan, "A Certain Mystery: How Can France Do Everything That It Does in Africa—and Get Away with It?" *African Affairs* 80 (January 1981): 3–11.

2. After years of silence, Foccart published some memoirs in the form of interviews with the journalist Philippe Gaillard: see *Foccart parle* (Paris: Fayard/Jeune Afrique, 1995). Later that year, upon the election of Jacques Chirac as president, Foccart again became a special adviser on and emissary to Africa.

3. For a table listing major and minor direct military interventions, see Edward Kolodziez and Bokanga Lokulutu, "Security Interests and French Arms-

Transfer Policy in Sub-Saharan Africa," in Bruce E. Arlinghaus, ed., *Arms for Africa* (Lexington, MA: Lexington Books, 1983), p. 138.

4. Jean-François Bayart, *La politique africaine de François Mitterrand* (Paris: Karthala, 1984), p. 27.

5. Kaye Whiteman, "President Mitterrand and Africa," *African Affairs* 82 (July 1983): 330.

6. Giscard had agreed to hold the 1981 summit in Kinshasa, a venue of some embarrassment to Mitterrand, who had criticized Giscard's close ties to the Mobutu regime. On the pretext that the first Franco-African summit of his term ought to be held in France, Mitterrand succeeded in evading Kinshasa, if only for a year. By 1982, *raison d'état* had reconciled Mitterrand to maintaining the tie with Congo.

7. The very growth in participation eventually annoyed the original partners. By 1985, the French decided to devote the first day of the conference *exclusively* to the francophone states, thereby to perpetuate an inner circle. It is noteworthy that Morocco attended for the first time in 1985 as a useful way to compensate for its boycott of the OAU. The institution evidently served a wide range of diplomatic needs.

8. Bayart, *La politique africaine*, p. 52.

9. *Le Monde*, June 22, 1990.

10. Edward T. Wilson, "Russia's Historic Stake in Black Africa," in David E. Albright, ed., *Communism in Africa* (Bloomington: Indiana University Press, 1980), p. 71.

11. Robert Legvold, *Soviet Policy in West Africa* (Cambridge, MA: Harvard University Press, 1970), p. 1.

12. Ibid., p. 65.

13. Ibid., p. 129.

14. Jiri Valenta, "Soviet Decision-Making on the Intervention in Angola," in Albright, *Communism in Africa*, p. 102.

15. Ibid., pp. 109–110.

16. Ibid., p. 116.

17. David E. Albright, "Moscow's African Policy of the 1970s," in Albright, *Communism in Africa*, p. 58.

18. Marina Ottaway, *Soviet and American Influence in the Horn of Africa* (New York: Praeger, 1982), p. 114.

19. Ellen Laipson, "Libya and the Soviet Union: Alliance at Arm's Length," in Walter Laqueur, ed., *The Pattern of Soviet Conduct in the Third World* (New York: Praeger, 1983), p. 133.

20. Robert Grey, "The Soviet Presence in Africa: An Analysis of Goals," *Journal of Modern African Studies* 22 (September 1984): 527.

21. Henry Jackson, *From the Congo to Soweto* (New York: Morrow, 1982), p. 55.

22. Clare Timberlake, the first U.S. ambassador to Congo, is reported to have remarked that "if Lumumba had walked into any gathering of Congolese politicians as a waiter with a tray on his head he would have come out as Prime Minister," according to Conor Cruise O'Brien, *To Katanga and Back* (New York: Grosset and Dunlap, 1966), p. 94. See O'Brien and Steven R. Weissman, *American Foreign Policy in the Congo* (Ithaca, NY: Cornell University Press, 1974), for thorough accounts of U.S. and UN policy.

23. The term is from Helen Kitchen, *U.S. Interests in Africa* (New York: Praeger, 1983), p. 2. See also Donald Rothchild and John Ravenhill, "Subordinating African Issues to Global Logic: Reagan Confronts Political Complexity," in Kenneth Oye, Robert J. Lieber, and Donald Rothchild, eds., *Eagle Resurgent?* (Boston: Little, Brown, 1987).

24. Steven Weissman, "The CIA and US Policy in Zaire and Angola," in René Lemarchand, ed., *American Policy in Southern Africa* (Washington, DC: University Press of America, 1978), p. 394.

25. Testimony to the Senate by the deputy assistant secretary of state for African affairs in 1975, as cited by Weissman, ibid., p. 395.

26. The quotations are from National Security Study Memorandum 39 and an accompanying document submitted to Nixon in January 1970, as cited in Gerald Bender "Kissinger in Angola: Anatomy of Failure," in Lemarchand, *American Policy in Southern Africa*, p. 68.

27. Ibid., pp. 76–77.

28. Anthony Lake, *The "Tar Baby" Option: American Policy Toward Southern Rhodesia* (New York: Columbia University Press, 1976); one of the classics on the bureaucratic politics of U.S. foreign policy decisionmaking, this book is likewise one of the best studies of U.S. policy toward southern Africa.

29. U.S. Department of State, *Department of State Bulletin* 74, no. 1927 (May 31, 1976): 5673–5674.

30. The quoted phrase appears in Chester Crocker, "South Africa: Strategy for Change," *Foreign Affairs* 59, no. 2 (Winter 1980–1981): 350. See also his *High Noon in Southern Africa: Making Peace in a Rough Neighborhood* (New York: Norton, 1992).

31. Cited by Allen D. Cooper, *U.S. Economic Power and Political Influence in Namibia, 1700–1982* (Boulder: Westview Press, 1982), p. 33. The speaker was George McGhee, assistant secretary of state for Near Eastern and African affairs.

32. The quotation is from a 1966 speech by Assistant Secretary Williams, cited in Cooper, *U.S. Economic Power*, p. 40.

33. *New York Times*, June 2, 1988.

34. Vernon V. Aspaturian, "Gorbachev's New Political Thinking and the Angolan Conflict," in Owen Ellison Kahn, ed., *Disengagement from Southwest Africa* (New Brunswick, NJ: Transaction Publishers, 1991), p. 18.

35. Herman J. Cohen, "A View from the Inside," in Harvey Glickman, ed., *Toward Peace and Security in Southern Africa* (New York: Gordon and Breach, 1990), p. 221.

36. Quoted in Hella Pick, "Namibia Independence Pact Signed," *Manchester Guardian Weekly* 140, no. 1 (January 1, 1989): 8. See also Crocker's remarks at the treaty signature in Kahn, *Disengagement from Southwest Africa*, pp. 225–226.

37. Chester A. Crocker, "Southern Africa: Eight Years Later," *Foreign Affairs* 68, no. 4 (Fall 1989): 158.

38. Remarks of Victor Goncharev of the Soviet Institute of African Studies as cited by Colin Legum, "Gorbachev's Policies on Southern Africa," in Kahn, *Disengagement from Southwest Africa*, p. 59.

39. Ibid., p. 60.

40. See Winrich Kuhne, "What Does the Case of Mozambique Tell Us About Soviet Ambivalence Toward Africa?" *CSIS Africa Notes*, no. 46 (August 30, 1985).

41. John Harbeson, "Africa in World Politics: Amid Renewal, Deepening Crisis," in John Harbeson and Donald Rothchild, eds., *Africa in World Politics: Post Cold-War Challenges* (Boulder: Westview Press, 1995), p. 14.

42. See Mohamed Sahnoun, *Somalia: The Missed Opportunities* (Washington: United States Institute of Peace Press, 1994) for a firsthand account of his mission.

43. Of these, U.S. forces numbered 25,426. Nineteen other states, including Botswana, Egypt, Morocco, Nigeria, Tunisia, and Zimbabwe, also contributed units to UNITAF.

44. John L. Hirsch and Robert B. Oakley, *Somalia and Operation Restore Hope* (Washington: United States Institute of Peace Press, 1995), p. 153.

45. Remarks of Ambassador Colin Keating of New Zealand, who led a Security Council mission to Somalia in October 1994, as reported in John Tessitore and Susan Woolfson, eds., *A Global Agenda* (Lanham, MD: University Press of America, 1995), p. 47.

46. Cited in Géraldine Faes, "Togo: l'effet Cohen," *Jeune Afrique*, July 2–8, 1992.

47. For a broader treatment and other examples of this rivalry, see Peter Schraeder, "From Berlin 1884 to Berlin 1989: Foreign Assistance and French, American, and Japanese Competition in Francophone Africa," *The Journal of Modern African Studies* 33, no. 4 (1995): 539–567.

48. Jean-Claude Willame, *L'ONU au Rwanda (1993-1995)*, (Paris: Maisonneuve et Larose, 1996), p. 144.

49. Olusegun Obasanjo, "A Balance Sheet of the African Region and the Cold War," in Keller and Rothchild, *Africa in the New International Order,* p. 24.

50. That a leader of the stature of Obasanjo should have been in prison on trumped-up charges during the Abacha dictatorship was a measure of the Nigerian regime's loss of credibility in international affairs. Released in 1998 after the death of Abacha, Obasanjo was reelected president of Nigeria in 1999.

51. George T. Yu, "Sino-Soviet Rivalry in Africa," in Albright, *Communism in Africa*, p. 181.

52. Michael Curtis, "Africa, Israel, and the Middle East," *Middle East Review* 17, no. 4 (Summer 1985): 7.

53. Victor T. LeVine and Timothy W. Luke, *The Arab-African Connection: Political and Economic Realities* (Boulder: Westview Press, 1979), pp. 24–25.

54. Dunstan M. Wai, "African-Arab Relations: Interdependence or Misplaced Optimism," *Journal of Modern African Studies* 21, no. 2 (June 1983): 187–213.

Part 5

POLITICAL FUTURES

13

South Africa:
The Possibilities and Limits of
Transforming State and Society

On April 26, 1994, South Africans voted in the first nonracial universal suffrage election in the country's violent history and elected Nelson Mandela president. The election culminated decades of popular struggle against apartheid, a system of racial domination whose hallmarks were racial violence and privilege. In 1960, Africa's "year of independence" in much of the continent, the ruling government in South Africa banned the leading nationalist movement, the African National Congress (ANC). Not until thirty years later would the government lift its ban on the ANC and other antiapartheid political parties. The intervening period saw recurrent outbursts of violent protest and ever growing black political mobilization within the country, and increasing international pressure against apartheid in the rest of the world. Mandela's election brought one chapter in the history of Africa to a close—the era of formal white domination of African states—and began a new era in South Africa's history: an era faced with the challenge of transforming a racist, ethnically dominated state and society into a nonracial democracy.

The 1990s have been a remarkable period in South Africa: in ten years the country has changed from international pariah to international model of racial and ethnic cooperation. The ANC has been transformed from liberation movement to governing party. It now faces the challenge of transforming a state and an economy designed to benefit its white population into institutions capable of harnessing the energy and resourcefulness of all of its peoples in ways that promote long-term equitable growth, free and fair political participation, and conflict resolution among previously hostile groups.

In this chapter we examine how a deeply divided society initiated a long-term process of conflict resolution, whose first result—the election of

Nelson Mandela—was seen by many as miraculous. To understand the enormity of this process, we examine the historical formation of a dual society in South Africa marked by vast inequalities between blacks and whites. We look at how black civil society successfully challenged white domination in the 1980s and prompted negotiations to end apartheid. We analyze the negotiations between the ANC and the National Party that created a new constitution and the first universal suffrage elections in South African history. Finally, we describe the legacies of apartheid for the South African state, society, and economy and speculate on whether South Africans will be able to overcome those legacies.

We devote a separate chapter to South Africa because the rest of the continent has an enormous stake in whether that country successfully transforms its state and society. South Africa faces many of the same problems that haunt the rest of the continent: incorporation into the global economy, a multiethnic character, and the need for responsive governance. South Africa, because of its experience in societal conflict resolution and its enormous capabilities, has the potential to serve as an example of how to overcome these problems.

■ THE HISTORICAL FORMATION OF A DUAL SOCIETY

State and society in contemporary South Africa have been forged by three and a half centuries of interaction between white colonial settlers and Africans. This formative history can be divided into three distinct eras.[1] The first era, from 1652 to the 1870s, focused on encounters between colonial settlers and Africans—the clash of different systems of governance and social structures. The second era, from 1870 to 1940, created an integrated political economy in South Africa centered on the need for cheap mine labor and the demands of white farmers to be protected from competition by their African counterparts. The third era, from 1948 to 1976, enshrined apartheid as the organizing principle for state and society.

■ Encountering the Other

In 1652, in what is now the Western Cape of South Africa, a small band of Dutch settlers arrived to establish a supply station for the Dutch East Indies Company. The settlers traded with the indigenous Khoisans—metal, tobacco, and liquor for Khoisan cattle—to provide East Indies–bound ships with food and provisions. Members of the settlement eventually moved inland, expropriating large tracts of land for grazing, along with any livestock on that land. The Boers (as they called themselves) clashed with the African inhabitants over the seizure of land and livestock. From the mid-1700s to the mid-1800s several wars were fought along the frontier of white expansion, first to the north and then to the east of the Cape. The intrusion of the settlers and their capture of land and cattle disrupted the already fragile carrying capacity of the South African ecology.

Even before the new intruders came, shortages of resources had fueled wars among African communities. Early frontier wars between the Boers and the Xhosas in the late 1700s were fought not only because the Boers were encroaching on Xhosa lands, but also because intra-Xhosa warfare drove some Xhosa toward Boer settlements. Recent studies have concluded that the *Mfecane,* or "Great Crushing"—a series of deadly wars fought in the 1820s between Africans in what is now KwaZulu/Natal—was an outcome of drought, overgrazing, and the need to find water and land for survival.[2]

Two patterns describe relations between Dutch settlers and Africans from 1650 to 1800. First, the early Cape Dutch East India economy was based on slavery, which bred a patriarchal master-servant relationship between Cape gentry and their slaves inside the colony.[3] That mode of slavery, although grounded ultimately on force, demanded reciprocity and obligations from the master. Boers who ventured to the frontier hoped to replicate such a relationship as a way to affirm their social status. On the other hand, relations between Boers and Africans on the frontier were frequently marked by acknowledged interdependence: "Proximity and intimacy achieved familiarity, sensual gratification, shared lifestyle and mutual convenience, but not tolerance or understanding."[4]

When the British seized the colony from the Dutch in 1806, tensions arose between the Boer settlers and the new colonial authorities. The Cape became part of the British empire during the most dynamic period of Britain's industrial revolution. Although the British seized the Cape to secure the sea route to Asia, on which so much of their trade depended, they quickly sought to establish a prosperous, capitalist colony there. Violence soon erupted between Boer slave-holding farmers and the British, who implemented legislation conducive to the free labor market requirements of the new era. The British colonial government crushed a series of minor rebellions by Boer farmers in the first three decades of the 1800s and abolished slavery in 1834.

British liberalism in the Cape contained contradictory impulses.[5] On the one hand, British liberalism valued free labor and conceived of education, wealth, and religious instruction as possible steps to racial equality, although that view was usually tempered by skepticism that Africans could ever achieve true equality. British liberalism outlawed slavery, and when it resurrected various prohibitions on free labor in the 1850s, it did so in nonracial terms. When Britain devolved a measure of self-government to the Cape colony, it insisted on a color-blind franchise with voting restrictions limited to property and legal employment. Although such restrictions limited

African participation in politics, they nonetheless kept the legal possibility alive.

On the other hand, British liberalism was capable of appalling atrocity. In the Eastern Frontier of the Cape, where interaction between whites and Africans was the most acute, the British settlers of Grahamstown in 1820 injected the most virulent racism known in South Africa. That racism arose when the Xhosa peoples refused to give up their traditional agricultural way of life to become wage laborers for the white economy. The settlers soon characterized Africans as the antithesis of progress, describing them as "libidinous, uncontrolled, lazy, and disrespectful of established authority."[6]

The British colonial army fought a series of wars in the Eastern Cape between 1811 and 1855. During that time the African was transformed, in British eyes, from noble savage awaiting religious and economic conversion to "irredeemable." These wars differed dramatically from the Boer-African wars and Xhosa wars of the 1700s, when rival groups fought limited conflicts over land, cattle, and resources. British military campaigns against the Xhosa and their allies eventually became total wars, with the Xhosa character at the root of the conflict, according to the British. By the 1850s, by using scorched-earth tactics, carrying out indiscriminate slaughter, and inducing famine, the British had destroyed the social order of the Xhosa peoples.

By depicting the Xhosa as the antithesis of progress, liberalism could justify atrocity. British colonial representatives thought destroying the Xhosa traditional institutions and way of life was necessary for the group's advancement. The British perception of the African that developed in the early nineteenth century became the chief justification for British colonialism throughout Africa in the late nineteenth century.

British state-building in the nineteenth century yielded another far-reaching legacy, that of using the state to enforce racial categorization and discrimination. The British colonial state in South Africa invented "pass laws," which restricted the movement of Africans in white areas, and "native reserves"—isolated, usually barren areas where Africans were forced to live. Such institutions were used repeatedly throughout the region in the twentieth century.[7]

■ The Creation of a Mining Economy

From 1750 to 1870 twenty-nine separate wars or skirmishes—between Boers and Africans, British and Africans, Boers and British, and Africans and Africans—were fought in what is now South Africa. No single victor emerged, and by 1870 a delicate balance of power existed in the region. The British colony in the Cape had about 180,000 European settlers; tensions still ran high along the Eastern Frontier. In Natal a small British presence lived uneasily with Zulus to the north. Two Boer republics, the Transvaal and the Orange Free State, with a combined population of about 30,000 settlers, maintained a fragile hold in the interior of South Africa. Population growth and resource scarcity (especially land for cattle grazing) ensured conflict and instability, but the lack of predominant military strength seemed to ordain a grudging coexistence between Africans and settlers.[8]

This equipoise was shattered when the discovery of diamonds in Kimberly in 1867 and of gold in the Witwatersrand in 1886 started a frenzied search for mineral wealth in the region. These finds offered new prospects for wealth, and colonists quickly set out to create the conditions needed to cheaply extract and produce minerals. The mineral revolution required transportation, capital, labor, exploration, and political control.

Until 1870 only 62 miles of railroad track had been laid in southern Africa, but between 1870 and 1915, 10,700 miles of railways were constructed in the region.[9] Johannesburg became the hub of the rapidly emerging regional economy. The lure of instant wealth brought an explosion of European immigration. In 1865 the European population of South Africa was about 200,000; by 1905 it had reached more than 1.1 million.[10]

The exploitation of South Africa's mineral wealth was equaled only by the exploitation of labor. The low quality of the gold in the Witswatersrand meant the ore could be mined profitably only with cheap labor. To ensure an adequate supply of cheap manual labor, colonial authorities forcibly dispossessed Africans of land and consequently of an independent means to earn a living.

Legislation to limit African landholding passed in all of the territories of South Africa between 1890 and 1913. In 1913 the Natives Land Act was passed, which cemented what would become a crucial distribution conflict for South Africa throughout the twentieth century. Driven by two demands—the need for cheap labor for the mines and protection of white farmers against black competition—the 1913 act set aside 93 percent of South Africa's land for white purchase only. The act crowded the African population onto small parcels of land that could not sustain the agricultural needs of so many. Destitution, disease, and death for Africans on the reserves were the inevitable result, which forced formerly productive landowning peasants to labor for white owners of large farms or, alternatively, for the mines.[11]

The demand for mineral wealth also altered relationships among white settlers. The British intervened militarily to stake their claim to the newfound riches. Thousands of troops were sent to vanquish the Zulu empire, and from 1899 to 1902 nearly 500,000 troops attempted to suppress Boer independence in the South African war (which the British refer to as the Boer war).

The war ended in 1902 with a British military victory and a political compromise between the British and the Boers. A treaty established the Union of South Africa in 1910. The various South African colonies were united under a single parliament based in the Cape and an executive civil service in Pretoria. Although the Cape retained its property-based, nonracial franchise, the British conceded to the Boers that the rest of the Union could deny Africans the vote. By doing so, the peace that concluded the South African war of 1899–1902 postponed for more than ninety years the resolution of the conflict over black political participation.

The dramatic displacements of the mineral revolution in South Africa created deep identity crises for many Africans. In the case of black South Africans the fragmentation of rural communities contributed to the creation of the African National Congress, which was formed in 1912 and called for national citizenship in South Africa as well as greater unity among all Africans. Among the white settlers, the displacements created a new intense ethnic identification—Afrikanerdom. A coherent and compelling mythology and group identity grew out of the war between Britain and the Boers in which entire Boer families were herded into concentration camps. The Boers' impoverishment and their bitter envy of British newcomers who enjoyed the riches of the mining revolution led to the establishment of secret organizations such as the Broederbond, which pledged to further the aims of Afrikaners.

■ The Creation of Apartheid

World War II transformed the position of Afrikaners in the South African state and society. Major domestic changes wrought by the war challenged racism in South Africa. Meeting the wartime needs of the Western Allies fostered a manufacturing boom in South Africa. South African industry grew tremendously and brought more and more blacks into the industrial workplace and urban communities. Even so, there was a shortage of labor during this growth period. Accordingly, black wages rose sharply, black trade unions made solid gains, and the number of blacks living in urban areas more than doubled.[12]

The increased economic strength of an African urban, organized, industrial workforce led to growing political strength for organizations that challenged white political domination in South Africa, notably the ANC and the South African Communist Party (SACP). These two groups worked together to organize nonviolent mass action campaigns to win basic political, economic, and social rights for blacks.

These domestic changes struck at the heart of Afrikanerdom. Afrikaner leaders feared the massing together of blacks in cities and bridled at black demands for political change. Afrikaner farmers wanted stricter controls on labor mobility because the departure of black farmworkers for the cities and for higher wages was creating a shortage of cheap labor in the countryside. Afrikaners' self-proclaimed racial superiority over black Africans was melting away, as blacks made economic gains despite racist legislation. Moreover, Afrikaners, whose place in the South African hierarchy was inferior to that of English-speaking whites, feared that English-dominated business would support African demands for reform. Afrikaners rallied behind the National Party (NP) in order to resist change, roll back black economic gains, and upgrade their own status vis-à-vis anglophone whites.

Apartheid came to South Africa when the NP won a plurality of seats in the 1948 elections. The party implemented a vigorous set of laws and policies that sought to regulate all relations between races in South Africa. Apartheid was distinguished from earlier economic, political, and legal domination by whites over blacks by "the completeness with which racial separation was sought, and in the locus within the state of racial control."[13]

In pursuing apartheid the NP had three aims: "(1) to create a completely segregated society, in keeping with the precepts of Afrikaner politico-religious doctrine, and in so doing to preserve Afrikaner identity; (2) to secure white political supremacy and its resulting economic privileges from potential internal and external threats (the former represented primarily by the black majority and the latter by an international community increasingly inhospitable to notions of racial rule); and (3) to move the Afrikaner community into a position of social and economic parity with the English-speaking community, which had dominated the modern economy and urban sector since the dawn of capitalist economic development in South Africa."[14]

To accomplish these goals the NP established a totalitarian police state to control blacks. Laws such as the Population Registration Act, the Prohibition of Mixed Marriages Act, the Immorality Act, the Reservation of Separate Amenities Act, and the Group Areas Act strictly segregated South Africa by race. Forced removal of entire communities led to the violent uprooting of over 3.5 million people.[15] Enforcement of laws restricting black movement within the country (pass laws) led to 5.8 million prosecutions in one decade alone.[16] The success of such draconian coercion depended on restricting violence to the black townships, thereby insulating white South Africans from the harshness their way of life inflicted on millions. The security of white South Africans came to rest on the insecurity of black South Africans.

Once the National Party had captured the South African state, it molded a bureaucracy, judiciary, police force, and military to serve the interests of the white minority, especially the Afrikaner population. The NP legislated away voting rights for coloured and Indian populations. Through the force of law and by packing the judiciary, the apartheid state effectively gave the government the right to arrest and detain anyone indefinitely. Rights to free speech and assembly did not exist for the African majority.

The National Party transformed the state into an employment agency for poor Afrikaners, which resulted in the South African government becoming a bloated bureaucracy with a vested interest in preventing any reform. In 1948, when the National Party took power, Afrikaners were mostly indigent farmers and blue-collar workers. By 1970 more than half of Afrikaners were state employees, and less than 10 percent were occupied in agriculture.[17] Eighty percent of state jobs were held by Afrikaners.[18] By 1977 Afrikaners held 90 percent of the top state executive and managerial positions.[19]

The National Party also established a welfare economy for Afrikaners and actively intervened to assist Afrikaner businesses. The state increased the amount of capital it placed in Afrikaner-owned banks by nearly 500 percent; it also awarded important contracts to Afrikaner businesses and established state-run industries with Afrikaner directors to compete with English-owned enterprises.[20]

The ANC spearheaded the opposition to apartheid. The ANC called for African self-determination in its 1949 Program of Action. In conjunction with the South African Indian Congress and the SACP, the party sponsored a "Freedom Day Strike" on May 1, 1950. Such political actions had led to independence elsewhere in Africa, although under extremely inhospitable conditions. In South Africa such activities provoked the NP government to pass the Suppression of Communism Act, which defined communism broadly enough to cover most forms of opposition to apartheid. In turn, the ANC initiated a Campaign for the Defiance of Unjust Laws, which involved holding peaceful demonstrations against the entire battery of pass, curfew, residency, and censorship laws. Thousands were arrested, greatly enhancing the reputation of the ANC.

The ANC, in alliance with various other groups, drafted the Freedom Charter in 1955—a call for equal rights, which the government treated as a "blueprint" for a communist state. Drafted by a multiracial coalition, the charter spelled out in simple eloquence a vision of a nonracial, democratic state:

> We, the people of South Africa, declare for all our country and the world to know:
>   That South Africa belongs to all who live in it, black and white, and that no government can justly claim authority, unless it is based on the will of all the people. . . .
>   And therefore, we, the people of South Africa, black and white together—equals, countrymen and brothers—adopt this Freedom Charter. And we pledge ourselves to strive together, sparing nothing of our strength and courage, until the democratic changes set out here have been won.[21]

The white government reacted by arresting and detaining ANC officials for about a year; upon their release leaders such as Nobel Peace Prize recipient

Albert Luthuli and Oliver Tambo mounted a campaign against the pass laws, which they called "the main pillar of our oppression and exploitation."[22] During this campaign the police killed sixty-seven demonstrators in the notorious Sharpeville massacre.

Sharpeville marked a turning point for the antiapartheid movement. Many Africans no longer believed it was possible to eradicate apartheid by peaceful means alone. In 1961, after long debate, the African National Congress abandoned its almost fifty-year commitment to nonviolent change and launched an armed struggle against the white regime.

The Sharpeville massacre riveted international attention on South Africa. The killing of unarmed demonstrators elicited worldwide condemnations and increased normative pressures against the white regime. The obvious potential for political instability drove international investors to look elsewhere to place their money.

The South African government responded immediately, quickly clamping down on the opposition. The government banned the ANC within days of the Sharpeville massacre and dramatically increased spending for the military, the police, and domestic arms production. Eventually, the government arrested and imprisoned Nelson Mandela. The government reacted to international condemnation by declaring South Africa a republic and pulling out of the Commonwealth.

The National Party also formulated a longer-term strategy. In an attempt to meet international demands for self-determination but still maintain the racial segregation embraced by most white South Africans, the government established Bantustans, or black homelands. Swaths of barren territory—about 13 percent of South Africa's land—were carved out, and millions of blacks were forced to move to them. Such "separate development," National Party leaders declared, would be akin to formal decolonization. From 1961 to the mid-1970s, when Pretoria formally recognized the Bantustans as "independent sovereign homelands," South Africa sought international acceptance of the homelands policy as a way out of its racial dilemma. Not one foreign government, however, recognized the homelands as independent states.

■ APARTHEID'S CONTRADICTIONS AND BLACK RESISTANCE

The clampdown produced a decade of stability before cracks appeared in the apartheid foundation. Between 1948 and 1970, South Africa possessed the second-fastest-growing economy in the world, which dramatically raised the living standards of Afrikaners.[23] By the 1970s, however, economic recession convinced white business leaders that the successful performance of South Africa's economy required the relaxation of apartheid's formal prohibitions on labor mobility and collective bargaining. The expansion of manufacturing required a more highly skilled black workforce, and thus the need to provide education for black laborers. The very success of apartheid, lifting Afrikaners into affluence, induced divisions in their ranks concerning the need for political change and created a movement within the National Party for basic reforms.

Economic stagnation in the 1970s also helped to create the conditions for black rebellion against apartheid. Mobilized by Stephen Biko and other adherents of the black consciousness movement and emboldened by the defeat of Portuguese colonialism in nearby Angola and Mozambique, students in Soweto went on strike on June 16, 1976, to protest the teaching of Afrikaans in the schools. As it had in Sharpeville sixteen years earlier, the South African state answered the peaceful demands of demonstrators with lethal force. This time, however, the protests spread across South Africa. Hundreds of blacks were killed during the student uprising, and thousands crossed the border into Mozambique to train to overthrow the white regime. The international community responded with a UN arms embargo on Pretoria and a worldwide movement to convince multinational corporations to divest from South Africa.

In 1978 P. W. Botha became prime minister and put in place what Robert Price has called South Africa's "security-driven agenda."[24] Apartheid was to be abandoned—reluctantly—to ensure continued white political and economic domination; in its place would be a program of social, economic, and political reforms aimed at drawing what state strategists dubbed "useful blacks" into a new supportive alliance. Purposeful repression would be used to lower black expectations about the extent of change and to alleviate whites' worries that reform would result in the majority coming to power. Although Botha's program made some concessions to the demands and grievances of the disenfranchised majority—for example, black trade unions were legalized, and local communities were given state permission to end petty discrimination if they desired—it resolutely maintained direct white minority control of the political system.

The centerpiece of the National Party's attempt to reform apartheid was a new tricameral constitution, approved in a whites-only referendum in November 1983. South Africans classified by apartheid as "coloureds" and "Asians" were to be represented in parliament, although in separate, racially exclusive chambers. A ratio of four votes for the white chamber to every two for the coloured and one for the Asian chamber ensured a white majority of votes on "general affairs." South Africans classified as "blacks" continued to be excluded from the parliament.

The tricameral scheme proved an important spur to mass protest campaigns. The majority of coloureds and Asians boycotted elections for the new parliament. The United Democratic Front (UDF)—a confederation of previously disparate antiapartheid organizations, local community associations in black townships, militant student groups, and organized labor—

was launched to campaign against the new constitution. In September 1984 an uprising in the townships surrounding Johannesburg triggered a countrywide wave of escalating strikes, protests, and riots that continued until June 1986.

The South African government declared states of emergency in various parts of the country, and the army was sent into the townships to restore order. In addition, the government began clandestine operations to assassinate UDF organizers, to establish black criminal groups to foment violence in the townships, and to train homeland forces to be used against UDF and ANC supporters.[25]

Western media coverage of South African police and military repression in the townships increased public demands in Europe and the United States for the imposition of tough economic sanctions. A speech by P. W. Botha to a federal congress of the National Party in August 1985 marked an important turning point in international efforts to isolate South Africa. Heralded in advance as a statement that would map out a new direction, Botha's speech instead demonstrated to a large international audience that the regime had no credible answers to the deepening crisis. Botha's xenophobic, threatening tone goaded foreign bankers into refusing to roll over South African short-term loans, which created what became known as the "debt standstill" crisis.

The increasing international isolation, especially the partial sanctions introduced by many countries in 1985–1986, exacerbated South Africa's long-standing, precarious economic situation. Transnational companies and international banks lost confidence in South Africa; Western commercial bankers also had grave doubts about the economy. A freeze on new lending was accompanied by a reluctance to renew credits. With prospects for profits dramatically diminished, private investors were disinclined to enter the South African market.

Botha's speech also fueled what had become all-out insurrection in the townships. Responding to a call by the ANC to render the townships ungovernable, youths enforced school and consumer boycotts and labor stayaways, targeted blacks thought to be collaborators, and used hit-and-run tactics to attack police and defense forces in the townships: "Between August 1984 and the end of 1986, four times more political work stoppages or 'stayaways' were staged than in the entire preceding three-and-one-half decades. . . . The workdays lost to strikes over 'economic' issues jumped over 200 percent between 1983 and 1984, then increased by 80 percent in 1985 and 93 percent in 1986. . . . Concurrently, the number of students boycotting school increased from approximately 10,000 in 1983 to almost 700,000 in 1985, swelling the ranks of militant youth available to 'man the barricades.'"[26]

The regime responded to the deepening crisis by intensifying repression and imposing a nationwide state of emergency in June 1986. Over the next six months the government detained more than 29,000 people without charge.[27] As the repression failed to restore order and international ostracism increased, executives of some of South Africa's largest business corporations began to meet unilaterally with the ANC at their headquarters in exile in Lusaka, Zambia, and elsewhere. The message from private citizens and business seemed to be that if the National Party was unwilling to make peace, they would have to do so themselves.

By the late 1980s the National Party's policies of limited reform and repression had reached a dead end. The accession to power of F. W. de Klerk in 1989 coincided with great changes in the world that emboldened him to seek a new direction. The collapse of communist regimes in Eastern Europe and the Soviet Union released the ideological stranglehold anticommunism held on the South African state. The continuing weakness of the South African economy led more and more businesspeople to urge face-to-face negotiations with the ANC. Many had met with the ANC while in exile and felt confident that a political solution could be reached that would address the fears of the white community. Afrikanerdom itself had gone through major changes; the major elite Afrikaner organization, the Broederbond, circulated a secret document in 1989 arguing that "the exclusion of effective black sharing in the political processes at the highest level had become 'a threat to the survival of the white man.' There could no longer be a white government and the head of government did not necessarily have to be white."[28]

In February 1990 de Klerk stunned South Africa by releasing Nelson Mandela from prison and lifting the ban on the ANC and the SACP. These bold moves initiated a process of difficult negotiations that would prove more protracted and deadly than anyone had anticipated. In part, the difficulty stemmed from the condition of the South African state and the NP, both of which were deeply fractured. The state contained military and police elements that had been involved in killings and severe human rights violations and were opposed to a settlement with the ANC. Homeland leaders feared negotiation would diminish their power and resources. The NP also contained opponents of negotiation. Even among party members who favored negotiation, there was a wide range of opinions concerning optimal and minimal settlement terms.

The ANC's willingness to negotiate a settlement was rooted in its long advocacy of racial reconciliation and the creation of a nonracial nation. A combination of liberal strands in the party's heritage, a strong degree of legalism in its makeup, and a history of linking armed struggle to negotiation created an organization disposed toward a negotiated transition of power.[29] Indeed, it was Nelson Mandela, writing from prison in 1986, who proposed meeting with P. W. Botha to find a peaceful method of resolving South Africa's crisis. This disposition—combined with an increasing consensus within the party that armed struggle was unlikely to bring down the regime in the short run, the loss of allies such as the Soviet Union and some

Eastern European countries, and positive responses by the international community to de Klerk's initiatives—diminished the ANC's range of alternatives away from the bargaining table.

The ANC also contained deep divisions, exacerbated by the different experiences of many of its members. In 1990 the ANC leadership consisted of long-term political prisoners in South Africa, exiles in Lusaka and elsewhere across the world, and civic association leaders who remained in South Africa and fought the regime as part of the UDF and the Mass Democratic Movement (MDM). Although the older leaders of the ANC were unified in their belief that armed struggle could not bring victory, younger rank-and-file members who had made the townships ungovernable felt mass action could topple the regime. Deeply distrustful of the South African government, the youth remained vigilant to any sign that their leadership might abandon them.

■ NEGOTIATIONS FOR A NEW CONSTITUTION

Many people hoped Nelson Mandela's release from prison and the unbanning of the African National Congress in February 1990 portended a quick march to new democratic institutions for South Africa. Instead, it took four years and nearly 13,000 deaths to bring South Africa to its first one-person, one-vote election. In 1993 Afrikaner commentator Max du Preez captured the folly of South Africans' early optimism: "Anyone who thought we would be able to change 300 years of white domination and 45 years of apartheid into a liberal democracy in a flash and without releasing considerable energy was naive."[30]

The leaders of South Africa faced multiple challenges in 1990. South Africa needed new political institutions that would include participation by the disenfranchised majority and be seen as legitimate by that group. At the same time, these institutions had to alleviate the fears of racial and ethnic minorities without crippling the ability of the state to confront the country's economic and social problems. Conflict resolution in a complex society such as South Africa depends on much more than formal agreement among political leaders. Elites cannot reach agreement on such weighty issues as constitutional reform and economic policies without first reducing the distance that separates them, which calls for debate, exchange, interaction, and information sharing among groups and individuals in society. This section examines attempts between 1990 and 1994 to create transitional and constitutional arrangements for a new South Africa.

▓ Negotiating About Negotiations

The eighteen months following the release of Nelson Mandela were spent laying the foundation for substantive negotiations. In May and August 1990, two formal summits were held between the ANC and the South African government. The protocols of these summits, the Groote Schuur and Pretoria minutes, are what political scientists call elite-based pacts. Such pacts consist of formalized rules of the game under which antagonists agree to moderate their competition during negotiations.[31] The Groote Schuur and Pretoria minutes committed the parties to peaceful negotiation and resulted in the ANC formally suspending its campaign of armed struggle. The meetings established preconditions for constitutional negotiations, release of remaining political prisoners, the safe return of political exiles, and the formal cessation of violence.

Unfortunately, although progress was made on establishing the preconditions for substantive talks, South Africa experienced a paradox: as the two largest parties—the NP and the ANC—reached agreement on the need to curtail violence, South Africa suffered from levels of political violence higher than those of the states of emergency in the 1980s. In part, this can be attributed to the presence of spoilers in the peace process— leaders and factions whose interests, worldview, and power are threatened by the prospect of a peace agreement.[32] In South Africa the leaders and groups with the most to lose from a negotiated settlement attacked the peace process in hopes of undermining it. Narrowly defined ethnic parties such as Mangosuthu Buthelezi's Inkatha movement in the homeland of KwaZulu and the Afrikaner Resistance Movement—a right-wing Afrikaner paramilitary group that opposed majority rule—joined with conservative elements in the South African police and military to foment terrorist violence that coincided with any progress in negotiations between the NP and the ANC.

Private citizens, church associations, and business corporations expressed concern that such violence could destroy the negotiations. With their prodding, the government, the ANC, and Inkatha signed a National Peace Accord in September 1991 that committed them to control violence by their followers. The accord also created mechanisms for monitoring political violence. Although violence continued, the peace accord mobilized thousands of South Africans to engage in dialogue with enemies and attempt to resolve conflicts nonviolently.[33]

Progress was also made on the negotiating front. The NP and the ANC both issued proposals for the transition to and creation of a new constitution. In April 1991 the ANC published its desired constitutional principles and structures. The constitution would be based on universal suffrage and a unified, nonracial, nonsexist nation. It would establish a far-reaching bill of rights that would "acknowledge the importance of securing minimum conditions of decent and dignified living for all South Africans; and include basic human rights to nutrition, shelter, education, health, employment and welfare." Constitutional structures would include a strong presidency (limited to two terms of office) and a two-house legislature (one for national representation, the other for regional representation) elected through proportional representation. An independent judiciary and constitutional court would interpret and rule on the constitutionality of proposed legislation.[34]

The ANC National Congress of July 2, 1991, hammered out proposals to guide the transition to democracy. An all-party conference would be held to establish broad constitutional principles and agreements on an interim government. A transitional government of national unity would rule for two to three years, during which time an elected constitutional assembly would draft the new constitution. When the new constitution was agreed on, elections would be held and a new, legitimate South African government would rule.[35]

The ANC's constitutional and transitional proposals differed dramatically from those of the NP. Although the NP did not specify its preferred plan for transition, members of its constitutional committee spoke of a ten-year transition period. The NP wanted the parties themselves—not an elected assembly—to negotiate the substance and details of a new constitution. The NP's constitutional proposals envisioned an extremely weak central government ruled by consociational principles—that is, by a committee of political parties, each with veto power over central decisions. One legislative house would be based on proportional representation; the other would consist of equal representation among parties that attained a low threshold of voter support. The latter house would also have veto power over legislation. At subnational levels, regions and communities would have their own tax bases and could curtail voting rights through property qualifications. The constitution would include a "charter of fundamental rights," but it would be limited to property rights and individual protections from government power—what are known in constitutional law as first-generation rights.[36]

The fundamental concerns of the two main parties in South Africa were clear. The ANC, believing it would gain a majority in a one-person, one-vote election, wanted a strong central government to redress societal and political inequalities forged by apartheid. The NP wanted arrangements that would protect the economic and political interests of the white population. Fearing the results of majority rule, the NP wanted "to dilute the strong drink of democracy."[37] By establishing a group veto, the NP could forestall economic redistribution and entrench the white advantage.

■ CODESA

The only real accord between the major parties was an agreement that all-parties talks should negotiate the path to and principles of a new South Africa. This slim reed of agreement led to the Convention for a Democratic South Africa (CODESA), formulated on December 21 and 22, 1991, which established a broad declaration of intent to guide the work toward a new constitution and created five working groups. The working groups were to establish a climate for free and fair political competition, devise constitutional principles and mechanisms, develop proposals for an interim government, plan the reincorporation of the homelands, and set a timetable for the transition to a new government.

CODESA lasted six months, failed to produce an agreement on any of the substantive issues under consideration, and provided tangible evidence of the difficulty of resolving South Africa's constitutional conflict. The two most powerful actors in the country were the ANC and the government; any settlement would require their active support. But these two parties combined did not represent all of South Africa. Since blacks had never voted in South Africa, no party (not even the ANC) could claim to represent anyone other than its own members. CODESA therefore incorporated all of the various claimants to authority in South Africa, including all homeland governments and any political party that demanded participation—nineteen organizations in all. Although the inclusive nature of CODESA gave it legitimacy, the sheer size of the negotiating forum caused problems. The ANC feared CODESA would never agree on anything if decisions were taken by strict consensus. On the other hand, majority rule would give equal weight to all CODESA participants, and not all organizations were equal within CODESA. In the end CODESA created a decision rule called "sufficient consensus," whereby in the case of outstanding differences over issues a judge could rule on whether an agreement existed to which most parties concurred. In essence, this plan created a veto for both the ANC and the NP, but it also required that they seek a wide range of acceptance for their proposals.

Although CODESA failed to produce an agreement, it nonetheless produced partial breakthroughs that would form the basis of a settlement between the ANC and the NP two years later. Transitional arrangements and a basis for a settlement—a constituent assembly to meet ANC demands and binding constitutional principles for the NP—resulted from CODESA. Many of the proposals the ANC would make during the next year to gain NP trust and approval stemmed from learning NP demands and needs through CODESA. Too often, conflict resolution in divided societies is expected to happen overnight; in the South African case a long-term process of bargaining, information sharing, and learning was necessary.

▓ Toward Compromise

As negotiations became bogged down at CODESA, an important debate occurred among ANC strategists. Joe Slovo, a member of the ANC executive council and former head of the South African Communist Party, argued that the ANC would have to make substantial concessions for negotiations to succeed. He reasoned that NP entrenchment in the state bureaucracy and security forces would undermine any settlement that did not address white fears and interests. The ANC's only alternative was to compromise on fundamental issues such as job security, retrenchment packages for the present administration, and general amnesty as part of a negotiated settlement. Slovo proposed the need for sunset clauses, laws that would extend for a fixed number of years protection of white privilege beyond any negotiated transfer of power to a majority government.[38]

Toward the end of 1992 and into January 1993, ANC and NP leaders participated in a series of private meetings to discuss a way out of their impasse. The ANC and the NP agreed that an election would produce a constitutional assembly that would write a new constitution and act as an interim government of national unity for five years; the assembly would elect a national president, and any party that received over 5 percent of the vote would place members in the cabinet. The party with the second-largest vote total would select a deputy vice-president. The ANC accepted that the constitutional assembly could be bound by arrangements established by prior negotiation. The ANC refused the NP demand for a collective presidency but agreed that a new constitution must establish regional and local governments, with some powers devolved to them. The new constitution would be ratified by a two-thirds vote of the assembly. The NP accepted that if the constitutional assembly could not agree on a new constitution within two years a deadlock-breaking mechanism, such as a referendum, would be needed. The ANC wanted an election date set within a year; during the run-up to the election an interim constitution would be drafted and a transitional executive council and independent election council put in place. The ANC and the NP would return to a CODESA-like forum, which would involve as many parties as possible in the transition, to draft the interim constitution and constitutional principles.

In February 1993 the NP and the ANC went public with their agreement and began the hard sell to their constituencies, which had not been privy to the deliberations. The ANC encountered tough opposition from militants within the party such as Winnie Mandela, Harry Gwala, and Peter Mokoba, then head of the ANC Youth League. They accused the top negotiators, in particular Cyril Ramaphosa, of selling out the goal of fundamental revolutionary change. Three years of violence and dashed expectations had embittered many youths in the ANC. Mokoba warned the leadership that if it failed to gain the support of the youth, they could destroy any settlement.

The NP was also beset by factionalism. A group of proreform members coalesced around Roelf Meyer, the chief negotiator for the party. As an architect of the compromise with the ANC, Meyer bore the brunt of charges that the NP had abandoned the veto in the new regime. Some NP officials used bureaucratic sabotage to undermine Meyer.

The convergence of the ANC and the NP on constitutional proposals raised the issue of how to bring parties such as Inkatha into negotiations. The problem was compounded by the formation of the Concerned South Africans Group (COSAG), an alliance among Inkatha, the homeland governments of Ciskei and Bophuthatswana, the Conservative Party (an Afrikaner right-wing party), and other Afrikaner militants. These groups, which objected to an ANC-NP deal and to their loss of power in a new South Africa, put forward radical proposals for a new constitution. Inkatha demanded a confederal state that would vest nearly total power in the regions and grant them autonomy. Some within the Afrikaner right demanded a sovereign white homeland.

The ANC could not concede on this issue because it feared that if regional constitutions took precedence over the national constitution apartheid could continue. If Inkatha won on this principle it could win an election in KwaZulu, Buthelezi's homeland, and write a regional constitution that would perpetuate its authoritarian rule. Likewise, if a white party won a regional election it could erect an apartheid constitution. The ANC insisted that a single national constitution would establish rights and obligations for every South African.

The ANC and the NP invited interested parties back to the negotiating table and promised to hear all of their concerns. The new Multiparty Negotiating Forum convened on March 5, 1993, with twenty-six parties representing various groups from South Africa. Very quickly, however, it bogged down in disputes among its participants. A new urgency was interjected into the process on April 19, when Chris Hani, former head of the ANC armed wing and leader of the South African Communist Party, was assassinated by a Polish emigrant to South Africa with ties to the Conservative Party. Hani's death brought South Africa close to the breaking point. Youth violence erupted throughout the country. Nelson Mandela appeared on the South Africa Broadcasting Service and appealed for calm. The crisis brought urgency to the ANC and NP negotiators, who could see that the likely price of a continued stalemate would be societal violence beyond the control of either party. On July 3, the ANC and the NP insisted that a date be set for South Africa's first nonracial election. Although COSAG objected, the presiding judge at the forum declared that sufficient consensus existed to set the election for April 27, 1994.

On July 26 a committee of constitutional experts chosen by the forum offered the first draft of an interim constitution. The draft established twenty-seven principles to bind the elected constitutional assembly, including multiparty democracy; proportional representation; an independent judiciary; fundamental human rights; due process before the law; a two-house parliament, of which one would represent provincial interests; and strong local and regional governments, which would have some concurrent and exclusive powers vis-à-vis the central government. The draft constitution established nine regional governments and put forward twelve functional areas in which those governments would have competence (including taxation within the region, housing, education, traditional law, and health and welfare). The final demarcation of central and regional powers would be established by a commission on regional government. Regions would be allowed to have their own constitutions as long as they were not at odds with the national constitution.

COSAG rejected the draft constitution and promised to boycott any election. Constitutional negotiators continued to revise the draft and hoped to win COSAG approval by strengthening the powers of the regions. A draft was finally accepted in November 1993, at which time a Transitional Executive Council was established to guide the country to the April elections. COSAG still renounced the negotiations. Even after the interim constitution was accepted, the ANC and the NP continued to make concessions to bring Inkatha and right-wing whites into the process.

All four groups that had promised to boycott the elections weakened. The homeland governments of Bophuthatswana and Ciskei were brought down by a strike by civil servants, police, and local defense forces. The Afrikaner right wing split into two factions when retired South African army general Constand Viljoen pledged to contest the election. Buthelezi's support in KwaZulu wavered at the prospect of boycotting the first non-racial election in South African history.

A combination of incentives and pressure brought Buthelezi into the elections.[39] A key role was played by a Kenyan mediator, Washington Okumu, who met privately with Buthelezi on April 16–17, about ten days before the elections were scheduled. Okumu warned that if Inkatha continued its electoral boycott, Buthelezi would be out of power in ten days; his only options would be complete capitulation or a protracted guerrilla war with no international support. Okumu pointed out that Nelson Mandela was willing to offer special considerations to preserve the Zulu monarchy in the new constitution—an issue that Buthelezi had made central to his cause. On April 19, Buthelezi signaled his willingness to join the elections.

The elections of April 26–28 brought South Africa's long-standing conflict over political participation to a close. Myriad logistical foul-ups created much confusion, but for the most part the election proceeded in a free and fair manner. Although there were many reports of fraud and intimidation in KwaZulu, the ANC, NP, and Inkatha negotiators hammered out a compromise on how the problem would be handled. Indeed, their close cooperation during the election gave rise to allegations that the three parties had rigged the election results to produce percentages of votes that would provide stability for the country. The ANC won the national election with 62.6 percent of the vote, enough to form the new government but short of the two-thirds threshold that would have enabled the party to write the constitution by itself. The NP and Inkatha, with 20.4 percent and 10.5 percent of the vote, respectively, performed well enough to win seats in the new cabinet, and the NP's performance also assured F. W. de Klerk one of the two deputy presidencies. Both parties also maintained regional bases of support, with the NP winning the Western Cape and Inkatha taking KwaZulu/Natal.

The two main parties to the conflict, the ANC and the NP, sacrificed much for a bargain. Although the ANC won its demand for a constituent assembly, it compromised on the principles that would guide the writing of a new constitution. It achieved its objective that a single president rule the new government, but it conceded much power to regional and local governments. The ANC also agreed to a much longer interim arrangement than it had wanted and accepted a five-year government of national unity. The National Party abandoned the idea of an executive by committee and a white veto on policy. In return, it won a commitment to strong regionalism, limited power sharing for the first five years, guarantees of civil servant pensions and jobs, and the enshrinement of property rights in a new constitution.

■ THE CHALLENGE OF TRANSFORMATION

We conclude this chapter by examining the most prominent challenges that have faced the attempt to transform South Africa's state and society. Having gained power in 1994, the ANC faces the enormous task of delivering basic services to its black population. Actors in civil society—including human rights groups, churches, and prodemocracy organizations—have put truth and reconciliation on South Africa's agenda and insisted that the elimination of apartheid's legacies depends on establishing accountability over the past. And finally, there is the challenge of consolidating democracy, an issue that has created a sharp debate over what constitutes the biggest threat to South Africa's new democracy: the inability of elected governments to fulfill South African citizens' expectations for social and economic change, or the accumulation of power by the ANC in a one-party–dominant state.

■ Apartheid's Legacies and State and Society

South Africa's tortured history of racism and violence has left enduring legacies for today's state and society. The capture of the South African state by Afrikaners in 1948 and their relentless hold on that state for over forty years pose major challenges for governance. First, Afrikaner dominance created a class of officeholders with a vested interest in opposing reforms. As a price of the negotiated settlement, these civil servants gained job security under a new government. This alone need not be bad, but when coupled with a second legacy—bureaucratic bloat—it established an overstaffed, underproductive bureaucracy that is difficult to streamline. Because the apartheid state insisted on ethnic and racial separation, it created multiple ministries and departments to provide each societal group with its own administration for policy issues. For example, in 1990 there were eighteen departments of housing and education, each with jurisdiction over different geographic areas and racial groups.[40]

Third, the present government must confront the legacy of the racist state in the everyday provision of security to citizens beset by crime and violence. The apartheid state used the police and the judiciary to foster insecurity among blacks. These institutions were known in South Africa for arbitrariness, coercion, amateurishness, and injustice toward blacks. This legacy fosters a profound mistrust of the police among black South Africans.

Fourth, apartheid as an economic system produced a massive distribution conflict, with great disparities between whites and blacks in wealth, income, health, education, housing, and land. The gap between rich and poor is rarely as wide as that in South Africa. South Africa's Gini coefficient—a measure of income inequality—is 0.62, among the highest in the world.[41] With an estimated annual per capita income of whites at $4,775.70 in 1989, South Africa would rank among the world's upper-income countries. The yearly per capita income of black South Africans—$417.80—would put South Africa into the category of low-income countries.[42] The South African government estimated in 1992 that 45 percent of South Africans— most of them black—were below a "minimum living level."[43]

Wealth and land follow the same pattern. In 1993, four South African corporations—Anglo-American, Old Mutual, Rembrandt, and Sanlam— controlled companies that held more than 80 percent of the assets of the Johannesburg Stock Exchange; Anglo-American alone controlled companies that owned 45.3 percent of those assets.[44] Land legislation in South Africa enacted in 1913 and 1936 gave 87 percent of the land to white farmers, relegating blacks to overcrowded reserves that had been farmed to death by the 1930s. Such legislation, combined with the establishment of homelands in the most arid areas, left a large African rural population barely able to eke out a living. In 1993 researchers estimated that "25 percent of children under the age of five suffer from stunting as a result of chronic malnutrition."[45]

The inadequate carrying capacity of the homelands forced illegal black migration to the cities in the 1970s and 1980s. The abolition of pass laws and the Group Areas Act further intensified urbanization and created a monumental housing crisis for poor blacks. South Africa's Urban Foundation estimates that between 1985 and 1990 the population of South Africa's urban and metropolitan areas grew by 3.4 million.[46] Estimates of the number of black families waiting for housing range from 1.1 million to 3.4 million.[47] In 1991 the average number of blacks per housing unit exceeded 16.[48]

Apartheid created a large gap in state expenses for education for white and black children. In 1988/89 the per capita expenditure was R3,082 for white pupils, R2,227 for Indians, and R1,360 for coloureds. Annual spending for African children ranged from R765 in the cities to R481 in the homelands. In 1991 blacks averaged forty pupils per teacher and more than fifty pupils per classroom, whereas whites averaged under twenty pupils per teacher and fewer than fifteen students per classroom. That same year, white schools in South Africa had 250,000 vacancies, and there were 400,000 more African students than spaces provided.[49] The same unequal system ruled in the health sector. In 1992, infant mortality for Africans was eight to ten times higher than that for whites and was significantly higher than rates in Zimbabwe, Zambia, and Botswana. Tuberculosis struck 780 of 10,000 black Africans, compared with only 13.5 of 10,000 whites.[50]

If the South African economy were healthy and growing at a steady rate, the distribution conflict would be more easily resolved since "it is easier to deal with difficult distributive issues . . . if the total size of the cake is increasing."[51] But by 1990 South Africa's economy had been in a prolonged slump. Although apartheid economic policies had contributed to rapid economic growth in the 1950s and 1960s, they became increasingly counterproductive in the early 1970s because of the rigidity of the labor market, massive state subsidies to white businesses, and protection of the manufacturing sector and commercial agriculture. Between 1975 and 1990 South Africa's economic performance was on a par with that of the least developed countries in the world. Gross domestic product (GDP) growth averaged 1.3 percent per year from 1980 through 1989.[52] Real GDP per capita declined 2 percent each year during that period. The decline in per capita GDP coincided with a sharp drop in fixed investment, from nearly 29 percent of GDP in 1980 to around 21 percent in 1990.[53]

The economic decline produced massive unemployment. Unemployment increased from 3.1 million in 1980 to 5 million in 1989, based on measures that broadly define employed as "anyone who was working for as little as five hours in a week."[54] Between 1986 and 1991 less than 13 percent of 400,000 first-time job seekers in South Africa found employment.[55] Unemployment disproportionately struck black youth: approximately 90 percent of those unemployed were under the age of thirty.[56]

◼ Meeting the Challenges

Although five years is too limited a period to serve as a comprehensive basis for evaluating a regime's performance, certain trends are visible. Not surprisingly, the ANC-led Government of National Unity has compiled a mixed record. In its first five years in power, the government has made spectacular gains in provision of access to water, electricity, basic health care services, and land. Between 1994 and 1999, 1.7 million people gained access to clean water, and 1.2 million households were provided with electricity. More than 300,000 new houses have been built. Free primary health care has been introduced at all public primary health care facilities. The Ministry of Land has redistributed nearly 2 million hectares of land.[57]

On the other hand, there is little to show on issues of unemployment and crime, both of which are related to the performance of the economy. Although the South African economy grew steadily from 1994 to 1998, it has not performed well enough to reduce unemployment. Estimates in 1996 suggest that as many as 55 percent of young black males were unemployed. Crime has not been stanched: in 1994 murder rates in South Africa were among the highest in the world, and they remain so today.[58]

South Africa also has a mixed record in confronting a different legacy of apartheid: human rights abuses by officials of the South African government during apartheid. South Africa's civil society insisted that an attempt be made to establish the truth of those years, to investigate the responsibility of leaders and officials for atrocities and abuses. People like Nobel Peace Prize winner Archbishop Desmond Tutu argued that only by confronting the past, establishing accountability for past actions, and asking for forgiveness could true reconciliation be reached between South African blacks and whites. Tutu was instrumental in creating South Africa's Truth and Reconciliation Commission (TRC), which had the legal power to subpoena witnesses, offer amnesty in exchange for confessions, and provide reparations to victims. The TRC has been instrumental in uncovering in ghastly detail political murders, assassinations, and torture of antiapartheid activists and the involvement of South African ministers, generals, and police in such abuses.

It is too early to know the ramifications of the TRC. Some victims of apartheid are disgruntled because so many perpetrators of crimes have received amnesty. For these critics, truth is a poor substitute for justice. TRC supporters, however, point out that a necessary condition of the negotiated transition to majority rule was an offer of amnesty to former government officials for their past actions. The absence of such assurance would have reinforced the "backs against the wall" attitude so long ingrained in South Africa's white population. Other observers see little evidence that revelations of truth have fostered reconciliation between former adversaries in South Africa. Yet it may be unfair to judge reconciliation in the short term; perhaps the fault lies with outside observers who expect too much from normal people who have lived through such hateful and abusive times.

Finally, what can be said of the future of democracy in South Africa? Some observers argue that the greatest threat to political stability and democracy in South Africa is the possibility that the ANC will become such a dominant party that all opposition will be vanquished. Such observers believe South Africa will fall into the authoritarianism mode that the rest of Africa has suffered with throughout its history.[59] Yet this analysis ignores the fact that South Africa possesses an immense wealth of nongovernmental and community-based organizations that can act as a check on any party that seeks to usurp all of the power in the country. Moreover, norms of human rights, constitutionalism, and accountability will likely act as safeguards against one-party rule.[60]

This brings us back to where we started: to the imperative for the new South African state to meet the needs and demands of its citizens. In a perceptive analysis Michael Bratton has written, "The threat to the South African miracle emanates not so much from a state that governs too much, as one that governs too little."[61] Future stability requires that the South African state address the long-standing concerns of its people—jobs, safety, and prosperity—to transform South Africa in ways that eradicate the vestiges of apartheid.

■ NOTES

1. This historical analysis draws from Thomas Ohlson and Stephen John Stedman, with Robert Davies, *The New Is Not Yet Born: Conflict Resolution in Southern Africa* (Washington, DC: Brookings Institution Press, 1994).

2. Elizabeth A. Eldridge, "Sources of Conflict in Southern Africa, ca. 1800–1830: The 'Mfecane' Revisited," *Journal of African History* 33 (1992): 1–35.

3. Clifton C. Crais, *The Making of the Colonial Order: White Supremacy and Black Resistance in the Eastern Cape, 1770–1865* (Johannesburg: Witswatersrand University Press, 1992), pp. 33–35.

4. Noel Mostert, *Frontiers: The Epic of South Africa's Creation and the Tragedy of the Xhosa People* (New York: Knopf, 1992), p. 232.

5. Martin Legassick, "The State, Racism, and the Rise of Capitalism in the Nineteenth-Century Cape Colony," *South African Historical Journal* 28 (1993): 329–368.

6. Crais, *Making of the Colonial Order,* p. 129.

7. Ibid., p. 3.

8. See A. Atmore and S. Marks, "The Imperial Factor in South Africa in the Nineteenth Century: Towards a Reassessment," *Journal of Imperial and Commonwealth History* 3 (1972–1973): 107–108.

9. A.J. Christopher, *Southern Africa* (Hamden, CT: Archon, 1976), p. 175.

10. Ibid., p. 248.

11. Colin Bundy, *The Rise and Fall of the South African Peasantry* (Berkeley: University of California Press, 1979).

12. Robert M. Price, *The Apartheid State in Crisis: Political Transformation in South Africa, 1975–1990* (New York: Oxford University Press, 1991), pp. 15–17.

13. Ibid., p. 19.

14. Ibid., p. 23.

15. Thompson, *History of South Africa* (New Haven: Yale University Press, 1990), p. 194.

16. Price, *Apartheid State,* p. 20.

17. Ibid., p. 25; and Heribert Adam and Hermann Giliomee, *Ethnic Power Mobilized: Can South Africa Change?* (New Haven: Yale University Press, 1979), p. 169.

18. Ibid., p. 25.

19. Thompson, *History of South Africa,* p. 199.

20. Dan O'Meara, *Volkskapitalisme. Class, Capital, and Ideology in the Development of Afrikaner Nationalism, 1934–1948* (Cambridge: Cambridge University Press, 1983), p. 250.

21. The text of the Freedom Charter appears in Commonwealth Group of Eminent Persons, *Mission to South Africa: The Commonwealth Report* (Harmondsworth: Penguin, 1986), pp. 157–160.

22. Bernard Magubane, *The Political Economy of Race and Class in South Africa* (New York: Monthly Review Press, 1979), p. 305.

23. O'Meara, *Volkskapitalisme,* p. 247.

24. Price, *Apartheid State,* p. 45.

25. Truth and Reconciliation Commission, *Final Report,* presented to President Nelson Mandela on October 29, 1998. The report can be downloaded from the Internet (www.polity.org.za/govdocs/commissions/1998/trc).

26. Price, *Apartheid State,* p.193.

27. Leonard Thompson, *A History of South Africa* (New Haven: Yale University Press, 1990), p. 236.

28. Hermann Giliomee, "Broedertwis: Intra-Afrikaner Conflicts in the Transition from Apartheid," *African Affairs* 91 (July 1992): 360.

29. Tom Lodge, "Perspectives on Conflict Resolution in South Africa," in Francis Deng and I. William Zartman, eds., *Conflict Resolution in Africa* (Washington, DC: Brookings Institution Press, 1991), pp. 125–130.

30. Quoted in *Cape Times,* July 2, 1993.

31. For an analysis of pact making in South Africa, see Timothy D. Sisk, *Democratization in South Africa: The Elusive Social Contract* (Princeton: Princeton University Press, 1995).

32. Stephen John Stedman, "Spoiler Problems in Peace Processes," *International Security* 22, no. 2 (Fall 1997): 5.

33. Peter Gastrow, *Bargaining for Peace: South Africa and the National Peace Accord* (Washington, DC: U.S. Institute of Peace Press, 1995).

34. Quotes in this paragraph, as well as the description of proposals, are based on African National Congress Constitutional Committee, *Discussion Document: Constitutional Principles and Structures for a Democratic South Africa* (Bellville, South Africa: Centre for Development Studies, University of the Western Cape, April 1991), pp. 15, 19.

35. "The 48th National Conference of the African National Congress," *Monitor* (June 1991): 82.

36. Federal Council of the National Party's Outline of Its Views Concerning a Constitution for a New South Africa, mimeo, no date.

37. Roger Southall, "The Contradictory State! The Proposals of the National Party for a New Constitution," *Monitor* (October 1991): 90.

38. Joe Slovo, "Negotiations: What Room for Compromise?" *African Communist* 130 (Third Quarter 1992): 36–40.

39. Donald Rothchild, *Managing Ethnic Conflict in Africa: Pressures and Incentives for Cooperation* (Washington, DC: Brookings Institutional Press, 1997), pp. 205–209.

40. Desmond Lachman and Kenneth Bercuson, eds., *Economic Policies for a New South Africa* (Washington, DC: International Monetary Fund, 1992), p. 19; and Gavin Maasdorp, "Meeting Expectations: The Policy Environment Facing the Post-Apartheid Government," in Robert Schrire, ed., *Wealth or Poverty? Critical Choices for South Africa* (Johannesburg: Oxford University Press, 1992), p. 600.

41. Servaas Van Der Berg, "Consolidating South African Democracy: The Political Arithmetic of Budgetary Redistribution," *African Affairs* 97 (1998): 255.

42. William F. Moses and Meg Vorhees, *Corporate Responsibility in Changing South Africa* (Washington, DC: Investor Responsibility Research Center, 1991), p. 32.

43. Andrew Donaldson, "Basic Needs and Social Policy: The Role of the State in Education, Health and Welfare," in Merle Lipton and Charles Simkins, eds., *State and Market in Post-Apartheid South Africa* (Johannesburg: Witwatersrand University Press, 1993), p. 273.

44. Jos Gerson, "Should the State Attempt to Reshape South Africa's Corporate and Financial Structures?" in Lipton and Simkins, eds., *State and Market,* pp. 164–165.

45. Heather Deegan, *South Africa Reborn: Building a New Democracy* (London: University College of London Press, 1999), p. 129.

46. Charles Simkins, "State, Market, and Urban Development in South Africa," in Lipton and Simkins, eds., *State and Market,* p. 335.

47. Lawrence Schlemmer, "Distribution and Redistribution Trade-offs," in Schrire, ed., *Wealth or Poverty?* p. 572.

48. Ronnie Bethlehem, "The Sensible Thing to Do," in *The Watershed Years: A Leadership Publication, 1991* (Johannesburg: Leadership Publications, 1991), pp. 102–106.

49. Expenditures are from South African Institute of Race Relations; class and teacher ratios and vacancies are from "South Africa: Growth Crisis . . . or Development Challenge?" in *Watershed Years,* p. 139.

50. Colin Bundy, "Development and Inequality in Historical Perspective," in Schrire, ed., *Wealth or Poverty?* p. 25.

51. Stephen R. Lewis Jr., *The Economics of Apartheid* (New York: Council on Foreign Relations, 1990), p. 136.

52. Bobby Godsell and Jim Buys, "Growth and Poverty," in Schrire, ed., *Wealth or Poverty?* p. 640.

53. Nicoli Nattrass, *Profits and Wages: The South African Economic Challenge* (Johannesburg: Penguin, 1992), p. 4.

54. Bob Tucker and Bruce R. Scott, eds., *South Africa: Prospects for a Successful Transition: Nedcor-Old Mutual Scenarios* (Kenwyn, South Africa: Juta, 1992), p. 53.

55. Colin Bundy, "At War with the Future? Black South African Youth in the 1990s," in Stephen John Stedman, ed., *South Africa: The Political Economy of Transformation* (Boulder: Lynne Rienner, 1994), p. 53.

56. Ibid.

57. Michael Bratton, "After Mandela's Miracle in South Africa," *Current History* 97, no. 619 (May 1998): 215–216.

58. Deegan, *South African Reborn,* p. 97.

59. An example of this kind of analysis is R. W. Johnson, "Fear in the Miracle Nations," *London Review of Books* (November 2, 1995).

60. Heribert Adam, Frederik Van Zyl Slabbert, and Kogila Moodley, *Comrades in Business: Post-Liberation Politics in South Africa* (Cape Town: Tafelberg, 1997).

61. Bratton, "After Mandela's Miracle in South Africa," p. 219.

14

Africa in the Twenty-First Century

As the world enters the twenty-first century, African states and societies are enmeshed in a process of global reordering. The terms we have used to describe contemporary African politics—"vibrant," "fluid," "rich," "complex"—are especially appropriate today. Despite the economic and social problems faced by most African governments, the continent is characterized by a tremendous political vitality. Indeed, as the 1990s so forcefully demonstrated, the very difficulties that Africans have faced since independence have prompted experimentation with new political forms and directions.

We hope that the political interaction approach that we have presented in this book has provided readers with a concept that captures the diversity of contemporary African politics. Our approach is far from deterministic. Although recognizing the severe constraints under which most African governments function, constraints that have been compounded by the increased marginalization of the continent in the wake of the end of the Cold War, we have emphasized that alternative options exist, and that Africans have begun to explore these possibilities with renewed vigor. Policy decisions have led not only to markedly different forms of regime, but also to a restructuring of economic life and to a reassessment of relations with foreign actors. Consequently, it is often misleading to talk in general terms about Africa as if it were a single entity. There are many Africas.

The fluidity of African politics and the variety of responses to the problems that have emerged since independence make any effort to predict the future extremely hazardous. Old certainties have disappeared. The naive optimism expressed by some modernization theorists—and resurrected briefly with the fall of so many authoritarian regimes in the beginning of the 1990s—would find little resonance among serious observers of the contemporary African scene. On the other hand, the pessimism and helplessness of underdevelopment theories have increasingly been regarded as inadequate for conveying the richness and diversity of the African experience. In our final chapter, we continue to emphasize the centrality of interaction in African politics. Rather than attempting to specify outcomes, we will identify some of the major dimensions on which change may be expected and pose questions as to which directions that change might take.

Less than fifty years have passed since the first black African country gained its independence from colonial rule. Although the popular saying is that a week is a long time in politics, four and a half decades is a relatively short period in political history. This is especially so when placed in the context of the centuries over which the states of Asia and Western Europe were consolidated or, indeed, the long period between the independence of the United States and the introduction of universal adult suffrage. It should come as no surprise, therefore, that African countries have only begun to contend with the enormous problems of state construction and societal consolidation they confront. State capabilities for penetrating society and carrying into effect public policies remain weak; governments are still often characterized by repression and personal rule. Yet, in many respects, state institutions and established procedures of governance have nevertheless become an integral part of daily life on the continent.

The challenges faced by Africans in the twenty-first century—whether these take the form of deteriorating commodity prices, population growth, shortage of land, porous borders, ethnic conflicts, or pressure from international agencies—sap limited state resources in a relentless manner. We can expect the gap between resource availability and the demands made on them to close only slowly. Even optimistic projections of economic performance into the twenty-first century leave most Africans well behind the levels of income achieved in numerous Latin American and Asian countries. Although some African states may experience windfalls that afford some breathing space—as oil did for Nigeria in the second half of the 1970s—the impact of such events is likely to be only temporary and may indeed complicate the process of development by creating unrealistic expectations and encouraging extravagant expenditures.

Given the continuing dilemmas confronting African countries, some governments have had remarkable success in the pursuit of at least some of their objectives. These achievements must be placed in the context of their limited inheritance at independence and the constraints, both domestic and international, that they have subsequently faced. There have been significant advances in the fields of education and health care, although new medical dangers, including the spread of AIDS, have emerged in recent years. In the political realm, rules and procedures for conflict management have gradually but steadily been established. Some African regimes—most notably Cameroon, Mozambique, and Tanzania—managed the difficult task of political succession under authoritarian rule. In others, such as Mauritius, regime changes have taken place peacefully in accordance with democratic rules. African states have become active participants on the international stage, playing an important role in regional and continental forums, as well as in the United Nations. Despite the complexities of their borders, African states (Chad/Libya, Mali/Burkina Faso, Tanzania/Uganda, Rwanda/Congo, Senegal/Mauritania, and Ethiopia/Eritrea notwithstanding) have for the most part been adept at avoiding boundary disputes. The continent's leaders and organizations responded creatively to the economic crises that beset Africa in the first half of the 1980s, just as most incumbents also accommodated to the political pressures of the 1990s.

While the economic malaise that characterizes much of contemporary Africa should not blind us to the very real accomplishments since independence, it would be naive to pretend that costly failures—in economic, political, and social terms—have not occurred. The lessons of mistaken policies, such as forced industrialization or the attempt to coerce the population into communal farming, should by now be sufficiently deeply inscribed on the minds of Africa's leaders that repetition will be avoided. Failures elsewhere have certainly made some policy paths much less attractive. In the early 1970s, for instance, Tanzania's strategy of self-reliance was widely praised and suggested as a model for other states to emulate. Today, few commentators would prescribe this course, because the ineffective way in which aspects of this policy were implemented has largely discredited the whole strategy. In these and other instances in which faulty implementation has damaged the credibility of otherwise potentially sound strategies, there may well be a risk of succumbing to the proverbial danger of throwing the baby out with the bathwater.

One thing is certain. The idealized "traditional" society, much beloved by theorists of modernization, has no counterpart in contemporary Africa. The continent has, of course, been penetrated by international traders for centuries, and the communications revolution of recent years has left few areas of the continent untouched by external influences. Processes of economic differentiation and class formation were well under way long before independence. Despite economic setbacks, these trends are continuing and may be expected to increase. Problems in agricultural production may well lead to more experiments with large-scale capital-intensive farming that will accentuate issues of land tenure that have already emerged in some countries; Ghana, Kenya, Nigeria, and Zimbabwe are some of the most notable examples.

The days when Africans could display their dissatisfaction with government policies by pursuing an "exit" option—a retreat into subsistence farming—may, in most countries, be increasingly less feasible. This narrowing of options has significant implications, not merely for the already rapid rate of urban growth and the emergence of a landless proletariat, but also for political participation and the forms of political conflict.[1] Although a growing land shortage may enhance the ability of governments to "capture" the peasantry, it may also generate new economic and social forces. Major changes can be expected in social relations if access to the land is lost by the children of existing farmers: the roles of the village and the local community, of such importance in the social and political life of many parts of Africa, might alter significantly. And the extended family will, perforce, have to undergo substantial adjustment. Continuing industrialization will accelerate the process of class formation. Whether the horizontal ties of class relations will become more important than the vertical links of patron-client ties remains to be seen. Will Africa's elites become self-perpetuating as a result of their own control of major resources and their children's privileged access to scarce educational opportunities?

In the political realm, the search for formulas for greater institutionalization is likely to continue. African states since independence have experimented with a wide array of regime types—from personal dictatorships and bureaucratic regimes to now largely defunct Marxist-Leninist parties and populist governments. And while multipartyism was the order of the day during most of the 1990s, the problem of establishing a tradition of responsible government remains. The 1990s witnessed the disappearance of almost the entire independence generation, marking the termination of the postcolonial phase of African history. Will their successors be able to create a new foundation for legitimacy now that the status of "father of the nation" is no longer available?

What mechanisms of political accountability will be devised? Will the new century see the regularization of political competition on the African continent? It is certain that the 1990s witnessed the founding of more parties than at any time since the last years of the decolonization period. But will these parties become anything more than hollow shells? Given the brief and unhappy experiences that many countries had with democratization in the immediate postindependence period, are there any grounds to believe that the prospects for democratic government are better today? The failure of early democratic experiments highlights the importance of strengthening the social foundations, and not only the institutional frameworks, of liberal government. How will the pluralism of African societies and the newfound voice of popular groups be expressed and channeled politically? What will be the basis of political mobilization? Now that the Marxist-Leninist model, so much an outgrowth of particular political circumstances, is no longer attractive, will ethnic, religious, and sectarian pressures increase? Is there a possibility that the populist institutional arrangements of direct participation—"social inclusion"—that came to the fore in the 1980s in countries such as Burkina Faso and Ghana will be revived in the next few years? What design will specific African countries invent to assure responsible participation and adequate representation of all major interests in the decisionmaking process? And is there a potential incompatibility between democratization and economic stabilization?

Not surprisingly, political uncertainties abound as the political patterns of the initial phase of independence are unraveling and most countries are at a political crossroads whose direction is unclear. How will political transitions take place in the first decades of the twenty-first century? Will the return to the ballot box persist? Will the instrument of national conferences developed as a means of moving from authoritarian to multiparty politics become the norm? Or will the military play a major role in African politics and economic activities? Will more states succumb to military intervention? Have those countries that have not experienced a military coup been blessed with favorable background factors, found a successful formula for containing military intervention, or just been plain lucky? How many states will collapse into various warring factions in the same manner as Chad and Uganda in the 1980s and Somalia, Liberia, Sierra Leone, and Congo in the 1990s? Can the colonially imposed state boundaries withstand the resurgence of ethnic and cultural sentiments in many parts of the continent? The experiences of some countries—Liberia, Congo, and Ethiopia stand out in this regard—have shown that the road back from state collapse is long and painful.

How will shifting economic and political conditions affect social organization? We can expect that frameworks will continue to be redefined as urbanization progresses and economic circumstances change. These developments will in all probability be accompanied by the continuation of ethnic-based demands and by the growth of powerful ideological and religious movements that have gathered considerable political momentum in recent years. We have shown how some governments have handled their ethnic and regional problems in a creative manner through various policies such as ethnic balancing and political decentralization. Urban-rural and interregional inequalities are almost certain to be exacerbated as economic development progresses. Will governments be able to continue to pursue innovative politics of regional and ethnic equity in an era of extreme scarcity of resources? Will one response to scarcity be the revival of destructive ethnic politics, as appears to be occurring not only in Rwanda, Burundi, and Sudan, but also in Kenya and Congo-Brazzaville? Or will demands be channeled through various class and interest groups?

Continuing conflict over resource allocation and disillusionment with the formal political process may also be expected to encourage the activities of voluntary organizations. Will these take the form primarily of groups whose principal purpose is to lobby governments, or organizations such as syncretist churches that offer a vent for frustrations largely outside the official political realm? Will the Islamic revival that began in parts of the Sahel and North Africa in the 1990s continue and assume increasingly political overtones in the twenty-first century? Will we see the emergence in Africa of an Islamic fundamentalist state comparable to Iran? Will the rise of Islam conflict with the growing political role of women on the continent and the increasing awareness among women in the general population of their disadvantaged position? Or, in stark contrast, will some of the new groups being formed throughout the continent lay the foundation for the consolidation of vibrant civil societies in Africa? Will international agencies succeed in their professed goal of fortifying voluntary activity and averting parochial and patriarchal trends?

The path of societal restructuring will depend heavily on the organization of African states in the years to come. What are the prospects that the African state will become more effective? There is little hope that significantly increased resources will become available: if the state is to enhance its capacity for policy implementation, then existing resources must be used more creatively and efficiently. Most observers assert that a significant reason why African states have been ineffective is that the implementation of policymaking is distorted by sectional and elitist interests. How can the penetrative capacity of African states be facilitated while decisionmaking procedures are streamlined and opened to closer public scrutiny? Early optimism that military governments would be able to resist pressures from special interests soon faded as it became obvious that they were as divided as the wider societies from which they were drawn. Similarly, Africa's handful of Marxist-Leninist governments did not succeed any more effectively than their Eastern European counterparts in turning themselves into organizational weapons that could overcome social divisions. It now remains to be seen whether multiparty competition can contain undue social pressures.

African governments have had to learn to live with greatly increased interference by the World Bank and the International Monetary Fund. Many questions still remain, however, at the end of the second decade of structural adjustment in Africa. Have the international financial institutions put forward viable programs that can provide the foundation for long-term growth in Africa? Will they, and other Western donors, supply additional financing to the degree necessary to enable these programs to have a reasonable chance for success? Will Western governments adopt a more sensible approach to resolving Africa's debt problems? How seriously will African governments pursue the painful and politically risky policies necessary for prolonged adjustment—especially if they are now faced with regular electoral challenges?

International agencies such as the World Bank and the IMF call for a greater reliance on market mechanisms to achieve a more efficient allocation of resources. Many commentators, however, question whether markets actually function effectively in Africa, where they are often dominated by a few large transnational corporations and where information flows are inefficient. There is also considerable controversy over the advocacy by international agencies of a reduced role for the state in African economies. Although many accept that the state has overextended itself, critics of the World Bank believe that it has misread twentieth-century economic history in general—and the recent experience of the newly industrializing countries in particular—in failing to perceive the leading role that the state has played in fostering economic growth through such devices as selective protectionism, the regulation of foreign enterprises, and the promotion of exports. Few would accept either the feasibility or the wisdom of the withdrawal of the African state from the global economy. But will the adoption of policies that emphasize market forces render African economies even more vulnerable to international influences and weaken the bargaining positions of African governments with transnational actors, just at the time when these governments are becoming more effective negotiators? Will decentralization of state activities, as advocated by many advisers, increase the effectiveness of the state or merely render it more vulnerable to capture by regional patron-client networks?

In the realm of international relations, will Africa sink into oblivion now that it is no longer a battleground for the superpowers? Or will there be a more sophisticated realization on the part of the international community that the disincorporation of the African continent carries dangers no less threatening to the security of the world than the conflicts that preoccupied external actors in the past? It appears that differential economic growth and patterns of political change in Africa will be translated into shifts in the continent's military balance. Will this lead to an increase in transborder adventurism, to growing interference in the domestic political affairs of neighboring states, as seen so dramatically in the military intervention in Congo? Will OAU norms regarding state sovereignty survive the current spate of interventions, or will new efforts to develop a sustainable normative order take place in the twenty-first century? Will differential economic performance facilitate the growth of regional cooperation by making it easier for the relatively well-off to subsidize services for poorer partners? Or will it intensify interstate jealousies and complicate the task of regional integration? Will Africa's regions become more clearly defined, or will the interactions that we have described in Chapter 11 become more genuinely continental, making any definition of regions more complex?

We do not pretend to have the answers to the questions posed here nor to the many others that have not been articulated in these pages. We can only hope that the ideas we have presented will provide readers with a basis from which to undertake a better-informed consideration of the alternative paths that African countries might take. But we can be sure that there will be new strategies adopted, new solutions devised by imaginative peoples and their leaders. That is why the study of contemporary African politics is so exciting.

■ NOTES

1. For the introduction of this terminology into the contemporary African debate see Goran Hyden, *Beyond Ujamaa in Tanzania: Underdevelopment and the Uncaptured Peasantry* (Berkeley: University of California Press, 1980).

Appendix 1: Acronyms

AAF-SAP	African Alternative Framework to Structural Adjustment Programmes
AAPC	All-African Peoples Conference
AAPSO	Afro-Asian People's Solidarity Organization
ACP Group	African, Caribbean, and Pacific Group
ADB	African Development Bank
ADP	agricultural development program
AEF	Afrique Equatoriale Française (French Equatorial Africa)
AIDS	Acquired Immune Deficiency Syndrome
ANC	African National Congress
AOF	Afrique Occidentale Française (French West Africa)
APEC	Asian-Pacific Economic Cooperation
AZAPO	Azanian Peoples' Organization
AZASO	Azanian Students' Organization
BCM	Black Consciousness Movement
BOSS	Bureau of State Security
CC	Chama Cha Mapinduzi
CEAO	Economic Community of West Africa
CFA	African Financial Community
CIA	Central Intelligence Agency
CIAS	Conference of Independent African States
CIEC	Conference on International Economic Cooperation
CODESA	Convention for a Democratic South Africa
COMECON	Council for Mutual Economic Assistance
COSAG	Concerned South Africans Group

COSAS	Congress of South African Students
COSATU	Congress of South African Trade Unions
CPP	Convention People's party
CUSA	Council of Unions of South Africa
DAC	Development Assistance Committee
DFI	direct foreign investment
DROC	Democratic Republic of Congo, typically referred to as Congo, or Congo-Kinshasa
EAC	East African Community
ECA	Economic Commission for Africa
ECCAS	Economic Community of Central African States
ECOMOG	ECOWAS Cease-Fire Monitoring Group
ECOWAS	Economic Community of West African States
EDF	European Development Fund
EEC	European Economic Community
ELF	Eritrean Liberation Front
EPZ	export processing zone
FLN	National Liberation Front
FNLA	National Front for the Liberation of Angola
FOSATU	Federation of South African Trade Unions
FRELIMO	Front for the Liberation of Mozambique
Frolinat	Front pour la Liberation Nationale du Tchad
GDP	gross domestic product
GNP	gross national product
GRAE	Angolan Revolutionary Government in Exile
GUNT	Transitional National Union Government
HIPC	Highly Indebted Poor Country
IFI	international financial institution
IMF	International Monetary Fund
ISI	import-substituting industrialization
KANU	Kenya African National Union
LDCs	less-developed countries
MDM	Mass Democratic Movement
MPLA	Popular Movement for the Liberation of Angola
MVA	manufacturing value-added

NAFTA	North American Free Trade Agreement
NAM	Nonaligned Movement
NANS	National Association of Nigerian Students
NF	National Forum
NGOs	nongovernmental organizations
NICs	newly industrializing countries
NIEO	New International Economic Order
NP	National Party (South Africa)
NUGS	National Union of Ghanaian Students
NUM	National Union of Mineworkers
OAU	Organization of African Unity
OCAM	Afro-Malagasy Common Organization
OECD	Organization for Economic Cooperation and Development
OMVS	Organisation pour la Mise en Valeur du Fleuve Sénégal (Organisation for the Development of the Senegal River)
ONUC	United Nations Operation in the Congo
OPEC	Organization of Petroleum Exporting Countries
PA	Program of Action
PAC	Pan-African Congress
PAMSCAD	Program to Mitigate the Social Costs of Adjustment
PDCI	Parti Démocratique du Côte d'Ivoire
PDG	Parti Démocratique de Guinée
PFP	Progressive Federal party
PLO	Palestine Liberation Organization
PMAC	Provisional Military Administrative Council
PNDC	Provisional National Defense Council
Polisario Front	Frente Popular para la Liberacion de Saguia el Hamra y Rio de Oro
PTA	Preferential Trade Area of East and Southern Africa
RCC	Revolutionary Command Council
RENAMO	Mozambique National Resistance Movement
SACC	South African Council of Churches
SACP	South African Communist Party
SACU	Southern African Customs Union
SADC	Southern African Development Community
SADCC	Southern African Development Coordination Conference
SADR	Saharan Arab Democratic Republic
SALT	Strategic Arms Limitation Treaty
SASO	South African Students' Organization

SONATRACH	Société Nationale de Transports et de Commercialisation des Hydrocarbures
STABEX	Stabilization of Export Earnings Scheme
SWAPO	South West African People's Organization
TANU	Tanzanian African National Union
TNCs	transnational corporations
TRC	Truth and Reconciliation Commission
UAM	Union of African States and Madagascar
UDAO	Customs Union of West Africa
UDEAO	Customs Union of West African States
UDF	United Democratic Front
UDI	Unilateral Declaration of Independence
UNCTAD	United Nations Conference on Trade and Development
UNECA	United Nations Economic Commission for Africa
UNESCO	United Nations Educational, Scientific, and Cultural Organization
UNICEF	United Nations International Children's Emergency Fund
UNIDO	United Nations Industrial Development Organization
UNITA	National Union for the Total Independence of Angola
UPA	Union of Angolan Peoples
WPE	Workers' Party of Ethiopia
WSLF	Western Somali Liberation Front
WTO	World Trade Organization
ZANU	Zimbabwe African National Union
ZAPU	Zimbabwe African People's Union
ZNP	Zanzibar Nationalist Party

Appendix 2:
Changes in Country Names

Present	*Previous*
Benin	Dahomey
Botswana	Bechuanaland
Burkina Faso	Upper Volta
Burundi[1]	Ruanda-Urundi
Cameroon	French Cameroons and British Southern Cameroons[2]
Cape Verde	Cape Verde Islands
Central African Republic	Oubangui Chari; Central African Empire
Congo, Democratic Republic of	Belgian Congo; later Congo; subsequently Zaïre; sometimes referred to as Congo-Kinshasa or Congo-Leopoldville
Congo, Republic of (Congo-Brazzaville)	French Congo
Côte d'Ivoire	Ivory Coast
Djibouti	French Territory of the Afars and Issas; French Somaliland
Equatorial Guinea	Spanish Guinea
Eritrea	Eritrea Autonomous Region in Ethiopia
Ghana	Gold Coast; British Togoland
Guinea	French Guinea
Guinea-Bissau	Portuguese Guinea
Lesotho	Basutoland

Present	*Previous*
Madagascar	Malagasy Republic
Malawi	Nyasaland
Mali	French Soudan
Namibia	South West Africa
Rwanda[1]	Ruanda-Urundi
Saharan Arab Democratic Republic[3]	Spanish Sahara; sometimes referred to as Western Sahara
Somali (Somali Democratic Republic)	British Somaliland and Italian Somaliland
Tanzania[4]	Tanganyika and Zanzibar
Togo	French Togoland
Zambia	Northern Rhodesia
Zimbabwe	Southern Rhodesia; Rhodesia

Notes:

1. Ruanda-Urundi was a Belgian-administered trust territory that became independent in 1960 as two separate states.

2. The Southern Cameroons, a British-administered UN trust territory, joined the Republic of Cameroon following a plebiscite in 1961; the people of the Northern Cameroons opted for integration with Nigeria.

3. Morocco has claimed this territory, a claim contested by the Polisario Front (the national liberation movement). Polisario refers to the territory as the Saharan Arab Democratic Republic (SADR).

4. The United Republic of Tanganyika and Zanzibar came into being on April 26, 1964, as a consequence of the union between Tanganyika and Zanzibar; the name "United Republic of Tanzania" was officially adopted a year later.

Sources: Adapted from William Tordoff, *Government and Politics in Africa* (Indiana University Press, 1993), and the 1998 *CIA World Factbook*.

Appendix 3:
Basic Political Data

Country and Date of Independence	Capital City	Rulers Since Independence	Major Political Parties
Algeria 3 July 1962	Algiers	1. Ahmed Ben Bella, president, 1962–June 1965 2. Col. Houari Boumedienne, president, June 1965–Dec. 1978 3. Col. Benjedid Chadli, president, Feb. 1979–Jan. 1992 4. Abd al-Malek Benhabiles, chairman, Constitutional Council, acting head of state, 12–14 Jan. 1992 5. High Committee of State appointed as collegiate presidency, Jan. 1992–Jan. 1994 6. Liamine Zéroual, head of state, Feb. 1994–1999 7. Abdelaziz Bouteflika elected president, Apr. 1999	National Liberation Front (FLN) Islamic Salvation Front (FIS) Movement for Democracy in Algeria (MDA) Socialist Forces Front (FFS)
Angola 11 Nov. 1975	Luanda	1. Antonio Agostinho Neto, founding president, 1975–Sept. 1979 2. José Eduardo dos Santos, president, 20 Sept. 1979–	Popular Movement for the Liberation of Angola (MPLA) National Union for the Total Independence of Angola (UNITA)
Benin 1 Aug. 1960 (formerly Republic of Dahomey 1960–1975)	Porto Novo	1. Hubert Maga, president, Jan. 1961–Oct. 1963	Benin People's Revolutionary Party (PRPB)

Country and Date of Independence	Capital City	Rulers Since Independence	Major Political Parties
Benin (continued)		2. Col. (later Gen.) Christophe Soglo, president, Oct. 1963–Jan. 1964	Union for the Triumph of Democratic Renewal (UTR) includes: UDFP, MOPS, ULD
		3. Sourou Migan Apithy, president, Jan. 1964–Nov. 1965	Our Common Cause (NCC)
		4. Tahirou Congacou, president, Nov. 1965–Dec. 1965	National Assembly for Democracy (RND)
		5. Gen. Christophe Soglo, president, Dec. 1965–Dec. 1967	Party for the Rebirth of Benin (PRB) Party of Democratic Renewal (PRD)
		6. Lt. Col. Alphonse Alley, president, Dec. 1967–July 1968	Action Front for Renewal and Development (FARD-Alafin)
		7. Emile-Derlin Zinsou (civilian), president, July 1968–Dec. 1969	
		8. Lt. Col. Paul Emile de Souza, president, Dec. 1969–May 1970	
		9. Hubert Maga, president, May 1970–May 1972	
		10. Justin Ahomadegbé, president, May 1972–Oct. 1972	
		11. Col. Mathieu Kerekou, president, Oct. 1972–Feb. 1991	
		12. Nicephore Soglo, Feb. 1991–Mar. 1996	
		13. Gen. Mathieu Kerekou, president, Mar. 1996–	
Botswana 30 Sept. 1966	Gaborone	1. Sir Seretse Khama, Sept. 1966–July 1980	Botswana Democratic Party
		2. Quett Masire, president, July 1980–Mar. 1998	Botswana People's Party Botswana Independence Party
		3. Following resignation of President Masire, Vice-President Festus Mogae assumed the presidency, April 1998–	Botswana National Front Botswana Progressive Union (BPU)
Burkina Faso 5 Aug. 1960 (formerly Upper Volta; renamed Burkina Faso, Aug. 1984)	Ouagadougou	1. Maurice Yaméogo, president, Apr. 1959–Jan. 1966	Organization for Popular Democracy–Labor Party (ODP–MT)
		2. Lt. Col. Sangoulé Lamizana, president, Jan. 1966–1980	Popular Front Movement for Tolerance & Progress (MTP)
		3. Col. Sayé Zerbo, 1980–1982	Union for Democracy & Social Progress (UDPS)
		4. NCO coup, Oct. 1982	

Country and Date of Independence	Capital City	Rulers Since Independence	Major Political Parties
Burkina Faso (continued)		5. Maj. Jean Baptiste Ouedraogo, president, Jan. 1983–Aug. 1983 6. Capt. Thomas Sankara, president, National Revolutionary Council (CNR), 1983–1987 7. Capt. Blaise Compaore, president, National Revolutionary Council, 1987–	National Convention of Progressive Patriots–Social Democratic Party (CNPP–PSD) Party for Democracy & Progress (PDP)
Burundi 1 July 1962	Bujumbura	1. (King) Mwami Mwambutsa II, 1915–1966; prime ministers: André Muhirwa, 1962–1963; Pierre Ngendandumwe, 1963; Albin Nyamoya, 1964–1965; Pierre Ngendandumwe, 1965 (assassinated Jan. 1965); Joseph Bamina, 1965; Leopold Biha, 1965; 2. Mwami Ntare V (deposed father, Mwambutsa II, as King), Capt. (later Col.) Michel Micombero, prime minister, July 1966–Nov. 1966 3. Micombero declared Burundi a republic with himself as president, Nov. 1966–Nov. 1976 4. Col. Jean-Baptiste Bagaza, president, Nov. 1976–Sept. 1987 5. Maj. Pierre Buyoya, chairman Military Committee for National Salvation, 1987–July 1993 6. Melchior Ndadaye, president, July 1993–Oct. 1993 (killed) 7. Council of Ministers exercised presidential power Oct. 1993–Feb. 1994 8. Cyprien Ntaryamira, president, Feb. 1994–Apr. 1994 9. Sylvestre Ntibantunganya, interim president, Apr. 1994, elected president, Sept. 1994–July 1996	Union for National Progress (UPRONA) Front for democracy in Burundi (FRODEBU) Burunidian People's Union (RPB)

Country and Date of Independence	Capital City	Rulers Since Independence	Major Political Parties
Burundi (continued)		10. Maj. Pierre Buyoya led coup ousting Ntibantunganya and named himself president, July 1996–	
Cameroon 1 Jan. 1960 (1960–1961: Republic of East Cameroon; Oct. 1961– 1972: Federal Republic of Cameroon, composed of East part of former French trust territory— and West part of former British trust territory; 1972–: United Cameroon Republic)	Yaounde	1. Ahmadou Ahidjo, president, May 1960– Nov. 1982 2. Paul Biya, president, 1982–	Cameroonian People's Democratic Union (RDPC) National Union for Democracy and Progress (UNDP) Union for Change (UPC) Movement for the Defense of the Republic (MDR)
Cape Verde July 1975 (in federation with Guinea-Bissau, 1975– Jan. 1981)	Praia	1. Aristides Pereira, president, 1975–Feb. 1991 2. Antonio Mascarenhas Monteiro, president, Feb. 1991–	African Party for the Independence of Cape Verde (PAICV) Movement for Democracy (MPD)
Central African Republic 13 Aug. 1960 (1976–1979: Central African Empire)	Bangui	1. David Dacko (formerly prime minister), president, Nov. 1960– Dec. 1965 2. Coup led by Field Marshal Jean-Bedel Bokassa, 31 Dec. 1965 3. Bokassa proclaimed "President for Life," Mar. 1972 4. Bokassa crowned emperor, Dec. 1977 5. Bokassa deposed in coup, David Dacko, president, Sept. 1979	Central African Democratic Assembly (RDC) Alliance for Democracy and Progress (ADP) Movement for the Liberation of the Central African People (MLPC) Patriotic Front for Progress (FPP) Liberal-Democratic Party (PLD)

Country and Date of Independence	Capital City	Rulers Since Independence	Major Political Parties
Central African Republic (continued)		6. Gen. André Kolingba established military regime, chairman of Military Committee for National Recovery, Sept. 1901 Oct. 1993 7. Ange-Félix Patassé, president, Oct. 1993–	
Chad 11 Aug. 1960	Ndjamena	1. Ngarta (formerly François) Tombalbaye, prime minister, head of state on independence; president, Apr. 1962–Apr. 1975 (killed in army coup) 2. Gen. Félix Malloum, president, Apr. 1975–1979 3. Hissene Habré appointed prime minister, Aug. 1978 4. Malloum and Habré resigned, Mar. 1979; Transitional Government of National Unity 5. Goukouni Oueddei, president, 1979–1982 6. Hissene Habré, president, 1982–Dec. 1990 7. Idris Déby, Dec. 1990–	Mouvement Patriotique du Salut (MPS) National Alliance for Democracy and Development (ANDD) Union for Democracy and the Republic (UDR) Comite de Sursaut National pour la paix et la democratie (CSNPD) Union for Democracy and Progress (RDP)
Comoros July 1975	Moroni	1. Ahmed Abdallah, president, July 1975–Aug. 1975 2. Coup led by Ali Soilih, Aug. 1975; president, 1976–1978 3. Ahmed Adballah, president, reinstated in coup by mercenaries under Bob Denard, 1978–27 Nov. 1989 (murdered) 4. Bob Denard, president, 27 Nov. 1989–Dec. 1989 5. Said Djohar, Dec. 1989–Sept. 1995 6. Coup led by Bob Denard, Djohar went into exile under French protection, Sept. 1995–Oct. 1995 following intervention by French troops	National Union for Democracy in Comoros (UNDC) Union for Change and Democracy (Rachade) Union of Democrats for Development (UDD) Union for Democracy and Renewal (RDR) Forum for National Redress (FRN)

Country and Date of Independence	Capital City	Rulers Since Independence	Major Political Parties
Comoros (continued)		7. Caabi Elyachroutu, prime minister under Djohar, became head of the Government of National Unity and interim president in Djohar's absence, Oct. 1995–Mar. 1996 8. Mohamed Taki Abdoulkarim, president, Mar. 1996–Apr. 1999 (ousted in coup) 9. Col. Assoumani Azzali led military coup, president, May 1999–	
Congo, Democratic Republic of 30 June 1960 (1960–1971: Congo-Kinshasa; Oct. 1971–May 1997: Zaïre; May 1997: named Democratic Republic of Congo)	Kinshasa	1. Patrice Lumumba, prime minister, June–Sept. 1960; Joseph Kasavubu, president, 1960–1965 2. Col. Joseph Mobutu suspended constitution, Sept. 1960; College of Commissioners ruled until Feb. 1961 3. Joseph Ileo, prime minister, Feb.–Aug. 1961 4. Cyrille Adoula, prime minister, Aug. 1961–July 1964 5. Moise Tshombe, prime minister, July 1964–Oct. 1965 6. Evariste Kimba, prime minister, Oct.–Nov. 1965 7. Military coup led by Gen. (later Marshal) Mobutu Sese Seko Kuku Ngbendu Wa Za Banga, president, 1965–17 May 1997 8. Rebellion against Mobutu; Laurent Kabila, president, 17 May 1997–	Alliance of Democratic Forces for the Liberation of Congo Popular Movement of the Revolution (MPR) Union for Democracy and Social Progress (UDPS) Social-Christian and Democratic Party (PDSC) Federal Union of Imdependent Republicans (UFERI) Congolese National Movement-Lumumba (MNC-Lumumba)
Congo, Republic of 15 Aug. 1960	Brazzaville	1. Foulbert Youlou, president under pre-independence constitution, Nov. 1959 2. Military coup Aug. 1963; Alphonse Massamba-Débat, president, Dec. 1963	Congolese Workers Party (PCT) Pan-African Union for Social Democracy (UPADS) Congolese Movement for Integral Democracy and Development (MCDDI) Union for Democracy and Development (RDD) Union for Democracy and Social Progress (RDPS)

Country and Date of Independence	Capital City	Rulers Since Independence	Major Political Parties
Congo, Republic of (continued)		3. Capt. Marien Ngouabi, chairman of Governing National Revolutionary Council; Maj. Alfred Raoul, prime minister and temporary head of state, Sept. 1968–Dec. 1968 4. Capt. Marien Ngouabi, president, Jan. 1969–Mar. 1977 (assassinated) 5. Col. (later Brig. Gen.) Joachim Yhombi-Opango, president, Mar. 1977–Feb. 1979 6. Col. Dennis Sassou Nguesso, president, Feb. 1979–Aug. 1992 7. Pascal Lissouba, president, Aug. 1992–Oct. 1997 (ousted in coup) 8. Dennis Sassou Nguesso, president, Oct. 1997	
Côte d'Ivoire 7 Aug. 1960	Yammoussoukro	1. Felix Houphouët-Boigny, prime minister, May 1959; president, Nov. 1960–Dec. 1993 (died) 2. Henri Konan Bédié, president, Dec. 1993–	Democratic Party of Côte d'Ivoire–African Democratic Union (PDCI–RDA) Ivoirian Popular Front Ivoirian Workers Party Republican Union (RDR)
Djibouti 27 June 1977	Djibouti	1. Hassan Gouled Aptidon, president, June 1977–	Popular Union for Progress (RPP) Party for Democratic Renewal (PRD) National Democratic Party (PND)
Egypt, Arab Republic of 28 Feb. 1922	Cairo	1. King Farouk to 1952 2. Coup led by Col. Gamal Abdel Nasser and Abdul-al-Hakim; Maj. Gen. Neguib, president, June 1953–Nov. 1954 3. Nasser, head of state, 1954–1970 (president from 1956) 4. Col. Anwar Sadat, president, 1970–Oct. 1981 5. Lt. Gen. Hosni Mubarak, president, Oct. 1981–	Liberal Socialist Party National Democratic Party National Progressive Unionist Party New Wafd Party Socialist Labour Party Ummah Party

Country and Date of Independence	Capital City	Rulers Since Independence	Major Political Parties
Equatorial Guinea 12 Oct. 1968	Malabo	1. Francisco Macias Nguema, president, Sept. 1968–Aug. 1979 2. Military coup led by Lt. Col. Teodoro Obiango Nguema Mbasogo, Aug. 1979 3. Lt. Col. (later Brig. Gen.) Teodoro Obiango Nguema Mbasogo, president, Oct. 1980–	Democratic Party of Equatorial Guinea (PDGE) Popular Socio-democratic Convention (CSDP) Democratic and Social Union of Equatorial Guinea (UDSGE)
Eritrea 24 May 1993	Asmara	1. Isaias Afewerki, president, June 1993–	People's Front for Democracy and Justice Eritrean Liberation Front Central Command Eritrean Liberation Front National Council Eritrean Liberation Front Revolutionary Council
Ethiopia	Addis Ababa	1. Succession of emperors 2. Emperor Haile Selassie, 1930–Sept. 1974 3. Lt. Gen. Aman Andom, chairman, PMAC (Provisional Military Administrative Council) thru Nov. 1974 4. Brig. Gen. Teferi Banti, chairman, PMAC (killed Feb. 1977); power actualy held by vice-chairman Maj. (later Col.) Mengistu Haile Mariam and Lt. Col. Atnafu Abate 5. Mengistu Haile Mariam, chairman of PMAC, head of state, 1977–May 1991 6. Meles Zenawi, president, May 1991–Aug. 1995 7. Dr. Negasso Gidada, president; Zenawi, prime minister, Aug. 1995–	Ethiopian People's Revolutionary Democratic Front (EPRDF) Tigre People's Liberation Front (TPLF) Coalition of Alternative Forces for Peace and Democracy in Ethiopia (CAFPDE)
Gabon 17 Aug. 1960	Libreville	1. Leon M'Ba, president, 1961–Nov. 1967 2. Omar (formerly Albert-Bernard) Bongo, president, Nov. 1967–	Gabonese Democratic Party (PDG) Gabonese Progressive Party (PGP) Morena-Original Union for Gabonese Socialism (UPSG) Circle for Renewal and Progress (CRP) National Woodcutters Union (RNB)

Country and Date of Independence	Capital City	Rulers Since Independence	Major Political Parties
Gambia 18 Feb. 1965	Banjul	1. Constitutional Monarchy with Dawda Jawara, prime minister, 1965–1970 2. Gambia became a republic, Apr. 1970; Dawda Jawara, first president, Apr. 1970–July 1994 3. Coup led by Capt. Yahya Jammeh, chairman of the Armed Forces Provisional Ruling Council, July 1994; elected president, Sept. 1996–	National Convention Party People's Progressive Party Gambia People's Party
Ghana 6 Mar. 1957	Accra	1. Constitutional monarchy, 1957–1960; Kwame Nkrumah, prime minister. Became a republic in 1960 2. Nkrumah, president, Feb. 1966 3. Lt. Gen. Joseph Ankrah, chairman of National Liberation Council, Feb. 1966–1969; replaced, 1969, by Brig. Gen. Akwasi Afrifa 4. Competitive Electoral Politics: Kofi Busia, prime minister, Sept. 1969–Jan. 1972 5. Lt. Col. (later Gen.) Ignatius Kutu Acheampong, chairman of National Redemption Council, replaced by Supreme Military Council, Jan. 1972–July 1978 6. Lt. Gen. Frederick Akuffo, chairman of Supreme Military Council, July 1978–June 1979 7. Flight Lt. Jerry Rawlings, chairman of Armed Forces Revolutionary Council, June 1979–Sept. 1979 8. Dr. Hilla Limann, president, Sept. 1979–Dec. 1981 9. Flight Lt. Jerry Rawlings, chairman of National Defence Council, Dec. 1981; elected president Nov. 1992, reelected Dec. 1996	National Democratic Congress (NDC) National Convention Party (NCP) EGLE (Every Ghanaian Living Everywhere) Party

Country and Date of Independence	Capital City	Rulers Since Independence	Major Political Parties
Guinea 2 Oct. 1958	Conakry	1. Ahmed Sekou Touré, president, 1958–Apr. 1984 2. Col. Lansana Conté, president, head of Comité Militaire de Redressement National, Apr. 1984; elected president, 1993–	Party for Unity and Progress (PUP) Guinea Popular Union Party for Renewal and Progress (PRP) Union for the New Republic (UNR)
Guinea-Bissau 10 Sept. 1974	Bissau	1. Luiz De Almeida Cabral, president, 1974–1980 2. Gen. João Bernardo Vieira, president of the Council of State, head of government, 1980; president, Aug. 1994–May 1999 3. Vieira ousted by rebels, May 1999 (Malan Bacai Sanha in line as interim president)	African Party for the Independence of Guinea and Cape Verde Islands (PAIGC) Guinea-Bissau Resistance–Bah Fatah Movement (RGD–MB) Party for Social Renovation (PRS) União para a Mudança (UM)
Kenya 12 Dec. 1963	Nairobi	1. Constitutional monarchy, 1963–1964; Jomo Kenyatta, prime minister 2. Kenyatta, president, 1964–11 Aug. 1978 3. Succeeded by Daniel arap Moi, president, Aug. 1978–	Kenya African National Union (KANU) Forum for the Restoration of Democracy-Asili Forum for the Restoration of Democracy-Kenya
Lesotho 4 Oct. 1966	Maseru	1. Constitutional monarchy under King Motlotlehi Moshoeshoe II 2. Chief Leabua Jonathan seized power in civilian coup, Jan. 1970–Jan. 1986 3. Maj. Gen. Justin Lekhanya, chairman, Military Council, 1986–Apr. 1991 4. Col. Elias Ramaema, chairman, Military Council, Apr. 1991–Apr. 1993 5. Dr. Ntsu Mokhehle, prime minister, Apr. 1993–Aug. 1994 6. King Letsie III dismissed Mokhehle government and assumed role of head of state, Aug. 1994–Sept. 1994 7. Mokhehle resumed post as prime minister, Sept. 1994–	Basotho Congress Party (BCP)

Country and Date of Independence	Capital City	Rulers Since Independence	Major Political Parties
Lesotho (continued)		8. King Moshoeshoe II restored to throne with no legislative or political powers, head of state, Jan. 1995–Jan. 1996 (died) 9. King Letsie III resumed throne, Feb. 1996–	
Liberia 26 July 1847	Monrovia	1. Until 1944, eighteen presidents 2. William V. S. Tubman, president, 1944–1971 3. William R. Tolbert, president 1971–Apr. 1980 4. M. Sgt. Samuel K. Doe, president, People's Redemption Council, 1980–Sept. 1990 (murdered) 5. Amos Sawyer, president of Interim Government of National Unity (IGNU), Nov. 1990–Mar. 1994 6. David Kpomakpor, chairman, Ruling Council of State, Mar. 1994–Sept. 1995 7. Prof. Wilton Sankawulo, chairman, Ruling Council of State, Sept. 1995–Sept. 1996 8. Ruth Perry, chairwoman, Ruling Council of State, Sept. 1996–Aug. 1997 9. Charles Taylor, president, Aug. 1997	Liberia Peace Council Lofa Defence Force National Patriotic Front of Liberia (NPFL) United Liberation Movement of Liberia for Democracy (Ulimo)
Libya 24 Dec. 1951 (from Mar. 1977 named Socialist People's Libyan Arab Jamahiriya)	Tripoli	1. King Idris, 1951–1969 2. Col. Muammar Mohammed Qaddafi, Leader of the Revolution, 1969–	None
Madagascar, Democratic Republic of 26 June 1960	Antananarivo	1. Philibert Tsiranana, president, 1960–May 1972 2. Gen. Gabriel Ramanantsoa, president, 1972–Feb.1975 3. Col. Ratsimandrava, Feb. 1975 (assassinated)	Cartel HVR Movement for the Progress of Madagascar (MPM) Leader-Fanilo Famima

Country and Date of Independence	Capital City	Rulers Since Independence	Major Political Parties
Madagascar, Democratic Republic of (continued)		4. Gen. Gilles Andria Mahazo, National Military Directorate, Feb. 1975 5. Lt. Comdr. Didier Ratsiraka, president, Mar. 1975–Oct. 1991; Guy Razanamasy, prime minister, Aug. 1991– 6. Prof. Albert Zafy, president, Mar. 1993–Sept. 1996 (impeached) 7. Norbert Ratsirahonana, interim president, Sept. 1996–Jan. 1997 8. Didier Ratsiraka, president, Jan. 1997	
Malawi 6 July 1964	Lilongwe	1. Constitutional monarchy, Hastings Kamuzu Banda, prime minister, 1964–1966 2. Banda, president, 1966 3. Banda, "President for Life," July 1971–Oct. 1993 4. Gwanda Chakuamba, chairman, Presidential Council, Oct.–Dec. 1993 5. Banda resumed powers, Dec. 1993–May1994 6. Bakili Muluzi, president, May 1994–	Malawi Congress Party United Democratic Front (UDF) Alliance for Democracy (AFORD)
Mali 22 Sept. 1960 (20 June 1960: independence of Mali Federation) (4 Apr. 1959–20 Aug. 1960: Mali Federation with Senegal)	Bamako	1. Modibo Keita, president of Mali Federation; president of Soudan government, Apr. 1959; president of Mali, 1960–1968 2. Lt. (later Brig. Gen.) Moussa Traoré, chairman of Military Committee of National Liberation, Nov. 1968–June 1979 3. Gen. Moussa Traoré, president, June 1979–Mar. 1991 4. Lt. Col. Amadou Toumany Toure, acting head of state, Mar. 1991–Apr. 1991 5. Soumana Sacko, prime minister, Apr. 1991–June 1992	Union Sudanaise–Section du RDA (US–RDA) Alliance pour la Democratie au Mali (ADEMA) Congrès National d'Initiative Démocratique (CNID) Parti Malien pour le Développement (PMD)

Country and Date of Independence	Capital City	Rulers Since Independence	Major Political Parties
Mali (continued)		6. Alpha Oumar Konaré, president, June 1992–	
Mauritania, Islamic Republic of 28 Nov. 1960	Nouakchott	1. Mokhtar Ould Daddah, president, 1961–July 1978 2. Lt. Col. Mustapha Ould Mohammed Salek, president of Comité Militaire de Redressement National (CMRN), July 1978–Apr. 1979 3. Lt. Col. Ahmed Ould Bouceif, prime minister, Apr. 1979–May 1979 (assassinated) 4. Lt. Col. Mohammed Khouna Haidalla, prime minister appointed by Salek, May 1979 5. CMSN (formerly CMRN) forced Salek to resign, June 1979; Lt. Col. Mohammed Mahmoud Ould Louly, president, June 1979–Jan. 1980 6. Haidalla ousted Louly, Jan. 1980; Haidalla became president, head of state, and chairman of CMSN, 1980–1984 7. Col. Maawiya Ould Sid'Ahmed Taya, president of the Republic, chairman of the Military Committee for National Salvation, 1984, president Jan. 1992–	Union for Democracy and National Unity (RDNU) Mauritania Party for Renewal (PMR) Democratic and Social Republican Party (DSRP)
Mauritius 12 Mar. 1968	Port Louis	1. Seewoosagur Ramgoolam, prime minister, 1968–1982 2. Anerood Jugnauth, prime minister, 1982–Dec. 1995 3. Navin Ramgoolam, prime minister, Dec. 1995–	Comité d'Action Musulman (CAM) Mauritian Labour Party Mouvement Militant Mauricien (MMM) Mouvement Socialiste Mauricien (MSM)
Morocco 2 Mar. 1956	Rabat	1. King Mohammed V, to 1961 2. King Hassan II, 1961–	Istiqlal Mouvement Populaire Parti Démocratique pour l'Independence Parti National Démocrate (PND) Rassemblement National des Indépendents (RNI)

Country and Date of Independence	Capital City	Rulers Since Independence	Major Political Parties
Morocco (continued)			Union Constitutionelle Union Socialiste des Forces Populaires (USFP) Mouvement National Populaire (MNP)
Mozambique 25 June 1975	Maputo	1. Samora Moisés Machel, president, June 1975–Nov. 1986 2. Joaquim Alberto Chissano, president, Nov. 1986	Front for the Liberation of Mozambique (FRELIMO) Mozambican National Resistence (Renamo) Democratic Union
Namibia 21 Mar. 1990	Windhoek	1. Sam Nujoma, president; Hage Geingob, prime minister, Mar. 1990–	South West African People's Organization (SWAPO) Democratic Turnhalle Alliance (DTA) United Democratic Front
Niger 8 Aug. 1960	Niamey	1. Hamani Diori, president, 1960–Apr. 1974 2. Maj. Gen. Seyni Kountché, head of state, president of Supreme Military Council, 1974–1987 3. Col. Ali Seibou, president of Supreme Military Council, head of state, Nov. 1987–Apr. 1993 4. Mahamane Ousmane, president, Apr. 1993–Jan. 1996 5. Coup led by Lt. Col. Ibrahim Mainassara Barre; Barre named self head of state, Jan. 1996; elected president, July 1996; killed in coup, Apr. 1999 6. Coup led by Major Daouda Malam Wanke; Wanke assumed powers as head of state, Apr. 1999–	National Movement for a Developing Society (MNSD-Nassara) Nigerien Party for Democracy and Socialism (PNDS) Democratic and Social Convention-Rahama (CDS-Rahama) Nigerien Alliance for Democracy & Social Progress (ANDPS-Zaman Lahiya)
Nigeria 1 Oct. 1960	Abuja	1. Alhaji Abubakar Tafawa Balewa, prime minister, 1960–1966; Nnamdi Azikiwe, president, 1963–1966 2. Gen. Johnson Aguiyi-Ironsi, head of Federal Military Government, Jan.–July 1966	All Nigerian Congress (ANC) Committee of National Consensus (CNC) National Consciousness Party (NCP) United Democratic Congress (UDC)

Country and Date of Independence	Capital City	Rulers Since Independence	Major Political Parties
Nigeria (continued)		3. Lt. Col. Yakubu Gowon, head of Federal Military Government, July 1966–July 1975 4. Gen. Murtala Mohammed, chief of Supreme Military Council, July 1975–Feb. 1976 5. Lt. Gen. Olusegun Obasanjo, Feb. 1976–Oct. 1979 6. Alhaji Shehu Shagari, president, Oct. 1979–Dec. 1983 7. Maj. Gen. Mohammed Duhari, president, Dec. 1983–Aug. 1985 8. Maj. Gen. Ibrahim Babangida, president, Aug. 1985–Aug. 1993 9. Ernest Shonekan, chairman of interim Federal Executive Council, later head of state, Aug. 1993–Nov. 1993 (resigned) 10. Gen. Sani Abacha, head of government and chairman of Provisional Ruling Council, Nov. 1993–June 1998 11. Gen. Abdulsalami Abubakar appointed head of state by Provisional Ruling Council, after death of Gen. Abacha, June 1998–May 1999 12. Olusegun Obasanjo elected president, inaugurated May 1999	
Rwanda 1 July 1962	Kigali	1. Grégoire Kayibanda, president, 1961–July 1973 2. Maj. Gen. Juvénal Habyarimana, president, July 1973–Apr. 1994 (killed) 3. Dr. Théodore Sindikubwabo, interim president, Apr. 1994–July 1994 4. Pasteur Bizimungu, president, July 1994–	Union du Peuple Rwandais (UPR) Republican Democratic Movement (MDR) Rwandan Patriotic Front Social Democratic Party Liberal Party (PL) Christian Democratic Party (PDC)

Country and Date of Independence	Capital City	Rulers Since Independence	Major Political Parties
Saharan Arab Democratic Republic (SADR) Feb. 1982 (admitted as 51st member of OAU) (Western Sahara: partitioned between Morocco and Mauritania in Apr. 1976; SADR declared by Polisario in exile, Feb. 1976)	Not applicable	1. Polisario formally proclaimed the creation of SADR and its government in exile, 1976 2. Mohammed Abdelaziz, president of Polisario government, 1982– 3. State is claimed and de facto administered by Morocco. A U.N.-brokered cease-fire has been in place since Sept. 1991. A U.N. team in Western Sahara is attempting to prepare the state for a referendum.	Frente Popular para la Liberación de Saguia el Hamra y Rio de Oro-Frente Polisario (Polisario Front)
São Tomé and Principe 12 July 1975	São Tomé	1. Dr. Manuel Pinto da Costa, president, 1975–Mar. 1991 2. Miguel Trovoada, president, Mar. 1991–	Movement for the Liberation of São Tomé and Principe Parti de la Convergence Démocratique Grupo de Reflexão Acçao Democrática Independente (ADI)
Senegal 20 Aug. 1960 (14 Apr. 1959–20 Aug. 1960: Mali Federation)	Dakar	1. Léopold Sédar Senghor, president, 1960–Jan. 1981 2. Abdou Diouf, president, Jan. 1981–	Senegal Democratic Party (PDS) Senegalese Socialist Party (PS)
Seychelles 29 June 1976	Victoria	1. James Mancham, president, June 1976–June 1977 2. Albert René, president, June 1977–	Seychelles People's Progressive Front (SPPF) Democratic Party (DP)
Sierra Leone 27 Apr. 1961	Freetown	1. Sir Milton Margai, prime minister, 1961–1964 2. Sir Albert Margai, prime minister, 1964–1967 3. Lt. Col. Andrew Juxon-Smith, chairman of National Reformation Council, Mar. 1967–Apr. 1968	All People's Congress (APC) Sierra Leone Democratic Party (SLDP) United Front of Political Movements (UNIFOM)

Country and Date of Independence	Capital City	Rulers Since Independence	Major Political Parties
Sierra Leone (continued)		4. Siaka Probyn Stevens, prime minister, Apr. 1968 5. Stevens became president of Republic, Apr. 1971–Oct. 1985 6. Maj. Gen. Dr. Joseph Saidu Momoh, president, Oct. 1985–Apr. 1992 7. Military coup led by Capt. Valentine Strasser; Strasser became chairman of the Supreme Council of State, May 1992–Jan. 1996 8. Military coup led by Brig. Gen. Julius Maada Bio; Bio became president, Jan. 1996–Mar. 1996 9. Ahmad Tejan Kabbah, president, Mar. 1996 May 1997 10. Military coup, led by Maj. Johnny Paul Koromah, chairman of Armed Forces Revolutionary Council, May 1997 11. Ahmad Tejan Kabbah reinstated following intervention of Nigerian-led West African (ECOMOG) force, March 1998–	
Somalia 1 July 1960	Mogadishu	1. Aden Abdulla Osman, president, 1960–1967; Abdirashid Ali Shirmarke, prime minister, 1960–1964; Abdirazak Hussein, prime minister, 1964–1967 2. Abdirashid Ali Shirmarke, president, 1967–1969; Mohammed Ibrahim Egal, prime minister, 1967–1969 3. Maj. Gen. Mohammed Siad Barre, president, 1969–Jan. 1991 4. Ali Mahdi Mohammed, president, Jan. 1991–Fall 1991	Somali Revolutionary Socialist Party (SRSP) United Somali Congress (USC) New President's Party

Country and Date of Independence	Capital City	Rulers Since Independence	Major Political Parties
Somalia (continued)		5. Civil war has resulted in the dissolution of all government structures and posts.	
South Africa 31 May 1961	Pretoria	1. Dr. Hendrik Verwoerd, prime minister, 1958–1966 2. B. J. Vorster, president and prime minister, 1966–1978 3. Pieter W. Botha, prime minister, then president, 1978–1989 4. Chris Heunis, acting president, Jan. 1989–Sept. 1989 5. Frederik W. de Klerk, president, Sept. 1989–May 1994 6. Nelson R. Mandela, president, May 1994–	African National Congress of South Africa (ANC) Democratic Party (DP) Freedom Front Inkatha Freedom Party (IFP) National Party (NP) Pan-Africanist Congress (PAC)
Sudan 1 Jan. 1956	Khartoum	1. Ismail al-Azhari, prime minister, 1956 2. Abdulla Khalil, prime minister, 1956–1958 3. Lt. Gen. Ibrahim Abboud, prime minister, 1958–1964 4. Sir el-Khatim el-Khalifah, prime minister, 1964–1965 5. Muhammed Ahmad Mahgoub, prime minister, 1965–1966 6. Sayed Sadiq el-Mahdi, prime minister, 1966–1967 7. Muhammed Ahmad Mahgoub, prime minister, 1967–1969 8. Abubakr Awadallah, prime minister, 1969 9. Field Marshal Gaafar Mohammed Nimeiri, president, May 1969–Apr. 1985 10. Coup, Apr. 1985. Lt. Gen. Abdel Rahman Swar al Dahab, chairman, Transitional Military Council	Baath Party Democratic Unionist Party Muslim Brotherhood National Alliance for Salvation (NAS) National Congress Party National Islamic Front National Unionist Party Southern Sudanese Political Association Sudan African National Union (SANU) Sudanese National Party Umma Party

Country and Date of Independence	Capital City	Rulers Since Independence	Major Political Parties
Sudan (continued)		11. Ahmed Ali el-Mirghani, president, Supreme Council 1986–June 1989 (military coup) 12. Omar Hassan Ahmed al-Bashir, prime minister, June 1989; appointed president, Oct. 1993	
Swaziland 6 Sept. 1968	Mbabane	1. King Sobhuza II, 1922–Sept. 1982; Queen Mother Dzeliwe, regent, Sept. 1982; Dzeliwe deposed Aug. 1983; Prince Makosetive named as King Mswati III, Apr. 1986–	Imbokodvo National Movement (INM) Confederation for Full Democracy in Swaziland
Tanzania 9 Dec. 1961 (of Tanganyika) 10 Dec. 1963 (of Zanzibar) (Tanganyika joined with Zanzibar to form United Republic of Tanzania in Apr. 1964)	Dar es Salaam	1. Julius Nyerere, prime minister, Dec. 1961–Jan. 1962 2. Rashidi M. Kawawa, prime minister, Jan. 1962–Dec. 1962 3. Tanzania became a republic, Dec. 1962; Julius Nyerere, president, Dec. 1962–Nov. 1985 4. Ali Hassan Mwinyi, president, Nov. 1985–Nov. 1995 5. Benjamin Mkapa, president, Nov. 1995–	Chama Cha Mapinduzi (CCM)
Togo 27 Apr. 1960	Lomé	1. Sylvanus Olympio, president, Apr. 1960–Jan. 1963 2. Military coup, Jan. 1963, led by Sgt. (later Gen.) Etienne Eyadema; Nicholas Grunitzky, president, 1963–Jan. 1967 3. Col. Kleber Dadjo, chairman of Comité de Réconciliation Nationale (CRN), Jan. 1967 (bloodless coup) 4. Gen. Gnassingbé Eyadema, president, Apr. 1967–	Rassemblement du Peuple Togolais (RPT) Togolese Union for Democracy (UTD) Comité d'Action pour le Renouveau (CAR) Union pour la justice et la Démocratie (UJD)

Country and Date of Independence	Capital City	Rulers Since Independence	Major Political Parties
Tunisia 20 Mar. 1956	Tunis	1. Habib Bourguiba, prime minister, 1956–July 1957 2. July 1957, became a republic; Habib Bourguiba, president, 1957–1987 3. Nov. 1987, Zine el Abidine Ben Ali acceeded to the presidency, 1987–	Socialist Democrat Movement (MDS) Rassemblement Constitutionnel Démocratique Mouvement de la Rénovation (MR) Union Démocratique Unioniste (UDU) Parti de l'Unité Populaire
Uganda 9 Oct. 1962	Kampala	1. Apollo Milton Obote, 1962—1971 (prime minister until 1966; then president) 2. Maj. Gen. Idi Amin, president, 1971–Apr. 1979 3. Yusuf Lule, president, Provisional Government, Apr.–June 1979 4. Godfrey Binaisa, chairman of Military Commission of Uganda National Liberation Front (UNLF) and president, June 1979– May 1980 5. Paulo Mwanga, chairman, UNLF, May–Dec. 1980 6. Obote, president, Dec. 1980–July 1985 7. Coup led by Lt. Gen. Tito Okello of Uganda National Liberation Army; president, July 1985–Jan. 1986 8. Coup led by Yoweri Museveni of National Resistance Army (NRA); president, Jan. 1986–	Political parties were ordered to suspend active operations following accession to power of the National Resistance Movement (NRM). The NRM government includes representatives of: Conservative Party (CP) Democratic Party (DP) National Resistance Movement (NRM) (the military wing of this is the NRA) National Liberal Party Uganda Freedom Movement Uganda Patriotic Movement Uganda People's Congress
Zambia 24 Oct. 1964	Lusaka	1. Kenneth Kaunda, president, 1964–Oct. 1991 2. Frederik Chiluba, president, Oct. 1991–	United National Independence Party Movement for Multiparty Democracy (MMD)

Country and Date of Independence	Capital City	Rulers Since Independence	Major Political Parties
Zimbabwe 18 Apr. 1980	Harare	1. Canaan Banana, president, head of state, 1980–1987; Robert Mugabe, prime minister, 1980–1987 2. Mugabe, president, 1988–	Conservative Alliance of Zimbabwe (CAZ) Independent Zimbabwe Group National Democratic Union United National Federal Party (UNFP) Zimbabwe African National Union–Patriotic Front (ZANU–PF) Zimbabwe African National Union-Ndonga (ZANU-Ndonga) Zimbabwe Democratic Party Zimbabwe National Front

Sources: Africa: South of the Sahara, 1998 (London: Europa Publications, Ltd., 1997); *The Middle East & North Africa, 1998* (London, Europa Publications, Ltd., 1997); *Africa Research Bulletin: Political Series* (Exeter: Africa Research, Ltd., Jan.–Sept. 1991); *Keesing Record of World Events* (London: Longman, Jan.–Dec. 1990 and Jan.–Apr. 1991); *Sub-Saharan Africa, Daily Report* (Washington, DC: Government Printing Office, Apr. 1–Nov. 27, 1991).

Index

About the Book

Recognized as *the* textbook on African politics, as well as an excellent resource for scholars, *Politics and Society in Contemporary Africa* analyzes the complexities and diversities of the African continent since independence.

The authors provide a basic knowledge of political events; political structures, processes, problems, and trends; political economy; and international relations. Clearly organized charts offer easy access to current political, economic, and social data. This new edition includes entirely new chapters on political economy and South Africa, and the enormous changes of the last seven years in Africa and in the post–Cold War world more generally are reflected in revised discussions of civil society, democratic transitions, decentralization, structural adjustment, and Africa in the world economy.

Broadly encompassing, challenging, and timely, the book is a major contribution to our understanding of the multiple forces at work on the continent.

Naomi Chazan is professor of political science and African studies at the Hebrew University of Jerusalem. **Peter Lewis** is assistant professor at the American University School of International Service. **Robert Mortimer** is professor of political science at Haverford College. **Donald Rothchild** is professor of political science at the University of California, Davis. **Stephen John Stedman** is senior research scholar at the Center for International Security and Cooperation, Stanford University.

THIRD EDITION

Politics and Society in Contemporary Africa

Naomi Chazan
Peter Lewis
Robert Mortimer
Donald Rothchild
Stephen John Stedman

LYNNE
RIENNER
PUBLISHERS

BOULDER

Published in the United States of America in 1999 by
Lynne Rienner Publishers, Inc.
1800 30th Street, Boulder, Colorado 80301

Library of Congress Cataloging-in-Publication Data
Politics and society in contemporary Africa / Naomi Chazan . . . [et
   al.]. — 3rd ed.
   Includes bibliographical references and index.
   ISBN 1-55587-668-4 (hc : alk. paper)
   ISBN 1-55587-679-X (pb : alk. paper)
   1. Africa—Politics and government—1960–   2. Africa—Social
conditions—1960–   3. Africa—Economic conditions—1960–   4. Africa—
Foreign relations—1960–   I. Chazan, Naomi, 1946–   .
JQ1875.P635   1999
320.96'09'045—dc21   99-24154
                                                               CIP

Published and distributed exclusively in Europe and nonexclusively
elsewhere excluding the Americas and Japan
by
PALGRAVE MACMILLAN
Houndmills, Basingstoke, Hampshire RG21 2XS and London
Companies and representatives throughout the world.

ISBN 0-333-69475-9

A catalogue record for this book is available from the
British Library.

Printed and bound in the United States of America

   The paper used in this publication meets the requirements
⊗ of the American National Standard for Permanence of
   Paper for Printed Library Materials Z39.48-1984.

   5 4 3 2